GUN TRADER'S GUIDE

EIGHTEENTH EDITION

STOEGER PUBLISHING COMPANY

COVER DESIGN AND PHOTOGRAPHS: Ray Wells

FRONT COVER: Firearm at left is a nickel-plated 44-40 caliber Colt Single Action Revolver with 7$1/2$-inch barrel and elaborate factory engraving. One of four identical revolvers shipped to Mexico City in 1883, it was fitted with ivory grips into which was carved the Mexican eagle/snake symbol. It is believed that the four revolvers were ordered for President Diaz. The Colt Single Action Revolver at right is a 45-caliber, nickel-plated version engraved by master factory engraver Gustav Young. With 7$1/2$-inch barrel, it was originally part of the Colt factory display at the St. Louis Exposition of 1876.

Published by Stoeger Publishing Company
5 Mansard Court
Wayne, New Jersey 07470

International Standard Book Number: 0-88317-182-1
Library of Congress Catalog Card No.: 85-641040

Manufactured in the United States of America

In the United States, distributed to the book trade and to the sporting goods trade by:
Stoeger Industries,
5 Mansard Court
Wayne, New Jersey 07470

In Canada, distributed to the book trade and to the sporting goods trade by:
Stoeger Canada Ltd.
1801 Wentworth Street, Unit 16
Whitby, Ontario, L1N 8R6, Canada

INTRODUCTION

Firearms are unique machines! Many are based on designs that are over 100 years old. Indeed, many firearms that are more than a century old are still being used today. How many other machines can boast this longevity? Compare a firearm to an automobile and the uniqueness of the former is highlighted to an even greater degree. After about five to seven years, an automobile is shot, and it's way past time to get a new one. After 50 or even 100 years, a firearm is still being shot, still used for its intended purpose, and in many cases, with the same or better efficiency than when it was new!

The unique status of firearms, coupled with anti-gun legislation, has created a market in which sales are booming, probably more so than at any other time since the Gun Control Act of 1968. Trading at gun shows and used-gun shops is healthy, because most buyers are now very aware of the fact that firearms are a lifetime investment, generally increasing in value over the years. But how much has the value of a particular gun appreciated as of today? How does its current condition affect its price? Is it likely that this firearm will increase even more in value over the next five years?

These and many more questions are answered directly and indirectly by GUN TRADER'S GUIDE, a publication whose usefulness and longevity seem to parallel that of the firearms themselves. In print for over 40 years, GUN TRADER'S GUIDE has been touted as the Wall Street Journal of the firearms industry. It has been widely accepted and consulted by everyone involved with firearms—gun dealers, collectors, gunsmiths, law-enforcement agencies, forensic experts, military personnel, museum curators, auctioneers, insurance adjusters, firearms appraisers, the general shooting public, and shooting editors and writers.

The format of GUN TRADER'S GUIDE is simple. It lists thousands of firearms that have been manufactured in the United States and abroad since 1900. Most listings include complete specifications, such as model, caliber/gauge, barrel length, overall length, weight, distinguishing features, and variations, plus the date of manufacture (when it can be accurately determined). Photos and drawings of many models accompany the text to help further identify certain guns.

Most important for many users is the current used-gun price, based on the national average. GUN TRADER'S GUIDE is revised annually to ensure that this information is the most accurate and current available. Again, prices are based on the national average, obtained by sampling many different gun dealers and not by some formula or equation, which could be way off the mark. The prices listed in this publication reflect the prices that are being charged nationwide at the time of publication. This past year, in particular, guns have witnessed extreme price fluctuations due, in part, to the anti-crime bill signed by President Clinton in September 1994. Keeping up with the price changes has been a challenge at best.

ORGANIZATION OF LISTINGS

In the early editions of GUN TRADER'S GUIDE, firearms were frequently organized chronologically by date of production within manufacturers' listings. Experienced firearms enthusiasts know that many firearms companies used the date that a particular model was introduced as the model number. For example, the Colt U.S. Model 1911 semiautomatic pistol was introduced in 1911; the Winchester Model 1892 lever-action rifle was introduced in 1892; the Savage Model 1899 was introduced in 1899, and so on. However, during the first quarter of this century, firearms manufacturers began giving their products names and numbers that had no significance to the date of introduction of manufacture. And as the number of firearms and variations multiplied through the years, it became increasingly difficult to track the various models—especially for the less experienced firearms enthusiasts.

To overcome any confusion and to provide the

most accurate reference source available, the organization of GUN TRADER'S GUIDE was radically rearranged to help simplify matters.

In today's GUN TRADER'S GUIDE, guns are:

• grouped by category first: Handguns, Rifles and Shotguns;
• arranged alphabetically by name of manufacturer or, in the case of some military weapons, by country;
• listed within each manufacturer's entries by *Model Numbers,* which appear first in consecutive numerical order (Model 1, Model 2, Model 3), followed by *Model Names* in alphabetical order (Ace, Delta, Xpert).

Additionally, models from the large manufacturers of handguns—Colt, Smith & Wesson, etc.—are further separated into groupings of Pistols (single shot and semiautomatic) and Revolvers. The index at the back of this book parallels these refinements, so you can see the exact order in which the listings appear for any particular manufacturer.

ACKNOWLEDGMENTS

The Publisher wishes to express special thanks to the numerous readers, collectors, dealers, manufacturers, shooting editors and others whose suggestions and advice always contribute to making this a better book.

A warm thank you is extended to the firearms manufacturers and distributors—their public relations and product personnel, and all the research people the Stoeger editors work with throughout the year; we are especially grateful to all of you for your assistance and cooperation in compiling information for GUN TRADER'S GUIDE and for allowing us to reproduce photographs and illustrations of your firearms. Thank you also to Triple K Manufacturing Co. for previous permission to use the pistol illustrations (indicated by *) from their catalog. In addition, thank you to all the readers who take the time to write in with comments, suggestions and queries about various firearms. It keeps us on our toes and ultimately results in a more accurate product that helps perpetuate the reputation of GUN TRADER'S GUIDE as a reliable resource.

HOW TO USE THIS GUIDE

When a gun enthusiast is ready to buy or sell a used gun, he inevitably turns to GUN TRADER'S GUIDE. He opens the book, then silently asks two questions: "How much will I be able to get (or expect to pay) for a particular gun?" and, "How was that price obtained?" This chapter strives to answer those questions so that all readers will understand the information in this book and know how to use it most effectively.

First, be aware that the prices contained in this book are "retail"; that is, the price the consumer may expect to pay for a similar item. However, many variables must be considered when buying or selling any gun. In general, scarcity, demand, geographical location, the buyer's position and the gun's condition will govern the selling price of a particular gun. Sentiment also enters into the value of an individual's gun, but cannot be logically cataloged.

To illustrate how the price of a particular gun may fluctuate, let's take the popular Winchester Model 94 and see what its value might be.

In general, the Model 1894 (94) is a lever action, solid-frame repeater. Round or octagon barrels of 26 inches were standard when the rifle was first introduced in 1894. However, half-octagon barrels were available for a slight increase in price. A full-length magazine, holding nine shots, was standard. Weight ran about 7¾ pounds.

Fancy grade versions in all Model 94 calibers were available with 26-inch round, octagon or half-octagon nickel-steel barrels. This grade used a checkered fancy walnut pistol-grip stock and forearm, and was available with either shotgun or rifle-type buttplates.

In addition, Winchester turned out this model in carbine-style with a saddle ring in the side of the receiver. The carbine had a 20-inch round barrel and full- or half-magazine. Some carbines were supplied with standard grade barrels, while others were made of nickel steel.

In later years, the rifle version was dropped and only the carbine remained. Eventually, the saddle ring was eliminated from this model and the carbine buttstock was replaced with a shotgun-type buttstock and shortened forend. After World War II, the finish on Winchester Model 94 carbines changed to strictly hot-caustic bluing; thus, pre-war models usually demand a premium over post-war models.

Then in 1964, beginning with serial number 2,700,000, the action on Winchester Model 94s was redesigned for easier manufacturing. Many collectors and firearms enthusiasts considered the change inferior to former models. Whether this is true or not is not the issue; the main reason for a price increase of pre-1964 models was that they were no longer available. This put them immediately in the "scarce" class and made them desirable to collectors.

Shortly after the 1964 transition, Winchester started producing Model 94 commemoratives in an almost endless number—further adding to the confusion on prices. If this were not enough, the Winchester Company was sold in the 1980s and the name changed to U.S. Repeating Arms Co. This firm still manufactured the Model 94 in both standard carbine and Big Bore, and later introduced its "Angle-Eject" model to allow for the mounting of telescopic sights directly over the action.

With the above facts in mind, let's see how to use GUN TRADER'S GUIDE to find out the approximate value of a particular Winchester Model 94. Let's say that you recently inherited a rifle that has the inscription "Winchester Model 94" on the barrel. You turn to the rifle section of this book and look under the W's until you find "Winchester." The Contents pages will also tell you that Winchester Rifles begin on page 372. Since the listings in GUN TRADER'S GUIDE are arranged within each manufacturer's entry first by Model Numbers in consecutive numerical order (followed by Model Names in alphabetical order), you brief through the pages until you come to "Model 94." If you prefer to use the Index at the back of the book, it will quickly tell you that Winchester Model 94 Carbines and Rifles begin on page 389. At first glance, you realize there are two pages of Model 94 listings, not including the commemoratives. Which of these is yours?

The first step is to try to match the appearance of your model with an illustration in the book. They may all look similar at first, but paying careful attention to detail will soon weed out the models that don't apply. You look at your gun and see that the buttplate is kind of curved, or crescent-shaped. Matching up the appearance leads you to the "Winchester Model 94 Lever Action Rifle."

You think you have your model, but, to be sure, you read through the specifications and see that the barrel on the rifle was 26 inches long—either round, octagonal or half-octagonal. Upon measuring, you find that yours is approximately 26 inches long, maybe a trifle under, and it is obviously round. (Please note that the guns are not always shown in proportion to one another; that is, a carbine might not appear shorter than a rifle.)

Your rifle is marked ".38-55"—the caliber designation. Since the caliber offerings include 38-55, you are further convinced. You read on to find that this rifle was manufactured from 1894 to 1937. After this date, only the shorter-barreled carbine was offered by Winchester and only in calibers 30-30, 32 Special and 25-35.

At this point you know you have a Winchester Model 94 rifle manufactured before World War II. You read the value as $795 and decide to take the rifle to your local dealer and collect your money. Here are some of the scenarios you may encounter:

1. If the rifle is in excellent condition—that is, if it contains at least 95 percent of its original finish on both the metal and wood and has a perfect bore— then the gun does have a retail value of $795. However, the dealer is in business to make some profit. If he pays you $795 for the gun, he will have to charge more than this when he sells it. If more is charged than the fair market value, then either the gun will not sell, or someone will pay more than the gun is worth. Therefore, an honest dealer will have to offer you less than the retail price for the gun to make a fair profit. However, the exact amount will vary from dealer to dealer and from situation to situation. For example, if this dealer already has a dozen or so of the same model on his shelf and they have been slow moving, the dealer's offer will probably be low. On the other hand, if the dealer does not have any rifles of this model in stock, but knows several collectors who want this model, chances are the dealer may raise his offer.

2. Perhaps you overlooked the rifle's condition. Although the gun apparently functions flawlessly, not much of the original bluing is left. Rather, there are several shiny bright spots mixed with a brown patina finish over the remaining metal. You also notice that much of the original varnish on the wood has disappeared. Consequently, your rifle is not in "excellent" condition, and you will have to settle for less than the value shown in this book.

3. So your Winchester Model 94 rifle looks nearly new, just out of the box, and the rifle works perfectly. Therefore, you are convinced that the dealer is going to pay you full value, less a reasonable profit of between 25% and 35%. When the dealer offers you about half of what you expected, you are shocked! Perhaps you were not aware that the gun had recently been refinished, and although the finish looks new to you, you did not notice the rounding of the formerly sharp edges on the receiver, or the slight funneling of some screw holes—all of which are a dead giveaway that the rifle had at one time been refinished. Therefore, your rifle has less than "book" value.

Now if you are somewhat of an expert and know for certain that your rifle has never been refinished or otherwise tampered with, and there is still at least 95% of its original finish left, and you believe you have a firearm that is worth full book value, a dealer will still offer you from 25% to 35% less; perhaps even less if he is overstocked with this model.

Another alternative is to advertise in a local newspaper, selling the firearm directly to a private individual. However, this approach may prove both frustrating and expensive. In addition, there are federal and local restrictions on the sale of firearms. Chances are, the next time you have a firearm to sell, you will be more than happy to sell to a dealer, letting him make his fair share of profit.

CONDITION

The condition of a firearm is a big factor in determining its value. In some rare collector models, a jump from one condition to another can mean a value difference of several thousand dollars. Therefore, it stands to reason that you must be able to determine condition before you can accurately evaluate firearms. Several sets of standards have been available over the years, with the National Rifle Association Standards of Condition of Modern Firearms probably being the most popular. However, in recent years, condition has been specified by percentage of original finish remaining on the firearm—both on the wood and metal. Let's see how these standards stack up against each other.

NATIONAL RIFLE ASSOCIATION STANDARDS OF CONDITION OF MODERN FIREARMS

- **New:** Not previously sold at retail, in same condition as current factory production

- **New, Discontinued:** Same as *New,* but discontinued model
- **Perfect:** In new condition in every respect; sometimes referred to as *mint*
- **Excellent:** New condition, used very little, no noticeable marring of wood or metal, bluing perfect (except at muzzle or sharp edges)
- **Very Good:** In perfect working condition, no appreciable wear on working surfaces, no corrosion or pitting, only minor surface dents or scratches
- **Good:** In safe working condition, minor wear on working surfaces, no broken parts, no corrosion or pitting that will interfere with proper functioning
- **Fair:** In safe working condition, but well worn, perhaps requiring replacement of minor parts or adjustments that should be indicated in advertisement; no rust, but may have corrosion pits that do not render the gun unsafe or inoperable
- **Poor:** Badly worn, rusty and battered, perhaps requiring major adjustment or repairs to place in operating condition

When a collector firearm has been expertly refinished to "excellent" condition, a rule of thumb is to deduct 50% from the value indicated in this book; if poorly done, deduct 90%.

For the purpose of assigning comparative values as a basis for trading, firearms listed in this book are assumed to be in "excellent" condition with 95% or better remaining overall finish, no noticeable marring of wood or metal, and bores excellent with no pits. To the novice, this means a practically new gun, almost as though you had removed it from the factory carton. The trained eye, however, will know the difference between "new or mint" condition, and "excellent."

From the above paragraph, any other defects, regardless of how minor, lower the value from those listed in this book. For example, if more than 5% of the original finish is gone and there are minor surface dents or scratches—regardless of how small—the gun is no longer in "excellent" condition; rather, it takes on the condition of "very good," provided the gun is in perfect working order. Even in this state, other than for the minor defects, the gun will still look relatively new to the uninitiated gun buyer.

If the gun is in perfect working condition—functions properly, does not jam and is accurate—but has minor wear on working surfaces, perhaps some bad scratches on the wood or metal, etc., then the gun takes on the condition of "good," one grade below "very good," according to the NRA Standards. Again, the price in this book for that particular firearm must be lowered more to obtain its true value.

The two remaining NRA conditions fall under the headings of "fair" and "poor," respectively.

Previous editions of GUN TRADER'S GUIDE gave multiplication factors to use for firearms in other than "excellent" condition. While these factors are still listed below, please be aware that they are not infallible. They are only one means of establishing a value.

TABLE OF MULTIPLICATION FACTORS FOR GUNS IN OTHER THAN EXCELLENT CONDITION

For guns in other than "excellent" condition, multiply the price in this book for the model in question by the following appropriate factors:

Condition	Multiplication Factor
• Mint or New	1.25
• Excellent	1.00
• Very Good	0.85
• Good	0.68
• Fair	0.35
• Poor	0.15

The above examples present some of the factors that influence firearms values. There are countless others, and the brief examples given here are meant only to provide you with a basic understanding of the process. Remember, the word "Guide" in GUN TRADER'S GUIDE should be taken literally. It is a *guide* only, not *gospel*. We sincerely hope, however, that it is helpful when you do decide to buy or sell a used firearm.

> **NOTE:** All prices shown in this book are for guns in excellent condition (almost new) and the prices are retail (what a dealer would normally charge for them). A dealer will seldom pay the full value shown in this book. If a gun is in any condition other than excellent, the price in this book must be multiplied by the appropriate factor to obtain a true value of the gun in question.

CONTENTS

Section II
RIFLES

Section III
SHOTGUNS

Section I
HANDGUNS

ACCU-TEK
Chino, California

Accu-Tek Model AT-25 Auto Pistol
Similar to Model AT-380, except for caliber 25 ACP with
7-shot magazine. Made from 1991 to date.
Lightweight w/aluminum frame **$115**
Satin Stainless Model **119**
Matte Black Stainless **120**

Accu-Tek Model AT-32SS Auto Pistol
Similar to Model AT-380, except in 32 ACP. Made from
1990 to date.
Satin Stainless Model **$129**
Matte Black Stainless **135**

Accu-Tek Model AT-380SS Auto Pistol
Caliber: 380 ACP. 5-shot magazine. 2³/₄-inch barrel. 5.6
inches overall. Weight: 20 oz. External hammer with slide
safety. Grooved black composition grips. Stainless finish.
Made from 1992 to date.
Satin Stainless Model **$135**
Matte Black Stainless **140**

Accu-Tek Model HC-380SS Auto Pistol **$165**
Caliber: 380 ACP. 13-shot magazine. 2.75-inch barrel. 6
inches overall. Weight: 28 oz. External hammer with slide
safety. Checkered black composition grips. Stainless finish. Made from 1993 to date.

Accu-Tek Model AT-40 Double Action Auto Pistol
Caliber: 40 S&W. 7-shot magazine. 3.2-inch barrel. 6.25
inches overall. Weight: 28 oz. Sights: fixed blade front;
adjustable rear w/3-dot system. Firing-pin block with no
external safety. Stainless or black over stainless finish.
Checkered black nylon grips. Made from 1992 to date.
Satin Stainless Model **$200**
Matte Black Stainless **205**

Accu-Tek AT-9mm

Accu-Tek Model AT-9 Double Action Auto Pistol
Same as Model AT-40, except chambered for caliber 9mm
Parabellum. Made from 1992 to date.
Satin Stainless Model **$195**
Matte Black Stainless **200**

> **NOTE:** The following abbreviations are used throughout
> the Handgun Section: *DA* = Double Action; *SA* = Single
> Action; *LR* = Long Rifle; *WMR* = Winchester Magnum Rim-
> fire; *adj.* = adjustable; *avail.* = available; *bbl.* = barrel.

ACTION ARMS
Philadelphia, Pennsylvania

See also listings under Brno Pistols.

**Action Arms AT-84
Double Action Pistol**

Action Arms AT-84 DA Automatic Pistol **$395**
Caliber: 9mm Parabellum. 15-shot magazine. 4³/₄-inch
barrel. 8 inches overall. Weight: 35 oz. Fixed front sight;
drift adjustable rear. Checkered walnut stocks. Blued finish. Made in Switzerland 1987–89.

ADVANTAGE ARMS
St. Paul, Minnesota

Advantage Arms Model 6 Double Derringer **$245**
Calibers: .410 and 45 Colt. 6-inch barrel. 8.2 inches overall.
Weight: 21 oz. Satin or high-polished stainless steel.

Advantage Arms Model 7 Ultra Lightweight
Calibers: 38 S&W, 380 Auto, 32 S&W Long, 32 Mag. 38
Special, 22 LR and 44 Mag. Same general specifications
as Model 6, except weighs 7¹/₂ oz. and chambered for different calibers.
38 S&W, 380 Auto and 32 S&W **$125**
32 Magnum **135**
38 Special **140**
22 Long Rifle **135**
44 Special **345**

**Advantage Arms
Model 422**

Advantage Arms Model 11 Lightweight **$140**
Same general specifications as Model 7, except weighs 11 oz. and chambered for 38 Special only.

Advantage Arms Model 422 . . . . **$220**
Calibers: 22 LR and 22 Mag. 4-cartridge capacity. Barrel: 2½ inches. 4½ inches overall. Weight: 15 oz. Fixed sights. Walnut grips. Blued or nickel finish. Discontinued 1986.

Advantage Arms Semmerling LM-4 Vest Pocket
Caliber: 45 ACP or 9mm. 5-shot capacity. 5 inches overall.
Blued Finish **$1050**
Stainless Finish **1250**

= S. A. ALKARTASUNA FABRICA DE ARMAS = Guernica, Spain

Alkartasuna Ruby

Alkartasuna "Ruby" Automatic Pistol **$250**
Caliber: 32 Automatic (7.65mm). 9-shot magazine. 3⅝-inch barrel. 6⅜ inches overall. Weight: about 34 oz. Fixed sights. Blued finish. Checkered wood or hard rubber stocks. Made 1917–1922. *Note:* Mfd. by a number of Spanish firms, the Ruby was a secondary standard service pistol of the French Army in World Wars I and II. Specimens made by Alkartasuna bear the "Alkar" trademark.

= AMERICAN ARMS = Kansas City, Missouri

American Arms CX 22

American Arms CX-22 DA Automatic Pistol **$125**
Similar to Model PX-22, except with 3.33-inch barrel. 8-shot magazine. 6.5 inches overall. Weight: 22 oz. Made from 1990 to date.

American Arms EP-380

American Arms EP-380 DA Automatic Pistol **$320**
Caliber: 380 Automatic. 7-shot magazine. 3.5-inch barrel. 6.5 inches overall. Weight: 25 oz. Fixed front sight; square-notch adjustable rear. Stainless finish. Checkered wood stocks. Discontinued 1991.

American Arms P-98

American Arms PK 22

American Arms P-98 DA Automatic Pistol $145
Caliber: 22 LR. 8-shot magazine. 5-inch barrel. 8¼ inches
overall. Weight: 25 oz. Fixed front sight; square-notch adj.
rear. Blued finish. Serrated black polymer stocks. (*See*
photo, preceding page.)

American Arms PK-22 DA Automatic Pistol $145
Caliber: 22 LR. 8-shot magazine. 3.33-inch barrel. 6.33
inches overall. Weight: 22 oz. Fixed front sight; V-notch
rear. Blued finish. Checkered black polymer stocks. Made
from 1989 to date. (*See* photo, preceding page.)

American Arms PX 22

American Arms PX-22 DA Automatic Pistol $135
Caliber: 22 LR. 7-shot magazine. 2.75-inch barrel. 5.33
inches overall. Weight: 15 oz. Fixed front sight; V-notch
rear. Blued finish. Checkered black polymer stocks. Made
from 1989 to date.

American Arms PX-25 DA Automatic Pistol $145
Same general specifications as the Model PX-22, except
chambered for 25 ACP. Made from 1991 to date.

American Arms Regulator

American Arms Regulator Single Action Revolver
Calibers: 357 Mag., 44-40, 45 Long Colt. 6-shot cylinder.
4.75- and 7.5-inch barrel. Blade front sight, fixed rear sight.
Brass trigger guard/backstrap Standard model. Case-
hardened steel Deluxe model. Made from 1992 to date.
Standard Model $215
Standard Combo Set
 (45 LC/45 ACP & 44-40/44 Spec.) 245
Deluxe Model 240
Deluxe Combo Set
 (45 LC/45 ACP & 44-40/44 Spec.) 275
Stainless Steel 265

American Arms Sabre

American Arms Sabre DA Automatic Pistol
Calibers: 9mm Luger, 40 S&W. 8-shot magazine in 9mm,
9-shot in 40 S&W. 3.75-inch barrel. 6.9 inches overall.
Weight: 26 oz. Fixed blade front sight; square notch ad-
justable rear. Black polymer stocks. Blued or stainless
finish. Made from 1991 to date.
Blued Finish $235
Stainless Steel 265

American Arms Woodmaster

American Arms Woodmaster SA Auto Pistol $140
Caliber: 22 LR. 10-shot magazine. 5.875-inch barrel. 10.5
inches overall. Weight: 31 oz. Fixed front sight; square-
notch adj. rear. Blued finish. Checkered wood stocks. Discontinued 1989.

AMERICAN DERRINGER CORPORATION
Waco, Texas

**American Derringer
Model 1**

HANDGUNS

American Derringer Model 1, Stainless

Single-action pocket pistol. 2-shot capacity. Barrel: 3 inches. 4.82 inches overall. Weight: 15 oz. Automatic barrel selection. Satin or high-polished stainless steel. Rosewood grips. Made from 1985 to date.

45 Colt, 44-40 Win., 44 Special	**$260**
45 Colt or 2½" .410, .410 × 2½" or 45 Colt	225
45 Win. Mag.	185
45-70, 44 Mag., 41 Mag., 30-30 Win., 223 Rem.	225
357 Max.	190
357 Mag.	185
38 Special, 32 Mag., 22 LR, 22 Rim. Mag.	175
38 Super, 380 Auto, 9mm Luger, 30 Luger	180

American Derringer Model 2 Steel "Pen" Pistol

Calibers: 22 LR, 25 Auto, 32 Auto (7.65mm). Single shot. 2-inch barrel. 5.6 inches overall (4.2 inches in pistol format). Weight: 5 oz. Stainless finish. Made 1993 to date.

22 Long Rifle	**$195**
25 Auto	205
32 Auto	225

American Derringer Model 3

American Derringer Model 3 Stainless Steel $75

Single Shot. Caliber: 38 Special. Barrel: 2½ inches. 4.9 inches overall. Weight: 8.5 oz. Rosewood grips. Made from 1984 to date.

American Derringer Model 4 Double Derringer .. $295

Calibers: 3-inch .410 shotshell or 45 Colt. Barrel: 4.1 inches. 6 inches overall. Weight: 16½ oz. Stainless steel. Stag horn grips. Made from 1984 to date.

American Derringer Model 6 .... $250

Caliber: .410 or 45 Colt. Barrel: 6 inches. 8.2 inches overall. Weight: 1 lb. 6 oz. Satin or high-polished stainless steel with rosewood grips. Made from 1986 to date.

American Derringer Model 7

Same general specifications as the Model 1, except high-strength aircraft aluminum is used to replace some of the stainless steel parts, which reduces its weight to 7½ oz. Made from 1986 to date.

22 Long Rifle, 22 Mag.	**$150**
38 Special, 32 Mag., 32 S&W Long	135
38 S&W, 380 Auto	135

American Derringer Model 10

Same general specifications as the Model 7, except chambered for 45 ACP or 45 Long Colt.

45 ACP	**$165**
45 Long Colt	180

American Derringer Model 11 .... $130

Same general specifications as Model 7, except chambered for .38 Special only, and weighs 11 oz. Made 1980 to date.

American Derringer 25 Automatic Pistol $310

Calibers: 25 ACP or 250 Mag. Barrel: 2.1 inches. 4.4 inches overall. Weight: 15½ oz. Smooth rosewood grips. Made from 1984 to date.

American Derringer Model 38 Double Action

American Derringer Model 38 Double Action Derringer

Hammerless, double action, double barrel (over/under). Calibers: 38 Special, 9mm Luger, 357 Mag., 40 S&W. 3-inch barrel. Weight: 14.5 oz. Made from 1990 to date.

38 Special	**$155**
9mm Luger	175
357 Mag.	210
40 S&W	220

American Derringer Alaskan Survival Model $225

Same general specifications as the Model 4, except upper barrel comes in 45-70 or 3-inch .410 and 45 Colt lower barrel. Also available in 45 Auto, 45 Colt, 44 Special, 357 Mag. and .357 Max. Made from 1985 to date.

American Derringer Cop DA Derringer $235

Hammerless, double action, four-barrel derringer. Caliber: 357 Mag. 3.15-inch barrel. 5.5 inches overall. Weight: 16 oz. Rosewood grips. Made from 1990 to date.

American Derringer Lady Derringer

American Derringer Lady Derringer

Same general specifications as Model 1, except with custom-tuned action fitted with scrimshawed synthetic ivory

American Derringer Lady Derringer (cont.)

grips. Calibers: 32 H&R Mag., 32 Special, 38 Special (additional calibers on request). Deluxe Grade engraved and highly polished with French fitted jewelry box. Made from 1991 to date.

Lady Derringer **$175**
Deluxe Engraved **560**

American Derringer Mini-Cop DA Derringer $195

Same general specifications as the American Derringer Cop, except chambered for 22 Magnum.

**American Derringer
Semmerling LM-4**

American Derringer Semmerling LM-4

Manually operated repeater. Calibers: 45 ACP or 9mm. 5-shot (45 ACP) or 7-shot magazine (9mm). 3.6-inch barrel. 5.2 inches overall. Weight: 24 oz. Made from 1986 to date. Limited availability.

Blued Finish **$2395**
Stainless Steel **2650**

American Derringer Texas Commemorative

Same general specifications as Model 1, except with solid brass frame, stainless barrels and rosewood grips. Calibers: 38 Special, 44-40 Win. or 45 Colt. Made 1991 to date.

38 Special **$175**
44-40 or 45 Colt **250**

AMERICAN FIREARMS MFG. CO., INC.
San Antonio, Texas

American 25 Auto Pistol

Caliber: 25 Auto. 8-shot magazine. 2.1-inch barrel. 4.4 inches overall. Weight: 14 1/2 oz. Fixed sights. Stainless or blued ordnance steel. Smooth walnut stocks. Made 1966–1974.

Stainless Steel Model **$170**
Blued Steel Model **135**

American 380 Auto Pistol **$325**

Stainless steel. Caliber: 380 Auto. 8-shot magazine. 3 1/2-inch barrel. 5 1/2 inches overall. Weight: 20 oz. Smooth walnut stocks. Made 1972–74.

American 380 Automatic

AMT (ARCADIA MACHINE & TOOL)
Irwindale, California

AMT 45 ACP Hardballer

Caliber: 45 ACP. 7-shot magazine. 5-inch barrel. 8 1/2 inches overall. Weight: 39 oz. Adjustable or fixed sights. Serrated matte slide rib. Wraparound rubber grips.

Hardballer Model **$375**
Government Model (fixed sights w/o rib) **335**
Hardballer Long Slide (w/2-inch longer bbl./
   slide) **395**

AMT 1911 Government Model Auto Pistol

Caliber: 45 ACP. 7-shot magazine. 5-inch barrel. 8 1/2 inches overall. Weight: 38 ounces. Fixed sights. Made from 1979 to date.

Standard Model **$325**
Hardballer Model (Millett sights/Matte rib) **345**
Hardballer Longslide (7-inch bbl./46 oz.) **370**
Stainless (Disc. 1991) **375**

AMT Automag II

AMT Automag II Automatic Pistol $225

Caliber: 22 WRF. 9-shot magazine. Barrel lengths: 3 3/8-, 4 1/2-, 6-inch. Weight: 32 oz. Fully adjustable Millett sights. Stainless finish. Smooth black composition stocks. Made from 1986 to date.

AMT Automag III Automatic Pistol $275

Calibers: 30 M1 and 9mm Win. 8-shot magazine. 6 3/8-inch barrel. 10 1/2 inches overall. Weight: 43 ounces. Millet

AMT Automag III Automatic Pistol (cont.)

adjustable sights. Stainless finish. Carbon fiber grips. Made from 1989 to date.

AMT Automag IV Automatic Pistol $450

Calibers: 10mm Mag., 45 Win. Mag. 7-shot magazine. $6^{1/2}$- or $8^{5/8}$-inch barrel. $10^{1/2}$ inches overall. Weight 46 oz. Millet adjustable sights. Stainless finish. Carbon fiber grips. Made from 1990 to date.

AMT Automag V Automatic Pistol $675

Caliber: 50 A.E. 5-shot magazine. 7-inch barrel. $10^{1/2}$ inches overall. Weight: 46 oz. Custom adjustable sights. Stainless finish. Carbon fiber grips. Made from 1994 to date.

AMT Bulls Eye Target Model

AMT Bulls Eye Target Model $290

Caliber: 40 S&W. 8-shot magazine. 5-inch barrel. $8^{1/2}$ inches overall. Weight: 38 oz. Millet adjustable sights. Wide adjustable trigger. Wraparound Neoprene grips. Made 1990–92.

AMT Hardball Automatic Pistol $325

Caliber: 45 ACP. 7-shot magazine. 5-inch barrel. 8.5 inches overall. Weight: 38 oz. Fixed front sight; Millett adjustable rear. Stainless finish. Wraparound Neoprene grips. Discontinued 1991.

AMT Javelina $425

Caliber: 10mm. 8-shot magazine. 7-inch barrel. $10^{1/2}$ inches overall. Weight: 48 oz. Long grip safety, beveled magazine well, wide adj. trigger. Millet adj. sights. Wraparound Neoprene grips. Stainless finish. Made 1991–93.

AMT Lightning Auto Pistol

Caliber: 22 LR. 10-shot magazine. 5-, $6^{1/2}$-, $8^{1/2}$-, 10-inch barrels. $10^{3/4}$ inches overall w/$6^{1/2}$-inch barrel. Weight: 45 oz. w/$6^{1/2}$-inch barrel. Millett adj. sights. Checkered rubber grips. Stainless finish. Made 1984–87.
Standard Model $185
Bull's-Eye Model 275

AMT Backup

AMT Backup Automatic Pistol $165

Caliber: 380. 5-shot magazine. $2^{1/2}$-inch barrel. 5 inches overall. Weight: 18 oz. Open sights. Carbon fiber grips. Made from 1990 to date.

AMT Backup DAO

AMT Backup DAO Auto Pistol $170

Similar to the AMT Backup, except double action only with re-contoured slide and enlarged trigger guard. Made from 1992 to date.

AMT On Duty Auto Pistol

AMT On Duty Double Action Pistol

Calibers: 40 S&W, 9mm Luger, 45 ACP. 15-shot (9mm), 13-shot (40 S&W) or 9-shot (45 ACP) magazine. $4^{1/2}$-inch barrel. $7^{3/4}$ inches overall. Weight: 32 oz. Hard anodized

AMT On Duty Double Action Pistol (cont.)

aluminum frame. Stainless steel slide and barrel. Carbon fiber grips. Introduced in 1991.

9mm or 40 S&W **$325**
45 ACP **380**

AMT Skipper Auto Pistol

AMT Skipper Auto Pistol **$300**

Calibers: 40 S&W and 45 ACP. 7-shot magazine. 4¼-inch barrel. 7½ inches overall. Weight: 33 oz. Millet adj. sights. Walnut grips. Matte finish stainless steel. Made 1990–92.

ANSCHUTZ PISTOLS
Ulm, Germany
Mfd. by J.G. Anschutz GmbH Jagd und Sportwaffenfabrik

Anschutz Exemplar

Anschutz Exemplar Bolt Action Pistol

Calibers: 22 LR, 22 Magnum, 22 Hornet. 5-shot clip. 10- or 14-inch barrel. 19 inches overall (w/10-inch bbl.). Weight: 3⅓ lbs. Match 64 action. Slide safety. Hooded ramp post front sight; adjustable open notched rear. European walnut contoured grip. Made from 1990 to date.

22 LR with 10-inch bbl. **$300**
22 LR with 14-inch bbl. **345**

Anschutz Exemplar Hornet

Anschutz Exemplar Hornet **$595**

Same general specifications as the standard Exemplar Pistol, except a centerfire version with Match 54 action, wing safety, tapped and grooved for scope mounting. Made from 1990 to date.

Anschutz Exemplar XIV

Anschutz Exemplar XIV **$325**

Same general specifications as the standard Exemplar Bolt Action Pistol, except with 14-inch barrel, weight 4.15 lbs. Made from 1990 to date.

ASTRA PISTOLS
Guernica, Spain
Manufactured by Unceta y Compania

Astra Model 41 Double Action Revolver **$200**

Same gen. specifications as Model 44, except in 41 Mag.

Astra Model 44 Revolver

Astra Model 44 Double Action Revolver **$225**

Similar to Astra 357, except chambered for 44 Magnum. Barrels: 6-, 8½-inch. 11½ inches overall with 6-inch barrel. Weight: 44 oz. with 6-inch barrel. Made 1980–87.

Astra Model 45 Double Action Revolver **$220**

Similar to Astra 357, except chambered for 45 Colt or 45 ACP. Barrels: 6- or 8½-inch. 11½ inches overall w/6-inch bbl. Weight: 44 oz. w/6-inch bbl. Made 1980–87.

Astra Model 200 Firecat

Astra Model 200 Firecat Vest Pocket Auto Pistol $175
Caliber: 25 Automatic (6.35mm). 6-shot magazine. 2¼-inch barrel. 4³/₈ inches overall. Weight: 11³/₄ oz. Fixed sights. Blued finish. Plastic stocks. Made from 1920 to date; U.S. importation discontinued in 1968.

Astra Model 800 Condor

Astra 357, 3-inch barrel

Astra 357 Double Action Revolver **$190**
Caliber: 357 Magnum. 6-shot cylinder. Barrels: 3-, 4-, 6-, 8½-inch. 11¼ inches overall w/6-inch bbl. Weight: 42 oz. w/6-inch bbl. Ramp front sight, adjustable rear sight. Blued finish. Checkered wood stocks. Made 1972–1988.

Astra Model 800 Condor Military Auto Pistol **$895**
Similar to Models 400 and 600, except has an external hammer. Caliber: 9mm Luger. 8-shot magazine. 5¼-inch barrel. 8¼ inches overall. Weight: 32½ oz. Fixed sights. Blued finish. Plastic stocks. Made 1958–1965.

Astra Model 400

Astra Model 2000 Camper

Astra Model 600

Astra Model 2000 Camper Automatic Pistol **$255**
Same as Model 2000 Cub, except chambered for 22 Short only, has 4-inch barrel; overall length, 6¼ inches; weight, 11½ oz. Made 1955–1960.

Astra Model 400 Auto Pistol **$260**
Caliber: 9mm Bayard Long (38 ACP, 9mm Browning Long, 9mm Glisenti, 9mm Luger and 9mm Steyr cartridges may be used interchangeably in this pistol because of its chamber design). 9-shot magazine. 6-inch barrel. 10 inches overall. Weight: 35 oz. Fixed sights. Blued finish. Plastic stocks. Made 1922–1945. *Note:* This pistol, as well as Astra Models 600 and 3000, is a modification of the Browning Model 1912.

Astra Model 2000 Cub

Astra Model 600 Mil./Police Type Auto Pistol . . . **$300**
Calibers: 32 Automatic (7.65mm), 9mm Luger. Magazine: 10- (32 cal.) or 8-shot (9mm). 5¼-inch barrel. 8 inches overall. Weight: about 33 oz. Fixed sights. Blued finish. Checkered wood or plastic stocks. Made 1944–45.

Astra Model 2000 Cub Pocket Auto Pistol **$200**
Calibers: 22 Short, 25 Auto. 6-shot magazine. 2¼-inch barrel. 4½ inches overall. Weight: about 11 oz. Fixed sights. Blued or chromed finish. Plastic stocks. Made from 1954 to date; U.S. importation discontinued in 1968.

Astra Model 3000

Astra Model 3000 Pocket Auto Pistol **$265**
Calibers: 22 LR, 32 Automatic (7.65mm), 380 Auto (9mm
Short). 10-shot magazine (22 cal.), 7-shot (32 cal.), 6-shot
(380 cal.). 4-inch barrel. 6³/₈ inches overall. Weight: about
22 oz. Fixed sights. Blued finish. Plastic stocks. Made
1947–1956.

Astra Model 4000 Falcon

Astra Model 4000 Falcon Auto Pistol **$350**
Similar to Model 3000, except has an external hammer.
Calibers: 22 LR, 32 Automatic (7.65mm), 380 Auto (9mm
Short). 10-shot magazine (22 LR), 8-shot (32 Auto), 7-
shot (380 Auto). 3²/₃-inch barrel. 6¹/₂ inches overall.
Weight: 20 oz. (22 cal.) or 24³/₄ oz. (32 and 380). Fixed
sights. Blued finish. Plastic stocks. Made 1956–1971.

Astra Model A-60 DA Automatic Pistol **$265**
Similar to the Constable, except in 380 only, with 13-shot
magazine and slide-mounted ambidextrous safety. Blued
finish only. Made 1980–1991.

Astra Model A-70 Compact Auto Pistol
Calibers: 9mm Parabellum, 40 S&W. 8-shot (9mm) or 7-
shot (40 S&W) magazine. 3.5-inch barrel. 6.5 inches over-
all. Blued, nickel or stainless finish. Weight: 29.3 oz. Made
from 1992 to date.
Blued Finish **$255**
Nickel Finish 275
Stainless Finish 295

Astra Model A-75 Decocker Auto Pistol
Similar to the Model 70, except in 9mm, 40 S&W and 45
ACP with decocking system and contoured pebble-tex-
tured grips. Made from 1993 to date.
Blued Finish, 9mm or 40 S&W **$295**
Nickel Finish, 9mm or 40 S&W 325

Astra Model A-75 Decocker Auto Pistol (cont.)
Stainless, 9mm or 40 S&W **$375**
Blued Finish, 45 ACP 325
Nickel Finish, 45 ACP 360
Stainless, 45 ACP 395

Astra Model A-75 Ultralight **$385**
Similar to the standard Model 75, except 9mm only with
24-oz. alloy frame. Made from 1994 to date.

Astra Model A-80

Astra Model A-80 Auto Pistol **$280**
Calibers: 9mm Parabellum, 38 Super, 45 ACP. 15-shot
magazine or 9-shot (45 ACP). Barrel: 3³/₄ inches. 7 inches
overall. Weight: 36 oz. Made 1982–89.

Astra Model A-90

Astra Model A-90 DA Automatic Pistol **$295**
Calibers: 9mm Parabellum, 45 ACP. 15-shot (9mm) or 9-
shot (45 ACP) magazine. 3.75-inch barrel. 7 inches overall.
Weight: about 40 oz. Fixed sights. Blued finish. Checkered
plastic stocks. Made 1985–1990.

Astra Model A-100 Double Action Auto Pistol
Same general specifications as the Model A-90, except
selective double action chambered for 9mm Luger, 40
S&W or 45 ACP. Made in 1991.
Blued Finish **$295**
Nickel Finish 330
For Night Sights, **add** 100

Astra Cadix

**Auto-Ordnance 1911A1
Gov't. Automatic Pistol**

Astra Cadix Double Action Revolver **$150**
Calibers: 22 LR, 38 Special. 9-shot (22 LR) or 5-shot (38 cal.) cylinder. Barrels: 4- or 6-inch. Weight: about 27 oz. w/6-inch barrel. Ramp front sight, adjustable rear sight. Blued finish. Plastic stocks. Made 1960–68.

Auto-Ordnance 1911A1 40 S&W Pistol **$325**
Similar to the Model 1911A1, except has 4^1/$_2$-inch barrel with 7^3/$_4$-inch overall length. 8-shot magazine. Weight: 37 oz. Blade front and adjustable rear sights with 3-dot system. Checkered black rubber wraparound grips. Made from 1991 to date.

Auto-Ordnance 1911 "The General" **$295**
Caliber: 45 ACP. 7-shot magazine. 4^1/$_2$-inch barrel. 7^3/$_4$ inches overall. Weight: 37 oz. Blued nonglare finish. Made from 1992 to date.

Auto-Ordnance 1927 A-5 Semiautomatic Pistol
See listing under Thompson Pistol.

Auto-Ordnance Pit Bull Automatic Pistol **$285**
Caliber: 45 ACP. 7-shot magazine. 3^1/$_2$-inch barrel. 7 inches overall. Weight: 32 oz. Fixed front sight; square notch rear. Blued finish. Checkered plastic stocks. Made from 1991 to date.

Astra Constable

Astra Constable Double Action Auto Pistol
Calibers: 22 LR, 32 Automatic (7.65mm), 380 Auto (9mm Short). Magazine capacity: 10-shot (22 LR), 8-shot (32), 7-shot (380). 3^1/$_2$-inch barrel. 6^1/$_2$ inches overall. Weight: about 24 oz. Blade front sight, windage adjustable rear. Blued or chromed finish. Made 1965–1992.
Stainless Finish **$290**
Blued or Chrome **235**

Auto-Ordnance ZG-51

═══ **AUTO-ORDNANCE CORPORATION** ═══
West Hurley, New York

Auto-Ordnance 1911A1 Government Auto Pistol
Calibers: 9mm Para., 38 Super, 10mm, 45 ACP. 9-shot (9mm, 38 Super) or 7-shot (10mm, 45 ACP) magazine. 5-inch barrel. 8^1/$_2$ inches overall. Weight: 39 oz. Fixed blade front sight; rear adjustable. Blued finish. Checkered plastic stocks.
45 ACP Caliber **$270**
9mm, 10mm, 38 Super **305**

Auto-Ordnance ZG-51 Government Auto Pistol . . **$290**
Caliber: 45 ACP. 7-shot magazine. 3^1/$_2$-inch barrel. 7^1/$_4$ inches overall. Weight: 36 oz. Fixed blade front sight; drift adjustable rear. Blued finish. Checkered plastic stocks. Made 1989–1990.

BAUER FIREARMS CORPORATION
Fraser, Michigan

Bauer 25 Automatic

Bauer 25 Automatic Pistol **$125**
Stainless steel. Caliber: 25 Automatic. 6-shot magazine. 2¹⁄₈-inch barrel. 4 inches overall. Weight: 10 oz. Fixed sights. Checkered walnut or simulated pearl stocks. Made 1972–1984.

BAYARD PISTOLS
Herstal, Belgium
Mfd. by Anciens Etablissements Pieper

Bayard Model 1908*

Bayard Model 1908 Pocket Automatic Pistol . . . **$175**
Calibers: 25 Automatic (6.35mm), 32 Automatic (7.65mm), 380 Automatic (9mm Short). 6-shot magazine. 2¹⁄₄-inch barrel. 4⁷⁄₈ inches overall. Weight: about 16 oz. Fixed sights. Blued finish. Hard rubber stocks.

Bayard Model 1923 Pocket Automatic Pistol . . . **$155**
Caliber: 25 Automatic (6.35mm). 2¹⁄₈-inch barrel. 4⁵⁄₁₆ inches overall. Weight: 12 oz. Fixed sights. Blued finish. Checkered hard rubber stocks.

Bayard Model 1923 Pocket Automatic Pistol . . . **$185**
Calibers: 32 Automatic (7.65mm), 380 Automatic (9mm Short). 6-shot magazine. 3⁵⁄₁₆-inch barrel. 5¹⁄₂ inches overall. Weight: about 19 oz. Fixed sights. Blued finish. Checkered hard rubber stocks.

Bayard Model 1930

Bayard Model 1930 Pocket 25 Automatic Pistol . . . **$190**
This is a modification of the Model 1923, which it closely resembles.

BEEMAN PRECISION ARMS, INC.
Santa Rosa, California

Beeman Mini P08 Automatic Pistol **$265**
Caliber: Same general specifications as P08, except shorter 3¹⁄₂-inch barrel, 7.4 inches overall and weight of 20 oz. Imported 1986–1991.

Beeman P08 Automatic Pistol

Beeman P08 Automatic Pistol **$270**
Caliber: 22 LR. 10-shot magazine. 3.8-inch barrel. 7.8 inches overall. Weight: 25 oz. Fixed sights. Blued finish. Checkered hardwood grips. Imported 1986–1991.

Beeman SP Deluxe Metallic Silhouette
Caliber: 22 LR. Single shot. Barrel: 6, 8, 10 or 15 inches. Adjustable rear sight; receiver ground for scope mount. Walnut target grips w/adj. palm rest. Made 1985–86.
With 8-or 10-inch bbl. **$195**
With 12-inch bbl. **215**
With 15-inch bbl. **235**

Beeman/FAS 601 Semiautomatic
Caliber: 22 Short. 9¼-inch sight radius. Weight: about 41 oz. Top loading magazine. Ventilated with gas vents. Adjustable, removable trigger.
Right **$650**
Left.. **675**

Beeman/FAS 602 Semiautomatic
Caliber: 22 LR. 8½-inch sight radius. Weight: 40 oz.
Right **$620**
Left.. **650**

**Beeman/Hämmerli Model 150
Free Pistol**

Beeman/Hämmerli Model 150 Free Pistol $1300
Caliber: 22 LR. Free-floating precision barrel w/low axis relative to hand. Martini-type locking action w/side-mounted locking lever. Sight radius 14.8 inches. Micrometer rear sight adjustable for windage and elevation. Select walnut grip with handrest. Made from 1990 to date.

Beeman/Hämmerli Model 152 Electronic Pistol
Same general specifications as Model 150, except with electronic trigger.
Right Hand **$1400**
Left Hand **1450**

Beeman/Hämmerli Model 208S Target Pistol .. $1095
Caliber: 22 LR. 8-shot magazine. 6-inch barrel. 10.2 inches overall. Weight: 37.3 oz. Micrometer rear sight, ramp front sight. Blued finish. Stippled walnut stocks with adjustable heel plate. Imported from 1990 to date.

Beeman/Hämmerli Model 212

Beeman/Hämmerli Model 212 Hunter Pistol $925
Caliber: 22 LR. 8-shot magazine. 5-inch barrel. 8.6 inches overall. Weight: 31 oz. Blade front sight, square notched rear. Blued finish. Checkered walnut stocks. Imported from 1990 to date.

Beeman/Hämmerli Model 215 Target Pistol $910
Same general specifications as Model 208S, except with fewer deluxe features. Imported from 1990 to date.

Beeman/Hämmerli Model 232 Rapid Fire Pistol . $995
Caliber: 22 Short. 6-shot magazine. 5.2-inch barrel. 10.5 inches overall. Weight: 44 oz. Fully adjustable target sights. Blued finish. Stippled walnut wraparound target stocks. Imported from 1990 to date.

**Beeman/Hämmerli Model 280
Sport Pistol**

Beeman/Hämmerli Model 280 Sport Pistol $1095
Calibers: 22 LR, 32 S&W. 5-shot (32 S&W) or 6-shot (22LR) clip. 4½-inch barrel. Weight: 35 to 39 oz. Handrest grip. Made from 1990 to date.

Beeman/Korth Revolver

Beeman/Korth Revolver $2195
Calibers: 357 Mag. or 22 LR with interchangeable combo cylinders of 357 Mag./9mm Para or 22 LR/22 WMR. Barrel: 6-inch target; 3-, 4-inch combat. Walnut grips. Discontinued 1993.

Beeman/Korth Semiauto Pistol

Beeman/Korth Semiauto Pistol $1895
Calibers: 30 Luger, 9mm Para. 14-shot magazine. 4- or 5-

Beeman/Korth Semiauto Pistol (cont.)

inch barrel. All-steel construction; recoil-operated. Adjustable rear sight. Imported from 1990 to date.

Beeman/Unique 32U Rapid Fire Pistol

Caliber: 32 S&W Long (wadcutter). 5.9-inch barrel. Weight: 40 oz. Blade front, adj. rear target sights. Trigger adjustable for weight and position. Blued finish. Stippled handrest grips. Imported from 1990 to date.

Right-Hand Model . . . . **$ 970**
Left-Hand Model **1025**

Beeman/Unique DES/69-U

Beeman/Unique DES/69-U Target Pistol

Caliber: 22 LR. 5-shot magazine. 5.9-inch barrel. Trigger adjusts for position and pull weight. Comes with 250 gm counterweight. Weight: about 36 oz. Adjustable grips. Imported 1990–93.

Right-Hand Model **$950**
Left-Hand Model **975**

Beeman/Unique 2000-U
Target Pistol

Beeman/Unique 2000-U Match Pistol

Caliber: 22 Short. Designed for rapid fire. Weight: 2.7 lbs. Special light alloy frame, solid steel slide and shock absorber. Five vents for recoil reduction. Handrest grip. Imported 1990–93.

Right-Hand Model **$695**
Left-Hand Model **750**

BEHOLLA PISTOL
Suhl, Germany
Mfd. by both Becker and Holländer and Stenda-Werke GmbH

Beholla Pocket Automatic Pistol **$175**

Caliber: 32 Automatic (7.65mm). 7-shot magazine. 2.9-inch barrel. 5½ inches overall. Weight: 22 oz. Fixed sights.

Beholla Pocket Pistol*

Beholla Pocket Automatic Pistol (cont.)

Blued finish. Serrated wood or hard rubber stocks. Made by Becker and Holländer 1915–1920, by Stenda-Werke circa 1920–25. *Note:* Essentially the same pistol was manufactured concurrently with the Stenda version as the "Leonhardt" by H. M. Gering and as the "Menta" by August Menz.

BERETTA USA CORP.
Accokeek, Maryland

Beretta pistols are manufactured by Fabbrica D'Armi Pietro Beretta S.p.A. in the Gardone Valtrompia (Brescia), Italy. This prestigious firm has been in business for over 300 years. Since the late 1970s, many of the models sold in the U.S. have been made at the Accokeek (MD) plant.

Beretta Model 20 Double Action Auto Pistol **$135**

Caliber: 25 ACP. 8-shot magazine. 2.5-inch barrel. 4.9 inches overall. Weight: 10.9 oz. Plastic or walnut grips. Fixed sights. Made 1984–85.

Beretta Model 21

Beretta Model 21 Double Action Auto Pistol

Calibers: 22 LR and 25 ACP. 7-shot (22 LR) or 8-shot (25 ACP) magazine. 2½-inch barrel. 4.9 inches overall.

Beretta Model 21 Double Action Auto Pistol (cont.)

Weight: about 12 oz. Blade front sight; V-notch rear. Walnut grips. Made from 1985 to date.

Blued Finish **$160**
Nickel Finish (22 LR only) **200**
Model 21EL Engraved Model **205**

Beretta Model 71

Beretta Model 70

Beretta Model 70 Automatic Pistol $195

Improved version of Model 1935. Steel or lightweight alloy. Calibers: 32 Auto (7.65mm), 380 Auto (9mm Short). 8-shot (32) or 7-shot (380) magazine. 3½-inch barrel. 6½ inches overall. Weight: steel, 22¼ oz.; alloy, 16 oz. Fixed sights. Blued finish. Checkered plastic stocks. Made 1959–1985. *Note:* Formerly marketed in U.S. as "Puma" (alloy model in 32) and "Cougar" (steel model in 380).

Beretta Model 70S $215

Similar to Model 70T, except chambered for 22 Auto and 380 Auto. Longer barrel guide, safety lever blocking hammer; front and rear sight blade fixed on breechblock. Weight: 1 lb. 7 oz. Made 1977–1985.

Beretta Model 71 Automatic Pistol $225

Same general specifications as alloy Model 70. Caliber: 22 LR. 6-inch barrel. 8-round magazine. Adjustable rear sight. Medium frame. Single action. Made 1959–1989. *Note:* Formerly marketed in U.S. as the "Jaguar Plinker."

Beretta Model 72

Beretta Model 72 .... $220

Same as Model 71, except has 6-inch barrel, weighs 18 oz. Made from 1959 to date. *Note:* Formerly marketed in U.S. as "Jaguar Plinker." Discontinued.

Beretta Model 76

Beretta Model 70T

Beretta Model 70T Automatic Pistol $250

Similar to Model 70. Caliber: 32 Automatic (7.65mm). 9-shot magazine. 6-inch barrel. 9½ inches overall. Weight: 19 oz. Adjustable rear sight, blade front sight. Blued finish. Checkered plastic stocks. Introduced in 1959. Discont.

Beretta Model 76 Auto Target Pistol

Caliber: 22 LR. 10-shot magazine. 6-inch barrel. 8.8 inches overall. Weight: 33 oz. Adjustable rear sight, front sight with interchangeable blades. Blued finish. Checkered plastic or wood grips (Model 76W). Made 1966–1985. *Note:* Formerly marketed in the U.S. as the "Sable."

Model 76 w/Plastic Grips **$330**
Model 76W w/Wood Grips **345**

Beretta Model 81

Beretta Model 81 Double Action Auto Pistol $250
Caliber: 32 Automatic (7.65mm). 12-shot magazine. 3.8-inch barrel. 6.8 inches overall. Weight: 23.5 oz. Fixed sights. Blued finish. Plastic stocks. Made principally for the European market 1975–1984, with similar variations to the Model 84.

Beretta Model 84 Double Action Auto Pistol $365
Same as Model 81, except made in caliber 380 Automatic with 13-shot magazine. 3.82-inch barrel. 6.8 inches overall. Weight: 23 oz. Fixed front and rear sights. Made from 1975 to about 1982.

**Beretta Model 84B
Double Action Pistol**

Beretta Model 84B DA Auto Pistol $385
Improved version of Model 84 with strengthened frame and slide, and firing-pin block safety added. Ambidextrous, reversible magazine release. Blued or nickel finish. Checkered black plastic or wood grips. Other specifications same. Made about 1982–84.

Beretta Model 84BB Double Action Auto Pistol
Improved version of Model 84B, with further strengthened slide, frame and recoil spring. Caliber: 380 ACP. 13-shot magazine. Barrel: 3.82 inches. 6.8 inches overall. Weight: 23 oz. Checkered black plastic or wood grips. Blued or nickel finish. Fixed sights. Made c. 1984 to date.

Beretta Model 84BB Double Action Auto Pistol (cont.)
Blued Finish **$350**
Blued w/Wood Grips 375
Nickel Finish 390

Beretta Model 85 Double Action Auto Pistol $295
This is basically the same gun as the Model 84 and has seen a similar evolution. However, this 8-shot version has no ambidextrous magazine release, has a slightly narrower grip and weighs 21.8 oz. It was introduced a little later than the Model 84.

Beretta Model 85B DA Auto Pistol $315
Improved version of the Model 85. Made about 1982–85.

**Beretta Model 85BB
Double Action Pistol**

Beretta Model 85BB Double Action Pistol
Improved version of the Model 85B, with strenthened frame and slide. Caliber: 380 ACP. 8-shot magazine. 3.82-inch barrel. 6.8 inches overall. Weight: 21.8 oz. Blued or nickel finish. Checkered black plastic or wood grips. Made from 1985 to date.
Blued Finish w/Plastic Grips **$325**
Blued Finish w/Wood Grips 345
Nickel Finish 360

Beretta Model 85F Double Action Pistol
Similar to the Model 85BB, except has re-contoured trigger guard and manual ambidextrous safety with decocking device. Made in 1990.
Blued Finish w/Plastic Grips **$360**
Blued Finish w/Wood Grips 380
Nickel Finish w/Wood Grips 410

Beretta Model 86

Beretta Model 86 Double Action Auto Pistol **$355**
Caliber: 380 auto. 8-shot mag. Barrel: 4.33 inches, tip-up.
7.33 inches overall. Weight: 23 oz. Made 1986–89.

Beretta Model 87BB

Beretta Model 87BB Auto Pistol
Similar to the Model 85, except in 22 LR with 8-shot
magazine and optional extended 6-inch barrel (in single
action). Overall length: 6.8 inches; 8.9 w/6-inch bbl.
Weight: 20.8 oz.; 23 oz. w/6-inch bbl. Checkered wood
grips. Made from 1977 to date.
Blued Finish (Double Action) **$340**
Long Barrel (Single Action) **350**

Beretta Model 89 Target Automatic Pistol **$485**
Caliber: 22 LR. 8-shot magazine. 6-inch barrel. 9.5 inches
overall. Weight: 41 oz. Adjustable target sights. Blued finish. Target-style walnut stocks. Made 1990–92.

Beretta Model 90

Beretta Model 90 Double Action Auto Pistol **$220**
Caliber: 32 Auto (7.65mm). 8-shot magazine. 3⅝-inch
barrel. 6⅝ inches overall. Weight: 19½ oz. Fixed sights.
Blued finish. Checkered plastic grips. Made 1969–1975.

Beretta Model 92 Double Action Auto Pistol **$395**
Caliber: 9mm Luger. 15-shot magazine. 4.9-inch barrel.
8.5 inches overall. Weight: 33.5 oz. Fixed sights. Blued
finish. Plastic stocks. Made from 1976 to date.

Beretta Model 92

Beretta Model 92D Double Action Auto Pistol
Same general specifications as Model 92F, except DA only
with bobbed hammer and 3-Dot Sight.
Model 92D **$420**
Model 92D w/Triticon Sight **470**

Beretta Model 92F Compact DA Auto **$375**
Caliber: 9mm Parabellum. 12-shot magazine. 4.3-inch
barrel. 7.8 inches overall. Weight: 31.5 oz. Wood grips.
Square-notched bar rear sight; blade front sight, integral
with slide. Made from 1986 to date.

Beretta Model 92F Double Action Auto Pistol
Same general specifications as Model 92, except with slide-
mounted safety and repositioned magazine release. Replaced Model 92SB. Blued or stainless finish. Made from
1985 to date.
Blued Finish **$410**
Stainless Finish **495**

Beretta Model 92F-EL Double Action Auto Pistol
Deluxe version of Model 92F with gold trim and logo inlay.
Deluxe walnut stocks.
Model 92F-EL Gold **$595**
Model 92F-EL Stainless **930**

Beretta Model 92SB Double Action Auto Pistol . . . **$395**
Same general specifications as standard Model 92, except
has slide-mounted safety and repositioned magazine release. Discontinued 1985.

Beretta Model 92 SB-F

Beretta Model 92 SB-F DA Auto Pistol **$415**
Caliber: 9mm Parabellum. 15-shot magazine. Barrel:
4.9 inches. 8½ inches overall. Weight: 34 oz. Plastic or

Beretta Model 92 SB-F DA Auto Pistol (cont.)

wood grips. Square-notched bar rear sight; blade front sight, integral with slide. This model, also called **Model 92S-1**, the standard-issue sidearm for the U.S. Armed Forces. Made from 1985 to date.

Beretta Model 96 Double Action Auto Pistol

Same general specifications as Model 92F, except in 40 S&W. 10-shot magazine (9-shot in Compact Model).

Model 96 Standard **$425**
Model 96 Centurion (Compact) **435**
Model 96 D (DA only) **420**
Model 96 w/Triticon Sights **485**

Beretta Model 101 . . . . **$215**

Same as Model 70T, except caliber 22 LR, has 10-shot magazine. Introduced in 1959. Discontinued.

Beretta Model 318 (1934)*

Beretta Model 318 (1934) Auto Pistol **$255**

Caliber: 25 Automatic (6.35mm). 8-shot magazine. 2½-inch barrel. 4½ inches overall. Weight: 14 oz. Fixed sights. Blued finish. Plastic stocks. Made from 1934 to c. 1939.

Beretta Model 949 Olimpionico

Beretta Model 949 Olimpionico Auto Pistol **$525**

Calibers: 22 Short, 22 LR. 5-shot magazine. 8¾-inch barrel. 12½ inches overall. Weight: 38 oz. Target sights. Adjustable barrel weight. Muzzle brake. Checkered walnut stocks with thumbrest. Made 1959–1964.

Beretta Model 950B Auto Pistol **$125**

Same general specifications as Model 950CC, except caliber 25 Auto, has 7-shot magazine. Made from 1959 to date. *Note:* Formerly marketed in the U.S. as "Jetfire."

Beretta Model 950B

Beretta Model 950 BS 22 Short

Beretta Model 950 BS Single Action Semiautomatic

Calibers: 25 ACP or 22 Short. Magazine capacity: 7 rounds (22 short); 8 rounds (25 ACP). 2½- or 4-inch barrel. 4½ inches overall (2½-inch bbl.) Weight: about 10 oz. Blade front sight; V-notch in rear. Checkered black plastic grips. Made from 1987 to date.

Blued Finish **$125**
Nickel Finish **160**
With 4-inch bbl. (22 short) **140**
Model 950 EL gold-etched version **210**

Beretta Model 950CC

Beretta Model 950CC Auto Pistol **$125**

Caliber: 22 Short. 6-shot magazine. Hinged, 2⅜-inch barrel. 4¾ inches overall. Weight: 11 oz. Fixed sights. Blued finish. Plastic stocks. Made from 1959 to date. *Note:* Formerly marketed in the U.S. as "Minx M2."

Beretta Model 950CC Special

Beretta Model 950CC Special Auto Pistol **$130**
Same general specifications as Model 950CC Auto, except has 4-inch barrel. Made from 1959 to date. *Note:* Formerly marketed in the U.S. as "Minx M4."

Beretta Model 951 (1951)

Beretta Model 951 (1951) Military Auto Pistol . . . **$245**
Caliber: 9mm Luger. 8-shot magazine. 4¹/₂-inch barrel. 8 inches overall. Weight: 31 oz. Fixed sights. Blued finish. Plastic stocks. Made from 1952 to date. *Note:* This is the standard pistol of the Italian Armed Forces; also used by Egyptian and Israeli armies and by the police in Nigeria. Egyptian and Israeli models usually command a premium. Formerly marketed in the U.S. as the "Brigadier."

Beretta Model 1915

Beretta Model 1915 Auto Pistol **$285**
Calibers: 9mm Glisenti and 32 ACP (7.65mm). 8-shot magazine. 4-inch barrel. 6.7 inches overall (9mm), 5.7 inches (32 ACP). Weight: 30 oz. (9mm), 20 oz. (32 ACP). Fixed sights. Blued finish. Wood grips. Made 1915–1922. An improved postwar 1915/1919 version in caliber 32 ACP was later offered for sale in 1922 as the Model 1922.

Beretta Model 1923

Beretta Model 1923 Auto Pistol **$565**
Caliber: 9mm Glisenti (Luger). 8-shot magazine. 4-inch barrel. 6¹/₂ inches overall. Weight: 30 oz. Fixed sights. Blued finish. Plastic stocks. Made from 1923 to c. 1936.

Beretta Model 1934

Beretta Model 1935

Beretta Model 1934 Auto Pistol
Caliber: 380 Automatic (9mm Short). 7-shot magazine. 3³/₈-inch barrel. 5⁷/₈ inches overall. Weight: 24 oz. Fixed sights. Blued finish. Plastic stocks. Official pistol of the Italian Armed Forces. Wartime pieces not as well made and finished as commercial models. Made 1934–1959. (*See* photo, preceding page.)
Commercial Model **$265**
War Model **325**

Beretta Model 1935 Auto Pistol
Caliber: 32 ACP (7.65mm). 8-shot magazine. 3¹/₂-inch barrel. 5³/₄ inches overall. Weight: 24 oz. Fixed sights. Blued finish. Plastic stocks. A roughly finished version of this pistol was produced during WW II. Made 1935–1959. (*See* photo, preceding page.)
Commercial Model **$245**
War Model **225**

Bernardelli Model 80

VINCENZO BERNARDELLI, S.P.A.
Gardone V. T. (Brescia), Italy

Bernardelli Model 60

Bernardelli Model 60 Pocket Automatic Pistol .. **$185**
Calibers: 22 LR, 32 Auto (7.65mm), 380 Auto (9mm Short). 8-shot magazine (22 and 32), 7-shot (380). 3¹/₂-inch barrel. 6¹/₂ inches overall. Weight: about 25 oz. Fixed sights. Blued finish. Bakelite stocks. Made 1959–1990.

Bernardelli Model 68 Automatic Pistol **$120**
Caliber: 6.35. 5- and 8-shot magazine. 2¹/₈-inch barrel. 4¹/₈ inches overall. Weight: 10 oz. Fixed sights. Blued or chrome finish. Bakelite or pearl stocks. This model, like its smaller bore 22-counterpart, was known as the "Baby" Bernardelli.

Bernardelli Model 69 Automatic Target Pistol ... **$385**
Caliber: 22 LR. 10-shot magazine. 5.9-inch barrel. 9 inches overall. Weight: 2.2 lbs. Fully adjustable target sights. Blued finish. Stippled right- or left-hand wrap-around walnut grips. Made from 1987 to date. *Note:* This was previously Model 100.

Bernardelli Model 80 Automatic Pistol **$165**
Calibers: 22 LR, 32 ACP (7.65mm), 380 Auto (9mm Short). Magazine capacity: 10-shot (22), 8-shot (32), 7-shot (380). 3¹/₂-inch barrel. 6¹/₂ inches overall. Weight: 25.6 oz. Adjustable rear sight, white dot front sight. Blued finish.

Bernardelli Model 80 Automatic Pistol (cont.)
Plastic thumbrest stocks. *Note:* Model 80 is a modification of Model 60 designed to conform with U.S. import regulations. Made 1968–1988.

Bernardelli Model 90

Bernardelli Model 90 Sport Target **$175**
Same as Model 80, except has 6-inch barrel, is 9 inches overall, weighs 26.8 oz. Made 1968–1990.

Bernardelli Model 100

Bernardelli Model 100 Target Automatic Pistol . . **$315**
Caliber: 22 LR. 10-shot magazine. 5.9-inch barrel. 9 inches overall. Weight: 37¾ oz. Adjustable rear sight, interchangeable front sights. Blued finish. Checkered walnut thumbrest stocks. Made 1969–1986: *Note:* Formerly Model 69.

Bernardelli Sporter

Bernardelli "Baby"

Bernardelli "Baby" Automatic Pistol **$175**
Calibers: 22 Short, 22 Long. 5-shot magazine. 2⅛-inch barrel. 4⅛ inches overall. Weight: 9 oz. Fixed sights. Blued finish. Bakelite stocks. Made 1949–1968.

Bernardelli Model P010 Automatic Pistol **$405**
Caliber: 22 LR. 5- and 10-shot magazine. 5.9-inch barrel with 7.5-inch sight radius. Weight: 40.0 oz. Interchangeable front sight; adjustable rear. Blued finish. Textured walnut stocks. Discontinued 1990.

Bernardelli P018 Compact Model **$395**
Slightly smaller version of the Model P018 standard DA automatic, except has 14-shot magazine and 4-inch barrel. 7.68 inches overall. Weight: 33 oz. Walnut grips only. Imported 1987–1991.

Bernardelli Vest Pocket

Bernardelli Sporter Automatic Pistol **$245**
Caliber: 22 LR. 8-shot magazine. Barrel lengths: 6-, 8-, and 10-inch. 13 inches overall with 10-inch barrel. Weight: about 30 oz. with 10-inch barrel. Target sights. Blued finish. Walnut stocks. Made from 1949 to 1968.

Bernardelli Vest Pocket Automatic Pistol **$190**
Caliber: 25 Auto (6.35mm). 5- or 8-shot magazine. 2⅛-inch barrel. 4⅛ inches overall. Weight: 9 oz. Fixed sights. Blued finish. Bakelite stocks. Made 1945–1968.

**Bernardelli P018 DA
Auto Pistol**

Bernardelli P018 Double Action Automatic Pistol
Caliber: 9mm Parabellum. 16-shot magazine. 4¾-inch barrel. 8½ inches overall. Weight: 36 oz. Fixed combat sights. Blued finish. Checkered plastic or walnut stocks. Imported 1987–1991.
With Plastic Grips **$370**
With Walnut Grips **380**

=== **BERSA PISTOLS** ===
Imported from Argentina by Eagle Imports

Bersa firearms have been imported by other distributors, including Interarms and Outdoor Sports Headquarters.

Bersa Model 23

Bersa Model 23 Double Action Auto Pistol

Caliber: 22 LR. 10-shot magazine. 4-inch barrel. Fixed front sight; square-notch adj. rear. Blued or satin nickel finish. Textured wood stocks. Imported 1989 to date. (*See* photo, preceding page.)

Blued Finish **$185**
Satin Nickel **200**

Bersa Model 83

Bersa Model 83 Double Action Auto Pistol

Caliber: 380 ACP. 7-shot magazine. 3½-inch barrel. Front blade sight integral on slide; square-notch rear adjustable for windage. Blued or satin nickel finish. Custom wood stocks. Imported 1990 to date.

Blued Finish **$185**
Satin Nickel **205**

Bersa Model 85

Bersa Model 85 Double Action Auto Pistol

Same general specifications as Model 83, except 13-shot magazine. Imported 1990 to date.

Blued Finish **$230**
Satin Nickel **275**

Bersa Model 86 Double Action Auto Pistol

Same general specifications as Model 85, except available in matte blue finish and with neoprene grips.

Matte Blue Finish **$235**
Nickel Finish **265**

Bersa Model 97

Bersa Model 97 Auto Pistol **$275**

Caliber: 380 ACP. 7-shot magazine. 3½-inch barrel. 6½ inches overall. Weight: 28 oz. Introduced 1982; disc.

Bersa Model 223

Same general specifications as Model 383, except in 22 LR w/10-round magazine capacity. Discontinued 1987.

Double Action **$170**
Single Action **160**

Bersa Model 224

Caliber: 22 LR. 10-shot magazine. 4-inch barrel. Weight: 26 oz. Front blade sight; square-notched rear adj. for windage. Blued finish. Checkered nylon or custom wood grips. Made from 1984; SA discontinued 1986.

Double Action **$170**
Single Action **165**

Bersa Model 226

Same general specifications as Model 224, but with 6-inch barrel. Discontinued.

Double Action **$170**
Single Action **160**

Bersa Model 383 Auto Pistol

Caliber: 380 Auto. 7-shot magazine. 3½-inch barrel. Front blade sight integral on slide; square-notched rear sight adjustable for windage. Custom wood grips on double action; nylon grips on single action. Blued or satin nickel finish. Made from 1984; SA discontinued 1989.

Double Action **$145**
Single Action **125**
Satin Nickel **155**

Bersa Model 622

Bersa Model 622 Auto Pistol **$125**

Caliber: 22 LR. 7-shot magazine. 4- or 6-inch barrel. 7 or 9 inches overall. Weight: 2¼ pounds. Blade front sight; square-notch rear adj. for windage. Blued finish. Nylon grips. Made 1982–87.

Bersa Model 644

**Brno CZ 75 DA
Automatic Pistol**

Bersa Model 644 Auto Pistol **$135**
Caliber: 22 LR. 10-shot magazine. 3.5-inch barrel. Weight: 26½ oz. 6½ inches overall. Adjustable rear sight, blade front. Contoured black nylon grips. Made 1980 to date.

Brno CZ 83 Double Action Automatic Pistol **$310**
Calibers: 32 ACP, 380 ACP. 15-shot (32 ACP) or 13-shot (380 ACP) magazine. 3¾-inch barrel. 6¾ inches overall. Weight: 26½ oz. Fixed sights. Blued finish. Checkered black plastic stocks.

Brno CZ 85 Combat DA Automatic Pistol
Similar to the standard CZ 85 Model, except with 13-shot magazine, combat-style hammer, fully adjustable rear sight and walnut grips.
Black Polymer Finish **$415**
High-Polish Blued Finish 465
Matte Blued Finish 440

Bersa Thunder 9 Pistol

Brno CZ 85 Double Action Automatic Pistol
Same as CZ 75, except with ambidextrous slide release and safety. Calibers: 9mm Parabellum, 7.65mm. Made from 1986 to date.
Black Polymer Finish **$400**
High-Polish Blued Finish 450
Matte Blued Finish 425

Bersa Thunder 9 Auto Pistol **$295**
Caliber: 9mm Parabellum. 15-shot magazine. 4-inch barrel. 7⅜ inches overall. Weight: 30 oz. Blade front sight, adjustable rear w/3-dot system. Ambidextrous safety and decocking devise. Matte blued finish. Checkered black polymer grips. Made from 1993 to date.

=== **BRONCO PISTOL** ===
Eibar, Spain
Manufactured by Echave y Arizmendi

Bronco Model 1918*

=== **BRNO PISTOLS** ===

Manufactured in Czechoslovakia

Brno CZ 75 Double Action Automatic Pistol
Caliber: 9mm Parabellum. 15-shot magazine. 4¾-inch barrel. 8 inches overall. Weight: 35 oz. Fixed sights. Blued or black polymer finish. Checkered wood or high-impact plastic stocks.
Black Polymer Finish **$365**
High-Polish Blued Finish 395
Matte Blue Finish 375

Bronco Model 1918 Pocket Automatic Pistol . . . **$115**
Caliber: 32 ACP (7.65mm). 6-shot magazine. 2½-inch barrel. 5 inches overall. Weight: 20 oz. Fixed sights. Blued finish. Hard rubber stocks. Made circa 1918–1925.

BROWNING PISTOLS
Morgan, Utah

The following Browning pistols have been manufactured by Fabrique Nationale d'Armes de Guerre (now Fabrique Nationale Herstal) of Herstal, Belgium; by Arms Technology Inc. of Salt Lake City; and by J. P. Sauer & Sohn of Eckernförde, W. Germany. (*See* also FN Browning and J.P. Sauer & Sohn listings.)

Browning 380 Automatic Standard Model (1955-Type)

Browning 9mm Gold Classic

Browning 380 Automatic Standard Model (1971-Type)

Browning 9mm Classic
Same general specifications as 9mm Auto (Hi-Power), except for high-grade engraving, finely checkered walnut grips with double border, and limited to 5000 production. Gold Classic limited to 500 production. Made 1985–86.
Gold Classic **$1695**
Standard Classic **895**

Browning 380 Automatic Pistol, 1971 Type
Same as 380 Automatic, 1955 Type, except has longer slide, 4⁷/₁₆-inch barrel, is 7¹/₁₆ inches overall, weighs 23 oz. Rear sight adjustable for windage and elevation, plastic thumbrest stocks. Made 1971–75.
Standard Model **$295**
Renaissance Model **795**

Browning 25 Automatic Standard Model

Browning BDA Automatic

Browning 25 Automatic Pistol
Same general specifications as FN Browning Baby (see separate listing). Standard Model, blued finish, hard rubber grips. Lightweight Model, nickel-plated, Nacrolac pearl grips. Renaissance Engraved Model, nickel-plated, Nacrolac pearl grips. Made by FN 1955–1969.
Standard Model **$260**
Lightweight Model **355**
Renaissance Model **695**

Browning 380 Automatic Pistol, 1955 Type
Same general specifications as FN Browning 380 Pocket Auto. Standard Model, Renaissance Engraved Model, as furnished in 25 Automatic. Made by FN 1955–1969.
Standard Model **$325**
Renaissance Model **895**

Browning BDA Double Action Automatic Pistol . . **$375**
Similar to SIG-Sauer P220. Calibers: 9mm Luger, 38 Super Auto, 45 Auto. 9-shot magazine (9mm and 38), 7-shot (45 cal). 4.4-inch barrel. 7.8 inches overall. Weight: 29.3 oz. Fixed sights. Blued finish. Plastic stocks. Made from 1977–79 by J. P. Sauer.

Browning BDA-380 Double Action Automatic Pistol
Caliber: 380 Auto. 13-shot magazine. Barrel length: 3¹³/₁₆ inches. 6¾ inches overall. Weight: 23 oz. Fixed blade front sight, square notch drift adjustable rear sight. Made from 1982 to date.
Blued finish **$335**
Nickel finish **350**

**Browning BDA-380
Nickel**

**Browning BDM 9mm
Double Action**

Browning BDM 9mm DA Automatic Pistol **$395**
Caliber: 9mm Luger. 15-shot magazine. 4.73-inch barrel. 7.85 inches overall. Weight: 31 oz. Low-profile removable blade front sight and windage-adjustable rear sight w/3-Dot system. Matte blue finish. Features selectable shooting mode. Made from 1991 to date.

Browning Buck Mark 22 Automatic Pistol **$155**
Caliber: 22 LR. 10-shot magazine. Barrel: 5½ inches. 9½ inches overall. Weight: 32 oz. Black molded grips. Adjustable rear sight. Made from 1985 to date.

**Browning Buck Mark
Micro 22**

Browning Buck Mark 22 Field Auto **$165**
Same general specifications as the standard Buck Mark 22, except with hoodless ramp-style front and low-profile rear sights. Contoured walnut grips. Made 1991 to date.

Browning Buck Mark 22 Micro
Same general specifications as standard Buck Mark 22, except with 4-inch barrel. 8 inches overall. Weight: 32 oz. Molded composite grips. Ramp front sight; Pro Target rear sight. Made from 1992 to date.
Blued Finish **$145**
Nickel finish **180**

Browning Buck Mark 22 Plus **$175**
Same general specifications as standard Buck Mark 22, except for black molded, impregnated hardwood grips. Made from 1987 to date.

**Browning Buck Mark 22
Silhouette**

Browning Buck Mark 22 Silhouette **$250**
Same general specifications as standard Buck Mark 22, except for 9⅞-inch barrel, 53-oz. weight, target sights mounted on full-length scope base, and laminated hardwood grips and forend. Made from 1987 to date.

Browning Buck Mark 22 Target 5.5 .... **$235**
Same general specifications as Buck Mark 22, except 5½-inch barrel, 35½-oz. weight and target sights mounted on full-length scope base. Made from 1989 to date.

Browning Buck Mark 22 Target 5.5 (Gold) **$255**
Caliber: 22 LR. 10-shot magazine. 5½-inch barrel. 9⅝ inches overall. Weight: 35 oz. Hooded blade front sight; adjustable rear sight. Contoured walnut grips. Made from 1991 to date.

Browning Buck Mark 22 Unlimited Silhouette ... **$295**
Same general specifications as standard Buck Mark 22 Silhouette, except with 14-inch barrel. 18¹¹⁄₁₆ inches overall. Weight: 64 oz. Interchangeable post front sight and Pro Target rear. Nickel finish. Made 1992 to date.

Browning Buck Mark 22 Varmint Auto Pistol **$225**
Same general specifications as standard Buck Mark 22, except for 9⅞-inch barrel, 48-oz. weight, no sights, full-length scope base, and laminated hardwood grips. Made from 1987 to date.

Browning Challenger Automatic Pistol
Caliber: 22 LR. 10-shot magazine. Barrel lengths: 4½- and 6¾-inch. 11⁷⁄₁₆ inches overall w/6¾-inch bbl. Weight: 38 oz. w/6¾-inch bbl. Removable blade front sight, screw adjustable rear. Standard finish, blue; also furnished gold-inlaid (Gold Model) and engraved and chrome-plated (Renaissance Model). Checkered walnut stocks; finely figured and carved stocks on Gold and Renaissance Models. Standard made by FN 1962–1975, higher grades intro.

Browning Challenger Standard Model

Browning Challenger III

Browning Challenger Gold Model

Browning Challenger III Sporter 22

Browning Challenger Renaissance Model

Browning Challenger III Automatic Pistol $175
Same general description as Challenger II, except has 5½-inch bull barrel, alloy frame and new sight system. Weight: 35 oz. Made 1982–84. **Sporter Model** w/6¾-inch barrel made 1984–86.

Browning Challenger Automatic Pistol (cont.)
in 1971; discontinued.
Standard Model .... $ 275
Gold Model 995
Renaissance Model 1095

Browning 9mm Hi-Power Ambidextrous Safety

Browning Challenger II

Browning Challenger II Automatic Pistol $185
Same general specifications as Challenger Standard Model with 6¾-inch barrel, changed grip angle and impregnated hardwood stocks. Original Challenger design modified for lower production costs. Made by ATI 1976–1983.

Browning Hi-Power 9mm Ambidextrous Safety . $345
Same general specifications as standard 9mm Hi-Power (see below), except with matte blued finish and ambidextrous safety. Made from 1987 to date.

Browning Hi-Power 9mm Automatic Pistol
Same general specifications as FN Browning Model 1935 (see separate listing). DA or SA. 13-shot. Barrel: about 5 inches. 7¾ inches overall. Weight: 32 oz. Fixed sights; also available with rear sight adjustable for windage and elevation and ramp front sight. Standard Model, blued finish, checkered walnut or contour-molded stocks. Re-

Browning Hi-Power SA
w/Contour Molded Grips

Browning International Medalist

Browning 9mm Hi-Power
Standard Model
(Fixed Sights, Walnut Grips)

Browning Hi-Power 9mm Automatic Pistol (cont.)

naissance Engraved Model, chrome-plated, Nacrolac pearl
stocks. Made by FN from 1955 to date.

Standard Model, fixed sights	**$335**
Standard Model, adjustable sights	**375**
Renaissance Model, fixed sights	**725**
Renaissance Model, adjustable sights	**765**

Browning Hi-Power 40 S&W Auto Pistol $395

Similar to the standard 9mm Hi-Power, except in caliber
40 S&W with 10-shot magazine. 4⁵/₈-inch barrel. 7³/₄
inches overall. Weight: 35 oz. Matte blued finish. Molded
Polyamide grips. Made from 1993 to date.

Browning HP Practical

Browning HP Practical Hi-Power Automatic Pistol

Similar to the standard Hi-Power, except has silver-
chromed frame and blued slide with Commander-style
hammer. Made from 1991 to date.

With Fixed Sights	**$395**
With Adjustable Sights	**445**

Browning International Medalist Automatic
Target Pistol $575

Modification of Medalist to conform with International
Shooting Union rules; has 5.9-inch barrel, smaller grip,
no forearm. Weight: 42 oz. Made 1970–73.

**Browning Medalist
Renaissance Model**

**Browning Medalist
Standard Model**

Browning Medalist Automatic Target Pistol

Caliber: 22 LR. 10-shot magazine. 6³/₄-inch barrel w/vent
rib. 11¹⁵/₁₆ inches overall. Weight: 46 oz. Removable blade
front sight, click-adjustable micrometer rear. Standard
finish, blue; also furnished gold-inlaid (Gold Model) and
engraved and chrome-plated (Renaissance Model).
Checkered walnut stocks with thumbrest (for right- or
left-handed shooter); finely figured and carved stocks on
Gold and Renaissance Models. Made by FN 1962–1975;
higher grades introduced in 1971.

Standard Model	**$ 585**
Gold Model	**1200**
Renaissance Model	**1650**

Browning Nomad

Browning Nomad Automatic Pistol **$265**
Caliber: 22 LR. 10-shot magazine. Barrel lengths: 4¹/₂-
and 6³/₄-inch. 8¹⁵/₁₆ inches overall w/4¹/₂-inch bbl. Weight:
34 oz. (4¹/₂-inch bbl.). Removable blade front sight, screw
adjustable rear. Blued finish. Plastic stocks. Made by FN
1962–1974.

**Browning Renaissance 9mm, 25 Auto and 380
Auto (1955) Engraved Models, Cased Set** **$3595**
One pistol of each of the three models in a special walnut
carrying case; all chrome-plated with Nacrolac pearl
stocks. Made by FN 1955–1969.

BUDISCHOWSKY PISTOL
Mt. Clemens, Michigan
Mfd. by Norton Armament Corporation

Budischowsky TP-70

Budischowsky TP-70 Double Action Automatic Pistol
Calibers: 22 LR, 25 Auto. 6-shot magazine. 2.6-inch barrel.
4.65 inches overall. Weight: 12.3 oz. Fixed sights. Stainless
steel. Plastic stocks. Made 1973–77.
22 Long Rifle **$365**
25 Automatic **250**

CALICO LIGHT WEAPONS SYSTEMS
Bakersfield, California

Calico Model 110 Auto Pistol **$285**
Caliber: 22 LR. 100-shot magazine. 6-inch barrel. 17.9
inches overall. Weight: 3³/₄ lbs. Sights: adjustable post
front; fixed U-notch rear. Black finish aluminum frame.
Molded composition grip. Made 1986–1994.

Calico Model M-950 Auto Pistol **$395**
Caliber: 9mm Parabellum. 50- or 100-shot magazine. 7¹/₂-
inch barrel. 14 inches overall. Weight: 2¹/₄ lbs. Sights:
adjustable post front; fixed U-notch rear. Glass-filled
polymer grip. Made 1989–1994.

CHARTER ARMS CORPORATION
Stratford, Connecticut

AUTOMATIC PISTOLS

> **NOTE:** For ease in finding a particular Charter Arms hand-
> gun, the listings are divided into two groupings: Automatic
> Pistols (below) and Revolvers, which follows. For a complete
> listing of Charter Arms handguns, please refer to the Index.

Charter Arms Model 40 Automatic Pistol **$235**
Caliber: 22 RF. 8-shot magazine. 3.3-inch barrel. 6.3 inches
overall. Weight: 21¹/₂ oz. Fixed sights. Checkered walnut
grips. Stainless steel finish. Made 1985–86.

Charter Arms Model 79K Automatic Pistol **$295**
Calibers: 380 or 32 Auto. 7-shot magazine. 3.6-inch barrel.
6.5 inches overall. Weight: 24¹/₂ oz. Fixed sights. Checkered walnut grips. Stainless steel finish. Made 1985–86.

Charter Arms Explorer II

**Charter Arms Explorer II
Silvertone w/Optional Barrels**

Charter Arms Explorer II Semiauto Survival Pistol

Caliber: 22 RF. 8-shot magazine. 6-, 8- or 10-inch barrel. 13½ inches overall w/6-inch barrel. Weight: 28 oz. Finishes: black, heat cured, semigloss textured enamel or silvertone anticorrosion. Discontinued 1987.

Standard Model **$75**
Silvertone (w/optional 6- and 10-inch bbls.) **85**

REVOLVERS

NOTE: The following section contains only Charter Arms Revolvers. Pistols may be found in the preceding section. For a complete listing of Charter Arms handguns, please refer to the Index.

Charter Arms Bonnie

Charter Arms Clyde

Charter Arms Bonnie and Clyde Set **$395**

Matching pair of shrouded 2½-inch barrel revolvers, chambered for 32 Magnum and 38 Special. Blued finish with scrolled name on barrels.

Charter Arms Bulldog 44

Charter Arms Bulldog 44 Double Action Revolver

Caliber: 44 Special. 5-shot cylinder. 3-inch barrel. 7½ inches overall. Weight: 19 oz. Fixed sights. Blued or nickel-plated finish. Checkered walnut Bulldog or square butt-stocks. Made from 1973 to date.

Blued Finish/Pocket Hammer (2½″) **$190**
Blued Finish/Bulldog Grips (3″) **195**
Stainless Steel/Bulldog Grips **210**
Neoprene Grips/Pocket Hammer **205**

Charter Arms Bulldog 357

Charter Arms Bulldog 357 DA Revolver **$165**

Caliber: 357 Magnum. 5-shot cylinder. 6-inch barrel. 11 inches overall. Weight: 25 oz. Fixed sights. Blued finish. Square, checkered walnut grips. Intro. 1977; discontinued.

Charter Arms Bulldog New Police DA Revolver

Same general specifications as Bulldog Police, except chambered for 44 Special. 5-shot cylinder. 2½- or 3½-inch barrel. Made 1990–92.

Blued Finish **$180**
Stainless Finish (2½-inch barrel only) **220**

**Charter Arms Police Bulldog
Old Model**

**Charter Arms Police Bulldog
New Model**

**Charter Arms Police Bulldog
32 H&R Magnum**

Charter Arms Bulldog Police Double Action Revolver

Caliber: 38 Special or 32 H&R Magnum. 6-shot cylinder. 4-inch barrel. 8½ inches overall. Weight: 20½ oz. Adjustable rear sight, ramp front. Blued or stainless finish. Square checkered walnut grips. Made from 1976 to date. Shroud dropped on new model.

Blued Finish **$160**
Stainless Finish **195**
32 H&R Magnum (Discontinued 1992) **210**

Charter Arms Bulldog Pug

Charter Arms Bulldog Pug Double Action Revolver

Caliber: 44 Special. 5-shot cylinder. 2½-inch barrel. 7¼ inches overall. Weight: 20 oz. Blued or stainless finish. Fixed ramp front sight; fixed square-notch rear. Checkered neoprene or walnut grips. Made from 1988 to date.

Blued Finish **$195**
Stainless Finish **220**

Charter Arms Bulldog Target

Charter Arms Bulldog Target DA Revolver

Calibers: 357 Magnum, 44 Special (latter introduced in 1977). 4-inch barrel. 8½ inches overall. Weight: in 357, 20½ oz. Adjustable rear sight, ramp front. Blued finish. Square checkered walnut grips. Made 1976–1992.

Blued Finish **$180**
Stainless Steel **225**

Charter Arms Bulldog Tracker

Charter Arms Bulldog Tracker DA Revolver **$165**

Caliber: 357 Mag. 5-shot cylinder. 2½-, 4- or 6-inch barrel. 11 inches overall w/6-inch barrel. Weight: 21 oz., 2½-inch barrel. Adjustable rear sight, ramp front. Checkered walnut grips. Blued finish. 4- and 6-inch barrels discontinued 1986.

Charter Arms Off-Duty Double Action Revolver

Calibers: 22 LR or 38 Special. 6-shot (22 LR) or 5-shot (38 Spec.) cylinder. 2-inch barrel. 6¼ inches overall. Weight: 16 oz. Fixed rear sight, Patridge-type front sight. Plain walnut grips. Matte black, electroless nickel or stainless steel finish.

Matte Black Finish **$130**
Electroless Nickel **185**
Stainless Steel **175**

**Charter Arms Pathfinder
New Model**

**Charter Arms Pathfinder
Old Model**

**Charter Arms Pathfinder
Stainless**

**Charter Arms Undercover
32 S&W Long**

Charter Arms Pathfinder Double Action Revolver
Calibers: 22 LR, 22 WMR. 6-shot cylinder. Barrel lengths: 2-, 3-, 6-inch. 7$^1/_8$ inches overall w/3-inch barrel and regular stocks. Weight: 18$^1/_2$ oz. w/3-inch barrel. Adjustable rear sight, ramp front. Blued or stainless finish. Plain walnut regular, checkered Bulldog or square buttstocks. Made from 1970 to date. *Note:* Originally designated "Pocket Target," name was changed in 1971 to "Pathfinder." Grips changed in 1984. Disc. 1993.
Blued Finish **$145**
Stainless Finish **175**

Charter Arms Pitbull Double Action Revolver
Calibers: 9mm, 357 Magnum, 38 Special. 5-shot cylinder. 2$^1/_2$-, 3$^1/_2$- or 4-inch barrel. 7 inches overall w/2$^1/_2$-inch barrel. Weight: 21$^1/_2$ to 25 oz. All stainless steel frame. Fixed ramp front sight; fixed square-notch rear. Checkered neoprene grips. Blued or stainless finish. Made 1989–1993.
Blued Finish **$175**
Stainless Finish **195**

Charter Arms Undercover 32 H&R Mag./S&W L (cont.)
has 6-shot cylinder and 2$^1/_2$" barrel.
32 H&R Magnum (Blued) **$140**
32 H&R Magnum (Stainless) **180**
32 S&W Long (Blued) Disc. 1989 . . . . **125**

Charter Arms Undercover Pocket Police Double Action Revolver
Same general specifications as standard Undercover, except has 6-shot cylinder and pocket-type hammer. Blued or stainless steel finish.
Blued Finish **$150**
Stainless Steel **180**

**Charter Arms Undercover
Stainless**

**Charter Arms Undercover Police
38 Special**

**Charter Arms Undercover Police
32 H&R Magnum**

Charter Arms Undercover Double Action Revolver
Caliber: 38 Special. 5-shot cylinder. Barrel lengths: 2-, 3-, 4-inch. 6$^1/_4$ inches overall w/2-inch barrel and regular grips. Weight: 16 oz. w/2-inch barrel. Fixed sights. Plain walnut, checkered Bulldog or square buttstocks. Made 1965–1994.
Blued or Nickel-plated Finish **$155**
Stainless Finish **185**

Charter Arms Undercover 32 H&R Magnum or S&W Long
Same general specifications as standard Undercover, except chambered for 32 H&R Magnum or 32 S&W Long,

Charter Arms Undercover Police Double Action Revolver

Same general specifications as standard Undercover, except has 6-shot cylinder. (*See* photos, preceding page.)

Blued, 38 Special **$165**
Stainless, 38 Special **195**
32 H&R Magnum **160**

Charter Arms Undercoverette

Charter Arms Undercoverette DA Revolver **$135**

Same as Undercover model with 2-inch barrel, except caliber 32 S&W Long, 6-shot cylinder, blued finish only; weighs 16½ oz. Made 1972–1983.

COLT MANUFACTURING CO., INC.
Hartford, Connecticut

Previously Colt Industries, Firearms Division. Production of some Colt handguns spans the period from before World War II to the postwar years. Values shown for these models are for earlier production. Those manufactured c. 1946 and later generally are less desirable to collectors, and values are approximately 30 percent lower.

AUTOMATIC PISTOLS

NOTE: For ease in finding a particular firearm, Colt handguns are grouped into three sections: Automatic Pistols (below), Single Shot Pistols and Deringers (page 50), and Revolvers (page 51). For a complete listing, please refer to the Index.

Colt Model 1900 38 Automatic Pistol **$4500**

Caliber: 38 ACP (*modern high-velocity cartridges should not be used in this pistol*). 7-shot magazine. 6-inch barrel. 9 inches overall. Weight: 35 oz. Fixed sights. Blued finish. Plain walnut stocks. Sharp-spur hammer. Combination rear sight and safety. Made 1900–1903.

Colt Model 1902 Military 38 Automatic Pistol . . . **$1250**

Caliber: 38 ACP (*modern high-velocity cartridges should not be used in this pistol*). 8-shot magazine. 6-inch barrel. 9 inches overall. Weight: 37 oz. Fixed sights, knife-blade and V-notch. Blued finish. Checkered hard rubber stocks. Round back hammer, changed to spur type in 1908. No safety. Made 1902–1929.

Colt Model 1902 Military

Colt Model 1902 Sporting 38 Automatic Pistol . **$1395**

Caliber: 38 ACP (*modern high-velocity cartridges should not be used in this pistol*). 7-shot magazine. 6-inch barrel. 9 inches overall. Weight: 35 oz. Fixed sights, knife-blade and V-notch. Blued finish. Checkered hard rubber stocks. Round back hammer. No safety. Made 1902–1908.

Colt Model 1903 Pocket*

Colt Model 1903 Pocket 38 Automatic Pistol . . . **$475**

Caliber: 38 ACP (*modern high-velocity cartridges should not be used in this pistol*). Similar to Model 1902 Sporting 38, but with 4½-inch barrel. 7½ inches overall. Weight: 31 oz. Fixed sights, knife-blade and V-notch. Blued finish. Checkered hard rubber stocks. Round back hammer, changed to spur type in 1908. No safety. Made 1903–1929.

Colt Model 1905 Military*

Colt Model 1905 Military 45 Automatic Pistol ... **$750**
Caliber: 45 Automatic. 7-shot magazine. 5-inch barrel. 8 inches overall. Weight: 32¹/₂ oz. Fixed sights, knife-blade and V-notch. Blued finish. Checkered walnut stocks. Similar to Model 1902 38 Auto Pistol. Made 1905–1911.

Colt M1991 A1

Colt Model M1991 A1 Semiauto Pistol
Reissue of Model 1911A1 (*see* Government Model 45) with a continuation of the original serial number range from 1945. Caliber: 45 ACP. 7-shot magazine. 5-inch barrel. 8¹/₂ inches overall. Weight: 39 oz. Fixed blade front sight; square notch rear. Parkerized finish. Black composition stocks. Made from 1991 to date. (Commander and Compact variations introduced 1993).
Standard Model **$350**
Commander w/4¹/₂-inch bbl. 355
Compact w/3¹/₂-inch bbl. (6-shot) 360

Colt Ace Automatic

Colt All American Model 2000

Colt Ace Automatic Pistol **$795**
Caliber: 22 LR (regular or high speed). 10-shot magazine. Built on the same frame as the Government Model 45 Auto, with same safety features, etc. Hand-honed action, target barrel, adjustable rear sight. 4³/₄-inch barrel. 8¹/₄ inches overall. Weight: 38 oz. Made 1930–1940.

Colt All American Model 2000 DA Pistol **$375**
Caliber: 9mm Luger. 15-shot magazine. Semiautomatic. 4¹/₂-inch barrel. 7¹/₂ inches overall. Weight: 29 oz. Fixed blade front sight; square notch rear w/3-dot system. Blued slide with polymer receiver. Made 1992–94.

Colt Cadet 22

Colt Cadet 22 Automatic Pistol **$160**
Caliber: 22 LR. 11-shot magazine. 4¹/₂-inch vent-rib barrel. 8⁵/₈ inches overall. Weight: 48 oz. Sights: blade front; dovetailed rear. Stainless steel. Textured black polymer grips with Colt medallion. Made from 1993 to date.

Colt Challenger Automatic Pistol **$295**
Same basic design as Woodsman Target, Third Issue, but lacks some of the refinements. Fixed sights. Magazine catch on butt as in old Woodsman. Does not stay open on last shot. Lacks magazine safety. 4¹/₂- or 6-inch barrel. 9 to 10¹/₂ inches overall. Weight: 30 oz., 4¹/₂-inch bbl.; 31¹/₂ oz., 6-inch bbl. Blued finish. Checkered plastic stocks. Made 1950–55.

Colt Combat Commander

Colt Combat Commander Automatic Pistol **$425**
Same as Lightweight Commander, except has steel frame, available in blued, nickel-plated or stainless steel finish. Weighs 36 oz. Made from 1970 to date.

Colt Commander Lightweight

Colt Commander Lightweight Automatic Pistol . . $435
Same basic design as Government Model, but shorter and lighter in weight; receiver and mainspring housing are forged from a special lightweight metal, "Coltalloy." Calibers: 45 Auto, 38 Super Auto, 9mm Luger. 7-shot magazine in 45 cal., 9-shot in 38 Auto and 9mm Luger. 4 1/4-inch barrel. 8 inches overall. Weight: 26 1/2 oz. Fixed sights. Round spur hammer. Improved safety lock. Blued finish. Checkered plastic or walnut stocks. Made 1951 to date.

Colt Conversion Unit—22-45 . . . . $2000
Converts Service Ace 22 to National Match 45 Auto. Unit consists of match-grade slide assembly and barrel, bushing, recoil spring, recoil spring guide and plug, magazine and slide stop. Made 1938–1942.

Colt Conversion Unit—45-22 . . . . $295
Converts Government Model 45 Auto to a 22 LR target pistol. Unit consists of slide assembly, barrel, floating chamber (as in Service Ace), bushing, ejector, recoil spring, recoil spring guide and plug, magazine and slide stop. Made from 1938 to date. *Note:* Now designated "22 Conversion Unit," postwar model of this unit is also adaptable to the Super 38 pistols.

Colt Delta Elite Semiauto Pistol
Caliber: 10 mm. 5-inch barrel. 8 1/2 inches overall. 8-round cylinder. Weight: 38 oz., empty. Checkered rubber combat grips with Delta medallion. 3-dot, high-profile front and rear combat sights. Blued or stainless finish.
Blued Finish **$495**
Stainless Finish **615**

Colt Delta Gold Cup Stainless

Colt Delta Gold Cup Semiauto Pistol
Same general specifications as Delta Elite, except weighs 39 oz. with 6 3/4-inch sight radius. Adjustable rear sight. Made 1989 to date.
Blued Finish **$550**
Stainless Steel Finish **625**

Colt Gold Cup Mark III National Match $685
Similar to Gold Cup National Match 45 Auto, except chambered for 38 Special mid-range. 5-shot magazine. Made 1961–1974.

Colt Gold Cup National Match 45

Colt Gold Cup National Match 45 Auto $595
Match version of Government Model 45 Auto with same general specifications, except: match grade barrel with new design bushing, flat mainspring housing, long wide trigger with adjustable stop, hand-fitted slide with improved ejection port, adjustable rear sight, target front sight, checkered walnut grips with gold medallions. Weight: 37 oz. Made 1957–1970.

Colt Government Model 45 Commercial, M1911A1-Type

Colt Government Model 45 Automatic Pistol
U.S. Models 1911 and 1911A1. Caliber: 45 Auto. 7-shot magazine. 5-inch barrel. 8 1/2 inches overall. Weight: 39 oz. Fixed sights. Blued finish on Commercial Model, Parkerized or similar finish on most military pistols. Checkered walnut stocks (early production), plastic grips (later production). Checkered, arched mainspring housing and longer grip safety spur adopted in 1923 (on M1911A1). Made 1911–1970. Letter "C" precedes or follows serial number on Commercial Model 45s.
Note: During both World Wars, Colt licensed other firms to make these pistols under government contract: Ithaca Gun Co., North American Arms Co. Ltd. (Canada), Remington-Rand Co., Remington-UMC, Singer Sewing Machine Co., and Union Switch & Signal Co.; M1911 also produced at Springfield Armory.
U.S. Model 1911
Colt manufacture . . . . **$ 845**
North American manufacture **8500**
Remington-UMC manufacture **995**
Springfield manufacture **875**
Commercial Model M1911 Type **995**
U.S. Model 1911A1
Singer manufacture **9275**
Colt, Ithaca, Remington-Rand, Union Switch manufacture **610**
Commercial Model, M1911A1 Type **595**

Colt Huntsman

Colt Huntsman **$285**
Same specifications as the Challenger. Made 1955–1976.

Colt Match Target, Second Issue

Colt Match Target Auto Pistol, Second Issue . . . **$595**
Same basic design as Woodsman Target, Third Issue.
Caliber: 22 LR (reg. or high speed). 10-shot magazine. 6-inch flat-sided heavy barrel. 10^1/$_2$ inches overall. Weight:
40 oz. Click adjustable rear sight, ramp front. Blued finish.
Checkered plastic or walnut grips. Made 1948–1976.

Colt Match Target "4^1/$_2$" Automatic Pistol **$550**
Same as Match Target, 2nd Issue, except w/4^1/$_2$-inch bbl.
9 inches overall. Weight: 36 oz. Made 1950–1976.

**Colt MK II/Series '90 Double Eagle Combat
Commander** **$475**
Calibers: 40 S&W, 45 ACP. 7-shot magazine. 4^1/$_4$-inch
barrel. 7^3/$_4$ inches overall. Weight: 36 oz. Fixed blade front
sight; square notch rear. Checkered Xenoy® grips.
Stainless finish. Made from 1992 to date.

**Colt MKII/Series '90
Double Eagle 10mm**

Colt MK II/Series '90 Double Eagle DA Semiauto Pistol
Calibers: 38 Super, 9mm, 40 S&W, 10mm, 45 ACP. 7-shot

Colt MK II/Series '90 Double Eagle DA (cont.)
magazine. 5-inch barrel. 8^1/$_2$ inches overall. Weight: 39
oz. Fixed or Accro™ adjustable sights. Matte stainless
finish. Checkered Xenoy grips. Made from 1991 to date.
38 Super, 9mm, 40 S&W (Fixed Sights) **$450**
45 ACP (Adjustable Sights) **475**
45 ACP (Fixed Sights) **455**
10mm (Adjustable Sights) **470**
10mm (Fixed Sights) **450**

**Colt MK II/Series '90 Double Eagle Officer's
ACP** **$460**
Same general specifications as Double Eagle Combat
Commander, except chambered for 45 ACP only. 3^1/$_2$-inch
barrel. 7^1/$_4$ inches overall. Weight: 35 oz. Also available
in lightweight (25 oz.) with blued finish (same price).

Colt MK IV/Series '70 Combat Commander
Same general specifications as the Lightweight Commander, except made from 1970–1983.
Blued Finish **$355**
Nickel Finish **365**
Stainless **395**

**Colt MK IV/Series '70
Gold Cup National Match 45**

**Colt MK IV/Series '70
Government Model 45**

**Colt MK IV/Series '70 Gold Cup National
Match 45 Auto** **$595**
Match version of MK IV/Series '70 Government Model.

Colt MK IV/Series '70 Gold Cup National Match 45 Auto (cont.)

Caliber: 45 Auto only. Flat mainspring housing. Accurizor barrel and bushing. Solid rib, Colt-Elliason adj. rear sight, undercut front sight. Adj. trigger, target hammer. 8¾ inches overall. Weight: 38½ oz. Blued finish. Checkered walnut stocks. Made 1970–1984.

Colt MK IV/Series '70 Gov't. Auto Pistol $435

Calibers: 45 Auto, 38 Super Auto, 9mm Luger. 7-shot magazine in 45, 9-shot in 38 and 9mm. 5-inch barrel. 8⅜ inches overall. Weight: 38 oz., 45; 39 oz., 38 and 9mm. Fixed rear sight and ramp front sight. Blued or nickel-plated finish. Checkered walnut stocks. Made 1970–1984.

**Colt MK IV/Series '80
380 Govt., Bright Nickel**

Colt MK IV/Series '80 380 Automatic Pistol

Caliber: 380 ACP. 3.29-inch barrel. 6.15 inches overall. Weight: 21.8 oz. Composition grips. Fixed sights. Made from 1984 to date.

Blued Finish	$250
Bright Nickel	295
Satin Nickel	275
Stainless Finish	325
Pocketlite (Blued, 14.75 oz.)	305

**Colt MK IV/Series '80
Combat Commander**

Colt MK IV/Series '80 Combat Commander

Updated version of the MK IV/Series '70 with same general specifications. Blued or stainless steel with "pebbled" black neoprene wraparound grips.

Blued Finish	$405
Stainless Finish	460

Colt MK IV/Series '80 Combat Elite

Same general specifications as MK IV/Series '80 Combat Commander, except with Elite enhancements. Calibers: 38 Super, 40 S&W, 45 ACP. Stainless frame with blued steel slide. Accro™ adjustable sights and beavertail grip safety. Made from 1992 to date.

38 Super, 45 ACP	$495
40 S&W	485

**Colt MK IV/Series '80
Gold Cup National Match**

Colt MK IV/Series '80 Gold Cup National Match

Same general specifications as Match '70 version, except with additional finishes and "pebbled" wraparound neoprene grips.

Blued Finish	$525
Bright Blue Finish	575
Stainless Finish	585

**Colt MK IV/Series '80
Government Model, Blue**

Colt MK IV/Series '80 Government Model

Same general specifications as Government Model Series '70, except also chambered in 40 S&W, with "pebbled" wraparound neoprene grips; blue or stainless finish.

Blued Finish	$425
Bright Blue Finish	450
Bright Stainless Finish	510
Matte Stainless Finish	495

Colt MK IV/Series '80 Lightweight Commander . $475

Updated version of the MK IV/Series '70 with same general specifications.

Colt MK IV/Series '80 Mustang 380 Automatic

Caliber: 380 ACP. 5-round magazine. 2¾-inch barrel. 5.5 inches overall. Weight: 18½ oz. Black composition grips.

**Colt MK IV/Series '80
Mustang 380 Auto**

**Colt MK IV/Series '80
Officer's ACP, Satin Nickel**

Colt MK IV/Series '80 Mustang 380 Automatic (cont.)
Currently in production.

Blued Finish	**$275**
Nickel Finish	**305**
Stainless Finish	**295**

Colt MK IV/Series '80 Mustang Plus II
Caliber: 380 ACP. 7-round magazine. 2³/₄-inch barrel. 5.5 inches overall. Weight: 20 oz. Blued finish with checkered, black composition grips, full-length as the 380 Government Model. Made from 1988 to date.

Blued Finish	**$245**
Stainless Finish	**295**

Colt MK IV/Series '80 Officer's ACP (cont.)

Matte Finish	**$395**
Satin Nickel Finish	**415**
Stainless Steel	**435**

Colt National Match 45

Colt National Match Automatic Pistol
Identical with the Government Model 45 Auto, but with hand-honed action, match-grade barrel, adj. rear and ramp front sights or fixed sights. Made 1932–1940.

With adjustable sights	**$1425**
With fixed sights	**1195**

Colt NRA Centennial 45 Gold Cup National Match **$750**
2500 produced in 1971.

**Colt MK IV/Series '80
Mustang Pocketlite**

Colt MK IV/Series '80 Mustang Pocketlite
Same general specifications as the Mustang 380 Automatic, except weighs only 12¹/₂ oz. with aluminum alloy receiver. Blued or stainless finish. Optional wood grain grips. Made from 1988 to date.

Blued Finish	**$260**
Stainless Finish	**295**

Colt MK IV/Series '80 Officer's ACP Automatic Pistol
Calibers: 40 S&W and 45 ACP. 3⁵/₈-inch barrel. 7¹/₄ inches overall. Weight: 34 oz. Made from 1984 to date. 40 S&W discontinued 1992.

Colt Pocket 25 Automatic

Colt Pocket Model 25 (1908) Auto Pistol **$395**
Caliber: 25 Auto. 6-shot magazine. 2-inch barrel. 4¹/₂ inches overall. Weight: 13 oz. Flat-top front, square-notch rear sight in groove. Blued or nickel finish. Checkered hard rubber stocks on early models, checkered walnut on later type; special pearl stocks illustrated. Disconnector added in 1916 at pistol No. 141000. Made 1908–1941.

Colt Pocket 32 Automatic

Colt Service Model Ace*

Colt Pocket Model 32 (1903) Automatic Pistol
First Issue **$495**
Caliber: 32 Auto. 8-shot magazine. 4-inch barrel. 7 inches overall. Weight: 23 oz. Fixed sights. Blued finish. Checkered hard rubber stocks. Hammerless. Slide lock and grip safeties. Barrel-lock bushing similar to that on Government Model 45 Auto. Made 1903–1911.

Colt Pocket Model 32 Automatic Pistol
Second Issue **$440**
Same as First Issue but without barrel-lock bushing. Made 1911–1926.

Colt Pocket Model 32 Automatic Pistol
Third Issue **$375**
Caliber: 32 Auto. Similar to First and Second Issues, but has safety disconnector on all pistols above No. 468097 which prevents firing of cartridge in chamber if magazine is removed. 3³/₄-inch barrel. 6³/₄ inches overall. Weight: 24 oz. Fixed sights. Blued or nickel finish. Checkered walnut stocks. Made 1926–1945.

Colt Pocket Model 380 (1908) Automatic Pistol
Same as Pocket 32 Auto, First, Second and Third Issues, respectively, except chambered for caliber 380 Auto with 7-shot magazine.
First Issue (made 1908–1911) **$600**
Second Issue (made 1911–1926) **345**
Third Issue (Safety disconnector on all pistols
    above No. 92,894; made 1926–1945) **375**

Colt Pocket Junior

Colt Pocket Junior Model Automatic Pistol **$225**
Made in Spain by Unceta y Cia (Astra). Calibers: 22 Short, 25 Auto. 6-shot magazine. 2¹/₄-inch barrel. 4³/₄ inches overall. Weight: 12 oz. Fixed sights. Checkered walnut grips. Made 1958–1968.

Colt Service Model Ace Automatic Pistol **$1250**
Identical to National Match Model 45 Auto, except for caliber, magazine capacity and weight; has "floating chamber" amplifying recoil to four times that normal in

Colt Service Model Ace Automatic Pistol (cont.)
a 22. Caliber: 22 LR (reg. or high speed). 10-shot magazine. Weight: 42 oz. Made 1938–1942.

Colt Super 38

Colt Super 38 Automatic Pistol
Identical with Government Model 45 Auto, except for caliber and magazine capacity. Caliber: 38 Automatic. 9-shot magazine. Made 1928–1970.
Pre-war **$1225**
Post-war **550**

Colt Super Match 38 Automatic Pistol
Identical to Super 38 Auto, but with hand-honed action, match grade barrel, adjustable rear sight and ramp front sight or fixed sights. Made 1933–1940.
With Adjustable Sights **$1395**
With Fixed Sights **795**

Colt Targetsman

Colt Targetsman **$325**
Similar to Woodsman Target but has "economy" adj. rear sight, lacks automatic slide stop. Made 1959–1976.

**Colt Woodsman Match Target
First Issue**

**Colt Woodsman Target
First Issue**

**Colt Woodsman Match Target Automatic
Pistol, First Issue** **$725**
Same basic design as other Woodsman models. Caliber:
22 LR. 10-shot magazine. 6¹/₂-inch barrel, slightly tapered
with flat sides. 11 inches overall. Weight: 36 oz. Adjustable
rear sight. Blued finish. Checkered walnut one-piece stock
w/extended sides. Made 1938–1942.

**Colt Woodsman Target
Second Issue**

**Colt Woodsman Sport Model
First Issue**

**Colt Woodsman Target
Third Issue**

**Colt Woodsman Sport Model Automatic Pistol,
First Issue** **$495**
Caliber: 22 LR (reg. or high speed). Same as Woodsman
Target, Second Issue, except has 4¹/₂-inch barrel.
Adjustable rear sight; fixed or adjustable front sight.
Weight: 27 oz. 8¹/₂ inches overall. Made 1933–1948.

Colt Woodsman Target Model, First Issue (cont.)
sights. Blued finish. Checkered walnut stocks. Made 1915–
1932. *Note:* The mainspring housing of this model is not
strong enough to permit safe use of high-speed cartridges.
Change to a new heat-treated mainspring housing was
made at pistol No. 83,790. Many of the old models were
converted by installation of new housings. The new housing may be distinguished from the earlier type by the
checkering in the curve under the breech; new housing is
grooved straight across, while the old type bears a diag-
onally checkered oval.

**Colt Woodsman Sport Model
Second Issue**

**Colt Woodsman Target Model Automatic,
Second Issue** **$425**
Caliber: 22 LR (reg. or high speed). Same as original model,
except has heavier barrel and high-speed mainspring
housing. See note under Woodsman, First Issue. Weight:
29 oz. Made 1932–1948.

**Colt Woodsman Sport Model Automatic Pistol,
Second Issue** **$500**
Same as Woodsman Target, 3rd Issue, but with 4¹/₂-inch
barrel. 9 inches overall. Weight: 30 oz. Made 1948–1976.

**Colt Woodsman Target Model Automatic,
First Issue** **$495**
Caliber: 22 LR (reg. velocity). 10-shot magazine. 6¹/₂-inch
barrel. 10¹/₂ inches overall. Weight: 28 oz. Adjustable

**Colt Woodsman Target Model Automatic,
Third Issue** **$395**
Same basic design as previous Woodsman pistols, but with
longer grip, magazine catch on left side, larger thumb
safety, slide stop, slide stays open on last shot, magazine
disconnector, thumbrest stocks. Caliber: 22 LR (reg. or
high speed). 10-shot magazine. 6-inch barrel. 10¹/₂ inches
overall. Weight: 32 oz. Click adjustable rear sight, ramp
front sight. Blued finish. Checkered plastic or walnut
stocks. Made 1948–1976.

Colt WWI Commemorative
Deluxe Grade, Meuse Argonne

Colt WW II Commemorative
Pacific Theater

Colt World War II Commemorative 45 Auto (cont.)
engagements occurred during WW II, as well as specific
issue and theater identification. European model has oak
leaf motif on slide; palm leaf design frames the Pacific
issue. Cased. 11,500 of each model were produced. Made
in 1970. Value listed is for gun in new condition.

Colt WW I Commemorative
Standard, Second Battle of the Marne

SINGLE SHOT PISTOLS AND DERINGERS

> **NOTE:** For ease in finding a particular firearm, Colt handguns
> are grouped into three sections: Automatic Pistols (which
> precedes this one), this section, and Revolvers, which fol-
> lows. For a complete listing, please refer to the Index.

**Colt World War I 50th Anniversary Commemorative
Series 45 Auto**
Limited production replica of Model 1911 45 Auto engraved with battle scenes, commemorating Battles at
Chateau Thierry, Belleau Wood, Second Battle of the
Marne, Meuse Argonne. In special presentation display
cases. Production: 7,400 standard model, 75 deluxe, 25
special deluxe grade. Match numbered sets offered. Made
in 1967, 1968, 1969. Values indicated are for commemoratives in new condition.

Standard Grade	$ 595
Deluxe Grade	1350
Special Deluxe Grade	2600

Colt Camp Perry, First Issue

**Colt Camp Perry Model Single Shot Pistol,
First Issue** **$995**
Built on Officers' Model frame. Caliber: 22 LR (embedded
head chamber for high-speed cartridges after 1930). 10-
inch barrel. 13³/₄ inches overall. Weight: 34¹/₂ oz.
Adjustable target sights. Hand-finished action. Blued
finish. Checkered walnut stocks. Made 1926–1934.

Colt WW II Commemorative
European Theater

Colt Camp Perry, Second Issue

Colt World War II Commemorative 45 Auto **$695**
Limited production replica of Model 1911A1 45 Auto engraved with respective names of locations where historic

Colt Camp Perry Model, Second Issue **$915**
Same general specifications as First Issue, except has
shorter hammer fall and 8-inch barrel. 12 inches overall.
Weight: 34 oz. Made 1934–1941 (about 440 produced).

**Colt
Civil War Centennial
(Cased Pair)**

Colt Civil War Centennial Model Pistol

Single-shot replica, 7/8 scale, of Colt Model 1860 Army Revolver. Caliber: 22 Short. 6-inch barrel. Weight: 22 oz. Blued finish with gold-plated frame, grip frame, and trigger guard, walnut grips. Cased. 24,114 were produced. Made in 1961.

Single Pistol	**$150**
Pair with consecutive serial numbers	**350**

**Colt Deringer No. 4
(Cased Pair)**

Colt Deringer No. 4

Replica of Deringer No. 3 (1872). Single shot with side-swing barrel. Caliber: 22 Short. 2-1/2-inch barrel. 4-15/16 inches overall. Weight: 7-3/4 oz. Fixed sights. Gold-finished frame, blued barrel, walnut grips; also nickel-plated with simulated ivory grips. Cased. Made 1959–1963.

Single Pistol	**$125**
Pair with consecutive serial numbers	**250**

Colt Deringer No. 4 Commemorative Models

Limited production version of 22 Deringer issued, with appropriate inscription, to commemorate historical events.

1961 Issue
Geneseo, Illinois, 125th Anniversary
  (104 produced) **$600**

1962 Issue
Fort McPherson, Nebraska, Centennial
  (300 produced) **$300**

Colt Lord and Lady Deringers

Same as Deringer No. 4. Lord model is blued with gold-plated frame and walnut stocks. Lady model is gold-plated with simulated pearl stocks. Furnished in cased pairs. Made 1970–72.

Lord Deringer, pair in case	**$200**
Lady Deringer, pair in case	**200**
Lord and Lady Deringers, one each, in case	**200**

Colt Rock Island Arsenal Centennial Pistol **$250**

Limited production (550 pieces) version of Civil War Centennial Model single shot 22 pistol, made exclusively for Cherry's Sporting Goods, Geneseo, Illinois, to commemorate the centennial of the Rock Island Arsenal in Illinois. Cased. Made in 1962.

REVOLVERS

NOTE: This section of Colt handguns contains only revolvers. For automatic pistols or single shot pistols and deringers, please see the two sections that precede this. For a complete listing, please refer to the Index.

Colt Agent, First Issue

**Colt Agent,
Second Issue**

Colt Agent Double Action Revolver, First Issue . **$295**

Same as Cobra, First Issue, except has short-grip frame, 38 Special only, weighs 14 oz. Made 1962–1973.

Colt Agent DA Revolver, Second Issue **$250**

Same as Cobra, Second Issue, except has short service stocks, 6-5/8 inches overall, weighs 16 oz. Made 1973–1981.

Colt Anaconda

Colt Anaconda Double Action Revolver

Calibers: 44 Mag., 45 Colt. Barrel lengths: 4, 6 or 8 inches. 11-5/8 inches overall w/6-inch bbl. Weight: 53 oz. w/6-inch bbl. Adjustable white outline rear sight, red insert ramp-style front. Matte stainless finish. Black neoprene combat grips with finger grooves. Made from 1992 to date.

44 Magnum	**$415**
45 Colt (6-inch bbl. only)	**425**

Colt Army Special Double Action Revolver $395

41-caliber frame. Calibers: 32-20, 38 Special (41 Colt). 6-shot cylinder, right revolution. Barrel lengths: 4-, 4½-, 5- and 6-inch. 9¼ inches overall w/4-inch bbl. Weight: 32 oz. w/4-inch bbl. Fixed sights. Blued or nickel-plated finish. Hard rubber stocks. Made 1908–1927. *Note:* This model has a somewhat heavier frame than the New Navy, which it replaced. Serial numbers begin with 300,000. The heavy 38 Special High Velocity loads should not be used in 38 Special arms of this model.

Colt Bankers' Special

Colt Bankers' Special Double Action Revolver

This is the Police Positive with a 2-inch barrel, otherwise specifications same as that model; rounded butt introduced in 1933. Calibers: 22 LR (embedded head-cylinder for high speed cartridges introduced 1933), 38 New Police. 6½ inches overall. Weight: 23 oz. (22 LR); 19 oz. (38). Made 1926–1940.

38 Caliber **$525**
22 Caliber **995**

Colt Bisley

Colt Bisley Model Single Action Revolver

Variation of the Single Action Army, developed for target shooting; grips, trigger and hammer changed. Calibers: general specifications same as Single Action Army. Target Model made w/flat-topped frame and target sights. Made 1894–1915.

Standard Model **$3550**
Target Model **5950**

Colt Buntline Scout

Colt Buntline Scout $350

Same as Frontier Scout, except has 9½-inch barrel. Made from 1959–1971.

Colt Buntline Special

Colt Buntline Special 45 .... $695

Same as standard Single Action Army, except has 12-inch barrel, caliber 45 Long Colt. Made 1957–1975.

**Colt Cobra, Round Butt
First Issue**

Colt Cobra DA Revolver, Round Butt
First Issue $325

Lightweight Detective Special with same general specifications as that model, except with Colt-alloy frame. 2-inch barrel. Calibers: 38 Special, 38 New Police, 32 New Police. Weight: 15 oz., 38 cal. Blued finish. Checkered plastic or walnut stocks. Made 1951–1973.

Colt Cobra, Second Issue

Colt Cobra DA Revolver, Second Issue $270

Lightweight version of Detective Special, Second Issue; has aluminum alloy frame. 16½ oz. Made 1973–1981.

Colt Cobra DA Revolver Square Butt $285

Lightweight Police Positive Special with same general specifications, except has Colt-alloy frame. 4-inch barrel.

Colt Cobra DA Revolver Square Butt (cont.)

Calibers: 38 Special, 38 New Police, 32 New Police. Weight: 17 oz. in 38 caliber. Blued finish. Checkered plastic or walnut stocks. Made 1951–1973.

Colt Commando Special

Colt Commando Special DA Revolver $295

Caliber: 38 Special. 6-shot cylinder. 2-inch barrel; 6⅞ inches overall. Weight: 21½ oz. Fixed sights. Low-luster blue finish. Made 1982–86.

Colt Detective Special First Issue

Colt Detective Special, Second Issue

Colt Detective Special DA Revolver, First Issue $395

This is the Police Positive Special with 2-inch barrel, otherwise specifications same as that model; rounded butt intro. 1933. Originally supplied in 38 Special only; also made in calibers 32 New Police, 38 New Police. Weight: 17 oz. (38 cal.) 6¾ inches overall. Made 1926–1972.

Colt Detective Special DA Revolver, 2nd Issue

"D" frame, shrouded ejector rod. Caliber: 38 Special. 6-shot cylinder. 2-inch barrel. 6⅞ inches overall. Weight: 21½ oz. Fixed rear sight, ramp front. Blued or nickel-plated finish. Checkered walnut wraparound stocks. Made 1972–1984. Reintroduced in 1993 with checkered black composition grips.

Second Issue $295
Reissue 325

Colt Diamondback

Colt Diamondback Double Action Revolver $325

"D" frame, shrouded ejector rod. Calibers: 22 LR, 38 Special. 6-shot cylinder. Barrels: 2½-, 4-inch; vent rib. 9 inches overall w/4-inch bbl. Weight: w/4-inch bbl., 22 cal., 31¾ oz.; 38 cal., 28½ oz. Adjustable rear sight, ramp front. Blued or nickel finish. Checkered walnut stocks. Made 1966–1984.

Colt Double Action Army (Frontier)

Colt Double Action Army Revolver $1095

Also called Double Action Frontier. Similar in appearance to the smaller Lightning Model, but has heavier frame of different shape, round disc on left side of frame, lanyard loop in butt. Calibers: 38-40, 44-40, 45 Colt. 6-shot cylinder. Barrel lengths: 3½- and 4-inch without ejector; 4¾-, 5½- and 7½-inch with ejector. 12½ inches overall with 7½-inch bbl. Weight: 45 cal. with 7½-inch bbl., 39 oz. Fixed sights. Hard rubber bird'shead grips. Blued or nickel finish. Made 1878–1905.

Colt Frontier Scout Revolver

Single Action Army replica, ⅞ scale. Calibers: 22 Short, Long, LR; 22 WMR (interchangeable cylinder available.)

Colt Frontier Scout

**General Hood Centennial
1964 Issue**

Colt Frontier Scout Revolver (cont.)

6-shot cylinder. 4³/₄-inch barrel. 9¹⁵/₁₆ inches overall. Weight: 24 oz. Fixed sights. Plastic stocks. Originally made with bright alloy frame; since 1959 with steel frame, blued finish, also in all nickel finish with wood stocks. Made 1958–1971.

Blued Finish, plastic stocks	$295
Nickel Finish, wood stocks	315
Extra interchangeable cylinder	35

Colt Frontier Scout Revolver Commemorative Models

Limited production versions of Frontier Scout issued, with appropriate inscription, to commemorate historical events. Cased. *Note:* Values indicated are for commemoratives in new condition.

1961 Issues

Kansas Statehood Centennial (6201 produced)	$350
Pony Express Centennial (1007 produced)	460

1962 Issues

Columbus, Ohio, Sesquicentennial (200 produced)	$ 575
Fort Findlay, Ohio, Sesquicentennial (130 produced)	710
Fort Findlay Cased Pair, 22 Long Rifle and 22 Magnum (20 produced)	3170
New Mexico Golden Anniversary (1000 produced)	360
West Virginia Statehood Centennial (3452 produced)	345

**Montana Territory Centennial
1964 Issue**

**New Jersey Tercentenary
1964 Issue**

**Idaho Territorial Centennial
1963 Issue**

1963 Issues

Arizona Territorial Centennial (5355 produced)	$345
Battle of Gettysburg Centennial (1019 produced)	345
Carolina Charter Tercentenary (300 produced)	425
Fort Stephenson, Ohio, Sesquicentennial (200 produced)	575
General John Hunt Morgan Indiana Raid (100 produced)	675
Idaho Territorial Centennial (902 produced)	350

1964 Issues

California Gold Rush (500 produced)	$350
Chamizal Treaty (450 produced)	410
General Hood Centennial (1503 produced)	345
Montana Territorial Centennial (2300 produced)	350
Nevada "Battle Born" (981 produced)	350
Nevada Statehood Centennial (3984 produced)	350
New Jersey Tercentenary (1001 produced)	350
St. Louis Bicentennial (802 produced)	365
Wyoming Diamond Jubilee (2357 produced)	350

Colt Frontier Scout Commemoratives (cont.)

1965 Issues

Appomattox Centennial (1001 produced) **$350**
Forty-Niner Miner (500 produced) 350
General Meade Campaign (1197 produced) 350
Kansas Cowtown Series—Wichita
  (500 produced) 350
Old Fort Des Moines Reconstruction
  (700 produced) 375
Oregon Trail (1995 produced) 350
St. Augustine Quadricentennial (500 produced) . . . 375

**Indiana Sesquicentennial
1966 Issue**

1966 Issues

Colorado Gold Rush (1350 produced) **$350**
Dakota Territory (1000 produced) 350
Indiana Sesquicentennial (1500 produced) 350
Kansas Cowtown Series—Abilene
  (500 produced) 365
Kansas Cowtown Series—Dodge City
  (500 produced) 350
Oklahoma Territory (1343 produced) 350

1967 Issues

Alamo (4500 produced) **$350**
Kansas Cowtown Series—Coffeyville
  (500 produced) 365
Kansas Trail Series—Chisholm Trail
  (500 produced) 365
Lawman Series—Bat Masterson
  (3000 produced) 385

1968 Issues

Kansas Trail Series—Santa Fe Trail
  (501 produced) **$350**
Kansas Trail Series—Pawnee Trail
  (501 produced) 350
Lawman Series—Pat Garrett (3000 produced) . . . 385
Nebraska Centennial (7001 produced) 350

1969 Issues

Alabama Sesquicentennial (3001 produced) **$350**
Arkansas Territory Sesquicentennial
  (3500 produced) 350
California Bicentennial (5000 produced) 325
General Nathan Bedford Forrest
  (3000 produced) 365
Golden Spike (11,000 produced) 325
Kansas Trail Series—Shawnee Trail
  (501 produced) 365
Lawman Series—Wild Bill Hickock
  (3000 produced) 375

Colt Frontier Scout Commoratives (cont.)

**Golden Spike Centennial
1969 Issue**

1970 Issues

Kansas Fort Series—Fort Larned
  (500 produced) **$350**
Kansas Fort Series—Fort Hays (500 produced) . . 350
Kansas Fort Series—Fort Riley (500 produced) . . 350
Lawman Series—Wyatt Earp (3000 produced) . . . 425
Maine Sesquicentennial (3000 produced) 330
Missouri Sesquicentennial (3000 produced) 350

1971 Issues

Kansas Fort Series—Fort Scott (500 produced) . . **$365**

1972 Issues

Florida Territory Sesquicentennial
  (2001 produced) **$350**

1973 Issues

Arizona Ranger (3001 produced) **$325**

Colt King Cobra Revolver

Colt King Cobra Revolver
Caliber: 357 Mag. Barrel lengths: 2½-, 4-, 6- or 8-inch. 9
inches overall w/4-inch barrel. Weight: 42 oz., average.

Colt King Cobra Revolver (cont.)

Matte stainless steel finish. Black neoprene combat grips. Made from 1986 to date. 2½-inch barrel, and "Ultimate" bright or blued finish made 1988–1992.

Matte Stainless **$325**
Ultimate Bright Stainless **350**
Blued **295**

Colt Lawman MK III

Colt Lawman MK III Double Action Revolver **$200**

"J" frame, shrouded ejector rod on 2-inch barrel only. Caliber: 357 Magnum. 6-shot cylinder. Barrel lengths: 2-, 4-inch. 9⅜ inches overall with 4-inch barrel. Weight: with 4-inch bbl., 35 oz. Fixed rear sight, ramp front. Service trigger and hammer or target trigger and wide-spur hammer. Blued or nickel-plated finish. Checkered walnut service or target stocks. Made 1969–1982.

Colt Lawman MK V

Colt Metropolitan MK III

Colt Lawman MK V DA Revolver **$225**

Similar to Trooper MK V. Caliber: 357 Mag. 6-shot cylinder. 2- or 4-inch barrel; 9⅜ inches overall w/4-inch barrel. Weight: 35 oz. w/4-inch barrel. Fixed sights. Checkered walnut grips. Made 1983–85.

Colt Marine Corps Model (1905) DA Revolver . . . **$1425**

General specifications same as New Navy, Second Issue, except this has round butt, was supplied only in 38 caliber (38 Short & Long Colt, 38 Special) with 6-inch barrel. Made 1905–1909.

Colt Metropolitan MK III DA Revolver **$195**

Same as Official Police MK III, except has 4-inch barrel, service or target stocks; weighs 36 oz. Made 1969–1972.

Colt New Double Action (Lightning)

Colt New Double Action Central Fire Revolver **$995**

Also called Lightning Model. Calibers: 38 and 41 Centerfire. 6-shot cylinder. Barrel lengths: 2½-, 3½-, 4½- and 6-inch without ejector, 4½- and 6-inch w/ejector. 8½ inches overall w/3½-inch barrel. Weight: 38 cal. w/3½-inch bbl., 23 oz. Fixed sights. Blued or nickel finish. Hard rubber bird'shead grips. Made 1877–1909.

Colt New Frontier Buntline Special

Colt New Frontier Buntline Special **$650**

Same as New Frontier Single Action Army, except has 12-inch barrel. Made 1962–66.

Colt New Frontier Single Action Army

Colt New Frontier Single Action Army Revolver . . . **$595**

Same as Single Action Army, except has flat-top frame, adjustable target rear sight, ramp front sight, smooth walnut grips. 5½- or 7½-inch barrel. Calibers: 357 Magnum, 44 Special, 45 Colt. Made 1961–1986.

Colt New Frontier 22

Colt New Frontier Single Action 22 Revolver **$260**

Same as Peacemaker 22, except has flat-top frame, adjustable rear sight, ramp front sight. Made 1971–76.

Colt New Navy

Colt New Navy Double Action Revolver
First Issue **$875**

Also called New Army. Calibers: 38 Short & Long Colt, 41 Short & Long Colt. 6-shot cylinder, left revolution. Barrel lengths: 3-, 4½- and 6-inch. 11¼ inches overall w/6-inch bbl. Weight: 32 oz., 6-inch bbl. Fixed sights, knife-blade and V-notch. Blued or nickel-plated finish. Walnut or hard rubber grips. Made 1889–1894. *Note:* This model, which was adopted by both the Army and Navy, was Colt's first revolver of the solid frame, swing-out cylinder type. It lacks the cylinder-locking notches found on later models made on this 41 frame; ratchet on the back of the cylinder is held in place by a double projection on the hand.

Colt New Navy Double Action Revolver
Second Issue **$695**

Also called New Army. General specifications same as First Issue, except has double cylinder notches and double locking bolt. Calibers: 38 Special added in 1904 and 32-20 in 1905. Made 1892–1907. *Note:* The heavy 38 Special High Velocity loads should not be used in 38 Special arms of this model.

Colt New Pocket Double Action Revolver **$325**

Caliber: 32 Short & Long Colt. 6-shot cylinder. Barrel lengths: 2½-, 3½- and 6-inch. 7½ inches overall with 3½-inch barrel. Weight: 16 oz., 3½-inch bbl. Fixed sights, knife-blade and V-notch. Blued or nickel finish. Rubber stocks. Made 1893–1905.

Colt New Pocket

Colt New Police Double Action Revolver **$260**

Built on New Pocket frame, but with larger grip. Calibers: 32 Colt New Police, 32 Short & Long Colt. Barrel lengths: 2½-, 4- and 6-inch. 8½ inches overall w/4-inch barrel. Weight: 17 oz., 4-inch bbl. Fixed sights: knife-blade, V-notch. Blued or nickel finish. Rubber stocks. Made 1896–1905.

Colt New Police Target DA Revolver **$450**

Target version of the New Police with same general specifications. Target sights. 6-inch barrel. Blued finish only. Made 1896–1905.

Colt New Service

Colt New Service Double Action Revolver

Calibers: 38 Special, 357 Magnum (intro. 1936), 38-40, 44-40, 44 Russian, 44 Special, 45 Auto, 45 Colt, 450 Eley, 455 Eley, 476 Eley. 6-shot cylinder. Barrel lengths: 4-, 5- and 6-inch in 38 Special and 357 Magnum; 4½-, 5½- and 7½-inch in other calibers. 9¾ inches overall w/4½-inch bbl. Weight: 39 oz., 45 cal. w/4½-inch bbl. Fixed sights. Blued or nickel finish. Checkered walnut stocks. Made 1898–1942. *Note:* More than 500,000 of this model in caliber 45 Auto (designated "Model 1917 Revolver") were purchased by the U.S. Gov't. during WW I. These arms were later sold as surplus to National Rifle Association members through the Director of Civilian Marksmanship. Price was $16.15 plus packing charge. Supply exhausted during the early 1930s.

Commercial Model **$625**
Magnum **675**
1917 Army **795**

Colt New Service Target **$995**

Target version of the New Service; general specifications same as that model. Calibers: originally chambered for 44 Russian, 450 Eley, 455 Eley and 476 Eley; later models in 44 Special, 45 Colt and 45 Auto. Barrel lengths: 6- and

Colt New Service Target

Colt New Service Target (cont.)

7½-inch. 12¾ inches overall with 7½-inch bbl. Adjustable target sights. Hand-finished action. Blued finish. Checkered walnut stocks. Made 1900–1940.

Colt Officers' Model Match

Colt Officers' Model Match $395

Same general design as Officers' Model revolvers. Has tapered heavy barrel, wide hammer spur, Accro™ rear sight, ramp front sight, large target stocks of checkered walnut. Calibers: 22 LR, 38 Special. 6-inch barrel. 11¼ inches overall. Weight: 43 oz., 22 cal.; 39 oz., 38 cal. Blued finish. Made 1953–1970.

Colt Officers' Model Special $495

Target arm replacing Officers' Model, Second Issue; basically the same as that model, but with heavier, non-tapered barrel, redesigned hammer, ramp front sight and "Coltmaster" rear sight adj. for windage and elevation. Calibers: 22 LR, 38 Special. 6-inch barrel. 11¼ inches overall. Weight: 39 oz., 38 cal.; 43 oz., 22 cal. Blued finish. Checkered plastic stocks. Made 1949–1953.

Colt Officers' Model Target DA Revolver, First Issue $995

Caliber: 38 Special. 6-inch barrel. Hand-finished action. Adjustable target sights. Checkered walnut stocks. General specifications same as New Navy, Second Issue. Made 1904–1908.

Colt Officers' Model Target Second Issue

Colt Officers' Model Target, Second Issue $800

Calibers: 22 LR (intro. 1930, embedded head-cylinder for high-speed cartridges after 1932), 32 Police Positive (made 1932–1942), 38 Special. 6-shot cylinder. Barrel lengths: 4-, 4½-, 5-, 6- and 7½-inch in 38 Special; 6-inch only in 22 LR and 32 PP. 11¼ inches overall w/6-inch bbl. (38 Special). Adjustable target sights. Blued finish. Checkered walnut stocks. Hand-finished action. General features same as Army Special and Official Police of same date. Made 1908–1949 (with exceptions noted).

Colt Official Police

Colt Official Police Double Action Revolver

Calibers: 22 LR (intro. 1930, embedded head-cylinder for high-speed cartridges after 1932), 32-20 (discontinued 1942), 38 Special, 41 Long Colt (discontinued 1930). 6-shot cylinder. Barrel lengths: 4-, 5-, and 6-inch; 2-inch and 6-inch heavy barrel in 38 Special only, 22 LR w/4- and 6-inch barrels only. 11¼ inches overall. Weight: 36 oz. w/standard 6-inch bbl. in 38 Special. Fixed sights. Blued or nickel-plated finish. Checkered walnut stocks on all revolvers of this model, except some of postwar production had checkered plastic stocks. Made 1927–1969. *Note:* This model is a refined version of the Army Special, which it replaced in 1928 at about serial number 520,000. The Commando 38 Special was a wartime adaptation of the Official Police made to Government specifications. Commando can be identified by its sandblasted blued finish; serial numbers start with number 1 (1942).
Commercial Model $365
Commando Model 310

Colt Official Police MK III

Colt Official Police MK III DA Revolver $170

"J" frame, without shrouded ejector rod. Caliber: 38 Special. 6-shot cylinder. Barrel lengths: 4-, 5-, 6-inch. 9¼ inches overall with 4-inch bbl. Weight: 34 oz. w/4-inch bbl. Fixed rear sight, ramp front. Service trigger and

Colt Official Police MK III DA Revolver (cont.)

hammer or target trigger and wide-spur hammer. Blued or nickel-plated finish. Checkered walnut service stocks. Made 1969–1975.

Colt Peacekeeper

Colt Peacekeeper Double Action Revolver $265

Caliber: 357 Mag. 6-shot cylinder. 4- and 6-inch barrels; 11⅛ inches overall with 6-inch barrel. Weight: 46 oz. with 6-inch barrel. Adjustable white outline rear sight; red insert ramp-style front. Non-reflective matte blued finish. Made 1985–89.

**Colt Peacemaker 22
Second Amendment Commemorative**

Colt Peacemaker 22 Second Amendment Commemorative $350

Peacemaker 22 Single Action Revolver with 7½-inch barrel. Nickel-plated frame, barrel, ejector rod assembly, hammer and trigger; blued cylinder, backstrap and trigger guard. Black pearlite stocks. Barrel inscribed "The Right to Keep and Bear Arms." Presentation case. Limited edition of 3000 issued in 1977. Value is for revolver in new condition.

Colt Peacemaker 22

Colt Peacemaker 22 Single Action Revolver $250

Calibers: 22 LR and 22 WMR. Furnished with cylinder for each caliber. 6-shot. Barrel: 4⅜-, 6- or 7½-inch. 11¼ inches overall w/6-inch bbl. Weight: 30½ oz. w/6-inch bbl. Fixed sights. Black composite stocks. Made 1971–76.

Colt Pocket Positive

Colt Pocket Positive Double Action Revolver . . . $350

General specifications same as New Pocket, except this model has positive lock feature (see Police Positive). Calibers: 32 Short & Long Colt (discontinued 1914), 32 Colt New Police (32 S&W Short & Long). Fixed sights, flat top and square notch. Made 1905–1940.

Colt Police Positive, First Issue

Colt Police Positive Double Action Revolver, First Issue $340

Improved version of the New Police with the "Positive Lock," which prevents the firing pin from coming in contact with the cartridge except when the trigger is pulled. Calibers: 32 Short & Long Colt (discontinued 1915), 32 Colt New Police (32 S&W Short & Long), 38 New Police (38 S&W). 6-shot cylinder. Barrel lengths: 2½- (32 cal. only), 4-, 5- and 6-inch. 8½ inches overall w/4-inch bbl. Weight: 20 oz. w/4-inch bbl. Fixed sights. Blued or nickel finish. Rubber or checkered walnut stocks. Made 1905–1947.

Colt Police Positive, Second Issue

Colt Police Positive Double Action Revolver, Second Issue $205

Same as Detective Special, Second Issue, except has 4-inch barrel, is 9 inches overall, weighs 26½ oz. Introduced in 1977. *Note:* Original Police Positive (First Issue) has a shorter frame, is not chambered for 38 Special.

Colt Police Positive Special

Colt Police Positive Special DA Revolver $315
Based on the Police Positive with frame lengthened to permit longer cylinder. Calibers: 32-20 (discontinued 1942), 38 Special, 32 New Police and 38 New Police (introduced 1946). 6-shot cylinder. Barrel lengths: 4- (only length in current production), 5- and 6-inch. 8¾ inches overall w/4-inch bbl. Weight: 23 oz. (38 Special) w/4-inch bbl. Fixed sights. Checkered stocks of hard rubber, plastic or walnut. Made 1907–1973.

Colt Police Positive Target

Colt Police Positive Target DA Revolver $595
Target version of the Police Positive. Calibers: 22 LR (introduced 1910, embedded head-cylinder for high-speed cartridges after 1932), 22 WRF (intro. 1910, disc. 1935), 32 Short & Long Colt (disc. 1915), 32 New Police (32 S&W Short & Long). 6-inch barrel. Blued finish only. 10½ inches overall. Weight: 26 oz. in 22 cal. Adjustable target sights. Checkered walnut stocks. Made 1905–1940.

Colt Python—Early Model

Colt Python Double Action Revolver
"I" frame, shrouded ejector rod. Calibers: 357 Magnum, 38 Special. 6-shot cylinder. Barrels: 2½-, 4-, 6-, 8-inch; vent rib. 11¼ inches overall w/6-inch bbl. Weight: 44 oz. w/6-inch bbl. Adjustable rear sight, ramp front. Blued, nickel-plated or stainless finish. Checkered walnut target

Colt Python Ultimate Stainless

Colt Python Double Action Revolver (cont.)
stocks. Made from 1955 to date. Ultimate stainless finish made from 1985 to date.

Blued Finish	**$395**
Royal Blue Finish	**445**
Nickel Finish	**375**
Stainless Finish	**525**

Colt Sheriff's Model 45
Limited edition of replica of Storekeeper's Model in caliber 45 Colt, made exclusively for Centennial Arms Corp., Chicago, Illinois. Numbered from "1SM." Blued finish with casehardened frame or nickel-plated. Walnut stocks. 478 were produced in blue, 25 in nickel. Made in 1961.

Blued Finish	**$1650**
Nickel Finish	**4250**

Colt Shooting Master

Colt Shooting Master Double Action Revolver .. $795
Deluxe target arm based on the New Service model. Calibers: originally made only in 38 Special; 44 Special, 45 Auto and 45 Colt added in 1933, 357 Magnum in 1936. 6-inch barrel. 11¼ inches overall. Weight: 44 oz., 38 cal. Adj. target sights. Hand-finished action. Blued finish. Checkered walnut stocks. Rounded butt. Made 1932–1941.

Colt Single Action Army Revolver
Also called Frontier Six-Shooter and Peacemaker. Calibers: 22 Rimfire (Short, Long, LR), 22 WRF, 32 Rimfire, 32 Colt, 32 S&W, 32-20, 38 Colt, 38 S&W, 38 Special, 357 Magnum, 38-40, 41 Colt, 44 Rimfire, 44 Russian, 44 Special, 44-40, 45 Colt, 45 Auto, 450 Boxer, 450 Eley, 455 Eley, 476 Eley. 6-shot cylinder. Barrel lengths: 4¾, 5½ and 7½ inches with ejector; 3 and 4 inches w/o ejector. 10¼ inches overall w/4¾-inch barrel. Weight: 36 oz., 45 cal. w/4¾-inch barrel. Fixed sights. Also made in Target Model with flat top-strap and target sights. Blued finish with casehardened frame or nickel-plated. One-piece smooth walnut or checkered black rubber stocks.
  S.A. Army Revolvers with serial numbers above 165,000 (circa 1896) are adapted to smokeless powder; cylinder

Colt Single Action Army

Colt Single Action Army Revolver (cont.)

pin screw was changed to spring catch at about the same time. Made 1873–1942; production resumed in 1955 with serial number 1001SA. Current calibers: 357 Magnum, 44 Special, 45 Long Colt.

Frontier Six-Shooter, 44-40	**$2895**
Storekeeper's Model, 3-inch/4-inch bbl., w/o ejector	**2850**
Target Model, flat top-strap, target sights	**8500**
U.S. Artillery Model, 45 Colt, 5½-inch bbl.	**5995**
U.S. Cavalry Model, 45, 7½-inch bbl.	**7500**

(Above values apply only to original models, not to similar S.A.A. revolvers of recent manufacture.)

Standard Model, pre-1942	**$1495**
Standard Model (1955–1982)	**595**
Standard Model (Reissued 1992)	**795**

Colt Single Action Army—125th Anniversary . . . **$850**

Limited production deluxe version of Single Action Army issued in commemoration of Colt's 125th Anniversary. Caliber: 45 Long Colt. 7½-inch barrel. Gold-plated frame, trigger, hammer, cylinder pin, ejector rod tip, and stock medallion. Presentation case with anniversary medallion. Serial numbers from "50AM." 7368 were made in 1961.

Colt Single Action Army Commemorative Models

Limited production versions of Single Action Army 45 issued, with appropriate inscription to commemorate historical events. Cased. *Note:* Values indicated are for commemorative revolvers in new condition.

1963 Issues

Arizona Territorial Centennial (1280 produced)	**$995**
West Virginia Statehood Centennial (600 produced)	**950**

1964 Issues

Chamizal Treaty (50 produced)	**$1250**
Colonel Sam Colt Sesquicentennial Presentation (4750 produced)	**950**
Deluxe Presentation (200 produced)	**1995**
Special Deluxe Presentation (50 produced)	**3000**
Montana Territorial Centennial (851 produced)	**995**
Nevada "Battle Born" (100 produced)	**1200**
Nevada Statehood Centennial (1877 produced)	**950**
New Jersey Tercentenary (250 produced)	**995**
Pony Express Presentation (1004 produced)	**1100**
St. Louis Bicentennial (450 produced)	**950**
Wyatt Earp Buntline (150 produced)	**1925**

1965 Issues

Appomattox Centennial (500 produced)	**$950**
Old Fort Des Moines Reconstruction (200 produced)	**995**

Colt Single Action Army Commemoratives (cont.)

1966 Issues

Abercrombie & Fitch Trailblazer—Chicago (100 produced)	**$ 995**
Abercrombie & Fitch Trailblazer—New York (200 produced)	**995**
Abercrombie & Fitch Trailblazer—San Francisco (100 produced)	**995**
California Gold Rush (130 produced)	**1200**
General Meade (200 produced)	**950**
Pony Express Four Square (4 guns)	**4500**

1967 Issues

Alamo (1000 produced)	**$ 950**
Lawman Series—Bat Masterson (500 produced)	**1225**

1968 Issues

Lawman Series—Pat Garrett (500 produced) . . .	**$1025**

1969 Issues

Lawman Series—Wild Bill Hickok (500 produced)	**$995**

1970 Issues

Lawman Series—Wyatt Earp (501 produced) . . .	**$1695**
Missouri Sesquicentennial (501 produced)	**895**
Texas Ranger (1000 produced)	**2000**

1971 Issues

NRA Centennial, 357 or 45 (5001 produced)	**$910**

**Peacemaker Centennial 45
1975 Issue**

**Peacemaker Centennial 44-40
1975 Issue**

1975 Issues

Peacemaker Centennial 45 (1501 produced)	**$ 995**
Peacemaker Centennial 44-40 (1501 produced)	**1000**
Peacemaker Centennial Cased Pair (501 produced)	**2000**

1979 Issues

Ned Buntline 45 (3000 produced)	**$895**

Colt Three-Fifty-Seven Double Action Revolver

Heavy frame. Caliber: 357 Magnum. 6-shot cylinder. 4- or 6-inch barrel. Quick-draw ramp front sight, Accro™ rear sight. Blued finish. Checkered walnut stocks. 9¼ or 11¼ inches overall. Weight: 36 oz., 4-inch bbl.; 39 oz., 6-inch bbl. Made 1953–1961.

With standard hammer and service stocks **$325**
With wide-spur hammer and target stocks **375**

Colt Trooper

Colt Trooper Double Action Revolver

Same specifications as Officers' Model Match, except has 4-inch barrel with quick-draw ramp front sight, weighs 34 oz. in 38 caliber. Made 1953–1969.

With standard hammer and service stocks **$275**
With wide-spur hammer and target stocks **315**

Colt Trooper MK III

Colt Trooper MK V

Colt Trooper MK III Double Action Revolver **$225**

"J" frame, shrouded ejector rod. Calibers: 22 LR, 22 Magnum, 38 Special, 357 Magnum. 6-shot cylinder. Barrel lengths: 4-, 6-inch. 9½ inches overall w/4-inch bbl. Weight: 39 oz. w/4-inch bbl. Adjustable rear sight, ramp front. Target trigger and hammer. Blued or nickel-plated finish. Checkered walnut target stocks. Made 1969–1978.

Colt Trooper MK IV Double Action Revolver **$265**

Same general specifications as Trooper MK III with action modifications. Introduced in 1978; discontinued.

Colt Trooper MK V Revolver **$260**

Re-engineered Mark III for smoother, faster action. Caliber: 357 Magnum. 6-shot cylinder. Barrel lengths: 4-, 6-, 8-inch w/vent rib. Adjustable rear sight, ramp front, red insert. Checkered walnut stocks. Made 1982–86.

Colt U.S. Bicentennial Commemorative Set

Colt U.S. Bicentennial Commemorative Set **$2100**

Replica Colt 3rd Model Dragoon Revolver with accessories, Colt Single Action Army Revolver, and Colt Python Revolver. Matching roll-engraved unfluted cylinders, blued finish, and rosewood stocks with Great Seal of the United States silver medallion. Dragoon revolver has silver grip frame. Serial numbers 0001 to 1776; all revolvers in set have same number. Deluxe drawer-style presentation case of walnut, with book compartment containing a reproduction of "Armsmear." Issued in 1976. Value is for revolvers in new condition.

Colt Viper Double Action Revolver **$245**

Same as Cobra, Second Issue, except has 4-inch barrel, is 9 inches overall, weighs 20 oz. Made 1977–1984.

Colt Viper

**CZ Model 27
Automatic Pistol**

**CZ Model 38 DA
Automatic Pistol**

COONAN ARMS, INC.
St. Paul, Minnesota

Coonan Arms Model 357

CZ Model 27 Auto Pistol **$395**
Caliber: 32 Automatic (7.65mm). 8-shot magazine. 4-inch
barrel. 6 inches overall. Weight: 23½ oz. Fixed sights.
Blued finish. Plastic stocks. Made 1927–1951.

CZ Model 38 Double Action Auto Pistol **$375**
Caliber: 380 Automatic (9mm). 9-shot magazine. 3¾-inch
barrel. 7 inches overall. Weight: 26 oz. Fixed sights. Blued
finish. Plastic stocks. Made 1939–1945.

Coonan Arms Model 357 Magnum Auto Pistol
Caliber: 357 Mag. 7-round magazine. 5- or 6-inch barrel.
8.3 inches overall (w/5-inch bbl.). Weight: 42 oz. Front
ramp interchangeable sight; fixed rear sight, adjustable
for windage. Black walnut grips.
Competition Grade **$810**
Standard Grade w/5-inch Barrel 550
Standard Grade w/6-inch Barrel 575

Coonan Arms 357 Magnum Cadet Compact **$550**
Similar to the standard 357 Magnum Model, except with
3.9-inch barrel. 6-shot magazine and compact frame.
Weight: 39 oz. 7.8 inches overall. Made from 1993 to date.

CZ Model 1945 Pocket Auto

CZ Model 1945 DA Pocket Auto Pistol **$195**
Caliber: 25 Auto (6.35mm). 8-shot magazine. 2½-inch
barrel. 5 inches overall. Weight: 15 oz. Fixed sights. Blued
finish. Plastic stocks. Introduced 1945; discontinued.

CZ PISTOLS
Strakonice, Czechoslovakia
Mfd. by Ceska Zbrojovka-Nardoni Podnik
(formerly Böhmische Waffenfabrik A. G.)

After the German occupation, March 1939, Models 27 and
38 were marked with manufacturer code "fnh." Designation
of Model 38 was changed to "Pistole 39(t)."

CZ Duo Pocket Auto

CZ Duo Pocket Auto Pistol $195
Caliber: 25 Automatic (6.35mm). 6-shot magazine. 2¹/₈-inch barrel. 4¹/₂ inches overall. Weight: 14¹/₂ oz. Fixed sights. Blued or nickel finish. Plastic stocks. Made 1926 to c. 1960.

CZ New Model .006

CZ New Model .006 Double Action Auto Pistol .. $395
Caliber: 32 Automatic (7.65mm). 8-shot magazine. 3¹/₈-inch barrel. 6¹/₂ inches overall. Weight: 24 oz. Fixed sights. Blued finish. Plastic stocks. Introduced 1951. Discont. *Note:* Official designation of this pistol, used by the Czech National Police, is "VZ50." "New Model .006" is export designation.

DAEWOO PISTOLS
Seoul, Korea
Mfd. by Daewoo Precision Industries Ltd.

Daewoo Model DH40

Daewoo DH40 Auto Pistol $260
Caliber: 40 S&W. 12-shot magazine. 4.25-inch barrel. 7 inches overall. Weight: 28 oz. Sights: blade front; dove-tailed rear w/3-dot system. Blued finish. Checkered composition grips. DH/DP series feature a patented "fastfire" action with 5–6 lb. trigger pull. Made from 1994 to date.

Daewoo DH45 Auto Pistol $350
Caliber: 45 ACP. 13-shot magazine. 5-inch barrel. 8.1 inches overall. Weight: 35 oz. Sights: blade front; dove-tailed rear w/3-dot system. Blued finish. Checkered composition grips. Made from 1994 to date.

Daewoo Model DP51

Daewoo DP51 Auto Pistol $275
Caliber: 9mm Parabellum. 13-shot magazine. 4.1-inch barrel. 7.5 inches overall. Weight: 28 oz. Blade front and square-notch rear sights. Matte black finish. Checkered composition grips. Made from 1991 to date.

Daewoo Model DP52

Daewoo DP52 Auto Pistol $235
Caliber: 22 LR. 10-shot magazine. 3.8-inch barrel. 6.7 inches overall. Weight: 23 oz. Sights: blade front; dovetailed rear w/3-dot system. Blued finish. Checkered wood grips. Made from 1994 to date.

DAKOTA/E.M.F. CO.
Santa Ana, California

Dakota Model 1873

Dakota Model 1873 Single Action Revolver
Calibers: 22 LR, 22 Mag., 357 Mag., 45 Long Colt, 30 M1 carbine, 38-40, 32-20, 44-40. Barrel lengths: 3¹/₂, 4³/₄, 5¹/₂, 7¹/₂ inches. Blue or nickel finish. Engraved models avail.
Standard Model $295
With Extra Cylinder 395

Dakota Model 1875 Outlaw

Dakota Hartford Single Action
Scroll Engraved

Dakota Model 1875 Outlaw SA Revolver $325
Calibers: 45 Long Colt, 357 Mag., 44-40. 7½-inch barrel. Casehardened frame, blued finish. Walnut grips. This is an exact replica of the Remington #3 revolver produced 1875–1889.

Dakota Hartford Single Action Revolver (cont.)
Blued or nickel finish.
Standard Model $340
Engraved Model 495
Hartford Artillery, U.S. Cavalry Models 310

Dakota Model 1890 Remington
Police

Dakota Target Revolver

Dakota Model 1890 Remington Police
Calibers: 357 Mag., 44-40, 45 Long Colt. 5¾-inch barrel. Blue or nickel finish. Exact replica of Colt original with lanyard ring.
Standard Model $355
Nickel Model................................. 420
Engraved Model 465

Dakota Target Single Action Revolver $405
Calibers: 45 Long Colt, 357 Mag., 22 LR. 5½- or 7½-inch barrel. Polished, blued finish, casehardened frame. Walnut grips. Ramp front, blade target sight, adj. rear sight.

=== **DAVIS INDUSTRIES, INC.** ===
Chino, California

Davis Model D Derringer $55
Single-action double derringer. Calibers: 25 Auto, 22 LR, 32 Auto, 22 Mag. 2-shot capacity. 2.4-inch barrel. 4 inches overall. Weight: 9½ oz. Laminated wood grips. Black teflon or chrome finish. Made from 1987 to date.

Dakota Bisley SA Revolver

Dakota Bisley Single Action Revolver
Calibers: 44-40, 45 Long Colt, 357 Mag. 5½- or 7½-inch barrel. Discontinued 1992.
Standard Model $245
Target Model 295

Dakota Hartford Single Action Revolver
Calibers: 22 LR, 32-20, 357 Mag., 38-40, 44-40, 44 Special, 45 Long Colt. These are exact replicas of the original Colts, with steel backstraps, trigger guards and forged frames.

Davis Model P-32

Davis Model P-32 .... $70
Caliber: 32 Auto. 6-round magazine. 2.8-inch barrel. 5.4 inches overall. Weight: 22 oz. Black teflon or chrome finish. Laminated wood grips. Made from 1987 to date. (*See* photo, preceding page.)

Davis Model P-380

Davis Model P-380 .... $70
Caliber: 380 Auto. 5-shot magazine. 2.8-inch barrel. 5.4 inches overall. Weight: 22 oz. Black teflon or chrome finish. Made from 1990 to date.

=== **DESERT INDUSTRIES, INC.** ===
Las Vegas, Nevada

Desert Industries Double Deuce DA Pistol $285
Caliber: 22 LR. 6-shot magazine. $2^{1/2}$-inch barrel. $5^{1/2}$ inches overall. Weight: 15 oz. Matte-finish stainless steel. Rosewood grips.

Desert Industries Two-Bit Special Pistol $295
Similar to the Double Deuce Model, except chambered in 25 ACP with 5-shot magazine.

Desert Industries War Eagle DA Pistol $495
Calibers: 9mm Parabellum, 10mm, 40 S&W, 45 ACP. Magazine: 14-shot, 9mm/40 S&W; 13-shot, 10mm; and 12-shot, 45 ACP. 4-inch barrel. 7.5 inches overall. Weight: 35.5 oz. Fixed sights. Matte-finish stainless steel. Rosewood grips. Made from 1986 to date.

=== **DETONICS FIREARMS INDUSTRIES** ===
Bellevue, Washington

Detonics Combat Master
Calibers: 45 ACP, 451 Detonics Mag. 6-round magazine. $3^{1/2}$-inch barrel. $6^{3/4}$ inches overall. Combat-type with fixed or adjustable sights. Checkered walnut stock. Stainless steel construction. Discontinued 1992.
MK I matte blue, fixed sights. Discontinued **$460**
MK I stainless steel finish **480**
MK IV polished blue, adjustable sights.
    Discontinued **415**
MK V matte stainless steel, fixed sights.
    Discontinued **530**

Detonics Combat Master

Detonics Combat Master (cont.)
MK VI polished stainless steel, adjustable
    sights **$560**
MK VI in 451 Magnum **795**
MK VII matte stainless steel, no sights **750**
MK VII in 451 Magnum **995**

Detonics Pocket 9 .... $365
Calibers: 9mm Parabellum, 380. 6-round magazine. 3-inch barrel. $5^{7/8}$ inches overall. Fixed sights. Double- and single-action trigger mechanism. Discontinued 1986.

Detonics Scoremaster

Detonics Scoremaster $825
Calibers: 45 ACP, 451 Detonics Mag. 7-round magazine. 5- or 6-inch heavyweight match barrel. $8^{3/4}$ inches overall. Weight: 47 oz. Stainless steel construction, self-centering barrel system.

Detonics Service Master $495
Caliber: 45 ACP. 7-round magazine. $4^{1/4}$-inch barrel. Weight: 39 oz. Interchangeable front sight, millett rear sight. Discontinued 1986.

Detonics Service Master II $625
Same general specifications as standard Service Master, except comes in polished stainless steel with self-centering barrel system. Discontinued 1992.

=== **DREYSE PISTOLS** ===
Sommerda, Germany
Mfd. by Rheinische Metallwaren und Maschinenfabrik ("Rheinmetall")

Dreyse Model 1907*

DWM Pocket Automatic*

Dreyse Model 1907 Automatic Pistol **$200**
Caliber: 32 Auto (7.65mm). 8-shot magazine. 3½-inch barrel. 6¼ inches overall. Weight: about 24 oz. Fixed sights. Blued finish. Hard rubber stocks. Made 1907–c. 1914.

Dreyse Vest Pocket*

Dreyse Vest Pocket Automatic Pistol **$175**
Conventional Browning type. Caliber: 25 Auto (6.35mm). 6-shot magazine. 2-inch barrel. 4½ inches overall. Weight: about 14 oz. Fixed sights. Blued finish. Hard rubber stocks. Made from c. 1909–1914.

DWM PISTOL
Berlin, Germany
Mfd. by Deutsche Waffen-und-Munitionsfabriken

DWM Pocket Automatic Pistol **$595**
Similar to the FN Browning Model 1910. Caliber: 32 Automatic (7.65mm). 3½-inch barrel. 6 inches overall. Weight: about 21 oz. Blued finish. Hard rubber stocks. Made from c. 1921–1931.

ENFIELD REVOLVER
Enfield Lock, Middlesex, England
Manufactured by Royal Small Arms Factory

Enfield (British Service) No. 2 MK 1 Revolver . . . **$195**
Webley pattern. Hinged frame. Double action. Caliber: 380 British Service (38 S&W w/200-grain bullet). 6-shot cylinder. 5-inch barrel. 10½ inches overall. Weight: about 27½ oz. Fixed sights. Blued finish. Vulcanite stocks. First issued in 1932, this was the standard revolver of the British Army in WW II. Now obsolete. *Note:* This model also produced w/spurless hammer as No. 2 Mk 1* and Mk 1**.

ERMA-WERKE
Dachau, Germany

Erma Model ER-772 Match Revolver

Erma Model ER-772 Match Revolver **$795**
Caliber: 22 LR. 6-shot cylinder. 6-inch barrel. 12 inches overall. Weight: 47¼ oz. Adjustable micrometer rear sight and front sight blade. Adjustable trigger. Interchangeable walnut sporter or match grips. Polished blue finish. Made from 1991 to date.

Erma Model ER-773 Match Revolver **$795**
Same general specifications as Model 772, except chambered for 32 S&W. Made from 1991 to date.

Erma Model ER-777 Match Revolver **$775**
Caliber: 357 Magnum. 6-shot cylinder. 4- or 5½-inch barrel. 9.7 to 11.3 inches overall. Weight: 43.7 oz. w/5½-inch bbl. Micrometer adjustable rear sight. Checkered walnut

Erma Model ER-777 Match Revolver (cont.)

sporter or match-style grip (interchangeable). Made from 1991 to date.

**Erma Model ESP-85A
Competition Pistol**

Erma Model ESP-85A Competition Pistol

Calibers: 22 LR and 32 S&W Wadcutter. 8- or 5-shot magazine. 6-inch barrel. 10 inches overall. Weight: 40 oz. Adjustable rear sight; blade front sight. Checkered walnut grip with thumbrest. Made from 1991 to date.

Match Model	**$795**
Chrome Match	895
Sporting Model	815
Conversion Unit 22 LR	750
Conversion Unit 32 S&W	750

Erma-Werke Model KGP68

Erma-Werke Model KGP68 Automatic Pistol $250

Luger type. Calibers: 32 Auto (7.65mm), 380 Auto (9mm Short). 6-shot magazine in 32, 5-shot in 380. 4-inch barrel. 7³/₈ inches overall. Weight: 22¹/₂ oz. Fixed sights. Blued finish. Checkered walnut stocks. Made from 1968 to date.

Erma-Werke Model KGP69

Erma-Werke Model KGP69 Automatic Pistol $250

Luger type. Caliber: 22 LR. 8-shot magazine. 4-inch barrel. 7³/₄ inches overall. Weight: 29 oz. Fixed sights. Blued finish. Checkered walnut stocks. Made from 1969 to date.

EUROPEAN AMERICAN ARMORY
Hialeah, Florida

See also listings under Astra Pistols.

European American Armory Model 380 DA Auto Pistol

Similar to the standard European Model, except double action and chambered in 380 only. Made 1992 to date.

Blued Finish	**$125**
Chrome	135
Ladies Model	160

**European American Armory
Big Bore Bounty Hunter**

European American Armory Big Bore Bounty Hunter Single Action Revolver

Calibers: 357 Mag., 41 Mag., 44-40, 44 Mag., 45 Colt. Barrel lengths: 4⁵/₈, 5¹/₂, 7¹/₂ inches. Blade front and grooved topstrap rear sights. Blued or chrome finish with color-casehardened or gold-plated frame. Smooth walnut grips. Made from 1992 to date.

Blued Finish	**$295**
Blued w/Color-Casehardened Frame	315
Blued w/Gold-Plated Frame	335
Chrome Finish	340

European American Armory Bounty Hunter SA Revolver

Calibers: 22 LR, 22 WRF. Barrel lengths: 4³/₄, 6 or 9 inches. Blade front and dovetailed rear sights. Blued finish or blue with gold-plated frame. European hardwood grips. Made from 1991 to date.

Blued Finish (4³/₄-inch bbl.)	$ 90
Blued 22 LR/22 WRF Combo (4³/₄-inch bbl.)	100
Blued 22 LR/22 WRF Combo (6-inch bbl.)	110
Blued 22 LR/22 WRF Combo (9-inch bbl.)	115
For Gold-Plated Frame, **add**	10%

European American Armory EA22 Target Auto Pistol
.... **$290**

Caliber: 22 LR. 12-shot magazine. 6-inch barrel. 9.10 inches overall. Weight: 40 oz. Ramp front sight, fully adjustable rear. Blued finish. Checkered walnut grips with thumbrest.

European American Armory European Model Auto Pistol

Calibers: 32 ACP, 380 ACP. 7-shot magazine. 3.85-inch barrel. 7³/₈ inches overall. Weight: 26 oz. Blade front sight,

European American Armory European Model (cont.)

rear sight drift-adjustable for windage. Blued or chrome finish. European hardwood grips.

Blued Finish SA	$125
Chrome SA	150
Ladies Model SA	160
Blued Finish DA only	160

European American Armory FAB 92 Auto Pistol

Similar to the Witness Model, except chambered in 9mm only with slide-mounted safety and no cock-and-lock provision.

FAB 92 Standard	$260
FAB 92 Compact	245

European American Armory Standard Grade Revolver

Calibers: 22 LR, 22 WRF, 32 H&R Mag., 38 Special. 2-, 4- or 6-inch barrel. Blade front sight, fixed or adjustable rear. Blued finish. European hardwood grips with finger grooves. Made from 1991 to date.

22 LR (4-inch bbl.)	$135
22 LR (6-inch bbl.)	140
22 LR Combo (4-inch bbl.)	195
22 LR Combo (6-inch bbl.)	205
32 H&R, 38 Special (2-inch bbl.)	140
38 Special (4-inch)	150

European American Armory Tactical Grade Revolver

Similar to the Standard Model, except chambered in 38 Special only. 2- or 4-inch barrel. Fixed sights. Available with compensator. Made from 1991 to date.

Tactical Revolver	$160
Tactical Revolver w/Compensator	265

**European American Armory
Windicator**

European American Armory Windicator Target Revolver ... $295

Calibers: 22 LR, 38 Special, 357 Magnum. 8-shot cylinder in 22 LR; 6-shot in 38 Special/357 Magnum. 6-inch barrel w/barrel weights. 11.8 inches overall. Weight: 50.2 oz. Interchangeable blade front sight, fully adjustable rear. Walnut competition-style grips. Made from 1991 to date.

European American Armory Witness DA Auto Pistol

Similar to the Brno CZ-75 with a cocked-and-locked system. Double or single action. Calibers: 9mm Parabellum, 38 Super, 40 S&W, 10mm and 45 ACP. 16-shot magazine in 9mm; 12-shot in 38 Super/40 S&W; 10-shot in 10mm/45 ACP. 4.75-inch barrel. 8.10 inches overall. Weight: 35.33 oz. Blade front sight, rear sight adjustable for wind-

**European American Armory
Witness**

European American Armory Witness DA (cont.)

age with 3-dot sighting system. Blued, satin chrome, blue/chrome or stainless finish. Checkered rubber grips. Made from 1991 to date.

9mm Blue	$280
9mm Chrome or Blue/Chrome	290
9mm Stainless	335
38 Super and 40 S&W Blued	295
38 Super and 40 S&W Chrome or Blue/Chrome	325
38 Super and 40 S&W Stainless	360
10mm and 45 ACP Blued	375
10mm and 45 ACP Chrome or Blue/Chrome	380
10mm and 45 ACP Stainless	415

European American Armory Witness Subcompact DA Auto Pistol

Calibers: 9mm Parabellum and 40 S&W. 13-shot magazine in 9mm; 9-shot in 40 S&W. 3.66-inch barrel. 7.25 inches overall. Weight: 30 oz. Blade front sight, rear sight adj. for windage. Blued, satin chrome or blue/chrome finish.

9mm Blue	$270
9mm Chrome or Blue/Chrome	295
40 S&W Blue	295
40 S&W Chrome or Blue/Chrome	325

European American Armory Witness Target Pistol

Similar to standard Witness Model, except fitted with 2- or 3-port compensator, competition frame and S/A target trigger. Calibers: 9mm Parabellum, 9×21, 40 S&W, 10mm and 45 ACP. 5.25-inch match barrel. 10.5 inches overall. Weight: 38 oz. Square post front sight, fully adjustable rear or drilled and tapped for scope. Blued or hard chrome finish. Low-profile competition grips.

Silver Team (Blued w/2-Port Compensator)	$ 695
Gold Team (Chrome w/3-Port Compensator)	1295

FIALA OUTFITTERS, INC.
New York, New York

Fiala Repeating Pistol ... $395

Despite its appearance, which closely resembles that of the early Colt Woodsman and High-Standard, this arm is not an automatic pistol. It is hand-operated by moving the slide to eject, cock and load. Caliber: 22 LR. 10-shot magazine. Barrel lengths: 3-, 7½- and 20-inch. 11¼ inches overall w/7½-inch bbl. Weight: 31 oz. w/7½-inch bbl. Target sights. Blued finish. Plain wood stocks. Shoulder stock was originally supplied for use with 20-inch barrel. Made 1920–23. Value shown is for pistol with one barrel and no shoulder stock.

F.I.E. CORPORATION
Hialeah, Florida

The F.I.E. Corporation became QFI (Quality Firearms Corp.) of Opa Locka, Fl., about 1990, when most of F.I.E.'s models were discontinued.

F.I.E. Model A27BW

F.I.E. Model A27BW "The Best" Semiauto $95
Caliber: 25 ACP. 6-round magazine. 2 1/2-inch barrel. 6 3/4 inches overall. Weight: 13 oz. Fixed sights. Checkered walnut stock. Discontinued 1990.

**F.I.E. Arminius
Double Action Revolver**

F.I.E. Arminius Double Action Revolver
Calibers: 22 LR; 22 combo w/interchangeable cylinder; 32 S&W, 38 Special, 357 Magnum. 6, 7 or 8 rounds depending on caliber. Swingout cylinder. Barrel lengths: 2-, 3-, 4-, 6-inch. Vent rib on calibers other than 22. 11 inches overall w/6-inch barrel. Weight: 26 to 30 oz. Fixed or micro-adjustable sights. Checkered plastic or walnut stocks. Blued finish. Made in Germany; discontinued.

22 LR	$ 95
22 Combo	95
32 S&W	100
38 Special	105
357 Magnum	150

F.I.E. Buffalo Scout Single Action Revolver
Calibers: 22 LR, 22 WRF; 22 combo w/interchangeable cylinder. 4 3/4-inch barrel. 10 inches overall. Weight: 32 oz. Adjustable sights. Blued or chrome finish. Smooth

F.I.E. Buffalo Scout Single Action Revolver (cont.)
walnut or black checkered nylon grips. Made in Italy.

Blued Standard	$ 50
Blued Convertible	100
Chrome Standard	65
Chrome Convertible	110

F.I.E. Hombre Single Action Revolver $160
Calibers: 357 Magnum, 44 Magnum, 45 Colt. 6-shot cylinder. Barrel lengths: 6 or 7 1/2 inches. 11 inches overall w/6-inch barrel. Weight: 45 oz. w/6-inch barrel. Fixed sights. Blued barrel with color-casehardened receiver. Smooth walnut stocks. Made 1979–1990.

F.I.E. Little Ranger Single Action Revolver
Same as the Texas Ranger, except with 3 1/4-inch barrel and bird's-head grips. Made 1986–1990.

Standard	$80
Convertible	95

F.I.E. Super Titan II
Caliber: 32 ACP or 380 ACP. 3 1/4-inch barrel. Weight: 28 oz. Blued or chrome finish. Discontinued 1990.

32 ACP in Blue	$130
32 ACP in Chrome	145
380 ACP in Blue	160
380 ACP in Chrome	175

F.I.E. Texas Ranger Single Action Revolver
Calibers: 22 LR, 22 WRF; 22 combo w/interchangeable cylinder. Barrel lengths: 4 3/4-, 6 1/2-, 9-inch. 10 inches overall w/4 3/4-inch barrel. Weight: 32 oz. w/4 3/4-inch barrel. Fixed sights. Blued finish. Smooth walnut stocks. Made 1983–1990.

Standard	$65
Convertible	95

F.I.E. Titan Tiger

F.I.E. Titan Tiger Double Action Revolver $100
Caliber: 38 Special. 6-shot cylinder. 2- or 4-inch barrel. 8 1/4 inches overall w/4-inch barrel. Weight: 30 oz. w/4-inch barrel. Fixed sights. Blued finish. Checkered plastic or walnut stocks. Made in the U.S. Discontinued 1990.

F.I.E. Titan II Semiautomatic
Calibers: 22 LR, 32 ACP, 380 ACP. 10-round magazine. Integral tapered post front sight, windage-adjustable rear sight. European walnut grips. Blued or chrome finish. Discontinued 1990.

22 LR in Blue	$ 95
32 ACP in Blue	145
32 ACP in Chrome	175
380 ACP in Blue	165
380 ACP in Chrome	185

HANDGUNS

F.I.E. Titan II

Firearms International Model D

F.I.E. Model TZ75
Satin Chrome

Firearms International Regent

F.I.E. Model TZ75 DA Semiautomatic
Double action. Caliber: 9mm. 15-round magazine. 4¹/₂-inch barrel. 8¹/₄ inches overall. Weight: 35 oz. Ramp front sight, windage-adjustable rear sight. European walnut or black rubber grips. Discontinued 1989.
Blued Finish **$290**
Satin Chrome **325**

F.I.E. Yellow Rose Single Action Revolver
Same general specifications as the Buffalo Scout, except in 22 combo w/interchangeable cylinder and plated in 24 karat gold. Limited Edition with scrimshawed ivory polymer grips and American walnut presentation case. Made 1987–1990.
Yellow Rose 22 Combo **$100**
Yellow Rose Ltd. Edition **250**

FIREARMS INTERNATIONAL CORP.
Washington, D.C.

Firearms Int'l. Model D Automatic Pistol **$165**
Caliber: 380 Automatic. 6-shot magazine. 3¹/₈-inch barrel. 6¹/₈ inches overall. Weight: 19¹/₂ oz. Blade front sight, windage-adjustable rear sight. Blued, chromed, or military finish. Checkered walnut stocks. Made 1974–77.

Firearms Int'l. Regent Double Action Revolver ... **$80**
Calibers: 22 LR, 32 S&W Long. 8-shot cylinder (22 LR), 7-shot (32). Barrels: 3-, 4-, 6-inch (22 LR); 2¹/₂-, 4-inch (32). Weight: with 4-inch barrel, 28 oz. Fixed sights. Blue finish. Plastic stocks. Made 1966–1972.

FN BROWNING PISTOLS
Liege, Belgium
Mfd. by Fabrique Nationale Herstal

See also Browning Pistols.

FN Browning 6.35mm

FN Browning 6.35mm Pocket Auto Pistol **$295**
Same specifications as Colt Pocket Model 25 Automatic.

FN Browning Model 1900*

FN Browning Model 1900 Pocket Auto Pistol . . . $350
Caliber: 32 Automatic (7.65mm). 7-shot magazine. 4-inch barrel. 6³/₄ inches overall. Weight: 22 oz. Fixed sights. Blued finish. Hard rubber stocks. Made 1899–1910.

FN Browning Model 1903 Military Auto Pistol . . . $390
Caliber: 9mm Browning Long. 7-shot magazine. 5-inch barrel. 8 inches overall. Weight: 32 oz. Fixed sights. Blued finish. Hard rubber stocks. *Note:* Aside from size, this pistol is of the same basic design as the Colt Pocket 32 and 380 Automatic pistols. Made 1903–1939.

FN Browning Model 1910

FN Browning Model 1910 Pocket Auto Pistol . . . $500
Calibers: 32 Auto (7.65mm), 380 Auto (9mm). 7-shot magazine (32 cal.), 6-shot (380 cal.). 3¹/₂-inch barrel. 6 inches overall. Weight: 20¹/₂ oz. Fixed sights. Blued finish. Hard rubber stocks. Made 1910–1922.

FN Browning Model 1922

FN Browning Model 1922 Police/Military Auto . . . $255
Calibers: 32 Auto (7.65mm), 380 Auto (9mm). 9-shot magazine (32 cal.), 8-shot (380 cal.). 4¹/₂-inch barrel. 7 inches overall. Weight: 25 oz. Fixed sights. Blued finish. Hard rubber stocks. Made 1922–1959.

FN Browning Model 1935 Hi-Power

FN Browning Model 1935 Military Hi-Power Pistol
Variation of the Browning-Colt 45 Auto design. Caliber: 9mm Luger. 13-shot magazine. 4⁵/₈-inch barrel. 7³/₄ inches overall. Weight: about 35 oz. Adjustable rear sight and fixed front, or both fixed. Blued finish (Canadian manufacture Parkerized). Checkered walnut or plastic stocks. *Note:* Above specifications in general apply to both the original FN production and the pistols made by John Inglis Company of Canada for the Chinese Government. A smaller version, with shorter barrel and slide and 10-shot magazine, was made by FN for the Belgian and Rumanian Governments about 1937–1940. Both types were made at the FN plant during the German Occupation of Belgium.
With adjustable rear sight $625
FN manufacture, with fixed rear sight 545
Inglis manufacture, with fixed rear sight 630

FN Browning Baby

FN Browning Baby Auto Pistol $325
Caliber: 25 Automatic (6.35mm). 6-shot magazine. 2¹/₈-inch barrel. 4 inches overall. Weight: 10 oz. Fixed sights. Blued finish. Hard rubber stocks. Made 1931–1983.

FOREHAND & WADSWORTH
Worcester, Massachusetts

Forehand & Wadsworth Revolvers
See listings of comparable Harrington & Richardson and Iver Johnson revolvers for values.

LE FRANCAIS PISTOLS
St. Etienne, France
Produced by Manufacture Francaise d'Armes et Cycles

Le Francais Army Model Automatic Pistol **$995**
Similar in operation to the Le Francais 25 Automatics. Caliber: 9mm Browning Long. 8-shot magazine. 5-inch barrel. 7³/₄ inches overall. Weight: about 34 oz. Fixed sights. Blued finish. Checkered walnut stocks. Made from 1928–1938.

Le Francais Policeman*

Le Francais Policeman Model Automatic Pistol **$650**
DA. Hinged barrel. Caliber: 25 Automatic (6.35mm). 7-shot magazine. 3¹/₂-inch barrel. 6 inches overall. Weight: about 12 oz. Fixed sights. Blued finish. Hard rubber stocks. Intro. 1914; discontinued.

Le Francais Staff Officer*

Le Francais Staff Officer Model Automatic Pistol . . **$210**
Caliber: 25 Automatic. Similar to the "Policeman" Model, except does not have cocking-piece head, barrel is about an inch shorter and weight is an oz. less. Intro. 1914; disc.

FREEDOM ARMS
Freedom, Wyoming

**Freedom Arms Model 252
Silhouette Class**

Freedom Arms Model 252 Revolver
Calibers: 22 LR, 22 Mag. Barrel lengths: 7¹/₂ (Varmint Class) or 10 inches (Silhouette Class). Silhouette competition sights (Silhouette Class); removable front express blade sight; adjustable rear sight. Stainless finish. Black micarta (Silhouette) or black and green laminated hardwood grips (Varmint).
Silhouette Model **$1050**
Varmint Model **995**

**Freedom Arms Model 353
Field Grade**

Freedom Arms Model 353 Revolver
Caliber: 357 Mag. Single action. Barrel lengths: 7¹/₂ or 9 inches. Removable blade front sight; adjustable rear sight. Stainless finish. Pachmayr Presentation or impregnated hardwood grips (Premier Grade).
Field Grade . . . . **$ 895**
Premier Grade **1095**

**Freedom Arms
Model FA-454 Casull**

Freedom Arms Model FA-454AS Casull **$995**
Caliber: 454 Casull. Barrel lengths: 4³/₄, 6, 7¹/₂, 10, 12 inches. Adjustable sight. Hardwood grips. Brushed stainless steel finish.

Freedom Arms Model FA-454FS Revolver **$950**
Same general specifications as Model FA-454AS, except with fixed sight.

**Freedom Arms FA-454GAS
Field Grade**

Freedom Arms Model FA-454GAS Revolver **$895**
Field Grade version of Model FA-454AS, except not made
w/12-inch barrel. Matte stainless finish, Pachmayr presentation grips. Adj. sights; fixed sight on 4³/₄-inch bbl.

**Freedom Arms Model FA-BG-22LR
Mini-Revolver** **$120**
Caliber: 22 LR. 3-inch tapered barrel. Partial high-gloss
stainless steel finish. Discontinued 1987.

**Freedom Arms Model FA-BG-22M
Mini-Revolver** **$135**
Same general specifications as model FA-BG-22LR, ex-
cept in caliber 22 Win. Mag.

**Freedom Arms Model FA-BG-22P
Mini-Revolver** **$120**
Same general specifications as Model FA-BG-22LR, ex-
cept in 22 percussion. Discontinued 1987.

Freedom Arms Model FA-L-22LR Mini-Revolver .. **$85**
Caliber: 22 LR. 1³/₄-inch contoured barrel. Partial high-
gloss stainless steel finish. Bird's-head-type grips. Discontinued 1987.

Freedom Arms Model FA-L-22M Mini-Revolver .. **$120**
Same general specifications as Model FA-L-22LR, except
in caliber 22 Win. Mag. Discontinued 1987.

Freedom Arms Model FA-L-22P Mini-Revolver ... **$95**
Same general specifications as Model FA-L-22LR, except
in 22 percussion. Discontinued 1987.

**Freedom Arms
Model FA-S-22LR**

**Freedom Arms Model FA-S-22LR Mini-
Revolver** **$110**
Caliber: 22 LR. 1-inch contoured barrel. Partial high-gloss
stainless steel finish. Discontinued.

Freedom Arms Model FA-S-22M Mini-Revolver .. **$120**
Same general specifications as Model FA-S-22LR, except
in caliber 22 Win. Mag. Discontinued.

Freedom Arms Model FA-S-22P Mini-Revolver ... **$95**
Same general specifications as Model FA-S-22LR, except
in percussion. Discontinued.

FRENCH MILITARY PISTOL
Cholet, France
Mfd. by Société Alsacienne de
Constructions Mécaniques (S.A.C.M.)

French Model 1935A

French Model 1935A Automatic Pistol **$275**
Caliber: 7.65mm Long. 8-shot magazine. 4.3-inch barrel.
7.6 inches overall. Weight: 26 oz. Fixed sights. Blued finish.
Checkered stocks. Made 1935–1945. *Note:* This pistol was
used by French troops during WW II and in Indo-China
1945–1954.

FROMMER PISTOLS
Budapest, Hungary
Mfd. by Fémáru-Fegyver-és Gépgyár R.T.

Frommer Baby*

Frommer Baby Pocket Automatic Pistol **$155**
Similar to Stop model, except has 2-inch barrel, is about
4³/₄ inches overall, weighs about 17¹/₂ oz. Magazine capacity is one round less. Introduced shortly after WW I.

Frommer Liliput Pocket Automatic Pistol **$195**
Caliber: 25 Automatic (6.35mm). 6-shot magazine. 2.14-
inch barrel. 4.33 inches overall. Weight: 10¹/₂ oz. Fixed
sights. Blued finish. Hard rubber stocks. Made during
early 1920s. *Note:* Although similar in appearance to the
Stop and Baby, this pistol is blowback operated.

Frommer Liliput*

Frommer Stop Pocket Auto*

Frommer Stop Pocket Automatic Pistol $130

Locked-breech action, outside hammer. Calibers: 32 Automatic (7.65mm), 380 Auto (9mm short). 7-shot (32 cal.) or 6-shot (380 cal.) magazine. 3^{7}/$_{8}$-inch barrel. 6^{1}/$_{2}$ inches overall. Weight: about 21 oz. Fixed sights. Blued finish. Hard rubber stocks. Made 1912–1920.

=== **GALESI PISTOLS** ===
Collebeato (Brescia), Italy
Mfd. by Industria Armi Galesi

Galesi Model 6*

Galesi Model 6 Pocket Automatic Pistol $125

Calibers: 22 Long, 25 Automatic (6.35mm). 6-shot magazine. 2^{1}/$_{4}$-inch barrel. 4^{3}/$_{8}$ inches overall. Weight: about 11 oz. Fixed sights. Blued finish. Plastic stocks. Made from 1930 to date.

Galesi Model 9*

Galesi Model 9 Pocket Automatic Pistol

Calibers: 22 LR, 32 Auto (7.65mm), 380 Auto (9mm Short). 8-shot magazine. 3^{1}/$_{4}$-inch barrel. 5^{7}/$_{8}$ inches overall. Weight: about 21 oz. Fixed sights. Blued finish. Plastic stocks. Made from 1930 to date. *Note:* Specifications vary; those shown are for 32 Automatic of common type.

22 Long Rifle or 380 Automatic $160
32 Automatic 150

=== **GLISENTI PISTOL** ===
Carcina (Brescia), Italy
Mfd. by Societa Siderurgica Glisenti

Glisenti Model 1910*

Glisenti Model 1910 Italian Service Automatic .. $545

Caliber: 9mm, Glisenti. 7-shot magazine. 4-inch barrel. 8^{1}/$_{2}$ inches overall. Weight: about 32 oz. Fixed sights. Blued finish. Checkered wood. Hard rubber or plastic stocks. Adopted 1910 and used through WW II.

=== **GLOCK, INC.** ===
Smyrna, Georgia

Glock Model 17 DA Automatic Pistol $385

Caliber: 9mm Parabellum. 17-shot magazine. 4^{1}/$_{2}$-inch barrel. 7.2 inches overall. Weight: about 22 oz., empty.

Glock Model 17

Glock Model 17 DA Automatic Pistol (cont.)

Hi-tech polymer frame and receiver; steel barrel, slide and springs. Fixed or adjustable rear sights. Matte, nonglare finish. Made of only 33 components, including 3 internal safety devices. This gun received the "Best Pistol Award of Merit" in 1987 by the American Firearms Industry. Made in Austria from 1983 to date.

Glock Model 17L Competition $535

Same general specifications as Model 17, except weighs 23.35 oz. with 6-inch barrel; 8.85 inches overall. Currently manufactured.

Glock Model 19 Compact

Glock Model 20

Glock Model 19 Compact $395

Same general specifications as Model 17, except smaller version with 4-inch barrel, 6.85 inches overall and 21-oz. weight. Made from 1988 to date.

Glock Model 20 DA Auto Pistol $475

Caliber: 10mm. 15-shot. Hammerless. 4.6-inch barrel. 7.59 inches overall. Weight: 26.3 oz. Fixed or adj. sights. Matte, nonglare finish. Made from 1991 to date.

Glock Model 21 Automatic Pistol $470

Same general specifications as Model 17, except chambered in 45 ACP. 13-shot magazine. 7.59 inches overall. Weight: 25.2 oz. Made from 1991 to date.

Glock Model 22 Automatic Pistol $360

Same general specifications as Model 17, except chambered for 40 S&W. 15-shot magazine. 7.4 inches overall. Made from 1992 to date.

Glock Model 23 Automatic Pistol $415

Same general specifications as Model 19, except chambered for 40 S&W. 13-shot magazine. 6.97 inches overall. Made from 1992 to date.

Glock Desert Storm Commemorative $750

Same general specifications as Model 17, except "Operation Desert Storm, January 16–February 27, 1991" engraved on side of slide with list of coalition forces. Limited issue of 1,000 guns. Made in 1991.

GREAT WESTERN ARMS CO.
North Hollywood, California

Great Western Double Barrel Derringer $125

Replica of Remington Double Derringer. Caliber: 38 S&W. Double barrels (superposed), 3-inch. Overall length: 5 inches. Fixed sights. Blued finish. Checkered black plastic grips. Made 1953–1962.

Great Western Single Action

Great Western Single Action Frontier Revolver . $565

Replica of the Colt Single Action Army Revolver. Calibers: 22 LR, 357 Magnum, 38 Special, 44 Special, 44 Magnum, 45 Colt. 6-shot cylinder. Barrel lengths: 4³/₄-, 5¹/₂- and 7¹/₂-inch. Weight: 40 oz., 22 cal. w/5¹/₂-inch bbl. Overall length: 11¹/₈ inches w/5¹/₂-inch bbl. Fixed sights. Blued finish. Imitation stag grips. Made 1951–1962. *Note:* Value shown is for improved late model revolvers; early Great Westerns are variable in quality and should be evaluated accordingly. It should also be noted that, beginning about July 1956, these revolvers were offered in kit form; values of guns assembled from these kits will, in general, be lower than for factory-completed weapons.

GRENDEL, INC.
Rockledge, Florida

Grendel Model P-12

Grendel Model P-12 DA Automatic Pistol
Caliber: 380 ACP. 11-shot Zytel magazine. 3-inch barrel. 5.3 inches overall. Weight: 13 oz. Fixed sights. Polymer DuPont ST-800 grip. Made from 1991 to date.
Standard Model $125
Electroless Nickel 145

Grendel Model P-30

Grendel Model P-30 Automatic Pistol
Caliber: 22 WMR. 30-shot magazine. 5-or 8-inch barrel. 8.5 inches overall with 5-inch bbl. Weight: 21 oz. Blade front sight; fixed rear sight. Made from 1991 to date.
With 5-inch barrel $160
With 8-inch barrel 185

Grendel Model P-31 Automatic Pistol $235
Caliber: 22 WMR. 30-shot Zytel magazine. 11-inch barrel. 17.3 inches overall. Weight: 48 oz. Adjustable blade front sight; fixed rear sight. Checkered black polymer DuPont ST-800 grip and forend. Made from 1991 to date.

HÄMMERLI AG JAGD-UND SPORTWAFFENFABRIK
Lenzburg, Switzerland

Hämmerli Model 33MP

Hämmerli Model 33MP Free Pistol $800
System Martini single-shot action, set trigger. Caliber: 22 LR. 11½-inch octagon barrel. 16½ inches overall. Weight: 46 oz. Micrometer rear sight, interchangeable front sights. Blued finish. Walnut grips, forearm. Made 1933–1949.

Hämmerli Model 100 Free Pistol
Same general specifications as Model 33MP. Improved action and sights, redesigned stock. Standard model has plain stocks and forearm; deluxe model has carved stocks and forearm. Made 1950–56.
Standard Model $635
Deluxe Model 725

Hämmerli Model 101

Hämmerli Model 101 .... $615
Similar to Model 100, except has heavy round barrel with matte finish, improved action and sights, adjustable stocks. Weight: about 49 oz. Made 1956–1960.

Hämmerli Model 102 Deluxe

Hämmerli Model 102
Same as Model 101, except barrel has highly polished blued finish. Deluxe model (illustrated) has carved stocks and forearm. Made 1956–1960.
Standard Model $615
Deluxe Model 730

Hämmerli Model 103 .... $605
Same as Model 101, except has lighter octagon barrel (as in Model 100) with highly polished blued finish, stocks and forearm of select French walnut. Weight: about 46 oz. Made 1956–1960.

Hämmerli Model 104 . . . . $575
Similar to Model 102, except has lighter round barrel, improved action, redesigned stocks and forearm. Weight: 46 oz. Made 1961–65.

Hämmerli Model 105

Hämmerli Model 105 . . . . $690
Similar to Model 103, except has improved action, redesigned stocks and forearm. Made 1961–65.

Hämmerli Model 106

Hämmerli Model 106 . . . . $575
Similar to Model 104, except has improved trigger and stocks. Made 1966–1971.

Hämmerli Model 107 Deluxe

Hämmerli Model 107
Similar to Model 105, except has improved trigger and stock. Deluxe model (illustrated) has engraved receiver and barrel, carved stocks and forearm. Made 1966–1971.
Standard Model $675
Deluxe Model 900

Hämmerli Model 120 Heavy Barrel
Adjustable Stocks

Hämmerli Model 120 Heavy Barrel
Same as Models 120-1 and 120-2, except has 5.7-inch heavy barrel. Weight: 41 oz. Available with standard or adjustable stocks. Made from 1972 to date.
With standard stocks . . . . $ 415
With adjustable stocks 440

Hämmerli Model 120-1

Hämmerli Model 120-1 Single Shot Free Pistol . . $395
Side lever-operated bolt action. Adjustable single-stage or two-stage trigger. Caliber: 22 LR. 9.999-inch barrel. 14³/₄ inches overall. Weight: 44 oz. Micrometer rear sight, front sight on high ramp. Blued finish barrel and receiver, lever and grip frame anodized aluminum. Checkered walnut thumbrest stocks. Made from 1972 to date.

Hämmerli Model 120-2 . . . . $405
Same as Model 120-1, except has hand-contoured stocks with adjustable palm rest (available for right or left hand). Made from 1972 to date.

Hämmerli Model 150 Free Pistol

Hämmerli Model 150 Free Pistol $1425
Improved Martini-type action with lateral-action cocking lever. Set trigger adjustable for weight, length and angle of pull. Caliber: 22 LR. 11.3-inch round barrel, free-floating. 15.4 inches overall. Weight: 43 oz. (w/extra weights, 49¹/₂ oz.). Micrometer rear sight, front sight on high ramp. Blued finish. Select walnut forearm and stocks w/adj. palm shelf. Made 1972–1989.

Hämmerli Model 160 Free Pistol

Hämmerli Models 160/162 Free Pistols
Caliber: 22 LR. Single shot. 11⁵/₁₆-inch barrel. 17¹/₂ inches overall. Weight: 46.9 oz. Sights: interchangeable front blade; fully adjustable match rear. Match-style stippled walnut stocks w/adj. palm shelf. Made from 1993 to date.

Hämmerli Models 160/162 Free Pistols (cont.)
Model 160 w/mechanical set trigger $1095
Model 162 w/electronic trigger 1295

Hämmerli Model 208

Hämmerli Model 208 Standard Auto Pistol $1250
Caliber: 22 LR. 8-shot magazine. 5.9-inch barrel. 10 inches overall. Weight: 35 oz. (barrel weight adds 3 oz.). Micrometer rear sight, ramp front. Blued finish. Checkered walnut stocks w/adjustable heel plate. Made 1966–1988.

Hämmerli Model 211 . . . . $1095
Same as Model 208, except has standard thumbrest stocks. Made from 1966 to date.

Hämmerli Model 212 Hunter's Pistol $950
Caliber: 22 LR. 4⅞-inch barrel. 8½ inches overall. Weight: 31 oz. Fully adjustable sights. Blued finish. Checkered walnut stocks. Made 1984–1990.

Hämmerli Model 230-1 Rapid Fire Auto Pistol . . . $595
Caliber: 22 Short. 5-shot magazine. 6.3-inch barrel. 11.6 inches overall. Weight: 44 oz. Micrometer rear sight, post front. Blued finish. Smooth walnut thumbrest stocks. Made 1970–1983.

Hämmerli Model 230-2

**Hämmerli Model 232
Rapid Fire Pistol**

Hämmerli Model 230-2 . . . . $625
Same as Model 230-1, except has checkered walnut stocks with adjustable heel plate. Made 1970–1983.

Hämmerli Model 232 Rapid Fire Auto Pistol $995
Caliber: 22 LR. 5-shot magazine. 5.2-inch barrel. 10⅜ inches overall. Weight: 44 oz. Fully adjustable target sights. Blued finish. Stippled walnut wraparound target stocks. Made from 1984 to date.

Hämmerli Model 280 Target Pistol
Carbon-reinforced synthetic frame and barrel housing. Calibers: 22 LR, 32 S&W Long WC. 6-shot (22 LR) or 5-shot (32 S&W) magazine. 4½-inch barrel w/interchangeable metal or carbon fiber counterweights. 11⅞ inches overall. Weight: 39 oz. Micro-adjustable match sights w/ interchangeable elements.
22 Long Rifle . . . . $ 950
32 S&W Long WC 1125

Hämmerli International Model 206

Hämmerli International Model 206 Auto Pistol . . $525
Calibers: 22 Short, 22 LR. 6-shot (22 Short) or 8-shot (22 LR) magazine. 7¹⁄₁₆-inch barrel w/muzzle brake. 12½ inches overall. Weight: 33 oz. (22 Short); 39 oz. (22 LR), (supplementary weights add 5 and 8 oz.). Micrometer rear sight, ramp front. Blued finish. Standard thumbrest stocks. Made 1962–69.

Hämmerli International Model 207

Hämmerli International Model 207 . . . . $595
Same as Model 206, except has stocks with adjustable heel plate, weighs 2 oz. more. Made 1962–69.

Hämmerli International Model 209 Auto Pistol . . $650
Caliber: 22 Short. 5-shot mag. 4¾-inch barrel w/muzzle brake and gas-escape holes. 11 inches overall. Weight: 39 oz. (interchangeable front weight adds 4 oz.). Micrometer rear sight, post front. Blued finish. Standard thumbrest stocks of checkered walnut. Made 1966–1970.

Hämmerli International Model 210

Hämmerli International Model 210 . . . . $675
Same as Model 209, except has stocks with adjustable heel plate; is 0.8-inch longer and weighs 1 ounce more. Made 1966–1970.

Hämmerli Virginian

Hämmerli Virginian Single Action Revolver $495
Similar to Colt Single Action Army, except has base pin safety system (SWISSAFE). Calibers: 357 Magnum, 45 Colt. 6-shot cylinder. Barrels: 4⅝-, 5½-, 7½-inch. 11 inches overall w/5½-inch bbl. Weight: 40 oz. w/5½-inch bbl. Fixed sights. Blued barrel and cylinder, casehardened frame, chrome-plated grip frame and trigger guard. One-piece smooth walnut stock. Made 1973–76 for Interarms, Alexandria, Va.

**Hämmerli-Walther Olympia Model 200
1952-Type**

Hämmerli-Walther Olympia Model 200
Automatic Pistol, 1952-Type $595
Similar to 1936 Walther Olympia Funfkampf Model. Calibers: 22 Short, 22 LR. 6-shot (22 Short) or 10-shot (22 LR) magazine. 7.5-inch barrel. 10.7 inches overall. Weight: 27.7 oz. (22 Short, light alloy breechblock); 30.3 oz. (22 LR); supplementary weights provided. Adjustable target sights. Blued finish. Checkered walnut thumbrest stocks. Made 1952–58.

**Hämmerli-Walther Olympia Model 200
1958-Type, Standard Stocks**

Hämmerli-Walther Olympia Model 200,
1958-Type $600
Same as Model 200, 1952 Type, except has muzzle brake, 8-shot magazine (22 LR). 11.6 inches overall. Weight: 30 oz. (22 Short); 33 oz. (22 LR) Made 1958–1963.

Hämmerli-Walther Olympia Model 201 . . . . $590
Same as Model 200, 1952 Type, except has 9½-inch barrel. Made 1955–57.

Hämmerli-Walther Olympia Model 202 . . . . $600
Same as Model 201, except has stocks with adjustable heel plate. Made from 1955–57.

**Hämmerli-Walther Olympia
Model 203, 1958-Type**

Hämmerli-Walther Olympia Model 203
Same as corresponding Model 200 (1955-Type lacks muzzle brake), except has stocks with adjustable heel plate. Made 1955–1963.
1955-Type **$595**
1958-Type **615**

Hämmerli-Walther Olympia Model 204
American Model. Same as corresponding Model 200 (1956-Type lacks muzzle brake), except in 22 LR only, has slide stop and micrometer rear sight. Made 1956–1963.
1956-Type **$600**
1958-Type **645**

**Hämmerli-Walther Olympia
Model 205**

Hämmerli-Walther Olympia Model 205
American Model. Same as Model 204, except has stocks with adjustable heel plate. Made 1956–1963.

1956-Type	**$675**
1958-Type	**715**

SIG-Hämmerli Model P240

SIG-Hämmerli Model P240 Automatic Pistol
Caliber: 38 Special (wadcutter). 5-shot magazine. 6-inch barrel. 10 inches overall. Weight: 41 oz. Micrometer rear sight, post front. Blued finish. Smooth walnut thumbrest stocks. Accessory 22 LR conversion unit available. Made from 1975 to date.

Model P240	**$1095**
22 Conversion Unit	**500**

SIG-Hämmerli Model P240 Target Auto Pistol .. **$1035**
Same general specifications as Model P240 Automatic, except with fully adjustable target sights and stippled walnut wraparound target stocks. Weight: 49 oz.

═══ HARRINGTON & RICHARDSON, INC. ═══
Gardner, Massachusetts
(Now H&R 1871, Inc., Gardner, Mass.)

Formerly Harrington & Richardson Arms Co. of Worcester, Mass. One of the oldest and most distinguished manufacturers of handguns, rifles and shotguns, H&R had suspended operations in 1986; it was purchased by New England Firearms in the early 1990s.

H&R Self-Loading 25*

NOTE: For ease in finding a particular firearm, H&R handguns are grouped into Automatic/Single Shot Pistols, followed by Revolvers. For a complete listing, please refer to the Index.

Harrington & Richardson Self-Loading 25 Pistol .. **$350**
Modified Webley & Scott design. Caliber: 25 Auto. 6-shot magazine. 2-inch barrel. 4½ inches overall. Weight: 12 oz. Fixed sights. Blued finish. Black hard rubber stocks. Discontinued prior to 1942.

H&R Self-Loading 32*

Harrington & Richardson Self-Loading 32 Pistol .. **$315**
Modified Webley & Scott design. Caliber: 32 Auto. 8-shot magazine. 3½-inch barrel. 6½ inches overall. Weight: about 20 oz. Fixed sights. Blued finish. Black hard rubber stocks. Discontinued prior to 1942.

H&R USRA Model Single Shot

Harrington & Richardson USRA Model Single Shot Target Pistol **$395**
Hinged frame. Caliber: 22 LR. Barrel lengths: 7-, 8- and 10-inch. Weight: 31 oz. with 10-inch bbl. Adj. target sights. Blued finish. Checkered walnut stocks. Made 1928–1941.

REVOLVERS

NOTE: This section contains only H&R Revolvers. Pistols may be found in the preceding section. For a complete listing of H&R handguns, please refer to the Index.

H&R Model 4 (1904)
Double Action Revolver

Harrington & Richardson Model 4 (1904) DA **$75**
Solid frame. Calibers: 32 S&W Long, 38 S&W. 6-shot
cylinder (32 cal.), 5-shot (38 cal.). Barrel lengths: 2½-,
4½- and 6-inch. Weight: about 16 oz., 32 cal. Fixed sights.
Blued or nickel finish. Hard rubber stocks. Discontinued
prior to 1942. (*See* photo, preceding page)

H&R Model 5

Harrington & Richardson Model 5 (1905) DA **$80**
Solid frame. Caliber: 32 S&W. 5-shot cylinder. Barrel
lengths: 2½-, 4½- and 6-inch. Weight: about 11 oz. Fixed
sights. Blued or nickel finish. Hard rubber stocks. Discontinued prior to 1942.

H&R Model 6

Harrington & Richardson Model 6 (1906) DA **$85**
Solid frame. Caliber: 22 LR. 7-shot cylinder. Barrel
lengths: 2½-, 4½- and 6-inch. Weight: about 10 oz. Fixed
sights. Blued or nickel finish. Hard rubber stocks. Discontinued prior to 1942.

H&R 22 Special

Harrington & Richardson 22 Special DA **$140**
Heavy hinged frame. Calibers: 22 LR, 22 W.R.F. 9-shot
cylinder. 6-inch barrel. Weight: 23 oz. Fixed sights, front
gold-plated. Blued finish. Checkered walnut stocks. Recessed safety cylinder on later models for high-speed ammunition. Discontinued prior to 1942.

H&R Model 199 Sportsman

**Harrington & Richardson Model 199
Sportsman SA Revolver** **$150**
Hinged frame. Caliber: 22 LR. 9-shot cylinder. 6-inch
barrel. 11 inches overall. Weight: 30 oz. Adjustable target
sights. Blued finish. Checkered walnut stocks.
Discontinued 1951.

Harrington & Richardson Model 504 DA **$145**
Caliber: 32 H&R Magnum. 5-shot cylinder. 4- or 6-inch
barrel, square butt; 3- or 4-inch barrel, round butt. Made
1984–1986.

Harrington & Richardson Model 532 DA **$85**
Caliber: 32 H&R Magnum. 5-shot cylinder. 2½- or 4-inch
barrel. Weight: approx. 20 and 25 oz. respectively. Fixed
sights. American walnut grips. Lustre blue finish. Made
1984–86.

Harrington & Richardson Model 586 DA **$140**
Caliber: 32 H&R Magnum. 5-shot cylinder. Barrel lengths:
4½, 5½, 7½, 10 inches. Weight: 30 oz. average. Adjustable
rear sight, blade front. Walnut finished hardwood grips.
Made 1984–86.

Harrington & Richardson Model 603 Target **$110**
Similar to Model 903, except in 22 WMR 6-shot capacity
with unfluted cylinder. Made 1980–83.

Harrington & Richardson Model 604 Target **$135**
Similar to Model 603, except with 6-inch bull barrel.
Weight: 38 oz. Made 1980–83.

H&R Model 622

Harrington & Richardson Model 622/623 DA **$85**
Solid frame. Caliber: 22 Short, Long, LR. 6-shot cylinder.
Barrel lengths: 2½-, 4-, 6-inch. Weight: 26 oz. w/4-inch
bbl. Fixed sights. Blued finish. Plastic stocks. Made 1957–
1986. *Note:* **Model 623** is same, except chrome or nickel
finish.

**Harrington & Richardson Model 632/633
Guardsman Double Action Revolver** **$90**
Solid frame. Caliber: 32 S&W Long. 6-shot cylinder. Barrel
lengths: 2½- or 4-inch. Weight: with 2½-inch barrel, 19 oz.

H&R Model 632 Guardsman

Harrington & Richardson 632/633 Guardsman (cont.)
Fixed sights. Blued or chrome finish. Checkered Tenite stocks (round butt on 2½-inch, square butt on 4-inch). Made 1953–1986. *Note:* **Model 633** is the same, except for chrome or nickel finish.

H&R Model 649

H&R Model 650, Nickel Finish

Harrington & Richardson Model 649/650 DA **$115**
Solid frame. Side loading and ejection. Convertible model with two 6-shot cylinders. Calibers: 22 LR, 22 WMR. 5½-inch barrel. Weight: 32 oz. Adjustable rear sight, blade front. Blued finish. One-piece, Western-style walnut stock. Made 1976–1986. *Note:* **Model 650** is same, except nickel finish.

H&R Model 666

Harrington & Richardson Model 666 DA **$90**
Solid frame. Convertible model with two 6-shot cylinders. Calibers: 22 LR, 22 WMR. 6-inch barrel. Weight: 28 oz. Fixed sights. Blued finish. Plastic stocks. Made 1976–78.

H&R Model 676

Harrington & Richardson Model 676 DA **$120**
Solid frame. Side loading and ejection. Convertible model with two 6-shot cylinders. Calibers: 22 LR, 22 WMR. Barrel lengths: 4½-, 5½-, 7½-, 12-inch. Weight: 32 oz. w/5½-inch bbl. Adjustable rear sight, blade front. Blued finish, color-casehardened frame. One-piece, Western-style walnut stock. Made 1976–1980.

H&R Model 686

Harrington & Richardson Model 686 DA **$145**
Caliber: 22 LR and 22 WMR. Barrels: 4½-, 5½-, 7½-, 10- and 12-inches. 6-shot magazine. Adjustable rear sight, ramp and blade front. Blued, color-casehardened frame. Weight: 31 oz. w/4½-inch bbl. Made 1980–86.

H&R Model 733, Nickel Finish

Harrington & Richardson Model 732/733 DA **$80**
Solid frame, swing-out 6-shot cylinder. Calibers: 32 S&W, 32 S&W Long. Barrel lengths: 2½-, 4-inch. Weight: 26 oz.w/ 4-inch bbl. Fixed sights (windage adjustable rear on 4-inch bbl. model). Blue finish. Plastic stocks. Made 1958–1986. *Note:* **Model 733** is same, except nickel finish.

Harrington & Richardson Model 826 DA **$110**
Caliber: 22 WMR. 6-shot magazine. 3-inch bull barrel. Ramp and blade front sight, adjustable rear. American walnut grips. Weight: 28 oz. Made 1981–83.

H&R Model 830, Nickel Finish

H&R Model 904

Harrington & Richardson Model 829/830 DA
Same as Model 826, except in 22 LR caliber. 9-shot capacity. Made 1981–83. Model 829, Blued **$115**
Model 830, Nickel **120**

Harrington & Richardson Model 832/833 DA
Same as Model 826, except in 32 S&W Long. Blued or nickel finish. Made 1981–83.
Model 832, Blued **$125**
Model 833, Nickel **130**

Harrington & Richardson Model 904 Target $115
Similar to Model 903, except 4- and 6-inch bull barrels. 4-inch barrel weighs 32 oz. Made 1980–86.

H&R Model 900

H&R Model 905

Harrington & Richardson Model 900/901 DA $65
Solid frame, snap-out cylinder. Calibers: 22 Short, Long, LR. 9-shot cylinder. Barrel lengths: 2½-, 4-, 6-inch. Weight: 26 oz. w/6-inch bbl. Fixed sights. Blued finish. Blade Cycolac stocks. Made 1962–1973. *Note:* **Model 901** (discontinued in 1963) is the same, except has chrome finish and white Tenite stocks.

Harrington & Richardson Model 905 Target $130
Same as Model 904, except with 4-inch barrel only. Nickel finish. Made 1981–83.

H&R Model 922, First Issue

H&R Model 903

H&R Model 922, Second Issue

Harrington & Richardson Model 903 Target $125
Caliber: 22 LR. 9-shot capacity. SA/DA. 6-inch target-weight flat-side barrel. Swing-out cylinder. Weight: 35 oz. Blade front sight, adjustable rear. American walnut grips. Made 1980–83.

Harrington & Richardson Model 922 DA Revolver, First Issue **$150**
Solid frame. Caliber: 22 LR. 9-shot cylinder. Barrel: early model, 10-inch, octagon; later production, 6-inch, round. Weight: 26 oz. w/6-inch bbl. Fixed sights. Blued finish. Checkered walnut stocks. Safety cylinder on later models. Discontinued prior to 1942.

Harrington & Richardson Model 922/923 DA Revolver, Second Issue **$75**
Solid frame. Caliber: 22 LR. 9-shot cylinder. Barrel lengths: 2½-, 4-, 6-inch. Weight: 24 oz. w/4-inch bbl. Fixed sights. Blued finish. Plastic stocks. Made 1950–1986. *Note:* Second Issue Model 922 has a different frame from that of the First Issue. **Model 923** is same as Model 922, Second Issue, except for nickel finish.

H&R Model 929

H&R Model 925

Harrington & Richardson Model 925 Defender .. **$115**
DA. Hinged frame. Caliber: 38 S&W. 5-shot cylinder. 2½-inch barrel. Weight: 22 oz. Adjustable rear sight, fixed front. Blued finish. One-piece wraparound grip. Made 1964–1978.

H&R Model 926

Harrington & Richardson Model 926 DA **$115**
Hinged frame. Calibers: 22 LR, 38 S&W. 9-shot (22 LR) or 5-shot (38) cylinder. 4-inch barrel. Weight: 31 oz. Adjustable rear sight, fixed front. Blued finish. Checkered walnut stocks. Made 1968–1978.

Harrington & Richardson Model 929/930 Sidekick DA Revolver **$85**
Caliber: 22 LR. Solid frame, swing-out 9-shot cylinder. Barrel lengths: 2½-, 4-, 6-inch. Weight: 24 oz. w/4-inch

Harrington & Richardson 929/930 Sidekick (cont.)
bbl. Fixed sights. Blued finish. Checkered plastic stocks. Made 1956–1986. *Note:* **Model 930** is same, except nickel finish.

H&R Model 939

Harrington & Richardson Model 939/940 Ultra Sidekick DA Revolver **$95**
Solid frame, swing-out 9-shot cylinder. Safety lock. Calibers: 22 Short, Long, LR. Flat-side 6-inch barrel w/ vent rib. Weight: 33 oz. Adjustable rear sight, ramp front. Blued finish. Checkered walnut stocks. Made 1958–1986. *Note:* **Model 940** is same, except has round barrel.

H&R Model 949

H&R Model 950

Harrington & Richardson Model 949/950 Forty-Niner DA Revolver **$90**

Solid frame. Side loading and ejection. Calibers: 22 Short, Long, LR. 9-shot cylinder. 5½-inch barrel. Weight: 31 oz. Adjustable rear sight, blade front. Blue or nickel finish. One-piece, Western-style walnut grip. Made 1960–1986. *Note:* **Model 950** is same, except nickel finish. (*See* photos, preceding page.)

Harrington & Richardson Model 976 DA **$90**

Same as Model 949, except has color-casehardened frame, 7½-inch barrel, weighs 36 oz. Intro. 1977; discontinued.

**H&R Model 999 Sportsman
First Issue**

Harrington & Richardson Model 999 Sportsman DA Revolver, First Issue **$160**

Hinged frame. Calibers: 22 LR, 22 W.R.F. Same specifications as Model 199 Sportsman Single Action. Discontinued before 1942.

Harrington & Richardson Model 999 Sportsman DA Revolver, Second Issue **$175**

Hinged frame. Caliber: 22 LR. 9-shot cylinder. 6-inch barrel w/vent rib. Weight: 30 oz. Adjustable sights. Blued finish. Checkered walnut stocks. Made 1950–1986.

**H&R New Model 999
Sportsman Double Action**

Harrington & Richardson (New) Model 999 Sportsman DA Revolver **$170**

Hinged frame. Caliber: 22 Short, Long, LR. 9-shot cylinder. 6-inch barrel w/vent rib. Weight: 30 oz. Sights: Blade front adjustable for elevation; square-notched rear adjustable for windage. Blued finish. Checkered hardwood stocks. Reintroduced in 1992.

Harrington & Richardson American DA **$75**

Solid frame. Calibers: 32 S&W Long, 38 S&W. 6-shot (32 cal.) or 5-shot (38 cal.) cylinder. Barrel lengths: 2½-, 4½- and 6-inch. Weight: about 16 oz. Fixed sights. Blued or nickel finish. Hard rubber stocks. Discont. prior to 1942.

Harrington & Richardson Automatic Ejecting DA Revolver **$145**

Hinged frame. Calibers: 32 S&W Long, 38 S&W. 6-shot cylinder (32 cal.), 5-shot (38 cal.). Barrel lengths: 3¼-,

H&R Automatic Ejecting

Harrington & Richardson Auto Ejecting DA (cont.)

4-, 5- and 6-inch. Weight: about 16 oz., 32 cal.; 15 oz., 38 cal. Fixed sights. Blued or nickel finish. Black hard rubber stocks. Discontinued prior to 1942.

H&R Bobby

Harrington & Richardson Bobby DA **$250**

Hinged frame. Calibers: 32 S&W, 38 S&W. 6-shot cylinder (32 cal.), 5-shot (38 cal.). 4-inch barrel. 9 inches overall. Weight: 23 oz. Fixed sights. Blued finish. Checkered walnut stocks. Discontinued 1946. *Note:* Originally designed and produced for use by London's bobbies.

H&R Defender 38

Harrington & Richardson Defender 38 DA **$105**

Hinged frame. Based on the Sportsman design. Caliber: 38 S&W. Barrel lengths: 4- and 6-inch. 9 inches overall w/4-inch barrel. Weight: 25 oz., 4-inch bbl. Fixed sights. Blued finish. Black plastic stocks. Discontinued 1946. *Note:* This model was manufactured during WW II as an arm for plant guards, auxiliary police, etc.

Harrington & Richardson Expert Model DA **$150**

Same specifications as 22 Special, except has 10-inch barrel. Weight: 28 oz. Discontinued prior to 1942.

Harrington & Richardson Hammerless DA, Large Frame **$105**

Hinged frame. Calibers: 32 S&W Long, 38 S&W. 6-shot cylinder (32 cal.), 5-shot (38 cal.). Barrel lengths: 3¼-, 4-,

Harrington & Richardson Hammerless DA, Lg. (cont.)

5- and 6-inch. Weight: about 17 oz. Fixed sights. Blued or nickel finish. Hard rubber stocks. Discont. prior to 1942.

H&R Hammerless Small Frame

Harrington & Richardson Hammerless DA, Small Frame $105

Hinged frame. Calibers: 22 LR, 32 S&W. 7-shot (22 cal.), 5-shot (32 cal.) cylinder. Barrel lengths: 2-, 3-, 4-, 5- and 6-inch. Weight: about 13 oz. Fixed sights. Blued or nickel finish. Hard rubber stocks. Discont. prior to 1942.

H&R Hunter

Harrington & Richardson Hunter Model DA $105

Solid frame. Caliber: 22 LR. 9-shot cylinder. 10-inch octagon barrel. Weight: 26 oz. Fixed sights. Blued finish. Checkered walnut stocks. Safety cylinder on later models. *Note:* An earlier Hunter Model was built on the smaller 7-shot frame. Discontinued prior to 1942.

H&R New Defender

H&R Premier

Harrington & Richardson New Defender DA $185

Hinged frame. Caliber: 22 LR. 9-shot cylinder. 2-inch barrel. 6¼ inches overall. Weight: 23 oz. Adjustable sights. Blued finish. Checkered walnut stocks, round butt. *Note:* Basically, this is the Sportsman DA with a short barrel. Discontinued prior to 1942.

Harrington & Richardson Premier DA $90

Small hinged frame. Calibers: 22 LR, 32 S&W. 7-shot (22 LR) or 5-shot (32) cylinder. Barrel lengths: 2-, 3-, 4-, 5- and 6-inch. Weight: 13 oz. (22 LR); 12 oz. (32). Fixed sights. Blued or nickel finish. Black hard rubber stocks. Discontinued prior to 1942.

Harrington & Richardson Model STR 022
Blank Revolver $65

Caliber: 22 RF blanks. 9-shot cylinder. 2½-inch barrel. Weight: 19 oz. Satin blue finish.

Harrington & Richardson Model STR 032
Blank Revolver $75

Same general specifications as STR 022 except chambered for 32 S&W blank cartridges.

H&R Target Model

Harrington & Richardson Target Model DA $130

Small hinged frame. Calibers: 22 LR, 22 W.R.F. 7-shot cylinder. 6-inch barrel. Weight: 16 oz. Fixed sights. Blued finish. Checkered walnut stocks. Discont. prior to 1942.

H&R Trapper

Harrington & Richardson Trapper Model DA $115

Solid frame. Caliber: 22 LR. 7-shot cylinder. 6-inch octagon barrel. Weight: 12¼ oz. Fixed sights. Blued finish. Checkered walnut stocks. Safety cylinder on later models. Discontinued prior to 1942.

H&R Ultra Sportsman

Harrington & Richardson Ultra Sportsman **$175**
SA. Hinged frame. Caliber: 22 LR. 9-shot cylinder. 6-inch
barrel. Weight: 30 oz. Adjustable target sights. Blued finish. Checkered walnut stocks. This model has short action,
wide hammer spur; cylinder is length of a 22 LR cartridge.
Discont. prior to 1942. (*See* illus., preceding page.)

H&R Vest Pocket

Harrington & Richardson Vest Pocket DA **$75**
Solid frame. Spurless hammer. Calibers: 22 Rimfire, 32
S&W. 7-shot (22 cal.) or 5-shot (32 cal.) cylinder. 1¹/₈-
inch barrel. Weight: about 9 oz. Blued or nickel finish.
Hard rubber stocks. Discontinued prior to 1942.

H&R Young America

Harrington & Richardson Young America DA **$75**
Solid frame. Calibers: 22 Long, 32 S&W. 7-shot (22 cal.)
or 5-shot (32 cal.) cylinder. Barrel lengths: 2-, 4¹/₂- and
6-inch. Weight: about 9 oz. Fixed sights. Blued or nickel
finish. Hard rubber stocks. Discont. prior to 1942.

HARTFORD ARMS & EQUIPMENT CO.
Hartford, Connecticut

Hartford pistols were the forebears of the original High
Standard line, since High Standard Mfg. Corp. acquired
Hartford Arms & Equipment Co. in 1932. The High Standard
Model B is essentially the same as the Hartford Automatic.

Hartford Automatic

Hartford Automatic Target Pistol **$525**
Caliber: 22 LR. 10-shot magazine. 6³/₄-inch barrel. 10³/₄
inches overall. Weight: 31 oz. Target sights. Blued finish.
Black rubber stocks. This arm closely resembles the early
Colt Woodsman and High Standard pistols. Made 1929–
1930.

Hartford Repeating Pistol **$400**
Same general design as the automatic pistol of this manufacture, but this model is a hand-operated repeating pistol
on the order of the Fiala. Made 1929–1930.

Hartford Single Shot Target Pistol **$405**
Similar in appearance to the Hartford Automatic. Caliber:
22 LR. 6³/₄-inch barrel. 10³/₄ inches overall. Weight: 38
oz. Target sights. Mottled frame and slide, blued barrel.
Black rubber or walnut stocks. Made 1929–1930.

HAWES FIREARMS
Van Nuys, California

Hawes Deputy Denver Marshal

Hawes Deputy Denver Marshal
Same as Deputy Marshal SA, except has brass frame.
22 LR (plastic grips) **$75**
Combination, 22 LR/22 WMR (plastic) **85**
Extra for walnut stocks **5**

Hawes Deputy Marshal

Hawes Deputy Marshal Single Action Revolver
Calibers: 22 LR; also 22 WMR in two-cylinder combination. 6-shot cylinder. 5¹/₂-inch barrel. 11 inches overall.
Weight: 34 oz. Adjustable rear sight, blade front. Blued
finish. Plastic or walnut grips. Made from 1973 to date.
22 Long Rifle (plastic grips) **$70**
Combination, 22 LR/22 WMR (plastic) **75**
Extra for walnut stocks **5**

Hawes Deputy Montana Marshal

Hawes Deputy Montana Marshal
Same as Deputy Marshal, except has brass grip frame, walnut grips only.
22 Long Rifle **$75**
Combination, 22 LR/22 WMR **95**

Hawes Deputy Silver City Marshal

Hawes Deputy Silver City Marshal
Same as Deputy Marshal, except has chrome-plated frame, brass grip frame, blued cylinder and barrel.
22 Long Rifle (plastic grips) **$70**
Combination, 22 LR/22 WMR (plastic) **90**
Extra for walnut grips **5**

Hawes Deputy Texas Marshal

Hawes Favorite

Hawes Deputy Texas Marshal
Same as Deputy Marshal, except has chrome finish.
22 Long Rifle (plastic grips) **$70**
Combination, 22 LR/22 WMR (plastic) **85**
Extra for walnut grips **5**

Hawes Favorite Single Shot Target Pistol **$130**
Replica of Stevens No. 35. Tip-up action. Caliber: 22 LR. 8-inch barrel. 12 inches overall. Weight: 24 oz. Target sights. Chrome-plated frame. Blued barrel. Plastic or rosewood grips (add $5). Made 1968–1976.

Hawes Sauer Chief Marshal

Hawes Sauer Chief Marshal SA Target Revolver
Same as Western Marshal, except has adjustable rear sight and front sight, oversized rosewood grips. Not made in 22 caliber.
357 Magnum or 45 Colt **$200**
44 Magnum **225**
Combination, 357 Magnum and 9mm Luger,
   45 Colt and 45 Auto **250**
Combination, 44 Magnum and 44-40 . . . . **245**

Hawes Sauer Federal Marshal

Hawes Sauer Federal Marshal
Same as Western Marshal, except has color-casehardened frame, brass grip frame, one-piece walnut grip. Not made in 22 caliber.
357 Magnum or 45 Colt **$200**
44 Magnum **220**
Combination, 357 Magnum and 9mm Luger,
   45 Colt and 45 Auto **250**
Combination, 44 Magnum and 44-40 . . . . **245**

Hawes Sauer Montana Marshal
Same as Western Marshal, except has brass grip frame. 22 caliber discontinued.
357 Magnum or 45 Colt **$200**
44 Magnum **225**
Combination, 357 Magnum and 9mm Luger,
   45 Colt and 45 Auto **240**

Hawes Sauer Montana Marshal

Hawes Sauer Western Marshal

Hawes Sauer Montana Marshal (cont.)
Combination, 44 Magnum and 44-40 . . . . $250
22 LR 195
Combination, 22 LR and 22 WMR 210

Hawes Sauer Silver City Marshal

Hawes Sauer Western Marshal 22

Hawes Sauer Silver City Marshal
Same as Western Marshal, except has nickel-plated frame, brass grip frame, blued cylinder and barrel, pearlite grips.
44 Magnum $240
Combination, 357 Magnum and 9mm Luger,
45 Colt and 45 Auto 225
Combination, 44 Magnum and 44-40 260

Hawes Sauer Western Marshal Single Action Revolver
Calibers: 22 LR (discont.), 357 Magnum, 44 Magnum, 45 Auto. Also in two-cylinder combinations: 22 WMR (discont.), 9mm Luger, 44-40, 45 Auto. 6-shot cylinder. Barrel lengths: 5½-inch (discont.), 6-inch. 11¾ inches overall w/6-inch bbl. Weight: 46 oz. Fixed sights. Blued finish. Originally furnished with simulated stag plastic stocks; recent production has smooth rosewood stocks. Made 1968 to date by J. P. Sauer & Sohn, Eckernforde, Germany.
357 Magnum or 45 Colt $200
44 Magnum 205
Combination, 357 Magnum and 9mm Luger,
45 Colt and 45 Auto 225
Combination, 44 Magnum and 44-40 240
22 Long Rifle 195
Combination, 22 LR and 22 WMR 210

Hawes Sauer Texas Marshal

Hawes Sauer Texas Marshal
Same as Western Marshal, except nickel-plated, has pearlite grips. 22 caliber discontinued.
357 Magnum or 45 Colt $225
44 Magnum 240
Combination, 357 Magnum and 9mm Luger,
45 Colt and 45 Auto 260
Combination, 44 Magnum and 44-40 275
22 Long Rifle 195
Combination, 22 LR and 22 WMR 230

HECKLER & KOCH
Oberndorf/Neckar, West Germany, and Chantilly, Virginia

Heckler & Koch Model HK4 DA Auto Pistol
Calibers: 380 Automatic (9mm Short); also 22 LR, 25 Automatic (6.35mm), 32 Automatic (7.65mm) with conversion kits. 7-shot magazine in 380; 8-shot in other calibers. 3¹¹/₃₂-inch barrel. 6³/₁₆ inches overall. Weight: 18 oz. Fixed sights. Blued finish. Plastic stock. Discontinued 1984.
380 Automatic $475
380 Automatic with 22 conversion unit 425
380 Automatic with 22, 25, 32 conversion units . . . 750

Heckler & Koch Model P7K3 DA Auto Pistol
Caliber: 380 ACP. 8-round magazine. 3.8 inch-barrel. 6.3 inches overall. Weight: about 26 oz. Adjustable rear sight. Made from 1988 to date.
P7K3 in 380 Cal. $790
22 LR Conversion Kit 425

Heckler & Koch HK4

Heckler & Koch Model P7K3

Heckler & Koch Model P7M8

Heckler & Koch Model P7M8 . . . . **$750**
Caliber: 9mm. 8-shot magazine. 4.13-inch barrel. 6.73 inches overall. Weight: 29.9 oz. Matte black finish. Adjustable rear sight. Made 1985 to date.

Heckler & Koch Model P7M10
Caliber: 40 S&W. 9-shot magazine. 4.2-inch barrel. 6.9 inches overall. Weight: 43 oz. Sights: fixed front blade; adjustable rear w/3-dot system. Made from 1992 to date.
Blued Finish **$1115**
Nickel Finish **1225**

Heckler & Koch P7M13

Heckler & Koch Model P7M13 . . . . **$1075**
Caliber: 9mm. 13-shot magazine. 4.13-inch barrel. 6.65 inches overall. Weight: 34.42 oz. Matte black finish. Adjustable rear sight. Made 1985–89.

Heckler & Koch Model P7 (PSP)

Heckler & Koch Model P7(PSP) Auto Pistol . . . **$1125**
Caliber: 9mm Parabellum/Luger. 8-shot magazine. DA. 4.13-inch barrel. 6.54 inches overall. Weight: about 33.5 oz. Blue finish. Made 1983–85.

Heckler & Koch Model P9S DA Automatic Pistol
Calibers: 9mm Luger, 45 Automatic. 9-shot (9mm) or 7-shot (45 Auto) magazine. 4-inch barrel. 7⅝ inches overall. Weight: 32 ounces. Fixed sights. Blued finish. Plastic grips. Discontinued 1986.
9mm **$950**
45 Automatic **975**

Heckler & Koch Model P9S 45

Heckler & Koch Model P9S 9mm Target

Heckler & Koch Model P9S 9mm Target **$995**
Same as standard Model P9S 9mm, except has adjustable trigger, trigger stop, adjustable rear sight.

Heckler & Koch Model P9S 9mm Competition Kit

Heckler & Koch Model P9S 9mm Target Competition Kit
Same as Model P9S 9mm Target, except comes with extra 5½-inch barrel and barrel weight. Also available with walnut competition stock.
With Standard stock **$1195**
With Competition stock 1295

Heckler & Koch Model SP89 . . . . **$2100**
Semiautomatic, recoil-operated, delayed roller-locked bolt system. Caliber: 9mm Luger. 15-shot magazine. 4.5-inch barrel. 13 inches overall. Weight: 68 oz. Hooded front sight; adj. rotary-aperture rear. Made from 1989 to date.

Heckler & Koch Model USP Auto Pistol
Polymer integral grip/frame design with recoil reduction system. Calibers: 9mm Parabellum, 40 S&W. 15-shot (9mm) or 13-shot (40 S&W) magazine. 4¾-inch barrel. 6⅞ inches overall. Weight: 28 oz. Sights: blade front; adjustable rear w/3-dot system. Matte black finish. Stippled black polymer grip. Available in SA/DA or DAO. Made from 1993 to date.
Right-Hand Model **$595**
Left-Hand Model 615

Heckler & Koch Model VP'70Z

Heckler & Koch Model VP'70Z Auto Pistol **$495**
Caliber: 9mm Luger. 18-shot magazine. DA. 4½-inch barrel. 8 inches overall. Weight: 32½ oz. Fixed sights. Blued slide, plastic receiver and stock. Discontinued 1986.

HELWAN PISTOL
See Interarms.

HERITAGE MANUFACTURING
Opa Locka, Florida

Heritage Model HA25 Auto Pistol
Caliber: 25 ACP. 6-shot magazine. 2½-inch barrel. 4⅝ inches overall. Weight: 12 oz. Fixed sights. Blued or chrome finish. Made from 1993 to date.
Blued **$65**
Chrome 75

Heritage Rough Rider

Heritage Rough Rider SA Revolver
Calibers: 22 LR, 22 WRF. 6-shot cylinder. Barrel lengths: 3, 4³/₄, 6¹/₂, 9 inches. Weight: 31–38 oz. Sights: blade front; fixed rear. High-polished blued finish with gold accents. Smooth walnut grips. Made from 1993 to date.
22 Long Rifle . . . . **$ 75**
22 WRF **100**

Heritage Sentry DA

Heritage Sentry DA Revolver
Caliber: 38 Special. 6-shot cylinder. 2- or 4-inch barrel. 6¹/₄ inches overall w/2-inch bbl. Sights: ramp front; fixed rear. Blued or chrome finish. Checkered plastic grips. Made from 1993 to date.
Blued . . . . **$ 95**
Chrome **100**

══ HI-POINT FIREARMS ══
Mansfield, Ohio

Hi-Point JS Series 9mm

Hi-Point Model JS-9mm Auto Pistol **$110**
Caliber: 9mm Parabellum. 8-shot magazine. 4³/₄-inch barrel. 7³/₄ inches overall. Weight: 42 oz. Fixed low-profile sights. Matte black finish. Checkered plastic grips.

Hi-Point Model JS-9mm Compact Pistol **$100**
Similar to standard JS-9, except with 3¹/₂-inch barrel.

Hi-Point Model JS-40 Auto Pistol **$125**
Similar to Model JS-9mm, except in caliber 40 S&W.

Hi-Point Model JS-45 Auto Pistol **$125**
Similar to Model JS-9mm, except in caliber 45 ACP with 7-shot magazine.

══ J. C. HIGGINS HANDGUNS ══
See Sears, Roebuck & Company.

══ HIGH STANDARD SPORTING FIREARMS ══
East Hartford, Connecticut
Formerly High Standard Mfg. Co., Hamden, Connecticut

A long-standing producer of sporting arms, High Standard discontinued its operations in 1984.

AUTOMATIC PISTOLS

> **NOTE:** For ease in finding a particular firearm, High Standard handguns are grouped into three sections: Automatic Pistols (below), Derringers, and Revolvers, which follow. For a complete listing, please refer to the Index.

High Standard Model A

High Standard Model A Automatic Pistol **$495**
Hammerless. Caliber: 22 LR. 10-shot magazine. Barrel lengths: 4¹/₂, 6³/₄ inch. 11¹/₂ inches overall w/6³/₄-inch bbl. Weight: 36 oz. w/6³/₄-inch bbl. Adjustable target sights. Blued finish. Checkered walnut stocks. Made 1938–1942.

High Standard Model B

High Standard Model B Automatic Pistol **$395**
Original Standard pistol. Hammerless. Caliber: 22 LR.
10-shot magazine. Barrel lengths: 4½-, 6¾-inch. 10¾
inches overall w/6¾-inch bbl. Weight: 33 oz. w/6¾-inch
bbl. Fixed sights. Blued finish. Hard rubber stocks. Made
1932–1942. (*See* illustration, preceding page.)

High Standard Model C Automatic Pistol **$450**
Same as Model B, except in 22 Short. Made 1935–1942.

High Standard Model D

High Standard Model D Automatic Pistol **$420**
Same general specifications as Model A, but heavier barrel.
Weight: 40 oz. w/6¾-inch barrel. Made 1937–1942.

High Standard Dura-Matic

High Standard Dura-Matic Automatic Pistol **$295**
Takedown. Caliber: 22 LR. 10-shot magazine. Barrels: 4½-
or 6½-inch, interchangeable. 10⅞ inches overall w/6½-
inch bbl. Weight: 35 oz. w/6½-inch bbl. Fixed sights.
Blued finish. Checkered grips. Made 1952–1970.

High Standard Model E

High Standard Model E Automatic Pistol **$515**
Same general specifications as Model A, but with extra
heavy barrel and thumbrest stocks. Weight: 42 oz. w/6¾-
inch bbl. Made 1937–1942.

High Standard Field-King Automatic Pistol
Same general specifications as Sport-King, but with
heavier barrel and target sights. Late model 6¾-inch barrels have recoil stabilizer feature. Weight: 43 oz. w/6¾-
inch barrel. Made 1951–58.
With one barrel **$310**
With both barrels **345**

High Standard Flite-King Automatic Pistol—First Model
Same general specifications as Sport-King, except in cal-
iber 22 Short with aluminum alloy frame and slide; weighs
26 oz. w/6½-inch bbl. Made 1953–58.
With one barrel **$395**
With both barrels **440**

**High Standard Flite-King Automatic Pistol
Second Model** **$310**
Same as Sport-King—Second Model, except caliber 22
Short and weighs 2 oz. lighter. Made 1958–1966.

High Standard Model G-380

High Standard Model G-380 Automatic Pistol . . . **$495**
Lever takedown. Visible hammer. Thumb safety. Caliber:
380 Automatic. 6-shot magazine. 5-inch barrel. Weight:
40 oz. Fixed sights. Blued finish. Checkered plastic stocks.
Made 1943–1950.

High Standard Model G-B

High Standard Model G-B Automatic Pistol
Lever takedown. Hammerless. Interchangeable barrels.
Caliber: 22 LR. 10-shot magazine. Barrel lengths: 4½-,
6¾-inch. 10¾ inches overall w/6¾-inch bbl. Weight: 36
oz. w/6¾-inch bbl. Fixed sights. Blued finish. Checkered
plastic stocks. Made 1948–1951.
With one barrel **$425**
With both barrels **460**

High Standard Model G-D Automatic Pistol
Lever takedown. Hammerless. Interchangeable barrels.
Caliber: 22 LR. 10-shot magazine. Barrel lengths: 4½-,
6¾-inch. 11½ inches overall w/6¾-inch bbl. Weight: 41
oz. w/6¾-inch bbl. Target sights. Blued finish. Checkered
walnut stocks. Made 1948–1951.
With one barrel **$450**
With both barrels **510**

High Standard Model G-E Automatic Pistol
Same general specifications as Model G-D, but with extra
heavy barrel and thumbrest stocks. Weight: 44 oz. w/6¾-
inch barrel. Made 1949–1951.

HANDGUNS

High Standard Model G-E

High Standard Model G-E Automatic Pistol (cont.)
With one barrel **$560**
With both barrels **595**

High Standard Model H-A

High Standard Model H-A Automatic Pistol **$495**
Same as Model A, but with visible hammer, no thumb
safety. Made 1939–1942.

High Standard Model H-B

High Standard Model H-B Automatic Pistol **$400**
Same as Model B, but with visible hammer, no thumb
safety. Made 1940–42.

High Standard Model H-D Automatic Pistol **$420**
Same as Model D, but with visible hammer, no thumb
safety. Made 1939–1942.

High Standard Model H-DM Automatic Pistol . . . **$410**
Also called H-D Military. Same as Model H-D, but with
thumb safety. Made 1941–1951.

High Standard Model H-E

High Standard Model H-E Automatic Pistol **$635**
Same as Model E, but with visible hammer, no thumb
safety. Made 1939–1942.

High Standard Olympic, First Model

High Standard Olympic Automatic Pistol—First Model
Same general specifications as Model G-E, but in 22 Short
with light alloy slide. Made 1950–51.
With one barrel **$395**
With both barrels **465**

High Standard Olympic, Second Model

High Standard Olympic Automatic Pistol—Second Model
Same general specifications as Supermatic, but in 22 Short
with light alloy slide. Weight: 39 oz. w/6¾-inch barrel. Made
1951–58.
With one barrel **$495**
With both barrels **600**

**High Standard Olympic Automatic Pistol
Third Model** **$575**
Same as Supermatic Trophy with bull barrel, except in
caliber 22 Short. Made 1963–66.

High Standard Olympic Commemorative
Limited edition of Supermatic Trophy Military issued to
commemorate the only American-made rimfire target
pistol ever to win an Olympic Gold Medal. Highly engraved with Olympic rings inlaid in gold. Deluxe presentation case. Two versions issued: in 1992 (22 LR) and
1980 (22 Short). *Note:* Value shown is for pistol in new,
unfired condition.
1972 Issue **$1295**
1980 Issue **995**

High Standard Olympic I.S.U. **$750**
Same as Supermatic Citation, except caliber 22 Short,
6¾- and 8-inch tapered barrels with stabilizer, detachable

High Standard Olympic I.S.U.

High Standard Plinker

High Standard Olympic I.S.U. (cont.)
weights. Made from 1958 to date; 8-inch barrel discontinued in 1964.

High Standard Olympic I.S.U. Military

High Standard Sharpshooter

High Standard Olympic I.S.U. Military $725
Same as Olympic I.S.U., except has military grip and bracket rear sight. Introduced in 1965. Discontinued.

High Standard Sharpshooter Automatic Pistol . . **$410**
Takedown. Hammerless. Caliber: 22 LR. 10-shot magazine. 5½-inch bull barrel. 9 inches overall. Weight: 42 oz. Micrometer rear sight, blade front sight. Blued finish. Plastic stocks. Made 1971–1983.

High Standard Olympic Military

**High Standard Sport-King
First Model**

High Standard Olympic Military $625
Same as Olympic—Third Model, except has military grip and bracket rear sight. Made in 1965.

High Standard Plinker $395
Similar to Dura-Matic with same general specifications. Made 1971–73.

High Standard Sport-King Automatic Pistol—First Model
Takedown. Hammerless. Interchangeable barrels. Caliber: 22 LR. 10-shot magazine. Barrel lengths: 4½-, 6¾-inch. 11½ inches overall w/6¾-inch bbl. Weight: 39 oz. w/6¾-inch bbl. Fixed sights. Blued finish. Checkered plastic thumbrest stocks. Made 1951–58. *Note:* 1951–54 production has lever takedown as in "G" series; later version illustrated has push-button takedown.
With one barrel **$295**
With both barrels **375**

**High Standard Sport-King
Second Model**

High Standard Sport-King Automatic Pistol Second Model **$260**

Caliber: 22 LR. 10-shot magazine. Barrels: 4¹/₂- or 6³/₄-inch, interchangeable. 11¹/₄ inches overall w/6³/₄-inch bbl. Weight: 42 oz. w/6³/₄-inch bbl. Fixed sights. Blued finish. Checkered grips. Made 1958–1970.

**High Standard Sport-King
Third Model**

High Standard Sport-King Automatic Pistol Third Model **$300**

Similar to Sport-King—Second Model, with same general specifications. Blued or nickel finish. Introduced in 1974. Discontinued.

High Standard Sport-King Lightweight

Same as standard Sport-King, except has forged aluminum alloy frame, weighs 30 oz. with 6³/₄-inch barrel. Made 1954–1965.

With one barrel **$395**
With both barrels **450**

High Standard Supermatic

High Standard Supermatic Automatic Pistol

Takedown. Hammerless. Interchangeable barrels. Caliber: 22 LR. 10-shot magazine. Barrel lengths: 4¹/₂-, 6³/₄-inch. Late model 6³/₄-inch barrels have recoil stabilizer feature. Weight: 43 oz. w/6³/₄-inch bbl. 11¹/₂ inches overall w/6³/₄-

High Standard Supermatic Automatic Pistol (cont.)

inch bbl. Target sights. Elevated serrated rib between sights. Adjustable barrel weights add 2 or 3 oz. Blued finish. Checkered plastic thumbrest stocks. Made 1951–58.

With one barrel **$395**
With both barrels **445**

**High Standard Supermatic Citation
Bull Barrel**

High Standard Supermatic Citation

Same as Supermatic Tournament, except 6³/₄-, 8-, 10-inch tapered barrels with stabilizer and two removable weights. Also furnished with Tournament's 5¹/₂-inch bull barrel, adjustable trigger pull, recoil-proof click-adjustable rear sight (barrel-mounted on 8- and 10-inch barrels), checkered walnut thumbrest grips on bull barrel model. Currently mfd. with only bull barrel. Made 1958 to date.

With bull barrel **$510**
With tapered barrel **550**

**High Standard Supermatic Citation
Military Fluted Barrel**

High Standard Supermatic Citation Military

Same as Supermatic Citation, except has military grip and bracket rear sight, barrels as in Supermatic Trophy. Made from 1965 to date.

With bull barrel **$500**
With fluted barrel **540**

**High Standard Supermatic Tournament
Bull Barrel**

High Standard Supermatic Tournament $525

Takedown. Caliber: 22 LR. 10-shot magazine. Barrels (interchangeable): 5½-inch bull, 6¾-inch heavy tapered, notched and drilled for stabilizer and weights. 10 inches overall w/5½-inch bbl. Weight: 44 oz. w/5½-inch bbl. Click adjustable rear sight, undercut ramp front. Blued finish. Checkered grips. Made 1958–1966. (*See* photo, preceding page.)

High Standard
Supermatic Tournament Military
Tapered Barrel

High Standard Supermatic Tournament Military ... $575

Same as Supermatic Tournament, except has military grip. Made 1965–1971.

High Standard Supermatic Trophy
Bull Barrel

High Standard Supermatic Trophy

Same as Supermatic Citation, except 5½-inch bull barrel or 7¼-inch fluted barrel with detachable stabilizer and weights, extra magazine. High-luster blued finish, checkered walnut thumbrest grips. Made 1963–66.
With bull barrel $550
With fluted barrel 615

High Standard Supermatic Trophy
Military Fluted Barrel

High Standard Supermatic Trophy Military

Same as Supermatic Trophy, except has military grip and bracket rear sight. Made 1965–1984.
With bull barrel $540
With fluted barrel 600

High Standard Victor
Solid Rib Barrel

High Standard Victor Automatic Pistol $465

Takedown. Caliber: 22 LR. 10-shot magazine. Barrels: 4½-inch solid or vent rib, 5½-inch vent rib; interchangeable. 9¾ inches overall w/5½-inch bbl. Weight: 52 oz. kw/5½-inch bbl. Rib-mounted target sights. Blued finish. Checkered walnut thumbrest stocks. Standard or military grip configuration. Made from 1972 to date (standard-grip model, 1974–75).

DERRINGER

NOTE: High Standard Automatic Pistols can be found in the preceding section, while Revolvers immediately follow this Derringer listing.

High Standard Derringer

High Standard Derringer

Hammerless, double action, double barrel (over/under). Calibers: 22 Short, Long, LR; 22 Magnum Rimfire. 2-shot. 3½-inch barrels. 5 inches overall. Weight: 11 oz. Standard model has blued or nickel finish, plastic grips; presentation model is gold-plated in walnut case. Standard model made from 1963 (22 S-L-LR) and 1964 (22 MRF) to date; gold model, 1965–1983.
Gold Presentation, one derringer $280
Gold Presentation, matched pair, consecutive numbers 425
Standard Model 160

REVOLVERS

NOTE: Only High Standard Revolvers can be found in this section. For Automatic Pistols and Derringers, see the preceding sections. For a complete listing of High Standard handguns, please refer to the Index.

High Standard Camp Gun

High Standard Camp Gun **$200**
Same as Sentinel Mark I/Mark IV, except has 6-inch barrel, adjustable rear sight, target-style checkered walnut stocks. Caliber: 22 LR or 22 WMR. Made 1976–1983.

**High Standard Double-Nine Double Action
Revolver—Aluminum Frame** **$215**
Western-style version of Sentinel. Blued or nickel finish with simulated ivory, ebony or stag grips. 5½-inch barrel. 11 inches overall. Weight: 27¼ oz. Made 1959–1971.

High Standard Double-Nine Deluxe **$225**
Same as Double-Nine—Steel Frame, except has adjustable target rear sight. Introduced in 1971. Discontinued.

**High Standard Double-Nine—
Steel Frame**

High Standard Double-Nine—Steel Frame **$250**
Similar to Double-Nine—Aluminum Frame, with same general specifications, except has extra cylinder for 22 WMR, walnut stocks. Introduced in 1971. Discont.

High Standard Durango

High Standard Durango **$190**
Similar to Double-Nine—Steel Frame, except 22 LR only, available with 4½- and 5½-inch barrels. Made 1971–73.

High Standard High Sierra

High Standard High Sierra Double Action Revolver
Similar to Double-Nine—Steel Frame, except has 7-inch octagon barrel, gold-plated grip frame; fixed or adjustable sights. Made 1973–1983.
With fixed sights **$190**
With adjustable sights **250**

High Standard Hombre **$195**
Similar to Double-Nine—Steel Frame, except 22 LR only, lacks single-action type ejector rod and tube, has 4½-inch barrel. Made 1971–73.

High Standard Kit Gun

High Standard Kit Gun Double Action Revolver . **$175**
Solid frame, swing-out cylinder. Caliber: 22 LR. 9-shot cylinder. 4-inch barrel. 9 inches overall. Weight: 19 oz. Adjustable rear sight, ramp front. Blued finish. Checkered walnut stocks. Made 1970–73.

**High Standard Longhorn
Aluminum Frame**

High Standard Longhorn—Aluminum Frame
Similar to Double-Nine—Aluminum Frame. Longhorn hammer spur. Blued finish 4½-inch barrel with simulated

High Standard Longhorn—Aluminum Frame (cont.)

pearl grips; 5½-inch, simulated stag grips; 9½-inch, walnut grips. Latter model made 1960–1971; others made 1961–66.

With 4½- or 5½-inch barrel **$160**
With 9½-inch barrel **225**

High Standard Longhorn—Steel Frame

High Standard Longhorn—Steel Frame

Similar to Double-Nine—Steel Frame, except has 9½-inch barrel; available with fixed or adjustable sights. Made 1971–1983.

With fixed sights **$175**
With adjustable sights **295**

High Standard Natchez

High Standard Natchez **$120**

Similar to Double-Nine—Aluminum Frame, except 4½-inch barrel (10 inches overall, weighs 25¼ oz.), blued finish, simulated ivory bird'shead grips. Made 1961–66.

High Standard Posse

High Standard Posse **$130**

Similar to Double-Nine—Aluminum Frame, except 3½-inch barrel (9 inches overall, weighs 23¼ oz.), blued finish, brass-grip frame and trigger guard, walnut grips. Made 1961–66.

High Standard Sentinel

High Standard Sentinel DA Revolver **$300**

Solid frame, swing-out cylinder. Caliber: 22 LR. 9-shot cylinder. Barrels: 3-, 4- or 6-inch. 9 inches overall w/4-inch bbl. Weight: 19 oz. w/4-inch bbl. Fixed sights. Aluminum frame. Blued or nickel finish. Checkered grips. Made 1955–56.

High Standard Sentinel Deluxe

High Standard Sentinel Deluxe **$250**

Same as Sentinel, except 4- or 6-inch barrels only; has wide trigger, movable rear sight, two-piece square-butt grips. Made 1957–1974. *Note:* Designated Sentinel after 1971.

High Standard Sentinel Imperial **$235**

Same as Sentinel, except has onyx-black or nickel finish, two-piece checkered walnut grips, ramp front sight. Made 1962–65.

High Standard Sentinel I

High Standard Sentinel I Double Action Revolver

Steel frame. Caliber: 22 LR. 9-shot cylinder. Barrel lengths: 2-, 3-, 4-inch. 6⅞ inches overall w/2-inch bbl. Weight: 21½ oz. w/2-inch bbl. Ramp front sight, fixed or adjustable rear. Blued or nickel finish. Smooth walnut stocks. Made 1974–1983.

With fixed sights **$245**
With adjustable sights **265**

High Standard Sentinel Mark II

High Standard Sentinel Mark III

HOPKINS & ALLEN ARMS CO.
Norwich, Connecticut

Hopkins & Allen Revolvers
See listings of comparable Harrington & Richardson and Iver Johnson models for values.

INTERARMS
Alexandria, Virginia

See also Bersa Pistol.

Interarms/Helwan Brigadier

High Standard Sentinel Mark II DA Revolver **$295**
Caliber: 357 Magnum. 6-shot cylinder. Barrel lengths: 2¹/₂-, 4-, 6-inch. 9 inches overall with 4-inch bbl. Weight: 38 oz. w/4-inch bbl. Fixed sights. Blued finish. Walnut service or combat-style stocks. Made 1974–76.

High Standard Sentinel Mark III **$300**
Same as Sentinel Mark II, except has ramp front and adjustable rear sights. Made 1974–76.

High Standard Sentinel Mark IV
Same as Sentinel Mark I, except in caliber 22 WMR. Made 1974–1983.
With fixed sights **$250**
With adjustable sights **275**

Interarms/Helwan Brigadier Auto Pistol **$245**
Caliber: 9mm Parabellum. 8-shot magazine. 4¹/₂-inch barrel. 8 inches overall. Weight: 32 oz. Sights: blade front; dovetailed rear. Blued finish. Grooved plastic grips.

Interarms Virginian Dragoon
Adjustable Sights

High Standard Sentinel Snub

High Standard Sentinel Snub **$180**
Same as Sentinel Deluxe, except with 2³/₈-inch barrel (7¹/₄ inches overall, weighs 15 oz.), checkered bird'shead-type grips. Made 1957–1974.

Interarms Virginian Dragoon Single Action Revolver
Calibers: 357 Magnum, 44 Magnum, 45 Colt. 6-shot cylinder. Barrels: 5- (not available in 44 Magnum), 6-, 7¹/₂-, 8³/₈-inch (latter only in 44 Magnum w/adjustable sights). 11⁷/₈ inches overall w/6-inch bbl. Weight: 48 oz. w/6-inch bbl. Fixed sights or micrometer rear and ramp front sights. Blued finish with color-casetreated frame. Smooth walnut stocks. SWISSAFE base pin safety system. Manufactured by Interarms Industries Inc., Midland, VA. 1977–1984.
Standard Dragoon **$250**
Engraved Dragoon **475**
Deputy Model **250**

**Interarms Virginian Revolver
Silhouette Model**

Interarms Virginian Revolver Silhouette Model .. **$375**
Same general specifications as regular model except designed in stainless steel with untapered bull barrel lengths of 7½, 8⅜ and 10½ inches. Made 1985–86.

Interarms Virginian Single Action Revolver **$295**
See listing under Hämmerli (manufacturer).

═══ INTRATEC U.S.A. INC. ═══
Miami, Florida

Intratec Model Tec-9 Semiautomatic
Caliber: 9mm Luger/Parabellum. 20- or 36-round magazine. 5-inch barrel. Weight: 50-51 oz. Open fixed front sight, adjustable rear. Military nonglare blued or stainless finish.
Tec-9 w/Blued Finish **$245**
Tec-9 w/Electroless Nickel Finish **275**
Tec 9S w/Stainless Finish **295**

Intratec Model Tec-9M Semiautomatic
Same specifications as Model Tec-9, except has 3-inch barrel without shroud and 20-round magazine. Blued or stainless finish.
Tec-9M w/Blued Finish **$225**
Tec-9MS w/Stainless Finish **280**

Intratec Model Tec-22T Semiautomatic
Caliber: 22 LR. 10/22-type 30-shot magazine. 4-inch barrel. 11³⁄₁₆ inches overall. Weight: 30 oz. Protected post front sight; adjustable rear sight. Finish: Matte black or Tec-Kote. Made from 1989 to date.
Tec-22T Standard **$155**
Tec-22TK Tec-Kote **175**

Intratec Model Tec-25 DA Semiautomatic **$75**
Caliber: 25 ACP. 8-shot magazine. 2.5-inch barrel. 5 inches overall. Weight: 14 oz. Fixed sights. Wraparound composition grips. Finish: Matte black, satin grey or Tec-Kote. Made from 1991 to date.

Intratec Model Tec Double Derringer **$90**
Calibers: 22 WRF, 32 H&R Mag., 38 Special. 2-shot capacity. 3-inch barrel. 4⅝ inches overall. Weight: 13 oz. Fixed sights. Matte black finish.

═══ JAPANESE MILITARY PISTOLS ═══
Tokyo, Japan
Manufactured by Government Plant

Japanese Model 14 (1925) Automatic Pistol **$475**
Modification of the Nambu Model 1914, changes chiefly intended to simplify mass production. Standard round

Japanese Model 14 (1925)*

Japanese Model 14 (1925) Automatic Pistol (cont.)
trigger guard or oversized guard for use with gloves. Caliber: 8mm Nambu. 8-shot magazine. 4¾-inch barrel. 9 inches overall. Weight: about 29 oz. Fixed sights. Blued finish. Grooved wood stocks. Introduced 1925; mfd. through WW II.

Japanese Model 94*

Japanese Model 94 (1934) Automatic Pistol **$230**
Poorly design and constructed, this pistol can be fired merely by applying pressure on the sear, which is exposed on the left side. Caliber: 8mm Nambu. 6-shot magazine. 3⅛-inch barrel. 7⅛ inches overall. Weight: about 27 oz. Fixed sights. Blued finish. Hard rubber or wood stocks. Introduced in 1934, principally for export to Latin American countries, production continued thru WW II.

Japanese Nambu Model 1914 Automatic Pistol . **$460**
Original Japanese service pistol, resembles Luger in appearance and Glisenti in operation. Caliber: 8mm Nambu. 7-shot magazine. 4½-inch barrel. 9 inches overall. Weight: about 30 oz. Fixed front sight, adjustable rear sight. Blued finish. Checkered wood stocks. Made 1914–1925.

═══ JENNINGS FIREARMS INC. ═══
Irvine, California

Jennings Model J Auto Pistol
Calibers: 22 LR, 25 ACP. 6-shot magazine. 2½-inch barrel. About 5 inches overall. Weight: 13 oz. Fixed sights. Chrome, satin nickel or black Teflon finish. Walnut,

Jennings Model J Auto Pistol (cont.)
grooved black Cycolac or resin-impregnated wood grips. Made from 1981 to date.
Model J-22 . . . . **$65**
Model J-25 . . . . **50**

Jennings Model M38 Bryco Auto Pistol **$90**
Calibers: 32 ACP, 380 ACP. 6-shot magazine. 2^{13}/$_{16}$-inch barrel. 5^5/$_{16}$ inches overall. Weight: 15 oz. Fixed sights. Chrome, satin nickel or black Teflon finish. Walnut, grooved black Cycolac or resin-impregnated wood grips. Made from 1988 to date.

Jennings Model M48 Bryco Auto Pistol **$100**
Calibers: 380 ACP, 9mm. 7-shot magazine. 4-inch barrel. 6^{11}/$_{16}$ inches overall. Weight: 20 oz. Fixed sights. Chrome, satin nickel or black Teflon finish. Smooth wood or black Teflon grips. Made from 1989 to date.

Jennings Model M58 Bryco Auto Pistol **$110**
Caliber: 380 ACP. 13-shot magazine. 3^3/$_4$-inch barrel. 5^1/$_2$ inches overall. Weight: 30 oz. Fixed sights. Chrome, satin nickel, blued or black Teflon finish. Smooth wood or black Teflon grips. Made from 1993 to date.

Jennings Model M59 Bryco Auto Pistol **$120**
Caliber: 9mm Parabellum. 13-shot magazine. 4-inch barrel. 6^1/$_2$ inches overall. Weight: 33 oz. Fixed sights. Chrome, satin nickel, blued or black Teflon finish. Smooth wood or black Teflon grips. Made from 1994 to date.

IVER JOHNSON'S ARMS
Jacksonville, Arkansas

Operation of this company dates back to 1871, when Iver Johnson and Martin Bye partnered to manufacture metallic cartridge revolvers. Johnson became the sole owner and changed the name to Iver Johnson's Arms & Cycle Works, which it was known as for almost 100 years. Modern management shortened the name, and after several owner changes, the firm was moved from Massachusetts, its original base, to Jacksonville, Arkansas. It is now a division of the American Military Arms Corporation (AMAC).

Iver Johnson 9mm DA Automatic

AUTOMATIC PISTOLS

> **NOTE:** For ease in finding a particular firearm, Iver Johnson handguns are divided into two sections: Automatic Pistols (below) and Revolvers, which follows. For the complete handgun listing, please refer to the Index.

Iver Johnson 9mm Double Action Automatic . . . **$295**
Caliber: 9mm. 6-round magazine. 3-inch barrel. 6.5 inches overall. Weight: 26 oz. Sights: blade front; adjustable rear. Smooth hardwood grip. Blued or matte blued finish. Introduced in 1986.

Iver Johnson Compact 25 ACP **$150**
Bernardelli V/P design. Caliber: 25 ACP. 5-shot magazine. 2^1/$_8$-inch barrel. 4^1/$_8$ inches overall. Weight: 9.3 oz. Fixed sights. Checkered composition grips. Blued slide, matte blue frame and color casehardened trigger. Made from 1991 to date.

Iver Johnson Enforcer

Iver Johnson Enforcer **$345**
Caliber: 30. 5-, 15-, or 30-round magazine. Semiautomatic. 9^1/$_2$ inch barrel. Weight: 5^1/$_2$ pounds. Adjustable sights. Walnut stock. Made mid-1980s to date.

Iver Johnson PP30 Super Enforcer Automatic . . . **$375**
Caliber: 30 US Carbine. 15- or 30-shot magazine. 9^1/$_2$-inch barrel. 17 inches overall. Weight: 4 pounds. Adjustable peer rear sight, blade front. American walnut stock. Made 1984–86.

Iver Johnson Pony

Iver Johnson Pony Automatic Pistol **$265**
Caliber: 380 Auto. 6-shot magazine. 3.1-inch barrel. 6.1 inches overall. Blue, matte or nickel finish. Weight: 20 oz. Wooden grips. Smallest of the locked breech automatics. Made 1982–88.

Iver Johnson Model TP

Iver Johnson Model TP DA Automatic **$155**
Calibers: 22 LR, 25 ACP. 7-shot magazine. 2.85-inch barrel. 5.39 inches overall. Blue finish. Weight: 14.46 oz. Introduced in 1982. Discontinued.

Iver Johnson Model TP22 DA Pocket Pistol . . . **$150**
Double-action automatic. Caliber: 22 LR. 7-round magazine. 3-inch barrel. 5½ inches overall. Weight: 12 oz. Black plastic grips and blued finish. Discontinued 1990.

Iver Johnson Model TP25 Pocket Pistol **$115**
Same general specifications as the Model TP22, except made in 25 ACP caliber. Discontinued.

Iver Johnson Trailsman Automatic Pistol
Caliber: 22 LR. 10-shot magazine. 4½- or 6-inch barrel. 8¾ inches overall w/4½-inch bbl. Weight: 46 oz. Fixed target-type sights. Checkered composition grips. Made 1984–1990.
Standard Model **$175**
Deluxe Model **195**

REVOLVERS

NOTE: Only Iver Johnson Revolvers can be found in the section below. For Pistols, please see the preceding pages. For a complete listing, please refer to the Index.

Iver Johnson Model 55A

Iver Johnson Model 55A Target DA Revolver . . . **$115**
Solid frame. Caliber: 22 LR. 8-shot cylinder. Barrel lengths: 4½-, 6-inch. 10¾ inches overall (6-inch bbl.).

Iver Johnson Model 55A Target DA Revolver (cont.)
Weight: 30½ oz. (6-inch bbl.). Fixed sights. Blued finish. Walnut stocks. *Note:* Original model designation was 55, changed to 55A when loading gate was added in 1961. Made 1955–1977.

Iver Johnson Model 57A Target

Iver Johnson Model 57A Target DA Revolver . . . **$145**
Solid frame. Caliber: 22 LR. 8-shot cylinder. Barrel lengths: 4½-, 6-inch. 10¾ inches overall (6-inch bbl.). Weight: 30½ oz., 6-inch bbl. Adjustable sights. Blued finish. Walnut stocks. *Note:* Original model designation was 57, changed to 57A when loading gate was added in 1961. Made 1956–1975.

Iver Johnson Model 66 Trailsman

Iver Johnson Model 66 Trailsman DA Revolver . . **$95**
Hinged frame. Rebounding hammer. Caliber: 22 LR. 8-shot cylinder. 6-inch barrel. 11 inches overall. Weight: 34 oz. Adjustable sights. Blued finish. Walnut stocks. Made 1958–1975.

Iver Johnson Model 67 Viking

Iver Johnson Model 67 Viking DA Revolver **$100**
Hinged frame. Caliber: 22 LR. 8-shot cylinder. Barrel lengths: 4½- and 6-inch. 11 inches overall w/6-inch bbl. Weight: 34 oz. w/6-inch bbl. Adjustable sights. Walnut stocks w/thumbrest. Made 1964–1975.

Iver Johnson
Model 67S Viking Snub

Iver Johnson Model 67S Viking Snub Revolver $125
DA. Hinged frame. Calibers: 22 LR, 32 S&W Short and Long, 38 S&W. 8-shot cylinder in 22; 5-shot in 32 and 38 calibers. 2³/4-inch barrel. Weight: 25 oz. Adjustable sights. Tenite grips. Made 1964–1975.

Iver Johnson Model 1900
Double Action Revolver

Iver Johnson Model 1900 DA Revolver $110
Solid frame. Calibers: 22 LR, 32 S&W, 32 S&W Long, 38 S&W. 7-shot cylinder (22 cal.), 6-shot (32 S&W), 5-shot (32 S&W Long, 38 S&W). Barrel lengths: 2¹/2-, 4¹/2- and 6-inch. Weight: 12 oz., 32 S&W w/2¹/2-inch bbl. Fixed sights. Blued or nickel finish. Hard rubber stocks. Made 1900–1947.

Iver Johnson Model 1900 Target DA Revolver . . $150
Solid frame. Caliber: 22 LR. 7-shot cylinder. Barrel lengths: 6- and 9¹/2-inch. Fixed sights. Blued finish. Checkered walnut stocks. This earlier model does not have counterbored chambers as in the Target Sealed 8. Made 1925–1942.

Iver Johnson American Bulldog

Iver Johnson American Bulldog Double Action Revolver
Solid frame. Calibers: 22 LR, 22 WMR, 38 Special. 6-shot cylinder in 22, 5-shot in 38. Barrel lengths: 2¹/2-, 4-inch. 9 inches overall w/4-inch bbl. Weight: 30 oz. w/4-inch bbl. Adjustable sights. Blued or nickel finish. Plastic stocks. Made 1974–76.
38 Special **$145**
Other calibers **125**

Iver Johnson Armsworth Model 855 SA $135
Hinged frame. Caliber: 22 LR. 8-shot cylinder. 6-inch barrel. 10³/4 inches overall. Weight: 30 oz. Adjustable sights. Blued finish. Checkered walnut one-piece grip. Adjustable finger rest. Made 1955–57.

Iver Johnson Cadet Double Action Revolver $125
Solid frame. Calibers: 22 LR, 22 WMR, 32 S&W Long, 38 S&W, 38 Special. 6- or 8-shot cylinder in 22, 5-shot in other calibers. 2¹/2-inch barrel. 7 inches overall. Weight: 22 oz. Fixed sights. Blued finish; nickel finish also available in 32 and 38 Special models. Plastic stocks. *Note:* Loading gate added in 1961; 22 cylinder capacity changed from 8 to 6 rounds in 1975. Made 1955–1977.

Iver Johnson Cattleman

Iver Johnson Cattleman Single Action Revolver
Calibers: 357 Magnum, 44 Magnum, 45 Colt. 6-shot cylinder. Barrel lengths: 4³/4-, 5¹/2- (not available in 44), 6- (44 only), 7¹/4-inch. Weight: about 41 oz. Fixed sights. Blued barrel and cylinder, color-casehardened frame, brass grip frame. One-piece walnut stock. Made by Aldo Uberti, Brescia, Italy, 1973–78.
44 Magnum **$250**
Other calibers **195**

Iver Johnson Cattleman Buckhorn

Iver Johnson Cattleman Buckhorn SA Revolver
Same as standard Cattleman, except has adjustable rear and ramp front sights. Barrels: 4³/4- (44 only), 5³/4- (not

NOTE: For engraved Cattleman revolvers, add **$450** to values indicated.

Iver Johnson Cattleman Buckhorn SA Revolver (cont.)

available in 44), 6- (44 only), 7½-, 12-inch. Weight: almost 44 oz. Made 1973–78.

357 Magnum or 45 Colt, 12-inch barrel	**$300**
357 Magnum or 45 Colt, other barrels	330
44 Magnum, 12-inch barrel	300
44 Magnum, other barrels	330

Iver Johnson Cattleman Buntline

Iver Johnson Cattleman Buntline SA Revolver

Same as Cattleman Buckhorn, except has 18-inch barrel, walnut shoulder stock with brass fittings. Weight: about 56 oz. Made 1973–78.

44 Magnum	**$385**
Other calibers	325

Iver Johnson Cattleman Trailblazer

Iver Johnson Cattleman Trailblazer **$155**

Similar to Cattleman Buckhorn, except 22 caliber; has interchangeable 22 LR and 22 WMR cylinders, 5½- or 6½-inch barrel. Weight: about 40 oz. Made 1973–78.

Iver Johnson Champion

Iver Johnson Champion 22 Target SA **$185**

Hinged frame. Caliber: 22 LR. 8-shot cylinder. Single action. Counterbored chambers as in Sealed 8 models. 6-inch barrel. 10¾ inches overall. Weight: 28 oz. Adjustable target sights. Blued finish. Checkered walnut stocks, adjustable finger rest. Made 1938–1948.

Iver Johnson Deluxe Target **$160**

Same as Sportsman, except has adjustable sights. Made 1975–76.

Iver Johnson Deluxe Target

Iver Johnson Protector Sealed 8

Iver Johnson Protector Sealed 8 DA Revolver . . . **$135**

Hinged frame. Caliber: 22 LR. 8-shot cylinder. 2½-inch barrel. 7¼ inches overall. Weight: 20 oz. Fixed sights. Blued finish. Checkered walnut stocks. Made 1933–1949.

Iver Johnson Rookie

Iver Johnson Rookie Double Action Revolver **$95**

Solid frame. Caliber: 38 Special. 5-shot cylinder. 4-inch barrel. 9-inches overall. Weight: 30 oz. Fixed sights. Blued or nickel finish. Plastic stocks. Made 1975–77.

Iver Johnson Safety Hammer

Iver Johnson Safety Hammer DA Revolver **$100**
Hinged frame. Calibers: 22 LR, 32 S&W, 32 S&W Long, 38 S&W. 7-shot cylinder (22 cal.), 6-shot (32 S&W Long), 5-shot (32 S&W, 38 S&W). Barrel lengths: 2, 3, 3¼, 4, 5 or 6 inches. Weight with 4-inch bbl.: 15 oz., 22, 32 S&W; 19½ oz., 32 S&W Long; 19 oz., 38 S&W. Fixed sights. Blued or nickel finish. Hard rubber stocks, round butt; square butt, rubber and walnut stocks available. *Note:* 32 S&W Long and 38 S&W models built on heavy frame. Made 1892–1950.

Iver Johnson Safety Hammerless

Iver Johnson Safety Hammerless DA Revolver **$125**
Hinged frame. Calibers: 22 LR, 32 S&W, 32 S&W Long, 38 S&W. 7-shot cylinder (22 cal.), 6-shot (32 S&W Long), 5-shot (32 S&W, 38 S&W). Barrel lengths: 2, 3, 3¼, 4, 5 or 6 inches. Weight with 4-inch bbl.: 15 oz., 22, 32 S&W; 20½ oz., 32 S&W Long; 20 oz., 38 S&W. Fixed sights. Blued or nickel finish. Hard rubber stocks, round butt. Square butt, rubber and walnut stocks available. *Note:* 32 S&W Long & 38 S&W models built on heavy frame. Made 1895–1950.

Iver Johnson Sidewinder DA Revolver **$130**
Solid frame. Caliber: 22 LR. 6- or 8-shot cylinder. Barrel lengths: 4¾-, 6-inch. 11¼ inches overall w/6-inch bbl. Weight: 31 oz. w/6-inch bbl. Fixed sights. Blued or nickel finish w/plastic "staghorn" stocks; also color-casehardened frame with walnut stocks. *Note:* Cylinder capacity changed from 8 to 6 rounds in 1975. Made 1961 to date.

Iver Johnson Sidewinder "S" **$145**
Same as Sidewinder, except has interchangeable cylinders in 22 LR and 22 WMR, adjustable sights. Introduced 1974; discontinued.

Iver Johnson Sportsman DA Revolver **$95**
Solid frame. Caliber: 22 LR. 6-shot cylinder. Barrel lengths: 4¾-, 6-inch. 10¾ inches overall w/6-inch bbl. Weight: 30½ oz. w/6-inch bbl. Fixed sights. Blued finish. Plastic stocks. Made 1974–76.

Iver Johnson Supershot 9-Shot DA Revolver . . . **$135**
Same as Supershot Sealed 8, except has nine non-counterbored chambers. Made 1929–1949.

Iver Johnson Supershot 22 DA Revolver **$95**
Hinged frame. Caliber: 22 LR. 7-shot cylinder. 6-inch barrel. Fixed sights. Blued finish. Checkered walnut stocks. This earlier model does not have counterbored chambers as in the Supershot Sealed 8. Made 1929–1949.

Iver Johnson Supershot Model 844 DA **$225**
Hinged frame. Caliber: 22 LR. 8-shot cylinder. Barrel lengths: 4½- or 6-inch. 9¼ inches overall w/4½-inch bbl. Weight: 27 oz. w/4½-inch bbl. Adjustable sights. Blued finish. Checkered walnut one-piece grip. Made 1955–56.

Iver Johnson Supershot Sealed 8

Iver Johnson Supershot Sealed 8 DA Revolver . **$150**
Hinged frame. Caliber: 22 LR. 8-shot cylinder. 6-inch barrel. 10¾ inches overall. Weight: 24 oz. Adjustable target sights. Blued finish. Checkered walnut stocks. Postwar model does not have adjustable finger rest as earlier version. Made 1931–1957.

Iver Johnson Swing Out

Iver Johnson Swing Out Double Action Revolver
Calibers: 22 LR, 22 WMR, 32 S&W Long, 38 Special. 6-shot cylinder in 22, 5-shot in 32 and 38. Barrels: plain, 2-, 3-, 4-inch; vent rib, 4-, 6-inch. 8¾ inches overall w/4-inch bbl. Fixed or adjustable sights. Blued or nickel finish. Walnut stocks. Made in 1977.
With plain barrel, fixed sights **$125**
With ventilated rib, adjustable sights **160**

Iver Johnson Target 9-Shot DA Revolver **$110**
Same as Target Sealed 8, except has nine non-counterbored chambers. Made 1929–1946.

Iver Johnson Target Sealed 8

Iver Johnson Target Sealed 8 DA Revolver $130

Solid frame. Caliber: 22 LR. 8-shot cylinder. Barrel lengths: 6- and 10-inch. 10¾ inches overall w/6-inch barrel. Weight: 24 oz. w/6-inch bbl. Fixed sights. Blued finish. Checkered walnut stocks. Made 1931–1957. (*See* illustration, preceding page.)

Iver Johnson Trigger-Cocking

Iver Johnson Trigger-Cocking SA Target $150

Hinged frame. First pull on trigger cocks hammer, second pull releases hammer. Caliber: 22 LR. 8-shot cylinder, counterbored chambers. 6-inch barrel. 10¾ inches overall. Weight: 24 oz. Adjustable target sights. Blued finish. Checkered walnut stocks. Made 1940–47.

═══ KAHR ARMS ═══
Blauvelt, New York

Kahr K9 9mm

Kahr Model K9 DA Auto Pistol $510

Caliber: 9mm Parabellum. 8-shot magazine. 3½-inch barrel. 6 inches overall. Weight: 24 oz. Fixed sights. Blued finish. Wraparound smooth hardwood grips. Made from 1994 to date.

═══ LAHTI PISTOLS ═══
Mfd. by Husqvarna Vapenfabriks A. B. Huskvarna, Sweden, and Valtion Kivaar Tedhas ("VKT") Jyväskyla, Finland

Lahti Automatic Pistol

Caliber: 9mm Luger. 8-shot magazine. 4¾-inch barrel. Weight: about 46 oz. Fixed sights. Blued finish. Plastic

Lahti, Swedish Model

Lahti Automatic Pistol (cont.)

stocks. Specifications given are those of the Swedish Model 40 but also apply in general to the Finnish Model L-35, which differs only slightly. A considerable number of Swedish Lahti pistols were imported and sold in the U.S.; the Finnish Model, somewhat better made, is a rather rare pistol. Finnish Model L-35 adopted 1935; Swedish Model 40 adopted 1940; mfd. thru 1944.

Finnish Model. **$1100**
Swedish Model **465**

═══ L.A.R. MANUFACTURING, INC. ═══
West Jordan, Utah

**L.A.R. Mark I
Grizzly Win. Mag.**

L.A.R. Mark I Grizzly Win. Mag. Automatic Pistol

Calibers: 357 Mag., 45 ACP, 45 Win. Mag. 7-shot magazine. 6½-inch barrel. 10½ inches overall. Weight: 48 oz. Fully adjustable sights. Checkered rubber combat-style grips. Blued finish. Made from 1983 to date. 8-inch and 10-inch barrels made from 1987 to date.

357 Mag. (6½″ barrel) **$650**
45 Win. Mag. (6½″ barrel) **615**
8-inch barrel **900**
10-inch barrel **995**

L.A.R. Mark IV Grizzly Automatic Pistol $745

Same general specifications as the L.A.R. Mark I, except chambered for 44 Magnum; has 5.5- or 6.5-inch barrel, beavertail grip safety, matte blue finish. Made from 1991 to date.

HANDGUNS

LIGNOSE PISTOLS
Suhl, Germany
Aktien-Gesellschaft "Lignose" Abteilung

The following Lignose pistols were manufactured from 1920 to the mid-1930s. They were also marketed under the Bergmann name.

Lignose Model 2 Pocket Auto Pistol **$150**
Conventional Browning type. Same general specifications as Einhand Model 2A, but lacks the one-hand operation.

Lignose Einhand Model 2A*

Lignose Einhand Model 2A Pocket Auto Pistol . . **$215**
As the name implies, this pistol is designed for one-hand operation; pressure on a "trigger" at the front of the guard retracts the slide. Caliber: 25 Automatic (6.35mm). 6-shot magazine. 2-inch barrel. 4¾ inches overall. Weight: about 14 oz. Blued finish. Hard rubber stocks.

Lignose Einhand Model 3A

Lignose Einhand Model 3A Pocket Auto Pistol . . **$225**
Same as the Model 2A except has longer grip, 9-shot magazine, weighs about 16 oz.

LLAMA HANDGUNS
Mfd. by Gabilondo y Cia, Vitoria, Spain
Imported by S.G.S., Wanamassa, New Jersey

AUTOMATIC PISTOLS

NOTE: For ease in finding a particular Llama handgun, the listings are divided into two groupings: Automatic Pistols (below) and Revolvers, which follows. For a complete listing of Llama handguns, please refer to the Index.

Llama Model IIIA

**Llama Model IIIA Deluxe
Blue Engraved**

**Llama Model IIIA Deluxe
Chrome Engraved**

Llama Model IIIA Automatic Pistol $230
Caliber: 380 Auto. 7-shot magazine. 3¹¹/₁₆-inch barrel. 6¹/₂ inches overall. Weight: 23 oz. Adjustable target sights. Blued finish. Plastic stocks. Intro. 1951; discontinued. (*See* photo, preceding page.)

Llama Models IIIA, XA, XV Deluxe
Same as standard Model IIIA, XA and XV, except finish—chrome engraved or blue engraved—and simulated pearl stocks. Disc. 1984. (*See* photos, preceding page.)
Chrome-engraved Finish $250
Blue-engraved Finish **200**

Llama Model VIII

Llama Model VIII Automatic Pistol $295
Caliber: 38 Super. 9-shot magazine. 5-inch barrel. 8¹/₂ inches overall. Weight: 40 oz. Fixed sights. Blued finish. Wood stocks. Introduced in 1952; discontinued.

Llama Models VIII, IXA, XI Deluxe
Same as standard Models VIII, IXA and XI, except finish—chrome engraved or blue engraved—and simulated pearl stocks. Discontinued 1984.
Chrome-engraved Finish $325
Blue-engraved Finish **350**

Llama Model IXA Automatic Pistol $265
Same as Model VIII, except caliber 45 Automatic, 7-shot magazine.

Llama Model XA Automatic Pistol $200
Same as Model IIIA, except caliber 32 Automatic, 8-shot magazine.

Llama Model XI

Llama Model XI Automatic Pistol $245
Same as Model VIII, except caliber 9mm Luger.

Llama Model XV Automatic Pistol $220
Same as Model XA, except caliber 22 LR.

Llama Models BE-IIIA, BE-XA, BE-XV $250
Same as Models IIIA, XA and XV, except with blue-engraved finish. Made 1977–1984.

Llama Models BE-VIII, BE-IXA, BE-XI Deluxe . . . $320
Same as Models VIII, IXA and XI, except with blue-engraved finish. Made 1977–1984.

Llama Models C-IIIA, C-XA, C-XV $320
Same as Models IIIA, XA and XV, except in satin-chrome.

Llama Model C-XI

Llama Models C-VIII, C-IXA, C-XI $320
Same as Models VIII, IXA and XI, except in satin-chrome.

Llama Model CE-IIIA

Llama Models CE-IIIA, CE-XA, CE-XV $315
Same as Models IIIA, XA and XV, except w/chrome-engraved finish. Made 1977–1984.

Llama Models CE-VIII, CE-IXA, CE-XI $395
Same as Models VIII, IXA and XI, w/except chrome-engraved finish. Made 1977–1984.

Llama Compact Frame Auto Pistol $355
Calibers: 9mm Para., 38 Super, 45 Auto. 7-, 8- or 9-shot. 5-inch barrel. 7⁷/₈ inches overall. Weight: 34 oz. Blued, satin-chrome or Duo-Tone finishes. Made 1990 to date; Duo-Tone discontinued 1993.

**Llama Duo-Tone Automatic
Large Frame**

**Llama Duo-Tone Automatic
Small Frame**

Llama Duo-Tone Large Frame Auto Pistol $295
Caliber: 45 ACP. 7-shot magazine. 5-inch barrel. 8.5 inches overall. Weight: 36 oz. Adj. rear sight. Blued finished with satin chrome. Polymer black grips. Made 1990–93.

Llama Duo-Tone Small Frame Auto Pistol $285
Calibers: 22 LR, 32 and 380 Auto. 7- or 8-shot magazine. 3-11/16-inch barrel. 6-1/2 inches overall. Weight: 23 oz. Square-notch rear sight; Patridge-type front. Blued finish with chrome. Made 1990–93.

Llama Model G-IIIA Deluxe $800
Same as Model IIIA, except is gold-damascened w/simulated pearl stocks. Discontinued 1982.

Llama Large-Frame 45

Llama Large-Frame Automatic Pistol (IXA)
Caliber: 45 Auto. 7-shot magazine. 5-inch barrel. Weight: 2 lbs. 8 oz. Adjustable rear sight, Patridge-type front. Walnut grips; teakwood on satin chrome model; later models with polymer grips. Made from 1984 to date.
Blued Finish **$300**
Satin Chrome Finish **310**

**Llama M-82 9mm Double Action
Automatic**

Llama M-82 DA Automatic Pistol **$425**
Caliber: 9mm Parabellum. 15-shot magazine. 4-1/4-inch barrel. 8 inches overall. Weight: 39 oz. Drift adjustable rear sight. Matte blue finish. Matte black polymer grips. Made from 1988 to date.

Llama M-87 Comp Pistol **$745**
Caliber: 9mm Parabellum. 15-shot magazine. 5.5-inch barrel. 9-1/2 inches overall. Weight: 40 oz. Low-profile combat sights. Satin nickel finish. Matte black grip panels. Built-in ported compensator to minimize recoil and muzzle rise. Made 1989–1993.

Llama Omni

Llama Omni 9mm Double Action Automatic $350
Same general specifications as 45 Omni, except chambered for 9mm w/13-shot magazine. Discontinued 1986.

Llama Omni 45 Double Action Automatic Pistol . $375
Caliber: 45 Auto. 7-shot magazine. 4-1/4-inch barrel. 7-3/4 inches overall. Weight: 40 oz. Adjustable rear sight, ramp front. Highly polished deep blue finish. Made 1984–86.

Llama Single Action Automatic Pistol $345
Calibers: 38 Super, 9mm, 45 Auto. 9-shot magazine (7-shot for 45 Auto). 5-inch barrel. 8½ inches overall. Weight: 2 lbs. 8 oz. Introduced in 1981.

Llama Small-Frame Automatic

Llama Small-Frame Automatic Pistol
Calibers: 380 Auto (9mm); 7-shot magazine; 22 RF (8-shot magazine). 3¹¹/₁₆-inch barrel. Weight: 23 oz. Adjustable rear sight, Patridge-type front. Blued or satin-chrome finish.

Blued Finish **$265**
Satin-Chrome Finish **325**

REVOLVERS

NOTE: This section contains only Llama Revolvers. Pistols may be found on the preceding pages. For a complete listing of Llama handguns, please refer to the Index.

Llama Comanche I

Llama Comanche I Double Action Revolver $180
Same gen. specifications as Martial 22. Made 1977–1983.

Llama Comanche II $195
Same gen. specifications as Martial 38. Made 1977–1983.

Llama Comanche III Double Action Revolver ... $250
Caliber: 357 Magnum. 6-shot cylinder. 4-inch barrel. 9¼ inches overall. Weight: 36 oz. Adjustable rear sight, ramp front. Blued finish. Checkered walnut stocks. Made from 1975 to date. *Note:* Prior to 1977, this model was designated "Comanche."

Llama Comanche III Chrome

Llama Comanche III Chrome $295
Same gen. specifications as Comanche III, except has satin chrome finish, 4- or 6-inch barrels. Made 1979 to date.

Llama Martial Double Action Revolver

Llama Martial Double Action Revolver $215
Calibers: 22 LR, 38 Special. 6-shot cylinder. Barrel lengths: 4-inch (38 Special only), 6-inch. 11¼ inches overall w/6-inch barrel. Weight: about 36 oz. w/6-inch barrel. Target sights. Blued finish. Checkered walnut stocks. Made 1969–1976.

Llama Martial Deluxe, Gold Damascened

Llama Martial Double Action Deluxe
Same as standard Martial, except finish—satin chrome, chrome engraved, blue engraved, gold damascened; has simulated pearl stocks. Discontinued 1978.

Llama Martial Double Action Deluxe (cont.)
Satin-chrome Finish . . . . $ 275
Chrome-engraved Finish 325
Blue-engraved Finish 300
Gold-damascened Finish 1500

Llama Super Comanche IV

Llama Super Comanche IV DA Revolver $295
Caliber: 44 Magnum. 6-shot cylinder. 6-inch barrel. 11³/₄ inches overall. Weight: 3 lbs. 2 oz. Sights: adjustable rear, ramp front. Polished deep blue finish. Checkered walnut grips. Made from 1980 to date.

Llama Super Comanche V DA Revolver $275
Caliber: 357 Mag. 6-shot cylinder. 4-, 6- or 8¹/₂-inch barrel. Weight: 3 pounds. Sights: click-adjustable rear, ramped blade front.

═══ LUGER PISTOLS ═══
GERMANY and SWITZERLAND
Mfd. by Deutsche Waffen und Munitionsfabriken (DWM), Berlin, Germany; also by Königlich Gewehrfabrik Erfurt, Heinrich Krieghoff Waffenfabrik, Mauser-Werke, Simson & Co., Vickers Ltd., Waffenfabrik, Bern.

**Luger 1900
U.S. Army Pistol**

Luger 1900 American Eagle $2400
Caliber: 7.65mm. 8-shot magazine. Thin, 4³/₄-inch long, tapered barrel. 9¹/₂ inches overall . Weight: 32 oz. Fixed rear sight, dovetailed front sight. Grip safety. Checkered walnut grips. Early-style toggle, narrow trigger, wide guard, no stock lug. American Eagle over chamber. Estimated 8000 production.

Luger 1900 Commercial $1495
Same specifications as Luger 1900 American Eagle, except DWM on early-style toggle, no chamber markings. Estimated 8000 production.

Luger 1900 Swiss $2100
Same specifications as Luger 1900 American Eagle, except Swiss cross in sunburst over chamber. Estimated 9000 production.

Luger 1902 American Eagle $3750
Caliber: 9mm Luger. 8-shot magazine. 4-inch, heavy tapered barrel. 8³/₄ inches overall. Weight: 30 oz. Fixed rear sight, dovetailed front sight. Grip safety. Checkered walnut stocks. American Eagle over chamber, DWM on early-style toggle, narrow trigger, wide guard, no stock lug. Estimated 700 production.

Luger 1902 Carbine $6300
Caliber: 7.65mm. 8-shot magazine. 11³/₄-inch tapered barrel. 16¹/₂ inches overall. Weight: 46 oz. Adjustable 4-position rear sight, long ramp front sight. Grip safety. Checkered walnut stocks and forearm. DWM on early-style toggle, narrow trigger, wide guard, no chamber markings, stock lug. Estimated 3200 production.

Luger 1902 Cartridge Counter $8000
Caliber: 9mm Luger. 8-shot magazine. Heavy, tapered 4-inch barrel. 8³/₄ inches overall. Weight: 30 oz. Fixed rear sight, dovetailed front sight. Grip safety. Checkered walnut stocks. DWM on dished toggle with lock, American Eagle over chamber when marked; no stock lug. Estimated production unknown.

Luger 1902 Commercial $4480
Same basic specifications as Luger 1902 Cartridge Counter, except DWM on early-style toggle, narrow trigger, wide guard, no chamber markings, no stock lug. Estimated 400 production.

Luger 1903 American Eagle $5500
Same basic specifications as Luger 1902 Cartridge Counter, except American Eagle over chamber, DWM on early-style toggle, narrow trigger, wide guard, no stock lug. Estimated 700 production.

Luger 1904 GL "Baby"

Luger 1904 GL "Baby" $150,000
Caliber: 9mm Luger. 7-shot magazine. 3¹/₄-inch barrel. 7³/₄ inches overall. Weight: approx. 20 oz. Serial number 10077B. "GL" marked on rear of toggle. Georg Luger's personal sidearm. Only one made in 1904.

Luger 1904 Naval (Reworked) **$6500**
Caliber: 9mm Luger. 8-shot magazine. Barrel length altered to 4 inches. 8¾ inches overall. Weight: 30 oz. Adjustable two-position rear sight, dovetailed front sight. Thumb lever safety. Checkered walnut stocks. Heavy tapered barrel. DWM on new-style toggle with lock, 1902 over chamber. With or without grip safety and stock lug. Estimated 800 production.

Luger 1906 (11.35) **$45,000**
Caliber: 45 ACP. 6-shot magazine. 5-inch barrel. 9¾ inches overall. Weight: 36 oz. Fixed rear sight, dovetailed front sight. Grip safety. Checkered walnut stocks. GL monogram on rear toggle link, larger frame with altered trigger guard and trigger, no proofs, no markings over chamber. No stock lug. Estimated production 2.

Luger 1906 American Eagle (7.65) **$1400**
Caliber: 7.65mm. 8-shot magazine. Thin, 4¾-inch, tapered barrel. 9½ inches overall. Weight: 32 oz. Fixed rear sight, dovetailed front sight. Grip safety. Checkered walnut stocks. DWM on new-style toggle, American Eagle over chamber; no stock lug. Estimated 8000 production.

Luger 1906 American Eagle (9mm) **$2400**
Same basic specifications as the 7.65mm 1906, except in 9mm Luger with 4-inch barrel, 8¾ inches overall and weight of 30 ounces. Estimated 3500 production.

Luger 1906 Bern (7.65mm) **$750**
Same basic specifications as the 7.65mm 1906 American Eagle, except checkered walnut stocks with 3/8-inch borders, Swiss Cross on new-style toggle, Swiss proofs, no markings over chamber, no stock lug. Estimated 17,874 production.

Luger 1906 Brazilian (7.65mm) **$1300**
Same general specifications as the 7.65mm 1906 American Eagle, except with Brazilian proofs, no markings over chamber, no stock lug. Estimated 4500 production.

Luger 1906 Brazilian (9mm) **$1625**
Same basic specifications as the 9mm 1906 American Eagle, except with Brazilian proofs, no markings over chamber, no stock lug. Estimated production unknown.

Luger 1906 Commercial
Calibers: 7.65mm, 9mm. Same specifications as the 1906 American Eagle versions, above, except no chamber markings, no stock lug. Estimated production: 6000 (7.65mm); 3500 (9mm).
7.65mm **$1200**
9mm **1350**

Luger 1906 Dutch **$1425**
Caliber: 9mm Luger. Same specifications as the 9mm 1906 American Eagle, except tapered barrel with proofs, no markings over chamber, no stock lug. Estimated 3000 production.

Luger 1906 Loewe and Company **$3100**
Caliber: 7.65mm. 8-shot magazine. 6-inch tapered barrel. 10¾ inches overall. Weight: 35 oz. Adjustable two-position rear sight, dovetailed front sight. Grip safety. Checkered walnut stocks. Loewe & Company over chamber, Naval proofs, DWM on new-style toggle, no stock lug. Estimated production unknown.

Luger 1906 Naval **$2600**
Caliber: 9mm Luger. 8-shot magazine. 6-inch tapered barrel. 10¾ inches overall. Weight: 35 oz. Adjustable two-position rear sight, dovetailed front sight. Grip safety and thumb safety with lower marking (1st issue), higher marking (2nd issue). Checkered walnut stocks. No chamber markings, DWM on new-style toggle without lock; with stock lug. Estimated production: 8000 (1st issue); 12,000 (2nd issue).

Luger 1906 Naval Commercial **$2850**
Same basic specifications as the 1906 Naval, except lower marking on thumb safety, no chamber markings, DWM on new-style toggle, with stock lug and commercial proofs. Estimated 3000 production.

Luger 1906 Portuguese Army **$995**
Same specifications as the 7.65mm 1906 American Eagle, except with Portuguese proofs, crown and crest over chamber; no stock lug. Estimated 3500 production.

Luger 1906 Portuguese Naval **$7500**
Same specifications as the 9mm 1906 American Eagle, except with Portuguese proofs, crown and anchor over chamber; no stock lug. Estimated production unknown.

Luger 1906 Russian **$9500**
Same general specifications as the 9mm 1906 American Eagle, except thumb safety has markings concealed in up position, DWM on new-style toggle, DWM barrel proofs, crossed rifles over chamber. Est. prod. unknown.

Luger 1906 Swiss **$2200**
Same general specifications as the 7.65mm 1906 American Eagle Luger, except Swiss Cross in sunburst over chamber, no stock lug. Estimated 10,300 production.

Luger 1906 Swiss (Rework) **$3000**
Same basic specifications as the 7.65mm 1906 Swiss, except in barrel lengths of 3⅝, 4 and 4¾ inches, overall length 8⅜ inches and up, weight 32 oz. and up. DWM on new-style toggle, barrel with serial number and proof marks, Swiss Cross in sunburst or shield over chamber, no stock lug. Estimated production unknown.

Luger 1906 Swiss Police **$2400**
Same general specifications as the 7.65mm 1906 Swiss, except DWM on new-style toggle, Swiss Cross in matted field over chamber, no stock lug. Estimated 10,300 production.

Luger 1908 Bulgarian **$2145**
Caliber: 9mm Luger. 8-shot magazine. 4-inch tapered barrel. 8¾ inches overall. Weight: 30 oz. Fixed rear sight, dovetailed front sight. Thumb safety with lower marking concealed. Checkered walnut stocks. DWM chamber marking, no proofs, crown over shield on new-style toggle, lanyard loop, no stock lug. Estimated production unknown.

Luger 1908 Commercial **$995**
Same basic specifications as the 1908 Bulgarian, except higher marking on thumb safety. No chamber markings, commercial proofs, DWM on new-style toggle; no stock lug. Estimated 4000 production.

Luger 1908 Erfurt Military **$995**
Caliber: 9mm Luger. 8-shot magazine. 4-inch tapered barrel. 8¾ inches overall. Weight: 30 oz. Fixed rear sight, dovetailed front sight. Thumb safety with higher marking

Luger 1908 Erfurt Military (cont.)

concealed. Checkered walnut stocks. Serial number and proof marks on barrel, crown and Erfurt on new-style toggle, dated chamber; no stock lug. Estimated production unknown.

Luger 1908 Military

Same general specifications as the 9mm 1908 Erfurt Military Luger, except *1st and 2nd Issue* have thumb safety with higher marking concealed, serial number on barrel, no chamber markings, proofs on frame, DWM on new-style toggle; no stock lug. Estimated production: 10,000 (1st issue); 5000 (2nd issue). *3rd Issue* has serial number and proof marks on barrel, dates over chamber, DWM on new-style toggle; no stock lug. Estimated 3000 production.

1st Issue	**$1200**
2nd Issue	1400
3rd Issue	995

Luger 1908 Naval $3100

Same basic specifications as the 9mm 1908 Military Lugers, except with 6-inch barrel, adjustable two-position rear sight, no chamber markings, DWM on new-style toggle; with stock lug. Estimated 26,000 production.

Luger 1908 Naval (Commercial) $3750

Same specifications as the 1908 Naval Luger, except no chamber markings or date. Commercial proofs, DWM on new-style toggle; with stock lug. Est. 1900 produced.

**Luger 1914 Artillery
with Holster**

Luger 1914 Erfurt Artillery $1500

Caliber: 9mm Luger. 8-shot magazine. 8-inch tapered barrel. 12¾ inches overall. Weight: 40 oz. Artillery rear sight, dovetailed front sight. Thumb safety with higher marking concealed. Checkered walnut stocks. Serial number and proof marks on barrel, crown and Erfurt on new-style toggle, dated chamber, with stock lug. Estimated production unknown.

Luger 1914 Erfurt Military $795

Same specifications as the 1914 Erfurt Artillery, except with 4-inch barrel and corresponding length, weight, etc., and fixed rear sight. Estimated 3000 production.

Luger 1914 Naval $2195

Same specifications as 9mm 1914 Lugers, except has 6-inch barrel with corresponding length and weight, and adjustable two-position rear sight. Dated chamber, DWM on new-style toggle; with stock lug. Est. 40,000 produced.

Luger 1914-1918 DWM Artillery $1175

Caliber: 9mm Luger. 8-shot magazine. 8-inch tapered barrel. 12¾ inches overall. Weight: 40 oz. Artillery rear sight, dovetailed front sight. Thumb safety with higher marking concealed. Checkered walnut stocks. Serial number and proof marks on barrel, DWM on new-style toggle, dated chamber; with stock lug. Estimated 3000 production.

Luger 1914-1918 DWM Military $995

Same specifications as the 9mm 1914-1918 DWM Artillery, except with 4-inch tapered barrel and corresponding length, weight, etc., and fixed rear sight. Estimated production unknown.

Luger 1920 Carbine

Caliber: 7.65mm. 8-shot magazine. 11¾-inch tapered barrel. 15¾ inches overall. Weight: 44 oz. Four-position rear sight, long ramp front sight. Grip (or thumb) safety. Checkered walnut stocks and forearm. Serial numbers and proof marks on barrel, no chamber markings, various proofs, DWM on new-style toggle; with stock lug. Estimated production unknown.

Carbine With Forearm	**$7500**
Carbine Less Forearm	3500

Luger 1920 Commercial $610

Calibers: 7.65mm, 9mm Luger. 8-shot magazine. Barrel lengths: 3⅝, 3¾, 4, 4¾, 6, 8, 10, 12, 16, 18, 20 inches; tapered. Overall length: 8⅜ to 24¾ inches. Weight: 30 oz. and up. Varying rear sight configurations, dovetailed front sight. Thumb safety. Checkered walnut stocks. Serial numbers and proof marks on barrel, no chamber markings, various proofs, DWM or crown over Erfurt on new-style toggle; with stock lug. Est. production not documented.

Luger 1920 DWM and Erfurt Military $795

Caliber: 9mm Luger. 8-shot magazine. 4-inch tapered barrel. 8¾ inches overall. Weight: 30 oz. Fixed rear sight, dovetailed front sight. Thumb safety. Checkered walnut stocks. Serial numbers and proof marks on barrel, dated chamber, various proofs, DWM or crown over Erfurt on new-style toggle; with stock lug. Est. 3000 production.

Luger 1920 Police $900

Same specifications as 9mm 1920 DWM with some dated chambers, various proofs, DWM or crown over Erfurt on new-style toggle, identifying marks on grip frame; with stock lug. Estimated 3000 production.

Luger 1923 Commerical $695

Calibers: 7.65mm and 9mm Luger. 8-shot magazine. Barrel lengths: 3⅝, 3¾, 4, 6, 8, 12 and 16 inches; tapered. Overall length: 8⅜ inches and up. Weight: 30 oz. and up. Various rear sight configurations, dovetailed front sight. Thumb lever safety. Checkered walnut stocks. DWM on new-style toggle, serial number and proofs on barrel, no chamber markings, with stock lug. Estimated 15,000 production.

Luger 1923 Dutch Commerical $2000

Same basic specifications as 1923 Commercial Luger, with same caliber offerings, but only 3⅝- or 4-inch barrel. Fixed rear sight, thumb lever safety with arrow markings. Estimated production unknown.

Luger 1923 Krieghoff Commercial **$1600**
Same specifications as 1923 Commercial Luger, with same caliber offerings but barrel lengths of 3⁵/₈, 4, 6, and 8 inches. "K" marked on new-style toggle; serial number, proofs and Germany on barrel; no chamber markings; with stock lug. Estimated production unknown.

Luger 1923 Safe and Loaded **$1100**
Same caliber offerings, barrel lengths and specifications as the 1923 Commercial, except thumb lever safety with safe markings. Other markings the same; with stock lug. Estimated 10,000 production.

Luger 1923 Stoeger **$2900**
Same general specifications as the 1923 Commercial Luger, with the same caliber offerings and barrel lengths of 3³/₄, 4, 6, and 8 inches. Thumb lever safety. DWM on new-style toggle, serial number and/or proof marks on barrel, American Eagle over chamber usually; no stock lug. Estimated production unknown.

Luger 1926 "Baby" Prototype **$85,000**
Calibers: 7.65mm Browning and 9mm Browning (short). 5-shot magazine. 2¹⁵/₁₆-inch barrel. About 6¹/₄ inches overall. Small-sized frame and toggle assembly. Prototype for a Luger "pocket pistol," but never manufactured commercially. Checkered walnut grips, slotted for safety. Only four known to exist, but possibly as many as a dozen could have been made.

Luger 1929 Swiss **$1350**
Caliber: 7.65mm. 8-shot magazine. 4³/₄-inch tapered barrel. 9¹/₂ inches overall. Weight: 32 oz. Fixed rear sight, dovetailed front sight. Long grip safety and thumb lever with S markings. Stepped receiver and straight grip frame. Checkered plastic stocks. Swiss Cross in shield on new-style toggle, serial numbers and proofs on barrel, no markings over chamber; no stock lug. Est. 1900 prod.

Luger 1934 Krieghoff Commercial (Side Frame) **$6995**
Caliber: 7.65mm and 9mm Luger. 8-shot magazine. Barrel lengths: 4, 6, and 8 inches. Overall length: 8³/₄ inch and up. Weight: 30 oz. and up. Various rear sight configurations, dovetailed front sight. Thumb lever safety. Checkered brown plastic stocks. Anchor with H K Krieghoff Suhl on new-style toggle, no chamber markings, tapered barrel with serial number and proofs; with stock lug. Estimated 1700 production.

Luger 1934 Krieghoff S
Caliber: 9mm Luger. 8-shot magazine. 4-inch tapered barrel. 8³/₄ inches overall. Weight: 30 oz. Fixed rear sight, dovetailed front sight. Thumb lever safety. Anchor with H K Krieghoff Suhl on new-style toggle, S dated chamber, barrel proofs; stock lug. *Early Model:* Checkered walnut or plastic stocks. Estimated 2500 production. *Late Model:* Checkered brown plastic stocks. Est. 1200 production.
Early Model **$1695**
Late Model 1495

Luger 1934 byf **$895**
Caliber: 9mm Luger. 8-shot magazine. 4-inch tapered barrel. 8³/₄ inches overall. Weight: 30 oz. Fixed rear sight, dovetailed front sight. Thumb lever safety. Checkered walnut or plastic stocks. byf on new-style toggle, serial number and proofs on barrel, 41-42 dated chamber; stock lug. Estimated 3000 production.

Luger 1934 Mauser 42 . . . . **$1500**
Caliber: 9mm Luger. 8-shot magazine. 4-inch tapered barrel. 8³/₄ inches overall. Weight: 30 oz. Fixed rear sight, dovetailed front sight. Thumb lever safety. Checkered walnut or plastic stocks. 42 on new-style toggle, serial number and proofs on barrel, 1939-40 dated chamber markings; stock lug. Estimated 3000 production.

Luger 1934 Mauser 42 (Dated) **$2300**
Same specifications as Luger 1934 Mauser 42, above, except 41 dated chamber markings; stock lug. Estimated production unknown.

Luger 1934 Mauser Banner (Military) **$1495**
Same specifications as Luger 1934 Mauser 42, except Mauser in banner on new-style toggle, tapered barrel with serial number and proofs usually, dated chamber markings; stock lug. Estimated production unknown.

Luger 1934 Mauser Commercial **$2800**
Same specifications as Luger 1934 Mauser 42, except checkered walnut stocks. Mauser in banner on new-style toggle, tapered barrel with serial number and proofs usually, no chamber markings; stock lug. Estimated production unknown.

Luger 1934 Mauser Dutch **$1395**
Same specifications as Luger 1934 Mauser 42, except checkered walnut stocks. Mauser in banner on new-style toggle, tapered barrel with caliber, 1940 dated chamber markings; stock lug. Estimated production unknown.

Luger 1934 Mauser Latvian **$3000**
Caliber: 7.65mm. 8-shot magazine. 4-inch tapered barrel. 8³/₄ inches overall. Weight: 30 oz. Fixed, square-notched rear sight, dovetailed Patridge front sight. Thumb lever safety. Checkered walnut stocks. Mauser in banner on new-style toggle, 1937 dated chamber markings; stock lug. Estimated production unknown.

Luger 1934 Mauser (Oberndorf) **$2100**
Same specifications as Luger 1934 Mauser 42, except checkered walnut stocks. Oberndorf 1934 on new-style toggle, tapered barrel with proofs and caliber, Mauser in banner over chamber; stock lug. Est. 6000 produced.

Luger 1934 Simson-S Toggle **$1800**
Same specifications as Luger 1934 Mauser 42, except checkered walnut stocks. S on new-style toggle, tapered barrel with serial number and proofs, no chamber markings; stock lug. Estimated 10,000 production.

Luger 42 Mauser Banner **$1350**
Same specifications as Luger 1934 Mauser 42, except weight 32 oz.; Mauser in banner on new-style toggle, tapered barrel with serial number and proofs usually, dated chamber markings; stock lug. Estimated production unknown.

Luger Abercrombie and Fitch **$4795**
Calibers: 7.65mm and 9mm Luger. 8-shot magazine. 4³/₄-inch tapered barrel. 9¹/₂ inches overall. Weight: 32 oz. Fixed rear sight, dovetailed front sight. Grip safety. Checkered walnut stocks. DWM on new-style toggle, Abercrombie & Fitch markings on barrel, Swiss Cross in sunburst over chamber; no stock lug. Est. 100 production.

Luger Dutch Royal Air Force **$1150**
Caliber: 9mm Luger. 8-shot magazine. 4-inch tapered barrel. 8³/₄ inches overall. Weight: 30 oz. Fixed rear sight, dovetailed front sight. Grip safety and thumb safety with markings and arrow. Checkered walnut stocks. DWM on new-style toggle, barrel dated with serial number and proofs, no markings over chamber, no stock lug. Estimated 4000 production.

Luger DWM (G Date) **$825**
Caliber: 9mm Luger. 8-shot magazine. 4-inch tapered barrel. 8³/₄ inches overall. Weight: 30 oz. Fixed rear sight, dovetailed front sight. Thumb lever safety. Checkered walnut stocks. DWM on new-style toggle, serial number and proofs on barrel, G (1935 date) over chamber; with stock lug. Estimated production unknown.

Luger DWM and Erfurt **$895**
Caliber: 9mm Luger. 8-shot magazine. Barrel length: 4 or 6 inches, tapered. Overall length: 8³/₄, 10³/₄ inches. Weight: 30 or 38 oz. Fixed rear sight, dovetailed front sight. Thumb safety. Checkered walnut stocks. Serial numbers and proof marks on barrel, double dated chamber, various proofs, DWM or crown over Erfurt on new-style toggle; with stock lug. Estimated production unknown.

Luger Krieghoff 36 . . . . **$2150**
Caliber: 9mm Luger. 8-shot magazine. 4-inch tapered barrel. 8³/₄ inches overall. Weight: 30 oz. Fixed rear sight, dovetailed front sight. Thumb lever safety. Checkered brown plastic stocks. Anchor with H K Krieghoff Suhl on new-style toggle, 36 dated chamber, serial number and proofs on barrel; stock lug. Estimated 700 production.

Luger Krieghoff—Dated 1936-1945 . . . . **$1910**
Same specifications as Luger Krieghoff 36, except 1936-1945 dated chamber, barrel proofs. Est. 8600 production.

Luger Krieghoff (Grip Safety) **$3625**
Same specifications as Luger Krieghoff 36, except grip safety and thumb lever safety. No chamber markings, tapered barrel with serial number, proofs and caliber; no stock lug. Estimated production unknown.

Luger Mauser Banner (Grip Safety) **$2800**
Caliber: 7.65mm. 8-shot magazine. 4³/₄-inch tapered barrel. 9¹/₂ inches overall. Weight: 30 oz. Fixed rear sight, dovetailed front sight. Grip safety and thumb lever safety. Checkered walnut stocks. Mauser in banner on new-style toggle, serial number and proofs on barrel, 1939 dated chamber markings; no stock lug. Estimated production unknown.

Luger Mauser Banner 42 (Dated) **$1295**
Caliber: 9mm Luger. 8-shot magazine. 4-inch tapered barrel. 8³/₄ inches overall. Weight: 30 oz. Fixed rear sight, dovetailed front sight. Thumb lever safety. Checkered walnut or plastic stocks. Mauser in banner on new-style toggle, serial number and proofs on barrel usually, 42 dated chamber markings; stock lug. Est. production unknown.

Luger Mauser Banner (Swiss Proof) **$1800**
Same specifications as Luger Mauser Banner 42, above, except checkered walnut stocks and 1939 dated chamber.

Luger Mauser Freise **$3000**
Same specifications as Mauser Banner 42, except checkered walnut stocks, tapered barrel with proofs on sight block and Freise above chamber. Estimated production unknown.

**German Luger S/42
Dated 1936**

Luger S/42
Caliber: 9mm Luger. 8-shot magazine. 4-inch tapered barrel. 8³/₄ inches overall. Weight: 30 oz. Fixed rear sight, dovetailed front sight. Thumb lever safety. Checkered walnut stocks. S/42 on new-style toggle, serial number and proofs on barrel; stock lug. *Dated Model:* has dated chamber; estimated 3000 production. *G Date:* has G (1935 date) over chamber; estimated 3000 production. *K Date:* has K (1934 date) over chamber; prod. figures unknown.
Dated Model . . . . **$ 895**
G Date Model 825
K Date Model 1895

Luger Russian Commercial **$2000**
Caliber: 7.65mm. 8-shot magazine. 3⁵/₈-inch tapered barrel. 8³/₈ inches overall. Weight: 30 oz. Fixed rear sight, dovetailed front sight. Thumb lever safety. Checkered walnut stocks. DWM on new-style toggle, Russian proofs on barrel, no chamber markings; with stock lug. Estimated production unknown.

Luger Simson and Company **$1295**
Calibers: 7.65mm and 9mm Luger. 8-shot magazine. Weight: 32 oz. Fixed rear sight, dovetailed front sight. Thumb lever safety. Checkered walnut stocks. Simson & Company Suhl on new-style toggle, serial number and proofs on barrel, date over chamber usually; with stock lug. Estimated 10,000 production.

Luger Vickers-Dutch **$2450**
Caliber: 9mm Luger. 8-shot magazine. 4-inch tapered barrel. 8³/₄ inches overall. Weight: 30 oz. Fixed rear sight, dovetailed front sight. Grip safety and thumb lever with arrow markings. Checkered walnut stocks (coarse). Vickers LTD on new-style toggle, no chamber markings, dated barrel; no stock lug. Estimated 10,000 production.

LUNA FREE PISTOL
Zella-Mehlis, Germany
Originally mfd. by Ernst Friedr. Büchel and later by Udo Anschütz

Luna Model 300 Free Pistol

Luna Model 300 Free Pistol **$1150**
Single shot. System Aydt action. Set trigger. Caliber: 22 LR. 11-inch barrel. Weight: 40 oz. Target sights. Blued finish. Checkered and carved walnut stock and forearm; improved design with adjustable hand base on later models of Udo Anschütz manufacture. Made prior to WW II.

M.A.C./DEFENSE SYSTEMS INTL.
Marietta, Georgia

M.A.C. Ingram Model 10A1S

M.A.C. Ingram Model 10A1S Semiautomatic **$795**
Caliber: 9mm or 45 ACP. 30- or 32-round magazine. 5³⁄₄-inch barrel. 10¹⁄₂ inches overall. Weight: 6¹⁄₄ pounds. Front protected post sight, fixed aperture rear sight. Manually operated Garand-type safety in trigger guard. Based on Military Armament Corporation's Ingram 10 design.

MAGNUM RESEARCH INC.
Minneapolis, Minnesota

Magnum Research Baby Eagle Semiautomatic **$460**
DA. Calibers: 9mm, 40 S&W, 41 AE. 15-shot magazine (9mm), 9-shot magazine (40 S&W), 10-shot magazine (41 AE). 4.75-inch barrel. 8.15 inches overall. Weight: 35.4 oz. Combat sights. Matte blued finish.

Magnum Research Baby Eagle

Magnum Research Desert Eagle

Magnum Research Desert Eagle Semiautomatic
Calibers: 357 Mag., 41 Mag., 44 Mag., 50 Action Express (AE). 8- or 9-shot magazine. Gas-operated. Barrel lengths: 6 (standard), 10 and 14 inches; polygonal. 10.6 inches overall w/6-inch barrel. Weight (w/6-inch bbl.): 357 Mag.—52 oz. w/alum. alloy frame, 62 oz. w/steel frame; 41/44 Mag.—56 oz. w/alloy; 67 oz. w/steel. Fixed or adjustable combat sights. Combat-type trigger guard. Finish: Military black oxide, nickel, chrome, stainless or blued. Wraparound rubber stocks. Made by Israel Military Industries from 1984 to date.

357 Standard (steel) or Alloy (6-inch bbl.)	$ 595
357 Stainless Steel (6-inch bbl.)	725
41 Mag. Standard (steel) or Alloy (6-inch bbl.)	695
41 Mag. Stainless Steel (6-inch bbl.)	675
44 Mag. Standard (steel) or Alloy (6-inch bbl.)	650
44 Mag. Stainless Steel (6-inch bbl.)	710
50 AE Magnum Standard	1000
Add for 10-inch Barrel	100
Add for 14-inch Barrel	125

**Magnum Research
Mountain Eagle**

Magnum Research Mountain Eagle Semiautomatic $195
Caliber: 22 LR. 15-shot polycarbonate resin magazine. 6.5-inch injection-molded polymer and steel barrel. 10.6 inches overall. Weight: 21 oz. Sights: ramp blade front; adjustable rear. Injection-molded, checkered and textured grip. Matte black finish. Made from 1992 to date.

Magnum Research SSP-91 Lone Eagle Pistol
Single-shot action with interchangeable rotating breech-barrel assembly. Calibers: 22 LR, 22 Mag., 22 Hornet, 22-250, 223 Rem., 243 Rem., 6mm BR, 7mm-08, 7mm BR, 30-06, 30-30, 308 Win., 35 Rem., 357 Mag., 44 Mag., 444 Marlin. 14-inch interchangeable barrel assembly. 15 inches overall. Weight: 4½ lbs.

SSP-91 S/S Pistol (Complete)	$255
14-inch Barrel Assembly	190
Stock Assembly	65

═══ MAUSER PISTOLS ═══
Oberndorf, Germany
Waffenfabrik Mauser of Mauser-Werke A.G.

Mauser Model 80-SA

Mauser Model 80-SA Automatic $330
Caliber: 9mm Para. 13-shot magazine. 4.66-inch barrel. 8 inches overall. Weight: about 31.5 oz. Blued finish. Hardwood grips. Made 1991–94.

Mauser Model 90-DA

Mauser Model 90-DA Automatic $375
Caliber: 9mm Para. 14-shot magazine. 4.66-inch barrel. 8 inches overall. Weight: 35 oz. Blued finish. Hardwood grips. Made 1991–94.

Mauser Model 90 DAC Compact $395
Caliber: 9mm Para. 14-shot magazine. 4.13-inch barrel. 7.4 inches overall. Weight: 33¼ oz. Blued finish. Hardwood grips. Made 1991–94.

Mauser Model 1898 Military

Mauser Model 1898 Military Auto Pistol $2475
Caliber: 7.63mm Mauser; also chambered for 9mm Mauser and 9mm Luger; the latter is identified by a large red "9" in the stocks. Box magazine, 10-shot. 5¼-inch barrel. 12 inches overall. Weight: 45 oz. Adjustable rear sight. Blued finish. Walnut stocks. Made 1898–1945. *Note:* Specialist collectors recognize a number of variations at higher values. Price here is for more common type.

Mauser Model HSc

Mauser Model HSc Double Action Auto Pistol . . $450
Calibers: 32 Auto (7.65mm), 380 Auto (9mm Short). 8-shot (32) or 7-shot (380) magazine. 3.4-inch barrel. 6.4 inches overall. Weight: 23.6 oz. Fixed sights. Blued or nickel finish. Checkered walnut stocks. Made 1938–1945; from 1968 to date.

Mauser Luger Lange Pistole 08 . . . . $1995
Caliber: 9mm Para. 8-inch barrel. Checkered grips. Blued finish. Accessorized w/walnut shoulder stock, front sight tool, spare magazine, leather case. Currently in production. Commemorative version made in limited quantities w/ivory grips and 14-carat gold monogram plate. (*See* photo, next page.)

Mauser Luger Lange Pistole 08

Mauser WTP Model I

Mauser WTP Model II

Mauser Parabellum (Luger)

Mauser WTP Model II Auto Pistol **$550**
Similar to Model I, but smaller and lighter. Caliber: 25
Automatic (6.35mm). 6-shot magazine. 2-inch barrel. 4
inches overall. Weight: 9½ oz. Blued finish. Hard rubber
stocks. Made 1938–1940.

MITCHELL ARMS, INC.
Santa Ana, California

Mitchell Arms American Eagle Pistol **$525**
Stainless-steel re-creation of the American Eagle Parabellum auto pistol. Caliber: 9mm Parabellum. 7-shot
magazine. 4-inch barrel. 9.6 inches overall. Weight: 26.6
oz. Blade front sight, fixed rear. Stainless finish. Checkered walnut grips. Discontinued 1994.

Mauser Parabellum (Luger) Auto Pistol **$1000**
Current commercial model. Swiss pattern with grip safety.
Calibers: 7.65mm Luger, 9mm Luger. 8-shot magazine.
Barrel lengths: 4-, 6-inch. 8¾ inches overall w/4-inch bbl.
Weight: 30 oz. w/4-inch bbl. Fixed sights. Blued finish.
Checkered walnut stocks. Made from 1970 to date. *Note:*
Pistols of this model sold in the U.S. have the American
Eagle stamped on the receiver.

Mauser Pocket Model 1910 Auto Pistol **$345**
Caliber: 25 Auto (6.35mm). 9-shot magazine. 3.1-inch
barrel. 5.4 inches overall. Weight: 15 oz. Fixed sights.
Blued finish. Checkered walnut or hard rubber stocks.
Made 1910–1934.

Mauser Pocket Model 1914 Automatic **$325**
Similar to Pocket Model 1910. Caliber: 32 Auto (7.65mm).
8-shot magazine. 3.4-inch bbl. 6 inches overall. Weight:
21 oz. Fixed sights. Blued finish. Checkered walnut or
hard rubber stocks. Made 1914–1934.

**Mitchell Arms
Citation II**

Mauser Pocket Model 1934 . . . . **$345**
Similar to Pocket Models 1910 and 1914 in the respective
calibers. Chief difference is in the more streamlined one-
piece stocks. Made 1934–c. 1939.

Mauser WTP Model I Auto Pistol **$395**
"Westentaschen-Pistole" (Vest Pocket Pistol). Caliber:
25 Automatic (6.35mm). 6-shot magazine. 2½-inch barrel.
4½ inches overall. Weight: 11½ oz. Blued finish. Hard
rubber stocks. Made c. 1922–1937.

Mitchell Arms Citation II Auto Pistol **$340**
Re-creation of the High Standard Supermatic Citation
Military. Caliber: 22 LR. 10-shot magazine. 5.5-inch bull
barrel or 7.25 fluted barrel. 9.75 inches overall (5.5-inch
bbl.). Weight: 44.5 oz. Ramp front sight, slide-mounted
micro-adj. rear. Satin blue or stainless finish. Checkered
walnut grips w/thumbrest. Made from 1992 to date.

Mitchell Arms Olympic I.S.U. Auto Pistol $435

Similar to the Citation II Model, except chambered in 22 Short. 6.75-inch round tapered barrel with stabilizer and removable counterweights. Made from 1992 to date.

**Mitchell Arms
Victor II**

**Mitchell Arms
Sharpshooter II**

Mitchell Arms Victor II Auto Pistol (cont.)

oz.(5.5-inch bbl.) Rib-mounted target sights. Satin blue or stainless finish. Checkered walnut grips w/thumbrest.

MKE PISTOL
Ankara, Turkey
Mfd. by Makina ve Kimya Endüstrisi Kurumu

**MKE Kirikkale
Double Action Automatic***

Mitchell Arms Sharpshooter II Auto Pistol $275

Re-creation of the High Standard Sharpshooter. Caliber: 22 LR. 10-shot magazine. 5-inch bull barrel. 10.25 inches overall. Weight: 42 oz. Ramp front sight, slide-mounted micro-adj. rear. Satin blue or stainless finish. Checkered walnut grips w/thumbrest. Made from 1992 to date.

**Mitchell Arms
Single Action Army**

MKE Kirikkale Double Action Automatic Pistol . . $295

Similar to Walther PP. Calibers: 32 Auto (7.65mm), 380 Auto (9mm Short). 7-shot magazine. 3.9-inch barrel. 6.7 inches overall. Weight: 24 oz. Fixed sights. Blued finish. Checkered plastic stocks. Made 1948 to date. *Note:* This is a Turkish Army standard service pistol.

Mitchell Arms Single Action Army Revolver

Calibers: 357 Mag., 44 Mag., 45 Colt/45 ACP. 6-shot cylinder. Barrel lengths: 4³/₄, 5¹/₂, 7¹/₂ inches. Weight: 40–43 oz. Sights: blade front; grooved topstrap or adjustable rear. Blued or nickel finish w/color-casehardened frame. Brass or steel backstrap/trigger guard. Smooth one-piece walnut grips.

Standard Model w/Blued Finish	$320
Standard Model w/Nickel Finish	395
Standard Model w/Stainless Backstrap	420
45 Combo w/Blued Finish	445
45 Combo w/Nickel Finish	495

Mitchell Arms Trophy II Auto Pistol $395

Similar to the Citation II Model, except with gold-plated trigger and gold-filled markings. Made from 1992 to date.

Mitchell Arms Victor II Auto Pistol $350

Re-creation of the High Standard Victor with full-length vent rib. Caliber: 22 LR. 10-shot magazine. 4.5- or 5.5-inch barrel. 9.75 inches overall (5.5-inch bbl.). Weight: 52

MOA CORPORATION
Dayton, Ohio

MOA Maximum Pistol

MOA Maximum Single Shot Pistol **$450**
Calibers: 22 Hornet to 358 Win. 10- or 14-inch Douglas barrel. Weight: 3 lbs. 13 oz.–4 lbs. 3 oz. Smooth walnut grips. Currently in production. (*See* photo, preceding page.)

MOA Maximum Carbine Pistol **$425**
Similar to Maximum Pistol, but with 18-inch barrel. Currently in production.

=== **NAVY ARMS COMPANY** ===
Ridgefield, New Jersey

Navy Arms Model 1873 Single Action Revolver
Calibers: 44-40, 45 Colt. 6-shot cylinder. Barrel lengths: 3, 4³/₄, 5¹/₂, 7¹/₂ inches. 10³/₄ inches overall (5¹/₂-inch bbl.). Weight: 36 oz. Sights: blade front; grooved topstrap rear. Blued w/color-casehardened frame or nickel finish. Smooth walnut grips. Made from 1991 to date.
Blued Finish w/Brass Backstrap **$295**
U.S. Artillery Model w/5-inch bbl. **395**
U.S. Cavalry Model w/7-inch bbl. **400**

Navy Arms Model 1875

Navy Arms Model 1875 Single Action Revolver . **$325**
Replica of Remington Model 1875. Calibers: 357 Magnum, 44-40, 45 Colt. 6-shot cylinder. 7¹/₂-inch barrel. 13¹/₂ inches overall. Weight: about 48 oz. Fixed sights. Blued or nickel finish. Smooth walnut stocks. Made in Italy c. 1955–1980. *Note:* Originally marketed in the U.S. as Replica Arms Model 1875; that firm was acquired by Navy Arms Co.

Navy Arms Buntline Frontier

Navy Arms Buntline Frontier **$375**
Same as Target Frontier, except has detachable shoulder stock and 16¹/₂-inch barrel. Calibers: 357 Magnum and 45 Colt only. Made 1975–79.

Navy Arms Frontier SA Revolver **$230**
Calibers: 22 LR, 22 WMR, 357 Mag., 45 Colt. 6-shot cylinder. Barrel lengths: 4¹/₂-, 5¹/₂-, 7¹/₂-inch. 10¹/₄ inches overall w/4¹/₂-inch bbl. Weight: about 36 oz. w/4¹/₂-inch bbl. Fixed sights. Blued barrel and cylinder, color-case-

**Navy Arms Frontier
Standard Model**

Navy Arms Frontier SA Revolver (cont.)
hardened frame, brass grip frame. One-piece smooth walnut stock. Made 1975–79.

**Navy Arms Frontier
Target Model**

Navy Arms Frontier Target Model **$250**
Same as Standard Frontier, except has adjustable rear sight and ramp front sight. Made 1975–79.

Navy Arms Luger (Standard) Automatic **$165**
Caliber: 22 LR, standard or high velocity. 10-shot magazine. Barrel: 4.5 inches. 8.9 inches overall. Weight: 1 lb. 13¹/₂ oz. Square blade front sight w/square notch, stationary rear sight. Walnut checkered grips. Non-reflecting black finish. Discontinued 1983.

Navy Arms Rolling Block

Navy Arms Rolling Block Single Shot Pistol **$180**
Calibers: 22 LR, 22 Hornet, 357 Magnum. 8-inch barrel. 12 inches overall. Weight: about 40 oz. Adjustable sights. Blued barrel, color-casehardened frame, brass trigger guard. Smooth walnut stock/forearm. Made 1965–1980.

Navy Arms TT-Olympia Pistol **$250**
Reproduction of the Walther Olympia Target Pistol. Caliber: 22 LR. 4.6-inch barrel. 8 inches overall. Weight: 28 oz. Blade front sight, adjustable rear. Blued finish. Checkered hardwood grips. Made from 1992 to date.

NEW ENGLAND FIREARMS
Gardner, Massachusetts

**New England Firearms
Model R73**

New England Firearms Model R73 Revolver **$125**
Caliber: 32 H&R Mag. 5-shot cylinder. 2½- or 4-inch barrel. 8½ inches overall w/4-inch bbl. Weight: 26 oz. w/4-inch bbl. Fixed or adjustable sights. Blued or nickel finish. Walnut-finish hardwood stocks. Made from 1988 to date.

New England Firearms Model R92 Revolver **$110**
Same general specifications as Model R73, except chambered for 22 LR. 9-shot cylinder. Weight: 28 oz. with 4-inch barrel.

**New England Firearms
Ultra (Nickel)**

New England Firearms Ultra Revolver **$130**
Calibers: 22 LR, 22 WRF. 9-shot cylinder in 22 LR, 6-shot cylinder in 22 WRF. 4- or 6-inch ribbed bull barrel. 10⅝ inches overall w/6-inch bbl. Weight: 36 oz. w/6-inch bbl. Blade front sight; adjustable square-notched rear. Blued or nickel finish. Walnut-finish hardwood grips. Made from 1989 to date.

**New England Firearms
Lady Ultra**

New England Firearms Lady Ultra Revolver **$150**
Same basic specifications as the Ultra, except in 32 H&R Mag. w/5-shot cylinder and 3-inch ribbed bull barrel. 7½ inches overall. Weight: 31 oz. Made from 1992 to date.

NORTH AMERICAN ARMS
Spanish Fork, Utah

North American Arms Model 22LR

North American Arms Model 22LR **$125**
Same as Model 22S, except chambered for 22 LR, is 3⅞ inches overall, weighs 4½ oz. Made 1976 to date.

North American Arms Model 22S

**North American Arms Model 22S Mini
Revolver** **$155**
SA. Caliber: 22 Short. 5-shot cylinder. 1⅛-inch barrel. 3½ inches overall. Weight: 4 oz. Fixed sights. Stainless steel. Plastic stocks. Made from 1975 to date.

North American Arms 450 Magnum Express . . . **$850**
SA. Calibers: 450 Magnum Express, 45 Win. Mag. 7½-inch barrel. Matte stainless steel finish. Cased. Discontinued 1986.

North American Arms Model 454C

North American Arms Model 454C Single Action Revolver $745
Caliber: 454 Casull. 5-shot cylinder. 7½-inch barrel. 14 inches overall. Weight: 50 oz. Fixed sights. Stainless steel. Smooth hardwood stocks. Introduced 1977. (*See* photo, preceding page.)

**North American Arms
Black Widow**

North American Arms Black Widow Revolver
SA. Calibers: 22 LR, 22 WMR. 5-shot cylinder. 2-inch heavy vent barrel. 5⅞ inches overall. Weight: 8.8 oz. Fixed or adjustable sights. Full-size black rubber grips. Stainless steel brush finish. Made from 1990 to date.

Adjustable Sight Model	$210
Adjustable Sight Combo Model	220
Fixed Sight Model	195
Fixed Sight Combo Model....................	200

**North American Arms
Mini-Master**

North American Arms Mini-Master Revolver
SA. Calibers: 22 LR, 22 WMR. 5-shot cylinder. 4-inch heavy vent-rib barrel. 7¾ inches overall. Weight: 10¾ inches. Fixed or adjustable sights. Black rubber grips. Stainless steel brush finish. Made from 1990 to date.

Adjustable Sight Model	$205
Adjustable Sight Combo Model	250
Fixed Sight Model	210
Fixed Sight Combo Model....................	245

NORWEGIAN MILITARY PISTOLS
Mfd. by Kongsberg Vaapenfabrikk, the government arsenal at Kongsberg, Norway

Norwegian Model 1914

Norwegian Model 1914 Automatic Pistol $300
Similar to Colt Model 1911 45 Automatic with same general specifications, except has lengthened slide stop. Made 1919–1946.

Norwegian Model 1912 is same except has conventional slide stop. Since only 500 were made, this is a very rare collector's item.

ORTGIES PISTOLS
Erfurt, Germany
Manufactured by Deutsche Werke A.G.

Ortgies Pocket*

Ortgies Pocket Automatic Pistol $215
Calibers: 32 Automatic (7.65mm), 380 Automatic (9mm). 7-shot magazine (380 cal.), 8-shot (32 cal.). 3¼-inch barrel. 6½ inches overall. Weight: 22 oz. Fixed sights. Blued finish. Plain walnut stocks. Made in 1920s.

Ortgies Vest Pocket*

Ortgies Vest Pocket Automatic Pistol **$225**
Caliber: 25 Automatic (6.35mm). 6-shot magazine. 2³/₄-inch barrel. 5³/₁₆ inches overall. Weight: 13¹/₂ oz. Fixed sights. Blued finish. Plain walnut stocks. Made in 1920s.

PARA-ORDNANCE MFG., INC.
Scarborough, Ontario, Canada

Para-Ordnance P•12

Para-Ordnance P•12 Compact Auto Pistol
Caliber: 45 ACP. 11-shot magazine. 3.5-inch barrel. 7 inches overall. Weight: 24 oz. (alloy frame). Blade front sight, adjustable rear w/ 3-Dot system. Textured composition grips. Matte black alloy or steel finish. Made from 1990 to date.
Model P1245 (Alloy) **$560**
Model P1245C (Steel) 595

Para-Ordnance P•13 Auto Pistol
Same general specifications as Model P-12, except with 12-shot magazine. 4.5-inch barrel. 8 inches overall. Weight: 25 oz. (alloy frame). Blade front sight, adjustable rear w/ 3-dot system. Textured composition grips. Matte black alloy or steel finish. Made from 1990 to date.
Model P1345 (Alloy) **$520**
Model P1345C (Steel) 545

Para-Ordnance P•14 Auto Pistol
Caliber: 45 ACP. 13-shot magazine. 5-inch barrel. 8.5 inches overall. Weight: 28 oz. alloy frame. Blade front

Para-Ordnance P•14 Auto Pistol (cont.)
sight, adjustable rear w/ 3-dot system. Textured composition grips. Matte black alloy or steel finish. Made from 1990 to date.
Model P1445 (Alloy) **$495**
Model P1445C (Steel) 560

PLAINFIELD MACHINE COMPANY
Dunellen, New Jersey

The operation of this firm was discontinued about 1982.

Plainfield Model 71

Plainfield Model 71 Automatic Pistol
Calibers: 22 LR, 25 Automatic; conversion kit available. 10-shot magazine in 22, 8-shot in 25. 2¹/₂-inch barrel. 5¹/₈ inches overall. Weight: 25 oz. Fixed sights. Stainless steel frame/slide. Checkered walnut stocks. Made 1970–1982.
22 LR or 25 Auto only **$130**
With Conversion Kit 150

Plainfield Model 72

Plainfield Model 72
Same as Model 71, except has aluminum slide, 3¹/₂-inch barrel, is 6 inches overall. Made 1970–1982.
22 LR or 25 Auto only **$140**
With Conversion Kit 160

RADOM PISTOL
Radom, Poland
Manufactured by the Polish Arsenal

Radom P-35 Automatic

Radom P-35 Automatic Pistol **$610**
Variation of the Colt Government Model 45 Auto. Caliber: 9mm Luger. 8-shot magazine. 4³/₄-inch barrel. 7³/₄ inches overall. Weight: 29 oz. Fixed sights. Blued finish. Plastic stocks. Made 1935 thru WW II.

RECORD-MATCH PISTOLS
Zella-Mehlis, Germany
Manufactured by Udo Anschütz

Record-Match Model 200

Record-Match Model 210

Record-Match Model 200 Free Pistol **$910**
Basically the same as Model 210 except plainer, with different stock design and conventional set trigger, spur trigger guard. Made prior to WW II.

Record-Match Model 210 Free Pistol **$1295**
System Martini action, set trigger with button release. Caliber: 22 LR. Single shot. 11-inch barrel. Weight: 46 oz. Target sights, micrometer rear. Blued finish. Carved and checkered walnut stock and forearm, adjustable hand base. Also made with dural action (Model 210A); weight of this model, 35 oz. Made prior to WW II.

REISING ARMS CO.
Hartford, Connecticut

Reising Target Automatic*

Reising Target Automatic Pistol **$400**
Hinged frame. Outside hammer. Caliber: 22 LR. 12-shot magazine. 6¹/₂-inch barrel. Fixed sights. Blued finish. Hard rubber stocks. Made 1921–24.

REMINGTON ARMS COMPANY
Ilion, New York

Remington Model 51

Remington Model 51 Automatic Pistol **$525**
Calibers: 32 Auto, 380 Auto. 7-shot magazine. 3¹/₂-inch barrel. 6⁵/₈ inches overall. Weight: 21 oz. Fixed sights. Blued finish. Hard rubber stocks. Made 1918–1934.

**Remington Model 95 Double Derringer
Engraved Model**

Remington Model 95 Double Derringer
SA. Caliber: 41 Short Rimfire. 3-inch double barrels (superposed). 4⁷/₈ inches overall. Early models have long hammer spur and two-armed extractor; later production have short hammer spur and sliding extractor (a few have no extractor). Fixed sights: front blade integral with barrels, rear groove. Finish: all blued, blued w/nickel-plated frame, fully nickel-plated; also with factory engraving. Grips: walnut, checkered hard rubber, pearl, ivory. Weight: 11 oz. Made 1866–1935. Approximately 150,000 were

Remington Model 95 Double Derringer (cont.)

manufactured. *Note:* During the 70 years of its production, serial numbering of this model was repeated two or three times. Therefore, aside from hammer and extractor differences between the earlier and later models, the best clue to the age of a Double Derringer is the stamping of the company's name on the top of the barrel or side rib. Prior to 1888, derringers were stamped "E. Remington & Sons"; 1888–1910, "Remington Arms Co."; 1910–1935, "Remington Arms-U.M.C. Co."

Plain Model **$1000**
Factory-engraved Model with ivory or pearl
  grips **1895**

Remington New Model Single Shot Target Pistol **$1650**

Also called Model 1901 Target. Rolling-block action. Calibers: 22 Short, 22 LR, 44 S&W Russian. 10-inch barrel, half-octagon. 14 inches overall. Weight: 45 oz. (22 cal.). Target sights. Blued finish. Checkered walnut grips and forearm. Made 1901–1909.

Remington Model XP-100 Custom Pistol

Remington Model XP-100 Custom, Heavy Barrel

Remington Model XP-100 Custom Pistol **$695**

Bolt-action, single-shot, long-range pistol. Calibers: 223 Rem., 7mm-08 or 35 Rem. 14½-inch barrel, standard contour or heavy. Weight: about 4¼ pounds. Currently in production.

Remington Model XP-100 Silhouette

Remington Model XP-100 Silhouette **$330**

Same general specifications as Model XP-100, except chambered for 7mm BR Rem., 14¾-inch barrel and weighs 4⅛ pounds.

Remington Model XP-100 Single Shot Pistol **$280**

Bolt action. Caliber: 221 Rem. "Fire Ball." 10½-inch vent-rib barrel. 16¾ inches overall. Weight: 3¾ pounds. Adjustable rear sight, blade front; receiver drilled and tapped for scope mounts. Blued finish. One-piece brown nylon stock. Made 1963–1988.

Remington Model XP-100 Varmint Special

Remington Model XP-100 Varmint Special **$295**

Bolt-action, single-shot, long-range pistol. Calibers: 223 Rem., 7mm BR. 14½-inch barrel. 21¼ inches overall. Weight: about 4¼ pounds. One-piece Du Pont nylon stock with universal grips. Discontinued 1991.

Remington Model XP-100R KS Custom Repeater

Remington Model XP-100R KS Custom Repeater **$545**

Same general specifications as Model XP-100 Custom, except chambered for 22-250, 223 Rem., 250 Savage, 7mm-08 Rem., 308 Win., 35 Rem. and 350 Rem. Mag. Kevlar-reinforced synthetic stock with blind magazine and sling swivel studs. Made from 1990 to date.

Remington XP-22R Rimfire Repeater **$300**

Bolt-action clip repeater built on Model 541-style action. Caliber: 22 Short, Long, LR. 5-shot magazine. 14½-inch barrel. Weight: 4¼ pounds. Rem. synthetic stock. Made 1991–92.

RG REVOLVERS
Miami, Florida

RG Model 23

RG Model 23

SA/DA. 6-shot magazine, swing-out cylinder. Caliber: 22 LR. 1¾- and 3⅜-inch barrels. Overall length: 5⅛ and 7½ inches. Weight 16–17 oz. Fixed sights. Blued or nickel finish. Discontinued.

Blued Finish **$75**
Nickel Finish **80**

RG Model 38S

RG Model 38S
SA/DA. 6-shot magazine, swing-out cylinder. Caliber: 38 Special. 3- and 4-inch barrels. Overall length: 8 1/4 and 9 1/4 inches. Weight: 32–34 oz. Windage-adjustable rear sight. Blued finish. Discontinued.
With Plastic Grips **$100**
With Wood Grips **110**

ROSSI REVOLVERS
São Leopoldo, Brazil
Manufactured by Amadeo Rossi S.A.

Rossi Model 31 Double Action Revolver **$115**
Caliber: 38 Special. 5-shot cylinder. 4-inch barrel. Weight: 20 oz. Blue or nickel finish. Discontinued 1985.

Rossi Model 51 Double Action Revolver **$130**
Caliber: 22 LR. 6-shot cylinder. 6-inch barrel. Weight: 28 oz. Blued finish.

Rossi Model 68 . . . . **$135**
Caliber: 38 Special. 5-round magazine. 2- or 3-inch barrel. Overall length: 6 1/2 and 7 1/2 inches. Weight: 21–23 oz. Blued finish. Nickel finish available with 3-inch barrel.

Rossi Model 84 Revolver

Rossi Model 84 Double Action Revolver **$175**
Caliber: 38 Special. 6-shot. 3-inch barrel. 8 inches overall. Weight: 27 1/2 oz. Stainless steel finish. Made 1984–86.

Rossi Model 85 Double Action Revolver **$190**
Same as Model 84 except has ventilated rib.

Rossi Model 88 Double Action Revolver **$185**
Caliber: 38 Special. 5-shot cylinder. 2- or 3-inch barrel. Weight: 21 oz. Stainless steel finish.

Rossi Model 88/2 Double Action Revolver **$200**
Caliber: 38 Special. 5-shot cylinder. 2- or 3-inch barrel. 6 1/2 inches overall. Weight: 21 oz. Stainless steel finish. Made 1985–87.

Rossi Model 89 Revolver

Rossi Model 89 Double Action Revolver **$150**
Caliber: 32 S&W. 6-shot cylinder. 3-inch barrel. 7 1/2 inches overall. Weight: 17 oz. Stainless steel finish. Disc. 1986.

Rossi Model 94 Double Action Revolver **$165**
Caliber: 38 Special. 6-shot cylinder. 3-inch barrel. 8 inches overall. Weight: 29 oz. Discontinued 1986.

Rossi Model 95 Revolver **$165**
Caliber: 38 Special. 6-round magazine. 3-inch barrel. 8 inches overall. Weight: 27 1/2 oz. Ventilated rib. Blued finish. Discontinued 1986.

Rossi Model 515 Double Action Revolver **$185**
Calibers: 22 LR, 22 WRF. 6-shot cylinder. 4-inch barrel. 9 inches overall. Weight: 30 oz. Red ramp front sight; adjustable square-notched rear. Stainless finish. Checkered hardwood stocks. Made from 1992 to date.

Rossi Model 720 Double Action Revolver **$205**
Caliber: 44 Special. 5-shot cylinder. 3-inch barrel. 8 inches overall. Weight: 27.5 oz. Red ramp front sight; adjustable square-notched rear. Stainless finish. Checkered neoprene combat-style stocks. Made from 1992 to date.

Rossi Model 841 Revolver

Rossi Model 841 Double Action Revolver **$190**
Same general specifications as Model 84, except has 4-inch barrel (9 inches overall), weighs 30 oz. Made 1985–86.

Rossi Model 851 Double Action Revolver **$175**
Same general specifications as Model 85, except with 3-
or 4-inch barrel. 8 inches overall w/3-inch bbl. Weight:
27.5 oz. w/3-inch bbl. Red ramp front sight; adjustable
square-notched rear. Stainless finish. Checkered hardwood
stocks. Made from 1991 to date.

Rossi Model 941 Double Action Revolver **$150**
Caliber: 38 Special. 6-shot cylinder. 4-inch barrel. 9 inches
overall. Weight: 30 oz. Blue finish. Made 1985–86.

Rossi Model 951 Double Action Revolver **$185**
Same general specifications as Model 941 except has ventilated rib.

Rossi Model 971

Rossi Model 971 Double Action Revolver
Caliber: 357 Magnum. 6-shot cylinder. 2½-, 4- or 6-inch
barrel. 9 inches overall w/4-inch bbl. Weight: 36 oz. w/4-
inch bbl. Blade front sight; adjustable square-notched rear.
Blued or stainless finish. Checkered hardwood stocks.
Made from 1990 to date.
Blued Finish **$200**
Stainless Finish **235**

Rossi Double Action Revolver

Rossi Double Action Revolver **$120**
Calibers: 22 LR, 32 S&W Long, 38 Special. 5-shot (38) or
6-shot cylinder (other calibers). Barrel lengths: 3-, 6-inch.
Weight: 22 oz. w/3-inch bbl. Sights: adjustable rear, ramp
front. Blued or nickel finish. Wood or plastic stocks. Made
1965–1991.

Rossi Sportsman's 22

Rossi Sportsman's 22 . . . . **$180**
Caliber: 22 LR. 6-round magazine. 4-inch barrel. 9 inches
overall. Weight: 30 oz. Stainless steel finish. Disc. 1991.

RUBY PISTOL
**Manufactured by Gabilondo y Urresti, Eibar, Spain,
and others**

Ruby 7.65mm*

Ruby 7.65mm Automatic Pistol **$175**
Secondary standard service pistol of the French Army in
World Wars I and II. Essentially the same as the Alkartasuna (see separate listing). Other manufacturers: Ar-
menia Elgoibarresa y Cia., Eceolaza y Vicinai y Cia., Hijos
de Angel Echeverria y Cia., Bruno Salaverria y Cia., Zu-
laika y Cia., all of Eibar, Spain; Gabilondo y Cia., Elgoibar,
Spain; Ruby Arms Company, Guernica, Spain. Made
1914–1922.

RUGER HANDGUNS
Southport, Connecticut
Manufactured by Sturm, Ruger & Co.

Rugers made in 1976 are designated "Liberty" in honor
of the U.S. Bicentennial and bring a premium of approximately 25 percent in value over regular models.

AUTOMATIC/SINGLE SHOT PISTOLS

NOTE: For ease in finding a particular Ruger handgun, the
listings are divided into two groupings: Automatic/Single
Shot Pistols (below) and Revolvers, which follows. For a
complete listing, please refer to the Index.

Ruger Hawkeye

Ruger 22/45 Zytel Frame

Ruger Hawkeye Single Shot Pistol $1000
SA. Cylinder replaced by rotating breechblock; chamber is in barrel. Caliber: 256 Magnum. 8½-inch barrel. 14½ inches overall. Weight: 45 oz. Blued finish. Click adjustable rear sight, ramp front sight. Smooth walnut stocks. Made 1963–65.

Ruger Mark I Target

Ruger Mark II 22/45 Automatic Pistol
Same general specifications as Ruger Mark II 22 LR, except with stainless receiver and barrel in three lengths: 4¾-inch tapered w/fixed sights, 5¼-inch tapered w/adj. sights and 5½-inch bull. Fitted with Zytel grip frame of the same design as the Model 1911 45 ACP.
Model KP4 . . . . $165
Model KP512, KP514 210

Ruger Mark I Target Model Automatic Pistol
Caliber: 22 LR. 9-shot magazine. Barrels: 5¼- or 6⅞-inch heavy tapered, 5½-inch untapered bull barrel. 10⅞ inches overall w/6⅝-inch bbl. Weight: 42 oz. w/5½- or 6⅞-inch bbl. Sights: adjustable rear, under-cut target front. Blued finish. Hard rubber stocks or checkered walnut thumbrest stocks (add $10 to value for latter). Made 1951–1981.
Standard $180
With Red Medallion 495

Ruger Mark II Bull Barrel

Ruger Mark II Bull Barrel Automatic Pistol
Same as standard Mark II, except for bull barrel (5½- or 10-inch). Weight: about 2¾ pounds.
Blued Finish $195
Stainless Model, intro. 1985 250

**Ruger Mark II Stainless
22 Long Rifle**

**Ruger Mark II Government
Target Automatic**

Ruger Mark II Automatic Pistol
Caliber: 22 LR, standard or high velocity. 4¾- or 6-inch tapered barrel. 10-shot magazine. 8⁵⁄₁₆ w/4¾-inch bbl. Weight: 36 oz. Fixed front sight; square notch rear. Blued or stainless finish. Made 1982 to date.
Blued $165
Stainless 215
Bright Stainless (Ltd. prod. 5,000 in 1982) 350

Ruger Mark II Government Target Auto Pistol
Civilian version of the Mark II used by U.S. Armed Forces. Caliber: 22 LR rimfire. 10-shot magazine. 6⅞-inch bull

Ruger Mark II Government Target (cont.)
barrel. 11¹/₈ inches overall. Weight: 44 oz., empty. Made from 1986 to date.

Blued **$230**
Stainless Steel **275**

**Ruger Mark II Target Model
22 LR Stainless**

Ruger Mark II Target Pistol
Same as standard Mark II, except has 6⁷/₈-inch tapered barrel. Made from 1982 to date.

Blued Finish **$200**
Stainless Steel Finish **255**

**Ruger P-85
Double Action Pistol**

Ruger Model P-85 Automatic Pistol
Caliber: 9mm. DA, recoil-operated. 15-shot capacity. 4¹/₂-inch barrel. 7.84 inches overall. Weight: 32 oz. Fixed rear sight, square-post front. Available with decocking levers, ambidextrous safety or in DA only. Blued or stainless finish. Made 1987 to date.

Blued Finish **$265**
Stainless Steel Finish **290**

Ruger Model P-89 Automatic Pistol
Caliber: 9mm. DA with slide-mounted safety levers. 15-shot magazine. 4.5-inch barrel. 7.84 inches overall. Weight: 32 oz. Square post front sight, adjustable rear with 3-dot system. Blued or stainless steel finish. Grooved black Xenoy grips. Made from 1986 to date; stainless introduced in 1990.

P-89 Blued **$310**
P-89 Stainless **355**

Ruger Model P-89 DAC

Ruger Model P-89 DAC/DAO Auto Pistols
Similar to the standard Model P-89, except the P-89 DAC has ambidextrous decocking levers. The P-89 DAO operates in double-action-only mode, has stainless finish only and was introduced in 1991.

P-89 DAC Blued **$305**
P-89 DAC Stainless **355**
P-89 DAO Stainless **350**

Ruger Model P-90 Double Action Automatic Pistol
Caliber: 45 ACP. 7-shot magazine. 4¹/₂-inch barrel. 7⁷/₈ inches overall. Weight: 33¹/₂ oz. Square post front sight; adj. square-notched rear w/3-dot system. Grooved black Xenoy composition stocks. Stainless finish. DAC model has ambidextrous decocking levers. Made 1991 to date.

Model P-90 Standard **$315**
Model P-90 DAC (Decockers) **320**

Ruger Model P-91 Double Action Automatic Pistol
Same general specifications as the Model P-90, except chambered for 40 S&W with 12-shot double-column magazine. Made from 1992 to date.

Model P-91 Standard **$315**
Model P-91 DAC (Decockers) **320**
Model P-91 DAO (Double Action Only) **325**

Ruger Model P-93 Compact Auto Pistol
Similar to the standard Model P-89, except with 3.9-inch barrel (7.3 inches overall) and weighs 31 oz. Stainless steel finish. Made from 1993 to date.

Model P-93 DAC (Decocker) (Disc. 1994) **$395**
Model P-93 DAO (Double Action Only) **375**

**Ruger Standard Automatic
Pistol**

Ruger Standard Model Automatic Pistol

Caliber: 22 LR. 9-shot magazine. 4³/₄- or 6-inch barrel. 8³/₄ inches overall w/4³/₄-inch bbl. Weight: 36 oz. w/4³/₄-inch bbl. Fixed sights. Blued finish. Hard rubber or checkered walnut stocks. Made from 1949 to date. *Note:* In 1951, after the death of Alexander Sturm, the color of the eagle on the stock medallion was changed from red to black as a memorial. Known as the "Red Eagle Automatic," this early type is now a collector's item. Discontinued 1981. (*See* photo, preceding page.)

With Red Eagle Medallion	**$495**
With Black Eagle Medallion	145
Extra for Walnut Stocks	15

REVOLVERS

NOTE: This section contains only Ruger Revolvers. Automatic and Single Shot Pistols may be found on the preceding pages. For a complete listing of Ruger handguns, please refer to the Index.

Ruger Bearcat

Ruger Bearcat Single Action Revolver $295

Aluminum frame. Caliber: 22 LR. 6-shot cylinder. 4-inch barrel. 8⁷/₈ inches overall. Weight: 17 oz. Fixed sights. Blued finish. Smooth walnut stocks. Made 1958–1973.

Ruger Bisley, Large Frame

Ruger Bisley, Small Frame

Ruger Bisley SA Revolver, Large Frame $265

Calibers: 357 Mag., 41 Mag., 44 Mag., 45 Long Colt. 7¹/₂-inch barrel. 13 inches overall. Weight: 48 oz. Non-fluted or fluted cylinder, no engraving. Sights: adjustable rear, ramp front. Blued satin finish. Made from 1986 to date.

Ruger Bisley Single-Six Revolver, Small Frame ... $220

Calibers: 22 LR and 32 Mag. 6-shot cylinder. 6¹/₂-inch barrel. 11¹/₂ inches overall. Weight: 41 oz. Sights: fixed rear, blade front. Made from 1986 to date.

Ruger Blackhawk Single Action Convertible $285

Same as Blackhawk, except has extra cylinder. Caliber combinations: 357 Magnum and 9mm Luger, 45 Colt and 45 Automatic. Made 1967–1972.

Ruger Blackhawk

Ruger Blackhawk Single Action Revolver $230

Calibers: 30 Carbine, 357 Magnum, 41 Magnum, 45 Colt. 6-shot cylinder. Barrel lengths: 4⁵/₈-inch (357, 41, 45 caliber), 6¹/₂-inch (357, 41 caliber), 7¹/₂-inch (30, 45 caliber). 10¹/₈ inches overall (357 Mag. w/4⁵/₈-inch bbl.). Weight: 38 oz. (357 w/4⁵/₈-inch bbl.). Sights: adjustable rear, ramp front. Blued finish. Checkered hard rubber or smooth walnut stocks. Made 1956–1973.

Ruger Blackhawk 44

Ruger Blackhawk SA 44 Magnum Revolver

SA with heavy frame and cylinder. Caliber: 44 Magnum. 6-shot cylinder. 6¹/₂-inch barrel. 12¹/₈ inches overall. Weight: 40 oz. Adjustable rear sight, ramp front. Blued finish. Smooth walnut stocks. Made 1956–1973.

Standard	**$395**
Flat Top	625

Ruger GP-100 Double Action Revolver

Caliber: 357 Magnum. 4-inch heavy barrel, or 6-inch standard or heavy barrel. Overall length: 9³/₈ or 11³/₈ inches. Cushioned grip panels. Made from 1986 to date.

Blued Finish	**$240**
Stainless Steel Finish	280

HANDGUNS

Ruger GP-100 DA Revolver

Ruger New Model Single-Six SSM 32 Magnum

Ruger New Model Blackhawk Convertible **$240**
Same as New Model Blackhawk, except has extra cylinder; blued finish only. Caliber combinations: 357 Magnum and 9mm Luger, 45 Colt and 45 Automatic. 45 Colt and 45 Automatic discontinued 1983.

Ruger New Model Single-Six SSM Revolver **$190**
Same general specifications as standard Single-Six, except chambered for 32 H&R Magnum cartridge. Barrel length: 4⅝, 5½, 6½ or 9½ inches.

Ruger New Model Blackhawk

Ruger New Model Super Blackhawk

Ruger New Model Super Blackhawk Single Action Revolver **$275**
Interlocked mechanism. Caliber: 44 Magnum. 6-shot cylinder. 5½-inch, 7½-inch and 10½-inch bull barrel. 13⅜ inches overall. Weight: 48 oz. Adjustable rear sight, ramp front. Blued and stainless steel finish. Smooth walnut stocks. Made from 1973 to date. 5½-inch barrel made from 1987 to date.

Ruger New Model Blackhawk Stainless, 357 Magnum

Ruger New Model Super Single-Six Convertible

Ruger New Model Blackhawk Single Action Revolver
Interlocked mechanism. Calibers: 30 Carbine, 357 Magnum, 41 Magnum, 44 Magnum, 44 Special, 45 Colt. 6-shot cylinder. Barrel lengths: 4⅝-inch (357, 41, 45 Colt); 5½-inch (44 Mag., 44 Spec.); 6½-inch (357, 41, 45 Long Colt); 7½-inch (30, 45, 44 Special, 44 Mag.); 10½-inch in 44 Mag. 10⅜ inches overall in 357 Mag. w/4⅝-inch bbl. Weight: 40 oz. (357 w/4⅝-inch bbl.). Adjustable rear sight, ramp front. Blued finish or stainless steel; latter only in 357. Smooth walnut stocks. Made from 1973 to date.l
Blued finish **$210**
Stainless steel **290**
357 Maximum **270**
44 Magnum, intro. 1987 . . . . **250**

Ruger New Model Super Single-Six Convertible Revolver
SA with interlocked mechanism. Calibers: 22 LR and 22 WMR. Interchangeable 6-shot cylinders. Barrel lengths: 4⅝, 5½, 6½, 9½ inches. 10¹³⁄₁₆ inches overall w/4⅝-inch bbl. Weight: 33 oz. w/4⅝-inch bbl. Adjustable rear sight, ramp front. Blued finish or stainless steel; latter only with 5½- or 6½-inch bbl. Smooth walnut stocks. Made from 1972 to date.
Blued Finish **$185**
Stainless Steel **235**

**Ruger Police Service-Six
Stainless Steel**

Ruger Security-Six

Ruger Police Service-Six

Same general specifications as Speed-Six, except has square butt. Stainless steel models and 9mm Luger caliber available with only 4-inch barrel. Made 1971–1988.

38 Special, Blued Finish **$175**
38 Special, Stainless Steel **185**
357 Magnum or 9mm Luger, Blued Finish **190**
357 Magnum, Stainless Steel **215**

Ruger Security-Six Double Action Revolver

Caliber: 357 Magnum; handles 38 Special. 6-shot cylinder. Barrel lengths: 2³/₄-, 4-, 6-inch. 9¹/₄ inches overall w/4-inch bbl. Weight: 33¹/₂ oz. w/4-inch bbl. Adjustable rear sight, ramp front. Blued finish or stainless steel. Square butt. Checkered walnut stocks. Made 1971–1985.

Blued Finish **$195**
Stainless Steel **220**

**Ruger Redhawk Alloy Steel
Blued**

Ruger Single-Six

Ruger Redhawk Double Action Revolver **$265**

Calibers: 357 Mag., 41 Mag., 44 Mag. 6-shot cylinder. 5¹/₂- and 7¹/₂-inch barrel. 11 and 13 inches overall, respectively. Weight: about 52 oz. Adjustable rear sight, interchangeable front sights. Stainless finish. Made 1979 to date; 357 Mag. discontinued 1986. Alloy steel model with blued finish introduced in 1986 in 41 Mag. and 44 Mag. calibers.

Ruger Single-Six Single Action Revolver

Calibers: 22 LR, 22 WMR. 6-shot cylinder. Barrel lengths: 4⁵/₈, 5¹/₂, 6¹/₂, 9¹/₂ inches. 10⁷/₈ inches overall w/5¹/₂-inch bbl. Weight: about 35 oz. Fixed sights. Blued finish. Checkered hard rubber or smooth walnut grips. Made 1953–1973. *Note:* Pre-1956 model with flat loading gate is worth about twice as much as later version.

Standard **$195**
Convertible (w/2 cylinders, 22 LR/22 WMR) **215**

**Ruger Redhawk w/Integral
Scope Mounting System**

Ruger Single-Six Lightweight

Ruger Redhawk Stainless DA Scope-Ring Revolver **$345**

Same general specifications as standard Redhawk, except chambered for 44 Mag. only, and has integral scope mounting system.

Ruger Single-Six—Lightweight **$250**

Same general specifications as Single-Six, except has 4⁵/₈-inch barrel, lightweight alloy cylinder and frame, 10 inches overall length, weighs 23 oz. Made in 1956.

HANDGUNS

Ruger SP101 Double Action

Ruger SP101 Double Action Revolver
Calibers: 22 LR, 32 Mag., 9mm, 38 Special+P, 357 Mag. 5- or 6-shot cylinder. 2¼-, 3¹/₁₆- or 4-inch barrel. Weight: 25–34 oz. Stainless steel finish. Cushioned grips. Made from 1988 to date.
Standard Model **$270**
DAO Model (DA only, spurless hammer) **275**

Ruger Speed-Six

Ruger Speed-Six Double Action Revolver
Calibers: 38 Special, 357 Magnum, 9mm Luger. 6-shot cylinder. Barrel lengths: 2³/₄-, 4-inch; 9mm available only with 2³/₄-inch bbl. 7³/₄ inches overall w/2³/₄-inch bbl. Weight: 31 oz. w/2³/₄-inch bbl. Fixed sights. Blued or stainless steel finish; latter available in 38 Special w/2³/₄-inch bbl., 357 Magnum and 9mm with either barrel. Round butt. Checkered walnut stocks. Made 1973–1987.
38 Special, Blued Finish **$150**
38 Special, Stainless Steel **180**
357 Magnum or 9mm Luger, Blued Finish **215**
357 Magnum or 9mm Luger, Stainless Steel **245**

Ruger Super Bearcat

Ruger Super Bearcat $300
Same general specifications as Bearcat, except has steel frame. Weight: 25 oz. Made 1971–73.

Ruger Super Blackhawk

Ruger Super Blackhawk SA Revolver $250
Caliber: 44 Magnum. 6-shot cylinder. 7¹/₂-inch barrel. 13³/₈ inches overall. Weight: 48 oz. Click adjustable rear sight, ramp front. Blued finish. Steel or brass grip frame. Smooth walnut stocks. Made 1959–1973.

Ruger Super Redhawk

Ruger Super Redhawk Revolver $395
Caliber: 44 Magnum. 7¹/₂- or 9¹/₂-inch barrel. 13 or 15 inches overall. Weight: 53–58 oz. Cushioned grips. Satin polished stainless steel finish. Made from 1987 to date.

Ruger Super Single-Six Convertible

Ruger Super Single-Six Convertible Revolver
Same general specifications as Single-Six, except has ramp front, click-adj. rear sights with protective ribs integral with frame; 5¹/₂- or 6¹/₂-inch bbl. only; two interchangeable cylinders, 22 LR and 22 WMR. Made from 1973 to date.
Blued **$185**
Stainless Steel **235**

Ruger Vaquero SA Revolver
Calibers: 44-40, 44 Magnum, 45 Colt. 6-shot cylinder. Barrel lengths: 4⁵/₈, 5¹/₂, 7¹/₂ inches. 13⁵/₈ inches overall

Ruger Vaquero

Ruger Vaquero SA Revolver (cont.)
(7½-inch bbl.). Weight: 41 oz. (7½-inch bbl.). Sights: blade front; grooved topstrap rear. Blued with color-casehardened frame or polished stainless finish. Smooth rosewood grips w/Ruger medallion. Made 1993 to date.
Blued w/Color-casehardened Frame **$268**
Stainless Finish 268

RUSSIAN SERVICE PISTOL
Mfd. by Government plants at Tula and elsewhere

Tokarev-type pistols have also been made in Hungary, Poland, Yugoslavia, People's Republic of China, N. Korea.

Russian Tokarev*

Russian Model 30 Tokarev Service Automatic . . **$375**
Modified Colt-Browning type. Caliber: 7.62mm Russian Automatic (also uses 7.63mm Mauser Automatic cartridge). 8-shot magazine. 4½-inch barrel. 7¾ inches overall. Weight: about 29 oz. Fixed sights. Made 1930–mid-1950s. *Note:* A slightly modified version with improved locking system and different disconnector was adopted in 1933.

SAKO HANDGUNS
Riihimaki, Finland
Manufactured by Oy Sako Ab

Sako 22-32 Olympic Pistol
Calibers: 22 LR, 22 Short, 32 S&W Long. 5-round magazine. Barrels: 6 or 8.85 (22 Short) inches. Weight: about 46 oz. (22 LR); 44 oz. (22 Short); 48 oz. (32). Steel frame.

Sako 22-32 Olympic Pistol

Sako 22-32 Olympic Pistol (cont.)
ABS plastic, anatomically designed grip. Non-reflecting matte black upper surface and chromium-plated slide. Equipped w/carrying case and tool set. Made 1983–89.
Sako 22-32 Single Pistol **$1045**
Sako Triace, triple-barrel set w/wooden grip 1840

SAUER HANDGUNS
Mfd. through WW II by J. P. Sauer & Sohn, Suhl, Germany. Now mfd. by J. P. Sauer & Sohn, GmbH, Eckernförde, West Germany

See also listings under SIG-Sauer.

Sauer Model 1913*

Sauer Model 1913 Pocket Automatic Pistol **$260**
Caliber: 32 Automatic (7.65mm). 7-shot magazine. 3-inch barrel. 5⅞ inches overall. Weight: 22 oz. Fixed sights. Blue finish. Black hard rubber stocks. Made 1913–1930.

Sauer Model 1930 Pocket Automatic Pistol **$295**
Authority Model (Behorden Modell). Successor to Model 1913, has improved grip and safety. Caliber: 32 Auto (7.65mm). 7-shot magazine. 3-inch barrel. 5¾ inches overall. Weight: 22 oz. Fixed sights. Blued finish. Black hard rubber stocks. Made 1930–38. *Note:* Some pistols made with indicator pin showing when cocked. Also mfd. with dural slide and receiver; this type weighs about ⅓ less than the standard model.

Sauer Model 1930

Sauer Model H

Sauer Model H Double Action Automatic Pistol . $395
Calibers: 25 Auto (6.35mm), 32 Auto (7.65mm), 380 Auto (9mm). Specifications shown are for 32 Auto model. 7-shot magazine. 3¼-inch barrel. 6¼ inches overall. Weight: 20 oz. Fixed sights. Blued finish. Black plastic stocks. Also made in dural model weighing about ⅓ less. Made 1938–1945. *Note:* This pistol, designated Model 38, was mfd. during WW II for military use. Wartime models are inferior to earlier production, as some lack safety lever.

Sauer Pocket 25*

Sauer Pocket 25 Automatic Pistol $295
Smaller version of Model 1913, issued about same time as 32 caliber model. Caliber: 25 Auto (6.35mm). 7-shot magazine. 2½-inch barrel. 4¼ inches overall. Weight: 14½ oz. Fixed sights. Blued finish. Black hard rubber stocks. Made 1913–1930.

Sauer Single Action Revolvers
See listings under Hawes.

SAVAGE ARMS CO.
Utica, New York

Savage Model 101

Savage Model 101 SA Single Shot Pistol $150
Barrel integral with swing-out cylinder. Caliber: 22 Short, Long, LR. 5½-inch barrel. Weight: 20 oz. Blade front sight, slotted rear, adjustable for windage. Blued finish. Grips of compressed, impregnated wood. Made 1960–68.

Savage Model 1910

Savage Model 1910 Automatic Pistol $195
Calibers: 32 Auto, 380 Auto. 10-shot magazine (32 cal.), 9-shot (380 cal.). 3¾-inch barrel (32 cal.), 4½-inch (380 cal.). 6½ inches overall (32 cal.), 7 inch (380 cal.). Weight: about 23 oz. Fixed sights. Blued finish. Hard rubber stocks. Made in hammerless type with grip safety or with exposed hammer spur. Made 1910–17.

Savage Model 1917*

Savage Model 1917 Automatic Pistol $305
Same specifications as 1910 Model, except has spur-type hammer and redesigned heavier grip. Made 1917–1928.

SEARS, ROEBUCK & COMPANY
Chicago, Illinois

Sears/J.C. Higgins Model 80 Auto Pistol **$150**
Caliber: 22 LR. 10-shot magazine. 4½- or 6½-inch interchangeable barrel. 10⅞ inches overall w/6½-inch bbl. Weight: 41 oz. w/6½-inch bbl. Fixed Patridge sights. Blued finish. Checkered stocks with thumbrest.

Sears/J.C. Higgins Model 88 DA Revolver **$90**
Caliber: 22 LR. 9-shot cylinder. 4- or 6-inch barrel. 9½ inches w/4-inch bbl. Weight: 23 oz. w/4-inch bbl. Fixed sights. Blued or nickel finish. Checkered plastic stocks.

Sears/J.C. Higgins Ranger DA Revolver **$105**
Caliber: 22 LR. 9-shot cylinder. 5½-inch barrel. 10¾ inches overall. Weight: 28 oz. Fixed sights. Blued or chrome finish. Checkered plastic stocks.

SECURITY INDUSTRIES OF AMERICA
Little Ferry, New Jersey

Security Model PPM357

Security Model PM357 Double Action Revolver . **$195**
Caliber: 357 Magnum. 5-shot cylinder. 2½-inch barrel. 7½ inches overall. Weight: 21 oz. Fixed sights. Stainless steel. Walnut stocks. Introduced 1975; discontinued.

Security Model PPM357

Security Model PPM357 DA Revolver **$180**
Caliber: 357 Magnum. 5-shot cylinder. 2-inch barrel. 6⅛ inches overall. Weight: 18 oz. Fixed sights. Stainless steel. Walnut stocks. Made from 1976 to date. *Note:* Spurless hammer (illustrated) was discontinued in 1977; this model now has the same conventional hammer as other Security revolvers.

Security Model PSS38

Security Model PSS38 Double Action Revolver . **$175**
Caliber: 38 Special. 5-shot cylinder. 2-inch barrel. 6½ inches overall. Weight: 18 oz. Fixed sights. Stainless steel. Walnut stocks. Intro. 1973. Discontinued.

R. F. SEDGLEY, INC.
Philadelphia, Pennsylvania

Sedgley Baby Hammerless Ejector Revolver . . . **$395**
DA. Solid frame. Folding trigger. Caliber: 22 Long. 6-shot cylinder. 4 inches overall. Weight: 6 oz. Fixed sights. Blued or nickel finish. Rubber stocks. Made c. 1930–39.

SHERIDAN PRODUCTS, INC.
Racine, Wisconsin

Sheridan Knocabout

Sheridan Knocabout Single Shot Pistol **$140**
Tip-up type. Caliber: 22 LR, Long, Short. 5-inch barrel. 6¾ inches overall. Weight: 24 oz. Fixed sights. Checkered plastic stocks. Blue finish. Made 1953–1960.

HANDGUNS

SIG PISTOLS
Neuhausen am Rheinfall, Switzerland
Mfd. by SIG Schweizerische Industrie-Gesellschaft

See also listings under SIG-Sauer.

SIG Model P210-1

SIG Model P210-1 Automatic Pistol **$1495**
Calibers: 22 LR, 7.65mm Luger, 9mm Luger. 8-shot magazine. 4³/₄-inch barrel. 8¹/₂ inches overall. Weight: 33 oz. (22 cal.); 35 oz. (7.65mm, 9mm). Fixed sights. Polished blued finish. Checkered wood stocks. Made 1949–1986.

SIG Model P210-2 . . . . **$1250**
Same as Model P210-1, except has sandblasted finish, plastic stocks; not avail. in 22 LR. Discontinued 1987.

SIG Model P210-5 Target Pistol **$1495**
Same as Model P210-2, except has 6-inch barrel, micrometer adjustable rear sight, target front sight, adjustable trigger stop. 9.7 inches overall. Weight: about 38.3 oz. Discontinued.

SIG Model P210-6

SIG Model P210-6 Target Pistol **$1495**
Same as Model P210-2, except has micrometer adjustable rear sight, target front sight, adjustable trigger stop. Weight: about 37 oz. Discontinued 1987.

SIG P210 22 Conversion Unit **$595**
Converts P210 pistol to 22 LR. Consists of barrel with recoil spring, slide and magazine.

SIG-Hämmerli Model P240 Automatic Pistol . . . **$1095**
For data see listing under Hämmerli. Discont. 1986.

SIG-SAUER HANDGUNS
Mfd. by J. P. Sauer & Sohn of West Germany, SIG of Switzerland, and other manufacturers

SIG-Sauer Model P220

SIG-Sauer Model P220 DA Automatic Pistol **$545**
Calibers: 9mm Luger, 38 Super, 45 Automatic. 7-shot in 45, 9-shot in other calibers. 4.4-inch barrel. 8 inches overall. Weight: 9mm, 26.5 oz. Fixed sights. Blued finish. Checkered plastic stocks. Made from 1976 to date. *Note:* Also sold in U.S. as Browning BDA.

SIG-Sauer Model P225

SIG-Sauer Model P225 DA Automatic **$560**
Caliber: 9mm Parabellum. 8-shot magazine. 3.85-inch barrel. 7 inches overall. Weight: 26.1 oz. Blue finish.

SIG-Sauer Model P226 DA Automatic **$550**
Caliber: 9mm Parabellum. 15-shot magazine. 4.4-inch barrel. 7³/₄ inches overall. Weight: 26.5 oz. Blue finish. Made from 1985 to date.

SIG-Sauer Model P228 DA Automatic
Same general specifications as Model P226, except with 3.86-inch barrel. 7¹/₈ inches overall. Blued or K-Kote finish. Made from 1990 to date.
Blued Finish **$525**
K-Kote Finish 570
For Siglite Nite Sights, **add** 80

Sig-Sauer Model P229 DA Automatic

Same general specifications as Model P226, except chambered in 40 S&W with 12-shot magazine. 3.86-inch barrel. 7^1/$_8$ inches overall. Weight: 30.5 oz. Blued finish. Made from 1991 to date.

Blued Finish **$650**
Blued Finish DAO (double action only) **650**
For Siglite Nite Sights, **add** **80**

SIG-Sauer Model P230

SIG-Sauer Model P230 DA Automatic Pistol

Calibers: 22 LR, 32 Automatic (7.65mm), 380 Automatic (9mm Short), 9mm Police. 10-shot magazine in 22, 8-shot in 32, 7-shot in 9mm. 3.6-inch barrel. 6.6 inches overall. Weight: 32 Auto, 18.2 oz. Fixed sights. Blued or stainless finish. Plastic stocks. Made from 1976 to date.

Blued Finish **$350**
Stainless Finish **395**

SMITH & WESSON, INC.
Springfield, Massachusetts

AUTOMATIC/SINGLE SHOT PISTOLS

> **NOTE:** For ease in locating a particular S&W handgun, the listings are divided into two groupings: Automatic/Single Shot Pistols (below) and Revolvers (page 146). For a complete handgun listing, please refer to the Index.

S&W 32 Automatic

Smith & Wesson 32 Automatic Pistol **$1300**

Caliber: 32 Automatic. Same general specifications as 35 caliber model, but barrel is fastened to the receiver instead of hinged. Made 1924–1937.

S&W 35 Automatic

Smith & Wesson 35 Automatic Pistol **$675**

Caliber: 35 S&W Automatic. 7-shot magazine. 3^1/$_2$-inch barrel (hinged to frame). 6^1/$_2$ inches overall. Weight: 25 oz. Fixed sights. Blued or nickel finish. Plain walnut stocks. Made 1913–1921.

S&W Model 39

Smith & Wesson Model 39 9mm DA Auto Pistol

Caliber: 9mm Luger. 8-shot magazine. 4-inch barrel. Overall length: 7^7/$_{16}$ inches. Weight: 26^1/$_2$ oz. Click adjustable rear sight, ramp front. Blued or nickel finish. Checkered walnut stocks. Made 1954–1982. *Note:* Between 1954 and 1966, 927 pistols of this model were made w/ steel instead of alloy frames.

With Steel Frame **$795**
With Alloy Frame **315**

S&W Model 41

Smith & Wesson Model 41 22 Automatic Pistol . . **$625**

Caliber: 22 LR, 22 Short (not interchangeably). 10-shot magazine. Barrel lengths: 5-, 5^1/$_2$-, 7^3/$_8$-inch; latter has detachable muzzle brake. 12 inches overall (7^3/$_8$-inch bbl.). Weight: 43^1/$_2$ oz. (7^3/$_8$-inch bbl.). Click adj. rear sight, undercut Patridge front. Blued finish. Checkered walnut stocks w/thumbrest. Made from 1957 to date.

S&W Model 46

S&W Model 61

Smith & Wesson Model 46 22 Automatic Pistol . **$495**
Caliber: 22 LR. 10-shot magazine. Barrel lengths: 5, 5$^1\!/_2$, 7 inches. 10$^9\!/_{16}$ inches overall (7-inch bbl.). Weight: 42 oz. (7-inch bbl.). Click adjustable rear sight, undercut Patridge front. Blue finish. Molded nylon stocks w/thumb-rest. Only 4,000 produced. Made 1957–1966.

Smith & Wesson Model 61 Escort Pocket Automatic Pistol **$245**
Caliber: 22 LR. 5-shot magazine. 2$^1\!/_8$-inch barrel. 4$^{13}\!/_{16}$ inches overall. Weight: 14 oz. Fixed sights. Blued or nickel finish. Checkered plastic stocks. Made 1970–74.

S&W Model 52

S&W Model 422

Smith & Wesson Model 52 38 Master Auto **$750**
Caliber: 38 Special (midrange wadcutter only). 5-shot magazine. 5-inch barrel. Overall length: 8$^5\!/_8$ inches. Weight: 41 oz. Micrometer click rear sight, Patridge front, on ramp base. Blued finish. Checkered walnut stocks. Made 1961–1994.

Smith & Wesson Model 422 SA Auto Pistol
Caliber: 22 LR. 10-shot magazine. 4$^1\!/_2$- or 6-inch barrel. 7$^1\!/_2$ inches overall w/4$^1\!/_2$-inch bbl. Weight: 22–23$^1\!/_2$ oz. Fixed or adjustable sights. Checkered plastic or walnut grips. Blued finish. Made from 1987 to date.
Standard Model **$190**
Target Model 215

S&W Model 59

S&W Model 439

Smith & Wesson Model 59 9mm DA Auto **$335**
Similar specifications as Model 39, except has 14-shot magazine, checkered nylon stocks. Made 1971–1991.

Smith & Wesson Model 439 9mm Automatic ... $325

DA. Caliber: 9mm Luger. Two 8-round magazines. 4-inch barrel. 7⁷/₁₆ inches overll. Weight: 30 oz. Serrated ramp square front sight, square notch rear. Checkered walnut grips. Blue or nickel finish. Discontinued 1988. (*See* photo, preceding page.)

S&W Model 639

S&W Model 459

Smith & Wesson Model 459 DA Automatic

Caliber: 9mm Luger. Two 14-round magazines. 4-inch barrel. 7⁷/₁₆ inches overall. Weight: 28 oz. Blued or nickel finish. Discontinued 1988.

Standard Model	$340
FBI Model	550

Smith & Wesson Model 639 Automatic $340

Caliber: 9mm Luger Parabellum. Two 12-round magazines. 3¹/₂-inch barrel. 6.9 inches overall. Weight: 26 oz. Nonglare blued finish. Discontinued 1988.

S&W Model 645

S&W Model 469

Smith & Wesson Model 469 9mm Automatic ... $350

DA. Caliber: 9mm Luger. Two 12-round magazines. 3¹/₂-inch barrel. 6⁷/₈ inches overall. Weight: 26 oz. Yellow ramp front sight, dovetail mounted square notch rear. Sandblasted blue finish. Optional ambidextrous safety. Discontinued 1988.

Smith & Wesson Model 645 DA Automatic $375

Caliber: 45 ACP. 8-shot. 5-inch barrel. Overall length: 8¹/₂ inches. Weight: Approx. 38 oz. Red ramp front, fixed rear sights. Stainless. Made 1986–88.

Smith & Wesson Model 622 SA Auto Pistol

Same general specifications as Model 422, except with stainless finish. Made from 1990 to date.

Standard Model	$200
Target Model	230

S&W Model 659 Stainless

Smith & Wesson Model 659 9mm Automatic . . . $365
DA. Similar to S&W Model 459, except weight is 39¹/₂ oz. and finish is satin stainless steel. Discontinued 1988.

Smith & Wesson Model 669 Automatic $335
Caliber: 9mm. 12-shot magazine. Barrel: 3¹/₂ inches. 6.9 inches overall. Weight: 26 oz. Serrated ramp front sight with red bar, fixed rear. Nonglare stainless-steel finish. Made 1986–88.

S&W Model 1026

**S&W Model 745
Automatic Pistol**

Smith & Wesson Model 745 Automatic Pistol
Caliber: 45 ACP. 8-shot magazine. 5-inch barrel. 8⁵/₈ inches overall. Weight: 38³/₄ oz. Fixed sights. Blued slide, stainless frame. Checkered walnut grips. Similar to the model 645, but w/o DA capability. Made 1987–1990.
With Standard Competition Features $525
IPSC Commemorative (first 5,000) 545

Smith & Wesson Model 1000 Series DA Auto (cont.)
slide and frame. Made 1990–94.

Model 1006 (Fixed Sights, 5″ bbl.) $505
Model 1006 (Adj. Sights, 5″ bbl.) 525
Model 1026 (Fixed Sights, 5″ bbl.,
   Decocking Lever) 525
Model 1066 (Fixed Sights, 4¹/₄″ bbl.) 515
Model 1076 (Fixed Sights, 4¹/₄″ bbl.,
   Frame-mounted Decocking Lever, Straight
   Backstrap) 520
Model 1076 (same as above w/Tritium Night
   Sight) 535
Model 1086 (same as Model 1076 in DA only) 515

Smith & Wesson Model 2206 SA Automatic Pistol
Similar to Model 422, except w/stainless-steel slide and frame, weighs 35–39 oz., has Patridge front sight on adj. sight model; post w/white dot on fixed sight model, plastic grips.
Standard Model $250
Target Model 275

Smith & Wesson Model 2214 Sportsman Auto . . $200
Same general specifications as Model 422, except with 8-shot magazine. 3-inch barrel. Patridge front sight, fixed square-notched rear with 3-Dot system. Matte blue finish. Made from 1990 to date.

Smith & Wesson Model 915

S&W Model 3906

Smith & Wesson Model 915 Auto Pistol $395
DA. Caliber: 9mm Luger. 15-shot magazine. 4-inch barrel. 7¹/₂ inches overall. Weight: 28¹/₂ oz. Post front sight, fixed square-notched rear w/3-dot system. Xenoy wraparound grip. Blued steel slide and alloy frame. Made 1992 to date.

Smith & Wesson Model 1000 Series DA Auto
Caliber: 10mm. 9-shot magazine. 4¹/₄- or 5-inch barrel. 7⁷/₈ or 8⁵/₈ inches overall. Weight: about 38 oz. Post front sight, adjustable or fixed square-notched rear w/3-dot system. One-piece Xenoy® wraparound grips. Stainless

Smith & Wesson Model 3904/3906 DA Auto Pistol
Caliber: 9mm. 8-shot magazine. 4-inch barrel. 7¹/₂ inches overall. Weight: 25¹/₂ oz. (Model 3904); 34 oz. (Model 3906). Fixed or adj. sights. Delrin one-piece wraparound, checkered grips. Alloy frame w/blued carbon steel slide

Smith & Wesson Model 3904/3906 DA Auto Pistol (cont.)

(Model 3904) or satin stainless (Model 3906). Made 1989–1991.

Model 3904 w/Adjustable Sights	$365
Model 3904 w/Fixed Sights	325
Model 3904 w/Novak LC Sight	360
Model 3906 w/Adjustable Sights	410
Model 3906 w/Novak LC Sight	400

S&W Model 3914

Smith & Wesson Model 3913/3914 DA Automatic

Caliber: 9mm Parabellum (Luger). 8-shot magazine. 3½-inch barrel. 6⅞ inches overall. Weight: 25 oz. Post front sight; fixed or adjustable square-notched rear. One-piece Xenoy® wraparound grips w/straight backstrap. Alloy frame with stainless or blued slide. Made 1990 to date.

Model 3913 Stainless	$395
Model 3913LS Lady Smith Stainless w/contoured Trigger Guard	415
Model 3914 Blued	375

Smith & Wesson Model 3953/3954 DA Auto Pistol

Same general specifications as Model 3913/3914, except double action only. Made from 1991 to date.

Model 3953 Stainless, Double Action Only	$395
Model 3954 Blued, Double Action Only	350

S&W Model 4046

Smith & Wesson Model 4000 Series DA Auto

Caliber: 40 S&W. 11-shot magazine. 4-inch barrel. 7⅞ inches overall. Weight: 28–30 oz. (alloy frame); 36 oz.

Smith & Wesson Model 4000 Series DA Auto (cont.)

(stainless frame). Post front sight; adjustable or fixed square-notched rear w/2 white dots. Straight backstrap. One-piece Xenoy® wraparound grips. Blued or stainless finish. Made between 1990/1992 to date.

Model 4003 Stainless w/Alloy Frame	$475
Model 4004 Blued w/Alloy Frame	450
Model 4006 Stainless Frame, Fixed Sights	395
Model 4006 Stainless Frame, Adj. Sights	495
Model 4026 w/Decocking Lever (disc. 1994)	535
Model 4043 DA only, Stainless w/Alloy Frame	465
Model 4044 DA only, Blued w/Alloy Frame	440
Model 4046 DA only, Stainless Frame, Fixed Sights	400
Model 4046 DA only, Stainless Frame, Tritium Night Sight	565

Smith & Wesson Model 4013/4014 DA Automatic

Caliber: 40 S&W. 8-shot capacity. 3½-inch barrel. 7 inches overall. Weight: 26 oz. Post front sight; fixed Novak LC rear w/3-dot system. One-piece Xenoy® wraparound grips. Stainless or blued slide w/alloy frame. Made 1991 to date.

Model 4013 w/Stainless Slide	$565
Model 4014 w/Blued Slide	525

Smith & Wesson Model 4053/4054 DA Auto Pistol

Same general specifications as Model 4013/4014, except double action only. Alloy frame fitted with blued steel slide. Made from 1991 to date.

Model 4053 DA only w/Stainless Slide	$565
Model 4054 DA only w/Blued Slide	515

S&W Model 4506 With Fixed Sights

Smith & Wesson Model 4500 Series DA Automatic

Caliber: 45 ACP. 7-shot magazine (Model 4516); 8-shot magazine (Model 4506). Barrel lengths: 3¾, 4¼ or 5 inches. 7⅛ to 8⅝ inches overall. Weight: 34½ to 38½ oz. Post front sight; fixed Novak LC rear w/2-Dot system or adj. One-piece Xenoy® wraparound grips. Satin stainless finish. Made from 1990 to date.

Model 4506 w/Fixed Sights, 5-inch bbl.	$545
Model 4506 w/Novak LC Sight, 5-inch bbl.	550
Model 4516 w/3¾-inch bbl.	475
Model 4526 w/5-inch bbl., Alloy Frame, Decocking Lever, Fixed Sights	425
Model 4536 w/Anodized frame, Decocking Lever	415
Model 4556 w/3¾-inch bbl., DA only, Alloy Frame	395
Model 4566 4¼-inch bbl., Ambidextrous Safety, Fixed Sights	520

Smith & Wesson Model 4500 Series (cont.)
Model 4576 w/4¼-inch bbl., Decocking Lever **$510**
Model 4586 w/4¼-inch bbl., DA only **525**

**S&W Model 5904
9mm Double Action**

Smith & Wesson Model 5900 Series DA Automatic
Caliber: 9mm. 15-shot magazine. 4-inch barrel. 7½ inches overall. Weight: 26–38 oz. Fixed or adjustable sights. One-piece Xenoy® wraparound grips. Alloy frame w/stainless-steel slide (Model 5903) or blued slide (Model 5904); stainless-steel frame and slide (Model 5906). Made from 1989/1990 to date.
Model 5903 w/Adjustable Sights **$455**
Model 5903 w/Novak LC Rear Sight........... **445**
Model 5904 w/Adjustable Sights **450**
Model 5904 w/Novak LC Rear Sight........... **425**
Model 5906 w/Adjustable Sights **460**
Model 5906 w/Novak LC Rear Sight........... **425**
Model 5906 w/Tritium Night Sight **550**
Model 5924 Anodized frame, Blued Slide **375**
Model 5926 Stainless frame, Decocking Lever **500**
Model 5943 Alloy Frame/Stainless Slide,
DA only **475**
Model 5944 Alloy Frame/Blued Slide,
DA only **420**
Model 5946 Stainless Frame/Slide,
DA only **495**

**S&W Model 6906
With Tritium Night Sight**

Smith & Wesson Model 6900 Compact Series
Double action. Caliber: 9mm. 12-shot magazine. 3½-inch barrel. 6⅞ inches overall. Weight: 26½ oz. Ambidextrous safety. Post front sight; fixed Novak LC rear w/3-Dot system. Alloy frame w/blued carbon steel slide (Model 6904) or stainless steel slide (Model 6906). Made from 1989 to date.
Model 6904 .... **$495**
Model 6906 w/Fixed Sights................. **450**
Model 6906 w/Tritium Night Sight **525**
Model 6926 Same as Model 6906 w/Decocking
Lever **440**
Model 6944 Same as Model 6904 in DA only **420**
Model 6946 Same as Model 6906 in DA only, Fixed
Sights **450**
Model 6946 w/Tritium Night Sight **525**

**S&W Model 1891
Single Shot Pistol**

Smith & Wesson Model 1891 Single Shot Target Pistol, First Model
Hinged frame. Calibers: 22 LR, 32 S&W, 38 S&W. Barrel lengths: 6-, 8- and 10-inch. Approx. 13½ inches overall w/10-inch bbl. Weight: about 25 oz. Target sights, barrel catch rear adj. for windage and elevation. Blued finish. Square butt, hard rubber stocks. Made 1893–1905. *Note:* This model was available also as a combination arm w/ accessory 38 revolver barrel and cylinder enabling conversion to a pocket revolver. It has the frame of the 38 SA Revolver Model 1891 w/side flanges, hand and cylinder stop slots.
Single-shot Pistol, 22 LR .... **$ 300**
Single-shot Pistol, 32 S&W or 38 S&W **1150**
Combination Set, Revolver and Single-shot
Barrel **1295**

Smith & Wesson Model 1891 Single Shot Target Pistol, Second Model **$460**
Basically the same as the First Model, except side flanges, hand and stop slots eliminated, cannot be converted to revolver, redesigned rear sight. Caliber: 22 LR only. 10-inch barrel only. Made 1905–1909.

Smith & Wesson Perfected Single Shot Target Pistol
Also called Olympic Model. Similar to 1891 Single Shot Second Model, except has double-action lockwork. Caliber: 22 LR only. 10-inch barrel. Checkered walnut stocks, extended square butt target type. Made 1909–1923. *Note:* In 1920 and thereafter, this model was made w/barrels having bore diameter of .223 instead of .226 and tight, short chambering. The first group of these pistols was produced for the U.S. Olympic Team of 1920, thus the designation Olympic Model.
Pre-1920 Type **$495**
Olympic Model **675**

S&W Straight Line

Smith & Wesson Straight Line Single Shot
Target Pistol **$1200**
Frame shaped like that of an automatic pistol, barrel swings to the left on pivot for extracting and loading, straight line trigger and hammer movement. Caliber: 22 LR. 10-inch barrel. 11 1/4 inches overall. Weight: 34 oz. Target sights. Blued finish. Smooth walnut stocks. Supplied in metal case with screwdriver and cleaning rod. Made 1925–1936.

REVOLVERS

> **NOTE:** This section contains only S&W Revolvers. Pistols, both automatic and single shot, may be found on the preceding pages. For a complete listing of S&W handguns, please refer to the Index.

Smith & Wesson Model 1

Smith & Wesson Model 1 Hand Ejector
Double Action Revolver **$360**
First Model. Forerunner of the current 32 Hand Ejector and Regulation Police models, this was the first S&W revolver of the solid-frame, swing-out cylinder type. Top strap of this model is longer than those of later models, and it lacks the usual S&W cylinder latch. Caliber: 32 S&W Long. Barrel lengths: 3 1/4-, 4 1/4-, and 6-inch. Fixed sights. Blued or nickel finish. Round butt, hard rubber stocks. Made 1896–1903.

S&W No. 3 Frontier

Smith & Wesson No. 3 SA Frontier $1450
Caliber: 44-40 Winchester. Barrel lengths: 4-, 5- and 6 1/2-inch. Fixed or target sights. Blued or nickel finish. Round, hard rubber or checkered walnut grips. Made 1885–1908.

Smith & Wesson No. 3 SA (New Model) $1295
Hinged frame. 6-shot cylinder. Caliber: 44 S&W Russian. Barrel lengths: 4-, 5-, 6-, 6 1/2-, 7 1/2- and 8-inch. Fixed or target sights. Blued or nickel finish. Round, hard rubber or checkered walnut grips. Made 1878–1908. *Note:* Value shown is for standard model. Specialist collectors recognize numerous variations with a range of higher values.

Smith & Wesson No. 3 SA Target $1695
Hinged frame. 6-shot cylinder. Calibers: 32/44 S&W, 38/44 S&W Gallery & Target. 6 1/2-inch barrel only. Fixed or target sights. Blued or nickel finish. Round, hard rubber or checkered walnut grips. Made 1887–1910.

**S&W Model 10 M & P
Model of 1905**

S&W Model 10, Round Butt

Smith & Wesson Model 10 38 Military & Police DA
Also called Hand Ejector Model of 1902, Hand Ejector Model of 1905, Model K. Manufactured substantially in its present form since 1902, this model has undergone numerous changes, most of them minor. Round or square-butt models, the latter introduced in 1904. Caliber: 38 Special. 6-shot cylinder. Barrel lengths: 2- (introduced 1933), 4-, 5-, 6- and 6 1/2-inch (latter discontinued 1915), also 4-inch heavy barrel (introduced 1957). 11 1/8 inches overall in square-butt model w/6-inch barrel. Round-butt model is 1/4-inch shorter, weighs about 1/2 oz. less. Fixed sights. Blued or nickel finish. Checkered walnut stocks, hard rubber available in round-butt style. Current Model 10 has short action. Made 1902 to date. *Note:* S&W Victory Model, wartime version of the M & P 38, was produced for the U.S. Government from 1940 to the end of the war. A similar revolver, designated 38/200 British Service Revolver, was produced for the British Government during the same period. These arms have either brush-polish or sandblast blue finish, and most of them have plain, smooth walnut stocks, lanyard swivels.
Model of 1902 (1902–05) **$450**
Model of 1905 (1905–1940) **395**

Smith & Wesson Model 10 38 M&P (cont.)

38/200 British Service (1940–45)	**$295**
Victory Model (1942–45)	**225**
Model of 1944 (1945–48)	**165**
Model 10 (1948–date)	**170**

S&W Model 10, Heavy Barrel

Smith & Wesson Model 10 38 Military & Police Heavy Barrel **$185**

Same as standard Model 10, except has heavy 4-inch barrel, weighs 34 oz. Made from 1957 to date.

S&W Model 12

Smith & Wesson Model 12 38 M & P Airweight . . **$205**

Same as standard Military & Police, except has light alloy frame, furnished with 2- or 4-inch barrel only, weighs 18 oz. (with 2-inch barrel). Made 1952–1986.

Smith & Wesson Model 13 357 Military/Police . . **$190**

Same as Model 10 38 Military & Police Heavy Barrel, except chambered for 357 Magnum and 38 Special with 3- or 4-inch barrel. Made 1974 to date.

S&W Model 13, Heavy Barrel

Smith & Wesson Model 13 (Heavy Barrel) Double Action Revolver **$205**

Calibers: 357 Mag. and 38 S&W Special. DA. 6-shot cylinder. Barrel lengths: 3 and 4 inches. 9¼ inches overall. Weight: 34 oz. Square notch rear sight, ramp front.

S&W Model 14 Single Action

Smith & Wesson Models 14 (K38) and 16 (K32) Masterpiece Revolvers

Calibers: 22 LR, 22 Magnum Rimfire, 32 S&W Long, 38 Special. 6-shot cylinder. DA/SA. Barrel lengths: 4- (22 MRF only), 6-, 8³/8-inch (latter not available in K32). 11¹/8 inches overall (6-inch bbl.). Weight: 38½ oz. w/6-inch bbl. Click adjustable rear sight, Patridge front. Blued finish. Checkered walnut stocks. Made 1947 to date. (Model 16 discontinued 1974, with only 3,630 produced; reissued 1990–93.)

Model 14 (K-38, Double Action)	**$215**
Model 14 (K-38, Single Action, 6-inch bbl.)	**235**
Model 14 (K-38, Single Action, 8³/8-inch bbl.)	**250**
Model 16 (K-32, Double Action)	**225**

S&W Model 15 Double Action

Smith & Wesson Models 15 (38) and 18 (22) Combat Masterpiece Double Action Revolvers

Same as K-22 and K-38 Masterpiece but with 2- (38) or 4-inch barrel and Baughman quick-draw front sight. 9¹/8 inches overall with 4-inch bbl. Weight: 34 oz. (38 cal.). Introduced 1950; Model 18 discontinued 1985.

Model 15	**$235**
Model 18	**255**

S&W Model 17 K-22 Masterpiece

Smith & Wesson Model 17 K-22 Masterpiece Double Action Revolver **$230**

Caliber: 22 LR. 6-shot cylinder. Barrel lengths: 4, 6 or

Smith & Wesson Model 17 K-22 Masterpiece (cont.)

$8^3/_8$ inches. $11^1/_8$ inches overall w/6-inch barrel. Weight: $38^1/_2$ oz. w/6-inch barrel. Patridge-type front sight; S&W micrometer click rear. Checkered walnut Service grips w/ S&W monogram. S&W blued finish. Made 1947 to date.

S&W Model 21

S&W Model 19 Round Butt

S&W Model 19

Smith & Wesson Model 19 357 Combat Magnum Double Action Revolver **$245**

Caliber: 357 Magnum. 6-shot cylinder. Barrel lengths: $2^1/_2$ (round butt), 4, 6 inches. $9^1/_2$ inches overall (4-inch bbl.). Weight: 35 oz. (4-inch bbl.). Click adj. rear sight, ramp front. Blued or nickel finish. Target stocks of checkered Goncalo Alves. Made from 1956 to date.

S&W Model 20

Smith & Wesson Model 20 38/44 Heavy Duty DA

Caliber: 38 Special. 6-shot cylinder. Barrel lengths: 4, 5 and $6^1/_2$ inches. $10^3/_8$ inches overall w/5-inch bbl. Weight: 40 oz. w/5-inch bbl. Fixed sights. Blued or nickel finish. Checkered walnut stocks. Short action after 1948. Made 1930–1967.
Pre-World War II **$550**
Postwar **240**

Smith & Wesson Model 21 1950 44 Military Double Action Revolver **$1250**

Postwar version of the 1926 Model 44 Military with same general specifications, except redesigned hammer. Made 1950–1967.

S&W Model 22

Smith & Wesson Model 22 1950 Army DA **$895**

Postwar version of the 1917 Army w/same general specifications, except redesigned hammer. Made 1950–1967.

S&W 22/32 Kit Gun

Smith & Wesson 22/32 Kit Gun **$495**

Same as 22/32 Target, except has 4-inch barrel, round grips, 8 inches overall, weighs 21 oz. Made 1935–1953.

Smith & Wesson 22/32 Target DA Revolver **$695**

Also known as the Bekeart Model. Design based upon "32 Hand Ejector." Caliber: 22 LR (recessed head cylinder for high-speed cartridges introduced 1935). 6-shot cylinder. 6-inch barrel. $10^1/_2$ inches overall. Weight: 23 oz. Adjustable target sights. Blued finish. Checkered walnut stocks. Made 1911–1953. *Note:* In 1911, San Francisco gun dealer Phil Bekeart, who suggested this model, re-

S&W 22/32 Target

S&W Model 27

Smith & Wesson 22/32 Target DA (cont.)
ceived 292 pieces. These are the true "Bekeart Model" revolvers worth about double the value shown for the standard 22/32 Target.

S&W Model 23

Smith & Wesson Model 23 38/44 Outdoorsman Double Action Revolver
Target version of the 38/44 Heavy Duty. 6½-inch barrel only. Weight: 41¾ oz. Target sights, micrometer-click rear on postwar models. Blued finish only. 1950 model has ribbed barrel, redesigned hammer. Made 1930–1967.

Prewar **$595**
Postwar **465**

S&W Model 24

Smith & Wesson Model 24 1950 44 Target DA Revolver
. . . . **$565**
Postwar version of the 1926 Model 44 Target w/same specifications, except has redesigned hammer, ribbed barrel, micrometer click rear sight. Made 1950–1967.

Smith & Wesson Model 25 1950 45 Target DA Revolver
. . . . **$345**
Same as 1950 Model 44 Target but chambered for 45 Automatic cartridge. Made 1950 to date.

Smith & Wesson Model 27 357 Magnum DA
Caliber: 357 S&W Magnum. 6-shot cylinder. Barrel lengths: 3½-, 5-, 6-, 6½- and 8⅜-inch. 11⅜ inches overall w/6-inch bbl. Weight: 44 oz. w/6-inch bbl. Adjustable target sights, Baughman quick-draw ramp front sight on 3½-inch barrel. Blued or nickel finish. Checkered walnut stocks. Made 1935 to date. *Note:* Until 1938, the 357 Magnum was custom made in any barrel length from 3½-inch to 8¾-inch; each of these revolvers was accompanied by a registration certificate and has its registration number stamped on the inside of the yoke. Postwar Magnums have a redesigned hammer with shortened fall and the new S&W micrometer click rear sight.

Prewar Registered Model **$825**
Prewar Model without Registration Number **495**
Current Model with 8⅜-inch Barrel **325**
Current Model, other barrel lengths **295**

S&W Model 28

Smith & Wesson Model 28 Highway Patrolman Double Action Revolver
. . . . **$225**
Caliber: 357 Magnum. 6-shot cylinder. Barrel lengths: 4- or 6-inch. 11¼ inches overall w/6-inch bbl. Weight: 44 oz. w/6-inch bbl. Adjustable rear sight, ramp front. Blued finish. Checkered walnut stocks, Magna or target type. Made 1954–1986.

Smith & Wesson Model 29 44 Magnum DA Revolver
Caliber: 44 Magnum. 6-shot cylinder. Barrel lengths: 4-, 6½-, 8⅜-inch. 11⅞ inches overall (6½-inch bbl.). Weight: 47 oz., 6½-inch bbl. Click adjustable rear sight, ramp front. Blued or nickel finish. Checkered Goncalo Alves target stocks. Made 1956–1991.

With 8⅜-inch barrel **$335**
Other barrel lengths **300**

Smith & Wesson Model 30 32 Hand Ejector Double Action Revolver
. . . . **$225**
Caliber: 32 S&W Long. 6-shot cylinder. Barrel lengths: 2- (introduced 1949), 3-, 4- and 6-inch. 8 inches overall

S&W Model 30

Smith & Wesson Model 30 32 Hand Ejector DA (cont.)

w/4-inch bbl. Weight: 18 oz. w/4-inch bbl. Fixed sights. Blued or nickel finish. Round, checkered walnut or hard rubber stocks. Made 1903–1976. Numerous changes, mostly minor, as in M & P model.

S&W Model 31 Regulation Police

Smith & Wesson Models 31 & 33 Regulation Police Double Action Revolver $190

Same basic type as 32 Hand Ejector, except has square buttstocks. Calibers: 32 S&W Long (Model 31), 38 S&W (Model 33). 6-shot cylinder in 32 caliber, 5-shot in 38 caliber. Barrel lengths: 2- (introduced 1949), 3-, 4- and 6-inch in 32 cal.; 4-inch only in 38 cal. 8 1/2 inches overall w/4-inch bbl. Weight: 18 oz., 38 cal. w/4-inch barrel; 32 cal., 3/4-oz. heavier. Fixed sights. Blued or nickel finish. Checkered walnut stocks. Made from 1917. Model 33 discontinued in 1974; Model 31 discontinued in 1992.

S&W Model 32 Double Action

Smith & Wesson 32 Double Action Revolver . . . $195

Hinged frame. Caliber: 32 S&W. 5-shot cylinder. Barrel lengths: 3-, 3 1/2- and 6-inch. Fixed sights. Blued or nickel finish. Hard rubber stocks. Made 1880–1919. *Note:* Value shown applies generally to the several varieties. Exception is the rare first issue of 1880 (identified by squared side-plate and serial no. 1 to 30) valued at **$2,000.**

Smith & Wesson Model 32 Terrier DA $250

Caliber: 38 S&W. 5-shot cylinder. 2-inch barrel. 6 1/4 inches overall. Weight: 17 oz. Fixed sights. Blued or nickel finish. Checkered walnut or hard rubber stocks. Built on 32 Hand Ejector frame. Made 1936–1974.

Smith & Wesson 32-20 Military & Police DA

Same as M & P 38, except chambered for 32-20 Winchester cartridge. First introduced in the 1899 model, M & P Revolvers were produced in this caliber until about 1940. Values same as for corresponding M & P 38 models.

S&W Model 34

Smith & Wesson Model 34 1953 22/32 Kit Gun . . $250

Same general specifications as previous 22/32 Kit Gun, except with 2-inch or 4-inch barrel and round or square buttstocks, blue or nickel finish. Made 1953–1991.

S&W Model 35

Smith & Wesson Model 35 1953 22/32 Target . . $295

Same general specifications as previous model 22/32 Target, except has micrometer-click rear sight, Magna-type target stocks, weighs 25 oz. Made 1953–1974.

S&W Model 36 Chiefs Special

Smith & Wesson Model 36 Chiefs Special DA . . $225

Based on 32 Hand Ejector with frame lengthened to permit longer cylinder for 38 Special cartridge. Caliber: 38 Special. 5-shot cylinder. Barrel lengths: 2- or 3-inch. 6 1/2 inches overall w/2-inch bbl. Weight: 19 oz. Fixed sights. Blued or nickel finish. Checkered walnut stocks, round or square butt. Made 1952–1991.

Smith & Wesson Model 37 Airweight Chiefs Special $215

Same general specifications as standard Chiefs Special, except has light alloy frame, weighs 12 1/2 oz. with 2-inch bbl., blued finish only. Made 1954 to date.

Smith & Wesson Model 38 Airweight DA $235
Caliber: 38 Special. 5-shot cylinder. Barrel length: 2 or 4 inches. 6⅞ inches (2-inch barrel) overall. Weight: 18 oz. Square notch rear sight, ramp front sight.

S&W Model 38 Bodyguard Airweight

Smith & Wesson Model 38 Bodyguard Airweight Double Action Revolver $220
"Shrouded" hammer. Light alloy frame. Caliber: 38 Special. 5-shot cylinder. 2-inch barrel. 6⅜ inches overall. Weight: 14½ oz. Fixed sights. Blued or nickel finish. Checkered walnut stocks. Made 1955 to date.

Smith & Wesson 38 Double Action Revolver . . . $850
Hinged frame. Caliber: 38 S&W. 5-shot cylinder. Barrel lengths: 4-, 4¼-, 5-, 6-, 8- and 10-inch. Fixed sights. Blued or nickel finish. Hard rubber stocks. Made 1880–1911. *Note:* Value shown applies generally to the several varieties. Exceptions are the first issue of 1880 (identified by squared sideplate and serial no. 1 to 4,000) and the 8- and 10-inch barrel models of the third issue (1884–1895).

Smith & Wesson Model 38 Hand Ejector DA $670
Military & Police—First Model. Resembles Colt New Navy in general appearance, lacks barrel lug and locking bolt common to all later S&W hand ejector models. Caliber: 38 Long Colt. 6-shot cylinder. Barrel lengths: 4-, 5-, 6- and 6½-inch. 11½ inches overall w/6½-inch bbl. Fixed sights. Blued or nickel finish. Round, checkered walnut or hard rubber stocks. Made 1899–1902.

S&W 38 M&P Target

Smith & Wesson 38 Military & Police Target DA
Target version of the Military & Police with standard features of that model. Caliber: 38 Special. 6-inch barrel. Weight: 32¼ oz. Adj. target sights. Blued finish. Checkered walnut stocks. Made 1899–1940. For values, add **$75** to those shown for corresponding M&P 38 models.

Smith & Wesson Model 38 Perfected DA $550
Hinged frame. Similar to earlier 38 Double Action Model, but heavier frame, side latch as in solid-frame models, improved lockwork. Caliber: 38 S&W. 5-shot cylinder. Barrel lengths: 3¼-, 4-, 5- and 6-inch. Fixed sights. Blued or nickel finish. Hard rubber stocks. Made 1909–1920.

S&W Model 40 Centennial

Smith & Wesson Model 40 Centennial Double Action Hammerless Revolver $350
Similar to Chiefs Special, but has Safety Hammerless-type mechanism with grip safety. 2-inch barrel. Weight: 19 oz. Made 1953–1974.

Smith & Wesson Model 42 Centennial Airweight $395
Same as standard Centennial model, except has light alloy frame, weighs 13 oz. Made 1954–1974.

S&W Model 43

Smith & Wesson Model 43 1955 22/32 Kit Gun Airweight $395
Same as Model 34 Kit Gun, except has light alloy frame, furnished with 3½-inch barrel only, weighs 14¼ oz., square buttstock. Made 1954–1974.

Smith & Wesson Model 44 1926 Military DA Revolver
Basically the same as the early New Century model, having the extractor rod casing but lacking the "Triple Lock" feature. Caliber: 44 S&W Special. 6-shot cylinder. Barrel lengths: 4, 5 and 6½ inches. 11¾ inches overall w/6½-inch bbl. Weight: 39½ oz., 6½-inch bbl. Fixed sights. Blued or nickel finish. Checkered walnut stocks. Made 1926–1941.

Standard Model **$695**
Target Model w/6½-inch bbl., Target Sights, Blued **995**

Smith & Wesson 44 Double Action Revolver
Also called Wesson Favorite (lightweight model), Frontier (caliber 44-40). Hinged frame. 6-shot cylinder. Calibers: 44 S&W Russian, 38-40, 44-40. Barrel lengths: 4-, 5-, 6- and 6½-inch. Weight: 37½ oz. w/6½-inch bbl. Fixed

Smith & Wesson 44 DA (cont.)

sights. Blued or nickel finish. Hard rubber stocks. Made 1881–1913; Frontier discontinued 1910.

Standard Model, 44 Russian	$ 850
Standard Model, 38-40	1995
Frontier Model	1350
Favorite Model	3595

S&W 44 Hand Ejector Second Model

Smith & Wesson 44 Hand Ejector Second Model Double Action Revolver $695

Basically the same as New Century, except crane lock ("Triple Lock" feature) and extractor rod casing eliminated. Calibers: 44 S&W Special, 44-40 Win., 45 Colt. Barrel lengths: 4-, 5-, 6½- and 7½-inch. 11¾ inches overall w/6½-inch bbl. Weight: 38 oz. w/6½-inch bbl. Fixed sights. Blued or nickel finish. Checkered walnut stocks. Made 1915–1937.

Smith & Wesson Model 48 (K-22) Masterpiece M.R.F. Double Action Revolver $295

Caliber: 22 Mag. and 22 RF. 6-shot cylinder. Barrel lengths: 4 and 6 inches. 11⅛ inches overall. Weight: 39 oz. Adjustable rear sight, ramp front.

Smith & Wesson Model 49 Bodyguard $245

Same as Model 38 Bodyguard Airweight, except has steel frame, weighs 20½ oz. Made 1959 to date.

S&W Model 51

S&W Model 53

Smith & Wesson Model 51 1960 22/32 Kit Gun . . $395

Same as Model 34 Kit Gun, except chambered for 22 WMR; has 3½-inch barrel, weighs 24 oz. Made 1960–74.

Smith & Wesson Model 53 22 Magnum DA $575

Caliber: 22 Rem. Jet C.F. Magnum. 6-shot cylinder (inserts permit use of 22 Short, Long, or LR cartridges). Barrel lengths: 4-, 6-, 8⅜-inches. 11¼ inches w/6-inch bbl. Weight: 40 oz. w/6-inch bbl. Micrometer-click rear sight, ramp front. Checkered walnut stocks. Made 1960–1974.

Smith & Wesson Model 57 41 Magnum DA Revolver

Caliber: 41 Magnum. 6-shot cylinder. Barrel lengths: 4-, 6-, 8⅜-inches. Weight: with 6-inch barrel, 40 oz. Micrometer click rear sight, ramp front. Target stocks of checkered Goncalo Alves. Made 1964 to date.

With 8⅜-inch barrel	$365
Other barrel lengths	300

S&W Model 58 41 M&P

Smith & Wesson Model 58 41 Military & Police Double Action Revolver $295

Caliber: 41 Magnum. 6-shot cylinder. 4-inch barrel. 9¼ inches overall. Weight: 41 oz. Fixed sights. Checkered walnut stocks. Intro. 1964; discontinued.

S&W Model 60 Lady Smith

Smith & Wesson Model 60 Stainless DA $275

Caliber: 38 Special. 5-shot cylinder. Barrel length: 2 or 3 inches (Lady Smith Model). 6½ or 7½ inches overall. Weight: 19 oz. Square notch rear sight, ramp front. Satin finish stainless steel. Made 1965 to date.

Smith & Wesson Model 63 (1977) Kit Gun Double Action Revolver $250
Caliber: 22 LR. 6-shot cylinder. Barrel length: 4 inches. 6½ inches overall. Weight: 24½ oz. Adj. rear sight, ramp front.

Smith & Wesson Model 64 38 Military & Police Stainless $200
Same as standard Model 10, except satin-finished stainless steel; available w/square butt and 4-inch heavy barrel or round butt w/2-inch barrel. Made 1970 to date.

S&W Model 65 357 M&P

Smith & Wesson Model 65 357 Military/Police Stainless $215
Same as Model 13, except satin-finished stainless steel. Made 1974 to date.

S&W Model 66 357 Combat Magnum

Smith & Wesson Model 66 357 Combat Magnum Stainless $265
Same as Model 19, except satin-finished stainless steel. Made 1971 to date.

S&W Model 67 Combat Masterpiece

Smith & Wesson Model 67 38 Combat Masterpiece Stainless $225
Same as Model 15, except satin-finished stainless steel; available only with 4-inch barrel. Made 1972–1988.

S&W 125th Anniversary Commemorative, Deluxe Edition

Smith & Wesson 125th Anniversary Commemorative
Issued to celebrate the 125th anniversary of the 1852 partnership of Horace Smith and Daniel Baird Wesson. Standard Edition is Model 25 revolver, caliber 45 Colt, with 6½-inch barrel, bright blued finish, gold-filled barrel roll mark "Smith & Wesson 125th Anniversary," sideplate marked with gold-filled Anniversary seal, smooth Goncalo Alves stocks, in presentation case with nickel silver Anniversary medallion and book, *125 Years with Smith & Wesson,* by Roy Jinks. Deluxe Edition is same, except revolver is Class A engraved with gold-filled seal on sideplate, ivory stocks; Anniversary medallion is sterling silver and book is leather bound; limited to 50 units. Total issue is 10,000 units, of which 50 are Deluxe Edition and two are a Custom Deluxe Edition not for sale. Made in 1977. Values are for revolvers in new condition.
Standard Edition .... $ 595
Deluxe Edition 1600

Smith & Wesson Model 486 DA Revolver $265
Caliber: 357 Mag. 6-shot cylinder. Barrel length: 4, 6 or 8⅜ inches. 13¹³⁄₁₆ inches overall (w/8⅜-inch bbl.). Weight: 53 oz. Adjustable rear sight, ramp front.

Smith & Wesson Model 547 DA Revolver $250
Caliber: 9mm. 6-shot cylinder. Barrel length: 3 or 4 inches. 7⁵⁄₁₆ inches overall. Weight: 32 oz. Square notch rear sight, ramp front. Discontinued 1986.

Smith & Wesson Models 581 Revolver
Caliber: 357 Magnum. Barrel: 4 inches. Weight: 34 oz. Serrated ramp front sight, square notch rear. Checkered walnut grips.
Blued Finish $195
Nickel Finish 225

S&W Model 586 Distinguished Combat Magnum

Smith & Wesson Model 586 Distinguished Combat Magnum $275
Caliber: 357 Magnum. 6-shot. Barrel lengths: 4, 6 and 8⅜

Smith & Wesson Model 586 (cont.)

inches. Overall length: 9¾ inches w/4-inch bbl.; 13¹³/₁₆ inches w/8³/₈-inch bbl. Weight: 42, 46, 53 oz., respectively. Red ramp front sight, micrometer-click adjustable rear. Checkered grip. S&W blue or nickel finish.

Smith & Wesson Model 610 DA Revolver $385

Similar to Model 625, except in caliber 10mm. Magna-classic grips.

Smith & Wesson Model 617 Double Action Revolver

Similar to Model 17, except in stainless. Made 1992–93.
Semi-Target Model with 4- or 6-inch bbl. $275
Target Model with 6-inch bbl. 295
Target Model with 8³/₈-inch bbl. 315

Smith & Wesson Model 624 Double Action Revolver

Same general specifications as Model 24, except satin-finished stainless steel. Limited production of 10,000 made in 1985 only.
Standard Model $375
Semi-target Model 315
Target Model 395

S&W Model 625

Smith & Wesson Model 625 DA Revolver $355

Same general specifications as Model 25, except 3-, 4- or 5-inch barrel, round-butt Pachmayr grips and satin stainless steel finish. Made from 1989 to date.

Smith & Wesson Model 627 DA Revolver $345

Same general specifications as Model 27, except satin stainless steel finish. Made 1989–1991.

S&W Model 629

Smith & Wesson Model 629 Double Action Revolver

Same as Model 29 in 44 Magnum, except in stainless steel. Classic made from 1990 to date.
Model 629 (4- and 6-inch bbl.) $365
Model 629 (8³/₈-inch bbl.) 385

Smith & Wesson Model 629 DA (cont.)

Model 629 Classic (5- and 6½-inch bbl.) $395
Model 629 Classic (8³/₈-inch bbl.) 415

Smith & Wesson Model 631 Double Action Revolver

Similar to Model 31, except chambered for 32 H&R Mag. Goncalo Alves combat grips. Made 1991–92.
Fixed Sights, 2-inch bbl. $250
Adjustable Sights, 4-inch bbl. 275

Smith & Wesson Model 632 Centennial DA $295

Same general specifications as Model 640, except chambered for 32 H&R Mag. 2-inch barrel. Weight: 15½ oz. Stainless slide with alloy frame. Santoprene combat grips. Made in 1991.

Smith & Wesson Model 640 Centennial DA $325

Caliber: 38 Special. 5-shot cylinder. 2- or 3-inch barrel. 6⁵/₁₆ inches overall. Weight: 20–22 oz. Fixed sights. Stainless finish. Smooth hardwood service stocks. Made 1990 to date.

S&W Model 642 Centennial Airweight

Smith & Wesson Model 642 Centennial Airweight Double Action Revolver $315

Same general specifications as Model 640, except with 2-inch barrel only; weight of 15.8 oz. with stainless steel/aluminum alloy frame and finish. Santoprene combat grips. Made 1990–93.

Smith & Wesson Model 648 DA Revolver $295

Same general specifications as Models 17/617, except in stainless and chambered for 22 Magnum. Made 1992–93.

Smith & Wesson Model 649 Bodyguard DA $250

Caliber: 38 Special. 5-shot cylinder. Barrel length: 2 inches. 6¼ inches overall. Weight: 20 oz. Square notch rear sight, ramp front. Stainless frame and finish.

Smith & Wesson Model 650 Revolver $275

Caliber: 22 Mag. 6-shot cylinder. 3-inch barrel. 7 inches overall. Weight: 23½ oz. Serrated ramp front sight, fixed square notch rear. Round butt, checkered walnut monogrammed stocks. Stainless steel finish. Made 1983–85.

Smith & Wesson Model 651 Stainless DA $270

Caliber: 22 Mag. Rimfire. 6-shot cylinder. Barrel length: 3 and 4 inches. 7 and 8⁵/₈ inches, respectively, overall. Weight: 24½ oz. Adjustable rear sight, ramp front.

Smith & Wesson Model 657 Revolver

Caliber: 41 Mag. 6-shot cylinder. Barrel: 4, 6 or 8.4 inches. 9.6, 11.4, and 13.9 inches overall. Weight: 44.2, 48 and 52.5 oz. Serrated black ramp front sight on ramp base; click rear, adjustable for windage and elevation. Satin-finished stainless steel.

With 4- or 6-inch barrel **$295**
With 8.4-inch barrel **340**

S&W K-22 Outdoorsman

S&W Model 681

Smith & Wesson Model 681 . . . . **$215**

Same as S&W Model 581, except in stainless finish only.

Smith & Wesson Model 686 . . . . **$275**

Same as S&W Model 586 Distinguished Combat Magnum, except in stainless finish w/additional 2½-inch barrel.

Smith & Wesson Model 940 Centennial DA **$340**

Same general specifications as Model 640, except chambered for 9mm. 2- or 3-inch barrel. Weight: 23 oz. w/2-inch bbl. Santoprene combat grips. Made 1991 to date.

Smith & Wesson Model 1891 Single Action Revolver

Hinged frame. Caliber: 38 S&W. 5-shot cylinder. Barrel lengths: 3¼-, 4-, 5- and 6-inch. Fixed sights. Blued or nickel finish. Hard rubber stocks. Made 1891–1911. *Note:* Until 1906, an accessory single-shot target barrel (see Model 1891 Single Shot Target Pistol) was available for this revolver.

Revolver only . . . . **$ 695**
Set with 22 single-shot barrel **1295**

Smith & Wesson 1917 Army Double Action Revolver

Caliber: 45 Automatic, using 3-cartridge half-moon clip; 45 Auto Rim, without clip. 6-shot cylinder. 5½-inch barrel. 10¾ inches overall. Weight: 36¼ oz. Fixed sights. Blued finish (blue-black finish on commercial model, brush polish on military). Checkered walnut stocks (commercial model, smooth on military). Made under U.S. Government contract 1917–19; produced commercially 1919–1941. *Note:* About 175,000 of these revolvers were produced during WWI. The DCM sold these to NRA members during the 1930s at $16.15 each.

Commercial Model **$395**
Military Model **425**

Smith & Wesson K-22 Masterpiece DA **$795**

Improved version of K-22 Outdoorsman with same specifications but with micrometer-click rear sight, short action and antibacklash trigger. Manufactured in 1940.

Smith & Wesson K-22 Outdoorsman DA **$475**

Design based on the 38 Military & Police Target. Caliber: 22 LR. 6-shot cylinder barrel. 11⅛ inches overall. Weight: 35 oz. Adjustable target sights. Blued finish. Checkered walnut stock. Made 1931–1940.

Smith & Wesson K32 and K38 Heavy Masterpiece Double Action Revolvers

Same as K32 and K38 Masterpiece, but with heavy barrel. Weight: 38½ oz. Made 1950–53. *Note:* All K32 and K38 revolvers made after September 1953 have heavy barrels and the "Heavy Masterpiece" designation was discontinued. Values for Heavy Masterpiece models are the same as shown for Models 14 and 16. (See separate listing).

Smith & Wesson K-32 Target DA Revolver **$975**

Same as 38 Military & Police Target, except chambered for 32 S&W Long cartridge, slightly heavier barrel. Weight: 34 oz. Only 98 produced. Made 1938–1940.

**S&W Ladysmith
First Model**

Smith & Wesson Ladysmith (Model M Hand Ejector) Double Action Revolver

Caliber: 22 LR. 7-shot cylinder. Barrel lengths: 2¼-, 3-, 3½- and 6-inch (Third Model only). Approximately 7 inches overall w/3½-inch bbl. Weight: about 9½ oz. Fixed sights, adjustable target sights available on Third Model. Blued or nickel finish. Round butt, hard rubber stocks on First and Second Model; checkered walnut or hard rubber square buttstocks on Third Model. First Model—1902 to 1906: cylinder locking bolt operated by button on left side of frame, no barrel lug and front locking bolt. Second Model—1906 to 1911: rear cylinder latch eliminated, has barrel lug, forward cylinder lock with draw-bolt fastening. Third Model—1911 to 1921: same as Second Model except has square buttstocks, target sights and 6-inch barrel available. *Note:* Legend has it that a straight-laced D.B. Wesson ordered discontinuance of the Ladysmith when he learned of the little revolver's reputed popularity with ladies of the evening. The story, which undoubtedly has enhanced the appeal of this model to collectors, is not true: Wesson Ladysmith was discontinued because of dif-

**S&W Ladysmith
Second Model**

**S&W Ladysmith
Third Model**

S&W Safety Hammerless

Smith & Wesson Ladysmith (cont.)
ficulty of manufacture and high frequency of repairs.

First Model	$1195
Second Model	1025
Third Model, fixed sights, 3- or 3½-inch barrel	995
Third Model, fixed sights, 2¼- or 6-inch barrel	1150
Third Model, adjustable sights, 6-inch barrel	1195

Smith & Wesson New Century Model Hand Ejector Double Action Revolver $895
Also called "Triple Lock" because of its third cylinder lock at the crane. 6-shot cylinder. Calibers: 44 S&W Special, 450 Eley, 455 Mark II. Barrel lengths: 4-, 5-, 6½- and 7½-inch. Weight: 39 oz. w/6½-inch bbl. Fixed sights. Blued or nickel finish. Checkered walnut stocks. Made 1907–1915.

S&W Regulation Police Target

Smith & Wesson Regulation Police Target DA . . $360
Target version of the Regulation Police with standard features of that model. Caliber: 32 S&W Long. 6-inch barrel. 10¼ inches overall. Weight: 20 oz. Adjustable target sights. Blued finish. Checkered walnut stocks. Made about 1917–1940.

Smith & Wesson Safety Hammerless Revolver . $375
Also called New Departure Double Action. Hinged frame. Calibers: 32 S&W, 38 S&W. 5-shot cylinder. Barrel lengths: 32 cal.—2-, 3- and 3½-inch; 38 cal.—2-, 3¼-, 4-, 5- and 6-inch. Length overall: 6¾ inches, 32 cal. w/3-inch bbl.; 7½ inches, 38 cal. w/3¼-inch bbl. Weight: 14¼ oz., 32 cal. w/3-inch bbl.; 18¼ oz., 38 cal. w/3¼-inch bbl. Fixed

Smith & Wesson Safety Hammerless (cont.)
sights. Blued or nickel finish. Hard rubber stocks. 32 cal. made 1888–1937; 38 cal. 1887–1941. Various minor changes.

S&W Texas Ranger Commemorative

Smith & Wesson Texas Ranger Commem. $895
Issued to honor the 150th anniversary of the Texas Rangers. Model 19 357 Combat Magnum with 4-inch barrel, sideplate stamped with Texas Ranger Commemorative Seal, smooth Goncalo Alves stocks. Special Bowie knife. In presentation case. 8,000 sets made in 1973. Value is for set in new cond.

SPRINGFIELD, INC.
Colona, Illinois
(Formerly Springfield Armory of Geneseo, Ill.)

**Springfield Armory
Model 1911-A1 Auto Pistol**

Springfield Armory 1911-A1 Automatic Pistol

Calibers: 9mm Parabellum, 38 Super, 40 S&W, 45 ACP. 7-, 8- or 10-shot magazine. 5-inch barrel. 8½ inches overall. Weight: 36 oz. Fixed combat sights. Blued or parkerized finish. Checkered walnut stocks. *Note:* This is an exact duplicate of the Colt M1911-A1 that was used to the U.S. Armed Forces for many years.

Blued Finish **$395**
Parkerized Finish **350**

Springfield Armory Lynx

Springfield Armory Bobcat

Springfield Armory Panther

Springfield Armory Bobcat Automatic Pistol **$340**

Caliber: 380 ACP. 13-shot magazine. 3.5-inch barrel. 6.6 inches overall. Weight: 21.95 oz. Blade front sight; rear adjustable for windage. Textured composition grip. Matte blue finish. Made 1991–93.

Springfield Armory Panther Automatic Pistol (cont.)

all. Weight: 28.95 oz. Blade front sight; rear adjustable for windage w/3-dot system. Checkered walnut grip. Matte blue finish. Made 1991–93.

Springfield Armory Model P9

Springfield Armory Firecat

Springfield Armory Firecat Automatic Pistol

Calibers: 9mm, 40 S&W. 8-shot magazine (9mm); 7-shot magazine (40 S&W). 3.5-inch barrel. 6.5 inches overall. Weight: 25.75 oz. Fixed sights with 3-Dot system. Checkered walnut grip. Matte blue finish. Made 1991–93.

9mm **$370**
40 S&W **390**

Springfield Armory Lynx Automatic Pistol **$190**

Caliber: 25 ACP. 7-shot magazine. 2.25-inch barrel. 4.45 inches overall. Weight: 10.55 oz. Blade front sight; rear adjustable for windage with 3-Dot system. Checkered composition grip. Matte blue finish. Made 1991–93.

Springfield Armory Panther Automatic Pistol . . . **$455**

Calibers: 9mm, 40 S&W. 15-shot magazine (9mm); 11-shot magazine (40 S&W). 3.8-inch barrel. 7.5 inches over-

Springfield Armory Model P9 DA Automatic Pistol

Calibers: 9mm, 40 S&W, 45 ACP. Magazine capacity: 15-shot (9mm); 11-shot (40 S&W); 10-shot (45 ACP). 4.75-inch barrel. 8 inches overall. Weight: 32 oz. Fixed sights with 3-Dot system. Checkered walnut grip. Finishes: Matte blue, Parkerized or stainless. Made 1990–94.

9mm Blued **$395**
9mm Parkerized **415**
9mm Stainless **425**

Springfield Armory Model P9 DA Auto (cont.)
40 S&W or 45 ACP Blued **$410**
40 S&W or 45 ACP Parkerized **400**
40 S&W or 45 ACP Stainless **450**

Springfield Armory Model P9 Ultra LPS Pistol
Same general specifications as Model P9, except with dual port compensator system, extended safety and magazine release.
9mm Bi-Tone **$515**
9mm Stainless **525**
40 S&W Bi-Tone **535**
40 S&W Stainless **540**
45 ACP Bi-Tone **545**
45 ACP Stainless **550**

STAR PISTOLS
Eibar, Spain
Star, Bonifacio Echeverria, S.A.

Star Model 30M

Star Model 30M Double Action Auto Pistol **$335**
Caliber: 9mm Parabellum. 15-shot magazine. 4³/₈-inch barrel. 8 inches overall. Weight: 40 oz. Steel frame with combat features. Adjustable sights. Checkered composition stocks. Blued finish. Made 1984–1991.

Star Model 30PK

Star Model 30PK Double Action Auto Pistol **$320**
Same gen. specifications as Star Model 30M, except 3.8-inch barrel, 30-oz. weight and alloy frame. Made 1984–89.

Star Model 31P Double Action Auto Pistol
Same general specifications as Model 30M, except removable backstrap houses complete firing mechanism. Weight: 39.4 oz. Made 1990 to date.
Blued Finish **$275**
Starvel Finish **375**

Star Model 31PK Double Action Auto Pistol **$285**
Same general specifications as Model 31P, except with alloy frame. Weight: 30 oz. Made 1990 to date.

Star Model A Automatic Pistol **$205**
Modification of the Colt Government Model 45 Auto, which it closely resembles; lacks grip safety. Caliber: 38 Super. 8-shot magazine. 5-inch barrel. 8-inches overall. Weight: 35 oz. Fixed sights. Blued finish. Checkered stocks. Made 1934 to date. No longer imported.

Star Model AS

Star Models AS, BS, PS **$285**
Same as Models A, B and P, except have magazine safety. Made in 1975.

Star Model B **$230**
Same as Model A, except in 9mm Luger. Made 1934–1975.

Star Model BKM **$230**
Similar to Model BM, except has aluminum frame and weight 25.6 oz. Made 1976–1992.

Star Model BKS

Star Model BKS Starlight Automatic Pistol **$225**
Light alloy frame. Caliber: 9mm Luger. 8-shot magazine. 4¹/₄-inch bbl. 7 inches overall. Weight: 25 oz. Fixed sights. Blued or chrome finish. Plastic grips. Made 1970–1981.

Star Model BM Automatic Pistol
Caliber: 9mm. 8-shot magazine. 3.9-inch barrel. 6.95 inches overall. Weight: 34.5 oz. Fixed sights. Checkered walnut stocks. Blued or Starvel finish. Made 1976–1992.
Blued Finish **$225**
Starvel Finish **250**

Star Model CO Pocket Automatic Pistol **$175**
Caliber: 25 Automatic (6.35mm). $2^{3}/_{4}$-inch barrel. $4^{1}/_{2}$ inches overall. Weight: 13 oz. Fixed sights. Blued finish. Plastic stocks. Made 1941–1957.

Star Model FM

Star Model CU Starlet*

Star Model FM **$165**
Similar to Model FR, except has heavier frame with web in front of trigger guard, $4^{1}/_{4}$-inch heavy barrel; weighs 32 oz. Made 1972–1991.

Star Model FR **$175**
Similar to Model F with same general specifications, but restyled, has slide stop and adjustable rear sight. Made 1967–1972.

Star Model CU Starlet Pocket Automatic Pistol **$180**
Light alloy frame. Caliber: 25 Automatic (6.35mm). 8-shot magazine. $2^{3}/_{8}$-inch barrel. $4^{3}/_{4}$ inches overall. Weight: $10^{1}/_{2}$ oz. Fixed sights. Blued or chrome-plated slide; frame anodized in black, blue, green, gray or gold. Plastic stocks. Made 1957 to date. U.S. importation discont. 1968.

Star Model FRS

Star Model F Automatic

Star Model FRS **$170**
Same as Model FR, except has 6-inch barrel, weighs 28 oz.; also available in chrome finish. Made 1967–1991.

Star Model FS

Star Model F Automatic Pistol **$165**
Caliber: 22 LR. 10-shot magazine. $4^{1}/_{2}$-inch barrel. $7^{1}/_{4}$ inches overall. Weight: 25 oz. Fixed sights. Blued finish. Plastic stocks. Made 1942–1967.

Star Model F Olympic Rapid-Fire **$295**
Caliber: 22 Short. 9-shot magazine. 7-inch barrel. $11^{1}/_{16}$ inches overall. Weight: 52 oz. with weights. Adjustable target sight. Adjustable 3-piece barrel weight. Aluminum alloy slide. Muzzle brake. Plastic stocks. Made 1942–1967.

Star Model FS **$175**
Same as regular Model F, but with 6-inch barrel and adjustable sights. Weight: 27 oz. Made 1942–1967.

Star Model H*

Star Model H $175
Same as Model HN except caliber 32 Automatic (7.65mm).
7-shot magazine. Weight: 20 oz. Made 1934–1941.

Star Model HK Lancer*

Star Model HK Lancer Automatic Pistol $210
Similar to Starfire with same general specifications, except
caliber 22 LR. Made 1955–1968.

Star Model HN Automatic Pistol $155
Caliber: 380 Automatic (9mm Short). 6-shot magazine.
2³/₄-inch barrel. 5⁹/₁₆ inches overall. Weight: 20 oz. Fixed
sights. Blued finish. Plastic stocks. Made 1934–1941.

Star Model I*

Star Model I Automatic Pistol $170
Caliber: 32 Automatic (7.65mm). 9-shot magazine. 4¹³/₁₆-
inch barrel. 7¹/₂ inches overall. Weight: 24 oz. Fixed sights.
Blued finish. Plastic stocks. Made 1934–36.

Star Model IN $175
Same as Model I, except caliber 380 Automatic (9mm
Short), 8-shot magazine, weighs 24¹/₂ oz. Made 1934–36.

Star Model M Military

Star Model M Military Automatic Pistol $295
Modification of the Colt Government Model 45 Auto,
which it closely resembles; lacks grip safety. Calibers: 9mm
Bergmann, 38 Super, 9mm Luger. 8-shot magazine, except
7-shot in 45 caliber. 5-inch barrel. 8¹/₂ inches overall.
Weight: 36 oz. Fixed sights. Blued finish. Checkered
stocks. Made 1934–39.

Star Models M40, M43, M45 Firestar Auto Pistols
Calibers: 9mm, 40 S&W, 45 ACP. 7-shot magazine (9mm);
6-shot (other calibers). 3.4-inch barrel. 6.5 inches overall.
Weight: 30.35 oz. Blade front sight, adjustable rear w/3
Dot system. Checkered rubber grips. Blued or Starvel fin-
ish. Made 1990 to date.
M40 Blued (40 S&W) $255
M40 Starvel (40 S&W) 285
M43 Blued (9mm) 250
M43 Starvel (9mm) 275
M45 Blued (45 ACP) 295
M45 Starvel (45 ACP) 325

Star Megastar Automatic Pistol
Calibers: 10mm, 45 ACP. 12-shot magazine. 4.6-inch bar-
rel. 8.44 inches overall. Weight: 47.6 oz. Sights: blade front;
adjustable rear. Checkered composition grip. Finishes:
Blued or Starvel. Made from 1992 to date.
Blued Finish, 10mm or 45 ACP $365
Starvel Finish, 10mm or 45 ACP 395

Star Model P $290
Same as Model A, except caliber 45 Automatic; has 7-shot
magazine. Made 1934–1975.

Star Model PD Automatic Pistol
Caliber: 45 Automatic. 6-shot magazine. 3³/₄-inch barrel.
7 inches overall. Weight: 25 oz. Adjustable rear sight, ramp
front. Blued or Starvel finish. Checkered walnut stocks.
Made 1975–1992.
Blued Finish $235
Starvel Finish 265

Star Model PD

Star Model S

Star Model S **$170**
Same as Model SI except caliber 380 Automatic (9mm),
7-shot magazine, weighs 19 oz. Made 1941–1965.

Star Model SI

Star Model SI Automatic Pistol **$215**
Reduced-size modification of the Colt Government Model
45 Auto; lacks grip safety. Caliber: 32 Automatic (7.65mm).
8-shot magazine. 4-inch barrel. 6½ inches overall. Weight:
20 oz. Fixed sights. Blued finish. Plastic stocks. Made
1941–1965.

Star Starfire Automatic Pistol **$355**
Light alloy frame. Caliber: 380 Automatic (9mm Short).
7-shot magazine. 3⅛-inch barrel. 5½ inches overall.
Weight: 14½ oz. Fixed sights. Blued or chrome-plated
slide; frame anodized in black, blue, green, gray or gold.
Plastic stocks. Made 1957 to date. U.S. importation discont. 1968.

Star Models Super A, Super B, Super P **$230**
Same as Models A, B and P, except with improvements
described under Super Star. Made c. 1946–1989/1990.

Star Models Super SI, Super S **$235**
Same general specifications as the regular Model SI and
S, except with improvements described under Super Star.
Made c. 1946–1972.

Star Model Super SM

Star Model Super SM **$230**
Similar to Model Super S, except has adjustable rear sight,
wood stocks. Made 1973–1981.

Super Star Automatic

Super Star Automatic Pistol **$285**
Improved version of the Model M with same general specifications; has disarming bolt permitting easier takedown,
indicator of cartridge in chamber, magazine safety, takedown magazine, improved sights with luminous spots for
aiming in darkness. Calibers: 38 Super, 9mm Luger. This
is the standard service pistol of the Spanish Armed Forces,
adopted 1946.

Super Star Target Model **$395**
Same as regular Super Star, except with adjustable target
rear sight. Discontinued.

STENDA-WERKE PISTOL
Suhl, Germany

Stenda Pocket Automatic Pistol **$230**
Essentially the same as the Beholla; see listing of that
pistol for specifications. Made c. 1920–25. *Note:* This pistol
may be marked "Beholla" along w/the Stenda name and
address.

STERLING ARMS CORPORATION
Gasport, New York

Sterling Model 283

Sterling Model 284

Sterling Model 285

Sterling Model 283 Target 300 Auto Pistol **$135**
Caliber: 22 LR. 10-shot magazine. Barrel lengths: 4½-, 6-, 8-inch. 9 inches overall with 4½-inch bbl. Weight: with 4½-inch bbl., 36 oz. Adjustable sights. Blued finish. Plastic stocks. Made 1970–71.

Sterling Model 284 Target 300L **$150**
Same as Model 283, except has 4½- or 6-inch "Luger"-type barrel. Made 1970–71.

Sterling Model 285 Husky **$150**
Same as Model 283, except has fixed sights, 4½-inch barrel only. Made 1970–71.

NOTE: Total production of Models 283, 284, 285 and 286 was 2700 pieces.

Sterling Model 286

Sterling Model 300

Sterling Model 286 Trapper **$145**
Same as Model 284, except w/fixed sights. Made 1970–71.

Sterling Model 287 PPL-380 Automatic Pistol **$90**
Caliber: 380 Automatic. 6-shot magazine. 1-inch barrel. 5⅜ inches overall. Weight: 22½ oz. Fixed sights. Blued finish. Plastic stocks. Made 1971–72.

Sterling Model 300 Automatic Pistol **$115**
Caliber: 25 Automatic. 6-shot magazine. 2⅓-inch barrel. 4½ inches overall. Weight: 13 oz. Fixed sights. Blued or nickel finish. Plastic stocks. Made 1972–1983.

Sterling Model 300S **$105**
Same as Model 300, except in stainless steel. Made 1976–1983.

Sterling Model 302 .... **$115**
Same as Model 300, except in 22 LR. Made 1973–1983.

Sterling Model 302S **$125**
Same as Model 302, except in stainless steel. Made 1976–1983.

Sterling Model 400 DA Automatic Pistol **$195**
Caliber: 380 Automatic. 7-shot magazine. 3½-inch barrel. 6½ inches overall. Weight: 24 oz. Adjustable rear sight. Blued or nickel finish. Checkered walnut stocks. Made 1975–1983.

Sterling Model 400

Sterling Model 400S **$235**
Same as Model 400, except stainless steel. Made 1977–1983.

Sterling Model 450

Sterling Model PPL-22

Sterling Model 450 DA Auto Pistol **$295**
Caliber: 45 Automatic. 8-shot magazine. 4-inch barrel. 7$\frac{1}{2}$ inches overall. Weight: 36 oz. Adjustable rear sight. Blued finish. Smooth walnut stocks. Made 1977–1983.

Sterling Model PPL-22 Automatic Pistol **$150**
Caliber: 22 LR. 10-shot magazine. 1-inch barrel. 5$\frac{1}{2}$ inches overall. Weight: about 24 oz. Fixed sights. Blued finish. Wood stocks. *Note:* Only 382 made 1970–71.

J. STEVENS ARMS & TOOL CO.
Chicopee Falls, Mass.

This firm was established in Civil War days by Joshua Stevens, for whom the company was named. In 1936 it became a subsidiary of Savage Arms.

Stevens No. 10

Stevens No. 10 Single Shot Target Pistol **$250**
Caliber: 22 LR. 8-inch barrel. 11$\frac{1}{2}$ inches overall. Weight: 37 oz. Target sights. Blued finish. Hard rubber stocks. In external appearance this arm resembles an automatic pistol; it has a tip-up action. Made 1919–1939.

Stevens No. 35

Stevens No. 35 Offhand Model Single Shot Target Pistol **$340**
Tip-up action. Caliber: 22 LR. Barrel lengths: 6, 8, 10, 12$\frac{1}{4}$ inches. Weight: 24 oz. with 6-inch bbl. Target sights. Blued finish. Walnut stocks. *Note:* This pistol is similar to the earlier "Gould" model. No. 35 was also supplied chambered for .410 shotshell. Made 1907–1939.

STEYR PISTOLS
Steyr, Austria

Steyr GB Semiautomatic Pistol **$495**
Caliber: 9mm Parabellum. 18-round magazine. 5.4-inch barrel. 8.9 inches overall. Weight: 2.9 pounds. Post front

Steyr GB Semiautomatic

Stoeger Standard Luger

Steyr GB Semiautomatic Pistol (cont.)
sight; fixed, notched rear. Double, gas-delayed, blow-back action. Made 1981–88.

Steyr-Hahn M12

Steyr-Hahn M12 Automatic Pistol **$445**
Caliber: 9mm Steyr. 8-shot fixed magazine, charger loaded. 5.1-inch barrel. 8.5 inches overall. Weight: 35 oz. Fixed sights. Blued finish. Checkered wood stocks. Made 1911–19. Adopted by the Austro-Hungarian Army in 1912. *Note:* Confiscated by the Germans in 1938, an estimated 250,000 of these pistols were converted to 9mm Luger and stamped with an identifying "08" on the left side of the slide. Mfd. by Osterreichische Waffenfabrik-Gesellschaft.

STOEGER LUGERS
Formerly mfd. by Stoeger Industries, So. Hackensack, N.J.; then Classic Arms, Union City, N.J.

Stoeger Standard Luger 22 Automatic Pistol . . . **$150**
Caliber: 22 LR. 10-shot magazine. Barrels: $4\frac{1}{2}$, $5\frac{1}{2}$ inches. $8\frac{7}{8}$ inches overall w/$4\frac{1}{2}$-inch bbl. Weight: $29\frac{1}{2}$ oz. w/ $4\frac{1}{2}$-inch bbl. Fixed sights. Black finish. Smooth wood stocks. Made 1969–1986.

Stoeger Steel Frame Luger 22 Auto Pistol **$165**
Caliber: 22 LR. 10-shot magazine. $4\frac{1}{2}$-inch barrel. $8\frac{7}{8}$ inches overall. Blued finish. Checkered wood stocks. Features one-piece solidly forged and machined steel frame. Made 1980–86.

Stoeger Target Luger 22 Automatic Pistol **$195**
Same as Standard Luger 22, except has target sights. $9\frac{3}{8}$ inches overall with $4\frac{1}{2}$-inch bbl. Checkered wood stocks. Made 1975–1986.

TARGA PISTOLS
Italy
Manufactured by Armi Tanfoglio Guiseppe

Targa Model GT26S Automatic Pistol **$45**
Caliber: 25 ACP. 6-shot magazine. $2\frac{1}{2}$-inch barrel. $4\frac{5}{8}$ inches overall. Weight: 15 oz. Fixed sights. Checkered composition stocks. Blued or chrome finish. Disc. 1990.

Targa Model GT32 Automatic Pistol
Caliber: 32 ACP. 6-shot magazine. $4\frac{7}{8}$-inch barrel. $7\frac{3}{8}$ inches overall. Weight: 26 oz. Fixed sights. Checkered composition or walnut stocks. Blued or chrome finish.
Blued finish **$95**
Chrome finish **100**

Targa Model GT 380XE

Targa Model GT380 Automatic Pistol
Same as the Targa GT32, except chambered for 380 ACP.
Blued finish **$110**
Chrome finish **115**

Targa Model GT380XE Automatic Pistol **$135**
Caliber: 380 ACP. 11-shot magazine. 3³/₄-inch barrel. 7³/₈
inches overall. Weight: 28 oz. Fixed sights. Blued or satin
nickel finish. Smooth wooden stocks. Made 1980–1990.

FORJAS TAURUS S.A.
Porto Alegre, Brazil

**Taurus Model 65
Satin Nickel**

Taurus Model 65 Double Action Revolver
Caliber: 357 Magnum. 6-shot cylinder. 3- or 4-inch barrel.
Weight: 32 oz. Front ramp sight, square notch rear.
Checkered walnut target stock. Royal blue or satin nickel
finish. Currently in production.
Blue **$175**
Stainless **225**

Taurus Model 66

Taurus Model 66 Double Action Revolver
Calibers: 357 Magnum, 38 Special. 6-shot cylinder. Barrels: 3, 4 and 6 inches. Weight: 35 oz. Serrated ramp front
sight; rear click adjustable. Checkered walnut grips. Royal
blue or nickel finish. Currently in production.
Blue **$195**
Stainless **250**

Taurus Model 73 Double Action Revolver **$165**
Caliber: 32 Long. 6-shot cylinder. 3-inch heavy barrel.
Weight: 20 oz. Checkered grips. Blued or satin finish. Dis-
continued 1993.

Taurus Model 74

Taurus Model 74 Target Grade DA Revolver . . . **$145**
Caliber: 32 S&W Long. 6-shot cylinder. 3-inch barrel. 8¹/₄
inches overall. Weight: 20 oz. Adjustable rear sight, ramp
front. Blued or nickel finish. Checkered walnut stocks.
Made 1971–1990.

Taurus Model 80

Taurus Model 80 Double Action Revolver
Caliber: 38 Special. 6-shot cylinder. Barrel lengths: 3, 4
inches. 9¹/₄ inches overall with 4-inch bbl. Weight: with
4-inch bbl., 30 oz. Fixed sights. Blued or nickel finish.
Checkered walnut stocks. Made 1971 to date.
Blued **$150**
Stainless **185**

Taurus Model 82

Taurus Model 82 Heavy Barrel **$165**
Same as Model 80, except has heavy barrel. Weight: with
4-inch bbl., 33 oz. Made 1971 to date.

Taurus Model 83

Taurus Model 83 Heavy Barrel Target Grade
Same as Model 84, except has heavy barrel, weighs 34½ oz. Made 1977 to date.

Blued	**$165**
Stainless	195

Taurus Model 84

Taurus Model 84 Target Grade Revolver $200
Caliber: 38 Special. 6-shot cylinder. 4-inch barrel. 9¼ inches overall. Weight: 31 oz. Adjustable rear sight, ramp front. Blued or nickel finish. Checkered walnut stocks. Made 1971–1989.

Taurus Model 85

Taurus Model 85 Double Action Revolver
Caliber: 38 Special. 5-shot cylinder. Barrel. 2- or 3-inch Weight: 21 oz. Fixed sights. Checkered walnut grips. Blued, satin nickel or stainless-steel finish. Currently in production.

Blued or Satin Nickel	**$175**
Stainless Steel	210

Taurus Model 86

Taurus Model 86 Target Master DA Revolver ... $195
Caliber: 38 Special. 6-shot cylinder. 6-inch barrel. 11¼ inches overall. Weight: 34 oz. Adjustable rear sight, Patridge-type front. Blued finish. Checkered walnut stocks. Made 1971 to date.

Taurus Model 94 Target Grade
Same as Model 74, except caliber 22 LR, with 9-shot cylinder. 3- or 4-inch barrel. Weight: 25 oz. Blued or stainless finish. Made 1971 to date.

Blued Finish	**$185**
Stainless Finish	215

Taurus Model 96 Target Master $215
Same as Model 86, except in 22 LR. Made 1971 to date.

Tauras Model 431 Double Action Revolver
Caliber: 44 Spec. 5-shot cylinder. 3- or 4-inch solid-rib barrel with ejector shroud. Weight: 35 oz.with 4-inch bbl. Serrated ramp front sight, notched topstrap rear. Blued or stainless finish. Made 1992 to date.

Blued Finish	**$185**
Stainless Finish	225

Tauras Model 441 Double Action Revolver
Similar to the Model 431, except w/6-inch barrel and fully adj. target sights. Weight: 40 oz. Made 1991 to date.

Blued Finish	**$200**
Stainless Finish	250

Taurus Model 669VR

Tauras Model 669/669VR Double Action Revolver
Caliber: 357 Mag. 6-shot cylinder. 4- or 6-inch solid-rib barrel with ejector shroud; Model 669VR has vent-rib barrel. Weight: 37 oz. with 4-inch bbl. Serrated ramp front sight, micro-adjustable rear. Royal blue or stainless finish. Checkered Brazilian hardwood grips. Model 669 made 1989 to date; Model 669VR from 1990.

Model 669 Blued	**$195**
Model 669 Stainless	250
Model 669VR Blued	210
Model 669VR Stainless	260

Tauras Model 741/761 Double Action Revolver
Caliber: 32 H&R Mag. 6-shot cylinder. 3- or 4-inch solid-rib barrel with ejector shroud. Weight: 20 oz. with 3-inch bbl. Serrated ramp front sight, micro-adjustable rear. Blued or stainless finish. Checkered Brazilian hardwood grips. Made 1991 to date.

Model 741 Blued	**$190**
Model 741 Stainless	285
Model 761 (6-inch bbl., blued, 34 oz.)	245

Tauras Model 941 Target Revolver
Caliber: 22 Magnum. 8-shot cylinder. Solid-rib barrel with ejector shroud. Micro-adjustable rear sight. Brazilian hardwood grips. Blued or stainless finish.

Blued Finish	**$200**
Stainless Finish	240

Taurus Model PT 92AF

Taurus Model PT 22

Tauras Model PT 22 DA Automatic Pistol $135
Caliber: 22 LR. 9-shot magazine 2.75-inch barrel. Weight: 12.3 oz. Fixed open sights. Brazilian hardwood stocks. Blued finish. Made 1991 to date. **Model PT 25** same general specifications and price as Model PT 22, except in 25 ACP.

Tauras Model PT 92AF Semiautomatic Pistol
Caliber: 9mm Parabellum. 15-round magazine. Double action. Barrel: about 5 inches. 8½ inches overall. Weight: 34 oz. Blade front sight, notched bar rear. Smooth Brazilian walnut grips. Blued, satin nickel or stainless finish. Made 1991 to date.

Blued Finish	**$325**
Satin Nickel Finish	345
Stainless Finish	370

Tauras Model PT-92AFC Compact Pistol
Same general specifications as Model PT-92AF, except with 13-shot magazine. 4.25-inch barrel. 7.5 inches overall. Weight: 31 oz. Made 1991 to date.

Blued Finish	**$330**
Satin Nickel Finish	335
Stainless Finish	370

Taurus Model PT-58

Taurus Model PT 99AF

Tauras Model PT-58 Semiautomatic Pistol
Caliber: 380 ACP. 12-shot magazine. 4-inch barrel. 7.2 inches overall. Weight: 30 oz. Blade front sight; rear adj. for windage w/3-dot sighting system. Blued, satin nickel or stainless finish. Made 1988 to date.

Blued Finish	**$175**
Satin Nickel Finish	185
Stainless Finish	325

Tauras Model PT 99AF Semiautomatic Pistol ... $295
Same general specifications as Model PT 92AF, except rear sight is adjustable for elevation and windage, and finish is blued or satin nickel. Discontinued 1993.

Tauras Model PT 100 DA Automatic Pistol
Caliber: 40 S&W. 11-shot magazine. 5-inch barrel. Weight: 34 oz. Fixed front sight; adj. rear w/3-Dot system. Smooth hardwood grip. Blued, satin nickel or stainless finish. Made 1991 to date.

Blued Finish	**$330**
Satin Nickel Finish	360
Stainless Finish	385

Taurus Model PT 101 DA Automatic Pistol

Same general specifications as Model 100, except w/micrometer click adj. sights.

Blued	**$360**
Satin Nickel	**385**
Stainless	**415**

Taurus Model PT-908

Tauras Model PT-908 Semiautomatic Pistol

Caliber: 9mm Parabellum. 8-shot magazine. 3.8-inch barrel. 7 inches overall. Weight: 30 oz. Sights: drift-adjustable front; combat rear w/3-dot system. Blued, satin nickel or stainless finish. Made from 1993 to date.

Blued Finish	**$325**
Satin Nickel Finish	**340**
Stainless Finish	**370**

TEXAS ARMS
Waco, Texas

**Texas Arms
Defender Derringer**

Texas Arms Defender Derringer **$215**

Calibers: 9mm, 357 Mag., 44 Mag., 45 ACP, 45 Colt/.410. 3-inch barrel. 5 inches overall. Weight: 21 oz. Sights: blade front; fixed rear. Matte gun-metal grey finish. Smooth grips. Made from 1993 to date.

TEXAS LONGHORN ARMS
Richmond, Texas

Texas Longhorn Arms Keith No. 5 Single Action Revolver **$730**

Caliber: 44 Magnum. 6-shot. 5½-inch barrel. 11 inches overall. Weight: 44 oz. Adjustable rear sight, blade front. One-piece deluxe walnut stock. Blued finish. Intro. 1987.

Texas Longhorn Arms Sesquicentennial Single Action Revolver **$1875**

Same as South Texas Army Limited Edition, except engraved and nickel-plated with one-piece ivory stock. Introduced in 1986.

Texas Longhorn Arms Single Action Revolver Cased Set

Set contains one each of the Texas Longhorn Single Actions. Each chambered in the same caliber and with the same serial number. Introduced in 1984.

Standard Set	**$4300**
Engraved Set	**5700**

Texas Longhorn Arms South Texas Army Limited Edition Single Action Revolver **$1195**

Calibers: all popular centerfire pistol calibers. 6-shot cylinder. 4¾-inch barrel. 10¼ inches overall. Weight: 40 oz. Fixed sights. Color casehardened frame. One-piece deluxe walnut stocks. Blued barrel. Introduced in 1984.

Texas Longhorn Arms Texas Border Special Single Action Revolver **$1195**

Same as South Texas Army Limited Edition, except with 3½-inch barrel and bird's-head grips. Introduced in 1984.

Texas Longhorn Arms West Texas Flat Top Target Single Action Revolver **$1195**

Same as South Texas Army Limited Edition, except with choice of barrel lengths from 7½ to 15 inches. Same special features with flat-top style frame and adjustable rear sight. Introduced in 1984.

THOMPSON PISTOL
West Hurley, New York
Mfd. by Auto-Ordnance Corporation

Thompson Model 27A-5 w/Drum Magazine

Thompson Model 27A-5 Semiautomatic Pistol

Similar to Thompson Model 1928A submachine gun, except has no provision for automatic firing, does not have detachable buttstock. Caliber: 45 Automatic. 20-shot detachable box magazine (5-, 15- and 30-shot box magazines, 39-shot drum also available). 13-inch finned barrel. Overall length: 26 inches. Weight: about 6¾ pounds. Adj. rear sight, blade front. Blued finish. Walnut grips. Intro. 1977.

With box magazine	**$ 995**
With drum magazine (as illustrated)	**1195**

THOMPSON/CENTER ARMS
Rochester, New Hampshire

**Thompson/Center Contender
Standard Model, 1967-Type**

**Thompson/Center Contender
Early Bull Barrel Model w/Scope**

**Thompson/Center Contender
Vent-Rib Model**

**Thompson/Center Contender
Bull Barrel—New Model**

Thompson/Center Contender Single Shot Pistol

Break frame, underlever action. Calibers: (rimfire) 22 LR, 22 WMR, 5mm RRM; (standard centerfire), 218 Bee, 22 Hornet, 22 Rem. Jet, 221 Fireball, 222 Rem., 25-35, 256 Win. Mag., 30 M1 Carbine, 30-30, 38 Auto, 38 Special, 357 Mag./Hot Shot, 9mm Luger, 45 Auto, 45 Colt, 44 Magnum/Hot Shot; (wildcat centerfire) 17 Ackley Bee, 17 Bumblebee, 17 Hornet, 17 K Hornet, 17 Mach IV, 17-222, 17-223, 22 K Hornet, 30 Herrett, 357 Herrett, 357-4 B&D. Interchangeable barrels: 8³/₄- or 10-inch standard octagon (357 Mag., 44 Mag. and 45 Colt available with detachable choke for use with Hot Shot cartridges); 10-inch with ventilated rib and detachable internal choke tube for Hot Shots, 357 and 44 Magnum only; 10-inch bull barrel, 30 or 357 Herrett only. 13¹/₂ inches overall with 10-inch bbl. Weight: with standard 10-inch bbl., about 43 oz. Adj. rear sight, ramp front; vent-rib model has folding rear sight, adjustable front; bull barrel available with or w/o sights; Lobo 1¹/₂ X scope and mount (add $40 to value). Blued finish. Receiver photoengraved. Checkered walnut thumbrest stock and forearm (pre-1972 model has different stock with silver grip cap). Made 1967 to date, with the following revisions and variations.

Standard Model	$210
Ventilated-Rib Model	240
Bull Barrel Model, with sights	245
Bull Barrel Model, without sights	215
Extra standard barrel	85
Extra ventilated rib or bull barrel	90

Thompson/Center Contender—Bull Barrel $250

Caliber offerings of the bull barrel version expanded in 1973, with another bump in 1978, making it the Contender model with the widest range of caliber options: 22 LR, 22 Win. Mag., 22 Hornet, 223 Rem., 7mm T.C.U., 7×30 Waters, 30 M1 Carbine, 30-30 Win., 32 H&R Mag., 32-20 Win., 357 Rem. Max., 357 Mag., 10mm Auto, 44 Magnum, 445 Super Magnum. 10-inch heavy barrel. Patridge-style iron sights. Contoured Competitor™ grip. Blued finish.

Thompson/Center Contender—Internal Choke Model

Originally made in 1968–69 with octagonal barrel, this Internal Choke version in 45 Colt/.410 caliber only was reintroduced in 1986 with 10-inch bull barrel. Vent rib also available. Iron sights: fixed rear, bead front. Detachable choke screws into muzzle. Blued finish. Contoured American black walnut Competitor™ Grip, also introduced in 1986, has nonslip rubber insert permanently bonded to back of grip.

With Bull Barrel	$280
With Vent Rib	325

**Thompson Center Contender
Octagon Barrel**

Thompson/Center Contender—Octagon Barrel $245

The original Contender design, this octagonal barrel version began to see the discontinuance of caliber offerings in 1980, so that now it is available in 22 LR only. 10-inch octagonal barrel. Patridge-style iron sights. Contoured Competitor™ Grip. Blued finish.

Thompson/Center Contender—Stainless

Similar to the standard Contender Models, except stainless steel with blued sights. Black Rynite forearm and ambidextrous finger-groove grip. Made from 1993 to date.

Standard SS Model (10-inch bbl.)	$315
SS Super 14	325
SS Super 16	335

Thompson/Center Contender Super 14

Thompson/Center Contender Super 14 . . . . **$275**
Calibers: 22 LR, 222 Rem., 223 Rem., 6mm T.C.U., 6.5mm T.C.U., 7mm T.C.U., 7×30 Waters, 30 Herrett, 30-30 Win., 357 Herrett, 357 Rem. Max., 35 Rem., 10mm Auto, 44 Mag., 445 Super Mag. 14-inch bull barrel. 18 inches overall. Weight: 56 oz. Patridge-style ramp front sight, adjustable target rear. Blued finish. Made 1978 to date.

Unique Model B/cf

Thompson/Center Contender T/C Alloy II with Vent Rib

Thompson/Center Contender TC Alloy II
Calibers: 22 LR, 223 Rem., 357 Magnum, 357 Rem. Max., 44 Magnum, 7mm T.C.U., 30-30 Win.; 45 Colt/.410 with internal choke; 35 Rem. and 7×30 Waters (14-inch bbl.). 10- or 14-inch bull barrel or 10-inch vent-rib barrel (w/ internal choke). All metal parts permanently electroplated with T/C Alloy II, which is harder than stainless steel, ensuring smoother action, 30 percent longer barrel life. Other design specifications the same as late model Contenders. Made 1986–89.
T/C Alloy II 10-inch Bull Barrel **$305**
T/C Alloy II Vent-rib Barrel w/Choke **340**
T/C Alloy II Super 14 . . . . **350**

Unique Model D6

Unique Model D6 Automatic Pistol **$215**
Caliber: 22 LR. 10-shot magazine. 6-inch bbl. 9¼ inches overall. Weight: about 26 oz. Adjustable sights. Blued finish. Plain or thumbrest plastic stocks. Introduced in 1954; disccontinued.

=== **UNIQUE PISTOLS** ===
Hendaye, France
Mfd. by Manufacture d'Armes des Pyrénées Francaises

Unique Model B/cf Automatic Pistol **$200**
Calibers: 32 Auto (7.65mm), 380 Auto (9mm Short). 9-shot (32) or 8-shot (380) magazine. 4-inch barrel. 6.6 inches overall. Weight: 24.3 oz. Blued finish. Plain or thumbrest plastic stocks. Intro. 1954; discontinued.

Unique Model D2 . . . . **$235**
Same as Model D6, except has 4¼-inch barrel, 7½ inches overall, weighs 24½ oz. Made 1954 to date.

Unique Model DES/69

Unique Model DES/69 Standard Match Automatic Pistol **$875**
Caliber: 22 LR. 5-shot magazine. 5.9-inch barrel. 10.6 inches overall. Weight: 35 oz. (barrel weight adds about 9 oz.). Click adjustable rear sight, ramp front. Blued finish. Checkered walnut thumbrest stocks w/adj. handrest. Made 1969 to date.

Unique Model DES/VO

Unique Model DES/VO Rapid Fire Match Automatic Pistol $710
Caliber: 22 Short. 5-shot magazine. 5.9-inch barrel. 10.4 inches overall. Weight: 43 oz. Click adjustable rear sight, blade front. Checkered walnut thumbrest stocks w/adj. handrest. Trigger adjustable for length of pull. Made from 1974 to date.

Unique Kriegsmodell

Unique Model L

Unique Kriegsmodell Automatic Pistol $225
Caliber: 32 Automatic (7.65mm). 9-shot magazine. 3.2-inch barrel. 5.8 inches overall. Weight: 26.5 oz. Fixed

Unique Kriegsmodell Automatic Pistol (cont.)
sights. Blued finish. Plastic stocks. Mfd. during German occupation of France 1940–45. *Note:* Bears the German military acceptance marks and may have stocks marked "7.65m/m 9 SCHUSS."

Unique Model L Automatic Pistol $215
Calibers: 22 LR, 32 Auto (7.65mm), 380 Auto (9mm Short). 10-shot magazine in 22, 7 in 32, 6 in 380. 3.3-inch barrel. 5.8 inches overall. Weight: about 16½ oz. (380) w/light alloy frame; 23 oz. with steel frame. Fixed sights. Blued finish. Plastic stocks. Introduced 1955; discontinued.

Unique Model Mikros

Unique Model Mikros Pocket Automatic Pistol . . $150
Calibers: 22 Short, 25 Auto (6.35mm). 6-shot magazine. 2¼-inch barrel. 4⁷⁄₁₆ inches overall. Weight: 9½ oz. w/light alloy frame; 12½ oz. w/steel frame. Fixed sights. Blued finish. Plastic stocks. Intro. 1957; discontinued.

Unique Model Rr

Unique Model Rr Automatic Pistol $165
Postwar commercial version of WWII Kriegsmodell with same general specifications. Intro. 1951; discontinued.

UNITED STATES ARMS CORPORATION
Riverhead, New York

U.S. Arms Abilene

U.S. Arms Abilene Single Action Revolver
Safety Bar action. Calibers: 357 Magnum, 41 Magnum, 44 Magnum, 45 Colt; also 9mm Luger and 357 convertible model with two cylinders. 6-shot cylinder. Barrel lengths: $4^5/_8$-, $5^1/_2$-, $6^1/_2$-inch; $7^1/_2$- and $8^1/_2$-inch in 44 Magnum only. Weight: about 48 oz. Adjustable rear sight, ramp front. Blued finish or stainless steel. Smooth walnut stocks. Made 1976 to date.

44 Magnum, blued finish	**$250**
44 Magnum, stainless steel	275
Other calibers, blued finish	225
357 Magnum, stainless steel	240
Convertible, 357 Mag./9mm Luger, blued finish	215

UNIVERSAL FIREARMS CORPORATION
Hialeah, Florida

This company was purchased by Iver Johnson's Arms in the mid-1980s, when the Enforcer listed below was discontinued. An improved version was issued under the Iver Johnson name (*see* separate listing).

Universal Enforcer

Universal Enforcer Semiautomatic Pistol $275
M-1 Carbine-type action. Caliber: 30 Carbine. 5-, 15- or 30-shot clip magazine. $10^1/_4$-inch barrel. $17^3/_4$ inches overall. Weight: $4^1/_2$ pounds w/30-shot magazine. Adj. rear sight, blade front. Blued finish. Walnut stock with pistol grip and handguard. Made 1964–1983.

UZI PISTOLS
Mfd. by Israel Military Industries, Israel

Uzi 9mm Semiautomatic

Uzi Semiautomatic Pistol $995
Caliber: 9mm Parabellum. 20-round magazine. $4^1/_2$-inch barrel. About $9^1/_2$ inches overall. Weight: 3.8 pounds. Front post-type sight; rear open-type, both adjustable. Disc.

WALTHER PISTOLS
Manufactured by German, French and Swiss firms

The following Walther pistols were made before and during World War II by Waffenfabrik Walther, Zella-Mehlis (Thür.), Germany.

Walther Model 1*

Walther Model 1 Automatic Pistol $375
Caliber: 25 Auto (6.35mm). 6-shot. 2.1-inch barrel. 4.4 inches overall. Weight: 12.8 oz. Fixed sights. Blued finish. Checkered hard rubber stocks. Intro. 1908.

HANDGUNS

Walther Model 2

Walther Model 6

Walther Model 2 Automatic Pistol **$395**
Caliber: 25 Auto (6.35mm). 6-shot magazine. 2.1-inch barrel. 4.2 inches overall. Weight: 9.8 oz. Fixed sights. Blued finish. Checkered hard rubber stocks. Intro. 1909.

Walther Model 3 Automatic Pistol **$995**
Caliber: 32 Auto (7.65mm). 6-shot magazine. 2.6-inch barrel. 5 inches overall. Weight: 16.6 oz. Fixed sights. Blued finish. Checkered hard rubber stocks. Intro. 1910.

Walther Model 7

Walther Model 4

Walther Model 7 Automatic Pistol **$425**
Caliber: 25 Auto. (6.35mm). 8-shot magazine. 3-inch barrel. 5.3 inches overall. Weight: 11.8 oz. Fixed sights. Blued finish. Checkered hard rubber stocks. Made 1917–1918.

Walther Model 8*

Walther Model 4 Automatic Pistol **$250**
Caliber: 32 Automatic (7.65mm). 8-shot magazine. 3.5-inch barrel. 5.9 inches overall. Weight: 18.6 oz. Fixed sights. Blued finish. Checkered hard rubber stocks. Made 1910–1918.

Walther Model 5 Automatic Pistol **$290**
Improved version of Model 2 with same general specifications, distinguished chiefly by better workmanship and appearance. Introduced in 1913.

Walther Model 6 Automatic Pistol **$1995**
Caliber: 9mm Luger. 8-shot magazine. 4 3/4-inch barrel. 8 1/4 inches overall. Weight: 34 oz. Fixed sights. Blued finish. Checkered hard rubber stocks. Made 1915–1917. *Note:* Since the powerful 9mm Luger cartridge is too much for the simple blow-back system of this pistol, firing is not recommended.

Walther Model 8 Automatic Pistol **$335**
Caliber: 25 Auto. (6.35mm). 8-shot magazine. 2 7/8-inch barrel. 5 1/8 inches overall. Weight: 12 3/8 oz. Fixed sights. Blued finish. Checkered plastic stocks. Made 1920–1945.

Walther Model 8 Lightweight Automatic Pistol . . **$390**
Same as standard Model 8 except about 25 percent lighter due to use of aluminum alloys.

Walther Model 9

Walther Model 9 Vest Pocket Automatic Pistol . . $350
Caliber: 25 Automatic (6.35mm). 6-shot magazine. 2-inch barrel. 3¹⁵/₁₆ inches overall. Weight: 9 oz. Fixed sights. Blue finish. Checkered plastic stocks. Made 1921–1945.

Walther Model HP

Walther Model HP Double Action Automatic . . . $1050
Prewar commercial version of the P38. "HP" is abbreviation of "Heeres Pistole" (Army Pistol). Caliber: 9mm Luger. 8-shot magazine. 5-inch barrel. 8³/₈ inches overall. Weight: about 34¹/₂ oz. Fixed sights. Blued finish. Checkered wood or plastic stocks. The Model HP is distinguished by its notably fine material and workmanship. Made 1937–1944.

Walther Olympia Funfkampf

Walther Olympia Funfkampf Model Automatic . . $895
Caliber: 22 LR. 10-shot magazine. 9.6-inch barrel. 13 inches overall. Weight: 33 oz., less weight. Set of 4 detachable weights. Adjustable target sights. Blued finish. Checkered stocks. Introduced 1936.

Walther Olympia Hunting Model Automatic $695
Same general specifications as Olympia Sport Model, but with 4-inch barrel. Weight: 28¹/₂ oz.

Walther Olympia Rapid Fire Model Automatic . . $795
Caliber: 22 Short. 6-shot magazine. 7.4-inch barrel. 10.7 inches overall. Weight: without 12³/₈ oz. detachable muzzle weight, 27¹/₂ oz. Adjustable target sights. Blued finish. Checkered stocks. Made about 1936–1940.

Walther Olympia Sport Model Automatic $995
Caliber: 22 LR. 10-shot magazine. 7.4-inch barrel. 10.7 inches overall. Weight: 30¹/₂ oz., less weight. Adjustable target sights. Blued finish. Checkered stocks. Set of four detachable weights was supplied at extra cost. Made about 1936–1940.

Walther Model P38 (WW II)

Walther P38 Military DA Automatic $625
Modification of the Model HP adopted as an official German Service arm in 1938 and produced throughout WW II by Walther (code "ac"), Mauser (code "byf") and a few other manufacturers. General specifications same as Model HP, but with a vast difference in quality, the P38 being a mass-produced military pistol; some of the late wartime models were very roughly finished and tolerances were quite loose.

Walther Model PP (Prewar)

Walther Model PP DA Automatic Pistol
Polizeipistole (Police Pistol). Calibers: 22 LR (5.6mm), 25 Auto (6.35mm), 32 Auto (7.65mm), 380 Auto (9mm). 8-shot magazine, 7-shot in 380. 3⁷/₈-inch barrel. 6⁵/₁₆ inches overall. Weight: 23 oz. Fixed sights. Blued finish. Checkered plastic stocks. *Note:* Wartime models are inferior in quality to prewar commercial pistols. Made 1929–1945.

Walther Model PP (cont.)

22 caliber, commercial model	$475
25 caliber, commercial model	495
32 and 380 caliber, commercial model	810
Wartime model	400

Walther Model PP Lightweight

Same as standard Model PP, except about 25 percent lighter due to use of aluminum alloys. Values 50 percent higher.

Walther Model PP 7.65mm Presentation $1400

Made of soft aluminum alloy in green-gold color, these pistols were not intended to be fired.

Walther Model PPK (WW II)

Walther Model PPK Double Action Automatic Pistol

Polizeipistole Kriminal (Detective Pistol). Calibers: 22 LR (5.6mm), 25 Auto (6.35mm), 32 Auto (7.65mm), 380 Auto (9mm). 7-shot magazine, 6-shot in 380. 3¼-inch barrel. 5⅞ inches overall. Weight: 19 oz. Fixed sights. Blued finish. Checkered plastic stocks. *Note:* Wartime models are inferior in workmanship to prewar commercial pistols. Made 1931–1945.

25, commercial model	$ 795
32, commercial model	475
22 LR & 380	1500

Walther Model PPK Lightweight

Same as standard Model PPK, except about 25 percent lighter due to aluminum alloys. Values 50 percent higher.

Walther Model PPK 7.65mm Presentation $1095

Made of soft aluminum alloy in green-gold color, these pistols were not intended to be fired.

Walther Self-Loading Sport

Walther Self-Loading Sport Pistol $610

Caliber: 22 LR. 10-shot magazine. Barrel lengths: 6- and 9-inch. 9⅞ inches overall with 6-inch barrel. Target sights. Blued finish. One-piece, wood or plastic stocks, checkered. Introduced in 1932.

> **NOTE:** The following Walther pistols are now manufactured by Carl Walther Waffenfabrik, Ulm/Donau, Germany.

Walther Model GSP, 22 LR

**Walther Model GSP
32 S&W Long Wadcutter**

Walther Model GSP Target Automatic Pistol

Calibers: 22 LR, 32 S&W Long Wadcutter. 5-shot magazine. 4.5-inch barrel. 11.8 inches overall. Weights: 44.8 oz., 22 cal.; 49.4 oz., 32 cal. Adj. target sights. Black finish. Walnut thumbrest stocks w/adj. handrest. Made 1969–1994.

22 Long Rifle	$ 995
32 S&W Long Wadcutter	1250
Conversion unit, 22 Short or 22 LR extra	1000

Walther Model OSP

Walther Model OSP Rapid Fire Target Pistol .. $1095

Caliber: 22 Short. 5-shot magazine. 4.5-inch barrel. 11.8 inches overall. Weight: 42.3 oz. Adj. target sights. Black finish. Walnut thumbrest stocks w/adj. handrest. 22 LR conversion unit available (add $275). Made 1968–1994.

Walther Model P4

Walther Model P4 (P38-IV) DA Pistol $425
Similar to P38, except has an uncocking device instead of a manual safety. Caliber: 9mm Luger only. 4.3-inch barrel. 7.9 inches overall. Other general specifications same as for current model P38. Made 1974–1982.

Walther Model P38 (Current)

Walther Model P38K

Walther Model P38 (P1) Double Action Automatic
Postwar commercial version of the P38, has light alloy frame. Calibers: 22 LR, 7.65mm Luger, 9mm Luger. 8-shot magazine. Barrel lengths: 5.1-inch in 22 caliber, 4.9-inch in 7.65mm and 9mm. 8.5 inches overall. Weight: 28.2 oz. Fixed sights. Nonreflective black finish. Checkered plastic stocks. Made 1957–1989. *Note:* The "P1" is W. German Armed Forces official pistol.

22 Long Rifle	**$575**
Other calibers	**445**

Walther Model P38 Deluxe Engraved Pistol
Elaborately engraved. Available in blued, chrome-, silver- or gold-plated finish.

Blued finish	**$1095**
Chrome-plated	**1110**
Silver-plated	**1195**
Gold-plated	**1600**

Walther Model P38K $595
Short-barreled version of current P38, the "K" standing for *kurz* (short). Same general specifications as standard model, except 2.8-inch barrel, 6.3 inches overall, weighs 27.2 oz., front sight is slide mounted. Caliber: 9mm Luger only. Made 1974–1980.

**Walther Model P 88
9mm Double Action**

Walther Model P 88 Double Action Automatic ... $795
Caliber: 9mm Luger. 15-shot magazine. 4-inch barrel. 7.38 inches overall. Weight: 31.5 oz. Blade front sight; adjustable rear. Checkered black composition grip. Ambidextrous decocking levers. Blued finish. Made 1987 to date.

Walther Model P 88 DA Compact $895
Similar to the standard P 88 Model, except with 13-shot magazine. 3.8-inch barrel. 7.1 inches overall. Weight: 29 oz. Blued finish.

Walther Model PP (Current)

Walther Model PP Double Action Automatic Pistol
Calibers: 22 LR, 32 Auto (7.65mm), 380 Auto (9mm Short). 8-shot magazine in 22 and 32, 7-shot in 380. 3.9-inch barrel. 6.7 inches overall. Weight: 32 cal., 23.3 oz. Fixed sights.

Walther Model PP DA (cont.)

Blued finish. Checkered plastic stocks. Made 1963 to date.

22 Long Rifle **$355**
Other calibers **325**

Walther Model PPK/S

Walther Model PP Super

Walther Model PP Super DA Pistol **$425**

Caliber: 9×18mm. 7-shot magazine. 3.6-inch barrel. 6.9 inches overall. Weight: 30 oz. Fixed sights. Blued finish. Checkered plastic stocks. Made 1974–1981.

Walther Model PPK/S DA Auto Pistol (cont.)

6.1 inches. Weight: 23 oz. Other specifications are the same as those of standard PPK, except steel frame only. German-made 1971 to date. U.S. version made by Interarms 1979 to date.

22 Long Rifle **$315**
Other calibers **295**

Walther Models PP, PPK, PPK/S Deluxe Engraved

These elaborately engraved models are available in blued finish, chrome-, silver- or gold-plated.

Blued finish . . . . **$ 875**
Chrome-plated **995**
Silver-plated **1000**
Gold-plated **1145**
Add for 22 Long Rifle **50**

Walther Model PPK (Current)

Walther Model TPH

Walther Model PPK Double Action Automatic Pistol

Steel or dural frame. Calibers: 22 LR, 32 Auto (7.65mm), 380 Auto (9mm Short); latter caliber not available in model with dural frame. 3.3-inch barrel. 6.1 inches overall. Weight (32 caliber): with steel frame, 20.8 oz.; with dural frame, 16.6 oz. Fixed sights. Blued finish. Checkered plastic stocks. German-made 1963 to date; U.S. importation discontinued in 1968. U.S. version made by Interarms since 1986, incl. a stainless-steel model.

22 Long Rifle **$650**
Other calibers **595**

Walther Model PPK/S Double Action Automatic Pistol

Designed to meet the requirements of the U.S. Gun Control Act of 1968, this model has the frame of the PP and the shorter slide and barrel of the PPK. Overall length:

Walther Model TPH DA Pocket Pistol **$325**

Light alloy frame. Calibers: 22 LR, 25 ACP (6.35mm). 6-shot magazine. 2¼-inch barrel. 5⅜ inches overall. Weight: 14 oz. Fixed sights. Blued finish. Checkered plastic stocks. Made 1968 to date. *Note:* Few Walther-made models reached the U.S. because of import restrictions; a U.S.-made version has been mfd. by Interarms since 1986.

NOTE: The following Mark IIs have been made in France since 1950 by Manufacture de Machines du Haut-Rhin (MANURHIN) at Mulhouse-Bourtzwiller. The designation "Mark II" is used here to distinguish between these and the prewar models. Early (1950–54) production bears MANURHIN trademark on slide and grips. Later models are marked "Walther Mark II." U.S. importation discontinued.

Walther Mark II Model PP Auto Pistol $410
Same general specifications as prewar Model PP.

Walther Mark II Model PPK Auto Pistol $475
Same general specifications as prewar Model PPK.

Walther Mark II Model PPK Lightweight $510
Same as standard PPK except has dural receiver. Calibers: 22 LR and 32 Auto.

NOTE: The Walther Olympia Model pistols were manufactured 1952–1963 by Hämmerli AG Jagd-und Sportwaffen-fabrik, Lenzburg, Switzerland, and marketed as "Hämmerli-Walther." See Hämmerli listings for specific data.

Hämmerli-Walther Olympia Model 200 Auto Pistol, 1952 Type $575
Similar to 1936 Walther Olympia Funfkampf Model.

Hämmerli-Walther Olympia Model 200, 1958 Type $595
Hämmerli-Walther Olympia Model 201 . . . . $575
Hämmerli-Walther Olympia Model 202 . . . . $550
Hämmerli-Walther Olympia Model 203
1955 Type $625
1958 Type 625

Hämmerli-Walther Olympia American Model 204
1956 Type $695
1958 Type 650

Hämmerli-Walther Olympia American Model 205
1956 Type $750
1958 Type 675

WARNER PISTOL
Norwich, Connecticut
Warner Arms Corp. (or Davis-Warner Arms Co.)

Warner Infallible*

Warner Infallible Pocket Automatic Pistol $275
Caliber: 32 Automatic. 7-shot magazine. 3-inch barrel. 6½ inches overall. Weight: about 24 oz. Fixed sights. Blued finish. Hard rubber stocks. Made 1917–19.

WEBLEY & SCOTT LTD.
London and Birmingham, England

Webley 9mm M&P

Webley 9mm Military & Police Auto Pistol $795
Caliber: 9mm Browning Long. 8-shot magazine. 8 inches overall. Weight: 32 oz. Fixed sights. Blued finish. Checkered vulcanite stocks. Made 1909–1930.

Webley 25 Hammer

Webley 25 Hammer Model Automatic Pistol $225
Caliber: 25 Automatic. 6-shot magazine. Overall length: 4¾ inches. Weight: 11¾ oz. No sights. Blued finish. Checkered vulcanite stocks. Made 1906–1940.

Webley 25 Hammerless

Webley 25 Hammerless Model Auto Pistol $220
Caliber: 25 Automatic. 6-shot magazine. Overall length: 4¼ inches. Weight: 9¾ oz. Fixed sights. Blued finish. Checkered vulcanite stocks. Made 1909–1940.

Webley Mark I 455 Automatic*

Webley Mark IV 38 M&P

Webley Mark I 455 Automatic Pistol $995
Caliber: 455 Webley Automatic. 7-shot magazine. 5-inch barrel. 8½ inches overall. Weight: about 39 oz. Fixed sights. Blued finish. Checkered vulcanite stocks. Made 1913–1931. Reissued during WWII. Total production about 9,300. *Note:* **Mark I No. 2** is same pistol with adjustable rear sight and modified manual safety.

Webley Mark IV 38 Military & Police Revolver . . $250
Hinged frame. DA. Caliber: 38 S&W. 6-shot cylinder. Barrel lengths: 3-, 4- and 5-inch. 9⅛ inches overall w/5-inch bbl. Weight: 27 oz. w/5-inch bbl. Fixed sights. Blued finish. Checkered stocks. Made 1929–c. 1957.

Webley Mark III

Webley Mark VI No. 1 455

Webley Mark III 38 Military & Police Revolver . . . $275
Hinged frame. DA. Caliber: 38 S&W. 6-shot cylinder. Barrel lengths: 3- and 4-inch. 9½ inches overall w/4-inch bbl. Weight: 21 oz. w/4-inch bbl. Fixed sights. Blued finish. Checkered walnut or vulcanite stocks. Made 1897–1945.

Webley Mark VI No. 1 British Service Revolver . . $275
DA. Hinged frame. Caliber: 455 Webley. 6-shot cylinder. Barrel lengths: 4-, 6- and 7½-inch. 11¼ inches overall w/6-inch bbl. Weight: 38 oz. w/6-inch bbl. Fixed sights. Blued finish. Checkered walnut or vulcanite stocks. Made 1915–1947.

Webley Mark IV 22LR

Webley Mark VI 22

Webley Mark IV 22 Caliber Target Revolver $345
Same frame and general appearance as Mark IV 38. Caliber: 22 LR. 6-shot cylinder. 6-inch barrel. 10⅛ inches overall. Weight: 34 oz. Target sights. Blued finish. Checkered stocks. Discontinued. 1945.

Webley Mark VI 22 Target Revolver $250
Same frame and general appearance as the Mark VI 455. Caliber: 22 LR. 6-shot cylinder. 6-inch barrel. 11¼ inches overall. Weight: 40 oz. Target sights. Blued finish. Checkered walnut or vulcanite stocks. Discontinued 1945.

Webley Metropolitan Police

Webley Metropolitan Police Automatic Pistol ... **$675**
Calibers: 32 Auto, 380 Auto. 8-shot (32) or 7-shot (380) magazine. 3½-inch barrel. 6¼ inches overall. Weight: 20 oz. Fixed sights. Blued finish. Checkered vulcanite stocks. Made 1906–1940 (32); 1908–1920 (380).

Webley RIC Model

Webley RIC Model Revolver **$295**
Royal Irish Constabulary or Bulldog Model. Double action. Solid frame. Caliber: 455 Webley. 5-shot cylinder. 2¼-inch barrel. Weight: 21 oz. Fixed sights. Blued finish. Checkered walnut or vulcanite stocks. Discontinued.

Webley "Semiautomatic" Single Shot Pistol **$225**
Similar in appearance to the Webley Metropolitan Police Automatic, this pistol is "semiautomatic" in the sense that the fired case is extracted and ejected and the hammer cocked as in a blow-back automatic pistol; it is loaded singly and the slide manually operated in loading. Caliber: 22 Long. Barrel lengths: 4½- and 9-inch. 10¾ inches overall w/9-inch bbl. Weight: 24 oz. w/9-inch bbl. Adj. sights. Blued finish. Checkered vulcanite stocks. Made 1911–1927.

Webley Single Shot Target

Webley Single Shot Target Pistol **$250**
Hinged frame. Caliber: 22 LR. 10-inch barrel. 15 inches overall. Weight: 37 oz. Fixed sights on earlier models, current production has adjustable rear sight. Blued finish. Checkered walnut or vulcanite stocks. Made 1909 to date.

Webley-Fosbery Automatic Revolver

Webley-Fosbery Automatic Revolver **$2500**
Hinged frame. Recoil action revolves cylinder and cocks hammer. Caliber: 455 Webley. 6-shot cylinder. 6-inch barrel. 12 inches overall. Weight: 42 oz. Fixed sights. Blued finish. Checkered walnut stocks. Made 1901–1939. *Note:* A few were produced in caliber 38 Colt Auto with an 8-shot cylinder; this is a very rare collector's item.

=== **WESSON FIREARMS CO., INC.** ===
Palmer, Massachusetts
Formerly Dan Wesson Arms, Inc.

Dan Wesson Model 8 Service
Same general specifications as Model 14, except caliber 38 Special. Made 1971–75. Values same as for Model 14.

Dan Wesson Model 8-2 Service
Same general specifications as Model 14-2, except caliber 38 Special. Made 1975 to date. Values same as for Model 14-2.

Dan Wesson Model 9 Target
Same as Model 15, except caliber 38 Special. Made 1971–75. Values same as for Model 15.

Dan Wesson Model 9-2 Target
Same as Model 15-2, except caliber 38 Special. Made 1975 to date. Values same as for Model 15-2.

Dan Wesson Model 9-2H Heavy Barrel
Same as Model 15-2H, except caliber 38 Special. Made 1975 to date. Values same as for Model 15-2H. Discontinued 1983.

Dan Wesson Model 9-2HV Vent-Rib Heavy Barrel
Same as Model 15-2HV, except caliber 38 Special. Made 1975 to date. Values same as for Model 15-2HV.

Dan Wesson Model 9-2V Ventilated Rib
Same as Model 15-2V, except caliber 38 Special. Made 1975 to date. Values same as for Model 15-2H.

Dan Wesson Model 11

Dan Wesson Model 11 Service Double Action Revolver
Caliber: 357 Magnum. 6-shot cylinder. Barrel lengths: 2¹/₂-, 4-, 6-inch; interchangeable barrel assemblies. 9 inches overall w/4-inch bbl. Weight: 38 oz. w/4-inch bbl. Fixed sights. Blued finish. Interchangeable stocks. Made 1970–71. *Note:* The Model 11 has an external barrel nut.

With one barrel assembly and stock	**$175**
Extra barrel assembly	50
Extra stock	25

Dan Wesson Model 12

Dan Wesson Model 12 Target
Same general specifications as Model 11, except has adjustable sights. Made 1970–71.

With one-barrel assembly and stock	**$195**
Extra barrel assembly	50
Extra stock	25

Dan Wesson Model 14

Dan Wesson Model 14 Service Double Action Revolver
Caliber: 357 Magnum. 6-shot cylinder. Barrel lengths: 2¹/₄-, 3³/₄-, 5³/₄-inch; interchangeable barrel assemblies. 9 inches overall w/3³/₄-inch bbl. Weight: 36 oz. w/3³/₄-inch bbl. Fixed sights. Blued or nickel finish. Interchangeable stocks. Made 1971–75. *Note:* Model 14 has recessed barrel nut.

With one-barrel assembly and stock	**$200**
Extra barrel assembly	50
Extra stock	25

Dan Wesson Model 14-2

Dan Wesson Model 14-2 Service DA Revolver
Caliber: 357 Magnum. 6-shot cylinder. Barrel lengths: 2¹/₂-, 4-, 6-, 8-inch; interchangeable barrel assemblies. 9¹/₄ inches overall w/4-inch bbl. Weight: 34 oz. w/4-inch. Fixed sights. Blued finish. Interchangeable stocks. Made 1975 to date. *Note:* Model 14-2 has recessed barrel nut.

W/one-barrel assembly (8″) and stock	**$190**
W/one-barrel assembly (other lengths) and stock . . .	175
Extra barrel assembly, 8″	65
Extra barrel assembly, other lengths	50
Extra stock	25

Dan Wesson Model 15 Target
Same general specifications as Model 14, except has adjustable sights. Made 1971–75.

With one-barrel assembly and stock	**$210**
Extra barrel assembly	50
Extra stock	25

Dan Wesson Model 15

Dan Wesson Model 15-2

Dan Wesson Model 15-2 Target

Same general specifications as Model 14-2, except has adjustable rear sight and interchangeable blade front; also avail. with 10-, 12- and 15-inch barrels. Made 1975 to date.

With one-barrel assembly (8") and stock	**$240**
With one-barrel assembly (10") and stock	245
With one-barrel assembly (12")/stock. Disc.	250
With one-barrel assembly (15")/stock. Disc.	270
With one-barrel assembly (other lengths)/stock	190
Extra barrel assembly (8")	75
Extra barrel assembly (10")	95
Extra barrel assembly (12"). Discontinued.	100
Extra barrel assembly (15"). Discontinued.	115
Extra barrel assembly (other lengths)	50
Extra stock	20

Dan Wesson Model 15-2H
Interchangeable Heavy Barrel Assemblies

Dan Wesson Model 15-2H Heavy Barrel

Same as Model 15-2, except has heavy barrel assembly; weight, with 4-inch barrel, 38 oz. Made 1975–1983.

With one-barrel assembly (8") and stock	**$240**
With one-barrel assembly (10") and stock	245
With one-barrel assembly (12") and stock	265
With one-barrel assembly (15") and stock	295
With one-barrel assembly (other lengths)/stock	250
Extra barrel assembly (8")	80
Extra barrel assembly (10")	100
Extra barrel assembly (12")	110
Extra barrel assembly (15")	125
Extra barrel assembly (other lengths)	60
Extra stock	20

Dan Wesson Model 15-2HV Vent-Rib Heavy Barrel

Same as Model 15-2, except has ventilated-rib heavy barrel assembly; weight, with 4-inch barrel, 37 oz. Made 1975 to date.

With one-barrel assembly (8") and stock	**$265**
With one-barrel assembly (10") and stock	280
With one-barrel assembly (12") and stock	295
With one-barrel assembly (15") and stock	325
With one-barrel assembly (other lengths) and stock	260
Extra barrel assembly (8")	90
Extra barrel assembly (10")	110
Extra barrel assembly (12")	125
Extra barrel assembly (15")	140
Extra barrel assembly (other lengths)	70
Extra stock	20

Dan Wesson Model 15-2V Ventilated Rib

Same as Model 15-2, except has vent-rib barrel assembly, weighs 35 oz. w/4-inch barrel. Made 1975 to date. Values same as for 15-2H.

Dan Wesson Hunter Pacs

Dan Wesson Hunter Pacs are offered in all Magnum calibers and include heavy vent 8-inch shroud barrel revolver, Burris scope mounts, barrel changing tool in a case.

HP22M-V	**$515**
HP22M-2	475
HP722M-V	565
HP722M-2	525
HP32-V	515
HP32-2	455
HP732-V	550
HP732-2	515
HP15-V	515
HP15-2	475
HP715-V	555
HP715-2	515
HP41-V	450
HP741-V	595
HP741-2	515
HP44-V	585
HP44-2	515
HP744-V	645
HP744-2	625
HP40-V	395
HP40-2	565
HP740-V	675
HP740-2	625
HP375-V	375
HP375-2	565
HP45-V	495

WHITNEY FIREARMS COMPANY
Hartford, Connecticut

Whitney Wolvervine*

Whitney Wolverine Automatic Pistol **$325**

Dural frame/shell contains all operating components. Caliber: 22 LR. 10-shot magazine. 4⅝-inch barrel. 9 inches overall. Weight: 23 oz. Patridge-type sights. Blue or nickel finish. Plastic stocks. Made 1955–1962.

WICHITA ARMS
Wichita, Kansas

Wichita Classic Pistol

Caliber: Chambered to order. Bolt-action, single shot. 11¼-inch octagonal barrel. 18 inches overall. Weight: 78 oz. Open micro sights. Custom-grade checkered walnut stock. Blued finish. Made 1980 to date.

Standard	**$2195**
Presentation Grade (engraved)	3595

Wichita Hunter Pistol **$450**
Bolt-action, single shot. Calibers: 22 LR, 22 WRF, 7mm Super Mag., 7-30 Waters, 30-30 Win., 32 H&R Mag., 357 Mag., 357 Super Mag. 10½-inch barrel. 16½ inches overall. Weight: 60 oz. No sights (scope mount only). Stainless-steel finish. Walnut stock. Made 1983 to date.

Wichita International Pistol

Wichita International Pistol **$490**
Top-break, single-shot. SA. Calibers: 7-30 Waters, 7mm Super Mag., 7R (30-30 Win. necked to 7mm), 30-30 Win., 357 Mag., 357 Super Mag., 32 H&R Mag., 22 Mag. RF, 22 LR. 10- and 14-inch barrel (10½" for centerfire calibers). Weight: 50–71 oz. Patridge front sight; adjustable rear. Walnut forend and grips.

Wichita MK-40 Silhouette Pistol **$800**
Calibers: 22-250, 7mm IHMSA, 308 Win. Bolt-action, single shot. 13-inch barrel. 19½ inches overall. Weight: 72 oz. Wichita Multi-Range sight system. Aluminum receiver with blued barrel. Gray fiberthane glass stock. Made 1981 to date.

**Wichita Silhouette Pistol
w/Center Grip**

Wichita Silhouette Pistol **$800**
Calibers: 22-250, 7mm IHMSA, 308 Win. Bolt-action, single shot. 14 15/16-inch barrel. 21 3/8 inches overall. Weight: 72 oz. Wichita Multi-Range sight system. Blued finish. Walnut or gray fiberthane glass stock. Walnut center or rear grip. Made 1979 to date.

WILKINSON ARMS
Parma, Idaho

Wilkinson "Linda" Semiautomatic Pistol **$275**
Caliber: 9mm Luger Parabellum. 31-shot magazine. 8¼-inch barrel. 12¼ inches overall. Weight: 77 oz., empty. Rear peep sight with blade front. Blued finish. Checkered composition stocks.

Wilkinson "Sherry"

Wilkinson "Sherry" Semiautomatic Pistol **$135**
Caliber: 22 LR. 8-shot magazine. 2 1/8-inch barrel. 4 3/8 inches overall. Weight: 9¼ oz., empty. Crossbolt safety. Fixed sights. Blued or blue-gold finish. Checkered composition stocks. Made 1985 to date.

Section II
RIFLES

Action Arms Timber Wolf

Alpha Arms Alaskan

Alpha Arms Custom

ACTION ARMS
Philadelphia, Pennsylvania

Action Arms Timber Wolfe Repeating Rifle
Calibers: 357 Magnum, 38 Special, 44 Magnum. Slide action. Tubular magazine holds 10 (357 Mag./38 Spec.) or 8 shots (44 Mag.). 18½-inch barrel. 36½ inches overall. Weight: 5½ pounds. Fixed blade front sight; adj. rear. Receiver w/integral scope mount. Checkered walnut stock.
Blued Model **$245**
Chrome Model **295**

ALPHA ARMS, INC.
Dallas, Texas

Alpha Alaskan Bolt Action Rifle **$1125**
Same as Custom model, except w/stainless-steel barrel and receiver and all other parts coated with Nitex; sling swivel stud attached to barrel. Left-hand model available. Made 1984–89.

Alpha Custom Bolt Action Rifle **$1025**
Calibers: 17 Rem. thru 338 Win. Mag. Three action lengths w/three-lug locking system and 60-degree bolt rotation. 20- to 24-inch barrel; round or octagonal. Weight: 6 to 7¼ pounds. No sights. Pistol-grip stock of presentation-grade California claro walnut; hand-rubbed oil finish. Custom inletted sling swivel stud attached to forend. Ebony forend tip. Left-hand models avail. Made 1984–89.

Alpha Grand Slam Bolt Action Rifle **$925**
Same as Custom model, except w/Alphawood (fiberglass and wood) classic- style stock featuring Niedner-style grip cap. Weight: 6½ pounds. Left-hand models. Made from 1984 to date.

AMT (ARCADIA MACHINE & TOOL)
Irwindale, California

AMT Lightning

AMT Lightning 25/22 Autoloading Rifle **$175**
Caliber: 22 LR. 25-shot magazine. 18-inch tapered or bull barrel. Weight: 6 pounds. 37 inches overall. Sights: adj. rear; ramp front. Folding stainless-steel stock with matte finish. Made 1984–1994.

AMT Small Game Hunter II

AMT Lightning Small Game Hunter II **$185**
Similar to the Lightning 25/22, except w/conventional black matte fiberglass/nylon stock, 22-inch heavy barrel, no sights, fitted with 4X scope, swivel studs. Weight: 6 pounds. 40½ inches overall. Made from 1987 to date.

AMT Magnum Hunter Auto Rifle **$290**
Similar to the Lightning Small Game Hunter II Model, except chambered in 22 WRF with 22-inch match-grade barrel. Made from 1993 to date.

Anschutz Model 54.18 MS

Anschutz Model 64MS

Anschutz Model 1403B

ANSCHUTZ RIFLES
Ulm, Germany
Mfd. by J.G. Anschutz GmbH Jagd und Sportwaffenfabrik

Anschutz Models 1407 ISU, 1408-ED, 1411, 1413, 1418, 1432, 1433, 1518 and 1533 were marketed in the U.S. by Savage Arms. Further, Anschutz Models 1403, 1416, 1422D, 1441, 1516 and 1522D were sold as Savage/Anschutz with Savage model designations. (See also listings under Savage Arms.) Precision Sales Int'l., Inc. of Westfield, Mass., is now the U.S. distributor for all Anschutz rifles.

Anschutz Model 54.18MS **$895**
Bolt action, single shot. Caliber: 22 LR. 22-inch barrel. European hardwood stock w/cheekpiece. Forend and Wundhammer swell pistol grip stipple checkered. Receiver grooved, drilled and tapped for scope blocks. Weight: 8³/8 pounds. Made 1982 to date.

Anschutz Model 64 MS Bolt Action Single Shot Rifle
Bolt action, single shot. Caliber: 22 LR. 21¹/4-inch barrel. European hardwood silhouette-style stock w/cheekpiece. Forend base and Wundhammer swell pistol grip stipple checkered. Adj. two-stage trigger. Receiver grooved, drilled and tapped for scope blocks. Weight: 8 pounds. Made 1982–1990.
Standard or Featherweight **$520**
Left-hand Model **535**

Anschutz Model 520/61 Semiautomatic **$245**
Caliber: 22 LR. 10-shot magazine. 24-inch barrel. Sights: folding leaf rear; hooded ramp front. Receiver grooved for scope mounting. Rotary-style safety. Monte Carlo stock and beavertail forend, checkered. Weight: 6¹/2 pounds. Imported 1982–83.

Anschutz Model 525 Autoloading Rifle **$355**
Caliber: 22 LR. 10-shot magazine. 24-inch barrel. 43 inches overall. Weight: 6¹/2 pounds. Adj. folding rear sight; hooded ramp front. Checkered European hardwood Monte Carlo style buttstock and beavertail forend. Sling swivel studs. Imported since 1982.

Anschutz Model 1403B **$695**
A lighter weight model designed for Biathlon competition. Caliber: 22 LR. 21¹/2-inch barrel. Adj. two-stage trigger. Adj. grooved wood buttplate, stipple-checkered deep thumbrest flute and straight pistol grip. Weight: about 9 pounds with sights. Made 1982–1992.

Anschutz Model 1403D Match Single Shot Target Rifle
Caliber: 22 LR. 25-inch barrel. 43 inches overall. Weight: 8.6 pounds. No sights, receiver grooved for Anschutz target sights. Walnut finished hardwood target stock w/adj. buttplate. Discontinued 1992.
Standard Model **$505**
W/Match Sights **695**

Anschutz Model 1407

Anschutz Model 1408-ED

Anschutz Model 1411

Anschutz Model 1413

Anschutz Model 1407 ISU Match 54 Rifle $415

Bolt action, single shot. Caliber: 22 LR. 26⁷/₈-inch barrel. Scope bases. Receiver grooved for Anschutz sights. Single-stage adj. trigger. Select walnut target stock w/deep forearm for position shooting, adj. buttplate, hand stop and swivel. Model 1407-L has left-hand stock. Weight: about 10 pounds. Made 1970, discontinued. Value is for rifle less sights; add $65 for Anschutz International sight set.

Anschutz Model 1408-ED Super Running Boar .. $360

Bolt action, single shot. Caliber: 22 LR. 23¹/₂-inch barrel w/sliding weights. No metallic sights. Receiver drilled and tapped for scope bases. Single-stage adj. trigger. Oversize bolt knob. Select walnut stock w/thumbhole, adj. comb and buttplate. Weight: about 9¹/₂ pounds. Introduced 1976; discontinued.

Anschutz Model 1411 Match 54 Rifle

Bolt action, single shot. Caliber: 22 LR. 27¹/₂-inch extra heavy barrel. Scope bases. Receiver grooved for Anschutz

Anschutz Model 1411 Match 54 Rifle (cont.)

sights. Single-stage adj. trigger. Select walnut target stock w/cheekpiece (adj. in 1973 and later production), full pistol grip, beavertail forearm, adj. buttplate, hand stop and swivel. Model 1411-L has left-hand stock. Weight: about 11 pounds. Discontinued.

W/non-adjustable cheekpiece	**$475**
W/adjustable cheekpiece	525
Extra for Anschutz International sight set	125

Anschutz Model 1413 Super Match 54 Rifle

Freestyle international target rifle w/specifications similar to those of Model 1411, except has special stock with thumbhole, adj. pistol grip, adj. cheekpiece in 1973 and later production, adj. hook buttplate, adj. palmrest. Model 1413-L has left-hand stock. Weight: about 15¹/₂ pounds. Discontinued.

W/non-adjustable cheekpiece	**$895**
W/adjustable cheekpiece	925
Extra for Anschutz International sight set	125

Anschutz Model 1416D **$375**
Bolt-action sporter. Caliber: 22 LR. 22½-inch barrel.
Sights: folding leaf rear; hooded ramp front. Receiver
grooved for scope mounting. Select European stock w/
cheekpiece, skip-checkered pistol grip and forearm.
Weight: 6 pounds. Made 1982 to date.

Anschutz Model 1416D Classic/Custom Sporters
Same as Model 1416D, except w/American classic-style
stock (Classic) or modified European-style stock w/Monte
Carlo rollover cheekpiece and schnabel forend (Custom).
Weight: 5½ pounds. (Classic); 6 pounds. (Custom). Made
1986 to date.
Model 1416D Classic **$450**
Model 1416D Classic, "True" Left-Hand **465**
Model 1416D Custom **425**

Anschutz Model 1418 Bolt Action Sporter **$395**
Caliber: 22 LR. 5- or 10-shot magazine. 19¾-inch barrel.
Sights: folding leaf rear; hooded ramp front. Receiver
grooved for scope mounting. Select walnut stock, Mannlicher type, w/cheekpiece, pistol grip and forearm skip
checkered. Weight: 5½ pounds. Intro. 1976; discontinued.

Anschutz Model 1418D Bolt Action Sporter **$545**
Caliber: 22 LR. 5- or 10-shot magazine. 19¾-inch barrel.
European walnut Monte Carlo stock, Mannlicher type,
w/cheekpiece, pistol grip and forend skip-line checkered,
buffalo horn schnabel tip. Weight: 5½ pounds. Made from
1982 to date.

Anschutz Model 1422D Classic/Custom Rifle
Bolt-action sporter. Caliber: 22 LR. 5-shot removable
straight-feed clip magazine. 24-inch barrel. Sights: folding
leaf rear; hooded ramp front. Select European walnut
stock, classic type (Classic); Monte Carlo w/hand-carved
rollover cheekpiece (Custom). Weight: 7¼ lbs. (Classic);
6½ lbs. (Custom). Made 1982–89.
Model 1422D Classic **$550**
Model 1422D Custom **595**

Anschutz Model 1427B Biathlon Rifle **$1095**
Bolt-action clip repeater. Caliber: 22 LR. 21½-inch barrel.
Two-stage trigger w/wing-type safety. Hardwood stock
w/deep fluting, pistol grip and deep forestock with adj.
hand stop rail. Weight: about 9 pounds w/sights. Made
from 1982 to date.

RIFLES

Anschutz Model 1416D

Anschutz Model 1418

Anschutz Model 1422D Classic

Anschutz Model 1427B

Anschutz Model 1430D Match

Anschutz Model 1432 Sporter

Anschutz Model 1432D Classic

Anschutz Model 1433

Anschutz Model 1430D Match **$525**
Improved version of Model 64S. Bolt action, single shot. Caliber: 22 LR. 26-inch medium heavy barrel. Walnut Monte Carlo stock w/cheekpiece, adj. buttplate, deep midstock tapered to forend. Pistol grip and contoured thumb groove w/stipple checkering. Single-stage adj. trigger. Weight: 8³/₈ pounds. Made 1982–83.

Anschutz Model 1432 Bolt Action Sporter **$895**
Caliber: 22 Hornet. 5-shot box magazine. 24-inch barrel. Sights: folding leaf rear; hooded ramp front. Receiver grooved for scope mounting. Select walnut stock w/Monte Carlo comb and cheekpiece, pistol grip and forearm skip checkered. Weight: 6³/₄ pounds. Made 1974–1989.

Anschutz Model 1432D Classic/Custom Rifle
Bolt-action sporter similar to Model 1422D, except chambered for 22 Hornet. 4-shot magazine. 23¹/₂-inch barrel. Weight: 7³/₄ lbs. (Classic); 6¹/₂ lbs. (Custom). Classic stock on Classic model; fancy-grade Monte Carlo w/hand-carved rollover cheekpiece (Custom). Made 1982–89.
Model 1432D Classic **$895**
Model 1432D Custom **920**

Anschutz Model 1433 Bolt Action Sporter **$760**
Caliber: 22 Hornet. 5-shot box magazine. 19³/₄-inch barrel. Sights: folding leaf rear; hooded ramp front. Receiver grooved for scope mounting. Single-stage or double-set trigger. Select walnut Mannlicher stock; cheekpiece, pistol grip and forearm skip checkered. Weight: 6¹/₂ pounds. Made 1976–1986.

Anschutz Model 1449 . . . . **$185**
Bolt-action sporter version of Model 2000. Caliber: 22 LR. 5-shot box magazine. 16¹/₄-inch barrel. Weight: 3¹/₂ pounds. Hooded ramp front sight, adjustable rear. Walnut-finished hardwood stock. Made 1989–1992.

Anschutz Model 1516D Bolt Action Sporter **$460**
Same as Model 1416D, except chambered for 22 Magnum RF. Made from 1982 to date.

Anschutz Model 1516D Classic/Custom Rifle
Same as Model 1516D, except w/American classic-style stock (Classic) or modified European-style stock w/Monte Carlo rollover cheekpiece and schnabel forend (Custom). Weight: 5¹/₂ lbs. (Classic); 6 lbs. (Custom). Made from 1986 to date.
Model 1516D Classic **$520**
Model 1516D Custom **525**

Anschutz Models 1518/1518D Sporting Rifle

Same as Model 1418, except chambered for 22 Magnum RF, 4-shot box magazine. Model 1518 introduced 1976; discontinued. Model 1518D has full Mannlicher-type stock; made from 1982 to date.

Model 1518 . . . . **$515**
Model 1518D **635**

Anschutz Model 1522D Classic/Custom Rifle

Same as Model 1422D, except chambered for 22 Magnum RF, 4-shot magazine. Weight: 6½ pounds (Custom). Classic stock on Classic Model; fancy-grade Monte Carlo stock w/hand-carved rollover cheekpiece (Custom). Made 1982–89.

Model 1522D Classic **$775**
Model 1522D Custom **720**

Anschutz Model 1532D Classic/Custom Rifle

Same as Model 1432D, except chambered for 222 Rem. 3-shot mag. Weight: 6½ lbs. (Custom). Classic stock on Classic Model; fancy-grade Monte Carlo stock w/hand-carved rollover cheekpiece (Custom). Made 1982–89.

Model 1532D Classic **$625**
Model 1532D Custom **795**

Anschutz Model 1533 . . . . **$750**

Same as Model 1433 except chambered for 222 Rem. 3-shot box magazine. Introduced 1976; discontinued.

Anschutz Model 1700 Series Bolt Action Repeater

Match 54 Sporter. Calibers: 22 LR, 22 Magnum, 22 Hornet, 222 Rem. Removable straight-feed clip magazine. 24-inch barrel. 43 inches overall. Weight: 7½ pounds. Folding leaf rear sight; hooded ramp front. Select European walnut stock w/cheekpiece and schnabel forend tip. Made from 1989 to date.

Standard Model 1700 Bavarian—RF calibers . . . **$ 820**
Standard Model 1700 Bavarian—CF calibers . . . **985**
Model 1700D Classic (Classic stock, 6¾ lbs.)
  Rimfire calibers **845**
Model 1700D Classic—Centerfire calibers **975**
Model 1700D Custom (Select walnut stock w/rollover cheekpiece) Rimfire calibers **825**
Model 1700D Custom—Centerfire calibers **995**

Anschutz Model 1700 Series (cont.)

Model 1700D Graphite Custom (McMillian graphite-reinforced stock, 22″ bbl., intro. 1991) . . . . **$ 865**
Model 1700 FWT Featherweight (6½ lbs.)
  Rimfire calibers **885**
Model 1700 FWT—Centerfire calibers **1025**

Anschutz Model 1803D Match Single Shot Target Rifle

Caliber: 22 LR 25½-inch barrel. 43¾ inches overall. Weight: 8½ pounds. No sights, receiver grooved, drilled and tapped for scope mounts. Blonde or walnut-finished hardwood stock with adj. cheekpiece, stippled grip and forend. Left-hand version. Imported 1987–1992.

Right-hand Model **$685**
Left-hand Model **750**

Anschutz Model 1807 ISU Standard Match **$825**

Bolt action, single shot. Caliber: 22 LR. 26-inch barrel. Improved Super Match 54 action. Two-stage match trigger. Removable cheekpiece, adj. buttplate, thumbpiece and forestock w/stipple checkered. Weight: 10 pounds. Imported 1982–88.

Anschutz Model 1808ED Super-Running Target

Bolt action, single shot. Caliber: 22 LR. 23½-inch barrel w/sliding weights. Improved Super Match 54 action. Heavy beavertail forend, adj. cheekpiece and buttplate. Adj. single-stage trigger. Weight: 9¼ pounds. Made from 1982 to date.

Right-Hand Model . . . . **$ 995**
Left-Hand Model **1035**

Anschutz Model 1810 Super Match II **$1295**

A less detailed version of the Super Match 1813 Model. Tapered forend w/deep receiver area. Select European hardwood stock. Weight: about 13½ pounds. Imported 1982–88.

Anschutz Model 1811 Prone Match **$995**

Bolt action, single shot. Caliber: 22 LR. 27¼-inch barrel. Improved Super Match 54 action. Select European hardwood stock w/beavertail forend, adj. cheekpiece, and deep thumb flute. Thumb groove and pistol grip w/stipple checkering. Adj. buttplate. Weight: about 11½ pounds. Imported 1982–88.

RIFLES

Anschutz Model 1700D Custom

Anschutz Model 1808 ED Super

Anschutz Super Match Model 1813

Anschutz Model 1913

Anschutz Model 2007 Special

Anschutz Achiever

Anschutz Model 1813 Super Match **$1250**
Bolt action, single shot. Caliber: 22 LR. 27¼-inch barrel. Improved Super Match 54 action w/light firing pin, one-point adj. trigger. European walnut thumbhole stock, adj. palmrest, forend and pistol grip stipple checkered. Adj. cheekpiece and hook buttplate. Weight: 15¼ pounds. Imported 1982–88.

Anschutz Model 1827 Biathlon Rifle
Bolt action. Caliber: 22 LR. 21½-inch barrel. 42½ inches overall. Weight: 8½ pounds w/sights. 6827 Sight Set w/snow caps; 10-click adj. Slide safety. European walnut stock w/cheekpiece, stippled pistol grip and forearm. Discontinued 1989.
Model 1827B w/Super Match 54 action **$1350**
Model 1827BT w/Fortner straight-pull bolt
  Right-hand **2595**
  Left-hand **2895**

Anschutz Model 1907 International Match Rifle
Same general specifications Model 1913, except w/26-inch barrel. 44½ inches overall. Weight: 11 pounds. Designed for ISU 3-position competition. Fitted w/vented blonde finished stock.
Right-hand Model **$1195**
Left-hand Model **1275**

Anschutz Model 1910 International Super Match Rifle
Same general specifications Model 1913, except w/less-detailed hardwood stock w/tapered forend. Weight: 13½ pounds.
Right-hand Model **$1695**
Left-hand Model **1845**

Anschutz Model 1911 Prone Match Rifle
Same general specifications Model 1913, except w/specialized prone match hardwood stock w/beavertail forend. Weight: 11½ pounds.
Right-hand Model **$1295**
Left-hand Model **1395**

Anschutz Model 1913 Super Match Rifle
Bolt action, single-shot Super Match. Caliber: 22 LR. 27¼-inch barrel. Weight: 15.2 pounds. Adj. two-stage trigger. Vented International thumbhole stock w/adj. cheekpiece, hand and palmrest; fitted w/10-way butthook. Made 1982 to date.
Right-hand Model **$1825**
Left-hand Model **1895**

Anschutz Model 2007 ISU Standard Rifle **$1595**
Bolt action, single shot. Caliber: 22 LR. 19¾-inch barrel. 43½ to 44½ inches overall. Weight: 10.8 pounds. Two-stage trigger. Standard ISU stock w/adj. cheekpiece. Made from 1992 to date.

Anschutz Model 2013 Super Match Rifle **$2595**
Bolt action, single shot. Caliber: 22 LR. 19¾-inch barrel. 43 to 45½ inches overall. Weight: 12½ pounds. Two-stage trigger. International thumbhole stock w/adj. cheekpiece, hand and palmrest; fitted w/10-way butthook. Made from 1992 to date.

Anschutz Achiever Bolt Action Rifle **$240**
Caliber: 22 LR. 5-shot magazine. Mark 2000-type repeating action. 19½-inch barrel. 36¼ inches overall. Weight: 5 pounds. Adj. open rear sight; hooded ramp front. Plain European hardwood target-style stock w/vented forend and adj. buttplate. Imported since 1987.

Anschutz Mark 2000

Anschutz Kadett Bolt Action Repeating Rifle . . . **$190**
Caliber: 22 LR. 5-shot detachable box magazine. 22-inch barrel. 40 inches overall. Weight: 5 1/2 pounds. Adj. folding leaf rear sight; hooded ramp front. Checkered European hardwood stock w/walnut finish. Imported 1987–88.

Anschutz Mark 2000 Match **$275**
Takedown. Bolt action, single shot. Caliber: 22 LR. 26-inch heavy barrel. Walnut stock w/deep-fluted thumb groove, Wundhammer swell pistol grip, beavertail-style forend. Adj. buttplate, single-stage adj. trigger. Weight: 8 1/2 pounds. Imported 1982–89.

ARMALITE INC.
Costa Mesa, California

Armalite AR-7 Custom Rifle **$130**
Same as AR-7 Survival Rifle, except has deluxe walnut stock w/cheekpiece and pistol grip. Weight: 3 1/2 pounds. Made 1964–1970.

Armalite AR-7 Explorer Survival Rifle **$100**
Takedown. Semiautomatic. Caliber: 22 LR. 8-shot box magazine. 16-inch cast aluminum barrel with steel liner. Sights: peep rear; blade front. Brown plastic stock, recessed to stow barrel, action, and magazine. Weight: 2 3/4 pounds. Will float, either stowed or assembled. Made 1959–1973. *Note:* Now manufactured by Charter Arms Corp., Stratford, Conn.

Armalite AR-180 Semiautomatic Rifle **$995**
Commercial version of full automatic AR-18 Combat Rifle. Gas-operated semiautomatic. Caliber: 223 Rem. (5.56mm). 5-, 20-, 30-round magazines. 18 1/4-inch barrel w/flash hider/muzzle brake. Sights: flip-up "L" type rear, adj. for windage; post front, adj. for elevation. Accessory 3× scope and mount (add $60 to value). Folding buttstock of black nylon, rubber buttplate, pistol grip, heat-dissipating fiberglass forend (hand guard), swivels, sling. 38 inches overall, 28 3/4 inches folded. Weight: 6 1/2 pounds. *Note:* Made by Armalite Inc. 1969–1972; manufactured for Armalite by Howa Machinery Ltd., Nagoya, Japan, 1972–73; by Sterling Armament Co. Ltd., Dagenham, Essex, England, 1976 to date.

RIFLES

Armalite AR-7 Explorer

Armalite Custom AR-7

Armalite AR-180

Armi Jager AP-74 Commando

Armi Jager Model AP-74

ARMI JAGER
Turin, Italy

Armi Jager AP-74 Commando **$185**
Similar to standard AP-74, but styled to resemble original
version of Uzi 9mm submachine gun w/wood buttstock;
lacks carrying handle and flash suppressor, has different
type front sight mount and guards, wood stock, pistol grip
and forearm. Made 1976 to date.

Armi Jager AP-74 Semiautomatic Rifle
Styled after U.S. M16 military rifle. Calibers: 22 LR, 32
Auto (pistol cartridge). Detachable clip magazine; capacity: 14 rounds 22 LR, 9 rounds 32 ACP. 20-inch barrel
with flash suppressor. Weight: about 6½ pounds. M16
type sights. Stock, pistol grip and forearm of black plastic,
swivels and sling. Made from 1974 to date.
22 LR **$225**
32 Automatic **250**

Armi Jager AP-74 with Wood Stock
Same as standard AP-74, except has wood stock, pistol
grip and forearm, weighs about 7 pounds.
22 LR **$250**
32 Automatic **285**

ARMSCOR PRECISION
San Mateo, California

Armscor Model 20 Auto Rifle
Caliber: 22 LR. 15-shot magazine. 21-inch barrel. 39¾
inches overall. Weight: 6½ pounds. Sights: hooded front;
adjustable rear. Checkered or plain walnut-finished ma-

Armscor Model 20 Auto Rifle (cont.)
hogany stock. Blued finish. Made 1990 to date.
Model 20 (checkered stock) **$110**
Model 20C (carbine-style stock) **105**
Model 20P (plain stock) **90**

Armscor Model AK22 Auto Rifle
Caliber: 22 LR. 15- or 30-shot magazine. 18½-inch barrel.
36 inches overall. Weight: 7 pounds. Sights: post front;
adjustable rear. Plain mahogany stock. Matte black finish.
Made 1987 to date.
Standard Model **$225**
Folding Stock Model **275**

Armscor Model 1600 Auto Rifle
Caliber: 22 LR. 15-shot magazine. 19½-inch barrel. 38
inches overall. Weight: 6 pounds. Sights: post front; ap-
erture rear. Plain mahogany stock. Matte black finish.
Made 1987 to date.
Standard Model **$150**
Retractable Stock Model **160**

A-SQUARE COMPANY INC.
Bedford, Kentucky

A-Square Caesar Bolt Action Rifle
Calibers: Same as Hannibal, Groups I, II and III. 20- to
26-inch barrel. Weight: 8½ to 11 pounds. Express 3-leaf
rear sight, ramp front. Synthetic or classic Claro oil-finished walnut stock w/flush detachable swivels and Coil-
Check recoil system. Three-way adj. target trigger; 3-po-
sition safety. Right- or left-hand. Made 1984 to date.
Synthetic Stock Model **$2800**
Walnut Stock Model **2550**

A-Square Hannibal Bolt Action Rifle

Calibers: *Group I:* 30-06; *Group II:* 7mm Rem. Mag., 300 Win. Mag., 416 Taylor, 425 Express, 458 Win. Mag.; *Group III:* 300 H&H, 300 Wby. Mag., 8mm Rem. Mag., 340 Wby. Mag., 375 H&H, 375 Wby. Mag., 404 Jeffery, 416 Hoffman, 416 Rem Mag., 450 Ackley, 458 Lott; *Group IV:* 338 A-Square Mag., 375 A-Square Mag., 378 Wby. Mag., 416 Rigby, 416 Wby. Mag., 460 Short Square Mag., 500 A-Square Mag. 20- to 26-inch barrel. Weight: 9 to 11¾ pounds. Express 3-leaf rear sight, ramp front. Classic Claro oil-finished walnut stock, or synthetic stock w/flush detachable swivels and Coil-Check recoil system. Adj. trigger with 2-position safety. Made 1983 to date.
Synthetic Stock Model **$1950**
Walnut Stock Model **1825**

AUSTRIAN MILITARY RIFLES
Steyr, Austria
Manufactured at Steyr Armory

Austrian Model 90 Steyr-Mannlicher Carbine . . . **$140**
Same general specifications as Model 95 Rifle, except has 19½-inch barrel, weighs about 7 pounds.

Austrian Model 95 Rifle

Austrian Model 95 Steyr-Mannlicher Service Rifle
. . . . **$130**
Straight-pull bolt action. Caliber: 8×50R Mannlicher (many of these rifles were altered during World War II to use the 7.9mm German service ammunition). 5-shot Mannlicher-type box magazine. 30-inch barrel. Weight: about 8½ pounds. Sights: blade front; rear adj. for elevation. Military-type full stock.

AUTO-ORDNANCE CORPORATION
West Hurley, New York

Auto-Ordnance Model 22-27A-3 Thompson **$395**
Small-bore version of Deluxe Model 27A-1. Same general specifications, except caliber 22 LR, has lightweight alloy receiver, weighs about 6½ pounds; magazines include 5-, 20-, 30- and 50-shot box types, 80-shot drum. Introduced 1977.

Auto-Ordnance Deluxe Thompson Model 27A-1
. . . . **$995**
Same as Standard Model 27A-1, except has finned barrel w/compensator, adj. rear sight, pistol-grip forestock, weighs about 15 pounds. Made 1976 to date.

Auto-Ordnance Standard Thompson Model 27A-1 Semiauto Carbine
. . . . **$875**
Similar to Thompson submachine gun ("Tommy Gun"), except has no provision for automatic firing. Caliber: 45 Automatic. 20-shot detachable box magazine (5-, 15- and 30-shot box magazines, 39-shot drum also available). 16-inch plain barrel. Weight: about 14 pounds. Sights: aperture rear; blade front. Walnut buttstock, pistol grip and grooved forearm, sling swivels. Made 1976–1986.

BARRETT FIREARMS MFG., INC.
Murfreesboro, Tennessee

Barrett Model 82 A-1 Semiautomatic Rifle **$5095**
Caliber: 50 BMG. 10-shot detachable box magazine. 29-inch recoiling barrel with muzzlebrake. 57 inches overall. Weight: 28½ lbs. Open iron sights and 10x scope. Composition stock with Sorbothane recoil pad and self-leveling bipod. Blued finish. Made 1985 to date.

Barrett Model 90 Bolt Action Rifle **$2995**
Caliber: 50 BMG. 5-shot magazine. 29-inch match barrel. 45 inches overall. Weight: 22 pounds. Composition stock with retractable bipod. Made 1990 to date.

Auto-Ordnance Deluxe Thompson Model 27A-1

Auto-Ordnance Standard Thompson Model 27A-1

RIFLES

BEEMAN PRECISION ARMS, INC.
Santa Rosa, California

Beeman/Weihrauch HW Models 60J and 60J-ST Bolt Action Rifles
Calibers: 22 LR (60J-ST), 222 Rem. (60J). 22 4/5-inch barrel. 41.7 inches overall. Weight: 6 1/2 lbs. Sights: hooded blade front; open adjustable rear. Blued finish. Checkered walnut stock with cheekpiece. Made 1988–1994.
Model 60J **$495**
Model 60J-ST **440**

Beeman/Weihrauch HW Model 60M Small Bore Rifle **$450**
Caliber: 22 LR. Single shot. 26 4/5-inch barrel. 45.7 inches overall. Weight: 10 4/5 lbs. Adjustable trigger with push-button safety. Sights: hooded blade front on ramp, precision aperture rear. Target-style stock with stippled forearm and pistol grip. Blued finish. Made 1988–1994.

Beeman/Weihrauch HW Model 660 Match Rifle . . **$595**
Caliber: 22 LR. 26-inch barrel. 45.3 inches overall. Weight: 10.7 pounds. Adjustable match trigger. Sights: globe front; precision aperture rear. Match-style walnut stock with adjustable cheekpiece and buttplate. Made 1988–1994.

Beeman/Feinwerkbau Model 2600 Target Rifle
Caliber: 22 LR. Single shot. 26.3-inch barrel. 43.7 inches overall. Weight: 10 3/5 lbs. Match trigger with fingertip weight adjustment dial. Sights: globe front; micrometer match aperture rear. Laminated hardwood stock with adjustable cheekpiece. Made 1988–1994.
Standard Model (left-hand) **$1195**
Standard Model (right-hand) **995**
Free Rifle Model (left-hand) **1595**
Free Rifle Model (right-hand) **1450**

BELGIAN MILITARY RIFLES
Mfd. by Fabrique Nationale D'Armes de Guerre, Herstal, Belgium; Fabrique D'Armes de L'Etat, Luttich, Belgium

Hopkins & Allen Arms Co. of Norwich, Conn., as well as contractors in Birmingham, England, also produced these arms during World War I.

Belgian Model 1889 Mauser Military Rifle **$125**
Caliber: 7.65mm Belgian Service (7.65mm Mauser). 5-shot projecting box magazine. 30 3/4-inch barrel w/jacket. Weight: about 8 1/2 pounds. Adj. rear sight, blade front. Straight-grip military stock. This and the carbine version were the principal weapons of the Belgian Army at the start of WWII. Made 1889 to c.1935.

Belgian Model 1916 Mauser Carbine **$180**
Same as Model 1889 Rifle, except has 20 3/4-inch barrel, weighs about 8 pounds and has minor differences in the rear sight graduations, lower band closer to the muzzle and swivel plate found on side of buttstock.

Belgian Model 1935 Mauser Military Rifle **$210**
Same general specifications as F.N. Model 1924; minor differences. Caliber: 7.65mm Belgian Service. Mfd. by Fabrique Nationale D'Armes de Guerre.

Belgian Model 1936 Mauser Military Rifle **$180**
An adaptation of the Model 1889 w/German M/98-type bolt, Belgian M/89 protruding box magazine. Caliber: 7.65mm Belgian Service. Mfd. by Fabrique Nationale D'Armes de Guerre.

BERETTA U.S.A. CORP.
Accokeek, Maryland
Manufactured by Fabbrica D'Armi Pietro Beretta S.p.A. in the Gardone Valtrompia (Brescia), Italy

Beretta 455 SxS Express Double Rifle
Sidelock action with removable sideplates. Calibers: 375 H&H, 458 Win. Mag., 470 NE, 500 NE (3 inches), 416 Rigby. Barrels: 23 1/2 or 25 1/2-inch. Weight: 11 lbs. Double triggers. Sights: blade front; V-notch folding leaf rear. Checkered European walnut forearm and buttstock with recoil pad. Color casehardened receiver with blued barrels. Made 1990 to date.
Model 455 . . . . **$27,000**
Model 455EELL **35,250**

Beretta 500 Bolt Action Sporter
Centerfire bolt-action rifle w/a Sako AI short action. Calibers: 222 Rem., 223 Rem. 5-shot magazine. 23 5/8-inch barrel. Weight: 6 1/2 pounds. No sights. Tapered dovetailed receiver. European walnut stock. Discontinued.
Standard . . . . **$ 475**
DL Model **1095**
Engraved **1175**

Beretta 501 Bolt Action Sporter
Same as Model 500, except w/Sako AII medium action. Calibers: 243 Win., 308 Win. Weight: 7 1/2 pounds. Disc.
Standard . . . . **$ 495**
Standard w/Iron Sights **515**
DL Model **1150**
Engraved **1225**

Beretta 502 Bolt Action Sporter
Same as Model 500, except w/Sako AIII long action. Calibers: 270 Win., 7mm Rem. Mag., 30.06, 375 H&H. Weight: 8 1/2 pounds. Discontinued.
Standard . . . . **$ 530**
DL Model **1200**
Engraved **1325**

Beretta AR-70 Semiautomatic

Beretta AR-70 Semiautomatic Rifle **$995**
Caliber: 223 Rem. (5.56mm). 30-shot magazine. 17 3/4-inch barrel. Weight: 8 1/4 pounds. Sights: rear peep adj. for windage and elevation; blade front. High-impact synthetic buttstock. Made 1984 to date. No longer imported.

Blaser Model R 84 Bolt Action

Beretta Small Bore Sporting Carbine **$240**
Semiautomatic w/bolt handle raised, conventional bolt-action repeater w/handle in lowered position. Caliber: 22 LR. 4-, 8-, or 20-shot magazines. 20½-inch barrel. Sights: 3-leaf folding rear; patridge front. Stock w/checkered pistol grip, sling swivels. Weight: 5½ pounds.

Beretta Express SSO O/U Double Rifle
Sidelock. Calibers: 375 H&H, 458 Win. Mag., 9.3×74R. Barrels: 25½-inch. Weight: 11 pounds. Double triggers. Sights: blade front, V-notch folding leaf rear. Checkered European walnut forearm with recoil pad. Color receiver with blued barrels. Made 1990 to date.
Model SS06 . . . . **$16,200**
Model SS06 Gold **17,000**

BLASER USA, INC.
Fort Worth, Texas

Blaser Model R84 Bolt Action Rifle
Calibers: 22-250, 243, 6mm Rem., 25-06, 270, 280 Rem., 30-06; 257 Wby. Mag., 264 Win. Mag., 7mm Rem Mag., 300 Win. Mag., 300 Wby. Mag., 338 Win. Mag., 375 H&H. Interchangeable barrels w/standard or Magnum bolt assemblies. Barrel length: 23 inches (standard); 24 inches (Magnum). 41 to 42 inches overall. Weight: 7 to 7¼ pounds. No sights. Barrel-mounted scope system. Two-piece Turkish walnut stock w/solid black recoil pad.
Right-hand Model **$1690**
Left-hand Model **1725**
Extra Barrel Assembly **430**

RIFLES

British S.M.L.E. No. 1 Mark III*

British No. 3 Mark I*

BRITISH MILITARY RIFLES
Mfd. at Royal Small Arms Factory, Enfield Lock, Middlesex, England, as well as private contractors

British Army Rifle No. 1 Mark III* **$165**
Short Magazine Lee-Enfield (S.M.L.E.). Bolt action. Caliber: 303 British Service. 10-shot box magazine. 25¼-inch barrel. Weight: about 8¾ pounds. Sights: adjustable rear; blade front w/guards. Two-piece, full-length military stock. *Note:* The earlier Mark III (approved 1907) is virtually the same as the Mark III* (adopted 1918) except for sights and different magazine cut-off that was eliminated on the latter.

British Army Rifle No. 3 Mark I* (Pattern '14) . . . **$170**
Modified Mauser-type bolt action. Except for caliber, 303 British Service, and long-range sights, this rifle is the same as U.S. Model 1917 Enfield. See listing of the latter for general specifications.

British Army Rifle No. 4 Mark I* **$150**
Post-World War I modification of the S.M.L.E. intended to simplify mass production. General specifications same as Rifle No. 1 Mark III* except weighs 9¼ pounds, has aperture rear sight, minor differences in construction.

British Army Light Rifle No. 4 Mark I* **$125**
Modification of the S.M.L.E. Caliber: 303 British Service. 10-shot box magazine. 23-inch barrel. Weight: about 6¾ pounds. Sights: micrometer click rear peep; blade front. One-piece military-type stock w/recoil pad. Made during WWII.

British Army Rifle No. 5 Mark I* **$175**
Jungle Carbine. Modification of the S.M.L.E. similar to Light Rifle No. 4 Mark I* except has 20½-inch barrel w/ flash hider, carbine-type stock. Made during WWII, originally designed for use in the Pacific Theater.

Brno Model II

Brno Model 21H

Brno Model 22F

Brno Hornet

BRNO SPORTING RIFLES
Brno, Czechoslovakia
Manufactured by Ceska Zbrojovka

Brno Model I Bolt Action Sporting Rifle **$475**
Caliber: 22 LR. 5-shot detachable magazine. 22³/₄-inch barrel. Weight: about 6 pounds. Sights: three-leaf open rear; hooded ramp front. Sporting stock w/checkered pistol grip, swivels. Discontinued.

Brno Model II **$495**
Same as Model I except w/deluxe grade stock. Discont.

Brno Model 21H Bolt Action Sporting Rifle **$550**
Mauser-type action. Calibers: 6.5×57mm, 7×57mm, 8×57mm. 5-shot box magazine. 20¹/₂-inch barrel. Double-set trigger. Weight: about 6³/₄ pounds. Sights: two-leaf open rear; hooded ramp front. Half-length sporting stock w/cheekpiece, checkered pistol grip and forearm, swivels. Discontinued.

Brno Model 22F **$795**
Same as Model 21H except has full-length Mannlicher-type stock, weighs about 6 lbs 14 oz. Discontinued.

Brno Hornet Bolt Action Sporting Rifle **$750**
Miniature Mauser action. Caliber: 22 Hornet. 5-shot detachable box magazine. 23-inch barrel. Double set trigger. Weight: about 6¹/₄ pounds. Sights: three-leaf open rear; hooded ramp front. Sporting stock w/checkered pistol grip and forearm, swivels. Discontinued. *Note:* This was also marketed in the U.S. as "Z-B Mauser Varmint Rifle."

Brno ZKB 527 Bolt Action Rifle
Calibers: 22 Hornet, 222 Rem. 223 Rem. 5-shot magazine. 23¹/₂-inch barrel. 42¹/₂ inches overall. Weight: 6³/₄ pounds. Adj. rear sight, hooded ramp front. Grooved receiver. Adj. double-set triggers. Synthetic or walnut stock w/Monte Carlo.
Synthetic Stock Model **$450**
Walnut Stock Model **490**

Brno ZKB 537 Sporter Bolt Action Rifle
Calibers: 270 Win., 308 Win., 30-06. 23¹/₂-inch barrel. 44³/₄ inches overall. Weight: 7¹/₂ pounds. Adj. folding leaf rear sight, hooded ramp front. Shrouded bolt and grooved. Synthetic or checkered walnut stock. Imported 1992.
Synthetic Stock Model **$450**
Walnut Stock Model **500**

Brno ZKB 680 Bolt Action Rifle **$350**
Calibers: 22 Hornet, 222 Rem. 5-shot detachable box magazine. 23¹/₂-inch barrel. Weight: 5³/₄ lbs. Double-set triggers. Adj. open rear sight, hooded ramp front. Walnut stock. No longer imported.

Brno Model ZKK 600

RIFLES

Brno ZKK 600 Bolt Action Rifle
Calibers: 270 Win., 7×57, 7×64, 30-06. 5-shot magazine. 23½-inch-barrel. Weight: 7½ pounds. Adj. folding-leaf rear sight, hooded ramp front. Pistol-grip walnut stock. Imported 1990 to date.
Standard Model **$475**
Deluxe Model **525**

Brno ZKK 601 Bolt Action Rifle
Similar to Model ZKK 600, except w/short action in calibers 223 Rem., 243 Win., 308 Win. 43 inches overall. Weight: 6 lbs. 13 oz. Checkered walnut pistol-grip stock w/Monte Carlo cheekpiece. Imported 1990 to date.
Standard Model **$395**
Deluxe Model **425**

Brno ZKK 602 Bolt Action Rifle
Similar to Model ZKK 600, except w/Magnum action in calibers 300 Win. Mag., 8×68S, 375 H&H, 458 Win. Mag. 25-inch barrel. 45.5 inches overall. Weight: 9¼ pounds. Imported 1990 to date.
Standard Model **$550**
Deluxe Model **625**

Brno ZKM 452 Bolt Action Repeating Rifle **$190**
Caliber: 22 LR. 5- or 10-shot magazine. 25-inch barrel. 43½ inches overall. Weight: 6 pounds. Adj. rear sight, hooded bead front. Checkered oil-finished beechwood stock. Currently imported.

Brown Precision "High Country"

Brown Precision "High Country" Bolt Action Sporter **$850**
Calibers: 243 Win., 25-06, 270 Win., 7mm Rem. Mag., 308 Win., 30-06. 5-shot magazine (except 4-shot in 7mm Magnum). Remington Model 700 action. 22- or 24-inch barrel. No sights. Fiberglass stock w/recoil pad and sling swivels. Weight: about 6½ pounds. Made 1975 to date. Add **$100** for stainless-steel barrel.

BROWN PRECISION COMPANY
Los Molinos, California

Browning 22 Automatic, Grade I

BROWNING RIFLES
Morgan, Utah

Mfd. for Browning by Fabrique Nationale d'Armes de Guerre (now Fabrique Nationale Herstal), Herstal, Belgium; Miroku Firearms Mfg. Co., Tokyo, Japan; Oy Sako Ab, Riihimaki, Finland

Browning 22 Automatic Rifle, Grade I
Similar to discontinued Remington Model 241A. Autoloading. Takedown. Calibers: 22 LR, 22 Short (not inter-

Browning 22 Automatic Rifle, Grade I (cont.)
changeably). Tubular magazine in buttstock holds 11 LR, 16 Short. Barrel lengths: 19¼-inch (22 LR), 22¼-inch (22 Short). Weight: about 4¾ lbs. (22 LR); 5 lbs. (Short). Receiver scroll engraved. Open rear sight, bead front. Checkered pistol-grip buttstock, semibeavertail forearm. Made 1965–1972 by FN; 1972 to date by Miroku. *Note:* Illustrations are of rifles manufactured by FN.
FN manufacture **$340**
Miroku manufacture **250**

Browning 22 Automatic Rifle, Grade II
Same as Grade I, except satin chrome-plated receiver engraved w/small game animal scenes, gold-plated trigger, select walnut stock and forearm. 22 LR only. Made 1972–1984.
FN manufacture **$495**
Miroku manufacture **295**

Browning 22 Automatic, Grade III

Browning 22 Auto
Grade VI

Browning 22 Automatic Rifle, Grade III

Same as Grade I, except satin chrome-plated receiver elaborately hand-carved and engraved w/dog and game-bird scenes, scrolls and leaf clusters: gold-plated trigger, extra-fancy walnut stock and forearm, skip-checkered. 22 LR only. Made 1972–1984.

FN manufacture **$1350**
Miroku manufacture **560**

Browning 22 Automatic, Grade VI **$515**

Same general specifications as standard 22 Automatic, except for engraving, high-grade stock with checkering and glossy finish. Made 1986 to date.

Browning Model 52
Limited Edition

Browning Model 53
Limited Edition

Browning Model 71
Grade I Rifle

Browning Model 52 Bolt Action Rifle **$425**

Limited Edition of the Winchester Model 52C Sporter. Caliber: 22 LR. 5-shot magazine. 24-inch barrel. Weight: 7 pounds. Micro-Motion trigger. No sights. Checkered select walnut stock w/rosewood forend and metal grip cap. Blued finish. Only 5000 made in 1991.

Browning Model 53 Lever Action Rifle **$450**

Limited Edition of the Winchester Model 53. Caliber: 32-20. 7-shot tubular half-magazine. 22-inch barrel. Weight: 6½ pounds. Adj. rear sight, bead front. Select walnut checkered pistol-grip stock w/high-gloss finish. Classic-style forearm. Blued finish. Made in 1991.

Browning Model 65 Grade I Lever Action Rifle . . **$450**

Caliber: 218 Bee. 7-shot tubular half-magazine. 24-inch barrel. Weight: 6¾ pounds. Sights: adj. buckhorn-style rear; hooded bead front. Select walnut pistol-grip stock

Browning Model 65 Grade I Rifle (cont.)

w/high-gloss finish. Semibeavertail forearm. Limited edition made in 1989 only.

Browning Model 65 High Grade Rifle **$795**

Same general specifications as Model 65 Grade I, except w/engraving and gold-plated animals on grayed receiver. Cut-checkering on pistol grip and forearm. Limited edition made in 1989 only.

Browning Model 71 Grade I Carbine **$425**

Same general specifications as Model 71 Grade I Rifle, except carbine has 20-inch round barrel. Disc. 1989.

Browning Model 71 Grade I Lever Action Rifle **$430**

Caliber: 348 Win. 4-shot magazine. 24-inch round barrel. Weight: 8 lbs. 2 oz. Open buckhorn sights. Select walnut straight grip stock with satin finish. Classic-style forearm, flat metal buttplate. Made 1986–89.

**Browning Model 71
High Grade Carbine**

**Browning Model 71
High Grade Rifle**

Browning Model 71 High Grade Carbine **$650**
Same general specifications as Model 71 High Grade Rifle,
except carbine has 20-inch round barrel. Disc. 1989.

Browning Model 71 High Grade Rifle **$675**
Caliber: 348 Win. 4-shot magazine. 24-inch round barrel.
Weight: 8 lbs. 2 oz. Engraved receiver. Open buckhorn
sights. Select walnut checkered pistol-grip stock w/high-
gloss finish. Classic-style forearm, flat metal buttplate.
Made 1987 only.

Browning 78 Bicentennial

Browning 78 Bicentennial Set **$2200**
Special Model 78 45-70 w/same specifications as standard
type, except sides of receiver engraved w/bison and eagle,
scroll engraving on top of receiver, lever, both ends of

Browning 78 Bicentennial Set (cont.)
barrel and buttplate; high-grade walnut stock and forearm.
Accompanied by an engraved hunting knife and stainless-
steel commemorative medallion, all in an alder wood presentation case. Each item in set has matching serial number beginning with "1776" and ending with numbers 1 to
1,000. Edition limited to 1,000 sets. Made in 1976. Value
is for set in new condition.

Browning 78 Single Shot Rifle **$450**
Falling-block lever action similar to Winchester 1885 High
Wall S.S. Calibers: 22-250, 6mm Rem., 243 Win., 25-06,
7mm Rem. Mag., 30-06, 45-70 Govt. 26-inch octagon or
heavy round barrel; 24-inch octagon bull barrel on 45-70
model. Weight: w/octagon barrel, about 7$\frac{3}{4}$ lbs.; w/round
barrel, 8$\frac{1}{2}$ lbs.; 45-70, 8$\frac{3}{4}$ lbs. Furnished without sights,
except 45-70 model has open rear sight, blade front.
Checkered fancy walnut stock and forearm. 45-70 model
has straight-grip stock w/curved buttplate; others have
stock w/Monte Carlo comb and cheekpiece, pistol grip w/
cap, recoil pad. Made 1973–1983 by Miroku.

Browning Model 1885 Single Shot Rifle **$525**
Calibers: 22-250, 270, 7mm Rem. Mag., 45-70 Govt. (223
and 30-06 scheduled for 1988). 28-inch octagonal barrel.
43$\frac{1}{2}$ inches overall. Weight: 8 lbs. 12 oz. Blued receiver.

Browning 78 Single Shot, 45-70

Browning 78 w/Monte Carlo Stock

Browning Model 1885
Single Shot Rifle

Browning Model 1886
Grade I Rifle

Browning Model 1886
High Grade Rifle

Browning Model 1895
High Grade Rifle

Browning Model 1885 Single Shot Rifle (cont.)
Gold-colored adj. trigger. Drilled and tapped for scope mounts, open sights on 45-70 Govt. caliber only. Walnut straight-grip stock and schnabel forearm w/cut checkering and high-gloss finish. Made 1985 to date.

Browning Model 1886 Grade I Lever Action Rifle . . **$595**
Caliber: 45-70 Govt. 8-round magazine. 26-inch octagonal barrel. 45 inches overall. Weight: 9 lbs. 5 oz. Deep blued finish on receiver. Open buckhorn sights. Straight-grip walnut stock. Classic-style forearm. Metal buttplate. Satin finish. Made in 1986 in limited issue 1 of 7,000 by Miroku.

Browning Model 1886 High Grade Lever Action . . **$1095**
Same general specifications as the Model 1886 Grade I, except receiver is grayed steel embellished with scroll; game scenes of elk and American bison engraving. High-gloss stock. Made in 1986 in limited issue 1 of 3,000 by Miroku.

Browning Model 1886 Montana Centennial Rifle **$1100**
Same general specifications as the Model 1886 High Grade Lever Action, except has specially engraved receiver designating Montana Centennial; also different stock design. Made in 1986 in limited issue 1 of 2,000 by Miroku.

Browning Model 1895 Grade I Lever Action Rifle **$495**
Caliber: 30-06, 30-40 Krag. 4-shot magazine. 24-inch round barrel. 42 inches overall. Weight: 8 pounds. French walnut stock and schnabel forend. Sights: rear buckhorn; gold bead on elevated ramp front. Made in 1984 in limited issue 1 of 6,000. The 30-40 Krag caliber made in 1985 in limited issue 1 of 2,000. Mfd. by Miroku.

Browning Model 1895 High Grade Lever Action Rifle **$850**
Same general specifications as Model 1895 Grade I except engraved receiver and Grade III French walnut stock and forend with fine checkering. Made in 1985 in limited issue 1 of 1,000 by Miroku.

Browning Model A-Bolt 22 Rifle
Calibers: 22 LR, 22 Magnum. 5- and 15-shot magazines. 22-inch round barrel. 40¼ inches overall. Weight: 5 lbs. 9 oz. Gold-colored adj. trigger. Laminated walnut stock with checkering. Rosewood forend grip cap; pistol grip. With or without sights. Ramp front and adj. folding leaf rear on open sight model. 22 LR made 1985 to date; 22 Magnum, 1990 to date.
Grade I 22 LR **$250**
Grade I 22 Magnum **285**
Deluxe Grade Gold Medallion **350**

Browning Model A-Bolt Euro-Bolt Rifle **$495**
Same general specifications as Model A-Bolt Hunter Rifle, except has checkered satin-finished walnut stock with continental-style cheekpiece, palm-swell grip and schna-

Browning Model 1895
Grade I Rifle

Browning Model A-Bolt 22
Rifle

Browning Model A-Bolt
Camo Stalker

Browning Model A-Bolt
Stainless Stalker

Browning Model A-Bolt
Pronghorn Antelope Rifle

Browning Model B-92
Lever Action Rifle

Browning Model A-Bolt Euro-Bolt (cont.)
bel forend. Mannlicher-style spoon bolt handle and re-contoured bolt shroud. Calibers: 270, 30-06 and 7mm Mag. only. Weight: 6³/₄ lbs. Made 1993 to date.

Browning Model A-Bolt Hunter Grade Rifle
Calibers: 22 Hornet, 223, 22-250, 243, 257 Roberts, 7mm-08, 308, (short action) 25-06, 270, 280, 30-06, 7mm Rem., 300 Win. Mag., 338 Win. 4-shot magazine (standard), 3-shot (Magnum). 22-inch barrel (standard); 24-inch (Magnum). Weight: 7¹/₂ lbs. (standard), 8¹/₂ lbs. (Magnum). No sights. Classic-style walnut stock. Produced in two action lengths w/nine locking lugs, fluted bolt w/60 degree rotation. Mfd. by Miroku since 1985.

Hunter Model	**$340**
Hunter Model (with sights)	**365**
Hunter Composite Model	**375**

Browning Model A-Bolt Medallion Grade Rifle
Same as Hunter Grade, except w/high-gloss deluxe stock, rosewood grip cap and forend, high-luster blued finish. Also in 375 H&H. w/open sights. Left Hand Models in 270, 30-06, 7mm Rem. Mag.

Big Horn Sheep Ltd. Ed. (600 made 1986, 270 Win.)	**$900**
Gold Medallion Deluxe Grade	**520**
Medallion Model, Standard	**415**
Medallion Model, Left Hand	**425**

Browning Model A-Bolt Medallion Grade (cont.)

Medallion Grade, 375 H&H	**$575**
Micro Medallion Model	**415**
Pronghorn Antelope Ltd. Ed. (500 made 1987, 243 Win.)	**850**

Browning Model A-Bolt Stalker Rifle
Same general specifications as Model A-Bolt Hunter Rifle, except w/checkered graphite-fiberglass composite stock and matte blued or stainless metal. Nonglare matte finish on all exposed metal surfaces. 3 models: Camo Stalker orig. with multi-colored laminated wood stock/matte blued metal; Composite Stalker w/graphite-fiberglass stock/matte blued metal; Stainless Stalker w/composite stock/stainless metal. Made 1987 to date.

Camo Stalker (orig. Laminated Stock)	**$425**
Composite Stalker	**430**
Stainless Stalker	**515**
Stainless Stalker Left-hand	**525**
Stainless Stalker 375 H&H	**600**

Browning Model B-92 Lever Action Rifle **$315**
Calibers: 357 Mag. and 44 Rem. Mag. 11-shot magazine. 20-inch round barrel. 37¹/₂ inches overall. Weight: 5¹/₂ lbs. to 6 lbs. 6 oz. Seasoned French walnut stock w/high-gloss finish. Cloverleaf rear sight; steel post front. Made 1979–1989 by Miroku.

Browning BAR, Grade I

Browning BAR, Grade II

Browning BAR-22

Browning BAR, Grade III

Browning BAR, Grade IV

Browning BAR, Grade V

Browning BAR, Grade II

Same as Grade I, except receiver engraved w/big-game heads (deer and antelope on standard-caliber rifles, ram and grizzly on Magnum-caliber) and scrollwork, higher grade wood. Made 1967–1974 by FN.
Standard calibers $610
Magnum calibers 640

Browning BAR, Grade III $1050

Same as Grade I, except receiver of grayed steel engraved w/big-game heads (deer and antelope on standard-caliber rifles, moose and elk on Magnum-caliber) framed in fine-line scrollwork, gold-plated trigger, stock and forearm of highly figured French walnut, hand-checkered and carved. Made 1971–74 by FN.

Browning BAR, Grade IV $1350

Same as Grade I, except receiver of grayed steel engraved w/full detailed rendition of running deer and antelope on standard-caliber rifles, moose and elk on Magnum-caliber, gold-plated trigger, stock and forearm of highly figured French walnut, hand checkered and carved. Made 1971–1986 by FN.

Browning BAR, Grade V $2600

Same as Grade I, except receiver w/complete big-game scenes executed by a master engraver and inlaid with 18K gold (deer and antelope on standard-caliber rifles, moose and elk on Magnum caliber), gold-plated trigger, stock and forearm of finest French walnut, intricately hand-checkered and carved. Made 1971–74 by FN.

Browning BAR Automatic Rifle, Grade I, Standard Calibers $450

Gas-operated semiautomatic. Calibers: 243 Win., 270 Win., 308 Win., 30-06. 4-round box magazine. 22-inch barrel. Weight: about 7½ pounds. Folding leaf rear sight, hooded ramp front. French walnut stock and forearm, checkered, QD swivels. Made 1967 to date by FN.

Browning BAR, Grade I, Magnum Calibers $595

Same as BAR in standard calibers, except chambered for 7mm Rem. Mag., 300 Win. Mag.; has 3-round box magazine, 24-inch barrel, recoil pad. Weight: about 8½ pounds. Made 1969 to date by FN.

Browning Model BAR Mark II Semiautomatic Rifle

Same general specifications as standard BAR Model, except has redesigned gas and buffer systems, new bolt release lever, removable trigger assembly and engraved receiver. Made 1993 to date.
Standard Calibers $495
Magnum Calibers 550

Browning BAR-22 Automatic Rifle

Semiautomatic. Caliber: 22 LR. Tubular magazine holds 15 rounds. 20¼-inch barrel. Weight: 6¼ pounds. Sights:

RIFLES

Browning BAR-22 (82 Model)

Browning BBR Lightning

Browning BL-22, Grade I

Browning BL-22, Grade II

Browning BLR

Browning BLR (81 Model)

Browning BAR-22 Automatic Rifle (cont.)

folding-leaf rear; gold bead front on ramp. Receiver grooved for scope mounting. French walnut pistol-grip stock and forearm, checkered. Made 1977–1981.
BAR-22, Standard Version **$235**
BAR-22, 1982 Version 6 lbs. (Made 1982–84) **215**

Browning BBR Lightning Bolt Action Rifle **$840**

Bolt-action rifle with short throw bolt of 60 degrees. Calibers: 25-06 Rem., 270 Win., 30-06, 7mm Rem. Mag., 300 Win. Mag. 24-inch barrel. Weight: 8 pounds. Made 1979–1984.

Browning BL-22 Lever Action Repeating Rifle

Short-throw lever action. Caliber: 22 LR, Long, Short. Tubular magazine holds 15 LR, 17 Long, 22 Short. 20-inch barrel. Weight: 5 pounds. Sights: folding leaf rear; bead front. Receiver grooved for scope mounting. Walnut straight-grip stock and forearm, barrel band. Made 1970 to date by Miroku.

Browning BL-22 Lever Action Repeating Rifle (cont.)

Grade I **$180**
Grade II w/Scroll Engraving **220**

Browning BLR Lever Action Repeating Rifle **$325**

Calibers: 243 Win., 308 Win., 358 Win. 4-round detachable box magazine. 20-inch barrel. Weight: about 7 pounds. Sights: windage and elevation adj. open rear; hooded ramp front. Walnut straight-grip stock and forearm, checkered, barrel band, recoil pad. Made 1971 by FN, 1972 to date by Miroku.

Browning BLR Model '81

Redesigned version of the Browning BLR. Calibers: 22-250 Rem., 243 Win., 308 Win., 358 Win; Long Action—270 Win., 7mm Rem. Mag., 30-06. 4-round detachable box magazine. 20-inch barrel. Weight: about 7 pounds. Walnut straight-grip stock and forearm, cut checkering, recoil pad. Made 1982 to date; Long Action introduced 1991.
BLR Model '81 Standard **$350**
BLR Model '81 Long Action **395**

Browning BPR-22

Browning High-Power, Medallion Grade

Browning High-Power, Olympian Grade

Browning High-Power, Safari Grade
Medium Action, Heavy Barrel

Browning High-Power, Safari Grade
Short Action, Heavy Barrel

Browning BPR-22 Pump Rifle **$200**
Hammerless slide-action repeater. Specifications same as
for BAR-22, except also available chambered for 22 Magnum RF; magazine capacity, 11 rounds. Made 1977–1982
by Miroku.

**Browning High-Power Bolt Action Rifle,
Medallion Grade** **$1125**
Same as Safari Grade, except receiver and barrel scroll
engraved, ram's head engraved on floorplate; select walnut
stock w/rosewood forearm tip, grip cap. Made 1961–1974.

**Browning High-Power Bolt Action Rifle,
Olympian Grade** **$2395**
Same as Safari Grade, except barrel engraved; receiver,
trigger guard and floorplate satin chrome-plated and
engraved with game scenes appropriate to caliber; finest
figured walnut stock with rosewood forearm tip and grip
cap, latter with 18K-gold medallion. Made 1961–1974.

**Browning High-Power Bolt Action Rifle,
Safari Grade, Medium Action** **$695**
Same as Standard, except medium action. Calibers: 22/
250, 243 Win., 264 Win. Mag., 284 Win. Mag., 308 Win.
Barrel: 22-inch lightweight barrel; 22/250 and 243 also
available w/24-inch heavy barrel. Weight: 6 lbs. 12 oz. w/
lightweight barrel; 7 lbs. 13 oz. w/heavy barrel. Made 1963–
1974 by Sako.

**Browning High-Power Bolt Action Rifle,
Safari Grade, Short Action** **$710**
Same as Standard, except short action. Calibers: 222 Rem.,
222 Rem. Mag. 22-inch lightweight or 24-inch heavy
barrel. No sights. Weight: 6 lbs. 2 oz. w/lightweight barrel;
7 1/2 lbs. w/heavy barrel. Made 1963–1974 by Sako.

**Browning High-Power Bolt Action Rifle,
Safari Grade, Standard Action** **$895**
Mauser-type action. Calibers: 270 Win., 30-06, 7mm Rem.
Mag., 300 H&H Mag., 300 Win. Mag., 308 Norma Mag.,

Browning High-Power, Safari Grade Standard Action

Browning "T-Bolt" T-1

Browning "T-Bolt" T-2

RIFLES

Browning "T-Bolt" T-1 22 Repeating Rifle $295
Straight-pull bolt action. Caliber: 22 LR. 5-shot clip magazine. 24-inch barrel. Sights: peep rear; blade/ramp front. Plain walnut stock w/pistol grip. Weight: 6 lbs. Also left-hand model. Made 1965–1974 by FN.

Browning "T-Bolt" T-2 . . . . $350
Same as T-1, except fancy-figured walnut stock, checkered. Discontinued 1974.

F.N. Browning Semiautomatic Rifle $2500
Same as F.N. FAL Semiautomatic Rifle. See listing of that rifle for specifications. Sold by Browning for a brief period c. 1960.

Browning High-Power, Safari Grade Standard (cont.)
338 Win. Mag., 375 H&H Mag., 458 Win. Mag. Cartridge capacity: 6 rounds in 270, 30-06; 4 in Magnum calibers. Barrel length: 22 in., 270, 30-06; 24 in., Magnum calibers. Weight: 7 lbs. 2 oz., 270, 30-06; 8¼ lbs., Mag. calibers. Folding leaf rear sight, hooded ramp front. Checkered stock w/pistol grip, Monte Carlo cheekpiece, QD swivels; recoil pad on Magnum models. Made 1959–1974 by FN.

BSA Model 12/15 Martini

=== **BSA GUNS LTD.** ===
Birmingham, England

BSA rifles are no longer imported.

BSA No. 12 Martini Single Shot Target Rifle $295
Caliber: 22 LR. 29-inch barrel. Weight: about 8¾ pounds. Parker-Hale Model 7 rear sight and Model 2 front sight. Straight-grip stock, checkered forearm. *Note:* This model was also available with open sights or with BSA No. 30 and 20 sights. Made before WWII.

BSA Model 12/15 Martini Heavy $325
Same as Standard Model 12/15 except has extra heavy barrel, weighs about 11 pounds.

BSA Model 12/15 Martini Single Shot Target Rifle $330
Caliber: 22 LR. 29-inch barrel. Weight: about 9 pounds. Parker-Hale No. PH-7A rear sight and No. FS-22 front sight. Target stock w/high comb and cheekpiece, beavertail forearm. *Note:* This is a post-WWII model; however, a similar rifle, the BSA-Parker Model 12/15, was produced c. 1938.

BSA No. 13 Martini

BSA Model 15 Martini

BSA CF-2 Stutzen Rifle

BSA CFT Target Rifle

BSA No. 13 Martini Single Shot Target Rifle **$275**
Caliber: 22 LR. Lighter version of the No. 12 w/same general specifications, except has 25-inch barrel, weighs 6½ pounds. Made before WWII.

BSA No. 13 Sporting Rifle
Same as No. 13 Target except fitted w/Parker-Hale "Sportarget" rear sight and bead front sight. Also available in caliber 22 Hornet. Made before WWII.
22 Long Rifle...................................... **$275**
22 Hornet **340**

BSA Model 15 Martini Single Shot Target Rifle .. **$320**
Caliber: 22 LR. 29-inch barrel. Weight: about 9½ pounds. BSA No. 30 rear sight and No. 20 front sight. Target stock w/cheekpiece and pistol grip, long semibeavertail forearm. Made before WWII.

BSA Centurion Model Match Rifle **$450**
Same general specifications as Model 15 except has "Centurion" match barrel, 1½-inch groups at 100 yards guaranteed. Made before WWII.

BSA CF-2 Bolt Action Hunting Rifle **$315**
Mauser-type action. Calibers: 7mm Rem. Mag., 300 Win. Mag. 3-shot magazine. 23.6-inch barrel. Weight: 8 pounds. Sights: adjustable rear; hooded ramp front. Checkered walnut stock w/Monte Carlo comb, rollover cheekpiece, rosewood forend tip, recoil pad, sling swivels. Made 1975–1987. *Note:* Also marketed in the U.S.A. as Ithaca-BSA CF-2. See Ithaca listings for that photo.

BSA CF-2 Stutzen Rifle **$375**
Calibers: 222 Rem., 22/250, 243 Win., 270 Win., 308 Win., 30-06. 4-round capacity (5 in 222 Rem.). 20.6-inch barrel. 41½ inches (approx.) overall length. Weight: 7½ to 8 lbs. Williams front and rear sights. Hand-finished European walnut stock. Monte Carlo cheekpiece and Wundhammer palmswell. Double-set triggers. Discontinued 1987.

BSA CFT Target Rifle **$695**
Single shot, bolt action. Caliber: 7.62mm. 26½-inch barrel. About 47½ inches overall. Weight: 11 pounds, incl. accessories. Barrel and action weight: 6 lbs. 12 oz. Discontinued 1987.

BSA Majestic Deluxe Featherweight Bolt Action Hunting Rifle
Mauser-type action. Calibers: 243 Win., 270 Win., 308 Win., 30-06, 458 Win. Mag. 4-shot magazine. 22-inch barrel with BESA recoil reducer. Weight: 6¼ lbs.; 8¾ lbs. in 458. Folding leaf rear sight, hooded ramp front. Checkered European-style walnut stock w/cheekpiece, pistol grip, schnabel forend, swivels, recoil pad. Made 1959–1965.
458 Win. Mag. caliber **$425**
Other calibers **265**

BSA Majestic Deluxe Standard Weight **$295**
Same as Featherweight Model, except heavier barrel without recoil reducer. Calibers: 22 Hornet, 222 Rem., 243 Win., 7×57mm, 308 Win., 30-06. Weight: 7¼ to 7¾ pounds. Discontinued.

RIFLES

BSA Martini-International ISU Match

BSA Martini-International Mark V

BSA Martini-International MK III

BSA Monarch Deluxe Varmint

BSA Martini-International ISU Match Rifle **$695**
Similar to MK III, but modified to meet International
Shooting Union "Standard Rifle" specifications. 28-inch
standard weight barrel. Weight: 10³/₄ pounds. Redesigned
stock and forearm; latter attached to barrel with "V" section alloy strut. Introduced 1968, discontinued.

BSA Martini-International Mark V Match Rifle . . . **$495**
Same as ISU model, except has heavier barrel. Weight:
12¹/₄ pounds. Introduced 1976, discontinued.

BSA Martini-International Match Rifle
Single Shot Heavy Pattern **$395**
Caliber: 22 LR. 29-inch heavy barrel. Weight: about 14
pounds. Parker-Hale "International" front and rear sights.
Target stock w/full cheekpiece and pistol grip, broad
beavertail forearm, handstop, swivels. Right- or left-hand
models. Mfd. 1950–53.

BSA Martini-International Match Rifle—
Light Pattern **$390**
Same general specifications as Heavy Pattern, except has
26-inch lighter weight barrel. Weight: about 11 pounds.
Discontinued.

BSA Martini-International MK II Match Rifle **$435**
Same general specifications as original model. Heavy and
Light Pattern. Improved trigger mechanism and ejection
system. Redesigned stock and forearm. Made 1953–59.

BSA Martini-International MK III Match Rifle **$495**
Same general specifications as MK II Heavy Pattern.
Longer action frame with I-section alloy strut to which

BSA Martini-International MK III Match Rifle (cont.)
forearm is attached; barrel is fully floating. Redesigned
stock and forearm. Made 1959–1967.

BSA Monarch Deluxe Bolt Action Hunting Rifle . **$325**
Same as Majestic Deluxe Standard Weight Model, except
has redesigned stock of U.S. style with contrasting hardwood forend tip and grip cap. Calibers: 222 Rem., 243
Win., 270 Win., 7mm Rem. Mag., 308 Win., 30-06. 22-
inch barrel. Weight: 7 to 7¹/₄ pounds. Made 1965–1974.

BSA Monarch Deluxe Varmint Rifle **$360**
Same as Monarch Deluxe, except has 24-inch heavy barrel
and weighs 9 pounds. Calibers: 222 Rem., 243 Win.

=== **CALICO LIGHT WEAPONS SYSTEMS** ===
Bakersville, California

Calico Model M-900 Semiautomatic Carbine . . . **$495**
Caliber: 9mm Parabellum. 50- or 100-shot magazine. 16.1-
inch barrel. 28.5 inches overall. Weight: 3.7 pounds. Post
front sight adjustable for windage and elevation, fixed
notch rear. Collapsible steel buttstock and glass-filled
polymer grip. Matte black finish. Made 1989 to date.

Calico Model M-951 Tactical Carbine
Similar to the Model 900, except with long compensator
and adjustable forward grip. Made 1990 to date.
Model 951 . . . . **$495**
Model 951-S **505**

CANADIAN MILITARY RIFLES
Quebec, Canada
Manufactured by Ross Rifle Co.

Canadian Model 1907 Mark II Ross Military Rifle $190
Straight-pull bolt action. Caliber: 303 British. 5-shot box magazine. 28-inch barrel. Weight: about 8½ pounds. Sights: adj. rear; blade front. Military-type full stock. *Note:* The Ross was originally issued as a Canadian service rifle in 1907. There were several variations; it was the official weapon at the start of WWI, but has been obsolete for many years. For Ross sporting rifle, see listing under Ross Rifle Co.

CHARTER ARMS CORPORATION
Stratford, Connecticut

Charter AR-7 Explorer
(Disassembled and Stowed in Stock)

Charter AR-7 Explorer Survival Rifle $135
Same as Armalite AR-7, except has black, instead of brown, "wood grain" plastic stock. See listing of that rifle for specifications. Made 1973–1990.

CHIPMUNK MANUFACTURING INC.
Medford, Oregon

Succeeded by Oregon Arms Co.

Chipmunk Bolt Action Single Shot Rifle
Calibers: 22 LR or 22 WMR. Barrel: 16⅛ inches. Weight: about 2½ pounds. Sights: peep rear; ramp front. Plain American walnut stock. Made 1982 to date.
Standard Model (Discontinued 1987) **$105**
Camouflage Model **125**
Deluxe Grade **150**

CHURCHILL, GUNMAKERS, LTD.
London, England

Churchill Highlander Bolt Action Rifle $360
Calibers: 243 Win., 25-06 Rem., 270 Win., 308 Win., 30-06, 7mm Rem. Mag., 300 Win. Mag. 4-shot magazine (standard); 3-shot (magnum). Barrel length: 22-inch (standard); 24-inch (magnum). 42½ to 44½ inches overall. Weight: 7½ pounds. Adj. rear sight, blade front. Checkered European walnut pistol-grip stock. Imported 1986–1991.

Churchill "One of One Thousand" Rifle $1195
Made for Interarms to commemorate that firm's 20th anniversary. Mauser-type action. Calibers: 270, 7mm Rem. Mag., 308, 30-06, 300 Win. Mag., 375 H&H Mag., 458 Win. Mag. 5-shot magazine (3-shot in Magnum calibers). 24-inch barrel. Weight: about 8 pounds. Classic-style French walnut stock w/cheekpiece, black forend tip, checkered pistol grip and forearm, swivel-mounted recoil pad w/cartridge trap, pistol-grip cap w/trap for extra front sight, barrel-mounted sling swivel. Issue limited to 1,000 rifles. Made in 1973.

Churchill Regent Bolt Action Rifle $410
Calibers: 243 Win., 25-06 Rem., 270 Win., 308 Win., 30-06, 7mm Rem. Mag., 300 Win. Mag. 4-shot magazine. 22-

Churchill Highlander

Churchill "One of One Thousand"

Churchill Regent

Clerke Hi-Wall

Churchill Regent Bolt Action Rifle (cont.)

inch round barrel. 42.5 inches overall. Weight: 7.5 pounds. Ramp front sight w/gold bead; adj. rear. Hand-checkered Monte Carlo-style stock of select European walnut; recoil pad. Made 1986–1990.

CLERKE RECREATION PRODUCTS
Santa Monica, California

Clerke Hi-Wall Single Shot Rifle **$220**
Falling-block lever action similar to Winchester 1885 High Wall S.S. Color casehardened investment-cast receiver. Calibers: 222 Rem., 22-250, 243 Rem., 6mm Rem., 25-06, 270 Win., 7mm Rem. Mag., 30-06, 45-70 Govt. 26-inch medium-weight barrel. Weight: about 8 pounds. Furnished without sights. Checkered walnut pistol-grip stock and schnabel forearm. Made 1972–74.

Clerke Deluxe Hi-Wall **$275**
Same as standard model, except has adj. trigger, half-octagon barrel, select wood, stock w/cheekpiece and recoil pad. Made 1972–74.

COLT INDUSTRIES, FIREARMS DIVISION
Hartford, Connecticut

Colt 22 Lightning Magazine Rifle **$1275**
Slide action. Caliber: 22 Rimfire (Short or Long). Tubular magazine holding 15 long or 16 short. 24-inch barrel, round or octagon. Weight: 5³/₄ pounds (round barrel). Sights: open rear, bead front. Walnut stock and forearm. Avail. in small, medium and large frames. Made 1887–1904.

Colt AR-15 Compact 9mm Carbine **$995**
Semiautomatic. Caliber: 9mm NATO. 20-round detachable magazine. Barrel: 16-inch round. Weight: 6.3 pounds. Adj. rear and front sights. Adj. buttstock. Ribbed round handguard. Made 1985–86.

Colt AR-15 Semiautomatic Sporter
Commercial version of U.S. M16 rifle. Gas-operated. Takedown. Caliber: 223 Rem. (5.56mm). 20-round magazine w/spacer to reduce capacity to 5 rounds. 20-inch barrel w/flash suppressor. Sights: rear peep w/windage adjustment in carrying handle; front adj. for windage. 3× scope and mount optional (add $70 to value). Black molded buttstock of high-impact synthetic material, rubber buttplate. Barrel surrounded by handguards of black fiberglass w/heat-reflecting inner shield. Swivels, black web sling strap. Weight: w/o accessories, 6.3 pounds. Made from

RIFLES

Colt AR-15 9mm Carbine

Colt AR-15 Sporter

Colt AR-15 Adjustable Stock

Colt AR-15 A2 Sporter II

Colt AR-15 Semiautomatic Sporter (cont.)
1964 to date.
Standard Sporter .... **$ 975**
With Adjustable Stock, redesigned forearm **1100**

Colt AR-15 A2 Sporter II **$1095**
Same general specifications as standard AR-15 Sporter except heavier barrel, improved pistol grip, weight of 7½ pounds and optional 3× or 4× scope. Made 1985–89.

Colt AR-15 Sporter Competition HBAR Rifle ... **$1050**
Similar to the AR-15 Sporter Target Model, except with integral Weaver-type mounting system on a flat-top receiver. 20-inch barrel with counter-bored muzzle and 1:9″ rifling twist. Made 1991 to date.

Colt AR-15 Sporter Competition HBAR (RS) Rifle **$1275**
Similar to the AR-15 Sporter Competition HBAR Model, except "Range Selected" for accuracy with 3×9 rubber-clad scope with mount. Carrying handle with iron sights. Made 1992 to date.

Colt AR-15 Sporter Target Rifle **$950**
Caliber: 223 Rem. 5-shot magazine. 20-inch barrel with flash suppressor. 39 inches overall. Weight: 7½ pounds. Black composition stock, grip and handguard. Sights: post

Colt AR-15 Sporter Target Rifle (cont.)
front; adjustable aperture rear. Matte black finish. Made 1993 to date.

Colt Lightning Carbine
Same as Lightning Magazine Rifle, except has 12-shot magazine, 20-inch barrel, weighs 6¼ pounds.
Carbine **$2195**
Baby Carbine (5½ pounds) **2995**

Colt Lightning Magazine Rifle **$1395**
Slide action. Calibers: 32-20, 38-40, 44-40. 15-shot tubular magazine. 26-inch barrel, round or octagon. Weight: 6¾ pounds (round barrel). Sights: open rear; bead or blade front. Walnut stock and forearm. Made 1884–1902.

Colt Stagecoach 22 Autoloader **$255**
Same as Colteer 22 Autoloader, except has engraved receiver, saddle ring, 16½-inch barrel. Weight: 4 lbs. 10 oz. Made 1965–1975.

Colteer 1-22 Single Shot Bolt Action Rifle **$220**
Caliber: 22 LR, Long, Short. 20- or 22-inch barrel. Sights: open rear; ramp front. Pistol-grip stock w/Monte Carlo comb. Weight: about 5 pounds. Made 1957–1967.

Colt Stagecoach

Colteer 1-22

Colteer 22 Autoloader

Coltsman Deluxe

Coltsman 1957 Standard

Coltsman 1961 Custom

Coltsman 1961 Standard

Colteer 22 Autoloader **$230**
Caliber: 22 LR. 15-round tubular magazine. 19³/₈-inch barrel. Sights: open rear; hooded ramp front. Straight-grip stock, Western carbine-style forearm with barrel band. Weight: about 4³/₄ pounds. Made 1964–1975.

Coltsman Custom Bolt Action Sporting Rifle **$385**
FN Mauser action, side safety, engraved floorplate. Calibers: 30-06, 300 H&H Mag. 5-shot box magazine. 24-inch barrel, ramp front sight. Fancy walnut stock, Monte Carlo comb, cheekpiece, pistol grip, checkered, QD swivels. Weight: about 7¹/₄ pounds. Made 1957–1961. Value shown is for rifle, as furnished by manufacturer, w/o rear sight.

Coltsman Deluxe Rifle **$620**
FN Mauser action. Same as Custom model except plain floorplate, plainer wood and checkering. Made 1957–1961. Value shown is for rifle, as furnished by manufacturer, without rear sight.

Coltsman Models of 1957 Rifles
Sako Medium action. Calibers: 243, 308. Weight: about 6³/₄ pounds. Other specifications similar to those of models w/FN actions. Made 1957–1961.

Coltsman Models of 1957 Rifles (cont.)
Custom **$575**
Deluxe **450**
Standard **395**

Coltsman Model of 1961, Custom Rifle **$460**
Sako action. Calibers: 222, 222 Mag., 223, 243, 264, 270, 308, 30-06, 300 H&H. 23-, 24-inch barrel. Sights: folding leaf rear; hooded ramp front. Fancy French walnut stock w/Monte Carlo comb, rosewood forend tip and grip cap, skip checkering, recoil pad, sling swivels. Weight: 6¹/₂ to 7¹/₂ pounds. Made 1963–65.

Coltsman Model of 1961, Standard Rifle **$395**
Same as Custom model, except plainer, American walnut stock. Made 1963–65.

Coltsman Standard Rifle **$395**
FN Mauser action. Same as Deluxe model except stock w/o cheekpiece, barrel length is 22 inches. Made 1957–1961. Value shown is for rifle, as furnished by manufacturer, w/o rear sight.

Colt-Sauer Grand African

Colt-Sauer Grand Alaskan

Colt-Sauer Short Action

Colt-Sauer Standard

NOTE: The following Colt-Sauer rifles are manufactured for Colt by J. P. Sauer & Sohn, Eckernförde, Germany.

Colt-Sauer Drillings
See Colt shotgun listings.

Colt-Sauer Grand African **$1200**
Same specifications as standard model, except caliber 458 Win. Mag., weighs 9½ pounds. Sights: adj. leaf rear; hooded ramp front. Magnum-style stock of Bubinga. Made 1973–1985.

Colt-Sauer Grand Alaskan **$1195**
Same specifications as standard model, except caliber 375 H&H, weighs 8½ pounds. Sights: adj. leaf rear; hooded ramp front. Magnum-style stock of walnut.

Colt-Sauer Magnum **$965**
Same specifications as standard model, except calibers 7mm Rem. Mag., 300 Win. Mag., 300 Weatherby. Weight: 8½ pounds. Made 1973–1985.

Colt-Sauer Short Action **$895**
Same specifications as standard model, except calibers 22-250, 243 Win., 308 Win. Weight: 7½ lbs.; 8¼ lbs. (22-250). Made 1973–1988.

Colt-Sauer Sporting Rifle, Standard Model **$925**
Sauer 80 nonrotating bolt-action. Calibers: 25-06, 270 Win., 30-06. 3-round detachable box magazine. 24-inch barrel. Weight: 7¾ lbs.; 8½ lbs. (25-06). Furnished w/o sights. American walnut stock w/Monte Carlo cheekpiece, checkered pistol grip and forearm, rosewood forend tip and pistol-grip cap, recoil pad. Made 1973–1988.

Commando Mark III

Commando Mark 9

Commando Mark 45

COMMANDO CARBINES
Knoxville, Tennessee
Manufactured by Volunteer Enterprises, Inc.

Commando Mark III Semiautomatic Carbine
Blow-back action, fires from closed bolt. Caliber: 45 ACP. 15- or 30-shot magazine. 16½-inch barrel w/cooling sleeve and muzzle brake. Weight: 8 pounds. Sights: peep rear; blade front. "Tommy Gun" style stock and forearm or grip. Made 1969–1976.
With horizontal forearm **$300**
With vertical foregrip **400**

Commando Mark 9
Same specifications as Mark III and Mark 45, except caliber 9mm Luger. Made 1976–1981.
With horizontal forearm **$350**
With vertical foregrip **360**

Commando Mark 45
Same specifications as Mark III. Has redesigned trigger housing and magazine. 5-, 15-, 30- and 90-shot magazines available. Made 1976 to date.
With horizontal forearm **$375**
With vertical foregrip **400**

CONTINENTAL RIFLES
Manufactured in Belgium for Continental Arms Corp., New York, N.Y.

Continental Double Rifle **$4750**
Calibers: 270, 303 Sav., 30-40, 348 Win., 30-06, 375 H&H, 400 Jeffrey, 465, 470, 475 No. 2, 500, 600. Side-by-side. Anson-Deeley reinforced boxlock action w/triple bolting lever-work. Two triggers. Nonautomatic safety. 24- or 26-inch barrels. Sights: express rear; bead front. Checkered cheekpiece stock and forend. Weight: from 7 pounds, depending on caliber.

CZECHOSLOVAKIAN MILITARY RIFLES
Brno, Czechoslovakia
Manufactured by Ceska Zbrojovka

Czech Model 1924 (VZ24) Mauser Military Rifle . . . **$185**
Basically the same as the German Kar., 98k and F.N. (Belgian Model 1924.) Caliber: 7.9mm Mauser. 5-shot box magazine. 23¼-inch barrel. Weight: about 8½ pounds. Sights: adj. rear; blade front w/guards. Military stock of Belgian-type, full handguard. Mfd. 1924 thru WWII. Many of these rifles were made for export. As produced during the German occupation, this model was known as Gewehr 24t.

Czech Model 1933 (VZ33) Mauser Military Carbine **$220**
Modification of the German M/98 action with smaller receiver ring. Caliber: 7.9mm Mauser. 19¼-inch barrel. Weight: about 7½ pounds. Sights: adj. rear; blade front w/guards. Military-type full stock. Mfd. 1933 thru WWII; a similar model, produced during the German occupation, was designated Gew., 33/40.

Daisy V/L Collector's Kit

Daisy V/L Standard

DAISY RIFLES
Rogers, Arkansas

Daisy V/L rifles carry the first and only commercial caseless cartridge system. These rifles are expected to appreciate considerably in future years. The cartridge, no longer made, is also a collector's item.

Daisy V/L Collector's Kit $295
Presentation-grade rifle w/gold plate inscribed w/owner's name and gun serial number mounted on the stock. Also includes a special gun case, pair of brass gun cradles for wall-hanging, 300 rounds of 22 V/L ammunition and a certificate signed by Daisy president Cass S. Hough. Approx. 1,000 manufactured 1968–69.

Daisy V/L Presentation Grade $265
Same specifications as standard model, except w/walnut stock. Approx. 4,000 manufactured 1968–69.

Daisy V/L Standard Rifle $160
Single shot, under-lever action. Caliber: 22 V/L (caseless cartridge; propellant ignited by jet of hot air). 18-inch barrel. Weight: 5 pounds. Sights: adj. open rear; ramp w/ blade front. Wood-grained Lustran stock (foam-filled). Approx. 19,000 manufactured 1968–69.

DAKOTA ARMS, INC.
Sturgis, South Dakota

Dakota Model 10 Single Shot Rifle $1650
Chambered for most commercially loaded calibers. 23-inch barrel. $39\frac{1}{2}$ inches overall. Weight: $5\frac{1}{2}$ pounds. Top tang safety. No sights. Checkered pistol-grip buttstock and semibeavertail forearm, QD swivels, rubber recoil pad. Made 1992 to date.

Dakota Model 10 Single Shot

Dakota 22 LR Sporter

Dakota Model 76 Classic Grade

Dakota 22 Bolt Action Sporter Rifle **$795**
Calibers: 22 LR, 22 Hornet. 5-shot magazine. 22-inch barrel. Weight: 6½ pounds. Adjustable trigger. Checkered classic-style Clara or English walnut stock w/black recoil pad. Made 1992 to date.

Dakota Model 76 African Bolt Action Rifle **$2625**
Same general specifications as Model 76 Safari. Calibers: 404 Jeffery, 416 Rigby, 416 Dakota, 450 Dakota. 24-inch barrel. Weight: 8 pounds. Checkered select walnut stock w/two crossbolts. Made 1989 to date.

Dakota Model 76 Alpine Bolt Action Rifle **$1450**
Same general specifications as Model 76 Classic, except short action w/blind magazine. Calibers: 22-250, 243, 6mm Rem., 250-3000, 7mm-08, 308. 21-inch barrel. Weight: 7½ pounds. Made 1989 to date.

Dakota Model 76 Classic Bolt Action Rifle **$1550**
Calibers: 257 Roberts, 270 Win., 280 Rem., 30-06, 7mm Rem. Mag., 300 Win. Mag., 338 Win. Mag., 375 H&H Mag., 458 Win. Mag. 21- or 23-inch barrel. Weight: 7½ pounds. Receiver drilled and tapped for sights. Adj. trigger. Classic-style checkered walnut stock w/steel grip cap and solid recoil pad. Right- and left-hand models. Made 1988 to date.

Dakota Model 76 Safari Bolt Action Rifle **$2215**
Calibers: 300 Win. Mag., 338 Win. Mag., 375 H&H Mag., 458 Win. Mag. 23-inch barrel w/barrel band swivel. Weight: 8½ pounds. Ramp front sight; standing leaf rear. Checkered fancy walnut stock w/ebony forend tip and solid recoil pad. Made 1988 to date.

=== **CHARLES DALY RIFLE** ===
Made by Franz Jaeger & Co., Suhl, Germany

Distributed in the U.S. by Outdoor Sports Headquarters, Inc., Dayton, Ohio.

Charles Daly Hammerless Drilling
See listing under Charles Daly shotguns.

Charles Daly Hornet Rifle **$895**
Same as Herold Rifle. See listing of that rifle for specifications. Imported during the 1930s.

=== **DESERT INDUSTRIES, INC.** ===
Las Vegas, Nevada

Desert Industries G-90 Single Shot Rifle **$390**
Falling-block action. Calibers: 22-250, 220 Swift 223, 243, 6mm, 257 Roberts, 25-06, 270 Win., 270 Wby., 280, 7×57, 7mm Rem. Mag., 30-06, 300 Win., 300 Wby., 338 Win. Mag., 375 H&H, 45-70, 458 Win. Mag. 20-, 22-, 24-, or 26-inch barrel in light, medium or heavy configuration. Weight: 7½ lbs. Checkered walnut stock. Blued finish. Made 1990 to date.

=== **EAGLE ARMS INC.** ===
Coal Valley, Illinois

Eagle Arms Model EA-15 Semiautomatic Rifle
Caliber: 223 Rem. (5.56mm). 30-shot magazine. 20-inch barrel. 39 inches overall. Winged post front sight; fully adj. rear. Weight: 7 pounds. Fixed black composition stock w/pistol-grip and barrel-shroud handguard. Black anodized receiver w/E2-style forward-assist mechanism. Made 1989 to date.
EA-15 Standard **$895**
EA-15 E2 H-Bar (20″ heavy barrel, 8¾ lbs.) **950**

Eagle Arms Model EA-15 Carbine
Same general specifications as EA-15 Standard, except w/16-inch barrel and collapsible buttstock. Weight: 5¾ pounds (E1); 6¼ pounds (E2 w/heavy bbl. & NM sights). Made 1989 to date.
E1 Carbine **$925**
E2 Carbine **975**

Eagle Arms Model EA-15 Golden Eagle Match Rifle **$1025**
Same general specifications as EA-15 Standard, except w/E2-style National Match sights. 20-inch Douglas Heavy Match barrel. NM trigger and bolt-carrier group. Weight: 12¾ pounds. Made 1991 to date.

Erma Model EG72

Erma Model EG712

Erma Model EGM1

Erma Model EM1 22

ERMA-WERKE
Dachau, Germany

Erma EG72 Pump Action Repeater **$115**
Visible hammer. Caliber: 22 LR. 15-shot magazine. 18 1/2-inch barrel. Weight: about 5 1/4 pounds. Sights: open rear; hooded ramp front. Receiver grooved for scope mounting. Straight-grip stock, grooved slide handle. Made 1970–76.

Erma Model EG73 . . . . **$190**
Same as Model EG712, except chambered for 22 WMR, has 12-shot tubular magazine, 19.3-inch barrel. Made 1973 to date.

Erma Model EG712 Lever Action Repeating Carbine **$195**
Styled after Winchester Model 94. Caliber: 22 LR, Long, Short. Tubular magazine holds 15 LR, 17 Long, 21 Short. 18 1/2-inch barrel. Weight: about 5 1/2 pounds. Sights: open rear; hooded ramp front. Receiver grooved for scope mounting. Western carbine-style stock and forearm w/ barrel band. Made 1976 to date. *Note:* A similar carbine of Erma manufacture is marketed in the U.S. as Ithaca Model 72 Saddlegun.

Erma Model EGM1 . . . . **$200**
Same as Model EM1, except has unslotted buttstock, ramp front sight, 5-shot magazine standard. Introduced 1970; discontinued.

Erma Model EM1 22 Semiautomatic Carbine . . . **$225**
Styled after U.S. Carbine Cal. 30 M1. Caliber: 22 LR. 10- or 15-round magazine. 18-inch barrel. Weight: about 5 1/2 pounds. Carbine-type sights. Receiver grooved for scope mounting. Military stock and handguard. Introduced 1966; discontinued.

FABRIQUE NATIONALE HERSTAL
Herstal, Belgium
Formerly Fabrique Nationale d'Armes de Guerre

F.N. Models 1924, 1934/30 and 1930 Mauser Military Rifles **$275**
Basically the same as the German Kar. 98k. Straight bolt handle. Calibers: 7mm, 7.65mm and 7.9mm Mauser. 5-shot box magazine. 23 1/2-inch barrel. Weight: about 8 1/2 pounds. Sights: adj. rear; blade front. Military stock of M/98 pattern w/slight modification. Model differences are minor. Also produced in a short carbine model with 17 1/4-inch barrel. *Note:* These rifles were manufactured under contract for Abyssinia, Argentina, Belgium, Bolivia, Brazil, Chile, China, Colombia, Ecuador, Iran, Luxembourg, Mexico, Peru, Turkey, Uruguay and Yugoslavia. Such arms usually bear the coat of arms of the country for which they were made, together with the contractor's name and the date of manufacture. Also sold commercially and exported to all parts of the world.

F.N. Model 1949 Semiautomatic Military Rifle . . . **$450**
Gas-operated. Calibers: 7mm, 7.65mm, 7.92mm, 30M2 (30-06). 10-round box magazine, clip fed or loaded singly. 23.2-inch barrel. Weight: 9½ pounds. Sights: tangent rear; shielded post front. Pistol-grip stock, handguard. *Note:* Adopted in cal. 30 by Belgium in 1949; also by Belgian Congo, Brazil, Colombia, Luxembourg, and Netherlands East Indies; Venezuela bought this rifle in 7mm, Egypt in 7.92mm. Approx. 160,000 were made.

F.N. Model 1950 Mauser Military Rifle **$295**
Same as previous F.N. models of Kar. 98k type, except chambered for 30-06.

F.N. Deluxe Mauser Bolt Action Sporting Rifle . . **$550**
American calibers: 220 Swift, 243 Win., 244 Rem., 250/3000, 257 Roberts, 270 Win., 7mm, 300 Sav., 308 Win., 30-06. *European calibers:* 7×57, 8×57JS, 8×60S, 9.3×62, 9.5×57, 10.75×68mm. 5-shot box magazine. 24-inch barrel. Weight: about 7½ lbs.; in 270, 8¼ lbs. American model is standard w/hooded ramp front sight and Tri-Range rear; Continental model has two-leaf rear. Checkered stock w/cheekpiece, pistol grip, swivels. Made 1947–1963.

F.N. Deluxe Mauser—Presentation Grade **$995**
Same as regular model, except has select grade stock; engraving on receiver, trigger guard, floorplate and barrel breech. Discontinued 1963.

F.N. Supreme Mauser Bolt Action Sporting Rifle . . **$540**
Calibers: 243, 270, 7mm, 308, 30-06. 4-shot magazine in 243 and 308; 5-shot in other calibers. 22-inch barrel in 308; 24-inch in other calibers. Sights: hooded ramp front; Tri-Range peep rear. Checkered stock w/Monte Carlo cheekpiece, pistol grip, swivels. Weight: about 7¾ pounds. Made 1957–1975.

F.N. Supreme Magnum Mauser **$595**
Calibers: 264 Mag., 7mm Mag., 300 Win. Mag. Specifications same as for standard-caliber model except 3-shot magazine capacity.

F.N.-FAL Semiautomatic Rifle **$1695**
Same as the standard FAL military rifle except w/o provision for automatic firing. Gas-operated. Caliber: 7.62mm NATO (.308 Win.). 10- or 20-round box magazine. 25½-inch barrel (including flash hider). Weight: about 9 pounds. Sights: post front; aperture rear. Wood buttstock, pistol grip, forearm/handguard; carrying handle, sling swivels. Made 1950 to date.

RIFLES

FN Model 1949 Semiautomatic Rifle

FN Model 1950 Mauser

FN Deluxe Mauser

FN Supreme Mauser

F.N.-FAL Semiautomatic Rifle

FEATHER INDUSTRIES, INC.
Boulder, Colorado

Feather Model AT-9 Semiautomatic Rifle
Caliber: 9mm Parabellum. 25-shot magazine. 17-inch barrel. 35 inches overall (extended). Hooded post front sight; adj. aperture rear. Weight: 5 pounds. Telescoping wire stock w/composition pistol-grip and barrel-shroud handguard. Matte black finish. Made 1988 to date.
Model AT-9 .... **$410**
Model F-9 (AT-9 w/Fixed Polymer Stock) **450**

Feather Model AT-22
Caliber: 22 LR. 20-shot magazine. 17-inch barrel. 35 inches overall (extended). Hooded post front sight; adj. aperture rear. Weight: 3 1/4 pounds. Telescoping wire stock w/composition pistol-grip and barrel-shroud handguard. Matte black finish.
Model AT-22 .... **$190**
Model F-22 (AT-22 w/Fixed Polymer Stock) **210**

FINNISH LION RIFLES
Jyväskylä, Finland
Manufactured by Valmet Oy, Tourula Works

Finnish Lion Champion Free Rifle **$475**
Bolt action, single shot. Double-set trigger. Caliber: 22 LR. 28 3/4-inch heavy barrel. Weight: about 16 pounds.

Finnish Lion Champion Free Rifle (cont.)
Sights: extension rear peep; aperture front. Walnut free-rifle stock w/full pistol grip, thumbhole, beavertail forearm, hook buttplate, palmrest, hand stop, swivel. Made 1965–1972.

Finnish Lion Standard ISU Target Rifle **$295**
Bolt action, single shot. Caliber: 22 LR. 27 1/2-inch barrel. Weight: about 10 1/2 pounds. Sights: extension rear peep; aperture front. Walnut target stock w/full pistol grip, checkered beavertail forearm, adj. buttplate, sling swivel. Made 1966–1977.

Finnish Lion Match Rifle **$410**
Bolt action, single shot. Caliber: 22 LR. 28 3/4-inch heavy barrel. Weight: about 14 1/2 pounds. Sights: extension rear peep; aperture front. Walnut free-rifle stock w/full pistol grip, thumbhole, beavertail forearm, hook buttplate, palmrest, hand stop, swivel. Made 1937–1972.

Finnish Lion Standard Target Rifle
Bolt action. Single shot. Caliber: 22 LR. 27 1/2-inch barrel. 44 1/2 inches overall. Weight: 10 1/2 pounds. No sights; micrometer rear and globe front International-style sights available. Select walnut stock in target configuration. Currently in production.
Standard Model **$650**
Thumbhole Stock Model **695**

Finnish Lion Match

Finnish Lion Champion

Finnish Lion Standard

Franchi Deluxe Centennial

French Model 1936 MAS

LUIGI FRANCHI, S.P.A.
Brescia, Italy

Franchi Centennial Automatic Rifle
Commemorates Franchi's 100th anniversary (1868–1968). Centennial seal engraved on receiver. Semiautomatic. Takedown. Caliber: 22 LR. 11-shot magazine in buttstock. 21-inch barrel. Weight: 5 1/8 pounds. Sights: open rear; goldbead front, on ramp. Checkered walnut stock and forend. Deluxe model has fully engraved receiver, premium grade wood. Made 1968.
Standard Model **$260**
Deluxe Model **325**

FRENCH MILITARY RIFLE
Saint Etienne, France

French Model 1936 MAS Military Rifle **$100**
Bolt action. Caliber: 7.5mm MAS. 5-shot box magazine. 22 1/2-inch barrel. Weight: about 8 1/4 pounds. Sights: adj.

French Model 1936 MAS Military Rifle (cont.)
rear; blade front. Two-piece military-type stock. Bayonet carried in forend tube. Made 1936–1940 by Manufacture Francaise d'Armes et de Cycles de St. Etienne (MAS).

GALIL RIFLES
Manufactured by Israel Military Industries, Israel

Galil AR Semiautomatic Rifle
Calibers: 308 Win. (7.62 NATO), 223 Rem. (5.56mm). 25-shot (308) or 35-shot (223) magazine. 16-inch (223) or 18 1/2-inch (308) barrel w/flash suppressor. Weight: 9 1/2 pounds. Folding aperture rear sight, post front. Folding metal stock w/carrying handle. Imported early 1980s.
Model 223 AR **$1295**
Model 308 AR **1350**

Galil Sporter Semiautomatic Rifle **$995**
Same general specifications as AR Model, except w/hardwood thumbhole stock and 5-shot magazine. Weight: 8 1/2 pounds. Made 1991 to date.

Galil Model 223 AR Semiauto Rifle

Garcia Bronco 22

GARCIA CORPORATION
Teaneck, New Jersey

Garcia Bronco 22 Single Shot Rifle **$85**
Swing-out action. Takedown. Caliber: 22 LR, Long, Short. 16 1/2-inch barrel. Weight: 3 pounds. Sights: open rear; blade front. One-piece stock and receiver, crackle finish. Introduced 1967; discontinued.

GERMAN MILITARY RIFLES
Mfd. by Ludwig Loewe & Co., Berlin, other contractors and by German arsenals and various plants under German Government control.

German Model 24T (Gew. 24T) Mauser Rifle . . **$295**
Same general specifications as the Czech Model 24 (VZ24) Mauser Rifle w/minor modifications, has laminated wood stock. Weight: about 9 1/4 pounds. Made in Czechoslovakia during German occupation; adopted 1940.

German Model 29/40 (Gew. 29/40) Mauser Rifle . . **$195**
Same general specifications as Kar. 98K, with minor differences. Made in Poland during German occupation; adopted 1940.

German Model 33/40 (Gew. 33/40) Mauser Rifle . . **$550**
Same general specifications as the Czech Model 33 (VZ33) Mauser Carbine with minor modifications, has laminated wood stock as found in war-time Model 98K carbines. Made in Czechoslovakia during German occupation; adopted 1940.

German Models 41 and 41-W (Gew. 41, Gew. 41-W) Semiautomatic Military Rifles **$1125**
Gas-operated, muzzle cone system. Caliber: 7.9mm Mauser. 10-shot box magazine. 22 1/2-inch barrel. Weight: about 10 3/4 pounds. Sights: adj. leaf rear; blade front.

German Models 41 and 41-W (cont.)
Military-type stock w/semi-pistol grip, plastic handguard. *Note:* Model 41 lacks bolt release found on Model 41-W; otherwise, the models are the same. A Walther design, these early models were mfd. in that firm's Zella-Mehlis plant. Made c.1941–43.

German Model 43 (Gew. 43, Kar. 43) Semiauto Military Rifles **$900**
Gas-operated, barrel vented as in Russian Tokarev. Caliber: 7.9mm Mauser. 10-shot detachable box magazine. 22- or 24-inch barrel. Weight: about 9 pounds. Sights: adj. rear; hooded front. Military-type stock w/semipistol grip, wooden handguard. *Note:* These rifles are alike except for minor details, have characteristic late WWII mfg. short cuts: cast receiver and bolt cover, stamped steel parts, etc. Gew. 43 may have either 22- or 24-inch barrel; the former length was standardized in late 1944, when weapon designation was changed to "Kar. 43." Made 1943–45.

German Model 1888 (Gew. 88) Mauser-Mannlicher Service Rifle **$165**
Bolt action, straight handle. Caliber: 7.9mm Mauser (8×57mm). 5-shot Mannlicher box magazine. 29-inch barrel with jacket. Weight: about 8 1/2 pounds. Fixed front sight, adjustable rear. Military-type full stock. Mfd. by Ludwig Loewe & Co., Haenel, Schilling and other contractors.

German Kar. 88

German Model 1888 (Kar. 88) Mauser-Mannlicher Carbine **$165**
Same general specifications as Gew. 88, except w/18-inch barrel, w/o jacket, flat turned-down bolt handle, weighs about 6 3/4 pounds. Mfd. by Ludwig Loewe & Co., Haenel, Schilling and other contractors.

German Gew. 33/40

German Gew. 43

German Gew. 98

German Kar. 98K

German Model 1898 (Gew. 98) Mauser Military Rifle $225
Bolt action, straight handle. Caliber: 7.9mm Mauser (8×57mm). 5-shot box magazine. 29-inch steeped barrel. Weight: 9 pounds. Sights: blade front; adj. rear. Military-type full stock w/rounded bottom pistol grip. Adopted 1898.

> **NOTE:** German Mauser Military Rifles (Gew. 98, Kar. 98) were made before and during WWI at the government arsenals at Amberg, Brunn, Danzig, Erfurt and Spandau; they were also manufactured by contractors such as Haenel, Loewe, Mauser, Schilling and Steyr. These rifles bear the Imperial Crown, maker's name and date of manufacture on the receiver ring. Post-WWI Kar. 98B bears maker's name and date. During WWII as well as the years immediately before (probably from c. 1935), a letter or number code was used to indicate maker. This code and date of manufacture will be found stamped on the receiver ring of rifles of this period. German Service Mausers also bear the model number (Gew. 98, Kar. 98K, G. 33/40, etc.) on the left side of the receiver. An exception is Model VK98, which usually bears no identifying marks. Gew. is abbreviation for *gewehr* (rifle), Kar. for *karabiner* (carbine).

German Model 1898A (Kar. 98A) Mauser Carbine $235
Same general specifications as Model 1898 (Gew. 98) Rifle, except has turned-down bolt handle, smaller receiver ring, light 23½-inch straight taper barrel, front sight guards, sling is attached to left side of stock, weighs 8 pounds. *Note:* Some of these carbines are marked "Kar. 98"; the true Kar. 98 is the earlier original M/98 carbine with 17-inch barrel and is rarely encountered.

German Model 1898B (Kar. 98B) Mauser Carbine $245
Same general specifications as Model 1898 (Gew. 98) Rifle, except has turned-down bolt handle and sling attached to left side of stock. This is post-WWI model.

German Model 1898K (Kar. 98K) Mauser Carbine $230
Same general specifications as Model 1898 (Gew. 98) Rifle, except has turned-down bolt handle, 23½-inch barrel, may have hooded front sight, sling is attached to left side of stock, weighs about 8½ pounds. Adopted in 1935, this was the standard German Service rifle of WWII. *Note:* Late-war models had stamped sheet steel trigger guards and many of the Model 98K carbines made during WWII had laminated wood stocks; these weigh about ½ to ¾ pound more than the previous Model 98K. Value shown is for earlier type.

German Model VK 98 People's Rifle ("Volksgewehr") $150
Kar. 98K-type action. Caliber: 7.9mm. Single shot or repeater (latter w/rough hole-in-the-stock 5-shot "magazine" or fitted w/10-shot clip of German Model 43 semiauto rifle). 20.9-inch barrel. Weight: 7 pounds. Fixed V-notch rear sight dovetailed into front receiver ring; front blade welded to barrel. Crude, unfinished, half-length stock w/o buttplate. Last ditch weapon made in 1945 for issue to German civilians. *Note:* Of value only as a military arms collector's item, this hastily made rifle should be regarded as *unsafe* to shoot.

═══ GÉVARM RIFLE ═══
Saint Etienne, France
Manufactured by Gévelot

Gévarm E-1 Autoloading Rifle $160
Caliber: 22 LR. 8-shot clip magazine. 19½-inch barrel. Sights: open rear; post front. Pistol-grip stock and forearm of French walnut.

Gévarm E-1

Golden Eagle Model 7000

GOLDEN EAGLE RIFLES
Houston, Texas
Mfd. by Nikko Firearms Ltd., Tochigi, Japan

Golden Eagle Model 7000 Grade I African **$550**
Same as standard model, except calibers 375 H&H Mag.
and 458 Win. Mag., 2-shot magazine in 458, weighs 8³/₄
lbs. in 375 and 10¹/₂ lbs. in 458, furnished with sights.
Introduced 1976; discontinued.

Golden Eagle Model 7000 Grade I Big Game . . . **$495**
Bolt action. Calibers: 22-250, 243 Win., 25-06, 270 Win.,
270 Weatherby Mag., 7mm Rem. Mag., 30-06, 300 Weath.
Mag., 300 Win. Mag., 338 Win. Mag. Magazine capacity:
4 rounds in 22-250, 3 rounds in other calibers. 24- or 26-
inch barrel (26-inch only in 338). Weight: 7 lbs., 22-250;
8³/₄ lbs., other calibers. Furnished w/o sights. Fancy
American walnut stock, skip checkered, contrasting wood
forend tip and grip cap w/gold eagle head, recoil pad. Introduced 1976; discontinued.

GREIFELT & CO.
Suhl, Germany

Greifelt Sport Model 22 Hornet Bolt Action Rifle . **$1150**
Caliber: 22 Hornet. 5-shot box magazine. 22-inch Krupp
steel barrel. Weight: 6 pounds. Sights: two-leaf rear; ramp
front. Walnut stock, checkered pistol grip and forearm. Made
before WWII.

CARL GUSTAF RIFLES
Eskilstuna, Sweden
Mfd. by Carl Gustafs Stads Gevärsfaktori

Carl Gustaf Model 2000 Bolt Action Rifle
Calibers: 243, 6.5×55, 7×64, 270, 308 Win., 30-06, 7mm
Rem. Mag., 300 Win. Mag. 3-shot magazine. 24-inch barrel. 44 inches overall. Weight: 7¹/₂ pounds. Receiver drilled
and tapped. Hooded ramp front sight; open rear. Adj. trigger. Checkered European walnut stock w/Monte Carlo
cheekpiece and Wundhammer palmswell grip. Made 1991
to date.
Model 2000 w/o Sights **$1250**
Model 2000 with Sights **1295**

Carl Gustaf Deluxe **$550**
Same specifications as Monte Carlo Standard. Calibers:
6.5×55, 308 Win., 30-06, 9.3×62. 4-shot magazine in
9.3×62. Jeweled bolt. Engraved floorplate and trigger
guard. Deluxe French walnut stock w/rosewood forend
tip. Made 1970–77.

Carl Gustaf Grand Prix Single Shot Target Rifle . . **$475**
Special bolt action with "world's shortest lock time." Single-
stage trigger adjusts down to 18 oz. Caliber: 22 LR. 26³/₄-
inch heavy barrel w/adj. trim weight. Weight: 9³/₄ lbs. Furnished w/o sights. Target-type Monte Carlo stock of French
walnut, adj. cork buttplate. Made 1970 to date.

Carl Gustaf Model 2000

Carl Gustaf Deluxe

Carl Gustaf Grand Prix

Carl Gustaf Monte Carlo Standard

Carl Gustaf Special

Carl Gustaf Sporter

Carl Gustaf Trofé

Carl Gustaf Monte Carlo Standard Bolt Action Sporting Rifle $350
Carl Gustaf 1900 action. Calibers: 6.5×55, 7×64, 270 Win., 7mm Rem. Mag., 308 Win., 30-06, 9.3×62. 5-shot magazine, except 4-shot in 9.3×62 and 3-shot in 7mm Rem. Mag. 23½-inch barrel. Weight: about 7 pounds. Sights: folding leaf rear; hooded ramp front. French walnut Monte Carlo stock w/cheekpiece, checkered forearm and pistol grip, sling swivels. Also available in left-hand model. Made 1970–77.

Carl Gustaf Special $395
Also designated "Grade II" in U.S. and "Model 9000" in Canada. Same specifications as Monte Carlo Standard. Calibers: 22-250, 243 Win., 25-06, 270 Win., 7mm Rem. Mag., 308 Win., 30-06, 300 Win. Mag. 3-shot magazine in Magnum calibers. Select wood stock w/rosewood forend tip. Left-hand model avail. Made 1970–77.

Carl Gustaf Sporter $475
Also designated "Varmint-Target" in U.S. Fast bolt action with large bakelite bolt knob. Trigger pull adjusts down to 18 oz. Calibers: 222 Rem., 22-250, 243 Win., 6.5×55. 5-shot magazine, except 6-shot in 222 Rem. 26¾-inch heavy barrel. Weight: about 9½ pounds. Furnished w/o sights. Target-type Monte Carlo stock of French walnut. Made 1970 to date.

Carl Gustaf Standard $425
Same specifications as Monte Carlo Standard. Calibers: 6.5×55, 7×64, 270 Win., 308 Win., 30-06, 9.3×62. Classic-style stock w/o Monte Carlo. Made 1970–77.

Carl Gustaf Trofé $595
Also designated "Grade III" in U.S. and "Model 8000" in Canada. Same specifications as Monte Carlo Standard. Calibers: 22-250, 25-06, 6.5×55, 270 Win., 7mm Rem. Mag., 308 Win., 30-06, 300 Win. Mag. 3-shot magazine in Magnum calibers. Furnished w/o sights. Fancy wood stock w/rosewood forend tip, high-gloss lacquer finish. Made 1970–77.

C.G. HAENEL
Suhl, Germany

Haenel '88 Mauser Sporter $395
Same general specifications as Haenel Mauser-Mann-licher, except has Mauser 5-shot box magazine.

Haenel Mauser-Mannlicher Bolt Action Sporting Rifle $365
Mauser M/88-type action. Calibers: 7×57, 8×57, 9×57mm. Mannlicher clip-loading box magazine, 5-shot. 22- or 24-inch half or full octagon barrel with raised matted rib. Double-set trigger. Weight: 7½ pounds. Sights: leaf-type open rear; ramp front. Sporting stock w/cheekpiece, checkered pistol grip, raised side-panels, schnabel tip, swivels.

Hämmerli Model 45

Hämmerli Model 503

Hämmerli Model 506

Hämmerli Olympia

HÄMMERLI AG JAGD-UND SPORTWAFFENFABRIK
Lenzburg, Switzerland

Hämmerli Model 45 Smallbore Bolt Action Single Shot Match Rifle **$495**
Calibers: 22 LR, 22 Extra Long. 27½-inch heavy barrel. Weight: about 15½ pounds. Sights: micrometer peep rear; globe front. Free-rifle stock w/cheekpiece, full pistol grip, thumbhole, beavertail forearm, palmrest, Swiss-type buttplate, swivels. Made 1945–1957.

Hämmerli Model 54 Smallbore Match Rifle **$475**
Bolt action, single shot. Caliber: 22 LR. 27½-inch heavy barrel. Weight: about 15 pounds. Sights: micrometer peep rear; globe front. Free- rifle stock w/cheekpiece, thumbhole, adj. hook buttplate, palmrest, swivel. Made 1954–57.

Hämmerli Model 503 Free Rifle **$460**
Bolt action, single shot. Caliber: 22 LR. 27½-inch heavy barrel. Weight: about 15½ pounds. Sights: micrometer peep

Hämmerli Model 503 Free Rifle (cont.)
rear; globe front. Free-rifle stock w/cheekpiece, thumbhole, adj. hook buttplate, palmrest, swivel. Made 1957–1962.

Hämmerli Model 506 Smallbore Match Rifle **$495**
Bolt action, single shot. Caliber: 22 LR. 26¾-inch heavy barrel. Weight: about 16½ pounds. Sights: micrometer peep rear; globe front. Free-rifle stock w/cheekpiece, thumbhole, adj. hook buttplate, palmrest, swivel. Made 1963–66.

Hämmerli Model Olympia 300 Meter Bolt Action Single Shot Free Rifle **$625**
Calibers: 30-06, 300 H&H Magnum for U.S.A.; ordinarily produced in 7.5mm, other calibers available on special order. 29½-inch heavy barrel. Double-pull or double-set trigger. Sights: micrometer peep rear; globe front. Free-rifle stock w/cheekpiece, full pistol grip, thumbhole, beavertail for-end, palmrest, Swiss-type buttplate, swivels. Made 1945–1959.

Hämmerli-Tanner 300M

Hämmerli-Tanner 300 Meter Free Rifle **$795**
Bolt action, single shot. Caliber: 7.5mm standard, available
in most popular centerfire calibers. 29½-inch heavy barrel.
Weight: about 16¾ pounds. Sights: micrometer peep rear;
globe front. Free-rifle stock w/cheekpiece, thumbhole, adj.
hook buttplate, palmrest, swivel. Introduced 1962; disc.

HARRINGTON & RICHARDSON, INC.
Gardner, Massachusetts
(Now H&R 1871, INC., Gardner, Mass.)

Formerly Harrington & Richardson Arms Co. of Worcester,
Mass. After a long and distinguished career in gunmaking
this firm suspended operation in 1986. However, in 1992,
the firm was bought by New England Firearms of Gardner,
Mass. Some models are mfd. under that banner as well as
H&R 1871, Inc.

**Harrington & Richardson Model 60 Reising
Semiautomatic Rifle** **$350**
Caliber: 45 Automatic. 12- and 20-shot detachable box
magazines. 18¼-inch barrel. Weight: about 7½ pounds.
Sights: open rear; blade front. Plain pistol-grip stock.
Made 1944–46.

**Harrington & Richardson Model 65 Military
Autoloading Rifle** **$250**
Also called "General." Caliber: 22 LR. 10-shot detachable
box magazine. 23-inch heavy barrel. Weight: about 9
pounds. Sights: Redfield 70 rear peep; blade front w/
protecting "ears." Plain pistol-grip stock, "Garand"
dimensions. Made 1944–46. *Note:* This model was used
as a training rifle by the U.S. Marine Corps.

**Harrington & Richardson Model 150
Leatherneck Autoloader** **$110**
Caliber: 22 LR only. 5-shot detachable box magazine. 22-
inch barrel. Weight: 7¼ pounds. Sights: open rear; blade
front, on ramp. Plain pistol-grip stock. Made 1949–1953.

Harrington & Richardson Model 151 . . . . **$125**
Same as Model 150 except with Redfield 70 rear peep
sight.

**Harrington & Richardson Model 155 Single
Shot Rifle** **$95**
Model 158 action. Calibers: 44 Rem. Mag., 45-70 Govt.
24- or 28-inch barrel (latter in 44 only). Weight: 7 or 7½
pounds. Sights: folding leaf rear; blade front. Straight-
grip stock, forearm with barrel band, brass cleaning rod.
Made 1972–1982.

RIFLES

H&R Model 60 Reising

H&R Model 65

H&R Model 155

H&R Model 157

H&R Model 158 Topper Jet

H&R Model 158C

H&R Model 163 Mustang

H&R Model 165 Leatherneck

Harrington & Richardson Model 157 Single Shot Rifle **$95**
Model 158 action. Calibers: 22 WMR, 22 Hornet, 30-30. 22-inch barrel. Weight: 6¼ pounds. Sights: folding leaf rear; blade front. Pistol-grip stock, full-length forearm, swivels. Made 1976–1986.

Harrington & Richardson Model 158 Topper Jet Single Shot Combination Rifle
Shotgun-type action w/visible hammer, side lever, auto ejector. Caliber: 22 Rem. Jet. 22-inch barrel (interchanges with 30-30, .410 ga., 20 ga. barrels). Weight: 5 pounds. Sights: Lyman folding adj. open rear; ramp front. Plain pistol-grip stock and forearm, recoil pad. Made 1963–67.
Rifle only **$120**
Interchangeable barrel—30-30, shotgun **35**

Harrington & Richardson Model 158C **$145**
Same as Model 158 Topper Jet, except calibers 22 Hornet, 30-30, 357 Mag., 357 Max., 44 Mag. Straight-grip stock. Made 1963–1986.

Harrington & Richardson Model 163 Mustang Single Shot Rifle **$110**
Same as Model 158 Topper except has gold-plated hammer and trigger, straight-grip stock and contoured forearm. Made 1964–67.

Harrington & Richardson Model 165 Leatherneck Autoloader **$125**
Caliber: 22 LR. 10-shot detachable box magazine. 23-inch barrel. Weight: about 7½ pounds. Sights: Redfield 70 rear peep; blade front, on ramp. Plain pistol-grip stock, swivels, web sling. Made 1945–1961.

Harrington & Richardson Model 171 . . . . **$275**
Model 1873 Springfield Cavalry Carbine replica. Caliber: 45-70. 22-inch barrel. Weight: 7 pounds. Sights: leaf rear; blade front. Plain walnut stock. Made 1972–1981.

Harrington & Richardson Model 171 Deluxe **$315**
Same as Model 171, except engraved action and different sights. Made 1972–1986.

Harrington & Richardson Model 172 . . . . **$995**
Same as Model 171 Deluxe, except silver-plated, has fancy walnut stock, checkered, with grip adapter; tang-mounted aperture sight. Made 1972–1986.

Harrington & Richardson Model 173 . . . . **$325**
Model 1873 Springfield Officer's Model replica, same as 100th Anniversary Commemorative, except w/o plaque on stock. Made 1972–1986.

Harrington & Richardson Model 174 . . . . **$335**
Little Big Horn Commemorative Carbine. Same as Model 171 Deluxe, except has tang-mounted aperture sight, grip adapter. Made 1972–1984. Value is for carbine in new, unfired condition.

Harrington & Richardson Model 178 . . . . **$325**
Model 1873 Springfield Infantry Rifle replica. Caliber: 45-70. 32-inch barrel. Weight: 8 lbs. 10 oz. Sights: leaf rear; blade front. Full-length stock with barrel bands, swivels, ramrod. Made 1973–1986.

Harrington & Richardson Model 250 Sportster
Bolt Action Repeating Rifle **$80**
Caliber: 22 LR. 5-shot detachable box magazine. 23-inch barrel. Weight: about 6½ pounds. Sights: open rear; blade front, on ramp. Plain pistol-grip stock. Made 1948–1961.

Harrington & Richardson Model 251 . . . . **$85**
Same as Model 250 except has Lyman 55H rear sight.

Harrington & Richardson Model 265 "Reg'lar"
Bolt Action Repeating Rifle **$80**
Caliber: 22 LR. 10-shot detachable box magazine. 22-inch barrel. Weight: about 6½ pounds. Sights: Lyman 55 rear peep; blade front, on ramp. Plain pistol-grip stock. Made 1946–49.

RIFLES

H&R Model 171

H&R Model 172

H&R Model 173

H&R Model 174
Little Big Horn Commemorative Carbine

H&R Model 265 "Reg'lar"

H&R Model 301 Carbine

H&R Model 317 Ultra Wildcat

H&R Model 317P

H&R Model 330 Hunter's Rifle

H&R Model 333

Harrington & Richardson Model 300 Ultra Bolt Action Rifle $395
Mauser-type action. Calibers: 22-250, 243 Win., 270 Win., 30-06, 308 Win., 7mm Rem. Mag., 300 Win. Mag. 3-round magazine in 7mm and 300 Mag. calibers, 5-round in others. 22- or 24-inch barrel. Sights: open rear; ramp front. Checkered stock w/rollover cheekpiece and full pistol grip, contrasting wood forearm tip and pistol grip, rubber buttplate, swivels. Weight: 7¼ pounds. Made 1965–1982.

Harrington & Richardson Model 301 Carbine ... $375
Same as Model 300, except has 18-inch barrel, Mannlicher-style stock, weighs 7¼ pounds; not available in caliber 22-250. Made 1967–1982.

Harrington & Richardson Model 317 Ultra Wildcat Bolt Action Rifle $495
Sako short action. Calibers: 17 Rem., 17/223 (handload), 222 Rem., 223 Rem. 6-round magazine. 20-inch barrel. No

Harrington & Richardson Model 317 (cont.)
sights, receiver dovetailed for scope mounts. Checkered stock w/cheekpiece and full pistol grip, contrasting wood forearm tip and pistol-grip cap, rubber buttplate. Weight: 5¼ pounds. Made 1968–1976.

Harrington & Richardson Model 317P Presentation Grade $595
Same as Model 317, except has select grade fancy walnut stock with basketweave carving on forearm and pistol grip. Made 1968–1976.

Harrington & Richardson Model 330 Hunter's Rifle $295
Similar to Model 300, but w/plainer stock. Calibers: 243 Win., 270 Win., 30-06, 308 Win., 7mm Rem. Mag., 300 Win. Mag. Weight: about 7⅛ pounds. Made 1967–1972.

Harrington & Richardson Model 333 .... $230
Plainer version of Model 300 with uncheckered walnut-finished hardwood stock. Calibers: 7mm Rem. Mag. and 30-06. 22-inch barrel. Weight: 7¼ pounds. No sights. Made in 1974.

Harrington & Richardson Model 340 . . . . **$295**
Mauser-type action. Calibers: 243 Win., 308 Win., 270 Win., 30-06, 7×57mm. 22-inch barrel. Weight: 7¼ pounds. Hand-checkered, American walnut stock. Made 1982–84.

Harrington & Richardson Model 360 Ultra Automatic Rifle **$325**
Gas-operated semiautomatic. Calibers: 243 Win., 308 Win. 3-round detachable box magazine. 22-inch barrel. Sights: open rear; ramp front. Checkered stock with rollover cheekpiece, full pistol grip, contrasting wood forearm tip and pistol-grip cap, rubber buttplate, sling swivels. Weight: 7½ pounds. Introduced 1965; discontinued 1978. (*Note:* Originally designated Model 308, changed to 360 in 1967).

Harrington & Richardson Model 361 . . . . **$355**
Same as Model 360, except has full rollover cheekpiece for right- or left-hand shooters. Made 1970–73.

Harrington & Richardson Model 365 Ace Bolt Action Single Shot Rifle **$100**
Caliber: 22 LR. 22-inch barrel. Weight: about 6½ pounds. Sights: Lyman 55 rear peep; blade front, on ramp. Plain pistol-grip stock. Made 1946–47.

Harrington & Richardson Model 370 Ultra Medalist **$395**
Varmint and target rifle based on Model 300. Calibers: 22-250, 243 Win., 6mm Rem. 5-round magazine. 24-inch varmint weight barrel. No sights. Target-style stock with semibeavertail forearm. Weight: 9½ pounds. Made 1968–1973.

Harrington & Richardson Model 422 Slide Action Repeater **$125**
Caliber: 22 LR, Long, Short. Tubular magazine holds 21 Short, 17 Long, 15 LR. 24-inch barrel. Weight: about 6 pounds. Sights: open rear; ramp front. Plain pistol-grip stock, grooved slide handle. Made 1956–58.

Harrington & Richardson Model 450 . . . . **$130**
Same as Model 451, except w/o front and rear sights.

Harrington & Richardson Model 451 Medalist Bolt Action Target Rifle **$155**
Caliber: 22 LR. 5-shot detachable box magazine. 26-inch barrel. Weight: about 10½ pounds. Sights: Lyman 524F extension rear; Lyman 77 front, scope bases. Target stock w/full pistol grip and forearm, swivels and sling. Made 1948–1961.

Harrington & Richardson Model 465 Targeteer Special Bolt Action Repeater **$140**
Caliber: 22 LR. 10-shot detachable box magazine. 25-inch barrel. Weight: about 9 pounds. Sights: Lyman 57 rear peep; blade front, on ramp. Plain pistol-grip stock, swivels, web sling strap. Made 1946–47.

Harrington & Richardson Model 700 Autoloader . . . **$175**
Caliber: 22 WMR. 5-shot magazine. 22-inch barrel. Weight: about 6½ pounds. Sights: folding leaf rear; blade front, on

H&R Model 340

H&R Model 360 Ultra Automatic

H&R Model 370 Ultra Medalist

H&R Model 465 Targeteer

H&R Model 700

H&R Model 700 Deluxe

H&R Model 750

H&R "New" Model 750

H&R Model 755 Sahara

Harrington & Richardson Model 700 Autoloader (cont.)
ramp. Monte Carlo-style stock of American walnut. Introduced 1977; discontinued.

Harrington & Richardson Model 700 Deluxe $275
Same as Model 700 Standard except has select custom polished and blued finish, select walnut stock, hand checkering, and no iron sights. Fitted with H&R Model 432 4× scope. Made 1980–86.

Harrington & Richardson Model 750 Pioneer Bolt Action Single Shot Rifle $90
Caliber: 22 LR, Long, Short. 22- or 24-inch barrel. Weight: about 5 pounds. Sights: open rear; bead front. Plain pistol-grip stock. Made 1954–1981; redesigned 1982; discont. 1985.

Harrington & Richardson Model 751 Single Shot Rifle $75
Same as Model 750, except has Mannlicher-style stock. Made 1971.

Harrington & Richardson Model 755 Sahara Single Shot Rifle $75
Blow-back action, automatic ejection. Caliber: 22 LR, Long, Short. 18-inch barrel. Weight: 4 pounds. Sights: open rear; military-type front. Mannlicher-style stock. Made 1963–1971.

Harrington & Richardson Model 760 Single Shot $80
Same as Model 755, except has conventional sporter stock. Made 1965–1970.

H&R Model 866

**H&R Model 1873
100th Anniversary Springfield Replica**

H&R Model 5200

Harrington & Richardson Model 765 Pioneer Bolt Action Single Shot Rifle **$60**
Caliber: 22 LR, Long, Short. 24-inch barrel. Weight: about 5 pounds. Sights: open rear; hooded bead front. Plain pistol-grip stock. Made 1948–1954.

Harrington & Richardson Model 800 Lynx Autoloading Rifle **$110**
Caliber: 22 LR. 5- or 10-shot clip magazine. 22-inch barrel. Open sights. Weight: 6 pounds. Plain pistol-grip stock. Made 1958–1960.

Harrington & Richardson Model 852 Fieldsman Bolt Action Repeater **$90**
Caliber: 22 LR, Long, Short. Tubular magazine holds 21 Short, 17 Long, 15 LR. 24-inch barrel. Weight: about 5½ pounds. Sights: open rear; bead front. Plain pistol-grip stock. Made 1952–53.

Harrington & Richardson Model 865 Plainsman Bolt Action Repeater **$85**
Caliber: 22 LR, Long, Short. 5-shot detachable box magazine. 22- or 24-inch barrel. Weight: about 5¼ pounds. Sights: open rear; bead front. Plain pistol-grip stock. Made 1949–1986.

Harrington & Richardson Model 866 Bolt Action Repeater **$85**
Same as Model 865, except has Mannlicher-style stock. Made 1971.

Harrington & Richardson Model 1873 100th Anniversary (1871–1971) Commemorative Officer's Springfield Replica **$595**
Model 1873 "trap door" single-shot action. Engraved breech block, receiver, hammer, lock, band and buttplate. Caliber: 45-70. 26-inch barrel. Sights: peep rear; blade

Harrington & Richardson Model 1873 (cont.)
front. Checkered walnut stock w/anniversary plaque. Ramrod. Weight: about 8 pounds. 10,000 made 1971. Value is for rifle in new, unfired condition.

Harrington & Richardson Model 5200 Sporter . . . **$425**
Turn-bolt repeater. Caliber: 22 LR. 24-inch barrel. Classic-style American walnut stock. Adj. trigger. Sights: peep receiver; hooded ramp front. Weight: 6½ pounds. Discontinued 1983.

Harrington & Richardson Model 5200 Match Rifle **$395**
Same action as 5200 Sporter. Caliber: 22 LR. 28-inch target weight barrel. Target stock of American walnut. Weight: 11 pounds. Made 1982–86.

Harrington & Richardson Custer Memorial Issue
Limited Edition Model 1873 Springfield Carbine replica, richly engraved and inlaid with gold, fancy walnut stock, in mahogany display case. Made 1973. Value is for carbine in new, unfired condition.
Officers' Model, limited to 25 pieces **$3500**
Enlisted Men's Model, limited to 243 pieces **2250**

Harrington & Richardson Targeteer Jr. Bolt Action Rifle **$110**
Caliber: 22 LR 5-shot detachable box magazine. 20-inch barrel. Weight: about 7 pounds. Sights: Redfield 70 rear peep; Lyman 17A front. Target stock, junior size with pistol grip, swivels and sling. Made 1948–1951.

Harrington & Richardson Ultra Varmint Rifle **$190**
Single shot break-open action with side-lever release. Calibers: 22-250, 223. 22-inch barrel. Weight: 7½ pounds. Drilled and tapped for scope mounts with no sights. Checkered curly maple stock with Monte Carlo. Made 1993 to date.

Heckler & Koch Model HK91 A-2

Heckler & Koch Model HK91 A-3

Heckler & Koch Model HK93 A-2

HECKLER & KOCH, GMBH
Oberndorf/Neckar, Germany

Heckler & Koch Model 911 Semiauto Rifle **$1025**
Caliber: 308 (7.62mm). 5-shot magazine. 19.7-inch bull
barrel. 42²/₅ inches overall. Sights: hooded post front; adjustable aperture rear. Weight: 11 pounds. Kevlar reinforced fiberglass thumbhole-stock.

Heckler & Koch Model HK91 A-2 Semiauto **$1995**
Delayed roller-locked blow-back action. Caliber: 7.62mm
× 51 NATO (308 Win.). 5- or 20-round box magazine. 19-inch barrel. Weight: w/o magazine, 9.37 pounds. Sights:
"V" and aperture rear; post front. Plastic buttstock and
forearm. No longer imported.

Heckler & Koch Model HK91 A-3 .... **$2495**
Same as Model HK91 A-2, except has retractable metal
buttstock, weighs 10.56 pounds. Currently manufactured.

Heckler & Koch Model HK93 Semiautomatic
Delayed roller-locked blow-back action. Caliber: 5.56mm ×
45 (223 Rem.). 5- or 20-round magazine. 16.13-inch barrel.
Weight: w/o magazine, 7.6 pounds. Sights: "V" and aperture
rear; post front. Plastic buttstock and forearm. Currently
manufactured.
HK93, A-2 . . . . **$1950**
HK93, A-3 with retractable stock 2450

Heckler & Koch Model HK94 Semiautomatic Carbine
Caliber: 9mm Para. 15-shot magazine. 16-inch barrel.
Weight: 6³/₄ pounds. Aperture rear sight, front post. Plastic
buttstock and forend or retractable metal stock. Made
1983 to date.
HK94-A2 w/Standard Stock **$2595**
HK94-A3 w/Retractable Stock 2795

Heckler & Koch Model HK300

Heckler & Koch Model HK630

Heckler & Koch Model HK770

Heckler & Koch Model KH940

RIFLES

Heckler & Koch Model HK300 Semiautomatic . . . **$525**
Caliber: 22 WMR. 5- or 15-round box magazine. 19.7-inch barrel. Weight: about 5¾ pounds. Sights: V-notch rear; ramp front. European walnut stock w/cheekpiece, checkered forearm and pistol grip. No longer imported.

Heckler & Koch Model HK630 Semiautomatic . . . **$650**
Caliber: 223 Rem. 4- or 10-round magazine. Overall length: 42 inches. Weight: 7 pounds. Sights: open rear; ramp front. European walnut stock w/Monte Carlo cheekpiece. Made 1983–1990.

Heckler & Koch Model HK770 Semiautomatic . . . **$850**
Caliber: 308 Win. 3- or 10-round magazine. Overall length: 44½ inches. Weight: 8 pounds. Sights: open rear; ramp front. European walnut stock w/Monte Carlo cheekpiece. Made 1983–1990.

Heckler & Koch Model HK940 Semiautomatic . . . **$995**
Caliber: 30-06 Springfield. 3- or 10-round magazine. Overall length: 47 inches. Weight: 8.8 pounds. Sights: open rear; ramp front. European walnut stock w/Monte Carlo cheekpiece. Made 1983–1990.

Heckler & Koch Model HK PSG-1 Marksman's Rifle **$7500**
Caliber: 308 (7.62mm). 5- and 20-shot magazine. 25.6-inch barrel. 47½ inches overall. Hensoldt 6×42 telescopic sight. Weight: 17.8 pounds. Matte black composition stock w/pistol grip. Made 1988 to date.

Heckler & Koch Model SR-9 Semiauto Rifle . . . **$1950**
Caliber: 308 (7.62mm). 5-shot magazine. 19.7-inch bull barrel. 42.4 inches overall. Hooded post front sight; adj. aperture rear. Weight: 11 pounds. Kevlar reinforced fiberglass thumbhole-stock w/wood grain finish.

Heckler & Koch Model SR-9 Target Rifle **$2595**
Same general specifications as standard SR-9, except w/PSG-1 trigger group and adj. buttstock. Made 1992–94.

═══ **HERCULES RIFLES** ═══
See listings under "W" for Montgomery Ward.

Herold Repeating Rifle

HEROLD RIFLE
Suhl, Germany
Made by Franz Jaeger & Company

Herold Bolt Action Repeating Sporting Rifle **$795**
"Herold-Repetierbüchse." Miniature Mauser-type action with unique 5-shot box magazine on hinged floorplate. Double-set triggers. Caliber: 22 Hornet. 24-inch barrel. Sights: leaf rear; ramp front. Weight: about 7¾ pounds. Fancy checkered stock. Made before WWII. *Note:* These rifles were imported by Charles Daly and A.F. Stoeger Inc. of New York City and sold under their own names.

HEYM AMERICA, INC.
Fort Wayne, Indiana

Currently imported by Heckler & Koch, Sterling, VA.

Heym Model 55B O/U Double Rifle
Kersten boxlock action with double cross bolt and cocking indicators. Calibers: 308 Win., 30-06, 375 H&H, 458 Win. Mag., 470 N.E. 25-inch barrel. 42 inches overall. Weight: 8¼ pounds. Sights: fixed V-type rear; front ramp with silver bead. Engraved receiver with optional sidelocks, interchangeable barrels and claw mounts. Checkered European walnut stock. Imported from Germany.

Model 55 (boxlock)	$8,250
Model 55 (sidelock)	9,550
Add for extra rifle barrels	4,500
Add for extra shotgun barrels	2,500

Heym Model 88B Double Rifle
Modified Anson & Deeley boxlock action with standing sears, double underlocking lugs and Greener extension w/ crossbolt. Calibers: 8×57 JRS, 9.3×74R, 30-06, 375 H&H, 458 Win. Mag., 470 Nitro Express, 500 Nitro Express. Weight: 8 to 10 pounds. Top tang safety and cocking indicators. Double triggers with front set. Fixed or 3-leaf

Heym Model 88B Double Rifle (cont.)
express rear sight; front ramp w/silver bead. Engraved receiver w/optional sidelocks. Checkered French walnut stock. Imported from Germany.

Model 88B Boxlock	from $ 8,775
Model 88B/SS Sidelock	from 11,500
Model 88B Safari (Magnum)	11,950

Heym Express Bolt Action Rifle
Same general specifications as Model SR-20 Safari, except w/modified Magnum Mauser action. Checkered AAA-grade European walnut stock w/cheekpiece, solid rubber recoil pad, rosewood forend tip and grip cap. Calibers: 338 Lapua Magnum, 375 H&H, 378 Wby. Mag., 416 Rigby, 450 Ackley, 460 Wby. Mag., 500 A-Square, 500 Nitro Express, 600 Nitro Express. Made 1989 to date.

Standard Express Magnum	$ 4,150
600 Nitro Express	7,950
Add for Left-hand Models	600

Heym SR-20 Bolt Action Rifle
Calibers: 243 Win., 270 Win., 308 Win., 30-06, 7mm Rem. Mag., 300 Win. Mag., 375 H&H. 5-shot (standard) or 3-shot (Magnum) magazine. Barrel length: 20½-inch (SR-20L); 24-inch (SR-20N); 26-inch (SR-20G). Weight: 7¾ pounds. Adj. rear sight, blade front. Checkered French walnut stock in Monte Carlo style (N&G Series) or full Mannlicher (L Series). Imported from Germany. Discontinued 1992.

SR-20L	$1050
SR-20N	1195
SR-20G	1395

Heym SR-20 Classic Bolt Action Rifles
Same as SR-20, except w/22-250 and 338 Win. Mag., plus metric calibers on request. 24-inch (standard) or 25-inch (Magnum) barrel. Checkered French walnut stock. Left-hand models. Imported from Germany since 1985; Sporter version from 1989–1993.

Classic (Standard)	$1395
Classic (Magnum)	1525

Heym Model 88B Safari Double Rifle

Heym Model SR-20 Standard

Heym Model SR-20 Trophy Series

Heym SR-20 Classic Bolt Action Rifles (cont.)
Left-hand Models, **add** . . . . $ 300
Classic Sporter (Std. w/22-inch bbl.) 1595
Classic Sporter (Mag. w/24-inch bbl.) 1650

Heym SR-20 Alpine, Safari and Trophy Series
Same general specifications as Model SR-20 Classic Sporter, except **Alpine Series** has 20-inch barrel, Mannlicher stock, chambered in standard calibers only; **Safari Series** has 24-inch barrel, 3-leaf express sights and mag-

Heym SR-20 Alpine, Safari and Trophy Series (cont.)
num action in calibers 375 H&H, 404 Jeffrey, 425 Express, 458 Win. Mag.; **Trophy Series** has Krupp-Special tapered octagon barrel with quarter rib and open sights, standard and Magnum calibers. All imported from Germany 1989–1993.
Alpine Series **$1450**
Safari Series 1525
Trophy Series (Standard Calibers) 1595
Trophy Series (Magnum Calibers) 1625

RIFLES

High Standard Flite-King Pump

High Standard Hi-Power Deluxe

High Standard Hi-Power Field

High Standard Sport-King Auto Carbine

J.C. HIGGINS RIFLES
See Sears, Roebuck & Company.

HIGH STANDARD SPORTING FIREARMS
East Hartford, Connecticut
Formerly High Standard Mfg. Co., Hamden, CT

A long-standing producer of sporting arms, High Standard discontinued its operations in 1984.

High Standard Flite-King Pump Rifle $110
Hammerless slide action. Caliber: 22 LR, 22 Long, 22 Short. Tubular mag. holds 17 LR, 19 Long, or 24 Short. 24-inch barrel. Weight: 5½ pounds. Sights: Patridge

High Standard Flite-King Pump Rifle (cont.)
rear; bead front. Monte Carlo stock w/pistol grip, serrated semibeavertail forearm. Made 1962–1975.

High Standard Hi-Power Deluxe Bolt Action Rifle **$275**
Mauser-type action, sliding safety. Calibers: 270, 30-06. 4-shot magazine. 22-inch barrel. Weight: 7 pounds. Sights: folding open rear; ramp front. Walnut stock w/checkered pistol grip and forearm, Monte Carlo comb, QD swivels. Made 1962–66.

High Standard Hi-Power Field Bolt Action Rifle . . **$225**
Same as Hi-Power Deluxe, except has plain field style stock. Made 1962–66.

High Standard Sport-King Autoloading Carbine . . **$130**
Same as Sport-King Field Autoloader, except has 18¼-inch barrel, Western-style straight-grip stock w/barrel band, sling and swivels. Made 1964–1973.

High Standard Sport-King Deluxe Auto

High Standard Sport-King Field Auto

High Standard Sport-King Special Auto

High Standard Sport-King Deluxe Autoloader ... **$155**
Same as Sport-King Special Autoloader, except has checkered stock. Made 1966–1975.

High Standard Sport-King Field Autoloader **$100**
Calibers: 22 LR, 22 Long, 22 Short (high speed). Tubular magazine holds 15 LR, 17 Long, or 21 Short. 22¼-inch barrel. Weight: 5½ pounds. Sights: open rear; beaded post front. Plain pistol-grip stock. Made 1960–66.

High Standard Sport-King Special Autoloader .. **$125**
Same as Sport-King Field, except stock has Monte Carlo comb and semibeavertail forearm. Made 1960–66.

HOLLAND & HOLLAND, LTD.
London, England

Holland & Holland No. 2 Model Hammerless Ejector Double Rifle **$12,500**
Same general specifications as Royal Model, except plainer finish. Discontinued 1960.

Holland & Holland Best Quality Magazine Rifle .. **$5995**
Mauser or Enfield action. Calibers: 240 Apex, 300 H&H Magnum, 375 H&H Magnum. 4-shot box magazine. 24-inch barrel. Weight: about 7¼ lbs., 240 Apex; 8¼ lbs., 300 Mag. and 375 Mag. Sights: folding leaf rear; hooded ramp front. Detachable French walnut stock w/cheekpiece, checkered pistol grip and forearm, swivels. Currently mfd. Specifications given are those of the present model; however, in general they apply also to prewar models.

Holland & Holland Deluxe Magazine Rifle **$5400**
Same specifications as Best Quality, except has exhibition grade stock and special engraving. Currently mfd.

Holland & Holland Royal Deluxe Double Rifle ... **$29,500**
Formerly designated "Modele Deluxe." Same specifications as Royal Model, except has exhibition grade stock and special engraving. Currently mfd.

Holland & Holland Royal Hammerless Ejector Double Rifle **$9300**
Sidelock. Calibers: 240 Apex, 7mm H&H Mag., 300 H&H Mag., 300 Win. Mag., 30-06, 375 H&H Mag., 458 Win. Mag., 465 H&H Mag. 24- to 28-inch barrels. Weight: from 7½ pounds. Sights: folding leaf rear; ramp front. Cheekpiece stock of select French walnut, checkered pistol grip and forearm. Currently mfd. Same general specifications apply to prewar model.

H & H Best Quality Magazine Rifle

H & H Royal Double Rifle

Howa Trophy Sporting Rifle

HOWA MACHINERY LTD.
Shinkawa-Chonear, Nagoya 452, Japan

Howa Model 1500 Lightning Bolt Action Rifle
Similar to the Trophy Model, except fitted with black
Bell & Carlson Carbelite stock with checkered grip and
forend. Weight: 7½ pounds. Made 1993 to date.
Standard Calibers **$330**
Magnum Calibers **355**

Howa Model 1500 Realtree Camo Rifle **$375**
Similar to the Trophy Model, except fitted with Camo
Bell & Carlson Carbelite stock with checkered grip and
forend. Weight: 8 pounds. Stock, action and barrel finished
in Realtree camo. Available in standard calibers only.
Made 1993 to date.

Howa Model 1500 Trophy/Varmint Bolt Action Rifle
Calibers: 22-250, 223, 243 Win., 270 Win., 308 Win., 30-
06, 7mm Mag., 300 Win. Mag., 338 Win. Mag. 22-inch
barrel (standard); 24-inch barrel (Magnum). 42½ inches
overall (standard). Weight: 7½ pounds. Adj. rear sight;
hooded ramp front. Checkered walnut stock w/Monte
Carlo cheekpiece. **Varmint Model** has 24-inch heavy barrel,
weight of 9½ pounds in calibers 22-250, 223 and 308 only.
Imported 1979 to date.
Trophy Standard **$340**
Trophy Magnum **365**
Varmint (Parkerized Finish) **425**

HUNGARIAN MILITARY RIFLES
Budapest, Hungary
Manufactured at Government Arsenal

**Hungarian Model 1935M Mannlicher Military
Rifle** **$200**
Caliber: 8×52mm Hungarian. Bolt action, straight handle.
5-shot projecting box magazine. 24-inch barrel. Weight:
about 9 pounds. Adj. leaf rear sight, hooded front blade.
Two-piece military-type stock. Made 1935–1940.

**Hungarian Model 1943M (German Gew. 98/40)
Mannlicher Military Rifle** **$240**
Modification, during German occupation, of the Model
1935M. Caliber: 7.9mm Mauser. Turned-down bolt handle
and Mauser M/98-type box magazine; other differences
are minor. Made 1940 to end of war in Europe.

HUSQVARNA VAPENFABRIK A.B.
Huskvarna, Sweden

**Husqvarna Model 456 Lightweight Full-Stock
Sporter** **$415**
Same as Series 4000/4100 except has sporting-style full
stock with slope-away cheekrest. Weight: 6½ pounds.
Made 1959–1970.

Husqvarna Series 1000 Super Grade **$440**
Same as 1951 Model, except has European walnut sporter
stock w/Monte Carlo comb and cheekpiece. Made 1952–56.

**Husqvarna Series 1100 Deluxe Model Hi-Power
Bolt Action Sporting Rifles** **$450**
Same as 1951 Model, except has "jeweled" bolt, European
walnut stock. Made 1952–56.

Husqvarna Model 456

Husqvarna 1100 Deluxe

RIFLES

Husqvarna 1951 Hi-Power

Husqvarna 3000 Crown Grade

Husqvarna 4100 Lightweight

Husqvarna 6000 Imperial Custom

Husqvarna 7000 Imperial Lightweight

Husqvarna 1950 Model Hi-Power Bolt Action Sporting Rifle $275
Mauser-type action. Calibers: 220 Swift, 270 Win., 30-06 (see note below), 5-shot box magazine. 23³/₄-inch barrel. Weight: about 7³/₄ pounds. Sights: open rear; hooded ramp front. Sporting stock of Arctic beech, checkered pistol grip and forearm, swivels. *Note:* Husqvarna sporters were first introduced in the U.S. about 1948; earlier models were also available in calibers 6.5×55, 8×57 and 9.3×57. Made 1946–1951.

Husqvarna 1951 Model $310
Same as 1950 Model, except has high-comb stock, low safety.

Husqvarna Series 3000 Crown Grade $430
Same as Series 3100, except has Monte Carlo comb stock.

Husqvarna Series 3100 Crown Grade $450
HVA improved Mauser action. Calibers: 243, 270, 7mm, 30-06, 308 Win. 5-shot box magazine. 23³/₄-inch barrel. Weight: 7¹/₄ pounds. Sights: open rear; hooded ramp front. European walnut stock, checkered, cheekpiece, pistol-grip cap, black foretip, swivels. Made 1954–1972.

Husqvarna Series 4000 Lightweight Rifle $450
Same as Series 4100, except has no rear sight and has Monte Carlo comb stock.

Husqvarna Series 4100 Lightweight Rifle $425
HVA improved Mauser action. Calibers: 243, 270, 7mm, 30-06, 308 Win. 5-shot box magazine. 20¹/₂-inch barrel. Weight: about 6¹/₄ pounds. Sights: open rear; hooded ramp front. Lightweight walnut stock w/cheekpiece, pistol grip, schnabel foretip, checkered, swivels. Made 1954–1972.

Husqvarna Series 6000 Imperial Custom Grade $595
Same as Series 3100, except fancy-grade stock, 3-leaf folding rear sight, adj. trigger. Calibers: 243, 270, 7mm Rem. Mag., 308, 30-06. Made 1968–1970.

Husqvarna Series 7000 Imperial Monte Carlo Lightweight $550
Same as Series 4000 Lightweight, except fancy-grade stock, 3-leaf folding rear sight, adj. trigger. Calibers: 243, 270, 308, 30-06. Made 1968–1970.

Husqvarna Model 8000 Imperial Grade Rifle $525
Same as Model 9000, except has jeweled bolt, engraved floorplate, deluxe French walnut stock, no sights. Made 1971–72.

Husqvarna 9000 Crown Grade

Husqvarna P-3000 Presentation Grade

Husqvarna Model 9000 Crown Grade Rifle **$395**
New design Husqvarna bolt action. Adj. trigger. Calibers: 270, 7mm Rem. Mag., 30-06, 300 Win. Mag. 5-shot box magazine, hinged floorplate. 23³/₄-inch barrel. Sights: folding leaf rear; hooded ramp front. Checkered walnut

Husqvarna Model 9000 Crown Grade Rifle (cont.)
stock w/Monte Carlo cheekpiece, rosewood forearm tip and pistol-grip cap. Weight: 7 lbs. 3 oz. Made 1971–72.

Husqvarna Series P-3000 Presentation Rifle . . . **$695**
Same as Crown Grade Series 3000, except w/selected stock, engraved action, adj. trigger. Calibers: 243, 270, 7mm Rem. Mag., 30-06. Made 1968–1970.

Interarms Mark X

Interarms Mark X Cavalier

INTERARMS RIFLES
Alexandria, Virginia

The following Mark X rifles are manufactured by Zavodi Crvena Zastava, Belgrade, Yugoslavia.

Interarms Mark X Alaskan **$410**
Same specifications as Mark X Sporter, except calibers 375 H&H Mag. and 458 Win. Mag., 3-round magazine, weighs 8¹/₄ pounds, has stock with recoil-absorbing cross bolt and heavy duty recoil pad. Made 1976–1984.

Interarms Mark X Bolt Action Sporter Series
Mauser-type action. Calibers: 22-250, 243, 25-06, 270, 7×57, 7mm Rem. Mag., 308, 30-06, 300 Win. Mag. 5-shot magazine (3-shot in Magnum calibers). 24-inch barrel. Weight: 7¹/₂ pounds. Sights: adj. leaf rear; ramp front, with hood. Classic-style stock of European walnut w/ Monte Carlo comb and cheekpiece, checkered pistol grip and forearm, black forend tip, QD swivels. Made 1972 to date.
American Field Model, Std. (Rubber recoil Pad) . **$465**
American Field, Magnum (Rubber recoil Pad) . . . **495**
Mark X Standard Model **295**

Interarms Mark X Cavalier **$325**
Same specifications as Mark X Sporter, except has contemporary-style stock with rollover cheekpiece, rosewood forend tip/grip cap, recoil pad. Introduced 1974; disc.

Interarms Mark X Continental Mannlicher Style Carbine **$375**
Same specifications as Mark X Sporter, except straight European-style comb stock w/sculptured cheekpiece. Precise double-set triggers and classic "butter-knife" bolt handle. French checkering. Weight: about 7¹/₄ pounds. Discontinued.

Interarms Mark X Marquis Mannlicher Style Carbine **$395**
Same specifications as Mark X Sporter, except has 20-inch barrel, full-length Mannlicher-type stock with metal forend/muzzle cap. Calibers: 270, 7×57, 308, 30-06. Made 1976 to date.

Interarms Mini-Mark X Bolt Action Rifle **$350**
Miniature M98 Mauser action. Caliber: 223 Rem. 5-shot magazine. 20-inch barrel. 39³/₄ inches overall. Weight: 6¹/₄ pounds. Adj. rear sight, hooded ramp front. Checkered hardwood stock. Imported 1987 to date.

Interarms Mark X Viscount

Interarms Whitworth Express

Interarms Mark X Viscount $325
Same specifications as Mark X Sporter, except has plainer field grade stock. Made 1974–1987.

Interarms Whitworth Express Rifle, African Series $495
Mauser-type bolt action. Calibers: 375 H&H Mag., 458 Win. Mag. 3-shot magazine. 24-inch barrel. Weight: about

Interarms Whitworth Express, African Series (cont.)
8 pounds. Sights: 3-leaf express open rear; ramp front, with hood. English-style stock of European walnut, w/ cheekpiece, black forend tip, checkered pistol grip and forearm, recoil pad, QD swivels. Made 1974 to date by Whitworth Rifle Co., England.

Italian Model 38

ITALIAN MILITARY RIFLES
Manufactured by Government plants at Brescia, Gardone, Terni and Turin, Italy

Italian Model 38 Military Rifle $95
Modification of Italian Model 1891 Mannlicher-Carcano Military Rifle w/turned-down bolt handle, detachable folding bayonet. Caliber: 7.35mm Italian Service (many arms of this model were later converted to the old 6.5mm caliber). 6-shot box magazine. 21¼-inch barrel. Weight: about 7½ pounds. Sights: adj. rear; blade front. Military straight-grip stock. Adopted 1938.

Ithaca Model 49 Deluxe

Ithaca Model 49 Presentation

ITHACA GUN COMPANY, INC.
King Ferry (formerly Ithaca), New York

Ithaca Model 49 Deluxe Saddlegun $95
Same as standard Model 49, except has gold-plated hammer and trigger, figured walnut stock, sling swivels. Made 1962–1975.

Ithaca Model 49 Magnum Saddlegun $100
Same as standard Model 49, except chambered for 22 WMR cartridge. Made 1962–1978.

Ithaca Model 49 Presentation Saddlegun $160
Same as standard Model 49 Saddlegun, except has gold-plated hammer and trigger, engraved receiver, full fancy-figured walnut stock w/gold nameplate. Available in 22 LR or 22 WMR. Made 1962–1974.

Ithaca Model 49

Ithaca Model 49R Repeater

Ithaca Model 72 Deluxe

Ithaca Model 72

Ithaca Model LSA-55 Deluxe

RIFLES

Ithaca Model 49 Saddlegun Lever Action Single Shot Rifle **$80**
Martini-type action. Hand-operated rebounding hammer. Caliber: 22 LR, Long, Short. 18-inch barrel. Open sights. Western carbine-style stock. Weight: 5 1/2 pounds. Made 1961–1978.

Ithaca Model 49 St. Louis Bicentennial Saddlegun **$180**
Same as Model 49 Deluxe, except has commemorative inscription. 200 made in 1964. Value is for rifle in new, unfired condition.

Ithaca Model 49 Youth Saddlegun **$85**
Same as standard Model 49, except shorter stock for young shooters. Made 1961–1978.

Ithaca Model 49R Saddlegun Repeating Rifle . . . **$140**
Similar in appearance to Model 49 Single Shot. Caliber: 22 LR, Long, Short. Tubular magazine holds 15 LR, 17 Long, 21 Short. 20-inch barrel. Weight: 5 1/2 pounds. Sights: open rear; bead front. Western-style stock, checkered grip. Made 1968–1971.

Ithaca Model 72 Deluxe **$180**
Same as standard Model 72, except has silver-finished and engraved receiver, octagon barrel, higher grade walnut stock and forearm. Made 1974–76.

Ithaca Model 72 Magnum **$175**
Same as standard Model 72, except chambered for 22 WMR, has 11-shot tubular magazine, 18 1/2-inch barrel. Made 1975–78.

Ithaca Model 72 Saddlegun Lever Action Repeating Carbine **$195**
Caliber: 22 LR, Long, Short. Tubular magazine holds 15 LR, 17 Long, 21 Short. 18 1/2-inch barrel. Weight: about 5 1/2 pounds. Soghts: open rear; hooded ramp front. Receiver grooved for scope mounting. Western carbine stock and forearm of American walnut. Made 1973–78. *Note:* Barrel and action are manufactured by Erma-Werke, Dachau, W. Germany; wood installed by Ithaca.

Ithaca Model LSA-55 Deluxe **$395**
Same as Model LSA-55 Standard Grade, except has roll-over cheekpiece, rosewood grip-cap and forend tip, skip checkering, high-luster blue, no iron sights, scope mount standard equipment. Made 1969–1977.

Ithaca Model LSA-55 Standard

Ithaca Model LSA-65 Standard

Ithaca Model X5-T

Ithaca Model X-15

Ithaca-BSA CF-2

Ithaca Model LSA-55 Heavy Barrel **$400**
Same as Model LSA-55, except calibers 222 Rem. and 22-250 only; has 23-inch heavy barrel, no sights, special stock with beavertail forearm, weighs about 8½ pounds. Made 1974–77.

Ithaca Model LSA-55 Standard Grade Bolt Action Repeating Rifle **$375**
Mauser-type action. Calibers: 222 Rem., 22-250, 6mm Rem., 243 Win., 308 Win. 3-shot detachable clip magazine. 22-inch barrel. Weight: 6½ pounds. Sights: folding leaf rear; hooded ramp front. Checkered walnut stock w/Monte Carlo cheekpiece, detachable swivels. Made 1969–1977. Mfd. by Oy Tikkakoski AB, Tikkakoski, Finland.

Ithaca Model LSA-65 Deluxe **$395**
Same as Model LSA-65 Standard Grade, except has special features of Model LSA-55 Deluxe. Made 1969–1977.

Ithaca Model LSA-65 Standard Grade **$355**
Same as Model LSA-55 Standard Grade, except calibers 25-06, 270, 30-06; 4-shot magazine, 23-inch barrel, weighs 7 pounds. Made 1969–1977.

Ithaca Model X5-C Lightning Autoloader Clip Repeating Rifle **$95**
Takedown. Caliber: 22 LR. 7-shot clip magazine. 22-inch barrel. Weight: 6 pounds. Sights: open rear; Raybar front. Pistol-grip stock, grooved forearm. Made 1958–1964.

Ithaca Model X5-T Lightning Autoloader Tubular Repeating Rifle **$105**
Same as Model X5-C except has 16-shot tubular magazine, stock with plain forearm. Made 1959–1963.

Ithaca Model X-15 Lightning Autoloader **$100**
Same general specifications as Model X5-C, except forearm is not grooved. Made 1964–67.

Ithaca-BSA CF-2 Bolt Action Repeating Rifle . . . **$325**
Mauser-type action. Calibers: 7mm Rem. Mag., 300 Win. Mag. 3-shot magazine. 23.6-inch barrel. Weight: 8 pounds. Sights: adj. rear; hooded ramp front. Checkered walnut stock w/Monte Carlo comb, rollover cheekpiece, rosewood forend tip, recoil pad, sling swivels. Made 1976–77. Mfd. by BSA Guns Ltd., Birmingham, England.

Japanese Model 38

Japanese Model 99

JAPANESE MILITARY RIFLES
Tokyo, Japan
Manufactured by Government Plant

Japanese Model 38 Arisaka Carbine **$130**
Same general specifications as Model 38 Rifle, except has 19-inch barrel, heavy folding bayonet, weighs about 7¼ pounds.

Japanese Model 38 Arisaka Service Rifle **$130**
Mauser-type bolt action. Caliber: 6.5mm Japanese. 5-shot box magazine. Barrel lengths: 25³/₈ and 31¼ inches. Weight: about 9¼ pounds w/long barrel. Sights: fixed front; adj. rear. Military-type full stock. Adopted in 1905, the 38th year of the Meiji reign; hence, the designation "Model 38."

Japanese Model 44 Cavalry Carbine **$150**
Same general specifications as Model 38 Rifle except has 19-inch barrel, heavy folding bayonet, weighs about 8½ pounds. Adopted in 1911, the 44th year of the Meiji reign; hence, the designation "Model 44."

Japanese Model 99 Service Rifle **$165**
Modified Model 38. Caliber: 7.7mm Japanese. 5-shot box magazine. 25³/₄-inch barrel. Weight: about 8³/₄ pounds. Sights: fixed front; adj. aperture rear; anti-aircraft sighting bars on some early models; fixed rear sight on some late WWII rifles. Military-type full stock, may have bipod. Takedown paratroop model was also made during WWII. Adopted in 1939, Japanese year 2599 from which the designation "Model 99" is taken. *Note:* The last Model 99 rifles made were of poor quality; some have cast steel receivers. Value shown is for earlier type.

Johnson Model 1941

JOHNSON AUTOMATICS, INC.
Providence, Rhode Island

Johnson Model 1941 Semiauto Military Rifle . . **$1000**
Short-recoil-operated. Removable, air-cooled, 22-inch barrel. Calibers: 30-06, 7mm Mauser. 10-shot rotary magazine. Two-piece, wood stock, pistol grip; perforated metal radiator sleeve over rear half of barrel. Sights: receiver peep; protected post front. Weight: 9½ pounds. *Note:* The Johnson M/1941 was adopted by the Netherlands Government in 1940–41 and the major portion of the production of this rifle, 1941–43, was on Dutch orders. A quantity was also bought by the U.S. Government for use by Marine Corps parachute troops (1943) and for Lend Lease. All these rifles were caliber 30-06; the 7mm Johnson rifles were made for a South American government.

IVER JOHNSON'S ARMS, INC.
Jacksonville, Arkansas
Formerly of Fitchburg, Massachusetts, and Middlesex, New Jersey

Iver Johnson Model 5100A1 Bolt Action Rifle . . **$3850**
Single-shot long-range rifle with removable bolt for breech loading. Caliber: 50BMG. Flutted 29-inch barrel with muzzle break. 51½ inches overall. Adj. composition stock w/folding bipod. Scope rings; no sights.

Iver Johnson Li'l Champ Bolt Action Rifle **$75**
Caliber: 22 S, L, LR. Single shot. 16¼-inch barrel. 32½ inches overall. Weight: 3¼ pounds. Adjustable rear sight, blade front. Synthetic composition stock. Made 1986–88.

Iver Johnson M1 Carbine

Iver Johnson PM.30

Iver Johnson Model SC30FS

Iver Johnson Survival Carbine

Iver Johnson Trailblazer

Iver Johnson Model 2X

Iver Johnson Model M-1 Semiautomatic Carbine
Similar to U.S. M-1 Carbine. Calibers: 9mm Parabellum, 30 U.S. Carbine. 15- or 30-shot magazine. 18-inch barrel. 35½ inches overall. Weight: 6½ pounds. Sights: blade front, with guards; adj. peep rear. Walnut, hardwood or collapsible wire stock. Parkerized finish.

Model M-1 (30 cal. w/hardwood)	$265
Model M-1 (30 cal. w/walnut)	290
Model M-1 (30 cal. w/wire)	350
Model M-1 (9mm w/hardwood)	345
Model M-1 (9mm w/walnut)	365
Model M-1 (9mm w/wire)	395

Iver Johnson Model PM.30 Semiautomatic Carbine $270
Similar to U.S. Carbine, Cal. .30 M1. 18-inch barrel. Weight: about 5½ pounds. 15- or 30-round detachable magazine. Both hardwood and walnut stock.

Iver Johnson Model SC30FS Semiautomatic Carbine $295
Similar to Survival Carbine except has folding stock. Made 1983 to date.

Iver Johnson Survival Semiautomatic Carbine .. $325
Similar to Model PM.30 except in stainless steel w/high-impact plastic, one-piece stock. Made 1983 to date. W/ folding high-impact plastic stock add $35.

Iver Johnson Trailblazer Semiauto Rifle $125
Caliber: 22 LR. 18-inch barrel. Weight: 5½ pounds. Sights: open rear; blade front. Hardwood stock. Made 1983–85.

Iver Johnson Model X Bolt Action Rifle $110
Takedown. Single shot. Caliber: 22 Short, Long and LR. 22-inch barrel. Weight: about 4 pounds. Sights: open rear; blade front. Pistol-grip stock w/knob forend tip. Made 1928–1932.

Iver Johnson Model XX (2X) Bolt Action $110
Improved version of the Model X, has heavier 24-inch barrel, larger stock (w/o knob tip), weighs about 4½ pounds. Made 1932–1955.

KDF Model K15 Bolt Action

K.D.F. INC.
Sequin, Texas

KDF Model K15 Bolt Action Rifle
Calibers: (Standard) 22-250, 243 Win., 6mm Rem., 25-06, 270 Win., 280 Rem., 7mm Mag., 30-06; (Magnum) 300 Wby., 300 Win., 338 Win., 340 Wby., 375 H&H, 411 KFD,

KDF Model K15 Bolt Action Rifle (cont.)
416 Rem., 458 Win. 4-shot magazine (standard), 3-shot (magnum). 22-inch (standard) or 24-inch (magnum) barrel. 44½ to 46½ inches overall. Weight: 8 pounds. Sights optional. Kevlar composite or checkered walnut stock in classic, European or thumbhole-style.

Standard Model	**$1295**
Magnum Model	**1350**

RIFLES

Kimber Model 82 Rimfire Sporter

Kimber Model 84 Sporter

Kimber Model 89 Big Game Rifle

KIMBER OF OREGON, INC.
Colton, Oregon

The firm's operation stopped in 1992, but as of 1993 the Kimber Model 82 Sporter was marketed by Nationwide Sports; the Q/D scope mounts are produced by Warne Manufacturing Co., owned and operated by Jack Warne, founder of Kimber, and his son Greg.

Kimber Model 82 Bolt Action Rifle
Small action based on the Kimber "A" Model 82 rimfire receiver with twin rear locking lugs. Calibers: 22 LR, 22 WRF, 22 Hornet, 218 Bee, 25-20. 5- or 10-shot magazine (22 LR); 5-shot magazine (22WRF); 3-shot magazine (22 Hornet). 218 Bee and 25-20 are single shot. 18- to 25-inch barrel. 37⅝ to 42½ inches overall. Weight: 6 lbs. (Light Sporter); 6½ lbs. (Sporter); 7½ lbs. (Varmint); 10¾ lbs. (Target). Right- and left-hand actions are available in distinctive stock styles.

Cascade (discontinued 1987)	**$ 640**
Classic (discontinued 1988)	**575**
Continental	**795**
Custom Classic (discontinued 1988)	**680**
Mini Classic	**475**
Super America	**875**
Super Continental	**1100**

Kimber Model 82 Bolt Action Rifle (cont.)
1990 Classifications

All-American Match	**$ 680**
Deluxe Grade (discontinued 1990)	**975**
Hunter (Laminated Stock)	**635**
Super America	**840**
Target (Government Match)	**450**

Kimber Model 84 Bolt Action Rifle
Compact medium action based on a "scaled down" Mauser-type receiver, designed to accept small base centerfire cartridges. Calibers: 17 Rem., 221 Fireball, 222 Rem., 223 Rem. 5-shot magazine. Same general barrel and stock specifications as Model 82.

Classic (discontinued 1988)	**$ 650**
Continental	**750**
Custom Classic (Discontinued 1988)	**850**
Super America (Discontinued 1988)	**965**
Super Continental (Discontinued 1988)	**1125**

1990 Classifications

Deluxe Grade (Discontinued 1990)	**895**
Hunter/Sporter (Laminated Stock)	**695**
Super America (discontinued 1991)	**995**
Super Varmint (discontinued 1991)	**1025**
Ultra Varmint (discontinued 1991)	**950**

Kimber Model 89 Big Game Rifle
A large action combining the best features of the pre-64 Model 70 Winchester and the Mauser 98. Three action lengths are offered in three stock styles. Calibers: 257 Roberts, 25-06, 7×57, 270 Win., 280 Win., 30-06, 7mm Rem. Mag., 300 Win. Mag., 300 H&H, 338 Win., 35 Whe-

Kimber Model 89 Big Game Rifle (cont.)

len, 375 H&H, 404 Jeffrey, 416 Rigby, 460 Wby., 505 Gibbs (308 cartridge family to follow). 5-shot magazine (standard calibers); 3-shot magazine (Magnum calibers). 22- to 24-inch barrel. 42 to 44 inches overall. Weight: 7½ to 10½ lbs. Model 89 African features express sights on contoured quarter rib, banded front sight. Barrel-mounted recoil lug w/integral receiver lug and twin recoil crosspins in stock.

BGR Long Action
Classic (discontinued 1988) . . . . $ 795
Custom Classic (discontinued 1988) 950
Super America 1095
1990 Classifications
Deluxe Grade
  Featherweight 1295
  Medium 1325
  375 H&H 1350
Hunter Grade (Laminated Stock)
  270 and 30-06 1025
  375 H&H 1150
Super America
  Featherweight 1495
  Medium 1570
  375 H&H 2000
African—All calibers 2695

══ KRICO RIFLES ══
Stuttgart-Hedelfingen, Germany
Mfd. by Sportwaffenfabrik Kriegeskorte GmbH

Krico rifles currently imported are available thru Beeman Precision Arms, Inc., Santa Rosa, CA.

Krico Model 311 Small Bore Rifle

Bolt action. Caliber: 22 LR. 5- or 10-shot clip magazine. 22-inch barrel. Weight: about 6 pounds. Single- or double-

Krico Model 311 Small Bore Rifle (cont.)

set trigger. Sights: open rear; hooded ramp front; available with factory-fitted Kaps 2½× scope. Checkered stock w/cheekpiece and pistol grip, swivels.
W/scope sight **$325**
W/iron sights only **280**

Krico Model 260 Semiautomatic Rifle **$500**
Caliber: 22 LR. 5-shot magazine. 19⅗-inch barrel. 38⅘ inches overall. Weight: 6⅗ pounds. Beech hardwood stock. Blued finish.

Krico Model 300 Bolt Action Rifle
Calibers: 22 LR, 22 WMR, 22 Hornet. 19.6-inch barrel (22 LR), 23.6-inch (22 Hornet). 38½ inches overall. Weight: 6.3 pounds. Double-set triggers. Sights: ramped blade front; adjustable open rear. Checkered walnut-finished hardwood stock. Blued finish. Made 1993 to date.
Model 300 Standard **$525**
Model 300 Deluxe **560**
Model 300 SA (Monte-Carlo walnut stock) **565**
Model 300 Stutzen (full-length walnut stock) **620**

Krico Model 320 Bolt Action Sporter **$545**
Caliber: 22 LR. 5-shot detachable box magazine. 19½-inch barrel. 38½ inches overall. Weight: 6 pounds. Adj. rear sight, blade ramp front. Checkered European walnut Mannlicher-style stock w/low comb and cheekpiece. Single or double-set triggers. Discontinued 1989.

Krico Model 340 Metallic Silhouette Bolt Action Rifle **$595**
Caliber: 22 LR. 5-shot magazine. 21-inch heavy, bull barrel. 39½ inches overall. Weight: 7½ pounds. No sights. Grooved receiver for scope mounts. European walnut stock in off-hand match-style configuration. Match or double-set triggers. Imported 1983–86.

Krico Model 311

Krico Model 320 Sporter

Krico Model 340 Metallic Silhouette Rifle

Krico Model 420 Bolt Action

Krico Model 640 Super Sniper

Krico Model 360S Biathlon Rifle **$1025**
Caliber: 22 LR. Five 5-shot magazines. 21¼-inch barrel with snow cap. 40½ inches overall. Weight: 9¼ pounds. Straight-pull action. Match trigger with 17½ oz. pull. Sights: globe front; adjustable match peep rear. Biathlon-style walnut stock with high comb and adjustable buttplate. Made 1991 to date.

Krico Model 360 S2 Biathlon Rifle **$950**
Similar to the Model 360S, except with pistol-grip activated action. Biathlon-style walnut stock with black epoxy finish. Made 1991 to date.

Krico Model 400 Bolt Action Rifle **$710**
Caliber: 22 Hornet. 5-shot detachable box magazine. 23½-inch barrel. Weight: 6¾ pounds. Adj. open rear sight, ramp front. European walnut stock. Discontinued 1990.

Krico Model 420 Bolt Action Rifle **$695**
Same as Model 400, except has full-length Mannlicher-style stock and double-set triggers. Scope optional, extra. Discontinued 1989.

Krico Model 440 S Bolt Action Rifle **$705**
Caliber: 22 Hornet. Detachable box magazine. 20-inch barrel. 36½ inches overall. Weight: 7½ pounds. No sights. French walnut stock w/ventilated forend. Discont. 1988.

Krico Model 500 Match Rifle **$3000**
Caliber: 22 LR. Single shot. 23.6-inch barrel. 42 inches overall. Weight: 9.4 pounds. Kricotronic electronic ignition system. Sights: globe front; match micrometer aperture rear. Match-style European walnut stock w/adj. butt.

Krico Model 600 Bolt Action Rifle **$1025**
Same general specifications as Model 700, except with short action. Calibers: 17 Rem., 222, 223, 22-250, 243, 5.6×50 Mag. and 308.

Krico Model 620 Bolt Action Rifle **$895**
Same as Model 600, except has short action chambered 308 Win. only and full-length Mannlicher-style stock with schnabel forend tip. 20¾-inch barrel. Weight: 6½ pounds. No longer imported.

Krico Model 640 Super Sniper Bolt Action Repeating Rifle **$1095**
Calibers: 223 Rem., 308 Win. 3-shot magazine. 26-inch barrel. 44¾ inches overall. Weight: 9½ pounds. No sights, drilled and tapped for scope mounts. Single or double-set triggers. Select walnut stock with adjustable cheekpiece and recoil pad. Discontinued 1989.

Krico Model 640 Varmint Rifle **$695**
Caliber: 222 Rem. 4-shot magazine. 23¾-inch barrel. Weight: 9½ pounds. No sights. European walnut stock. No longer imported.

Krico Model 700 Bolt Action Rifle
Calibers: 17 Rem., 222, 222 Rem. Mag., 223, 22-250, 5.6×50 Mag., 243, 5.6×57 RSW, 6×62, 6.5×55, 6.5×57, 6.5×68, 270 Win., 7×64, 7.5 Swiss, 7mm Mag., 30-06, 300 Win., 8×68S, 9.3×64. 24-inch (standard) or 26-inch (magnum) barrel. 44 inches overall (standard). Weight: 7½ pounds. Adj. rear sight; hooded ramp front. Checkered European-style walnut stock w/Bavarian cheekpiece and rosewood schnabel forend tip. Imported 1983 to date.
Model 700 . . . . **$ 750**
Model 700 Deluxe 770
Model 700 Deluxe S 1120
Model 700 Stutzen 970

Krico Model 720 Bolt Action Rifle
Same general specifications as Model 700, except in calibers 270 Win. and 30-06 with full-length Mannlicher-style stock and schnabel forend tip. 20¾-inch barrel. Weight: 6¾ pounds. Discontinued importing 1990.
Sporter Model . . . . **$ 950**
Ltd. Edition 1695

Krico Bolt Action Sporting Rifle

Krico Bolt Action Sporting Rifle $535
Miniature Mauser action. Single- or double-set trigger. Calibers: 22 Hornet, 222 Rem. 4-shot clip magazine. 22-, 24- or 26-inch barrel. Weight: about 6¼ pounds. Sights: open rear; hooded ramp front. Checkered stock w/cheek-

Krico Bolt Action Sporting Rifle (cont.)
piece, pistol grip, black forend tip, sling swivels. Made 1956–1962.

Krico Carbine $525
Same as Krico Sporting Rifle, except has 20- or 22-inch barrel, full-length Mannlicher-type stock.

Krico Special Varmint Rifle $550
Same as Krico Rifle, except has heavy barrel, no sights, weighs about 7¼ pounds. Caliber: 222 Rem. only.

Krieghoff Teck Over/Under

Krieghoff Ulm Over/Under

KRIEGHOFF RIFLES
Ulm (Donau), Germany
Mfd. by H. Krieghoff Jagd und Sportwaffenfabrik

See also combination guns under Krieghoff shotgun listings.

Krieghoff Teck Over/Under Rifle
Kersten action, double crossbolt, double underlugs. Box lock. Calibers: 7×57r5, 7×64, 7×65r5, 30-30, 308 Win., 30-06, 300 Win. Mag., 9.3×74r5, 375 H&H Mag., 458 Win. Mag. 25-inch barrels. Weight: 8 to 9½ pounds. Sights: express rear; ramp front. Checkered walnut stock and forearm. Made 1967 to date.
Standard calibers **$4250**
375 H&H Mag. (disc. 1988), 458 Win. Mag...... **5295**

Krieghoff Ulm Over/Under Rifle $6950
Same general specifications as Teck model, except has side locks with leaf arabesque engraving. Made 1963 to date.

Krieghoff ULM-Primus Over/Under Rifle $8450
Deluxe version of Ulm model, has detachable side locks, higher grade engraving and stock wood. Made 1963 to date.

LAKEFIELD ARMS LTD.
Ontario, Canada

Lakefield Model 64B Semiautomatic Rifle $120
Caliber: 22 LR. 10-shot magazine. 20-inch barrel. Weight: 5½ pounds. 40 inches overall. Bead front sight, adjustable

Lakefield Model 64B Semiautomatic Rifle (cont.)
rear. Grooved receiver for scope mounts. Checkered walnut-finished hardwood stock with Monte Carlo. Made 1990 to date.

Lakefield Model 90B Bolt Action Target Rifle ... $375
Caliber: 22 LR. 5-shot magazine. 21-inch barrel w/snow cap. 39⅝ inches overall. Weight: 8¼ pounds. Adj. receiver peep sight; globe front w/inserts. Receiver drilled and tapped for scope mounts. Biathlon-style natural finished hardwood stock w/shooting rails, hand stop and butthook. Made 1991 to date.

Lakefield Model 91T/91TR Bolt Action Target Rifle
Calibers: 22 Short, Long, LR. 25-inch barrel. 43⅝ inches overall. Weight: 8 pounds. Adj. rear peep sight; globe front w/inserts. Receiver drilled and tapped for scope mounts. Walnut finished hardwood stock w/shooting rails and hand stop. **Model 91TR** is a 5-shot clip-fed repeater. Made 1991 to date.
Model 91T Single Shot **$315**
Model 91TR Repeater (22 LR only) **335**

Lakefield Model 64B

Lakefield Model 92S

Lakefield Mark I

RIFLES

Lakefield Model 92S Target Rifle **$310**
Same general specifications as Model 90B, except with
conventional target-style stock. 8 pounds. No sights.

Lakefield Mark I Bolt Action Rifle **$90**
Calibers: 22 Short, Long, LR. Single-shot. 20½-inch barrel
(19-inch Youth Model); available in smoothbore. Weight:
5½ pounds. 39½ inches overall. Bead front sight; adj.

Lakefield Mark I Bolt Action Rifle (cont.)
rear. Grooved receiver for scope mounts. Checkered walnut-finished hardwood stock w/Monte Carlo and pistol
grip. Blued finish. Made 1990 to date.

Lakefield Mark II Bolt Action Rifle
Same general specifications as the Mark I, except in the
repeater version with 10-shot clip magazine in 22 LR only.
Mark II Standard . . . . **$ 95**
Mark II Youth (19-inch barrel) **95**
Mark II Left-hand **105**

Luna Single Shot Target Rifle

LUNA RIFLE
Mehlis, Germany
Manufactured by Ernst Friedr. Büchel

Luna Single Shot Target Rifle **$895**
Falling block action. Calibers: 22 LR, 22 Hornet. 29-inch
barrel. Weight: about 8¼ pounds. Sights: micrometer peep
rear tang; open rear; ramp front. Cheekpiece stock w/full
pistol grip, semibeavertail forearm, checkered, swivels.
Made before WWII.

Mannlicher Model L Carbine

MANNLICHER SPORTING RIFLES
Steyr, Austria
Manufactured by Steyr-Daimler-Puch, A.-G.

In 1967, Steyr-Daimler-Puch introduced a series of sporting
rifles with a bolt action that is a departure from the Mannlicher-Schoenauer system of earlier models. In the latter,
the action is locked by lugs symmetrically arranged behind
the bolt head as well as by placing the bolt handle ahead
of the right flank of the receiver, the rear section of which
is open on top for backward movement of the bolt handle.
The current action, made in four lengths to accommodate
different ranges of cartridges, has a closed-top receiver;
the bolt locking lugs are located toward the rear of the bolt
(behind the magazine), and the Mannlicher-Schoenauer rotary magazine has been redesigned as a detachable box
type of Makrolon.

Mannlicher Model L Carbine **$995**
Same general specifications as Model SL Carbine, except
has type "L" action, weighs about 6.2 pounds. Calibers
same as for Model L Rifle. Made 1968 to date.

Mannlicher Model L Rifle

Mannlicher Model M Carbine

Mannlicher Model M Professional

Mannlicher Model M Rifle

Mannlicher Left-handed Model M Rifle

Mannlicher Model L Rifle $1050
Same general specifications as Model SL Rifle, except has
type "L" action, weighs about 6.3 pounds. Calibers: 22-
250, 5.6×57 (discontinued 1991), 243 Win., 6mm Rem.,
308 Win. Made 1968 to date.

Mannlicher Model L Varmint Rifle $1065
Same general specifications as Model SL Varmint Rifle,
except has type "L" action. Calibers: 22-250, 243 Win.,
308 Win. Made 1969 to date.

Mannlicher Model Luxus Bolt Action Rifle
Same general specifications as Models L and M, except
with 3-shot detachable box magazine and single-set trigger. Full or half-stock with low-luster oil or high-gloss
lacquer finish.
Full stock $1325
Half stock 1295

Mannlicher Model M Carbine
Same general specifications as Model SL Carbine, except
has type "M" action, stock w/recoil pad, weighs about 6.8
pounds. Made 1969 to date. Left-hand version w/addi-
tional 6.5×55 and 9.3×62 calibers introduced in 1977.
Right-hand Carbine $1000
Left-hand Carbine 1250

Mannlicher Model M Professional Rifle $1025
Same as standard Model M Rifle, except has synthetic
(Cycolac) stock, weighs about 7½ pounds. Calibers:
6.5×55, 6.5×57, 270 Win., 7×57, 7×64, 7.5 Swiss, 30-06,
8×57JS, 9.3×62. Introduced 1977.

Mannlicher Model M Rifle
Same general specifications as Model SL Rifle, except w/
type "M" action, stock w/forend tip and recoil pad; weighs
about 6.9 pounds. Calibers: 6.5×57, 270 Win., 7×57, 7×64,

Mannlicher Model SL Carbine

**Mannlicher Model SL Rifle
Double-Set Trigger**

**Mannlicher Model SL Rifle
Single-Set Trigger**

**Mannlicher Model SSG
Match Target Rifle**

RIFLES

Mannlicher Model M Rifle (cont.)

30-06, 8×57JS, 9.3×62. Made 1969 to date. Left-hand version also in calibers 6.5 × 55 and 7.5 Swiss intr. 1977.
Right-hand Rifle **$865**
Left-hand Rifle **995**

Mannlicher Model S Rifle **$895**

Same general specifications as Model SL Rifle, except has type "S" action, 4-round magazine, 25⁵/₈-inch barrel, stock with forend tip and recoil pad, weighs about 8.4 pounds. Calibers: 6.5×68, 257 Weatherby Mag., 264 Win. Mag., 7mm Rem. Mag., 300 Win. Mag., 300 H&H Mag., 308 Norma Mag., 8×68S, 338 Win. Mag., 9.3×64, 37 H&H Mag. Made 1970 to date.

Mannlicher Model SL Carbine **$995**

Same general specifications as Model SL Rifle, except has 20-inch barrel and full-length stock, weighs about 6 pounds. Made 1968 to date.

Mannlicher Model SL Rifle **$960**

Steyr-Mannlicher SL bolt action. Calibers: 222 Rem., 222 Rem. Mag., 223 Rem. 5-shot rotary magazine, detachable. 23⁵/₈-inch barrel. Weight: about 6 pounds. Single- or double-set trigger (mechanisms interchangeable). Sights: open rear; hooded ramp front. Half stock of European walnut w/Monte Carlo comb and cheekpiece, skip-checkered forearm and pistol grip, rubber buttpad, QD swivels. Made 1967 to date.

Mannlicher Model SL Varmint Rifle **$995**

Same general specifications as Model SL Rifle, except caliber 222 Rem. only, has 25⁵/₈-inch heavy barrel, no sights, weighs about 7.92 pounds. Made 1969 to date.

Mannlicher Model SSG Match Target Rifle

Type "L" action. Caliber: 308 Win. (7.62×51 NATO). 5- or 10-round magazine, single-shot plug. 25¹/₂-inch heavy barrel. Weight: 10¹/₄ pounds. Single trigger. Sights: micrometer peep rear; globe front. Target stock, European walnut or synthetic, with full pistol grip, wide forearm w/ swivel rail, adj. rubber buttplate. Made 1969 to date.
W/walnut stock **$1495**
W/synthetic stock **1240**

Mannlicher Model S/T Rifle **$995**

Same as Model S Rifle, except has heavy 25⁵/₈-inch barrel, weighs about 9 pounds. Calibers: 9.3×64, 375 H&H Mag., 458 Win. Mag. Option of 23⁵/₈-inch barrel in latter caliber. Made 1975 to date.

> **NOTE:** Certain Mannlicher-Schoenauer models were produced before WWII. Manufacture of sporting rifles and carbines was resumed at the Steyr-Daimler-Puch plant in Austria in 1950 during which time the Model 1950 rifles and carbines were introduced.

Mannlicher-Schoenauer Model 1903
Sporting Carbine

Mannlicher-Schoenauer
Model 1905 Carbine

Mannlicher-Schoenauer
Model 1950 Rifle

Mannlicher-Schoenauer
Model 1950 Carbine

Mannlicher-Schoenauer
Model 1952 Carbine

Mannlicher-Schoenauer Model 1903 Bolt Action Sporting Carbine **$925**
Caliber: 6.5×53mm (referred to in some European gun catalogs as 6.7×53mm, following the Austrian practice of designating calibers by bullet diameter). 5-shot rotary magazine. 450mm (17.7-inch) barrel. Weight: about 6$\frac{1}{2}$ pounds. Double-set trigger. Sights: two-leaf rear; ramp front. Full-length sporting stock w/cheekpiece, pistol grip, trap buttplate, swivels. Pre-WWII.

Mannlicher-Schoenauer Model 1905 Carbine . . . **$895**
Same as Model 1903, except caliber 9×56mm and has 19.7-inch barrel, weighs about 6$\frac{3}{4}$ pounds. Pre-WWII.

Mannlicher-Schoenauer Model 1908 Carbine . . . **$925**
Same as Model 1905, except calibers 7×57mm and 8×56mm. Pre-WWII.

Mannlicher-Schoenauer Model 1910 Carbine . . **$1095**
Same as Model 1905, except in 9.5×57mm. Pre-WWII.

Mannlicher-Schoenauer Model 1924 Carbine . . . **$950**
Same as Model 1905, except caliber 30-06 (7.62×63mm). Pre-WWII.

Mannlicher-Schoenauer Model 1950 Bolt Action Sporting Rifle **$895**
Calibers: 257 Roberts, 270 Win., 30-06. 5-shot rotary magazine. 24-inch barrel. Weight: about 7$\frac{1}{4}$ pounds. Single trigger or double-set trigger. Redesigned low bolt handle, shot-gun-type safety. Sights: folding leaf open rear; hooded ramp front. Improved half-length stock w/cheekpiece, pistol grip, checkered, ebony forend tip, swivels. Made 1950–52.

Mannlicher-Schoenauer Model 1950 Carbine . . . **$850**
Same general specifications as Model 1950 Rifle except has 20-inch barrel, full-length stock, weighs about 7 pounds. Made 1950–52.

Mannlicher-Schoenauer Model 1950 6.5 Carbine **$820**
Same as other Model 1950 Carbines except caliber 6.5×53mm, has 18$\frac{1}{4}$-inch barrel, weighs 6$\frac{3}{4}$ pounds. Made 1950–52.

Mannlicher-Schoenauer Model 1952 Improved Carbine **$925**
Same as Model 1950 Carbine except has swept-back bolt handle, redesigned stock. Calibers: 257, 270, 7mm, 30-06. Made 1952–56.

RIFLES

Mannlicher-Schoenauer
Model 1956 Rifle

Mannlicher-Schoenauer
Model 1961-MCA Carbine

Mannlicher-Schoenauer
High Velocity Sporting Rifle

Mannlicher-Schoenauer
M72 Model L/M Carbine

Mannlicher-Schoenauer Model 1952 Improved 6.5 Carbine $825
Same as Model 1952 Carbine except caliber 6.5×53mm, has 18¼-inch barrel. Made 1952–56.

Mannlicher-Schoenauer Model 1952 Improved Sporting Rifle $675
Same as Model 1950 except has swept-back bolt handle, redesigned stock. Calibers: 257, 270, 30-06, 9.3×62mm. Made 1952–56.

Mannlicher-Schoenauer Model 1956 Custom Carbine $795
Same general specifications as Models 1950 and 1952 Carbines, except has redesigned stock with high comb. Calibers: 243, 6.5mm, 257, 270, 7mm, 30-06, 308. Made 1956–1960.

Mannlicher-Schoenauer Model 1956 Custom Sporting Rifle $650
Same general specifications as Models 1950 and 1952 except 22-inch barrel, redesigned stock with high comb. Calibers: 243 and 30-06. Made 1956–1960.

Mannlicher-Schoenauer Carbine, Model 1961-MCA $695
Same as Model 1956 Carbine, except has universal Monte Carlo design stock. Calibers: 243 Win., 6.5mm, 270, 308, 30-06. Made 1961–1971.

Mannlicher-Schoenauer Rifle, Model 1961-MCA . . $725
Same as Model 1956 Rifle, except has universal Monte Carlo design stock. Calibers: 243, 270, 30-06. Made 1961–1971.

Mannlicher-Schoenauer High Velocity Bolt Action Sporting Rifle $1200
Calibers: 7×64 Brenneke, 30-06 (7.62×63), 8×60 Magnum, 9.3×62, 10.75×68mm. 23.6-inch barrel. Weight: about 7½ pounds. Sights: British-style 3-leaf open rear; ramp front. Half-length sporting stock w/cheek-piece, pistol grip, checkered, trap buttplate, swivels. Also produced in takedown model. Pre-WWII.

Mannlicher-Schoenauer M72 Model L/M Carbine $895
Same general specifications as M72 Model L/M Rifle, except has 20-inch barrel and full-length stock, weighs about 7.2 pounds. Made 1972 to date.

Mannlicher-Schoenauer M72 Model L/M Rifle . . $950
M72 bolt action, type L/M receiver, front-locking bolt, internal rotary magazine (5-round). Calibers: 22-250, 5.6×57, 6mm Rem., 243 Win., 6.5×57, 270 Win., 7×57, 7×64, 308 Win., 30-06. 23⅝-inch barrel. Weight: about 7.3 pounds. Single- or double-set trigger (mechanisms interchangeable). Sights: open rear; hooded ramp front. Half stock of European walnut, checkered forearm and pistol grip, Monte Carlo cheekpiece, rosewood forend tip, recoil pad, QD swivels. Made 1972 to date.

Mannlicher-Schoenauer M72 Model S Rifle $895
Same general specifications as M72 Model L/M Rifle, except has Magnum action, 4-round magazine, 25⅝-inch barrel, weighs about 8.6 pounds. Calibers: 6.5×68, 7mm Rem. Mag., 8×68S, 9.3×64, 375 H&H Mag. Made 1972 to date.

Mannlicher-Schoenauer M72 Model S/T Rifle . . . $995
Same as M72 Model S Rifle, except has heavy 25⅝-inch barrel, weighs about 9.3 pounds. Calibers: 300 Win. Mag., 9.3×64, 375 H&H Mag., 458 Win. Mag. Option of 23⅝-inch barrel in latter caliber. Made 1975 to date.

MARLIN FIREARMS CO.
North Haven, Connecticut

Marlin Model 9 Semiautomatic Carbine
Calibers: 9mm Parabellum. 12-shot magazine. 16.5-inch barrel. 35½ inches overall. Weight: 6¾ pounds. Manual bolt hold-open. Sights: hooded post front; adj. open rear. Walnut-finished hardwood stock w/rubber buttpad. Blued or nickel-Teflon finish. Made 1985 to date.

Model 9 . . . . **$245**
Model 9N (Nickel-Teflon) **310**

Marlin Model 15Y **$90**
Bolt-action, single-shot "Little Buckaroo" rifle. Caliber: 22 Short, Long or LR. 16¼-inch barrel. Weight: 4¼ pounds. Thumb safety. Ramp front sight, adj. open rear. One-piece walnut Monte Carlo stock w/full pistol grip. Made 1984–88.

Marlin Model 18 Baby Slide Action Repeater . . . $225
Exposed hammer. Solid frame. Caliber: 22 LR, Long, Short. Tubular magazine holds 14 Short. 20-inch barrel, round or octagon. Weight: 3¾ pounds. Sights: 0pen rear;

Marlin Model 18 Baby Slide Action Repeater (cont.)
bead front. Plain straight-grip stock and slide handle. Made 1906–1909.

Marlin Model 20 Slide Action Repeating Rifle . . . $240
Exposed hammer. Takedown. Caliber: 22 LR, Long, Short. Tubular magazine: half-length holds 15 Short, 12 Long, 10 LR; full-length holds 25 Short, 20 Long, 18 LR. 24-inch octagon barrel. Weight: about 5 pounds. Sights: open rear; bead front. Plain straight-grip stock, grooved slide handle. Made 1907–1922. *Note:* After 1920 was designated "Model 20-S."

Marlin Model 25 Bolt Action Rifle $100
Caliber: 22 Short, Long or LR. 7-shot clip. 22-inch barrel. Weight: 5½ pounds. Ramp front sight, adj. open rear. One-piece walnut Monte Carlo stock w/full pistol grip. Mar-Shield finish. Made 1984–88.

Marlin Model 25 Slide Action Repeater $250
Exposed hammer. Takedown. Caliber: 22 Short (also handles 22 CB Caps). Tubular magazine holds 15 Short. 23-inch barrel. Weight: about 4 pounds. Sights: open rear; beaded front. Plain straight-grip stock and slide handle. Made 1909–1910.

**Marlin Model 9
9mm Carbine**

**Marlin Model 15Y
"Little Buckaroo"**

Marlin Model 20

**Marlin Model 25
Bolt Action Rifle**

Marlin Model 25M Bolt Action W/Scope $120
Caliber: 22 WMR. 7-shot clip. 22-inch barrel. Weight: 6 pounds. Ramp front sight w/brass bead, adj. open rear. Walnut-finished stock w/Monte Carlo styling and full pistol grip. Sling swivels. Made 1986–88.

**Marlin Model 25 MB
Midget Magnum**

Marlin Model 25MB Midget Magnum $115
Bolt action. Caliber: 22 WMR. 7-shot capacity. 16¼-inch barrel. Weight: 4¾ pounds. Walnut-finished Monte Carlo-style stock w/full pistol grip and abbreviated forend. Sights: ramp front w/brass bead, adj. open rear. Thumb safety. Made 1986–88.

Marlin Model 25MN/25N Bolt Action Rifle
Caliber: 22 WMR (Model 25MN) or 22 LR (Model 25N). 7-shot clip magazine. 22-inch barrel. 41 inches overall.

Marlin Model 25MN/25N Bolt Action Rifle (cont.)
Weight: 5½ to 6 pounds. Adj. open rear sight, ramp front; receiver grooved for scope mounts. One piece walnut-finished hardwood Monte Carlo stock w/pistol grip. Currently manufactured.
Marlin Model 25MN **$130**
Marlin Model 25N **115**

Marlin Model 27 Slide Action Repeating Rifle ... $240
Exposed hammer. Takedown. Calibers: 25-20, 32-20. ⅔ magazine (tubular) holds 7 shots. 24-inch octagon barrel. Weight: about 5¾ pounds. Sights: open rear; bead front. Plain straight-grip stock, grooved slide handle. Made 1910–1916.

Marlin Model 27S $250
Same as Model 27, except has round barrel, also chambered for 25 Stevens R.F. Made 1920–1932.

Marlin Model 29 Slide Action Repeater $260
Similar to Model 20, has 23-inch round barrel, half magazine only, weighs about 5¾ pounds. **Model 37** is same type except has 24-inch barrel and full magazine. Made 1913–1916.

Marlin Model 30AS Lever Action $215
Caliber: 30/30 Win. 6-shot tubular magazine. 20-inch barrel with Micro-Groove rifling. 38¼ inches overall. Weight: 7 pounds. Brass bead front sight, adj. rear. Solid top receiver, offset hammer spur for scope use. Walnut-finished hardwood stock w/pistol grip. Mar-Shield finish. Made 1984 to date.

RIFLES

Marlin Model 25M w/Scope

Marlin Model 27

Marlin Model 29

**Marlin Model 30AS
Lever Action Rifle**

Marlin Model 38

Marlin Model 39 Carbine

Marlin Model 39
90th Anniversary Carbine

Marlin 39 Century Ltd.

Marlin Model 39 Rifle

Marlin Model 32 Slide Action Repeater **$265**
Hammerless. Takedown. Caliber: 22 LR, Long, Short. 2/3 tubular magazine holds 15 Short, 12 Long, 10 LR; full magazine, 25 Short, 20 Long, 18 LR. 24-inch octagon barrel. Weight: about 5 1/2 pounds. Sights: open rear; bead front. Plain pistol-grip stock, grooved slide handle. Made 1914–1915.

**Marlin Model 36 Lever Action Repeating
Carbine** **$225**
Calibers: 30-30, 32 Special. 6-shot tubular magazine. 20-inch barrel. Weight: about 6 1/2 pounds. Sights: 0pen rear; bead front. Pistol-grip stock, semibeavertail forearm w/ carbine barrel band. Made 1936–1948. *Note:* In 1936, this was designated "Model 1936."

Marlin Model 36 Sporting Carbine **$325**
Same as Model 36A rifle except has 20-inch barrel, weighs 6 1/4 pounds.

Marlin Model 36A/36A-DL Lever Action Repeating Rifle
Same as Model 36 Carbine, except has 2/3 magazine holding 5 cartridges, 24-inch barrel, weighs 6 3/4 pounds, has hooded front sight, semibeavertail forearm. Model 36A-DL has deluxe checkered stock, swivels and sling. Made 1938–1948.
Model 36A Standard **$205**
Model 36A-DL (Deluxe) **280**

Marlin Model 38 Slide Action Repeating Rifle . . . **$245**
Hammerless. Takedown. Caliber: 22 LR, Long, Short. 2/3 magazine (tubular) holds 15 Short, 12 Long, 10 LR. 24-inch octagon barrel. Weight: about 5 1/2 pounds. Sights: open rear; bead front. Plain pistol-grip stock, grooved slide handle. Made 1920–1930.

Marlin Model 39 Carbine **$175**
Same as Model 39M, except has lightweight barrel, 3/4 magazine (capacity: 18 Short, 14 Long, 12 LR), slimmer forearm. Weight: 5 1/4 pounds. Made 1963–67.

Marlin Model 39 90th Anniversary Carbine **$575**
Carbine version of 90th Anniversary Model 39A. 500 made in 1960. Value is for carbine in new, unfired condition.

Marlin 39 Century Ltd. **$250**
Commemorative version of Model 39A. Receiver inlaid with brass medallion, Marlin Centennial 1870–1970. Square lever. 20-inch octagon barrel. Fancy walnut straight-grip stock and forearm; brass forend cap, buttplate, nameplate in buttstock. 35,388 made in 1970.

Marlin Model 39 Lever Action Repeater **$495**
Takedown. Casehardened receiver. Caliber: 22 LR, Long, Short. Tubular magazine holds 25 Short, 20 Long, 18 LR. 24-inch octagon barrel. Weight: about 5 3/4 pounds. Sights: open rear; bead front. Plain pistol-grip stock and forearm. Made 1922–1938.

Marlin Model 39A
90th Anniversary Rifle

Marlin 39A Article II Rifle

Marlin Model 39-ADL

Marlin Golden 39A Rifle

Marlin Model 39A Octagon

Marlin Model 39A **$225**
General specifications same as Model 39, except has blued receiver, round barrel, heavier stock with semibeavertail forearm, weighs about 6½ pounds. Made 1938–1960.

Marlin Model 39A 90th Anniversary Rifle
Commemorates Marlin's 90th anniversary. Same general specifications as Golden 39A, except has chrome-plated barrel and action, stock and forearm of select walnut, finely checkered, carved figure of a squirrel on right side of buttstock. 500 made in 1960. Value is for rifle in new, unfired condition.
Model 39A 90th Anniversary Rifle **$465**
Model 39-ADL (W/Blued Barrel/Action,
  made 1960–63) **200**

Marlin Model 39A Article II Rifle **$230**
Commemorates National Rifle Association Centennial 1871–1971. "The Right to Bear Arms" medallion inlaid in receiver. Similar to Model 39A. Magazine capacity: 26

Marlin Model 39A Article II Rifle (cont.)
Short, 21 Long, 19 LR. 24-inch octagon barrel. Fancy walnut pistol-grip stock and forearm; brass forend cap, buttplate. 6,244 made in 1971.

Marlin Golden 39A/39AS Rifle
Same as Model 39A, except has gold-plated trigger, hooded ramp front sight, sling swivels. Made 1960–1987 (39A); Model 39AS currently manufactured.
Golden 39A **$205**
Golden 39AS (W/Hammer Block Safety) **225**

**Marlin Model 39A "Mountie" Lever Action
Repeating Rifle** **$225**
Same as Model 39A, except has lighter, straight-grip stock, slimmer forearm. Weight: 6¼ pounds. Made 1953–1960.

Marlin Model 39A Octagon **$395**
Same as Golden 39A, except has octagon barrel, plain bead front sight, slimmer stock and forearm, no pistol-grip cap or swivels. Made 1973.

Marlin Model 39D

Marlin 39M Article II Carbine

Marlin Golden 39M Rifle

Marlin Model 39M Octagon

Marlin Model 45

Marlin Model 39D **$195**
Same as Model 39M, except has pistol-grip stock, forearm with barrel band. Made 1970–74.

Marlin 39M Article II Carbine **$225**
Same as 39A Article II Rifle, except has straight-grip buttstock, square lever, 20-inch octagon barrel, reduced magazine capacity. 3,824 made in 1971.

Marlin Golden 39M
Calibers: 22 Short, Long and LR. Tubular magazine holds 21 Short, 16 Long or 15 LR cartridges. 20-inch barrel. 36 inches overall. Weight: about 6 pounds. Gold-plated trigger. Hooded ramp front sight, adjustable folding semi-buckhorn rear. Two-piece, straight-grip American black walnut stock. Sling swivels. Mar-Shield finish. Made 1960–1987.
Golden 39M **$200**

Marlin Golden 39M (cont.)
Model 39M Octagon (octagonal barrel, plain bead front sight, no swivels, made 1973) **$250**

Marlin Model 39M "Mountie" Carbine **$220**
Same as Model 39A "Mountie" Rifle, except has 20-inch barrel and reduced magazine capacity: 21 Short, 16 Long, 15 LR. Weight: 6 pounds. Made 1954–1960.

Marlin Model 39TDS Carbine **$260**
Same general specifications as Model 39M, except take-down style with 16½-inch barrel and reduced magazine capacity. 32⅝ inches overall. Weight: 5¼ pounds. Made 1988 to date.

Marlin Model 45 . . . . **$250**
Semiautomatic action. Caliber: 45 Auto. 7-shot clip. 16½-inch barrel. 35½ inches overall. Weight: 6¾ pounds. Manual bolt hold-open. Sights: ramp front sight w/brass bead, adj. folding rear. Receiver drilled and tapped for scope mount. Walnut-finished hardwood stock. Made 1986 to date.

RIFLES

Marlin Model 49DL

Marlin Model 50

Marlin Model 56

Marlin Model 57

Marlin Model 62

Marlin Model 49/49DL Autoloading Rifle
Same as Model 99C, except has two-piece stock, checkered after 1970. Made 1968–1971. **Model 49DL** has scrollwork on sides of receiver, checkered stock and forearm; made 1971–78.
Model 49 . . . . **$120**
Model 49DL **130**

Marlin Model 50/50E Autoloading Rifle
Takedown. Caliber: 22 LR. 6-shot detachable box magazine. 22-inch barrel. Weight: about 6 pounds. Sights: open rear; bead front; **Model 50E** has peep rear sight, hooded front. Plain pistol-grip stock, forearm with finger grooves. Made 1931–34.
Model 50 . . . . **$130**
Model 50E **150**

Marlin Model 56 Levermatic Rifle **$135**
Same as Model 57 except clip-loading. Magazine holds eight rounds. Weight: about 5³/₄ pounds. Made 1955–1964.

Marlin Model 57 Levermatic Rifle **$150**
Lever action. Caliber: 22 LR, 22 Long, 22 Short. Tubular magazine holds 19 LR, 21 Long, 27 Short. 22-inch barrel. Weight: about 6¹/₄ pounds. Sights: open rear; hooded ramp front. Monte Carlo-style stock with pistol grip. Made 1959–1965.

Marlin Model 57M Levermatic **$190**
Same as Model 57, except chambered for 22 WMR cartridge, has 24-inch barrel, 15-shot magazine. Made 1960–69.

Marlin Model 62 Levermatic Rifle **$250**
Lever action. Calibers: 256 Magnum, 30 Carbine. 4-shot clip magazine. 23-inch barrel. Weight: 7 pounds. Sights: open rear; hooded ramp front. Monte Carlo-style stock w/pistol grip, swivels and sling. Made in 256 Magnum 1963–66; in 30 Carbine 1966–69.

Marlin Model 65 Bolt Action Single Shot Rifle . . . **$115**
Takedown. Caliber: 22 LR, Long, Short. 24-inch barrel. Weight: about 5 pounds. Sights: open rear; bead front. Plain pistol-grip stock with grooved forearm. Made 1932–38. **Model 65E** is same as Model 65, except has rear peep sight and hooded front sight.

Marlin Model 70HC

Marlin Model 70P
"Papoose"

Marlin Model 75C
Semiautomatic

Marlin Model 80C

Marlin Model 80DL

Marlin Model 70HC Semiautomatic $100
Caliber: 22 LR. 7- and 15-shot magazine. 18-inch barrel.
Weight: 5½ pounds. 36¾ inches overall. Ramp front sight,
adj. open rear. Grooved receiver for scope mounts. Walnut-
finished hardwood stock w/Monte Carlo and pistol grip.

Marlin Model 70P Semiautomatic $120
"Papoose" takedown. Caliber: 22 LR. 7-shot clip. 16¼-
inch barrel. 35¼ inches overall. Weight: 3¾ pounds.
Sights: ramp front; adj. open rear. Side ejection, manual
bolt hold-open. Cross-bolt safety. Walnut-finished hardwood stock w/abbreviated forend, pistol grip. Made 1984
to date.

Marlin Model 75C Semiautomatic $125
Caliber: 22 LR. 13-shot tubular magazine. 18-inch barrel.
36½ inches overall. Weight: 5 pounds. Side ejection.
Cross-bolt safety. Sights: ramp front; adj. open rear. Monte

Marlin Model 75C Semiautomatic (cont.)
Carlo-style walnut-finished hardwood stock w/pistol grip.
Made 1975 to date.

Marlin Model 80 Bolt Action Repeating Rifle
Takedown. Caliber: 22 LR, Long, Short. 8-shot detachable
box magazine. 24-inch barrel. Weight: about 6 pounds.
Sights: open rear; bead front. Plain pistol-grip stock. Made
1934–39. **Model 80E,** w/peep rear sight; hooded front,
made 1934–1940.
Model 80 Standard **$110**
Model 80E **105**

Marlin Model 80C/80DL Bolt Action Repeater
Improved version of Model 80. **Model 80C** has bead front
sight, semibeavertail forearm; made 1940–1970. **Model
80DL** has peep rear sight; hooded front, swivels; made
1940–1965.
Model 80C **$100**
Model 80DL **105**

Marlin Model 81DL

Marlin Model 88-C

Marlin Model 89-C

Marlin Model 93 Carbine

RIFLES

Marlin Model 81/81E Bolt Action Repeater

Takedown. Caliber: 22 LR, Long, Short. Tubular magazine holds 24 Short, 20 Long, 18 LR. 24-inch barrel. Weight: about 6¼ pounds. Sights: open rear; bead front. Plain pistol-grip stock. Made 1937–1940. **Model 81E** has peep rear sight; hooded front.

Model 81 . . . . **$120**
Model 81E **140**

Marlin Model 81C/81DL Bolt Action Repeater

Improved version of Model 81 with same general specifications. **Model 81C** has bead front sight, semibeavertail forearm; made 1940–1970. **Model 81DL** has peep rear sight; hooded front, swivels; discontinued 1965.

Model 81C **$120**
Model 81DL **130**

Marlin Model 88-C/88-DL Autoloading Rifle

Takedown. Caliber: 22 LR. Tubular magazine in buttstock holds 14 cartridges. 24-inch barrel. Weight: about 6¾ pounds. Sights: open rear; hooded front. Plain pistol-grip stock. Made 1947–1956. **Model 88-DL** has receiver peep sight, checkered stock and sling swivels; made 1953–56.

Model 88-C **$125**
Model 88-DL **125**

Marlin Model 89-C/89-DL Autoloading Rifle

Clip magazine version of Model 88-C. 7-shot clip (12-shot in later models); other specifications same. Made 1950–1961. **Model 89-DL** has receiver peep sight, sling swivels.

Model 89-C **$125**
Model 89-DL **160**

Marlin Model 92 Lever Action Repeating Rifle . . **$895**

Calibers: 22 Short, Long, LR; 32 Short, Long (rimfire or centerfire by changing firing pin). Tubular magazines: holding 25 Short, 20 Long, 18 LR (22); 17 Short, 14 Long (32); 16-inch barrel model has shorter magazine holding 15 Short, 12 Long, 10 LR. Barrel lengths: 16 (22 cal. only), 24, 26, 28 inches. Weight: with 24-inch bbl., about 5½ pounds. Sights: open rear; blade front. Plain straight-grip stock and forearm. Made 1892–1916. *Note:* Originally designated "Model 1892."

Marlin Model 93/93SC Carbine

Same as Standard Model 93 Rifle, except in calibers 30-30 and 32 Special only. **Model 93** has 7-shot magazine, 20-inch round barrel, carbine sights, weighs about 6¾ pounds. **Model 93SC** has ⅔ magazine holding 5 shots, weighs 6½ pounds.

Model 93 Carbine **$910**
Model 93SC Sporting Carbine **750**

Marlin Model 93 Rifle

Marlin Model 98

Marlin Model 99DL

Marlin Model 100

Marlin Model 93 Lever Action Repeating Rifle . . **$795**
Solid frame or takedown. Calibers: 25-36 Marlin, 30-30, 32 Special, 32-40, 38-55. Tubular magazine holds 10 cartridges. 26-inch round or octagon barrel standard; also made with 28-, 30- and 32-inch barrels. Weight: about 7¼ pounds. Sights: open rear; bead front. Plain straight-grip stock and forearm. Made 1893–1936. *Note:* Before 1915 designated "Model 1893."

Marlin Model 93 Musket **$1100**
Same as Standard Model 93, except has 30-inch barrel, angular bayonet, ramrod under barrel, musket stock, full-length military-style forearm. Weight: 8 pounds. Made 1893–1915.

Marlin Model 94 Lever Action Repeating Rifle . . **$895**
Solid frame or takedown. Calibers: 25-20, 32-20, 38-40, 44-40. 10-shot tubular magazine. 24-inch round or octagon barrel. Weight: about 7 pounds. Sights open rear; bead front. Plain straight-grip stock and forearm (also available with pistol-grip stock). Made 1894–1934. *Note:* Before 1906 designated "Model 1894."

Marlin Model 97 Lever Action Repeating Rifle . . **$925**
Takedown. Caliber: 22 LR, Long, Short. Tubular magazine; full length holds 25 Short, 20 Long, 18 LR; half length holds 16 Short, 12 Long and 10 LR. Barrel lengths: 16, 24, 26, 28 inches. Weight: about 6 pounds. Sights: open rear; bead front. Plain straight-grip stock and forearm (also avail. w/pistol-grip stock). Made 1897–1922. *Note:* Before 1905 designated "Model 1897."

Marlin Model 98 Autoloading Rifle **$150**
Solid frame. Caliber: 22 LR. Tubular magazine holds 15 cartridges. 22-inch barrel. Weight: about 6¾ pounds. Sights: open rear; hooded ramp front. Monte Carlo stock w/cheekpiece. Made 1950–1961.

Marlin Model 99 Autoloading Rifle **$165**
Caliber: 22 LR. Tubular magazine holds 18 cartridges. 22-inch barrel. Weight: about 5½ pounds. Sights: open rear; hooded ramp front. Plain pistol-grip stock. Made 1959–1961.

Marlin Model 99C **$170**
Same as Model 99 except has gold-plated trigger, receiver grooved for tip-off scope mounts, Monte Carlo stock (checkered in later production). Made 1962–1978.

Marlin Model 99DL **$200**
Same as Model 99 except has gold-plated trigger, jeweled breech bolt, Monte Carlo stock w/pistol grip, swivels and sling. Made 1960–65.

Marlin Model 99M1 Carbine **$210**
Same as Model 99C except styled after U.S. 30M1 Carbine; 9-shot tubular magazine, 18-inch barrel. Sights: open rear; military-style ramp front; carbine stock w/handguard and barrel band, sling swivels. Weight: 4½ pounds. Made 1966–1979.

Marlin Model 100 Bolt Action Single Shot Rifle . . **$100**
Takedown. Caliber: 22 LR, Long, Short. 24-inch barrel. Weight: about 4½ pounds. Sights: open rear; bead front. Plain pistol-grip stock. Made 1936–1960.

Marlin Model 122

Marlin Model 336 Marauder

Marlin Model 336 Sporting Carbine

Marlin Model 336 Zane Grey Century

RIFLES

Marlin Model 100SB **$175**
Same as Model 100 except smoothbore for use with 22 shot cartridges, shotgun sight. Made 1936–1941.

Marlin Model 100 Tom Mix Special **$500**
Same as Model 100 except has peep rear sight; hooded front; sling. Made 1936–1946.

Marlin Model 101 . . . . **$105**
Improved version of Model 100 with same general specifications except has stock with beavertail forearm, weighs about 5 pounds. Introduced 1951; discontinued.

Marlin Model 101DL **$130**
Same as Model 101 except has peep rear sight; hooded front, swivels. Discontinued.

Marlin Model 122 Single Shot Junior Target Rifle **$105**
Bolt action. Caliber: 22 LR, 22 Long, 22 Short. 22-inch barrel. Weight: about 5 pounds. Sights; open rear; hooded ramp front. Monte Carlo stock w/pistol grip, swivels, sling. Made 1961–65.

Marlin Model 322 Bolt Action Varmint Rifle **$350**
Sako short Mauser action. Caliber: 222 Rem. 3-shot clip magazine. 24-inch medium weight barrel. Checkered stock. Sights: two-position peep rear; hooded ramp front. Weight: about 7$\frac{1}{2}$ pounds. Made 1954–57.

Marlin Model 336 Marauder **$295**
Same as Model 336 Texan Carbine except has 16$\frac{1}{4}$-inch barrel, weighs about 6$\frac{1}{4}$ pounds. Made 1963–64.

Marlin Model 336 Micro Groove Zipper **$520**
General specifications same as Model 336 Sporting Carbine, except caliber 219 Zipper. Made 1955–1961.

Marlin Model 336 Octagon **$255**
Same as Model 336T, except chambered for 30-30 only, has 22-inch octagon barrel. Made 1973.

Marlin Model 336 Sporting Carbine **$225**
Same as Model 336A rifle, except has 20-inch barrel, weighs 6$\frac{1}{4}$ pounds. Made 1948–1963.

Marlin Model 336 Zane Grey Century **$325**
Similar to Model 336A, except has 22-inch octagonal barrel, caliber 30-30; Zane Grey Centennial 1872–1972 medallion inlaid in receiver; select walnut stock with classic pistol grip and forearm; brass buttplate, forend cap. Weight: 7 pounds. 10,000 produced (numbered ZG1 through ZG10,000). Made 1972.

Marlin Model 336A Rifle

Marlin Model 336A-DL

Marlin Model 336CS w/Scope

Marlin Model 336DT Deluxe Texan

Marlin Model 336T Texan

Marlin Model 336A Lever Action Rifle $220
Improved version of Model 36A Rifle with same general specifications, has improved action with round breech bolt. Calibers: 30-30, 32 Special (discontinued 1963), 35 Rem. (introduced 1952). Made 1948–1963; reintroduced 1973, discontinued 1980.

Marlin Model 336A-DL $350
Same as Model 336A Rifle except has deluxe checkered stock and forearm, swivels and sling. Made 1948–1963.

Marlin Model 336C Lever Action Carbine $225
Improved version of Model 36 Carbine with same general specifications, has improved action with round breech bolt. Made 1948–1983. *Note:* Cal. 35 Rem. introduced 1953. Cal. 32 Win. Spl. discontinued 1963.

Marlin Model 336CS W/Scope $295
Lever action with hammer block safety. Caliber: 30/30 Win. or 35 Rem. 6-shot tubular magazine. 20-inch barrel with Micro-Groove rifling. $38\frac{1}{2}$ inches overall. Weight: 7 pounds. Ramp front sight, adj. semibuckhorn folding rear. Solid top receiver for scope mount or receiver sight; offset hammer spur for scope use. American black walnut stock w/pistol grip, fluted comb. Mar-Shield finish. Made 1984 to date.

Marlin Model 336DT Deluxe Texan $250
Same as Model 336T, except has select walnut stock and forearm, hand-carved longhorn steer and map of Texas on buttstock. Made 1962–64.

Marlin Model 336T Texan Lever Action Carbine $200
Same as Model 336 Carbine, except has straight-grip stock and is not available in caliber 32 Special. Made 1953–1983. Caliber 44 Magnum made 1963–67.

RIFLES

Marlin Model 336TS Rifle

Marlin Model 444 Rifle

Marlin Model 444SS Rifle

Marlin Model 455 Sporter

Marlin Model 336TS **$240**
Lever action with hammer block safety. Caliber: 30/30 Win. 6-shot tubular magazine. 18½-inch Micro-Groove barrel. 37 inches overall. Weight: 6½ pounds. Ramp front sight, adjustable semibuckhorn folding rear. Straight-grip American black walnut stock. Made 1983–87.

Marlin Model 444 Lever Action Repeating Rifle . **$250**
Action similar to Model 336. Caliber: 444 Marlin. 4-shot tubular magazine. 24-inch barrel. Weight: 7½ pounds. Sights: open rear; hooded ramp front. Monte Carlo stock w/straight grip, recoil pad. Carbine-style forearm w/barrel band. Swivels, sling. Made 1965–1971.

Marlin 444 Sporter **$295**
Same as Model 444 Rifle, except has 22-inch barrel, pistol-grip stock and forearm as on Model 336A, recoil pad, QD swivels and sling. Made 1972–1983.

Marlin Model 444SS **$305**
Same general specifications as Model 444, except has hammer safety. Made 1984 to date.

Marlin Model 455 Bolt Action Sporter **$325**
FN Mauser action with Sako trigger. Calibers: 270, 30-06, 308. 5-shot box magazine. 24-inch medium weight stainless-steel barrel. Monte Carlo stock w/cheekpiece, checkered pistol grip and forearm. Lyman 48 receiver sight; hooded ramp front. Weight: about 8½ pounds. Made 1957–59.

Marlin Model 780

Marlin Model 781

Marlin Model 783

Marlin Model 882L

Marlin Model 883N

Marlin Model 780 Bolt Action Repeater Series

Caliber: 22 LR, Long, Short. 7-shot clip magazine. 22-inch barrel. Weight: 5½ to 6 pounds. Sights: open rear; hooded ramp front. Receiver grooved for scope mounting. Monte Carlo stock w/checkered pistol grip and forearm. Made 1971–1988.

Model 780 Standard . . . . $ 95
Model 781 (w/tubular magazine holding 17 LR,
  19 Long, 25 Short)   95
Model 782 (22 WMR, w/swivels, sling) 120
Model 783 (w/12-shot tubular magazine) 125

Marlin Model 880 Bolt Action Repeater Series

Caliber: 22 rimfire. 7-shot magazine. 22-inch barrel. 41 inches overall. Weight: 5½ to 6 pounds. Hooded ramp front sight; adj. folding rear. Grooved receiver for scope

Marlin Model 880 Bolt Action Repeater Series (cont.)

mounts. Checkered Monte Carlo-style walnut stock w/ QD studs and rubber recoil pad. Made 1989 to date.

Model 880 (22 LR) **$130**
Model 881 (w/Tubular Magazine of 17 LR, 19 Long
  or 25 Short) **135**
Model 882 (22 WMR) **140**
Model 882L (w/Laminated Hardwood Stock) **150**
Model 883 (22 WMR w/12-shot Tubular Maga-
  zine) **145**
Model 883N (w/Nickel-Teflon Finish) **165**
Model 883SS (Stainless w/Laminated Stock) **175**

Marlin Model 922 Magnum Self-Loading Rifle . . $240

Similar to the Model 9, except chambered for 22 WMR. 7-shot magazine. 20½-inch barrel. 39¾ inches overall. Weight: 6½ pounds. American black walnut stock with Monte Carlo. Blued finish. Made 1993 to date.

Marlin Model 980

Marlin Model 989

Marlin Model 989M2

Marlin Model 990
Semiautomatic

Marlin Model 990L
(Laminated Stock)

Marlin Model 995
Semiautomatic

RIFLES

Marlin Model 980 22 Magnum **$125**
Bolt action. Caliber: 22 WMR. 8-shot clip magazine. 24-inch barrel. Weight: about 6 pounds. Sights: open rear; hooded ramp front. Monte Carlo stock, swivels, sling. Made 1962–1970.

Marlin Model 989 Autoloading Rifle **$100**
Caliber: 22 LR. 7-shot clip magazine. 22-inch barrel. Weight: about 5½ pounds. Sights: open rear; hooded ramp front. Monte Carlo walnut stock w/pistol grip. Made 1962–66.

Marlin Model 989M2 Carbine **$110**
Same as Model 99M1, except clip-loading, 7-shot magazine. Made 1966–1979.

Marlin Model 990 Semiautomatic
Caliber: 22 LR. 17-shot tubular magazine. 22-inch barrel. 40¾ inches overall. Weight: about 5½ pounds. Side ejection. Cross-bolt safety. Ramp front sight w/brass bead; adj. semibuckhorn folding rear. Receiver grooved for scope mount. Monte Carlo-style American black walnut stock w/checkered pistol grip and forend. Made 1979–1987.
Model 990 Semiautomatic **$110**
Model 990L (w/14 Rounds, Laminated hardwood
    stock, QD studs, Black recoil pad; 1992 to date)   **135**

Marlin Model 995 Semiautomatic **$130**
Caliber: 22 LR. 7-shot clip magazine. 18-inch barrel. 36¾ inches overall. Weight: about 5 pounds. Cross-bolt safety. Sights: ramp front w/brass bead; adj. folding semibuckhorn rear. Monte Carlo-style American black walnut stock w/checkered pistol grip and forend. Made 1979 to date.

Marlin 1870-1970 Centennial Matched Pair

Marlin Model 1894 Carbine

Marlin Model 1894 Sporter

Marlin 1870–1970 Centennial Matched Pair, Models 336 and 39 . . . . **$1575**
Presentation grade rifles in luggage-style case. Matching serial numbers. Fancy walnut straight-grip buttstock and forearm, brass buttplate and forend cap. Engraved receiver w/inlaid medallion; square lever. 20-inch octagon barrel. Model 336: 30-30, 7-shot, 7 pounds. Model 39: 22 Short, Long, LR; tubular magazine holds 21 Short, 16 Long, 15 LR. 1,000 sets produced. Made 1970. Value is for rifles in new, unfired condition.

Marlin Model 1892 Lever Action Rifle
See Marlin Model 92.

Marlin Model 1893 Lever Action Rifle
See Marlin Model 93.

Marlin Model 1894 Carbine
Replica of original Model 94. Caliber: 44 Rem. 10-shot magazine. 20-inch round barrel. Weight: 6 pounds. Sights: open rear; ramp front. Straight-grip stock. Made 1969–1984.
Standard Model 1894 Carbine **$285**
Model 1894 Octagon (w/Octagon barrel, bead front
   sight; made 1973) **275**
Model 1894 Sporter (w/22-inch barrel, 6-shot
   magazine; made 1973 . . . . **310**

Marlin Model 1894 Lever Action Rifle
See Marlin Model 94.

RIFLES

Marlin Model 1894CS

Marlin Model 1894M

Marlin Model 1894S

Marlin Model 1895 45/70 Repeater

Marlin 1894CL Classic **$285**
Calibers: 218 Bee, 25-20 Win., 32-20 Win. 6-shot tubular magazine. 22-inch barrel. 38³/₄ inches overall. Weight: 6¹/₄ pounds. Adjustable semi-buckhorn folding rear sight, brass bead front. Receiver tapped for scope mounts. Straight-grip American black walnut stock with Mar-Shield® finish. Made 1988 to date.

Marlin Model 1894CS Lever Action **$275**
Caliber: 357 Magnum, 38 Special. 9-shot tubular magazine. 18¹/₂-inch barrel. 36 inches overall. Weight: 6 pounds. Side ejection. Hammer block safety. Square finger lever. Bead front sight, adj. semibuckhorn folding rear. Offset hammer spur for scope use. Two-piece straight-grip American black walnut stock w/white buttplate spacer. Mar-Shield® finish. Made 1984 to date.

Marlin Model 1894M Lever Action **$220**
Caliber: 22 WMR. 11-shot tubular magazine. 20-inch barrel. Weight: 6¹/₄ pounds. Sights: ramp front w/brass bead and Wide-Scan hood; adj. semibuckhorn folding rear. Offset hammer spur for scope use. Straight-grip American black walnut stock w/white buttplate spacer. Squared finger lever. Made 1986–88.

Marlin Model 1894S Lever Action **$275**
Calibers: 41 Mag., 44 Rem. Mag., 44 S&W Special, 45 Colt. 10-shot tubular magazine. 20-inch barrel. 37¹/₂ inches overall. Weight: 6 pounds. Sights and stock same as Model 1894M. Made 1984 to date.

Marlin 1895 45-70 Repeater **$275**
Model 336-type action. Caliber: 45-70 Government. 4-shot magazine. 22-inch barrel. Weight: about 7 pounds. Sights: open rear; bead front. Straight-grip stock, forearm w/metal end cap, QD swivels, leather sling. Made 1972–79.

Marlin Model 1895

Marlin Model 1895SS

Marlin Model 2000

Marlin Model A-1 Autoloader

Marlin-Glenfield Model 10

Marlin Model 1895 Lever Action Repeater **$1295**
Solid frame or takedown. Calibers: 33 WCF, 38-56, 40-65, 40-70, 40-82, 45-70. 9-shot tubular magazine. 24-inch round or octagon barrel standard (other lengths available). Weight: about 8 pounds. Sights: open rear; bead front. Plain stock and forearm (also available w/pistol-grip stock). Made 1895–1915.

Marlin 1895SS Lever Action **$295**
Caliber: 45/70 Govt. 4-shot tubular magazine. 22-inch barrel with Micro-Groove rifling. 40½ inches overall. Weight: 7½ pounds. Ramp front sight w/brass bead and Wide-Scan hood; adj. semibuckhorn folding rear. Solid top receiver tapped for scope mount or receiver sight. Off-set hammer spur for scope use. Two-piece American black walnut stock w/fluted comb, pistol grip, sling swivels. Made 1984 to date.

Marlin Model 1897 Lever Action Rifle
See Marlin Model 97.

Marlin Model 1936 Lever Action Carbine
See Marlin Model 36.

Marlin Model 2000 Target Rifle **$425**
Bolt-action single-shot. Caliber: 22 LR. Optional 5-shot adapter kit available. 22-inch barrel. 41 inches overall.

Marlin Model 2000 Target Rifle (cont.)
Weight: 8 pounds. Globe front sight, adj. peep rear. Textured composite Kevlar stock. Made 1991 to date.

Marlin Model A-1 Autoloading Rifle **$150**
Takedown. Caliber: 22 LR. 6-shot detachable box magazine. 24-inch barrel. Weight: about 6 pounds. Open rear sight. Plain pistol-grip stock. Made 1935–1946.

Marlin Model A-1C Autoloading Rifle **$160**
Improved version of Model A-1 w/same general specifications, stock w/semibeavertail forend. Made 1940–46.

Marlin Model A-1DL **$195**
Same as Model A-1C, except has peep rear sight; hooded front, swivels.

Marlin Model A-1E **$175**
Same as Model A-1, except has peep rear sight; hooded front.

Marlin-Glenfield Model 10 .... **$80**
Same as Marlin Model 101, except has walnut-finished hardwood stock. Made 1966–1979. *Note:* Later production has checkered pistol grip.

RIFLES

Marlin-Glenfield Model 20

Marlin-Glenfield Model 30A

Marlin-Glenfield Model 60

Marlin-Glenfield Model 70

Marlin-Glenfield Model 80G

Marlin-Glenfield Model 20 . . . . **$80**
Same as Marlin Model 80/780, except has bead front sight, walnut-finished hardwood stock. Made 1966 to date. *Note:* Recent production has checkered pistol grip.

Marlin-Glenfield Model 30 . . . . **$165**
Same as Marlin Model 336C, except chambered for 30-30 only, has 4-shot magazine, plainer stock and forearm of walnut-finished hardwood. Made 1966–68.

Marlin-Glenfield Model 30A **$175**
Same as Marlin Model 336C, except chambered for 30-30 only, has checkered stock of walnut-finished hardwood. Made 1969 to date.

Marlin-Glenfield Model 36G **$225**
Same as Marlin Model 336C, except chambered for 30-30 only, has 5-shot magazine, plainer stock. Made 1960–65.

Marlin-Glenfield Model 60 . . . . **$70**
Same as Marlin Model 99C, except has walnut-finished hardwood stock. Made 1966 to date.

Marlin-Glenfield Model 60SS **$145**
Same as the Marlin-Glenfield Model 60, except has stainless barrel, breech bolt and outer magazine tube. Black/gray laminated birch stock with Monte Carlo and rubber buttpad. Made 1993 to date.

Marlin-Glenfield Model 70 . . . . **$75**
Same as Marlin Model 989M2, except has walnut-finished hardwood stock, no handguard. Made 1966–69.

Marlin-Glenfield Model 80G **$80**
Same as Marlin Model 80C, except has plainer stock, bead front sight. Made 1960–65.

Marlin-Glenfield Model 81G

Marlin-Glenfield Model 81G **$80**
Same as Marlin Model 81C, except has plainer stock, bead
front sight. Made 1960–65.

Marlin-Glenfield Model 99G **$80**
Same as Marlin Model 99C, except has plainer stock, bead
front sight. Made 1960–65.

Marlin-Glenfield Model 101G **$70**
Same as Marlin Model 101, except has plainer stock. Made
1960–65.

Marlin-Glenfield Model 989G Autoloading Rifle . . **$70**
Same as Marlin Model 989, except has plain stock, bead
front sight. Made 1962–64.

MAUSER SPORTING RIFLES
Oberndorf am Neckar, Germany
Manufactured by Mauser-Werke GmbH

Before the end of WWI, the name of the Mauser firm was
"Waffenfabrik Mauser A.-G." Shortly after WWI, it was
changed to "Mauser-Werke A.-G." This may be used as
a general clue to the age of genuine Original-Mauser sporting rifles made before WWII, because all bear either of these
firm names as well as the "Mauser" banner trademark.
    The first four rifles listed were manufactured before WWI.
Those that follow were produced between World Wars I
and II. The early Mauser models can generally be identified
by the pistol grip, which is rounded instead of capped, and
the M/98 military-type magazine floorplate and catch; the
later models have hinged magazine floorplate with lever or
button release.

PRE-WORLD WAR I MODELS

Mauser Bolt Action Sporting Carbine **$695**
Calibers: 6.5×54, 6.5×58, 7×57, 8×57, 957mm. 19³/₄-inch
barrel. Weight: about 7 pounds. Full-stocked to muzzle.
Other specifications same as for standard rifle.

Mauser Bolt Action Sporting Rifle **$595**
Calibers: 6.5×55, 6.5×58, 7×57, 8×57, 9×57, 9.3×62,
10.75×68. 5-shot box magazine, 23¹/₂-inch barrel. Weight:
7 to 7¹/₂ pounds. Double-set trigger. Sights: tangent curve
rear; ramp front. Pistol-grip stock, forearm w/schnabel
tip, swivels.

**Mauser Bolt Action Sporting Rifle, Military
Type** **$495**
So called because of "stepped" M/98-type barrel, military
front sight and double-pull trigger. Calibers: 7×57, 8×57,
9×57mm. Other specifications same as for standard rifle.

Mauser Bolt Action Sporting Rifle, Short Model . **$595**
Calibers: 6.5×54, 8×51mm. 19³/₄-inch barrel. Weight:
about 6¹/₄ pounds. Other specifications same as for standard rifle.

PRE-WORLD WAR II MODELS

**Mauser Model DSM34 Bolt Action Single Shot
Sporting Rifle** **$350**
Also called "Sport-model." Caliber: 22 LR. 26-inch barrel.
Weight: about 7³/₄ pounds. Sights: tangent curve open
rear; barleycorn front. M/98 military-type stock, swivels.
Intro. c. 1935.

> **NOTE:** The "B" series of Mauser 22 rifles (Model MS350B,
> etc.) were improved versions of their corresponding models
> and were introduced about 1935.

**Mauser Model EL320 Bolt Action Single Shot
Sporting Rifle** **$315**
Caliber: 22 LR. 23¹/₂-inch barrel. Weight: about 4¹/₄
pounds. Sights: adj. open rear; bead front. Sporting stock
w/checkered pistol grip, swivels.

**Mauser Model EN310 Bolt Action Single Shot
Sporting Rifle** **$300**
Caliber: 22 LR. ("22 Lang für Büchsen.") 19³/₄-inch barrel.
Weight: about 4 pounds. Sights: fixed open rear; blade
front. Plain pistol-grip stock.

**Mauser Model ES340 Bolt Action Single Shot
Target Rifle** **$350**
Caliber: 22 LR. 25¹/₂-inch barrel. Weight: about 6¹/₂
pounds. Sights: tangent curve rear; ramp front. Sporting
stock w/checkered pistol grip and grooved forearm,
swivels.

**Mauser Model ES340B Bolt Action Single Shot
Target Rifle** **$375**
Caliber: 22 LR. 26³/₄-inch barrel. Weight: about 8 pounds.
Sights: tangent curve open rear; ramp front. Plain pistol-
grip stock, swivels.

Mauser Model ES340B

Mauser Model MM410B

Mauser Model MS350B

Mauser Model MS420B

Mauser Standard Model

Mauser Model ES350 Bolt Action Single Shot Target Rifle **$495**
"Meistershaftsbüchse" (Championship Rifle). Caliber: 22 LR. 27½-inch barrel. Weight: about 7¾ pounds. Sights: open micrometer rear; ramp front. Target stock w/ checkered pistol grip and forearm, grip cap, swivels.

Mauser Model ES350B Bolt Action Single Shot Target Rifle **$445**
Same general specifications as Model MS350B except single shot, weighs about 8¼ pounds.

Mauser Model KKW Bolt Action Single Shot Target Rifle **$395**
Caliber: 22 LR. 26-inch barrel. Weight: about 8¾ pounds. Sights: tangent curve open rear; barleycorn front. M/98 military-type stock, swivels. *Note:* This rifle has an improved design Mauser 22 action w/separate nonrotating bolt head. In addition to being produced for commercial sale, this model was used as a training rifle by the German armed forces; it was also made by Walther and Gustloff. Introduced just before WWII.

Mauser Model M410 Bolt Action Repeating Sporting Rifle **$425**
Caliber: 22 LR. 5-shot detachable box magazine. 23½-inch barrel. Weight: about 5 pounds. Sights: tangent curve open rear; ramp front. Sporting stock w/checkered pistol grip, swivels.

Mauser Model MM410B Bolt Action Repeating Sporting Rifle **$695**
Caliber: 22 LR. 5-shot detachable box magazine. 23½-inch barrel. Weight: about 6¼ pounds. Sights: tangent

Mauser Model M410B Bolt Action Repeater (cont.)
curve open rear; ramp front. Lightweight sporting stock w/checkered pistol grip, swivels.

Mauser Model MS350B, Bolt Action Repeating Target Rifle **$645**
Caliber: 22 LR. 5-shot detachable box magazine. Receiver and barrel grooved for detachable rear sight or scope. 26¾-inch barrel. Weight: about 8½ pounds. Sights: micrometer open rear; ramp front. Target stock w/checkered pistol grip and forearm, grip cap, sling swivels.

Mauser Model MS420 Bolt Action Repeating Sporting Rifle **$695**
Caliber: 22 LR. 5-shot detachable box magazine. 25½-inch barrel. Weight: about 6½ pounds. Sights: tangent curve open rear; ramp front. Sporting stock w/checkered pistol grip, grooved forearm swivels.

Mauser Model MS420B Bolt Action Repeating Target Rifle **$625**
Caliber: 22 LR. 5-shot detachable box magazine. 26¾-inch barrel. Weight: about 8 pounds. Sights: tangent curve open rear; ramp front. Target stock w/checkered pistol grip, grooved forearm, swivels.

Mauser Standard Model Rifle **$475**
Refined version of the German Service Kar. 98k. Straight bolt handle. Calibers: 7mm Mauser (7×57mm), 7.9mm Mauser (8×57mm). 5-shot box magazine. 23½-inch barrel. Weight: about 8½ pounds. Sights: blade front; adj. rear. Walnut stock of M/98 military-type. *Note:* These rifles were made for commercial sale and are of the high quality found in the Oberndorf Mauser sporters. They bear the Mauser trademark on the receiver ring.

Mauser Type "A" British Model

Mauser Type B Normal Model

Mauser Type M

Mauser Type "A" Bolt Action Sporting Rifle $895
Special British Model. Calibers: 7×57, 30-06 (7.62×63), 8×60, 9×57, 9.3×62mm. 5-shot box magazine. 23¹/₂-inch round barrel. Weight: about 7¹/₄ pounds. Military-type single trigger. Sights: express rear; hooded ramp front. Circassian walnut sporting stock w/checkered pistol grip and forearm, with or w/o cheekpiece, buffalo horn forend tip and grip cap, detachable swivels. Variations: octagon barrel, double-set trigger, shotgun-type safety, folding peep rear sight, tangent curve rear sight, three-leaf rear sight.

Mauser Type "A" Bolt Action Sporting Rifle, Magnum Model $950
Same general specifications as standard Type "A," except has Magnum action, weighs 7¹/₂ to 8¹/₂ pounds. Calibers: 280 Ross, 318 Westley Richards Express, 10.75×68mm, 404 Nitro Express.

Mauser Type "A" Bolt Action Sporting Rifle, Short Model $850
Same as standard Type "A," except has short action, 21¹/₂-inch round barrel, weighs about 6 pounds. Calibers: 250-3000, 6.5×54, 8×51mm.

Mauser Type "B" Bolt Action Sporting Rifle $825
Normal Model. Calibers: 7×57, 30-06 (7.62×63), 8×57, 8×60, 9×57, 9.3×62, 10.75×68mm. 5-shot box magazine. 23¹/₂-inch round barrel. Weight: about 7¹/₄ pounds. Double-set trigger. Sights: three-leaf rear; ramp front. Fine walnut stock w/checkered pistol grip, schnabel forend tip, cheekpiece, grip cap, swivels. Variations: octagon or half-octagon barrel, military-type single trigger, shotgun-type trigger, shotgun-type safety, folding peep rear sight, tangent curve rear sight, telescopic sight.

Mauser Type "K" Bolt Action Sporting Rifle $975
Light Short Model. Same specifications as Normal Type "B" model except has short action, 21¹/₂-inch round barrel, weighs about 6 lbs. Calibers: 250-3000, 6.5×54, 8×51mm.

Mauser Type "M" Bolt Action Sporting Carbine $725
Calibers: 6.5×54, 7×57, 30-06 (7.62×63), 8×51, 8×60, 9×57mm. 5-shot box magazine. 19³/₄-inch round barrel. Weight: 6 to 6³/₄ pounds. Double-set trigger, flat bolt handle. Sights: three-leaf rear; ramp front. Stocked to muzzle, cheekpiece, checkered pistol grip and forearm, grip cap, steel forend cap, swivels. Variations: military-type single trigger, shotgun-type trigger, shotgun-type safety, tangent curve rear sight, telescopic sight.

Mauser Type "S" Bolt Action Sporting Carbine . $775
Calibers: 6.5×54, 7×57, 8×51, 8×60, 9×57mm. 5-shot box magazine. 19³/₄-inch round barrel. Weight: about 6 to 6³/₄ pounds. Double-set trigger. Sights: three-leaf rear; ramp front. Stocked to muzzle, schnabel forend tip, cheekpiece, checkered pistol grip w/cap, swivels. Variations: same as listed for Normal Model Type "B."

> **NOTE:** Production of original Mauser sporting rifles (66 Series) resumed at the Oberndorf plant in 1965 by Mauser-Jagdwaffen GmbH, now Mauser-Werke Oberndorf GmbH. The Series 2000-3000-4000 rifles, however, were made for Mauser by Friedrich Wilhelm Heym Gewehrfabrik, Muennerstadt, West Germany.

Mauser Model 66S Deluxe

POST-WORLD WAR II MODELS

Mauser Model 66S Deluxe
On special order, Model 66S rifles and carbines are available with elaborate engraving, gold and silver inlays and

Mauser Model 66S Standard

Mauser Model 66SP Super Match Target Rifle

Mauser Model 66ST Carbine

Mauser Model 66S Deluxe (cont.)
carved stocks of the finest select walnut. Added value is upward of $1000.

Mauser Model 66S Standard Bolt Action Sporting Rifle
Telescopic short action. Barrels interchangeable within caliber group. Single- or double-set trigger (interchangeable). Calibers: 243 Win., 6.5×57, 270 Win., 7×64, 308 Win., 30-06. 3-round magazine. 23.6-inch barrel (25.6-inch in 7×64). Weight: about 7.3 pounds (7.5 pounds in 7×64). Sights: adj. open rear; hooded ramp front. Select European walnut stock, Monte Carlo w/cheekpiece, rosewood forend tip and pistol-grip cap, skip checkering, recoil pad, sling swivels. Made 1965 to date; export to U.S. discontinued 1974. *Note:* U.S. designation, 1971–73, was "Model 660."
With one barrel **$1095**
Extra barrel assembly **300**

Mauser Model 66S Ultra
Same general specifications as Model 66S Standard, except has 20.9-inch barrel, weighs about 6.8 pounds. **$1295**
With one barrel
Extra barrel assembly **300**

Mauser Model 66SG Big Game
Same general specifications as Model 66S Standard, except has 25.6-inch barrel, weighs about 9.3 pounds. Calibers: 375 H&H Mag., 458 Win. Mag. *Note:* U.S. designation, 1971–73, was "Model 660 Safari."

Mauser Model 66SG Big Game (cont.)
With one barrel **$1350**
Extra barrel assembly **325**

Mauser Model 66SH High Performance
Same general specifications as Model 66S Standard, except has 25.6-inch barrel, weighs about 7.5 pounds (9.3 pounds in 9.3×64). Calibers: 6.5×68, 7mm Rem. Mag., 7mm S.E.v. Hofe, 300 Win. Mag., 8×68S, 9.3×64.
With one barrel **$995**
Extra barrel assembly **300**

Mauser Model 66SP Super Match Bolt Action Target Rifle **$1150**
Telescopic short action. Adjustable single-stage trigger. Caliber: 308 Win. (chambering for other cartridges available on special order). 3-shot magazine. 27.6-inch heavy barrel with muzzle brake, dovetail rib for special scope mount. Weight: about 12 pounds. Target stock with wide and deep forearm, full pistol grip, thumbhole, adjustable cheekpiece, adjustable rubber buttplate.

Mauser Model 66ST Carbine
Same general specifications as Model 66S Standard, except has 20.9-inch barrel, full-length stock, weighs about 7 pounds.
With one barrel **$1050**
Extra barrel assembly **300**

Mauser Model 83 Bolt Action Rifle **$1890**
Centerfire single-shot, bolt-action rifle for 300-meter competition. Caliber: 308 Win. 25½-inch fluted barrel. Weight: 10½ pounds. Adj. micrometer rear sight, globe front. Fully adj. competition stock. Discontinued 1988.

Mauser Model 99

Mauser Model 201

Mauser Model 3000

Mauser Model 4000

Mauser Model 99 Classic Bolt Action Rifle
Calibers: 243 Win., 25-06, 270 Win., 30-06, 308 Win., 257 Wby., 270 Wby., 7mm Rem. Mag., 300 Win., 300 Wby., 375 H&H. 4-shot magazine (standard), 3-shot (Magnum). Barrel: 24-inch (standard) or 26-inch (Magnum). 44 inches overall (standard). Weight: 8 pounds. No sights. Checkered European walnut stock with rosewood grip cap available in Classic and Monte Carlo styles with High-Luster or oil finish. Discontinued importing 1994.

Standard Classic or Monte Carlo (Oil Finish) . . .	$ 895
Magnum Classic or Monte Carlo (Oil Finish) . . .	945
Standard Classic or Monte Carlo (H-L Finish) . .	925
Magnum Classic or Monte Carlo (H-L Finish) . .	995

Mauser Model 107 Bolt Action Rifle $280
Caliber: 22 LR. Mag. 5-shot magazine. 21 1/2-inch barrel. 40 inches overall. Weight: 5 pounds. Receiver drilled and tapped for rail scope mounts. Hooded front sight, adjustable rear. Discontinued importing 1994.

Mauser Model 201/201 Luxus Bolt Action Rifle
Calibers: 22 LR, 22 Win. Mag. 5-shot magazine. 21-inch barrel. 40 inches overall. Weight: 6 1/2 pounds. Receiver drilled and tapped for scope mounts. Sights optional. Checkered walnut-stained beech stock with Monte Carlo. **Model 201 Luxus** has checkered European walnut stock, QD swivels, rosewood forend and rubber recoil pad. Made 1989 to date. Discontinued importing 1994.

Mauser Model 201/201 Luxus Bolt Action Rifle (cont.)
Model 201 Standard	**$400**
Model 201 Magnum	450
Model 201 Luxus Standard	520
Model 201 Luxus Magnum	585

Mauser Model 2000 Bolt Action Sporting Rifle . . $295
Modified Mauser-type action. Calibers: 270 Win., 308 Win., 30-06. 5-shot magazine. 24-inch barrel. Weight: about 7 1/2 pounds. Sights: folding leaf rear; hooded ramp front. Checkered walnut stock w/Monte Carlo comb and cheekpiece, forend tip, sling swivels. Made 1969–1971. *Note:* Model 2000 is similar in appearance to Model 3000.

Mauser Model 3000 Bolt Action Sporting Rifle . . $445
Modified Mauser-type action. Calibers: 243 Win., 270 Win., 308 Win., 30-06. 5-shot magazine. 22-inch barrel. Weight: about 7 pounds. No sights. Select European walnut stock, Monte Carlo style w/cheekpiece, rosewood forend tip and pistol-grip cap, skip checkering, recoil pad, sling swivels. Made 1971–74.

Mauser Model 3000 Magnum $495
Same general specifications as standard Model 3000, except has 3-shot magazine, 26-inch barrel, weighs about 8 pounds. Calibers: 7mm Rem. Mag., 300 Win. Mag., 375 H&H Mag.

Mauser Model 4000 Varmint Rifle $395
Same general specifications as standard Model 3000, except w/smaller action, folding leaf rear sight; hooded ramp front, rubber buttplate instead of recoil pad, weighs about 6 3/4 pounds. Calibers: 222 Rem., 223 Rem.

RIFLES

McMillan Alaskan Bolt Action

McMillan Classic Sporter

McMillan Stainless Sporter

McMILLAN GUN WORKS
Phoenix, Arizona

McMillan Signature Alaskan Bolt Action Rifle .. **$2420**
Same general specifications as Classic Sporter, except with match-grade barrel. Rings and mounts. Sights: single-leaf rear; barrel band front. Checkered Monte Carlo stock w/ palmswell and solid recoil pad. Electroless nickel finish. Calibers: *LA (long)*—270 Win., 280 Rem., 30-06; *MA (Magnum)*—7mm Rem. Mag., 300 Win. Mag., 300 Wby. Mag., 340 Wby. Mag., 358 Win., 375 H&H Mag. Made 1989 to date.

McMillan Signature Classic Sporter
The "prototype" for McMillan's Signature Series, this bolt-action is available in three lengths: *SA (standard/short)*—22-250, 243 Win., 6mm Rem., 6mm BR, 7mm BR, 7mm-08, 284, 308, 350 Rem Mag.; *LA (long)*—25-06, 270 Win., 280 Rem., 30-06; *MA (Magnum)*—7mm STW, 7mm Rem. Mag., 300 Win. Mag., 300 Wby. Mag., 300 H&H Mag., 338 Win. Mag., 340 Wby. Mag., 375 H&H Mag., 416 Rem. Mag.
Four-shot or 3-shot (Magnum) magazine. Barrel lengths: 22, 24 or 26 inches. Weight: 7 pounds (short action). No sights; rings and bases provided. McMillan fiberglass stock, Fibergrain or wood stock optional. Stainless, matte black or black chrome sulfide finish. Available in right- and left-hand models. Made 1987 to date. Stainless introduced 1990. **Talon Sporter**, introduced 1991, has pre-64 Model 70-style action for dangerous game.
Classic Sporter Standard **$1695**
Classic Sporter Stainless **1750**
Talon Sporter **1795**

McMillan Signature Mountain Rifle **$1995**
Same general specifications as Classic Sporter, except w/ titanium action and graphite-reinforced fiberglass stock. Weight: 5½ pounds. Calibers: 270 Win., 280 Rem., 30-06, 7mm Mag., 300 Win. Mag. Made 1989 to date.

McMillan Talon Safari Rifle
Same general specifications as Classic Sporter, except w/ McMillan Safari-grade action, match-grade barrel and "Safari" fiberglass stock. Calibers: *Magnum*—300 H&H

McMillan Talon Safari Rifle (cont.)
Mag., 300 Win Mag., 300 Wby. Mag., 338 Win. Mag., 340 Wby. Mag., 375 H&H Mag., 404 Jeffrey, 416 Rem. Mag., 458 Win.; *Super Magnum*—300 Phoenix, 338 Lapua, 378 Wby. Mag., 416 Rigby, 416 Wby. Mag., 460 Wby Mag. Matte black finish. Made 1989 to date.
Safari Magnum **$2450**
Safari Super Magnum **2995**

McMillan Signature Super Varminter **$1495**
Same general specifications as Classic Sporter, except w/ heavy, contoured barrel, adj. trigger, fiberglass stock and field bipod. Calibers: 223, 22-250, 220 Swift, 243 Win., 6mm Rem., 25-06, 7mm-08, 308 Win., 350 Rem. Mag. Made 1989 to date.

GEBRÜDER MERKEL
Suhl, Germany

For Merkel combination guns and drillings, see listings under Merkel shotguns.

Merkel O/U Rifle Model 221

Merkel Over/Under Rifles ("Bock-Doppelbüchsen")
Calibers: 5.6×35 Vierling, 6.5×58r5, 7×57r5, 8×57JR, 8×60R Magnum, 9.3×53r5, 9.3×72r5, 9.3×74r5, 10.3×60R as well as most of the British calibers for African and Indian big game. Various barrel lengths, weights. In general, specifications correspond to those of Merkel over/under shotguns. Values of these over/under rifles (in calibers for which ammunition is obtainable) are about the same as those of comparable shotgun models. Currently

Merkel Over/Under Rifles (cont.)

manufactured. For more specific data, see Merkel shotgun models indicated below.

Model 220	$ 5,995
Model 220E	6,950
Model 221	2,750
Model 221E	7,995
Model 320	6,500
Model 320E	12,000
Model 321	13,250
Model 321E	14,000
Model 322	14,500
Model 323	15,500
Model 324	17,500

MEXICAN MILITARY RIFLE
Mfd. by Government Arsenal, Mexico, D.F.

Mexican Model 1936 Mauser Military Rifle $175
Same as the German Kar. 98k with minor variations, has U.S. M/1903 Springfield-type knurled cocking piece.

MITCHELL ARMS. INC.
Santa Ana, California

Mitchell AK-22 Semiautomatic Rifle **$270**
Replica of the AK-47 rifle. Calibers: 22 LR, 22 WMR. 20-shot magazine (22 LR), 10-shot (22 WMR). 18-inch barrel. 36 inches overall. Weight: 6 1/2 lbs. Sights: post front; open adj. rear. European walnut stock and forend. Matte black finish.

Mitchell CAR-15 22 Semiautomatic Rifle **$275**
Replica of the AR-15 CAR rifle. Caliber: 22 LR. 15-shot magazine. 16 1/4-inch barrel. 32 inches overall. Sights: adj. post front; adj. aperture rear. Telescoping buttstock and ventilated forend. Matte black finish. Made 1990 to date.

Mitchell Galil 22 Semiautomatic Rifle **$275**
Replica of the Israeli Galil rifle. Calibers: 22 LR, 22 WMR. 20-shot magazine (22 LR), 10-shot (22 WMR). 18-inch barrel. 36 inches overall. Weight: 6 1/2 lbs. Sights: adj. post front; rear adj. for windage. Folding metal stock with European walnut grip and forend. Matte black finish. Made 1987 to date.

Mitchell M-16A 22 Semiautomatic Rifle **$270**
Replica of the AR-15 rifle. Caliber: 22 LR. 15-shot magazine. 20 1/2-inch barrel. 38 1/2 inches overall. Weight: 7 pounds. Sights: adj. post front; adj. aperture rear. Black composition stock and forend. Matte black finish. Made 1990 to date.

Mitchell MAS 22 Semiautomatic Rifle **$275**
Replica of the French MAS bullpup rifle. Caliber: 22 LR. 20-shot magazine. 18-inch barrel. 28 inches overall. Weight: 7 1/2 pounds. Sights: adj. post front; folding aperture rear. European walnut buttstock and forend. Matte black finish. Made 1987 to date.

Mitchell PPS Semiautomatic Rifle
Caliber: 22 LR. 20-shot magazine, 50-shot drum. 16 1/2-inch barrel. 33 1/2 inches overall. Weight: 5 1/2 pounds. Sights: blade front; adjustable rear. European walnut stock with ventilated barrel shroud. Matte black finish. Made 1989 to date.

Model PPS (20-shot)	**$270**
Model PPS/50 (50-shot drum)	**350**

Mossberg Model 26B

O.F. MOSSBERG & SONS, INC.
North Haven, Connecticut

Mossberg Model 10 Bolt Action Single Shot Rifle . **$105**
Takedown. Caliber: 22 LR, Long, Short. 22-inch barrel. Weight: about 4 pounds. Sights: open rear; bead front. Plain pistol-grip stock w/swivels, sling. Made 1933–35.

Mossberg Model 14 Bolt Action Single Shot Rifle . **$110**
Takedown. Caliber: 22 LR, Long, Short. 24-inch barrel. Weight: about 5 1/4 pounds. Sights: peep rear; hooded ramp front. Plain pistol-grip stock with semibeavertail forearm, 1 1/4-inch swivels. Made 1934–35.

Mossberg Model 20 Bolt Action Single Shot Rifle . **$115**
Takedown. Caliber: 22 LR, Long, Short. 24-inch barrel. Weight: about 4 1/2 pounds. Sights: open rear; bead front. Plain pistol-grip stock and forearm with finger grooves, sling and swivels. Made 1933–35.

Mossberg Model 25/25A Bolt Action Single Shot Rifle
Takedown. Caliber: 22 LR, Long, Short. 24-inch barrel. Weight: about 5 pounds. Sights: peep rear; hooded ramp

Mossberg Model 25/25A Bolt Action (cont.)
front. Plain pistol-grip stock w/semibeavertail forearm. 1 1/4-inch swivels. Made 1935–36.

Model 25	**$100**
Model 25A (Improved Model 25, 1936-38)	**125**

Mossberg Model 26B/26C Bolt Action Single Shot
Takedown. Caliber: 22 LR, Long, Short. 26-inch barrel. Weight: about 5 1/2 pounds. Sights: Rear, micrometer click peep or open; hooded ramp front. Plain pistol-grip stock, swivels. Made 1938–1941.

Model 26B	**$125**
Model 26C (No rear sight/swivels)	**100**

Mossberg Model 30 Bolt Action Single Shot Rifle . **$100**
Takedown. Caliber: 22 LR, Long, Short. 24-inch barrel. Weight: about 4 1/2 pounds. Sights: peep rear; bead front, on hooded ramp. Plain pistol-grip stock, forearm with finger grooves. Made 1933–35.

Mossberg Model 34 Bolt Action Single Shot Rifle . **$100**
Takedown. Caliber: 22 LR, Long, Short. 24-inch barrel. Weight: 5 1/2 pounds. Sights: peep rear; hooded ramp front.

Mossberg Model 35

Mossberg Model L42A

Mossberg Model 42B

Mossberg Model 42C

RIFLES

Mossberg Model 34 Bolt Action (cont.)
Plain pistol-grip stock w/semibeavertail forearm, 1¼-inch swivels. Made 1934–35.

Mossberg Model 35 Target Grade Bolt Action Single Shot Rifle $220
Caliber: 22 LR. 26-inch heavy barrel. Weight: about 8¼ pounds. Sights: micrometer click rear peep; hooded ramp front. Large target stock w/full pistol grip, cheekpiece, full beavertail forearm, 1¼-inch swivels. Made 1935–37.

Mossberg Model 35A Bolt Action Single Shot Rifle $235
Caliber: 22 LR. 26-inch heavy barrel. Weight: about 8¼ pounds. Sights: micrometer click peep rear; hooded front. Target stock w/cheekpiece, full pistol grip and forearm, 1¼-inch sling swivels. Made 1937–38.

Mossberg Model 35A-LS $225
Same as Model 35A but with Lyman 57 rear sight, 17A front.

Mossberg Model 35B $200
Same specifications as Model 44B, except single shot. Made 1938–1940.

Mossberg Model 40 Bolt Action Repeater $95
Same specifications as Model 30, except has a tubular magazine (holds 16 LR) and weighs about 5 pounds. Made 1933–35.

Mossberg Model 42 Bolt Action Repeater $100
Takedown. Caliber: 22 LR, Long, Short. 7-shot detachable box magazine. 24-inch barrel. Weight: about 5 pounds. Sights: receiver peep, open rear; hooded ramp front. Pistol-grip stock. 1¼-inch swivels. Made 1935–37.

Mossberg Model 42A/L42A Bolt Action Repeaters
Takedown. Caliber: 22 LR, Long, Short. 7-shot detachable box magazine. 24-inch barrel. Weight: about 5 pounds. Sights: receiver peep, open rear; ramp front. Plain pistol-grip stock. Made 1937–38.
Model L42A, made 1937–1941, has left-hand action.
Model 42A **$115**
Model L42A **150**

Mossberg Model 42B/42C Bolt Action Repeaters
Takedown. Caliber: 22 LR, Long, Short. 5-shot detachable box magazine. 24-inch barrel. Weight: about 6 pounds. Sights: micrometer click receiver peep, open rear; hooded ramp front. Plain pistol-grip stock, swivels. Made 1938–1941.
Model 42B **$100**
Model 42C (No rear peep sight) **95**

Mossberg Model 42M Bolt Action Repeater $140
Caliber: 22 LR, Long, Short. 7-shot detachable box magazine. 23-inch barrel. Weight: about 6¾ pounds. Sights: microclick receiver peep, open rear; hooded ramp front. Two-piece Mannlicher-type stock w/cheekpiece and pistol grip, swivels. Made 1940–1950.

Mossberg Model L43

Mossberg Model 43B

Mossberg Model 44B

Mossberg Model 44US

Mossberg Model 45

Mossberg Model L45A

Mossberg Model 43/L43 Bolt Action Repeaters .. **$195**
Speedlock, adj. trigger pull. Caliber: 22 LR. 7-shot detachable box magazine. 26-inch heavy barrel. Weight: about 8¼ pounds. Sights: Lyman 57 rear; selective aperture front. Target stock w/cheekpiece, full pistol grip, beavertail forearm, adj. front swivel. Made 1937–38. **Model L43** is same as Model 43 except has left-hand action.

Mossberg Model 43B **$225**
Same as Model 44B, except with Lyman 57 receiver sight and 17A front sight. Made 1938–39.

Mossberg Model 44 Bolt Action Repeater **$135**
Takedown. Caliber: 22 LR, Long, Short. Tubular magazine holds 16 LR. 24-inch barrel. Weight: 6 pounds. Sights: peep rear; hooded ramp front. Plain pistol-grip stock w/ semibeavertail forearm, 1¼-inch swivels. Made 1934–35. *Note:* Do not confuse this rifle with the later Models 44B and 44US, which are clip repeaters.

Mossberg Model 44B Bolt Action Target Rifle . . **$200**
Caliber: 22 LR. 7-shot detachable box magazine. 26-inch heavy barrel. Weight: about 8 pounds. Sights: micrometer

Mossberg Model 44B Bolt Action Target Rifle (cont.)
click receiver peep; hooded front sight. Target stock w/ full pistol grip, cheekpiece, beavertail forearm, adj. swivel. Made 1938–1941.

Mossberg Model 44US Bolt Action Repeater . . . **$175**
Caliber: 22 LR. 7-shot detachable box magazine. 26-inch heavy barrel. Weight: about 8½ pounds. Sights: micrometer click receiver peep; hooded front. Target stock, swivels. Made 1943–48. *Note:* This model was used as a training rifle by the U.S. Armed Forces during WWII.

Mossberg Model 45 Bolt Action Repeater **$125**
Takedown. Caliber: 22 LR, Long, Short. Tubular magazine holds 15 LR, 18 Long, 22 Short. 24-inch barrel. Weight: about 6¾ pounds. Sights: rear peep; hooded ramp front. Plain pistol-grip stock, 1¼-inch swivels. Made 1935–37.

Mossberg Model 45A, L45A, 45AC Bolt Action Repeaters
Takedown. Caliber: 22 LR, Long, Short. Tubular magazine holds 15 LR, 18 Long, 22 Short. 24-inch barrel. Weight: about 6¾ pounds. Sights: receiver peep, open rear; hooded ramp front. Plain pistol-grip stock, 1¼-inch swivels. Made 1937–38.
Model 45A **$130**
Model L45A (Left-Hand Action) 175
Model 45AC (No receiver peep sight) 115

RIFLES

Mossberg Model 45B

Mossberg Model 46

Mossberg Model L46A-LS

Mossberg Model 46B

Mossberg Model 46M

Mossberg Model 45B/45C Bolt Action Repeaters
Takedown. Caliber: 22 LR, Long, Short. Tubular magazine holds 15 LR, 18 Long, 22 Short. 24-inch barrel. Weight: about 6¼ pounds. Open rear sight, hooded front. Plain pistol-grip stock, swivels. Made 1938–1940.
Model 45B **$125**
Model 45C (No sights, made 1935–37) **110**

Mossberg Model 46 Bolt Action Repeater **$125**
Takedown. Caliber: 22 LR, Long, Short. Tubular magazine holds 15 LR, 18 Long, 22 Short. 26-inch barrel. Weight: 7½ pounds. Sights: micrometer click rear peep; hooded ramp front. Pistol-grip stock w/cheekpiece, full beavertail forearm, 1¼-inch swivels. Made 1935–37.

Mossberg Model 46A, 46A-LS, L46A-LS Bolt Action Repeaters
Takedown. Caliber: 22 LR, Long, Short. Tubular magazine holds 15 LR, 18 Long, 22 Short. 26-inch barrel. Weight: about 7¼ pounds. Sights: micrometer click receiver peep, open rear; hooded ramp front. Pistol-grip stock w/cheekpiece and beavertail forearm, quick-detachable swivels. Made 1937–38.
Model 46A **$125**
Model 46A-LS (w/Lyman 57 Receiver Sight) **130**
Model L46A-LS (Left-hand Action) **165**

Mossberg Model 46B Bolt Action Repeater **$100**
Takedown. Caliber: 22 LR, Long, Short. Tubular magazine holds 15 LR, 18 Long, 22 Short. 26-inch barrel. Weight: about 7 pounds. Sights: micrometer click receiver peep, open rear; hooded front. Plain pistol-grip stock w/cheekpiece, swivels. *Note:* Postwar version of this model has full magazine holding 20 LR, 23 Long, 30 Short. Made 1938–1950.

Mossberg Model 46BT **$145**
Same as Model 46B, except has heavier barrel and stock, weighs 7¾ pounds. Made 1938–39.

Mossberg Model 46C **$115**
Same as Model 46 except has a heavier barrel and stock than that model, weighs 8½ pounds. Made 1936–37.

Mossberg Model 46M Bolt Action Repeater **$135**
Caliber: 22 LR, Long, Short. Tubular magazine holds 22 Short, 18 Long, 15 LR. 23-inch barrel. Weight: about 7 pounds. Sights: microclick receiver peep, open rear; hooded ramp front. Two-piece Mannlicher-type stock w/cheekpiece and pistol grip, swivels. Made 1940–1952.

Mossberg Model 50

Mossberg Model 51

Mossberg Model 51M

Mossberg Model 140B

Mossberg Model 140K

Mossberg Model 50 Autoloading Rifle **$130**
Same as Model 51, except has plain stock w/o beavertail, cheekpiece, swivels or receiver peep sight. Made 1939–1942.

Mossberg Model 51 Autoloading Rifle **$150**
Takedown. Caliber: 22 LR. 15-shot tubular magazine in buttstock. 24-inch barrel. Weight: about 7¼ pounds. Sights: micrometer click receiver peep, open rear; hooded ramp front. Cheekpiece stock w/full pistol grip and beavertail forearm, swivels. Made 1939 only.

Mossberg Model 51M Autoloading Rifle **$155**
Caliber: 22 LR. 15-shot tubular magazine. 20-inch barrel. Weight: about 7 pounds. Sights: microclick receiver peep, open rear; hooded ramp front. Two-piece Mannlicher-type stock w/pistol grip and cheekpiece, swivels. Made 1939–1946.

Mossberg Model 140B Sporter-Target Rifle **$140**
Same as Model 140K, except has peep rear sight, hooded ramp front sight. Made 1957–58.

Mossberg Model 140K Bolt Action Repeater . . . **$125**
Caliber: 22 LR, 22 Long, 22 Short. 7-shot clip magazine. 24½-inch barrel. Weight: 5¾ pounds. Sights: open rear;

Mossberg Model 140K Bolt Action Repeater (cont.)
bead front. Monte Carlo stock w/cheekpiece and pistol grip, sling swivels. Made 1955–58.

Mossberg Model 142-A Bolt Action Repeating Carbine **$150**
Caliber: 22 Short, Long, LR. 7-shot detachable box magazine. 18-inch barrel. Weight: about 5 pounds. Sights: peep rear; military-type front. Monte Carlo stock w/pistol grip, hinged forearm pulls down to form hand grip, sling swivels mounted on left side of stock. Made 1949–1957.

Mossberg Model 142K **$100**
Same as Model 142, except has open rear sight. Made 1953–57.

Mossberg Model 144 Bolt Action Target Rifle . . . **$190**
Caliber: 22 LR. 7-shot detachable box magazine. 26-inch heavy barrel. Weight: about 8 pounds. Sights: microclick receiver peep; hooded front. Pistol-grip target stock w/beavertail forearm, adj. hand stop, swivels. Made 1949–1954. *Note:* This model designation was resumed c.1973 for previous Model 144LS. See listing below. Disc. 1985.

Mossberg Model 144LS

Mossberg Model 146B

Mossberg Model 151K

Mossberg Model 151M

Mossberg Model 152

Mossberg Model 144LS **$225**
Same as Model 144 except has Lyman 57MS or Mossberg S331 receiver sight and Lyman 17A front sight. Made 1954 to date. *Note:* This model since c.1973 has been marketed as Model 144.

Mossberg Model 146B Bolt Action Repeater . . . **$135**
Takedown. Caliber: 22 LR, Long, Short. Tubular magazine holds 30 Short, 23 Long, 20 LR. 26-inch barrel. Weight: about 7 pounds. Sights: micrometer click rear peep, open rear; hooded front. Plain stock with pistol grip, Monte Carlo comb and cheekpiece, knob forend tip, swivels. Made 1949–1954.

Mossberg Model 151K **$145**
Same as Model 151M except has 24-inch barrel, weighs about 6 pounds, w/o peep sight, plain stock w/Monte Carlo

Mossberg Model 151K (cont.)
comb and cheekpiece, pistol-grip knob, forend tip, w/o swivels. Made 1950–51.

Mossberg Model 151M Autoloading Rifle **$155**
Improved version of Model 51M with same general specifications, complete action is instantly removable without use of tools. Made 1946–1958.

Mossberg Model 152 Autoloading Carbine **$150**
Caliber: 22 LR. 7-shot detachable box magazine. 18-inch barrel. Weight: about 5 pounds. Sights: peep rear; military-type front. Monte Carlo stock w/pistol grip, hinged forearm pulls down to form hand grip, sling mounted on swivels on left side of stock. Made 1948–1957.

Mossberg Model 152K **$120**
Same as Model 152, except w/open instead of peep rear sight. Made 1950–57.

Mossberg Model 320B

Mossberg Model 320K

Mossberg Model 333

Mossberg Model 340B

Mossberg Model 340K

Mossberg Model 341

Mossberg Model 320B Boy Scout Target Rifle . . **$125**
Same as Model 340K, except single shot w/auto. safety.
Made 1960–1971.

**Mossberg Model 320K Hammerless Bolt Action
Single Shot** **$100**
Same as Model 346K except single shot, has drop-in
loading platform, automatic safety. Weight: about 5¾
pounds. Made 1958–1960.

Mossberg Model 321B **$115**
Same as Model 321K, except has receiver peep sight. Made
1972–75.

Mossberg Model 321K Bolt Action Single Shot . . **$120**
Same as Model 341, except single shot. Made 1972–1980.

Mossberg Model 333 Autoloading Carbine **$130**
Caliber: 22 LR. 15-shot tubular magazine. 20-inch barrel.
Weight: about 6¼ pounds. Sights: open rear; ramp front.

Mossberg Model 333 Autoloading Carbine (cont.)
Monte Carlo stock w/checkered pistol grip and forearm,
barrel band, swivels. Made 1972–73.

Mossberg Model 340B Target Sporter **$135**
Same as Model 340K, except has peep rear sight, hooded
ramp front sight. Made 1958–1981.

**Mossberg Model 340K Hammerless Bolt
Action Repeater** **$130**
Same as Model 346K, except clip type, 7-shot magazine.
Made 1958–1971.

Mossberg Model 340M **$150**
Same as Model 340K, except has 18½-inch barrel, Mannlicher-style stock with swivels and sling. Weight: 5¼
pounds. Made 1970–71.

Mossberg Model 341 Bolt Action Repeater **$95**
Caliber: 22 Short, Long, LR. 7-shot clip magazine. 24-
inch barrel. Weight: 6½ pounds. Sights: open rear; ramp
front. Monte Carlo stock w/checkered pistol grip and
forearm, sling swivels. Made 1972 to date.

RIFLES

Mossberg Model 342K Carbine

Mossberg Model 346B

Mossberg Model 346K

Mossberg Model 350K Clip

Mossberg Model 351K Sporter

Mossberg Model 352K Carbine

Mossberg Model 342K Hammerless Bolt Action Carbine **$100**
Same as Model 340K, except has 18-inch barrel, stock has no cheekpiece, extension forend is hinged, pulls down to form hand grip; sling swivels and web strap on left side of stock. Weight: about 5 pounds. Made 1958–1974.

Mossberg Model 346B **$125**
Same as Model 346K, except has peep rear sight, hooded ramp front sight. Made 1958–1967.

Mossberg Model 346K Hammerless Bolt Action Repeater **$100**
Caliber: 22 Short, Long, LR. Tubular magazine holds 25 Short, 20 Long, 18 LR. 24-inch barrel. Weight: about 6½ pounds. Sights: open rear; bead front. Walnut stock w/ Monte Carlo comb, cheekpiece, pistol grip, sling swivels. Made 1958–1971.

Mossberg Model 350K Autoloading Rifle—Clip Type **$120**
Caliber: 22 Short (high speed), Long, LR. 7-shot clip magazine. 23½-inch barrel. Weight: about 6 pounds. Sights: open rear; bead front. Monte Carlo stock w/pistol grip. Made 1958–1971.

Mossberg Model 351C Automatic Carbine **$135**
Same as Model 351K, except has 18½-inch barrel, Western carbine-style stock w/barrel band and sling swivels. Weight: 5½ pounds. Made 1965–1971.

Mossberg Model 351K Automatic Sporter **$125**
Caliber: 22 LR. 15-shot tubular magazine in buttstock. 24-inch barrel. Weight: about 6 pounds. Sights: open rear; bead front. Monte Carlo stock w/pistol grip. Made 1960–1971.

Mossberg Model 352K Autoloading Carbine **$125**
Caliber: 22 Short, Long, LR. 7-shot clip magazine. 18-inch barrel. Weight: about 5 pounds. Sights: open rear; bead front. Monte Carlo stock w/pistol grip; extension forend of Tenite is hinged, pulls down to form hand grip; sling swivels, web strap. Made 1958–1971.

Mossberg Model 353 Carbine

Mossberg Model 377 Plinkster

Mossberg Model 380

Mossberg Model 400

Mossberg Model 402

Mossberg Model 353 Autoloading Carbine **$125**
Caliber: 22 LR. 7-shot clip magazine. 18-inch barrel.
Weight: about 5 pounds. Sights: open rear; ramp front.
Monte Carlo stock w/checkered pistol grip and forearm;
black Tenite extension forend pulls down to form hand
grip. Made 1972–1985.

Mossberg Model 377 Plinkster Autoloader **$145**
Caliber: 22 LR. 15-shot tubular magazine. 20-inch barrel.
Weight: about 6¼ pounds. 4X scope sight. Thumbhole
stock with rollover cheekpiece, Monte Carlo comb, checkered forearm; molded of modified polystyrene foam in
walnut finish; sling swivel studs. Introduced 1977.

Mossberg Model 380 Semiautomatic Rifle **$120**
Caliber: 22 LR. 15-shot buttstock magazine. 20-inch bar-
rel. Weight: 5½ pounds. Sights: open rear; bead front.
Made 1980–85.

**Mossberg Model 400 Palomino Lever Action
Rifle** **$165**
Hammerless. Caliber: 22 Short, Long, LR. Tubular
magazine holds 20 Short, 17 Long, 15 LR. 24-inch barrel.

Model 400 Palomino Lever Action (cont.)
Weight: about 5½ pounds. Sights: open rear; bead front.
Monte Carlo stock w/checkered pistol grip; beavertail
forearm. Made 1959–1964.

Mossberg Model 402 Palomino Carbine **$175**
Same as Model 400, except has 18½-inch (1961–64) or
20-inch barrel (1964–71), forearm with barrel band, swivels; magazine holds two less rounds. Weight: about 4¾
pounds. Made 1961–1971.

Mossberg Model 430 Automatic Rifle **$115**
Caliber: 22 LR. 18-shot tubular magazine. 24-inch barrel.
Weight: about 6¼ pounds. Sights: open rear; bead front.
Monte Carlo stock w/checkered pistol grip; checkered
forearm. Made 1970–71.

**Mossberg Model 432 Western-Style Auto
Carbine** **$120**
Same as Model 430 except has plain straight-grip carbine-
type stock and forearm, barrel band, sling swivels.
Magazine capacity: 15 cartridges. Weight: about 6 pounds.
Made 1970–71.

RIFLES

Mossberg Model 472 Brush Gun

Mossberg Model 472 Carbine
(Pistol Grip)

Mossberg Model 472 Carbine
(Straight Grip)

Mossberg Model 472
One in Five Thousand

Mossberg Model 640K

Mossberg Model 472 Brush Gun **$175**
Same as Model 472 Carbine with straight-grip stock, except has 18-inch barrel, weighs about 6½ pounds. Caliber: 30-30. Magazine capacity: 5 rounds. Made 1974–76.

Mossberg Model 472 Lever Action Carbine **$195**
Calibers: 30-30, 35 Rem. centerfire. 6-shot tubular magazine. 20-inch barrel. Weight: 6¾ to 7 pounds. Sights: open rear; ramp front. Pistol-grip or straight-grip stock, forearm w/barrel band; sling swivels on pistol-grip model, saddle ring on straight-grip model. Made 1972–79.

Mossberg Model 472 One in Five Thousand **$325**
Same as Model 472 Brush Gun, except has Indian scenes etched on receiver; brass buttplate, saddle ring and barrel

Mossberg Model 472 One in Five Thousand (cont.)
bands, gold-plated trigger; bright blued finish; select walnut stock and forearm. Limited edition of 5,000; serial numbered 1 to 5,000. Made in 1974.

Mossberg Model 472 Rifle **$165**
Same as Model 472 Carbine with pistol-grip stock, except has 24-inch barrel, 5-shot magazine, weighs about 7 pounds. Made 1974–76.

Mossberg Model 620K **$110**
Same as Model 640K, except single shot. Made 1960–64.

**Mossberg Model 640K Chuckster Hammerless
Bolt Action Rifle** **$125**
Caliber: 22 WMR. 5-shot detachable clip magazine. 24-inch barrel. Weight: about 6 pounds. Sights: open rear; bead front. Monte Carlo stock w/cheekpiece, pistol grip, sling swivels. Made 1959–1984.

Mossberg Model 640KS

Mossberg Model 640M

Mossberg Model 642K

Mossberg Model 800

Mossberg Model 800D

Mossberg Model 800M

Mossberg Model 640KS **$130**
Deluxe version of Model 640K, has select walnut stock,
hand checkering; gold-plated front sight, rear sight ele-
vator, and trigger. Made 1960–64.

Mossberg Model 640M **$165**
Similar to Model 640K, except chambered for 22 WMR;
has 20-inch barrel, Mannlicher-style stock w/Monte Carlo
comb and cheekpiece, swivels. Made 1967–1973.

Mossberg Model 642K **$125**
Same as Model 640K, except has 18½-inch barrel, forearm
with black Tenite extension that pulls down to form hand
grip. Made 1961–64.

**Mossberg Model 800 Bolt Action Centerfire
Rifle** **$165**
Calibers: 222 Rem., 22-250, 243 Win., 308 Win. 4-shot
magazine, 3-shot in 222. 22-inch barrel. Weight: about
7½ pounds. Sights: folding leaf rear; ramp front. Monte
Carlo stock w/cheekpiece, checkered pistol grip and
forearm, sling swivels. Made 1967–1979.

Mossberg Model 800D Super Grade **$295**
Deluxe version of Model 800; has stock w/rollover comb
and cheekpiece, rosewood forend tip and pistol-grip cap.
Weight: about 6¾ pounds. Not chambered for 222 Rem.
Made 1970–73.

Mossberg Model 800M **$300**
Same as Model 800, except has flat bolt handle, 20-inch
barrel, Mannlicher-style stock. Weight: 6½ pounds. Calibers: 22-250, 243 Win., 308 Win. Made 1969–1972.

Mossberg Model 800VT Varmint/Target **$275**
Similar to Model 800, except has 24-inch heavy barrel, no sights. Weight: about 9½ pounds. Calibers: 222 Rem., 22-250, 243 Win. Made 1968–1979.

Mossberg Model 810 Bolt Action Centerfire Rifle
Calibers: 270 Win., 30-06, 7mm Rem. Mag., 338 Win. Mag. Detachable box magazine (1970–75) or internal magazine with hinged floorplate (1972 to date). Capacity: 4-shot in 270 and 30-06, 3-shot in Magnums. 22-inch barrel in 270 and 30-06, 24-inch in Magnums. Weight: 7½ to 8 pounds. Sights: leaf rear; ramp front. Stock w/Monte Carlo comb and cheekpiece, checkered pistol grip and forearm, grip cap, sling swivels. Made 1970–79.
Standard calibers **$260**
Magnum calibers **295**

Mossberg Model 1500 Mountaineer Grade I Centerfire Rifle **$245**
Calibers: 223, 243, 270, 30-06, 7mm Mag. 22-inch or 24-inch (7mm Mag.) barrel. Weight: 7 lbs. 10 oz. Hardwood

Model 1500 Mountaineer Grade I (cont.)
walnut finished checkered stock. Sights: hooded ramp front w/gold bead; fully adj. rear. Drilled and tapped for scope mounts. Sling swivel studs. Made 1987–88.

Mossberg Model 1500 Varmint Bolt Action Rifle
Same as Model 1500 Grade I, except with 22-inch heavy barrel. Chambered in 222, 22-250, 223 only. High-luster blued finish or Parkerized satin finished stock. Imported from Japan 1982 to date.
High-Luster Blue **$300**
Parkerized Satin Finish **340**

Mossberg Model 1700LS Classic Hunter Bolt Action Rifle **$365**
Same as Model 1500 Grade I, except w/checkered classic-style stock and schnabel forend. Chambered in 243, 270, 30-06 only. Imported from Japan 1983 to date.

RIFLES

Mossberg Model 810

Mossberg Model K

Mossberg Model L

Mossberg Model B Bolt Action Rifle **$125**
Takedown. Caliber: 22 LR, Long, Short. Single shot. 22-inch barrel. Sights: open rear; bead front. Plain pistol-grip stock. Made 1930–32.

Mossberg Model K Slide Action Repeater **$195**
Hammerless. Takedown. Caliber: 22 LR, Long, Short. Tubular magazine holds 20 Short, 16 Long, 14 LR. 22-inch barrel. Weight: about 5 pounds. Sights: open rear; bead front. Plain straight-grip stock, grooved slide handle. Made 1922–1931.

Mossberg Models L42A, L43, L45A, L46A-LS
See Models 42A, 43, 45A and 46A-LS respectively; "L" refers to left-hand version of those rifles.

Mossberg Model L Single Shot Rifle **$300**
Martini-type falling-block lever action. Takedown. Caliber: 22 LR, Long, Short. 24-inch barrel. Weight: about 5 pounds. Sights: open rear; bead front. Plain pistol-grip stock and forearm. Made 1929–1932.

Mossberg Model M Slide Action Repeater **$200**
Specifications same as for Model K except has 24-inch octagon barrel, pistol-grip stock, weighs about 5½ pounds. Made 1928–1931.

Mossberg Model R Bolt Action Repeater **$195**
Takedown. Caliber: 22 LR, Long, Short. Tubular magazine. 24-inch barrel. Sights: open rear; bead front. Plain pistol-grip stock. Made 1930–32.

Musgrave Premier NR5

Musgrave RSA NR1

Musgrave Valiant NR6

MUSGRAVE MFRS. & DIST. (PTY) LTD.
Bloemfontein, South Africa

The following Musgrave bolt-action rifles were manufactured 1971–76.

Musgrave Premier NR5 Bolt Action Hunting Rifle **$350**
Calibers: 243 Win., 270 Win., 30-06, 308 Win., 7mm Rem. Mag. 5-shot magazine. $25\frac{1}{2}$-inch barrel. Weight: $8\frac{1}{4}$ pounds. Furnished w/o sights. Select walnut Monte Carlo stock w/cheekpiece, checkered pistol grip and forearm, contrasting pistol-grip cap and forend tip, recoil pad, swivel studs.

Musgrave RSA NR1 Bolt Action Single Shot Target Rifle **$345**
Caliber: 308 Win. (7.62mm NATO). 26.4-inch heavy barrel. Weight: about 10 pounds. Sights: aperture receiver; tunnel front. Walnut target stock w/beavertail forearm, handguard, barrel band, rubber buttplate, sling swivels.

Musgrave Valiant NR6 Hunting Rifle **$295**
Similar to Premier, except has 24-inch barrel; stock w/ straight comb, skip checkering, no grip cap or forend tip. Sights: leaf rear; hooded ramp front. Weight: $7\frac{3}{4}$ pounds.

Musketeer Mauser

MUSKETEER RIFLES
Washington, D.C.
Mfd. by Firearms International Corp.

Musketeer Mauser Sporter **$315**
FN Mauser bolt action. Calibers: 243, 25-06, 270, 264 Mag., 308, 30-06, 7mm Mag., 300 Win. Mag. Magazine holds 5 standard, 3 Magnum cartridges. 24-inch barrel. Weight: about $7\frac{1}{4}$ pounds. No sights. Monte Carlo stock w/checkered pistol grip and forearm, swivels. Made 1963–1972.

RIFLES

Navy Arms 45-70 Mauser Rifle

Navy Arms Model 1873 Carbine

Navy Arms Martini Target Rifle

NAVY ARMS CO.
Martinsburg, WV (formerly Ridgefield, NJ)

Navy Arms 45-70 Mauser Carbine **$175**
Same as 45-70 Mauser Rifle, except has 18-inch barrel, straight-grip stock with low comb, weighs about 7½ pounds. Discontinued.

Navy Arms 45-70 Mauser Rifle **$160**
Siamese Mauser bolt action. Caliber: 45-70 Gov't. 3-round magazine. 24- or 26-inch barrel. Weight: about 8½ pounds with 26-inch barrel. Sights: open rear; ramp front. Checkered stock w/Monte Carlo comb. Intro. 1973; discontinued.

Navy Arms 1873 Carbine **$535**
Similar to Model 1873 Rifle, except has blued receiver, 10-shot magazine, 19-inch round barrel, carbine-style forearm w/barrel band, weighs about 6¾ pounds. Discontinued. Reissued in 1991 in 44-40 or 45 Colt.

Navy Arms Model 1873 Lever Action Rifle **$560**
Replica of Winchester Model 1873. Casehardened receiver. Calibers: 22 LR, 357 Magnum, 44-40. 15-shot magazine. 24-inch octagon barrel. Weight: about 8 pounds. Sights: open rear; blade front. Straight-grip stock, forearm w/end cap. Discontinued. Reissued in 1991 in 44-40 or 45 Colt with 12-shot magazine. Discontinued 1994.

Navy Arms 1873 Trapper's Model **$600**
Same as Model 1873 Carbine, except has 16½-inch barrel, 8-shot magazine, weighs about 6¼ pounds. Discontinued.

Navy Arms Engraved Models
Yellowboy and Model 1873 rifles and carbines are available in deluxe models with select walnut stocks and forearms and engraving in three grades. Grade "A" has delicate scrollwork in limited areas. Grade "B" is more elaborate with about 40 percent coverage. Grade "C" has highest grade engraving. Add to value:
Grade "A" **$100**
Grade "B"   135
Grade "C"   350

Navy Arms Martini Target Rifle **$340**
Martini single-shot action. Calibers: 444 Marlin, 45-70. 26- or 30-inch half-octagon or full-octagon barrel. Weight: about 9 pounds with 26-inch barrel. Sights: Creedmore tang peep, open middle, blade front. Stock w/cheekpiece and pistol grip, forearm with schnabel tip, both checkered. Introduced 1972; discontinued.

Navy Arms Revolving Carbine **$395**
Action resembles that of Remington Model 1875 Revolver. Casehardened frame. Calibers: 357 Magnum, 44-40, 45 Colt. 6-shot cylinder. 20-inch barrel. Weight: about 5 pounds. Sights: open rear; blade front. Straight-grip stock, brass trigger guard and buttplate. Intro. 1968; discont.

Navy Arms Revolving Carbine

Navy Arms Rolling Block Baby Carbine

Navy Arms Rolling Block Buffalo Rifle

Navy Arms Yellowboy Carbine

Navy Arms Yellowboy, Grade "C" Engraving

Navy Arms Yellowboy Rifle

Navy Arms Rolling Block Baby Carbine **$195**
Replica of small Remington Rolling Block single-shot action. Casehardened frame, brass trigger guard. Calibers: 22 LR, 22 Hornet, 357 Magnum, 44-40. 20-inch octagon or 22-inch round barrel. Weight: about 5 pounds. Sights: open rear; blade front. Straight-grip stock, plain forearm, brass buttplate. Made 1968–1981.

Navy Arms Rolling Block Buffalo Carbine **$240**
Same as Buffalo Rifle, except has 18-inch barrel, weighs about 10 pounds.

Navy Arms Rolling Block Buffalo Rifle **$250**
Replica Remington Rolling Block single-shot action. Casehardened frame, brass trigger guard. Calibers: 444 Marlin, 45-70, 50-70. 26- or 30-inch heavy half-octagon or full-octagon barrel. Weight: 11 to 12 pounds. Sights: open rear; blade front. Straight-grip stock w/brass buttplate, forearm w/brass barrel band. Made 1971 to date.

Navy Arms Rolling Block Creedmoor Rifle **$495**
Same as Buffalo Rifle, except calibers 45-70 and 50-70 only, 28- or 30-inch heavy half-octagon or full-octagon barrel, Creedmoor tang peep sight.

Navy Arms Yellowboy Carbine **$425**
Similar to Yellowboy Rifle, except has 19-inch barrel, 10-shot magazine (14-shot in 22 Long Rifle), carbine-style forearm. Weight: about 6¾ pounds. Discontinued. Re-issued 1991 in 44-40 only.

Navy Arms Yellowboy Lever Action Repeater . . . **$510**
Replica of Winchester Model 1866. Calibers: 38 Special, 44-40. 15-shot magazine. 24-inch octagon barrel. Weight: about 8 pounds. Sights; folding leaf rear; blade front. Straight-grip stock, forearm w/end cap. Intro. 1966; discontinued. Reissued 1991 in 44-40 only w/12-shot magazine and adj. ladder-style rear sight.

Navy Arms Yellowboy Trapper's Model **$540**
Same as Yellowboy Carbine, except has 16½-inch barrel, magazine holds two fewer rounds, weighs about 6¼ pounds. Discontinued.

NEW ENGLAND FIREARMS
Gardner, Massachusetts

New England Firearms Handi-Rifle
Single-shot, break-open action with side-lever release. Calibers: 22 Hornet, 22-250, 223, 243, 270, 30-30, 30-06, 45-70. 22-inch barrel. Weight: 7 pounds. Sights: ramp front; folding rear. Drilled and tapped for scope mounts. Walnut-finished hardwood stock. Blued finish. Made 1989 to date.
22-250, 243, 270 and 30-06 . . . . **$150**
22 Hornet, 223, 30-30 and 45-70 . . . . **140**

NEWTON SPORTING RIFLES
Buffalo, New York
Mfd. by Newton Arms Co., Charles Newton Rifles Corp. and Buffalo Newton Rifle Co.

Buffalo Newton Sporting Rifle **$750**
Same general specifications as Standard Model—Second Type. Made c. 1922–32 by Buffalo Newton Rifle Co.

Newton-Mauser Sporting Rifle **$725**
Mauser (Oberndorf) action. Caliber: 256 Newton. 5-shot box magazine, hinged floorplate. Double-set triggers. 24-inch barrel. Open rear sight, ramp front sight. Sporting stock with checkered pistol grip. Weight: about 7 pounds. Made c. 1914 by Newton Arms Co.

**Newton Standard Model Sporting Rifle—
First Type** **$750**
Newton bolt action, interrupted screw-type breech-locking mechanism, double-set triggers. Calibers: 22, 256, 280, 30, 33, 35 Newton; 30-06. 24-inch barrel. Sights: open rear or cocking-piece peep; ramp front. Checkered pistol-grip stock. Weight: 7 to 8 pounds, depending on caliber. Made c. 1916–1918 by Newton Arms Co.

**Newton Standard Model Sporting Rifle—
Second Type** **$735**
Newton bolt action, improved design; distinguished by reversed-set trigger and 1917-Enfield-type bolt handle.

Newton Sporting Rifle—Second Type (cont.)
Calibers: 256, 30, 35 Newton; 30-06. 5-shot box magazine. 24-inch barrel. Sights: open rear; ramp front. Checkered pistol-grip stock. Weight: $7^3/_4$ to $8^1/_4$ pounds. Made c. 1921 by Charles Newton Rifle Corp.

NIKKO FIREARMS LTD.
Tochiga, Japan
See listings under Golden Eagle Rifles.

NOBLE MFG. CO.
Haydenville, Massachusetts

Noble Model 10 Bolt Action Single Shot Rifle **$65**
Caliber: 22 LR, Long, Short. 24-inch barrel. Plain pistol-grip stock. Sights: open rear; bead front. Weight: about 4 pounds. Made 1955–58.

Noble Model 20 Bolt Action Single Shot Rifle **$65**
Manually cocked. Caliber: 22 LR, Long, Short. 22-inch barrel. Weight: about 5 pounds. Sights: open rear; bead front. Walnut stock w/pistol grip. Made 1958–1963.

Noble Model 33 Slide Action Repeater **$70**
Hammerless. Caliber: 22 LR, Long, Short. Tubular magazine holds 21 Short, 17 Long, 15 LR. 24-inch barrel. Weight: 6 pounds. Sights: open rear; bead front. Tenite stock and slide handle. Made 1949–1953.

Noble Model 33A **$65**
Same general specifications as Model 33 except has wood stock and slide handle. Made 1953–55.

Noble Model 222 Bolt Action Single Shot Rifle . . . **$75**
Manually cocked. Caliber: 22 LR, Long, Short. Barrel integral w/receiver. Overall length: 38 inches. Weight: about 5 pounds. Sights: interchangeable V-notch and peep rear; ramp front. Scope mounting base. Pistol-grip stock. Made 1958–1971.

RIFLES

Noble Model 10

Noble Model 222

Noble Model 236

Noble Model 275

Noble Model 236 Slide Action Repeating Rifle . . . **$85**
Hammerless. Caliber: 22 Short, Long, LR. Tubular magazine holds 21 Short, 17 Long, 15 LR. 24-inch barrel. Weight: about 5½ pounds. Sights: open rear; ramp front. Pistol-grip stock, grooved slide handle. Made 1951 to date.

Noble Model 275 Lever Action Rifle **$100**
Hammerless. Caliber: 22 Short, Long, LR. Tubular magazine holds 21 Short, 17 Long, 15 LR. 24-inch barrel. Weight: about 5½ pounds. Sights: open rear; ramp front. Stock w/semipistol grip. Made 1958–1971.

PARKER-HALE LIMITED
Birmingham, England

Parker-Hale Model 81 African **$595**
Same general specifications as Model 81 Classic, except in caliber 375 H&H only. Sights: African express rear; hooded blade front. Barrel-band swivel. All-steel trigger guard. Checkered European walnut stock w/pistol grip and recoil pad. Engraved receiver. Imported since 1986.

Parker-Hale Model 81 Classic Bolt Action Rifle **$495**
Calibers: 22-250, 243 Win., 270 Win., 6mm Rem., 6.5×55, 7×57, 7×64, 308 Win., 30-06, 300 Win. Mag., 7mm Rem. Mag. 4-shot magazine. 24-inch barrel. Weight: 7¾ pounds. Sights: adj. open rear; hooded ramp front. Checkered pistol-grip stock of European walnut. Imported since 1984.

Parker-Hale Model 85 Sniper Rifle **$1325**
Caliber: 308 Win. 10- or 20-shot M-14-type magazine. 24¼-inch barrel. 45 inches overall. Weight: 12½ pounds. Blade front sight, folding aperture rear. McMillan fiberglass stock w/detachable bipod. Made 1992 to date.

Parker-Hale Model 87 Bolt Action Repeating Target Rifle **$950**
Calibers: 243 Win., 6.5×55, 308 Win., 30-06 Springfield, 300 Win. Mag. 5-shot detachable box magazine. 26-inch barrel. 45 inches overall. Weight: 10 pounds. No sights; grooved for target-style scope mounts. Stippled walnut stock w/adj. buttplate. Sling swivel studs. Parkerized finish. Folding bipod.

Parker-Hale Model 1000 Standard Rifle **$295**
Calibers: 22-250, 243 Win., 270 Win., 6mm Rem., 308 Win., 30-06. 4-shot magazine. Bolt action. 22-inch or 24-inch (22-250) barrel. 43 inches overall. 7¼ pounds. Checkered walnut Monte Carlo-style stock with satin finish. Imported 1984–88.

Parker-Hale Model 1100 Lightweight Bolt Action Rifle **$340**
Same general specifications as the Model 1000 Standard, except w/22-inch lightweight profile barrel, hollow bolt handle, alloy trigger guard and floorplate, 6½ pounds, schnabel forend. Imported since 1984.

Parker-Hale Model 81 Classic

Parker-Hale Model 1100 Lightweight

Parker-Hale 1200 Super

Parker-Hale 1200V Varmint

Parker-Hale Model 1100M African Magnum Rifle $595
Same as Model 1000 Standard, except w/24-inch barrel in calibers 404 Jeffery, 458 Win. Mag. Weight: 9½ pounds. Sights: adj. rear; hooded post front. Imported since 1984.

Parker-Hale Model 1200 Super Clip Bolt Action Rifle $425
Same as Model 1200 Super, except w/detachable box magazine in calibers 243 Win., 6mm Rem., 270 Win., 30-06 and 308 Win., 300 Win. Mag., 7mm Rem. Mag. Imported from England since 1984.

Parker-Hale 1200 Super Bolt Action Sporting Rifle $395
Mauser-type bolt action. Calibers: 22-250, 243 Win., 6mm Rem., 25-06, 270 Win., 30-06, 308 Win. 4-shot magazine. 24-inch barrel. Weight: 7¼ pounds. Sights: folding open rear; hooded ramp front. European walnut stock w/ rollover Monte Carlo cheekpiece, rosewood forend tip and pistol-grip cap, skip checkering, recoil pad, sling swivels. Made 1968 to date.

Parker-Hale 1200 Super Magnum $495
Same general specifications as 1200 Super, except calibers 7mm Rem. Mag. and 300 Win. Mag., 3-shot magazine.

Parker-Hale 1200P Presentation $395
Same general specifications as 1200 Super, except has scroll-engraved action, trigger guard and floorplate, no

Parker-Hale 1200P Presentation (cont.)
sights. QD swivels. Calibers: 243 Win. and 30-06. Made 1969–1975.

Parker-Hale 1200V Varmint $385
Same general specifications as 1200 Super, except has 24-inch heavy barrel, no sights, weighs 9½ pounds. Calibers: 22-250, 6mm Rem., 25-06, 243 Win. Made 1969 to date.

Parker-Hale Model 1300C Scout $445
Calibers: 243, 308 Win. 10-round magazine. 20-inch barrel w/muzzle brake. 41 inches overall. Weight: 8½ pounds. No sights, drilled and tapped for scope. Checkered laminated birch stock w/QD swivels. Made 1992 to date.

Parker-Hale Model 2100 Midland Bolt Action Rifle $295
Calibers: 22-250, 243 Win., 6mm Rem., 270 Win., 6.5×55, 7×57, 7×64, 308 Win., 30-06. 4-shot box magazine. 22-inch or 24-inch (22-250) barrel. 43 inches overall. Weight: 7 pounds. Sights: adj. folding rear; hooded ramp front. Checkered European walnut Monte Carlo stock w/pistol grip. Imported since 1984.

Parker-Hale Model 2700 Lightweight $310
Same general specifications as Model 2100 Midland, except w/tapered lightweight barrel and aluminum trigger guard. Weight: 6½ pounds. Made 1992 to date.

Parker-Hale Model 2800 Midland $290
Same general specifications as Model 2100, except w/ laminated birch stock. Made 1992 to date.

Pedersen Model 3000 Grade I

=== **PEDERSEN CUSTOM GUNS** ===
North Haven, Connecticut
Division of O.F. Mossberg & Sons, Inc.

Pedersen Model 3000 Grade I Bolt Action Rifle . $825
Richly engraved with silver inlays, full-fancy American black walnut stock. Mossberg Model 810 action. Calibers:

Pederson Model 3000 Grade I (cont.)
270 Win., 30-06, 7mm Rem. Mag., 338 Win. Mag. 3-shot magazine, hinged floorplate. 22-inch barrel in 270 and 30-06, 24-inch in Magnums. Weight: 7 to 8 pounds. Sights: open rear; hooded ramp front. Monte Carlo stock w/roll-over cheekpiece, wraparound hand checkering on pistol grip and forearm, rosewood pistol-grip cap and forend tip, recoil pad or steel buttplate with trap, detachable swivels. Made 1973–75.

Pedersen Model 3000 Grade III

Pedersen Model 3000 Grade II **$600**
Same as Model 3000 Grade I, except less elaborate engraving, no inlays, fancy grade walnut stock with recoil pad. Made 1973–75.

Pedersen Model 3000 Grade III **$495**
Same as Model 3000 Grade I, except no engraving or inlays, select grade walnut stock w/recoil pad. Made 1973–74.

**Pedersen Model 4700 Custom Deluxe Lever
Action Rifle** **$225**
Mossberg Model 472 action. Calibers: 30-30, 35 Rem. 5-shot tubular magazine. 24-inch barrel. Weight: 7½ pounds. Sights: open rear; hooded ramp front. Hand-finished black walnut stock and beavertail forearm, barrel band swivels. Made 1975.

J.C. PENNEY CO., INC.
Dallas, Texas

Firearms sold under the J.C. Penney label were mfd. by Marlin, High Standard, Stevens, Savage and Springfield.

J.C. Penney Model 2025 Bolt Action Repeater . . . **$50**
Takedown. Caliber: 22 RF. 8-shot detachable box magazine. 24-inch barrel. Weight: about 6 pounds. Sights: open rear; bead front. Plain pistol-grip stock. Mfd. by Marlin.

J.C. Penney Model 2035 Bolt Action Repeater . . . **$50**
Takedown. Caliber: 22 RF. 8-shot detachable box magazine. 24-inch barrel. Weight: about 6 pounds. Sights: open rear; bead front. Plain pistol-grip stock. Mfd. by Marlin.

J.C. Penney Model 2935 Lever Action Rifle **$145**
Same general specifications as Marlin Model 336.

**J.C. Penney Model 6400 Bolt Action Centerfire
Rifle** **$120**
Same general specifications as Savage Model 340.

J.C. Penney Model 6660 Autoloading Rifle **$75**
Caliber: 22 RF. Tubular magazine. 22-inch barrel. Weight: about 5½ pounds. Sights: open rear; hooded ramp front. Plain pistol-grip stock. Mfd. by Marlin.

Plainfield M-1 Carbine

Plainfield M-1 Carbine
Commando Model

PLAINFIELD MACHINE COMPANY
Dunellen, New Jersey

Plainfield M-1 Carbine **$150**
Same as U.S. Carbine, Cal. 30, M-1, except also available in caliber 5.7mm (22 with necked-down 30 Carbine car-

Plainfield M-1 Carbine (cont.)
tridge case). Current production has ventilated metal handguard and barrel band w/o bayonet lug; earlier models have standard military-type fittings. Made 1960–1977.

Plainfield M-1 Carbine, Commando Model **$175**
Same as M-1 Carbine, except has paratrooper-type stock w/telescoping wire shoulderpiece. Made 1960–1977.

**Plainfield M-1 Carbine
Military Sporter**

Plainfielder M-1 Deluxe Sporter

Plainfield M-1 Carbine, Military Sporter **$150**
Same as M-1 Carbine, except has unslotted buttstock and
wood handguard. Made 1960–1977.

Plainfielder M-1 Deluxe Sporter **$175**
Same as M-1 Carbine, except has Monte Carlo sporting
stock. Made 1960–1973.

Polish Model 1929

**Polish Model 1929 (Karabin 29, WZ29) Mauser
Military Rifle** **$175**
Same, except for minor details, as the Czech Model 24.
Mfd. 1929 thru WWII. A similar model produced during
German occupation was designated Gew. 29/40.

POLISH MILITARY RIFLES
Manufactured by Government Arsenals at Radom and Warsaw, Poland

**Polish Model 1898 (Karabin 98, WZ98A) Mauser
Military Rifle** **$110**
Same, except for minor details, as the German Gew. 98
used in WWI. Manufacture began c. 1921.

**Polish Model 1898 (Karabin 98, K98) Mauser
Military Carbine** **$175**
Same, except for minor details, as the German Kar. 98a.
First manufactured during early 1920s.

WILLIAM POWELL & SON LTD.
Birmingham, England

Powell No. 1 Best Grade Double-Barrel Rifle . . **$25,000**
Sidelock. Gauges: Made to order in any gauge, with 12,
16 and 20 the most common. Barrels: Made to order in
any length, but 28 inches the recommended length. Highest grade French walnut buttstock and forearm with fine
checkering. Metal is elaborately engraved. Imported by
Stoeger about 1938–1951.

Purdey Double Rifle

JAMES PURDEY & SONS LTD.
London, England

Purdey Double Rifle **$28,500**
Sidelock action, hammerless, ejectors. Calibers: 375
Flanged Magnum Nitro Express, 500/465 Nitro Express,

Purdy Double Rifle (cont.)
470 Nitro Express, 577 Nitro Express. 25½-inch barrels
(25-inch in 375). Weight: 9½ to 12¾ pounds. Sights:
folding leaf rear; ramp front. Cheekpiece stock, checkered
forearm and pistol grip, recoil pad, swivels. Currently
manufactured; same general specifications apply to pre-
WWII model.

Purdey Single Rifle

Purdey Single Rifle **$4500**
Mauser-type bolt action. Calibers: 7×57, 300 H&H Magnum, 375 H&H Magnum, 10.75×73. 3-shot magazine. 24-inch barrel. Weight: 7½ to 8¾ pounds. Sights: folding

Purdy Single Rifle (cont.)
leaf rear; hooded ramp front. Cheekpiece stock, checkered forearm and pistol grip, swivels. Currently manufactured; same general specifications apply to pre-WWII model.

Remington No. 2

Remington No. 3

Remington Model Four

REMINGTON ARMS COMPANY
Ilion, New York

Remington No. 2 Sporting Rifle
Single-shot, rolling-block action. Calibers: 22, 25, 32, 38, 44 rimfire or centerfire. Barrel lengths: 24, 26, 28 or 30 inches. Weight: 5 to 6 pounds. Sights: open rear; bead front. Straight-grip sporting stock and knobtip forearm of walnut. Made 1873–1910.
Calibers: 22, 25, 32 . . . . **$495**
Calibers: 38, 44 550

Remington Model 2C **$595**
Target Grade. Same as Model 12A, except has 24-inch octagon barrel, pistol-grip stock.

Remington No. 3 Creedmoor and Schuetzen Rifles . . . . **$5000+**
Produced in a variety of styles and calibers, these are collector's items and bring far higher prices than the sporting types. The Schuetzen Special, which has an under-lever action, is especially rare—perhaps less than 100 having been made.

Remington No. 3 High Power Rifle
Single shot. Hepburn falling-block action with side lever. Calibers: 30/30, 30/40, 32 Special, 32/40, 38/55, 38/72 (high-power cartridges). Barrel lengths: 26-, 28-, 30-inch.

Remington No. 3 High Power Rifle (cont.)
Weight: about 8 pounds. Open sporting sights. Checkered pistol-grip stock and forearm. Made 1893–1907.
Calibers: 30/30, 30/40, 32 Special, 32/40 . . . . . . **$1425**
Calibers: 38/55, 38/72 1750

Remington No. 3 Sporting Rifle **$1050**
Single shot. Hepburn falling-block action with side lever. Calibers: 22 WCF, 22 Extra Long, 25/20 Stevens, 25/21 Stevens, 25/25 Stevens, 32 WCF, 32/40 Ballard & Marlin, 32/40 Rem., 38 WCF, 38/40 Rem., 38/50 Rem., 38/55 Ballard & Marlin, 40/60 Ballard & Marlin, 40/60 WCF, 40/65 Rem. Straight, 40/82 WCF, 45/70 Gov., 45/90 WCF; also was supplied on special order in bottle-necked 40/50, 40/70, 40/90, 44/77, 44/90, 44/105, 50/70 Gov., 50/90 Sharps Straight. Barrel lengths: 26-inch (22, 25, 32 cal. only), 28-inch, 30-inch; half-octagon or full-octagon. Weight: 8 to 10 pounds. Sights: open rear; blade front. Checkered pistol-grip stock and forearm. Made 1880 to c. 1911.

Remington Model Four (4) Autoloading Rifle
Hammerless. Calibers: 6mm Rem., 243 Win., 270 Win., 7mm Express Rem., 30-06, 308 Win. 22-inch barrel. Weight: 7½ pounds. Sights: open rear; bead front, on ramp. Monte Carlo checkered stock and forearm. Made 1981–88.
Standard . . . . **$ 315**
Peerless Grade (Engr. receiver) 1235
Premier Grade (Engr. receiver, gold inlay) 3500

RIFLES

**Remington Model Four Limited Edition
One of Fifteen Hundred**

Remington No. 4

Remington No. 4S

Remington No. 5

Remington Model Six

Remington Model Four Diamond Anniversary Ltd. Edition
Same as Model Four Standard, except has engraved receiver w/inscription, checkered high-grade walnut stock and forend. Only 1,500 produced. Made 1981 only.

Standard Grade	**$ 895**
Peerless Grade	**1720**
Premier Grade	**3540**
Premier Gold Grade	**5250**

Remington No. 4 Single Shot Rifle $395
Rolling-block action. Solid frame or takedown. Calibers: 22 Short and Long, 22 LR, 25 Stevens R.F., 32 Short and Long R.F. 22½-inch octagon barrel, 24-inch available in 32 caliber only. Weight: about 4½ pounds. Sights: open rear; blade front. Plain walnut stock and forearm. Made 1890–1933.

Remington No. 4S Military Model 22 Single Shot Rifle $595
Rolling-block action. Calibers: 22 Short only, 22 LR only. 28-inch barrel. Weight: about 5 pounds. Sights: military-type rear; blade front. Military-type stock w/handguard, stacking swivel, sling. Has a bayonet stud on the barrel; bayonet and scabbard were regularly supplied. *Note:* At one time the "Military Model" was the official rifle of the Boy Scouts of America and was called the "Boy Scout Rifle." Made 1913–1933.

Remington No. 5 Special Rifle
Single shot. Rolling-block action. Calibers: 7mm Mauser, 30-30, 30-40 Krag, 303 British, 32-40, 32 Special, 38-55 (high-power cartridges). Barrel lengths: 24, 26 and 28 inches. Weight: about 7 pounds. Open sporting sights. Plain straight-grip stock and forearm. Made 1902–1918. *Note:* Models 1897 and 1902 Military Rifles, intended for the export market, are almost identical with the No. 5 except for 30-inch barrel, full military stock and weight (about 8½ pounds); a carbine was also supplied. The military rifles were produced in caliber 8mm Lebel for France, 7.62mm Russian for Russia and 7mm Mauser for the Central and South American government trade. At one time, Remington also offered these military models to retail buyers.

Sporting Model	**$395**
Military Model	**250**

Remington Model Six (6) Peerless Grade $1235
Same as Model Six Standard, except has engraved receiver. Made 1981–88.

Remington Model Six (6) Premier Grade $3500
Same as Model Six Standard, except has engraved receiver with gold inlay. Made 1981–88.

Remington Model Six (6) Slide Action Repeater .. $345
Hammerless. Calibers: 6mm Rem., 243 Win., 270 Win., 7mm Express Rem., 30-06, 308 Win. 22-inch barrel. Weight: 7½ pounds. Checkered Monte Carlo stock and forearm. Made 1981–88.

Remington No. 6

Remington Model Seven

Remington Model Seven FS

Remington Model Seven KS Custom Rifle

Remington No. 7 Target

Remington No. 6 Takedown Rifle **$310**
Single shot. Rolling-block action. Calibers: 22 Short, 22 Long, 22 LR, 32 Short and Long R.F. 20-inch barrel. Weight: about 4 pounds. Sights: open front and rear; tang peep. Plain straight-grip stock and forearm. Made 1901–1933.

Remington Model Seven (7) CF Bolt Action Rifle
Calibers: 17 Rem., 222 Rem., 223 Rem., 243 Win., 6mm Rem., 7mm-08 Rem., 308 Win. Magazine capacity: 5-shot in 17 Rem., 222 Rem., 223 Rem., 4-shot in other calibers. 18½-inch barrel. Weight: 6¼ pounds. Walnut stock, checkering, and recoil pad. Made 1983 to date. 223 Rem. added in 1984.
Standard calibers except 17 Rem. **$395**
Caliber 17 Rem. **415**

Remington Model Seven (7) FS Rifle **$325**
Calibers: 243, 7mm-08 Rem., 308 Win. 18½-inch barrel. 37½ inches overall. Weight: 5¼ pounds. Hand layup fiberglass stock, reinforced with DuPont Kevlar at points of bedding and stress. Made 1987–1990.

Remington Model Seven (7) KS Rifle **$620**
Calibers: 223 Rem., 7mm-08, 308, 35 Rem. and 350 Rem. Mag. 20-inch barrel. Custom made in Remington's Custom shop with Kevlar stock. Made 1987 to date.

Remington Model Seven (7) MS Custom Rifle . . **$695**
Similar to the standard Model 7, except fitted with a laminated full Mannlicher-style stock. Weight: 6¾ pounds. Calibers: 222 Rem., 22-250, 243, 6mm Rem., 7mm-08, 308, 350 Rem. Additional calibers available on special order. Made 1993 to date.

Remington Model Seven (7) Youth Rifle **$300**
Similar to the standard Model 7, except fitted with hardwood stock with a 12³/₁₆-inch pull. Calibers: 243, 6mm, 7mm-08 only. Made 1993 to date.

Remington No. 7 Target and Sporting Rifle **$695**
Single shot. Rolling-block Army Pistol frame. Calibers: 22 Short, 22 LR, 25 Stevens R.F. (other calibers as available in No. 2 Rifle were supplied on special order). Half-octagon barrels: 24-, 26-, 28-inch. Weight: about 6 pounds. Sights: Lyman combination rear; Beach combination front. Fancy walnut stock and forearm; Swiss buttplate available as an extra. Made 1903–1911.

Remington Model 8A

Remington Model 12A

Remington Model 14R

Remington Model 16

Remington Model 24A

RIFLES

Remington Model 8A Autoloading Rifle **$405**
Standard Grade. Takedown. Calibers: 25, 30, 32 and 35
Rem. Five-shot, clip-loaded magazine. 22-inch barrel.
Weight: 7¾ pounds. Sights: open rear; bead front. Plain
straight-grip stock and forearm of walnut. Made 1906–
1936.

Remington Model 12A, 12B, 12C, 12CS Slide Action Repeaters
Standard Grade. Hammerless. Takedown. Caliber: 22
Short, Long or LR. Tubular magazine holds 15 Short, 12
Long or 10 LR cartridges. 22- or 24-inch round or octagonal barrel. Open rear sight, bead front. Plain, half-pistol-grip stock and grooved slide handle of walnut. Made 1912–1935.
Model 12A **$295**
Model 12B (22 Short only w/octagon bbl.) **310**
Model 12C (w/24-inch octagon bbl.) **335**
Model 12CS (22 WRF w/24-inch octagon bbl.) . . . **295**

Remington Model 14A High Power Slide Action Repeating Rifle **$350**
Standard Grade. Hammerless. Takedown. Calibers: 25,
30, 32 and 35 Rem. 5-shot tubular magazine. 22-inch
barrel. Weight: about 6¾ pounds. Sights: open rear; bead
front. Plain, half-pistol-grip stock and grooved slide
handle of walnut. Made 1912–1935.

Remington Model 14R Carbine **$375**
Same as Model 14A except has 18½-inch barrel, straight-
grip stock, weighs about 6 pounds.

Remington Model 14½ Carbine **$725**
Same as Model 14½ Rifle, except has 9-shot magazine,
18½-inch barrel.

Remington Model 14½ Rifle **$750**
Similar to Model 14A, except calibers 38/40 and 44/40,
11-shot full magazine, 22½-inch barrel. Made 1912 to
early 1920s.

Remington Model 16 Autoloading Rifle **$225**
Takedown. Closely resembles the Winchester Model 03.
Calibers: 22 Short, 22 LR, 22 Rem. Auto. 15-shot tubular
magazine in buttstock. 22-inch barrel. Weight: 5¾ pounds.
Sights: open rear; bead front. Plain straight-grip stock
and forearm. Made 1914–1928. *Note:* In 1918 this model
was discontinued in all calibers except 22 Rem. Auto;
specifications given are for that.

Remington Model 24A Autoloading Rifle **$250**
Standard Grade. Takedown. Calibers: 22 Short only, 22
LR only. Tubular magazine in buttstock, holds 15 Short
or 10 LR. 21-inch barrel. Weight: about 5 pounds. Sights:
open rear; bead front. Plain walnut stock and forearm.
Made 1922–1935.

Remington Model 25R

Remington Model 30A

Remington Model 30R

Remington Model 30S

Remington Model 33

Remington Model 25A Slide Action Repeater . . . **$325**
Standard Grade. Hammerless. Takedown. Calibers:
25/20, 32/20. 10-shot tubular magazine. 24-inch barrel.
Weight: about 5½ pounds. Sights: open rear; bead front.
Plain, pistol-grip stock, grooved slide handle. Made 1923–
1936.

Remington Model 25R Carbine **$395**
Same as Model 25A, except has 18-inch barrel. 6-shot
magazine, straight-grip stock, weighs about 4½ pounds.

**Remington Model 30A Bolt Action Express
Rifle** **$395**
Standard Grade. Modified M/1917 Enfield Action.
Calibers: 25, 30, 32 and 35 Rem., 7mm Mauser, 30-06. 5-
shot box magazine. 22-inch barrel. Weight: about 7¼
pounds. Sights: open rear; bead front. Walnut stock w/
checkered pistol grip and forearm. Made 1921–1940. *Note:*
Early Model 30s had a slender forend with schnabel tip,
military-type double-pull trigger, 24-inch barrel.

Remington Model 30R Carbine **$495**
Same as Model 30A, except has 20-inch barrel, plain stock,
weighs about 7 pounds.

Remington Model 30S Sporting Rifle **$575**
Special Grade. Same action as Model 30A. Calibers: 257
Roberts, 7mm Mauser, 30-06. 5-shot box magazine. 24-
inch barrel. Weight: about 8 pounds. Lyman #48 Receiver
sight, bead front sight. Special high comb stock with long,
full forearm, checkered. Made 1930–1940.

**Remington Model 33 Bolt Action Single Shot
Rifle** **$120**
Takedown. Caliber: 22 Short, Long, LR. 24-inch barrel.
Weight: about 4½ pounds. Sights: open rear; bead front.
Plain, pistol-grip stock, forearm with grasping grooves.
Made 1931–36.

Remington Model 33 NRA Junior Target Rifle . . . **$150**
Same as Model 33 Standard, except has Lyman peep rear
sight, Patridge-type front sight, ⅞-inch sling and swivels,
weighs about 5 pounds.

Remington Model 34

Remington Model 37 (1937)

Remington Model 37 (1940)

Remington Model 40X Standard Rimfire

Remington Model 40-XB Centerfire

Remington Model 34 Bolt Action Repeater $125
Takedown. Caliber: 22 Short, Long, LR. Tubular magazine holds 22 Short, 17 Long or 15 LR. 24-inch barrel. Weight: 5¼ pounds. Sights: open rear; bead front. Plain, pistol-grip stock, forearm w/grasping grooves. Made 1932–36.

Remington Model 34 NRA Target Rifle $175
Same as Model 34 Standard, except has Lyman peep rear sight, Patridge-type front sight, 7/8-inch sling and swivels, weighs about 5¾ pounds.

Remington Model 37 Rangemaster Bolt Action Target Rifle (I)
Model of 1937. Caliber: 22 LR. 5-shot box magazine, single shot adapter also supplied as standard equipment. 28-inch heavy barrel. Weight: about 12 pounds. Remington front and rear sights, scope bases. Target stock, swivels, sling. *Note:* Original 1937 model had a stock with outside barrel band similar in appearance to that of the old-style Winchester Model 52; forearm design was modified and barrel band eliminated in 1938. Made 1937–1940.
With factory sights............................. **$375**
Without sights **325**

Remington Model 37 Rangemaster Bolt Action Target Rifle (II)
Model of 1940. Same as Model of 1937, except has "Miracle" trigger mechanism and Randle design stock with high comb, full pistol grip and wide beavertail forend. Made 1940–1954.

Remington Model 37 Rangemaster Bolt Action (II) (cont.)
With factory sights............................ **$495**
Without sights **415**

Remington Model 40X Centerfire Rifle $375
Specifications same as for Model 40X Rimfire (heavyweight). Calibers: 222 Rem., 222 Rem. Mag., 7.62mm NATO, 30-06 (others were available on special order). Made 1961–64. Value shown is for rifle w/o sights.

Remington Model 40X Heavyweight Bolt Action Target Rifle (Rimfire)
Caliber: 22 LR. Single shot. Action similar to Model 722. Click adjustable trigger. 28-inch heavy barrel. Redfield Olympic sights. Scope bases. High-comb target stock, bedding device, adj. swivel, rubber buttplate. Weight: 12¾ pounds. Made 1955–1964.
With sights **$410**
Without sights **325**

Remington Model 40-X Sporter $1150
Same general specifications as Model 700 C Custom (see that listing), except in caliber 22 LR. Made 1972–77.

Remington Model 40X Standard Barrel
Same as Model 40X Heavyweight except has lighter barrel. Weight: 10¾ pounds.
With sights **$345**
Without sights **310**

Remington Model 40-XB Centerfire Match Rifle $695
Bolt action, single shot. Calibers: 222 Rem., 222 Rem. Mag., 223 Rem., 22-250, 6×47mm, 6mm Rem., 243 Win.,

Remington Model 40-XB Rimfire

Remington Model 40-XB Varmint Special

Remington Model 40-XBBR

Remington Model 40-XC

Remington Model 40-XB Centerfire Match (cont.)
25-06, 7mm Rem. Mag., 30-06, 308 Win. (7.62mm NATO), 30-338, 300 Win. Mag. 27¼-inch standard or heavy barrel. Target stock w/adj. front swivel block on guide rail, rubber buttplate. Weight w/o sights: standard barrel, 9¼ lbs.; heavy barrel, 11¼ lbs. Value shown is for rifle without sights. Made 1964 to date.

Remington Model 40-XB Centerfire Repeater ... $795
Same as Model 40-XB Centerfire except 5-shot repeater. Calibers: 222 Rem., 222 Rem. Mag., 223 Rem., 22-250, 6×47mm, 6mm Rem., 243 Win., 308 Win. (7.62mm NATO). Heavy barrel only. Discontinued.

Remington Model 40-XB Rangemaster Centerfire
Single-shot target rifle with same basic specifications as Model 40-XB Centerfire Match. Additional calibers in 220 Swift, 6mm BR Rem. and 7mm BR Rem., and stainless barrel only. American walnut or Kevlar (weighs 1 lb. less) target stock with forend stop. Discontinued 1994.

Model 40-XB Right-hand Model	$790
Model 40-XB Left-hand Model	835
For 2-oz. Trigger, **add**	100
Model 40-XB KS (Kevlar Stock, R.H.)	905
Model 40-XB KS (Kevlar Stock, L.H.)	950
For 2-oz. trigger, **add**	100
For Repeater Model, **add**	80

Remington Model 40-XB Rangemaster Rimfire Match Rifle ... $650
Bolt action, single shot. Caliber: 22 LR. 28-inch standard or heavy barrel. Target stock with adjustable front swivel

Remington Model 40-XB Rangemaster Rimfire (cont.)
block on guide rail, rubber buttplate. Weight w/o sights: standard barrel, 10 lbs.; heavy barrel, 11¼ lbs. Value shown is for rifle without sights. Made 1964–1974.

Remington Model 40-XB Varmint Special Rifle ... $785
Same general specifications as Model 40-XB Repeater, except has synthetic stock of Kevlar. Made 1987–1994.

Remington Model 40-XBBR Bench Rest Rifle
Bolt action, single shot. Calibers: 222 Rem., 222 Rem. Mag., 223 Rem., 6×47mm, 308 Win. (7.62mm NATO). 20- or 26-inch unblued stainless-steel barrel. Supplied w/o sights. Weight: with 20-inch bbl., 9¼ lbs.; with 26-inch bbl., 12 lbs. (heavy Varmint class); 7¼ lbs. w/Kevlar stock (light Varmint class). Made 1969 to date.

Model 40-XBBR	$640
Model 40-XBBR KS (Kevlar Stock) (disc.)	960

Remington Model 40-XC National Match Course Rifle
Bolt-action repeater. Caliber: 308 Win. (7.62mm NATO). 5-shot magazine; clip slot in receiver. 24-inch barrel. Supplied w/o sights. Weight: 11 pounds. Thumb groove stock w/adj. hand stop and sling swivel, adj. buttplate. Made 1974 to date.

Model 40-XC	$795
Model 40-XC KS (Kevlar Stock) (disc. 1994)	960

Remington Model 40-XR Custom Sporter Rifle
Caliber: 22 RF. 24-inch contoured barrel. Supplied w/o sights. Made in four grades of checkering, engraving and

Remington Model 40-XR Custom Sporter, Grade II

Remington Model 40-XR Rimfire

Remington Model 41P

Remington Model 81A Woodsmaster

Remington Model 121A Fieldmaster

Remington Model 40-XR Custom Sporter Rifle (cont.)

other custom features. Made 1987 to date.

Grade I	$ 850
Grade II	1540
Grade III	2450
Grade IV	3800

Remington Model 40-XR Rimfire Position Rifle

Bolt action, single shot. Caliber: 22 LR. 24-inch heavy barrel. Supplied w/o sights. Weight: about 10 pounds. Position-style stock w/thumb groove, adj. hand stop and sling swivel on guide rail, adj. buttplate. Made 1974 to date.

| Model 40-XR | $895 |
| Model 40-XR KS (Kevlar Stock) | 950 |

Remington Model 41A Targetmaster Bolt Action Single Shot Rifle $155

Takedown. Caliber: 22 Short, Long, LR. 27-inch barrel. Weight: about 5½ pounds. Sights: open rear; bead front. Plain pistol-grip stock. Made 1936–1940.

Remington Model 41AS $175

Same as Model 41A, except chambered for 22 Remington Special (22 W.R.F.).

Remington Model 41P $100

Same as Model 41A, except has peep rear sight, hooded front sight.

Remington Model 41SB $200

Same as Model 41A, except smoothbore for use with shot cartridges.

Remington Model 81A Woodsmaster Auto-loader $350

Standard Grade. Takedown. Calibers: 30, 32 and 35 Rem., 300 Sav. 5-shot box magazine (not detachable). 22-inch barrel. Weight: 8¼ pounds. Sights: open rear; bead front. Plain, pistol-grip stock and forearm of walnut. Made 1936–1950.

Remington Model 121A Fieldmaster Slide Action Repeater $265

Standard Grade. Hammerless. Takedown. Caliber: 22 Short, Long, LR. Tubular magazine holds 20 Short, 15 Long or 14 LR cartridges. 24-inch round barrel. Weight: 6 pounds. Plain, pistol-grip stock and grooved semibeavertail slide handle. Made 1936–1954.

Remington Model 121S $295

Same as Model 121A, except chambered for 22 Remington Special (22 W.R.F.). Magazine holds 12 rounds. Disc.

Remington Model 121SB $395

Same as Model 121A, except smoothbore. Discontinued.

Remington Model 141A Gamemaster Slide Action Repeater $295

Standard Grade. Hammerless. Takedown. Calibers: 30, 32 and 35 Rem. 5-shot tubular magazine. 24-inch barrel. Weight: about 7³/₄ pounds. Sights: open rear; bead front, on ramp. Plain, pistol-grip stock, semibeavertail forend (slide-handle). Made 1936–1950.

Remington Model 241A Speedmaster Autoloader $260

Standard Grade. Takedown. Calibers: 22 Short only, 22 LR only. Tubular magazine in buttstock, holds 15 Short or 10 LR. 24-inch barrel. Weight: about 6 pounds. Sights; open rear; bead front. Plain walnut stock and forearm. Made 1935–1951.

Remington Model 341A Sportsmaster Bolt Action Repeater $135

Takedown. Caliber: 22 Short, Long, LR. Tubular magazine holds 22 Short, 17 Long, 15 LR. 27-inch barrel. Weight: about 6 pounds. Sights; open rear; bead front. Plain pistol-grip stock. Made 1936–1940.

Remington Model 341P $160

Same as Model 341A, except has peep rear sight, hooded front sight.

Remington Model 341SB $275

Same as Model 341A, except smoothbore for use with shot cartridges.

Remington Model 510A Targetmaster Bolt Action Single Shot Rifle $195

Takedown. Caliber: 22 Short, Long, LR. 25-inch barrel. Weight: about 5¹/₂ pounds. Sights: open rear; bead front. Plain pistol-grip stock. Made 1939–1962.

Remington Model 510P $150

Same as Model 510A, except has peep rear sight, Patridge front, on ramp.

Remington Model 510SB $275

Same as Model 510A, except smoothbore for use with shot cartridges, shotgun bead front sight, no rear sight.

Remington Model 510X Bolt Action Single Shot Rifle $160

Same as Model 510A, except improved sights. Mfd. 1964–66.

Remington Model 511A Scoremaster Bolt Action Box Magazine Repeater $140

Takedown. Caliber: 22 Short, Long, LR. 6-shot detachable box magazine. 25-inch barrel. Weight: about 5¹/₂ pounds. Sights: open rear; bead front. Plain pistol-grip stock. Made 1939–1962.

Remington Model 511P $125

Same as Model 511A, except has peep rear sight, Patridge-type blade front, on ramp.

Remington Model 141A Gamemaster

Remington Model 241A Speedmaster

Remington Model 341A Sportsmaster

Remington Model 510X

Remington Model 511A

Remington Model 511X Bolt Action Repeater . . . **$150**
Clip type. Same as Model 511A, except improved sights.
Made 1964–66.

Remington Model 512A Sportsmaster Bolt Action Repeater **$150**
Takedown. Caliber: 22 Short, Long, LR. Tubular magazine holds 22 Short, 17 Long, 15 LR. 25-inch barrel. Weight: about 5¾ pounds. Sights: open rear; bead front. Plain pistol-grip stock w/semibeavertail forend. Made 1940–1962.

Remington Model 512P **$195**
Same as Model 512A, except has peep rear sight, blade front, on ramp.

Remington Model 512X Bolt Action Repeater . . . **$210**
Tubular magazine type. Same as Model 512A, except has improved sights. Made 1964–66.

Remington Model 513S Bolt Action Sporting Rifle **$325**
Caliber: 22 LR. 6-shot detachable box magazine. 27-inch barrel. Weight: about 6¾ pounds. Marble open rear sight,

Remington Model 513S Bolt Action Sporter (cont.)
Patridge-type front. Checkered sporter stock. Made 1941–1956.

Remington Model 513TR Matchmaster Bolt Action Target Rifle **$250**
Caliber: 22 LR. 6-shot detachable box magazine. 27-inch barrel. Weight: about 9 pounds. Sights: Redfield No. 75 rear; globe front. Target stock. Sling and swivels. Made 1941–1969.

Remington Model 514 Bolt Action Single Shot . . **$135**
Takedown. Caliber: 22 Short, Long, LR. 24-inch barrel. Weight: 4¾ pounds. Sights: open rear; bead front. Plain pistol-grip stock. Made 1948–1971.

Remington Model 514BC Boy's Carbine **$175**
Same as Model 514, except has 21-inch barrel, 1-inch shorter stock. Made 1961–1971.

Remington Model 514P **$200**
Same as Model 514, except has receiver peep sight.

RIFLES

Remington Model 511X

Remington Model 512A Sportsmaster

Remington Model 513S

Remington Model 513TR Matchmaster

Remington Model 514BC

Remington Model 521TL

Remington Model 540-X

Remington Model 540-XR

Remington Model 541-S

Remington Model 541-T

Remington Model 521TL Junior Target Bolt Action Repeater $225
Takedown. Caliber: 22 LR. 6-shot detachable box magazine. 25-inch barrel. Weight: about 7 pounds. Sights: Lyman No. 57RS rear; blade front. Target stock. Sling and swivels. Made 1947–1969.

Remington Model 522 Viper $120
Calibers: 22 LR. 10-shot magazine. 20-inch barrel. 40 inches overall. Weight: 4⅝ pounds. Checkered black PET resin stock with beavertail forend. Dupont high-tech synthetic receiver. Matte black finish on all exposed metal. Made 1993 to date.

Remington Model 540-X Rimfire Target Rifle . . . $250
Bolt action, single shot. Caliber: 22 LR. 26-inch heavy barrel. Supplied w/o sights. Weight: about 8 pounds. Target stock w/Monte Carlo cheekpiece and thumb groove, guide rail for hand stop and swivel, adj. buttplate. Made 1969–1974.

Remington Model 540-XR Rimfire Position Rifle $280
Bolt action, single shot. Caliber: 22 LR. 26-inch medium-weight barrel. Supplied w/o sights. Weight: 8 lbs. 13 oz.

Remington Model 540-XR Rimfire Position (cont.)
Position-style stock w/thumb groove, guide rail for hand stop and swivel, adj. buttplate. Made 1974–1984.

Remington Model 540-XRJR $295
Same as Model 540-XR, except 1¾-inch shorter stock. Made 1974–1984.

Remington Model 541-S Custom Sporter $395
Bolt-action repeater. Scroll engraving on receiver and trigger guard. Caliber: 22 Short, Long, LR. 5-shot clip magazine. 24-inch barrel. Weight: 5½ pounds. Supplied w/o sights. Checkered walnut stock w/rosewood-finished forend tip, pistol-grip cap and buttplate. Made 1972–1984.

Remington Model 541-T Bolt Action Rifle
Caliber: 22 RF. Clip-fed, 5-shot. 24-inch barrel. Weight: 5⅞ pounds. Checkered walnut stock. Made 1986 to date; heavy barrel model introduced in 1993.
Model 541-T Standard $325
Model 541-T HB Heavy barrel 295

Remington Model 550A

Remington Model 552A

Remington Model 552BDL

Remington Model 572 Lightweight

Remington Model 572A

RIFLES

Remington Model 550A Autoloader **$135**
Has "Power Piston" or floating chamber, which permits interchangeable use of 22 Short, Long or LR cartridges. Tubular magazine holds 22 Short, 17 Long, 15 LR. 24-inch barrel. Weight: about 6¼ pounds. Sights: open rear; bead front. Plain, one-piece pistol-grip stock. Made 1941–1971.

Remington Model 550P **$150**
Same as Model 550A, except has peep rear sight, blade front, on ramp.

Remington Model 550-2G **$195**
"Gallery Special." Same as Model 550A, except has 22-inch barrel, screweye for counter chain and fired shell deflector.

Remington Model 552A Speedmaster Autoloader **$160**
Caliber: 22 Short, Long, LR. Tubular magazine holds 20 Short, 17 Long, 15 LR. 25-inch barrel. Weight: about 5½ pounds. Sights: open rear; bead front. Pistol-grip stock, semibeavertail forearm. Made 1957–1988.

Remington Model 552BDL Deluxe **$175**
Same as Model 552A, except has checkered walnut stock and forearm. Made 1966 to date.

Remington Model 552C Carbine **$160**
Same as Model 552A, except has 21-inch barrel. Made 1961–1977.

Remington Model 552GS Gallery Special **$175**
Same as Model 552A, except chambered for 22 Short only. Made 1957–1977.

Remington Model 572 Lightweight **$265**
Same as Model 572A, except has aluminum alloy receiver and outer barrel casing anodized in colors, chrome-plated magazine tube, trigger and trigger guard, checkered stock and forearm of light tan walnut. Weight: about 4 pounds. Colors: Buckskin Tan (Model 572BT), Teal Wing Blue (Model 572TWB), Crown Wing Black (Model 572CWB). Made 1958–1962.

Remington Model 572A Fieldmaster Slide Action Repeater **$150**
Hammerless. Caliber: 22 Short, Long, LR. Tubular magazine holds 20 Short, 17 Long, 15 LR. 23-inch barrel. Weight: about 5½ pounds. Sights: open rear; ramp front. Pistol-grip stock, grooved forearm. Made 1955–1988.

Remington Model 572BDL

Remington Model 580

Remington Model 581

Remington Model 581-S

Remington Model 582

Remington Model 591

Remington Model 572BDL Deluxe **$175**
Same as Model 572A, except has blade ramp front sight, sliding ramp rear; checkered stock and forearm. Made 1966 to date.

Remington Model 572SB Smooth Bore **$225**
Same as Model 572A, except smooth bore for 22 LR shot cartridges. Made 1961 to date.

Remington Model 580 Bolt Action Single Shot . . **$100**
Caliber: 22 Short, Long, LR. 24-inch barrel. Weight: 4³/₄ pounds. Sights: bead front; U-notch rear. Monte Carlo stock. Made 1967–1978.

Remington Model 580BR Boy's Rifle **$125**
Same as Model 580, except has 1-inch shorter stock. Made 1971–78.

Remington Model 580SB Smooth Bore **$145**
Same as Model 580, except smooth bore for 22 Long Rifle shot cartridges. Made 1967–1978.

Remington Model 581 Clip Repeater
Same general specifications as Model 580, except has 5-shot clip magazine. Made 1967–1984.
Model 581 . . . . **$125**
Model 581 Left Hand (made 1969–1984) **150**

Remington Model 581-S Bolt Action Rifle **$150**
Caliber: 22 RF. Clip-fed, 5-shot. 24-inch barrel. Weight: about 4³/₄ pounds. Plain walnut-colored stock. Made 1987–1992.

Remington Model 582 Tubular Repeater **$135**
Same general specifications as Model 580, except has tubular magazine holding 20 Short, 15 Long, 14 LR. Weight: about 5 pounds. Made 1967–1984.

Remington Model 591 Bolt Action Clip Repeater . **$225**
Caliber: 5mm Rimfire Magnum. 4-shot clip magazine. 24-inch barrel. Weight: 5 pounds. Sights: bead front; U-notch rear. Monte Carlo stock. Made 1970–73.

Remington Model 592

Remington Model 600

Remington Model 600
Montana Territorial Centennial

Remington Model 660

Remington Model 660 Magnum

Remington Model 700 ADL

RIFLES

Remington Model 592 Tubular Repeater **$200**
Same as Model 591, except has tubular magazine holding
10 rounds, weighs 5½ pounds. Made 1970–73.

Remington Model 600 Bolt Action Carbine **$495**
Calibers: 222 Rem., 6mm Rem., 243 Win., 308 Win., 35
Rem. 5-shot box magazine (6-shot in 222 Rem.). 18½-
inch barrel with ventilated rib. Weight: 6 pounds. Sights:
open rear; blade ramp front. Monte Carlo stock w/pistol
grip. Made 1964–67.

Remington Model 600 Magnum **$595**
Same as Model 600, except calibers 6.5mm Rem. Mag.
and 350 Rem. Mag., 4-shot magazine, special Magnum-
type barrel with racket for scope back-up, laminated
walnut-and-beech stock w/recoil pad. QD swivels and
sling; weight: about 6½ pounds. Made 1965–67.

**Remington Model 600 Montana Territorial
Centennial** **$725**
Same as Model 600, except has commemorative medallion
embedded in buttstock. Made 1964. Value is for rifle in
new, unfired condition.

Remington Model 660 Bolt Action Carbine **$425**
Calibers: 222 Rem., 6mm Rem., 243 Win., 308 Win. 5-
shot box magazine (6-shot in 222). 20-inch barrel. Weight:
6½ pounds. Sights: open rear; bead front, on ramp. Monte
Carlo stock, checkered, black pistol-grip cap and forend
tip. Made 1968–1971.

Remington Model 660 Magnum **$575**
Same as Model 660, except calibers 6.5mm Rem. Mag.
and 350 Rem. Mag., 4-shot magazine, laminated walnut-
and-beech stock with recoil pad, QD swivels and sling.
Made 1968–1971.

**Remington Model 700 ADL Centerfire Bolt
Action Rifle** **$285**
Calibers: 22-250, 222 Rem., 25-06, 6mm Rem., 243 Win.,
270 Win., 30-06, 308 Win., 7mm Rem. Mag. Magazine
capacity: 6-shot in 222 Rem.; 4-shot in 7mm Rem. Mag.;
5-shot in other calibers. Barrel lengths: 24-inch in 22-250,
222 Rem., 25-06, 7mm Rem. Mag.; 22-inch in other
calibers. Weight: 7 lbs. standard; 7½ lbs. in 7mm Rem.
Mag. Sights: ramp front; sliding ramp open rear. Monte
Carlo stock w/cheekpiece, skip checkering, recoil pad on
Magnum. Made 1962–1993.

Remington Model 700 BDL

Remington Model 700 BDL Left Hand

Remington Model 700 BDL Varmint Special

Remington Model 700 Classic

Remington Model 700 Classic Magnum

Remington Model 700 BDL Custom Deluxe

Same as Model 700 ADL, except has hinged floorplate, hooded ramp front sight, stock w/black forend tip and pistol-grip cap, cut checkering, QD swivels and sling. Additional calibers: 17 Rem., 223 Rem., 264 Win. Mag., 7mm-08, 280, 300 Sav., 300 Win. Mag., 8mm Rem. Mag., 338 Win. Mag., 35 Whelen. All have 24-inch barrels. Magnums have 4-shot magazine, recoil pad, weigh 7½ pounds; 17 Rem. has 6-shot magazine, weighs 7 pounds. Made 1962 to date. Left-hand version available in calibers 270 Win., 30-06, 7mm Rem. Mag.; made 1973 to date.

Standard calibers except 17 Rem.	**$385**
Magnum calibers and 17 Rem.	**425**
Left-hand, 270 Win. and 30-06	**395**
Left-hand, 7mm Rem. Mag.	**400**

Remington Model 700 BDL European Rifle

Same general specifications as Model 700 BDL, except has oil-finished walnut stock. Calibers: 243, 270, 7mm-08, 7mm Mag., 280 Rem., 30-06. Made 1993 to date.

Standard Calibers	**$395**
Magnum Calibers	**415**

Remington Model 700 BDL Varmint Special

Same as Model 700 BDL, except has 24-inch heavy barrel, no sights, weighs 9 lbs. (8¾ lbs. in 308 Win.). Calibers: 22-250, 222 Rem., 223 Rem., 25-06, 6mm Rem., 243 Win., 308 Win. Made 1967 to date. Synthetic stock version (black/grey) w/alum. bedding block made 1992 to date.

Model 700 BDL Varmint Special	**$415**
Model 700 VS (Varmint Synthetic)	**470**

Remington Model 700 Classic

Same general specifications as Model 700 BDL, except has "Classic" stock of high-quality walnut with full-pattern cut checkering, special satin wood finish; schnabel forend. Brown rubber buttpad. Hinged floorplate. No sights. Weight: 7 pounds. Also chambered for "Classic" cartridges such as 257 Roberts and 250-3000. Intro. 1981.

Standard Calibers	**$345**
Magnum Calibers	**385**

Remington Model 700 Custom
Rifle, Grade I

Remington Model 700 Custom
Rifle, Grade IV

Remington Model 700 KS Custom

Remington Model 700 RS

Remington Model 700 Safari

RIFLES

Remington Model 700 Custom Bolt Action Rifle
Same general specifications as Model 700 BDL, except custom built, and available in choice of grades—each with higher quality wood, different checkering patterns, engraving, high-gloss blued finish. Introduced in 1965.

Model 700 C Grade I	$ 850
Model 700 C Grade II	1540
Model 700 C Grade III	2450
Model 700 C Grade IV	3800
Model 700 D Peerless	1195
Model 700 F Premier	2495

Remington Model 700 FS Bolt Action Rifle $420
Calibers: 243, 270 Win., 30-06, 308 and 7mm Rem. Mag. 22-inch barrel. Weight: 6$1/4$ pounds. Straight-line fiberglass stock with solid black English-style buttpad and sling swivels. Made 1987–1990.

Remington Model 700 KS Custom Mountain Rifle
Calibers: 270 Win., 280 Rem., 30-06, 7mm Rem. Mag., 300 Win. Mag., 338 Win. Mag., 8mm Rem. Mag. and 375 H&H. 22-inch barrel. Weight: 6$3/4$ pounds. Available in both right- and left-hand models. Synthetic stock with Kevlar aramid fiber. Made 1987–1993.

Remington Model 700 KS Custom Mountain (cont.)

Standard Model	**$745**
Left-hand Model	775
Stainless Model	825

Remington Model 700 Mountain Rifle $390
Lightweight version (6$3/4$ pounds) of Model 700, with 22-inch barrel, checkered straight-comb satin-finished stock in calibers 243 Win., 270 Win., 280 Rem., 7mm-08 Rem., 30-06 and 308 Win. Made 1986 to date.

Remington 700 MTRSS Bolt Action Rifle $400
Similar to the Model 700 Mountain Rifle, except in stainless steel with black textured synthetic stock. Calibers: 25-06, 270, 280 Rem., 30-06. Weights 6$1/4$ pounds. Made 1993–94.

Remington Model 700 RS Bolt Action Rifle $370
Calibers: 270 Win., 280 Rem. and 30-06. 22-inch barrel. Weight: 7$1/4$ pounds. Stock made of Du Pont Rynite. Made 1987–1990.

Remington Model 700 Safari Grade
Magnum version of Model 700 BDL, except in calibers 8mm Rem. Mag., 375 H&H Mag., 416 Rem. Mag. and 458

Remington Model 700 Safari Grade (cont.)

Win. Mag., has heavier 24-inch barrel and stock, weighs 9 pounds. Made 1962 to date.

Safari Classic/Monte Carlo	$665
Safari KS (Kevlar Stock) intro. 1989	765
Safari KS (Wood-grain) intro. 1992	845
Safari Left-hand, add	50

Remington Model 700 Stock Variations

The following rifles have the same general specifications as Model 700 BDL, except with different stock options and finishes.

Model 700 AS (Black fiberglass-reinforced resin stock; nonreflective black matte finish) Standard calibers	$395
Model 700 AS, Magnum calibers	410
Model 700 CS (Mossy Oak Bottomland Camo Synthetic Stock w/black matte finish) Standard calibers	425
Model 700 CS, Magnum calibers	440
Model 700 LS (Multi-colored laminated stock) Standard calibers	365
Model 700 LS, Magnum calibers	385
Model 700 SS (Matte stainless barrel and action, Black synthetic stock) Standard calibers (discontinued 1994)	400
Model 700 SS Magnum calibers	420

Remington Model 720A Bolt Action High Power Rifle $895

Modified M/1917 Enfield action. Calibers: 257 Roberts, 270 Win., 30-06. 5-shot box magazine. 22-inch barrel. Weight: about 8 pounds. Sights: open rear; bead front, on ramp. Pistol-grip stock, checkered. **Model 720R** has 20-inch barrel; **Model 720S** has 24-inch barrel. Made 1941.

Remington Model 721A Standard Grade Bolt Action High Power Rifle $295

Calibers: 264 Win., 270 Win., 30-06. 4-shot box magazine. 24-inch barrel. Weight: about 7¼ pounds. Sights: open rear; bead front, on ramp. Plain sporting stock. Made 1948–1962.

Remington Model 721A 300 Magnum Standard Grade $510

Caliber: 300 H&H Magnum. Same as standard model, except has 26-inch heavy barrel, 3-shot magazine, recoil pads, weighs 8¼ pounds.

Remington Model 721ADL/BDL Deluxe

Same as Model 721A Standard or Magnum, except has deluxe checkered stock and/or select wood.

Model 721ADL Deluxe Grade	$335
Model 721ADL 300 Magnum Deluxe	475
Model 721BDL Deluxe Special Grade	395
Model 721BDL 300 Magnum Deluxe	410

Remington Model 722A Standard Grade Sporter

Same as Model 721A Bolt Action, except shorter action in calibers 257 Roberts, 308 Win., 300 Savage, weighs 7 pounds. Made 1948–1962. Caliber 222 Rem. (26-inch barrel, 5-shot magazine, 8 lbs.) introduced in 1950; caliber 244 Rem. (4-round capacity) introduced 1955.

Standard calibers	$260
222 Rem. Standard Grade	250
244 Rem. Standard Grade	275

Remington Model 722ADL Deluxe Grade

Same as Model 722A, except has deluxe checkered stock.

Standard Calibers	$300
222 Rem. Deluxe Grade	335
244 Rem. Deluxe Grade	350

Remington Model 722BDL Deluxe Special Grade

Same as Model 722ADL, except select wood.

Standard Calibers	$365
222 Rem. Deluxe Special Grade	395
244 Rem. Deluxe Special Grade	425

Remington Model 725 Kodiak Magnum Rifle . . $1995

Similar to Model 725ADL. Calibers: 375 H&H Mag., 458 Win. Mag. 3-shot magazine. 26-inch barrel with recoil reducer built into muzzle. Weight: about 9 pounds. Deluxe, reinforced Monte Carlo stock with recoil pad, black forend tip, swivels, sling. Less than 100 made in 1961.

Remington Model 720A

Remington Model 721A

Remington Model 725 Kodiak

**Remington Model 725ADL Bolt Action
Repeating Rifle** **$600**
Calibers: 222, 243, 244, 270, 280, 30-06. 4-shot box
magazine (5-shot in 222). 22-inch barrel (24-inch in 222).
Weight: about 7 pounds. Sights: open rear; hooded ramp
front. Monte Carlo comb stock w/pistol grip, checkered,
swivels. Made 1958–1961.

**Remington Model 740A Woodsmaster
Autoloader Rifle** **$295**
Standard Grade. Gas-operated. Calibers: 30-06 or 308. 4-
shot detachable box magazine. 22-inch barrel. Weight:
about 7½ pounds. Plain pistol-grip stock, semibeavertail
forend with finger grooves. Sights: open rear; ramp front.
Made 1955–1960.

Remington Model 740ADL/BDL Deluxe
Same as Model 740A, except has deluxe checkered stock,
standard or high comb, grip cap, sling swivels. Model
740BDL also has select wood. Made 1955–1960.
Model 740ADL Deluxe Grade. **$325**
Model 740BDL Deluxe Special Grade **350**

**Remington Model 742 Bicentennial
Commemorative** **$550**
Same as Model 742 rifle, except has commemorative
inscription on receiver. Made 1976.

Remington Model 742 Canadian Centennial **$565**
Same as Model 742 rifle, except has commemorative inscription on receiver. Made 1967. Value is for rifle in new,
unfired condition.

Remington Model 742 Carbine **$340**
Same as Model 742 Rifle, except made in calibers 30-06
and 308 only, has 18½-inch barrel, weighs 6¾ pounds.
Made 1961–1980.

**Remington Model 742 Woodsmaster
Automatic Big Game Rifle** **$300**
Gas-operated semiautomatic. Calibers: 6mm Rem., 243
Win., 280 Rem., 30-06, 308 Win. 4-shot clip magazine.
22-inch barrel. Weight: 7½ pounds. Sights: open rear; bead
front, on ramp. Checkered pistol-grip stock and forearm.
Made 1960–1980.

RIFLES

Remington Model 740A

Remington Model 742
Bicentennial Commemorative

Remington Model 742 Carbine

Remington Model 742
Woodsmaster

Remington Model 742BDL Custom Deluxe **$350**
Same as Model 742 Rifle, except made in calibers 30-06 and 308 only, has Monte Carlo cheekpiece stock, forearm with black tip, basket-weave checkering. Available in left-hand model. Made 1966–1980.

Remington Model 742D Peerless Grade **$945**
Same as Model 742 except scroll engraved, fancy wood. Made 1961–1980.

Remington Model 742F Premier Grade **$1995**
Same as Model 742 except extensively engraved with game scenes and scroll, finest grade wood. Also available with receiver inlaid with gold; adds 50 percent to value. Made 1961–1980.

Remington Model 760 Bicentennial Commemorative **$550**
Same as Model 760, except has commemorative inscription on receiver. Made 1976.

Remington Model 760 Carbine **$325**
Same as Model 760 Rifle, except made in calibers 270 Win., 280 Rem., 30-06 and 308 Win. only, has 18½-inch barrel, weighs 7¼ pounds. Made 1961–1980.

Remington Model 760 Gamemaster Standard Grade Slide Action Repeating Rifle **$300**
Hammerless. Calibers: 223 Rem., 6mm Rem., 243 Win., 257 Roberts, 270 Win., 280 Rem., 30-06, 300 Sav., 308 Win., 35 Rem. 22-inch barrel. Weight: about 7½ pounds. Sights: open rear; bead front, on ramp. Plain pistol-grip stock, grooved slide handle on early models; current production has checkered stock and slide handle. Made 1952–1980.

Remington Model 760ADL Deluxe Grade **$395**
Same as Model 760, except has deluxe checkered stock, standard or high comb, grip cap, sling swivels. Made 1953–1963.

Remington Model 742BDL

Remington Model 742F

Remington Model 760 Bicentennial Commemorative

Remington Model 760 Carbine

Remington Model 760 Standard

Remington Model 760ADL

Remington Model 760BDL Custom Deluxe **$325**
Same as Model 760 Rifle, except made in calibers 270, 30-06 and 308 only, has Monte Carlo cheekpiece stock, forearm with black tip, basket-weave checkering. Available also in left-hand model. Made 1953–1980.

Remington Model 760D Peerless Grade **$1100**
Same as Model 760, except scroll engraved, fancy wood. Made 1953–1980.

Remington Model 760F Premier Grade **$2370**
Same as Model 760, except extensively engraved with game scenes and scroll, finest grade wood. Also available with receiver inlaid with gold; adds 50 percent to value. Made 1953–1980.

Remington Model 788 Centerfire Bolt Action
Calibers: 222 Rem., 22-250, 223 Rem., 6mm Rem., 243 Win., 308 Win., 30-30, 44 Rem. Mag. 3-shot clip magazine (4-shot in 222 and 223 Rem.). Weight: 7 1/2 lbs. with 24-inch bbl.; 7 1/4 lbs. with 22-inch bbl. Sights: blade front, on ramp; U-notch rear. Plain Monte Carlo stock. Made 1967–1984.
Standard R.H. Model **$275**

Remington Model 788 Centerfire Bolt Action (cont.)
Left Hand (6mm Rem. and 308 Win. only; made 1972–79) **$295**

Remington Model 7400 Autoloader **$385**
Similar to Model Four, except has lower grade finishes. Made 1981 to date.

Remington Model 7400 Special Purpose **$395**
Same general specification as the Model 7400, except chambered only in 270 or 30-06. Special Purpose matte black finish on metal; American walnut stock with SP nonglare finish.

Remington Model 7600 Carbine **$340**
Same general specifications as Model 7600 Rifle, except has 18 1/2-inch barrel and weighs 7 1/4 pounds. Made 1987 to date.

Remington Model 7600 Rifle **$345**
Similar to Model Six, except has lower grade finishes. Made 1981 to date.

Remington Model 7600 Special Purpose **$360**
Same general specification as the Model 7600, except chambered only in 270 or 30-06. Special Purpose matte black finish on all exposed metal. American walnut stock with SP nonglare finish.

RIFLES

Remington Model 760BDL

Remington Model 788

Remington Model 788 Left Hand

Remington Model 7400

Remington Model 7600 Rifle

Remington International Free Rifle

Remington International Match

Remington Nylon 11

Remington Nylon 12

Remington Nylon 66 Apache Black

Remington Nylon 66 Bicentennial Commemorative

Remington International Free Rifle **$695**
Same as Model 40-XB rimfire and centerfire, except has
"free rifle" -type stock with adj. buttplate and hook, adj.
palmrest, movable front sling swivel, 2-oz. trigger. Weight:
about 15 pounds. Made 1964–1974. Value shown is for
rifle with professionally finished stock, no sights.

Remington International Match Free Rifle **$810**
Calibers: 22 LR, 222 Rem., 222 Rem. Mag., 7.62mm
NATO, 30-06 (others were available on special order).
Model 40X-type bolt action, single shot. 2-oz. adj. trigger.
28-inch heavy barrel. Weight: about 15½ pounds. "Free
rifle" -style stock with thumbhole (furnished semifinished
by mfr.); interchangeable and adj. rubber buttplate and
hook buttplate, adj. palmrest, sling swivel. Made 1961–
64. Value shown is for rifle with professionally finished
stock, no sights.

**Remington Nylon 10 Bolt Action Single Shot
Rifle** **$85**
Same as Nylon 11 except single shot. Made 1962–66.

Remington Nylon 11 Bolt Action Repeater **$90**
Clip type. Caliber: 22 Short, Long, LR. 6- or 10-shot clip
mag. 19⅝-inch barrel. Weight: 4½ pounds. Sights: open
rear; blade front. Nylon stock. Made 1962–66.

Remington Nylon 12 Bolt Action Repeater **$90**
Same as Nylon 11 except has tubular magazine holding
22 Short, 17 Long, 15 LR. Made 1962–66.

Remington Nylon 66 Apache Black **$120**
Same as Nylon 66 Mohawk Brown, except barrel and receiver cover chrome-plated, black stock. Made 1962–1984.

**Remington Nylon 66 Bicentennial
Commemorative** **$110**
Same as Nylon 66, except has commemorative inscription
on receiver. Made 1976.

RIFLES

Remington Nylon 66 GS Gallery Special **$95**
Same as Nylon 66 Mohawk Brown except chambered for
22 Short only. Made 1959–1980.

Remington Nylon 66MB Autoloading Rifle **$125**
Similar to the early production Nylon 66 Black Apache,
except with blued barrel and receiver cover. Made 1978
to date.

Remington Nylon 66 Mohawk Brown Autoloader . **$95**
Caliber: 22 LR. Tubular magazine in buttstock holds 14
rounds. 19½-inch barrel. Weight: about 4 pounds. Sights:
open rear; blade front. Brown nylon stock and forearm.
Made 1959 to date.

Remington Nylon 76 Lever Action Repeater . . . **$270**
Short-throw lever action. Other specifications same as for
Nylon 66. Made 1962–64.

Remington Nylon 77 Clip Repeater **$150**
Same as Nylon 66, except has 5-shot clip magazine. Made
1970–71.

Remington Sportsman 78 Bolt Action Rifle **$250**
Similar to Model 700 ADL, except with straight-comb
walnut-finished hardwood stock in calibers 223 Rem., 243
Win., 270 Win., 30-06 Springfield and 308 Win. 22-inch
barrel. Weight: 7 pounds. Adj. sights. Made 1984–1991.

Remington Nylon 66 Mohawk Brown

Remington Nylon 76

Remington Nylon 77

Rigby 275 Magazine Sporting Rifle (cont.)
w/half-pistol grip, checkered. Specifications given are
those of current model; however, in general, they apply
also to prewar model.

Rigby 350 Magnum

JOHN RIGBY & CO.
London, England
**Rigby 275 Lightweight Model Magazine
Rifle** . . . . **$4000+**
Same as standard 275 rifle, except has 21-inch barrel and
weighs only 6¾ pounds.

Rigby 275 Magazine

Rigby 275 Magazine Sporting Rifle . . . . **$5000+**
Mauser action. Caliber: 275 High Velocity or 7×57mm.
5-shot box magazine. 25-inch barrel. Weight: about 7½
pounds. Sights: folding leaf rear; bead front. Sporting stock

Rigby 350 Magnum Magazine Sporting Rifle . . . **$3595**
Mauser action. Caliber: 350 Magnum. 5-shot box magazine. 24-inch barrel. Weight: about 7¾ pounds. Sights:
folding leaf rear; bead front. Sporting stock with full pistol
grip, checkered. Currently mfd.

Rigby 416 Big Game Magazine Sporting Rifle . . **$6000+**
Mauser action. Caliber: 416 Big Game. 4-shot box magazine. 24-inch barrel. Weight: 9 to 9¼ pounds. Sights:
folding leaf rear; bead front. Sporting stock with full pistol
grip, checkered. Currently manufactured.

Rigby Best Quality Double Rifle

Rigby Best Quality Hammerless Ejector Double Rifle $35,000
Side locks. Calibers: 275 Magnum, 350 Magnum, 470 Nitro Express. 24- to 28-inch barrels. Weight: 7½ to 10½ pounds. Sights: folding leaf rear; bead front. Checkered pistol-grip stock and forearm.

Rigby Second Quality Double Rifle

Rigby Second Quality Hammerless Ejector Double Rifle $15,000
Same general specifications as Best Quality double rifle, except boxlock.

Rigby Third Quality Hammerless Ejector Double Rifle $9500
Same as Second Quality double rifle, except plainer finish and not of as high quality.

ROSS RIFLE CO.
Quebec, Canada

Ross Model 1910 Bolt Action Sporting Rifle $210
Straight-pull bolt action with interrupted-screw-type lugs. Calibers: 280 Ross, 303 British. 4-shot or 5-shot magazine. Barrel lengths: 22, 24, 26 inches. Sights: two-leaf open rear; bead front. Checkered sporting stock. Weight: about 7 pounds. Made c. 1910 to end of World War I. *Note:* Most firearm authorities agree that this and other Ross models with interrupted-screw-type lugs are unsafe to fire.

Rossi Gallery Model

ROSSI RIFLES
Sao Leopoldo, Brazil
Manufactured by Amadeo Rossi, S.A.

Rossi 62 Gallery Model SAC Carbine
Same as standard Gallery Model, except in 22 LR only with 16¼-inch barrel; weighs 5½ pounds. Made 1975 to date.
Blued Finish $160
Nickel Finish 170

Rossi 62 Gallery Model Magnum $145
Same as standard Gallery Model, except chambered for 22 WMR, 10-shot magazine. Made 1975 to date.

Rossi 62 Gallery Model Slide Action Repeater
Similar to Winchester Model 62. Calibers: 22 LR, Long, Short or 22 WMR. Tubular magazine holds 13 LR, 16

Rossi 62 Gallery Model Slide Action Repeater (cont.)
Long, 20 Short. 23-inch barrel. 39¼ inches overall. Weight: 5¾ pounds. Sights: open rear; bead front. Straight-grip stock, grooved slide handle. Blued or nickel finish. Made 1970 to date.
Blued Finish $170
Nickel Finish 180

Rossi Lever Action Carbine Engraved Model . . . $250
Same as standard model, except has engraved action. Made 1981 to date.

Rossi Lever Action Carbine $225
Similar to Winchester Model 92. Caliber: 357 Mag. Tubular magazine. 20-inch barrel. Weight: 5¾ pounds. Sights: open rear; bead front. Straight-grip walnut stock. Made 1978 to date.

Ruger No. 1 Light Sporter

RUGER RIFLES
Southport, Connecticut
Manufactured by Sturm, Ruger & Co.

Ruger Number One (1) Light Sporter $395
Same as No. 1 Standard, except has 22-inch barrel, folding leaf rear sight on quarter-rib and ramp front sight, Henry pattern forearm, front swivel on barrel band. Weight: 7¼ pounds. Calibers: 243 Win., 270 Win., 7×57mm, 30-06. Made 1966–1983.

Ruger Number One (1) Medium Sporter **$375**
Same as No. 1 Light Sporter, except has 26-inch barrel (22-inch in 45-70); weight is 8 pounds (7¼ pounds in 45-70). Calibers: 7mm Rem. Mag., 300 Win. Mag., 45-70. Made 1966 to date.

Ruger Number One (1) "North Americans" Presentation Rifle **$50,000**
Same general specifications as the Ruger No. 1 Standard, except highly customized with elaborate engravings, carvings, fine-line checkering and gold inlays. A series of 21 is planned, each rifle depicting a North American big-game animal, chambered in the caliber appropriate to the game. Stock is of Northern California English walnut. Comes in trunk-style Huey case with Leupold scope and other accessories.

Ruger Number One (1) RSI International Single Shot Rifle **$375**
Similar to the No. 1 Light Sporter, except with lightweight 20-inch barrel and full Mannlicher-style forend, in calibers 243 Win., 270 Win., 7×57mm, 30-06. Weight: 7¼ pounds.

Ruger Number One (1) Special Varminter **$425**
Same as No. 1 Standard, except has heavy 24-inch barrel with target scope bases, no quarter-rib. Weight: 9 pounds. Calibers: 22-250, 25-06, 7mm Rem. Mag., 300 Win. Mag. Made 1966 to date.

Ruger Number One (1) Standard Rifle **$375**
Falling-block single-shot action with Farquharson-type lever. Calibers: 22-250, 243 Win., 6mm Rem., 25-06, 270 Win., 30-06, 7mm Rem. Mag., 300 Win. Mag. 26-inch barrel. Weight: 8 pounds. No sights, has quarter-rib for scope mounting. Checkered pistol-grip buttstock and semibeavertail forearm, QD swivels, rubber buttplate. Made 1966 to date.

Ruger Number One (1) Tropical Rifle **$450**
Same as No. 1 Light Sporter, except has heavy 24-inch barrel; calibers are 375 H&H Mag. and 458 Win. Mag. Weight: 8¼ lbs. for 375; 9 lbs. for 458. Made 1966–1994.

Ruger Number Three (3) Single Shot Carbine . . . **$225**
Falling-block action with American-style lever. Calibers: 22 Hornet, 30-40, 45-70. 22-inch barrel. Weight, 6 pounds. Sights: folding leaf rear; gold bead front. Carbine-style stock w/curved buttplate, forearm with barrel band. Made 1972–1986.

RIFLES

Ruger No. 1 Medium Sporter

Ruger No. 1 Special Varminter

Ruger No. 1 Standard Rifle

Ruger No. 3 Single Shot Carbine

Ruger Model 10/22 Standard Autoloading Carbine

Caliber: 22 LR. Detachable 10-shot rotary magazine. 181/2-inch barrel. Weight: 5 pounds. Sights: folding leaf rear; bead front. Carbine-style stock with barrel band and curved buttplate (walnut stock discontinued 1980). Made 1964 to date. International and Sporter versions discontinued 1971.

10/22 Standard Carbine (Walnut stock) **$175**
10/22 Int'l (w/Mannlicher-style stock, swivels)
  Discontinued 1971 . . . . **425**
10/22 RB (Birch stock, Blued) **125**
K10/22 RB (Birch stock, Stainless **150**
10/22 Sporter (Monte Carlo stock, flat buttplate
  Sling swivels) Discontinued 1971 . . . . **165**
10/22 SP Deluxe Sporter (w/Checkered stock,
  Flat buttplate, sling swivels; made since 1966) . . **185**

Ruger Model 44 Standard Autoloading Carbine

Gas-operated. Caliber: 44 Magnum. 4-shot tubular magazine (with magazine release button since 1967). 18 1/2-inch barrel. Weight: 53/4 pounds. Sights: folding leaf rear; gold bead front. Carbine-style stock w/barrel band and curved buttplate. Made 1961–1986. International and Sporter versions discontinued 1971.

Model 44 Standard Autoloading Carbine **$365**
Model 44 Int'l (w/Mannlicher-style stock,
  swivels) **550**
Model 44 Sporter (w/Monte Carlo stock, flat buttplate,
  Sling swivels **360**
Model 44RS Carbine (w/Rear peep sight,
  Sling swivels; disc. 1978) **345**

Ruger 10/22 International

Ruger 10/22 Sporter

Ruger 10/22 Standard

Ruger Model 10/22SP Deluxe Sporter

Ruger 44 Standard

Ruger 44 Sporter

RIFLES

Ruger Model 77 Magnum Action

Ruger Model 77 Round Top Receiver

Ruger Model 77 Short Action

Ruger Model 77RL Ultra Light

Ruger Model 77RSI International

Ruger Model 77 Bolt Action Rifle

Receiver with integral scope mount base or with round top. Short stroke or magnum length action (depending on caliber) in the former type receiver, magnum only in the latter. Calibers: 22-250, 220 Swift, 6mm Rem., 243 Win., 250-3000, 25-06, 257 Roberts, 270 Win., 7×57mm, 7mm Rem. Mag., 280 Rem., 308 Win., 30-06, 300 Win. Mag., 338 Win. Mag., 458 Win. Mag. 5-shot magazine standard, 4-shot in 220 Swift, 3-shot in magnum calibers. 22-, 24- or 26-inch barrel (depending on caliber). Weight: about 7 lbs.; 458 Mag. model, 8³/₄ lbs. Round-top model furnished w/folding leaf rear sight and ramp front; integral base model furnished w/scope rings,with or w/o open sights. Stock w/checkered pistol grip and forearm, pistol-grip cap, rubber recoil pad, QD swivel studs. Made 1968 to date.

Model 77, integral base, no sights	**$325**
Model 77, 338 Win. Mag.	375
Model 77RL Ultra Light, no sights, 20-inch ultralight bbl., 6 lbs. (1983 to date)	375
Model 77RS, integral base, open sights	375
Model 77RS, 338 Win. Mag., 458 Win. Mag. with standard stock	395

Ruger Model 77 Bolt Action Rifle (cont.)

Model 77RS, 458 Win. Mag. with fancy Circassian walnut stock	**$550**
Model 77RSI International, Mannlicher stock, short action, 18¹/₂-inch bbl., 7 lbs.	425
Model 77ST, round top, open sights	325
Model 77ST, 338 Win. Mag.	425

Ruger Model 77 (M-77) Ultra Light Carbine $340

Bolt action. Calibers: 270, 30-06, 243, 308. 18¹/₂-inch barrel. About 39 inches overall. Weight: 6 pounds. Hand-checkered American walnut stock with pistol grip. Open sights and equipped with Ruger Integral Scope bases with one-inch Ruger rings. Sling swivels. Made 1986 to date.

Ruger Model 77V, Varmint Rifle

Same as standard Model 77 with integral base receiver, except has heavy 24-inch (26-inch in 220 Swift) barrel drilled and tapped for target scope bases. Weight: 9 pounds. Calibers: 22-250, 220 Swift, 243 Win., 6mm Rem., 25-06, 308. Made 1968–1992. Model M77NV with laminated American stock introduced in 1992.

Model 77V	**$375**
Model 77NV	465

Ruger Model 77/22R

Ruger Mini-14 Semiautomatic

Ruger Mini-14 with Folding Stock

Ruger Mini-14/5

Ruger Model 77/22 Rimfire Bolt Action Rifle

Calibers: 22 LR or 22 WMR. 10-shot (22 LR) or 9-shot (22 WMR) rotary magazine. 20-inch barrel. 39³/₄ inches overall. Weight: 5³/₄ pounds. Integral scope bases; with or w/o sights. Checkered American walnut or Zytel injection-molded stock. Stainless or blued finish. Made 1983 to date. (Blued); stainless introduced 1989.

77/22 R, rings, no sights, walnut stock	**$265**
77/22 RS, rings, sights, walnut	275
77/22 RP, rings, no sights, synthetic stock	220
77/22 RSP, rings, sights, synthetic stock	235
K77/22 RP, s/s, rings, no sights, synthetic	275
K77/22 RSP, s/s, rings, sights, synthetic	285
77/22 RM, 22 WMR, rings, no sights, walnut	260
77/22 RSM, 22 WMR, rings, sights, walnut	275
K77/22 SMP, 22 WMR, s/s, rings, sights, syn.	290
K77/22 RMP, 22 WMR, s/s, no sights, syn.	315
K77/22 VBZ, 22 WMR, no sights, syn. (1993)	280

Ruger Model 77 Mark II All-Weather Rifle $360

Revised Model 77 action. Same general specifications as Model M-77 Mark II, except with stainless barrel and action. Zytel injection-molded stock. Calibers: 223, 243, 270, 308, 30-06, 7mm Mag., 300 Win. Mag., 338 Win. Mag. Made 1990 to date.

Ruger Model 77 Mark II Bolt Action Rifle

Revised Model 77 action. Same general specifications as Model M-77, except with new 3-position safety and fixed blade ejector system. Calibers 223 and 6.5×55 Swedish also available.

Model M77 MKIIR, SA, no sights	**$355**
Model M77 MKIIRS, SA, sights	395
Model M77 MKIIRL, SA, 20-inch bbl.	380
Model M77 MKIILR, LA, left-hand	365

Ruger Model 77 Mark II (V2B) Target Rifle $435

Similar to the Model 77 Varmint Rifle, except with laminated American hardwood stock with flat forearm and no checkering. Calibers: 22 PPC, 22-250, 220 Swift, 223, 6mm PPC, 25-06, 308. 26-inch barrel. 44 inches overall. Weight: 9¹/₄ pounds. Made 1992 to date.

Ruger Model 77 Mark II (EXP) Express Rifle ... $1050

Calibers: 270, 30-06, 7mm Rem. Mag., 300 Win. Mag. 4-shot magazine. 22-inch barrel with integral rib. Weight: 7¹/₂ lbs. Ramp front sight, adjustable leaf rear. Checkered walnut stock with steel grip cap and black recoil pad. Blued finish. Made 1991 to date.

Ruger Model 77 Mark II (RSM) Magnum Rifle .. $1095

Calibers: 375 H&H, 404 Jeffery, (4-shot magazine); 416 Rigby, 458 Win. Mag.(3-shot magazine). 26-inch barrel with integral rib. Weight: 9³/₄ lbs. (375, 404); 10¹/₄ lbs. (416, 458). Sights: ramp front; three-leaf Express rear. Checkered Circassian walnut stock with steel-grip cap and recoil pad. Blued finish. Made 1989 to date.

Ruger Mini-14 Semiautomatic Rifle

Gas-operated. Caliber: 223 Rem. (5.56mm). 5-, 10- or 20-shot box magazine. 18¹/₂-inch barrel. Weight: about 6¹/₂ pounds. Sights: peep rear; blade front. Pistol-grip stock w/curved buttplate, handguard. Made 1976 to date.

Mini-14/5 Blued	**$395**
K-Mini-14/5 Stainless Steel	400
Mini-14/5F Blued, Folding Stock	550
K-Mini-14/5F Stainless, Folding Stock	600
Mini-14 Ranch Rifle, Scope Model, 6¹/₄ lbs.	375
K-Mini-1H Ranch Rifle, Scope Model, Stainless	495

Ruger Mini-Thirty Autoloader

Ruger Mini-Thirty (30) Autoloader
Caliber: 7.62 × 39mm. 5-shot detachable magazine. 18½-inch barrel. 37¼ inches overall. Weight: 7 lbs. 3 oz. De-

Ruger Mini-Thirty (30) Autoloader (cont.)
signed for use with telescopic sights. Walnut stained stock. Blued or stainless finish. Made 1986 to date.
Blued Finish **$400**
Stainless Finish **435**

Russian Model 1891 Mosin

RUSSIAN MILITARY RIFLES
Principal U.S.S.R. Arms Plant is located at Tula

Russian Model 1891 Mosin Military Rifle **$95**
Nagant system bolt action. Caliber: 7.62mm Russian. 5-shot box magazine. 31½-inch barrel. Weight: about 9 pounds. Sights: open rear; blade front. Full stock w/ straight grip. Specifications given are for WWII version; earlier types differ slightly. *Note:* In 1916, Remington Arms Co. and New England Westinghouse Co. produced 250,000 of these rifles on a contract from the Imperial Rus-

Russian Model 1891 Mosin Military Rifle (cont.)
sian Government. Few were delivered to Russia and the balance bought by the U.S. Government for training in 1918. Eventually, many of these rifles were sold to N.R.A. members for about $3 each by the director of Civilian Marksmanship.

Russian Tokarev Model 40 Semiautomatic
Military Rifle **$495**
Gas-operated. Caliber: 7.62mm Russian. 10-shot detachable box magazine. 24½-inch barrel. Muzzle brake. Weight: about 9 pounds. Sights: leaf rear; hooded post front. Full stock w/pistol grip. Differences among Models 1938, 1940 and 1941 are minor.

Sako Model 73

Sako Model 74 Carbine

SAKO RIFLES
Riihimaki, Finland
Manufactured by Oy Sako Ab

Sako Model 72 . . . . **$645**
Single model designation replacing Vixen Sporter, Vixen Carbine, Vixen Heavy Barrel, Forester Sporter, Forester Carbine, Forester Heavy Barrel, Finnbear Sporter, and Finnbear Carbine, with same specifications except all but heavy barrel models fitted with open rear sight. Values same as for corresponding earlier models. Made 1972–74.

Sako Model 73 Lever Action Rifle **$750**
Same as Finnwolf, except has 3-shot clip magazine, flush floorplate; stock has no cheekpiece. Made 1973–75.

Sako Model 74 Carbine **$495**
Long Mauser-type bolt action. Caliber: 30-06. 5-shot magazine. 20-inch barrel. Weight: about 7½ pounds. No sights. Checkered Mannlicher-type full stock of European walnut, Monte Carlo cheekpiece. Made 1974–78.

Sako Model 74 Heavy Barrel Rifle, Long Action . . **$515**
Same specifications as with short action, except has 24-inch heavy barrel, weighs about 8¾ pounds; magnum has 4-shot magazine. Calibers: 25-06, 7mm Rem. Mag. Made 1974–78.

Sako Model 74 Super Sporter

Sako Model 78 Super Rimfire

Sako Classic

Sako Deluxe Lightweight

Sako Model 74 Heavy Barrel Rifle, Medium Action $525

Same specifications as with short action, except has 23-inch heavy barrel, weighs about 8¹/₂ pounds. Calibers: 220 Swift, 22-250, 243 Win., 308 Win. Made 1974–78.

Sako Model 74 Heavy Barrel Rifle, Short Action $550

Mauser-type bolt action. Calibers: 222 Rem., 223 Rem. 5-shot magazine. 23¹/₂-inch heavy barrel. Weight: about 8¹/₄ pounds. No sights. Target-style checkered European walnut stock w/beavertail forearm. Made 1974–78.

Sako Model 74 Super Sporter, Long Action $525

Same specifications as with short action, except has 24-inch barrel, weighs about 8 pounds; magnums have 4-shot magazine, recoil pad. Calibers: 25-06, 270 Win. 7mm Rem. Mag., 30-06, 300 Win. Mag., 338 Win. Mag., 375 H&H Mag. Made 1974–78.

Sako Model 74 Super Sporter, Medium Action . . $575

Same specifications as with short action, except weight is 7¹/₄ pounds. Calibers: 220 Swift, 22-250, 243 Win. Made 1974–78.

Sako Model 74 Super Sporter, Short Action $595

Mauser-type bolt action. Calibers: 222 Rem., 223 Rem. 5-shot magazine. 23¹/₂-inch barrel. Weight: about 6¹/₂ pounds. No sights. Checkered European walnut stock with Monte Carlo cheekpiece, QD swivel studs. Made 1974, now discontinued.

Sako Model 78 Super Hornet Sporter $395

Same specifications as Model 78 Rimfire, except caliber 22 Hornet, 4-shot magazine. Intro. 1977; disc. 1987.

Sako Model 78 Super Rimfire Sporter $325

Bolt action. Caliber: 22 LR. 5-shot magazine. 22¹/₂-inch barrel. Weight, about 6³/₄ pounds. No sights. Checkered European walnut stock, Monte Carlo cheekpiece. Introduced 1977; discontinued.

Sako Classic Bolt Action Rifle

Medium Action (243. Win.) or Long Action (270 Win., 30-06, 7mm Rem. Mag.). American walnut stock. Made 1980–86. Reintroduced in 1993 with matte lacquer finish stock, 22- or 24-inch barrel, overall length of 42 to 44 inches, weight 6⁷/₈ to 7¹/₄ lbs.
Standard Calibers $650
Magnum Caliber 675
Left-Hand Models 725

Sako Deluxe Grade AI $625

Same specifications as Standard Grade, except with 22 lines to the inch French checkering, rosewood grip cap and forend tip, semibeavertail forend.

Sako Deluxe Grade AII $650

Same specifications as Standard Grade, except with 22 lines per inch French checkering, rosewood grip cap and forend tip, semibeavertail forend.

Sako Deluxe Grade AIII $895

Same specifications as with standard, except with French checkering, rosewood grip cap and forend tip, semibeavertail forend.

Sako Deluxe Lightweight Bolt Action Rifle $845

Same general specifications as Hunter Lightweight, except has beautifully grained French walnut stock, superb high-gloss finish, fine hand-cut checkering, rosewood forend tip and grip cap. Introduced 1985.

RIFLES

Sako Fiberclass

Sako Finnbear Sporter

Sako Finnwolf

Sako Forester Sporter

Sako Golden Anniversary Model

Sako Fiberclass Bolt Action Rifle **$795**
All-weather fiberglass stock version of Sako barreled long action. Calibers: 25-06, 270, 30-06, 7mm Rem. Mag., 300 Win. Mag., 338 Win. Mag., 375 H&H Mag. Barrel length: 22¹/₂ inches. Overall length: 44¹/₄ inches. Weight: 7¹/₄ pounds. Made 1984 to date.

Sako Finnbear Carbine **$720**
Same as Finnbear Sporter, except has 20-inch barrel, Mannlicher-type full stock. Made 1971.

Sako Finnbear Sporter **$695**
Long Mauser-type bolt action. Calibers: 25-06, 264 Mag., 270, 30-06, 300 Win. Mag., 338 Mag., 7mm Mag., 375 H&H Mag. Magazine holds 5 standard or 4 magnum cartridges. 24-inch barrel. Weight: about 7 pounds. Hooded ramp front sight. Sporter stock w/Monte Carlo cheekpiece, checkered pistol grip and forearm, recoil pad, swivels. Made 1961–1971.

Sako Finnwolf Lever Action Rifle **$800**
Hammerless. Calibers: 243 Win., 308 Win. 4-shot clip magazine. 23-inch barrel. Weight: 6³/₄ pounds. Hooded ramp front sight. Sporter stock w/Monte Carlo cheekpiece, checkered pistol grip and forearm, swivels (available w/right- or left-hand stock). Made 1963–1972.

Sako Finsport 2700 . . . . **$720**
Bolt-action centerfire rifle. Calibers: 270, 30-06, 7mm Rem. Mag., 300 Win. Mag. Barrel length: 24 inches. Weight: 8 pounds. Made 1984–86.

Sako Forester Carbine **$610**
Same as Forester Sporter, except has 20-inch barrel, Mannlicher-type full stock. Made 1958–1971.

Sako Forester Heavy Barrel **$595**
Same as Forester Sporter, except has 24-inch heavy barrel, weighs 7¹/₂ pounds. Made 1958–1971.

Sako Forester Sporter **$580**
Medium-length Mauser-type bolt action. Calibers: 22-250, 243 Win., 308 Win. 5-shot magazine. 23-inch barrel. Weight: 6¹/₂ pounds. Hooded ramp front sight. Sporter stock w/Monte Carlo cheekpiece, checkered pistol grip and forearm, swivels. Made 1957–1971.

Sako Golden Anniversary Model **$1800**
Special presentation-grade rifle issued in 1973 to commemorate Sako's 50th anniversary. 1,000 (numbered 1 to 1,000) made. Same specifications as Deluxe Sporter, long action, 7mm Rem. Mag. Receiver, trigger guard and floorplate decorated w/gold oak leaf and acorn motif. Stock of select European walnut, checkering bordered w/hand-carved oak leaf pattern.

Sako Hunter Lightweight

Sako Mannlicher-Style Carbine

Sako Sporter Deluxe

Sako High-Power Mauser Sporting Rifle $550
FN Mauser action. Calibers: 270, 30-06. 5-shot magazine. 24-inch barrel. Sights: open rear leaf; Patridge front; hooded ramp. Checkered stock w/Monte Carlo comb and cheekpiece. Weight: about 7½ pounds. Made 1950-57.

Sako Hunter Lightweight Bolt Action Rifle
5- or 6-shot magazine. Barrel length: 21½ inches, AI; 22 inches, AII; 22½ inches, AIII. Overall length: 42¼-44½ inches. Weight: 5¾ lbs., AI; 6¾ lbs. AII; 7¼ lbs., AIII. Monte Carlo-style European walnut stock, oil finished. Hand-checkered pistol grip and forend. Introduced 1985. Left-hand version introduced 1987.

AI (Short Action) 17 Rem.	$ 595
222 Rem., 223 Rem.	600
AII (Medium Action)	
22-250 Rem., 243 Win., 308 Win.	520
AIII (Long Action)	
25-06 Rem., 270 Win., 30-06	580
338 Win. Mag.	650
375 H&H Mag.	700
Left-hand Model (Standard Cal.)	900
Magnum Calibers	1050

Sako Laminated Stock Bolt Action Rifles
Similar in style and specifications to the Hunter Grade, except with stock of resin-bonded, hardwood veneers. Available 18 calibers in AI (Short), AII (Medium) or AV action; left-handed version in 10 calibers, AV only. Introduced in 1987.

Short or Medium Action	$775
Long Action/Magnum	795

Sako Magnum Mauser $950
Same specifications as Standard Model, except has recoil pad. Calibers: 300 H&H Magnum, 375 H&H Magnum.

Sako Mannlicher-Style Carbine
Similar to the Hunter Model, except with full Mannlicher-style stock and 18½-inch barrel. Weights 7½ lbs. Cham-

Sako Mannlicher-Style Carbine (cont.)
bered in 243, 25-06, 270, 308, 30-06, 7mm Rem. Mag., 300 Win. Mag., 338 Win. Mag., 375 H&H. Introduced in 1977.

Standard Calibers	$850
Magnum Calibers (except 375)	875
375 H&H	900

Sako Safari Grade $1500
Classic bolt action. Calibers: 300 Win. Mag., 338 Mag., 375 H&H. Oil-finished European walnut stock with hand-checkering. Barrel band swivel, express-type sight rib; satin or matte blue finish. Introduced in 1980.

Sako Sporter Deluxe $710
Same as Vixen, Forester, Finnbear and Model 74, except has fancy French walnut stock w/skip checkering, rosewood forend tip and pistol-grip cap, recoil pad, inlaid trigger guard and floorplate.

Sako Standard Grade AI $520
Short bolt action. Calibers: 17 Rem., 222 Rem., 223 Rem. 5-shot magazine. 23½-inch barrel. Weight: about 6½ pounds. No sights. Checkered European walnut stock w/ Monte Carlo cheekpiece, QD swivel studs. Made 1978 to date.

Sako Standard Grade AII $550
Medium bolt action. Calibers: 22-250 Rem., 243 Win., 308 Win. 23½-inch barrel in 22-250; 23-inch barrel in other calibers. 5-shot magazine. Weight: about 7¼ pounds. Checkered European walnut stock w/Monte Carlo cheekpiece, QD swivel studs. Made 1978-1985.

Sako Standard Grade AIII $595
Long bolt action. Calibers: 25-06 Rem., 270 Win., 30-06, 7mm Rem. Mag., 300 Win. Mag., 338 Win. Mag., 375 H&H. 24-inch barrel. 4-shot magazine. Weight: 8 pounds. Made 1978-1984.

Sako Super Deluxe Rifle $1495
Available in AI, AII, AIII action calibers. Select European walnut stock, hand-checkered, deep oak leaf hand-engraved design.

RIFLES

Sako TRG-21 Target Rifle **$2800**
Caliber: 308 Win. 10-shot magazine. 25³/₄-inch stainless heavy barrel. 46¹/₂ inches overall. Weight: 10¹/₂ lbs. No sights. Optional Q/D scope mount with 1-inch or 30mm rings. Reinforced polyurethane stock w/adj. cheekpiece and buttplate. Two-stage adj. trigger. Introduced in 1993.

Sako TRG-S Bolt Action Rifle
Calibers: 243, 7mm-08, 270, 30-06, 7mm Rem. Mag., 300 Win. Mag., 338 Win. Mag. 5-shot magazine (standard calibers), 4-shot (magnum), 22- or 24-inch barrel. 45¹/₂ inches overall. Weight: 7³/₄ lbs. No sights. Reinforced polyurethane stock w/Monte Carlo. Introduced in 1993.
Standard Calibers **$490**
Magnum Calibers **550**

Sako Vixen Carbine **$710**
Same as Vixen Sporter, except has 20-inch barrel, Mannlicher-type full stock. Made 1947–1971.

Sako Vixen Heavy Barrel **$715**
Same as Vixen Sporter, except calibers 222 Rem., 222 Rem. Mag., 223 Rem., heavy barrel, target-style stock w/beavertail forearm. Weight: 7¹/₂ lbs. Made 1947–1971.

Sako Vixen Sporter **$725**
Short Mauser-type bolt action. Calibers: 218 Bee, 22 Hornet, 222 Rem., 222 Rem. Mag., 223 Rem. 5-shot magazine. 23¹/₂-inch barrel. Weight: 6¹/₂ pounds. Hooded ramp front sight. Sporter stock w/Monte Carlo cheekpiece, checkered pistol grip and forearm, swivels. Made 1946–1971.

Sako TRG 21

Sako TRG-S

Sako Vixen Carbine

Sako Vixen Heavy Barrel

Sako Vixen Sporter

J. P. SAUER & SOHN
Suhl, Germany
Imported by G.U., Inc. (Simmons Enterprises)

Sauer Mauser Bolt Action Sporting Rifle **$995**
Calibers: 7×57 and 8×57mm most common, but these rifles were produced in a variety of calibers, including most of the popular Continental numbers as well as our 30-06. 5-shot box magazine. 22- or 24-inch Krupp steel barrel, half-octagon with raised matted rib. Double-set trigger. Weight: about 7½ pounds. Sights: three-leaf open rear; ramp front. Sporting stock w/cheekpiece, checkered pistol grip, raised side-panels, schnabel tip, swivels. Also made w/20-inch barrel and full-length stock. Mfd before WWII.

Sauer Model S-90 Bolt Action Rifles
Calibers: 243 Win., 308 Win. (Short action); 25-06, 270 Win., 30-06 (Medium action); 7mm Rem. Mag., 300 Win. Mag., 300 Wby., 338 Win., 375 H&H (Magnum action). 4-shot (standard) or 3-shot magazine (magnum). Barrel length: 20-inch (Stutzen); 24-inch. Weight: 7 lbs. 6 oz. to 10 lbs. 12 oz. (Safari). Adj. open rear; ramp front. Checkered American or European walnut stock and pistol grip with matte (Safari—458 Win.), satin gloss (Lux—all actions, Stutzen—30-06, 270 Win.) or high-gloss finish (Supreme—all actions); Monte Carlo cheekpiece; sling swivels. Made 1986 to date.
S-90 Lux **$795**
S-90 Safari 895
S-90 Stutzen 850
S-90 Supreme 995

Sauer Model 200 Bolt Action Rifles
Calibers: 243 Win., 25-06, 270 Win., 30-06, 308 Win. Box magazine. 24-inch (American) or 26-inch (European) interchangeable barrel. Weight: 6¾ to 7¾ pounds. American Model has checkered European walnut straight stock w/ satin oil finish, no sights. European Model has Monte Carlo cheekpiece, contrasting forend and pistol grip cap w/high-gloss finish; with sights. Made late 1980s.

Sauer Model 200 Bolt Action Rifles (cont.)
American/European Models **$695**
Left-hand Model **750**

SAVAGE INDUSTRIES
Westfield, Massachusetts
Formerly of Utica, New York

Savage Model 3 Bolt Action Single Shot Rifle . . . **$125**
Takedown. Caliber: 22 Short, Long, LR. 26-inch barrel on prewar rifles, postwar production has 24-inch barrel. Weight: about 5 pounds. Sights: open rear; bead front. Plain pistol-grip stock. Made 1933–1952.

Savage Model 3S **$165**
Same as Model 3, except has peep rear sight, hooded front. Made 1933–1942.

Savage Model 3ST **$175**
Same as Model 3S, except fitted with swivels and sling. Made 1933–1942.

Savage Model 4 Bolt Action Repeater **$105**
Takedown. Caliber: 22 Short, Long, LR. 5-shot detachable box magazine. 24-inch barrel. Weight: about 5½ pounds. Sights: open rear; bead front. Checkered pistol-grip stock on prewar models, early production had grooved forearm; postwar rifles have plain stocks. Made 1933–1965.

Savage Model 4M **$125**
Same as Model 4, except chambered for 22 Rimfire Magnum. Made 1961–65.

Savage Model 4S **$135**
Same as Model 4, except has peep rear sight, hooded front. Made 1933–1942.

Savage Model 3
Bolt Action Single Shot Rifle

Savage Model 4

Savage Model 4M

Savage Model 5 Bolt Action Repeater **$125**
Same as Model 4, except has tubular magazine (holds 21 Short, 17 Long, 15 LR), weighs about 6 pounds. Made 1936–1961.

Savage Model 5S **$140**
Same as Model 5, except has peep rear sight, hooded front. Made 1936–1942.

Savage Model 6 Autoloading Rifle **$165**
Takedown. Caliber: 22 Short, Long, LR. Tubular magazine holds 21 Short, 17 Long, 15 LR. 24-inch barrel. Weight: about 6 pounds. Sights: open rear; bead front. Checkered pistol-grip stock on prewar models, postwar rifles have plain stocks. Made 1938–1968.

Savage Model 6S **$180**
Same as Model 6, except has peep rear sight, bead front. Made 1938–1942.

Savage Model 7 Autoloading Rifle **$150**
Same general specifications as Model 6, except has 5-shot detachable box magazine. Made 1939–1951.

Savage Model 7S **$175**
Same as Model 7, except has peep rear sight, hooded front. Made 1938–1942.

Savage Model 19 Bolt Action Target Rifle **$225**
Model of 1933. Speed lock. Caliber: 22 LR. 5-shot detachable box magazine. 25-inch barrel. Weight: about 8 pounds. Adj. rear peep sight, blade front on early models,

Savage Model 19 Bolt Action Target Rifle (cont.)
later production equipped w/extension rear sight, hooded front. Target stock w/full pistol grip and beavertail forearm. Made 1933–1946.

Savage Model 19 NRA Bolt Action Match Rifle . . . **$295**
Model of 1919. Caliber: 22 LR. 5-shot detachable box magazine. 25-inch barrel. Weight: about 7 pounds. Sights: adj. rear peep; blade front. Full military stock w/pistol grip. Made 1919–1933.

Savage Model 19H **$395**
Same as standard Model 19 (1933), except chambered for 22 Hornet, has Model 23D-type bolt mechanism, loading port and magazine. Made 1933–1942.

Savage Model 19L **$250**
Same as standard Model 19 (1933), except equipped w/ Lyman 48Y receiver sight, 17A front sight. Made 1933–1942.

Savage Model 19M **$295**
Same as standard Model 19 (1933), except has heavy 28-inch barrel with scope bases, weighs about $9\frac{1}{4}$ pounds. Made 1933–1942.

Savage Model 20-1926 Hi-Power Bolt Action Rifle **$365**
Same as Model 1920, except has 24-inch medium weight barrel, improved stock, Lyman 54 rear peep sight, weighs about 7 pounds. Made 1926–29.

RIFLES

Savage Model 5

Savage Model 6

Savage Model 19 NRA (1933)

Savage Model 20 (1926)

Savage Model 23A

Savage Model 23AA

Savage Model 23B

Savage Model 29

Savage Model 40

Savage Model 23A Bolt Action Sporting Rifle . . . $190
Caliber: 22 LR. 5-shot detachable box magazine. 23-inch barrel. Weight: about 6 pounds. Sights: open rear; blade or bead front. Plain pistol-grip stock with slender forearm and schnabel tip. Made 1923–1933.

Savage Model 23AA $250
Model of 1933. Improved version of the Model 23A with same general specifications, except has speed lock, improved stock, weighs about 6½ pounds. Made 1933–1942.

Savage Model 23B $215
Same as Model 23A, except caliber 25/20, has 25-inch barrel. Model of 1933 has improved stock w/full forearm instead of the slender forearm w/schnabel found on earlier production. Weight: about 6½ pounds. Made 1923–1942.

Savage Model 23C $225
Same as Model 23B, except caliber 32/20. Made 1923–1942.

Savage Model 23D $285
Same as Model 23B, except caliber 22 Hornet. Made 1933–1947.

Savage Model 25 Slide Action Repeater $325
Takedown. Hammerless. Caliber: 22 Short, Long, LR. Tubular magazine holds 20 Short, 17 Long, 15 LR. 24-inch octagon barrel. Weight: about 5¾ pounds. Sights: open rear; blade front. Plain pistol-grip stock, grooved slide handle. Made 1925–29.

Savage Model 29 Slide Action Repeater $300
Takedown. Hammerless. Caliber: 22 Short, Long, LR. Tubular magazine holds 20 Short, 17 Long, 15 LR. 24-inch barrel, octagon on prewar, round on postwar production. Weight: about 5½ pounds. Sights: open rear; bead front. Stock w/checkered pistol grip and slide handle on prewar, plain stock and grooved forearm on postwar production. Made 1929–1967.

Savage Model 40 Bolt Action Sporting Rifle $250
Standard Grade. Calibers: 250/3000, 300 Sav., 30/30, 30/06. 4-shot detachable box magazine. 22-inch barrel in calibers 250/3000 and 30/30; 24-inch in 300 Sav. and 30/06. Weight: about 7½ pounds. Sights: open rear; bead front, on ramp. Plain pistol-grip stock w/tapered forearm and schnabel tip. Made 1928–1940.

Savage Model 45

Savage Model 60

Savage Model 63K

Savage Model 71
"Stevens Favorite"

Savage Model 90

RIFLES

Savage Model 45 Super Sporter $350
Special Grade. Same as Model 40, except has checkered pistol grip and forearm, Lyman No. 40 receiver sight. Made 1928–1940.

Savage Model 60 Autoloading Rifle $115
Caliber: 22 LR. 15-shot tubular magazine. 20-inch barrel. Weight: 6 pounds. Sights: open rear; ramp front. Monte Carlo stock of walnut w/checkered pistol grip and forearm. Made 1969–1972.

Savage Model 63K Key Lock Bolt Action
Single Shot $75
Trigger locked with key. Caliber: 22 Short, Long, LR. 18-inch barrel. Weight: 4 pounds. Sights: open rear; hooded ramp front. Full-length stock w/pistol grip, swivels. Made 1970–72.

Savage Model 63KM $90
Same as Model 63K, except chambered for 22 WMR. Made 1970–72.

Savage Model 71 "Stevens Favorite" Single
Shot Lever Action Rifle $150
Replica of the original Stevens Favorite issued as a tribute to Joshua Stevens, "Father of 22 Hunting." Caliber: 22 LR. 22-inch full-octagon barrel. Brass-plated hammer and lever. Sights: open rear; brass blade front. Weight: 4½ pounds. Plain straight-grip buttstock and schnabel forend; brass commemorative medallion inlaid in buttstock, brass crescent-shaped buttplate. 10,000 produced. Made in 1971 only. Value is for new, unfired specimen.

Savage Model 90 Autoloading Carbine $120
Similar to Model 60, except has 16½-inch barrel, 10-shot tubular magazine, folding leaf rear sight, bead front, carbine-style stock of uncheckered walnut with barrel band and sling swivels. Weight: 5¾ pounds. Made 1969–1972.

Savage Model 99 Lever Action Repeater

Introduced in 1899, this model has been produced in a variety of styles and calibers. Original designation "Model 1899" was changed to "Model 99" c.1920. Earlier rifles and carbines—similar to Models 99A, 99B and 99H—were supplied in calibers 25-35, 30-30, 303 Sav., 32-40 and 38-55. Post-WWII Models 99A, 99C, 99CD, 99DE, 99DL, 99F and 99PE have top tang safety; other 99s have slide safety on right side of trigger guard. Models 99C and 99CD have detachable box magazine instead of traditional Model 99 rotary magazine.

Savage Model 99A (I) $525
Hammerless. Solid frame. Calibers: 30/30, 300 Sav., 303 Sav. Five-shot rotary magazine. 24-inch barrel. Weight: about 7 1/4 pounds. Sights: open rear; bead front, on ramp. Plain straight-grip stock, tapered forearm. Made 1920–1936.

Savage Model 99A (II) $350
Current model. Similar to original Model 99A, except has top tang safety, 22-inch barrel, folding leaf rear sight, no crescent buttplate. Calibers: 243 Win., 250 Sav., 300 Sav., 308 Win. Made 1971–1982.

Savage Model 99B $650
Takedown. Otherwise same as Model 99A, except weight about 7 1/2 pounds. Made 1920–1936.

Savage Model 99C $425
Current model. Same as Model 99F, except has clip magazine instead of rotary. Calibers: 243 Win., 284 Win., 308 Win. (4-shot detachable magazine holds one round less in 284). Weight: about 6 3/4 pounds. Made 1965 to date.

Savage Model 99CD $395
Deluxe version of Model 99C. Calibers: 243 Win., 250 Sav., 308 Win. Hooded ramp front sight. Weight: 8 1/4 pounds. Stock w/Monte Carlo comb and cheekpiece, checkered pistol grip, grooved forearm, swivels and sling. Made 1975 to 1981.

Savage Model 99DE Citation Grade $525
Same as Model 99PE, except has less elaborate engraving. Made 1968–1970.

Savage Model 99DL Deluxe $295
Postwar model. Calibers: 243 Win., 308 Win. Same as Model 99F, except has high comb Monte Carlo stock, sling swivels. Weight: about 6 3/4 pounds. Made 1960–1973.

Savage Model 99A

Savage Model 99A (current)

Savage Model 99C

Savage Model 99CD

Savage Model 99DE

Savage Model 99E Carbine (I) **$675**
Pre-WWII type. Solid frame. Calibers: 22 Hi-Power, 250/3000, 30/30, 300 Sav., 303 Sav. with 22-inch barrel; 300 Sav. 24-inch. Weight: about 7 pounds. Other specifications same as Model 99A. Made 1920–1936.

Savage Model 99E Carbine (II) **$275**
Current model. Solid frame. Calibers: 250 Sav., 243 Win., 300 Sav., 308 Win. 20- or 22-inch barrel. Checkered pistol-grip stock and forearm. Made 1960–1989.

Savage Model 99EG (I) **$535**
Pre-WWII type. Solid frame. Plain pistol-grip stock and forearm. Otherwise same as Model G. Made 1936–1941.

Savage Model 99EG (II) **$495**
Post-WWII type. Same as prewar model, except has checkered stock and forearm. Calibers: 250 Sav., 300 Sav.,

Savage Model 99EG (II) (cont.)
308 Win. (introduced 1955), 243 Win., and 358 Win. Made 1946–1960.

Savage Model 99F Featherweight (I) **$600**
Pre-WWII type. Takedown. Specifications same as Model 99E, except weight about 6½ pounds. Made 1920–1942.

Savage Model 99F Featherweight (II) **$325**
Postwar model. Solid frame. Calibers: 243 Win., 300 Sav., 308 Win. 22-inch barrel. Checkered pistol-grip stock and forearm. Weight: about 6½ pounds. Made 1955–1973.

Savage Model 99G **$595**
Takedown. Checkered pistol-grip stock and forearm. Weight: about 7¼ pounds. Other specifications same as Model 99E. Made 1920–1942.

RIFLES

Savage Model 99E (pre-WWII)

Savage Model 99E (current)

Savage Model 99EG (post-WWII)

Savage Model 99F (pre-WWII)

Savage Model 99G

Savage Model 99H

Savage Model 99K

Savage Model 99PE

Savage Model 99R (pre-WWII)

Savage Model 99R (post-WWII)

Savage Model 99RS (pre-WWII)

Savage Model 99H Carbine **$495**
Solid frame. Calibers: 250/3000, 30/30, 303 Sav. Carbine
stock and forearm. Weight: about 6½ pounds. Other
specifications same as Model 99A. Made 1931–1942.

Savage Model 99K **$1350**
Deluxe version of Model G with same specifications, ex-
cept has fancy stock and engraving on receiver and barrel,
Lyman peep rear sight, folding middle. Made 1931–1942.

Savage Model 99PE Presentation Grade **$1500**
Same as Model 99DL, except has engraved receiver (game
scenes on sides), tang and lever; fancy walnut Monte Carlo
stock and forearm with hand checkering, QD swivels.
Calibers: 243, 284, 308. Made 1968–1970.

Savage Model 99R (I) **$595**
Pre-WWII type. Solid frame. Calibers: 250/3000 with 22-
inch barrel; 300 Sav. with 24-inch barrel. Weight: about
7½ pounds. Special large pistol-grip stock and forearm,
checkered. General specifications same as other Model 99
rifles. Made 1936–1942.

Savage Model 99R (II) **$495**
Post-WWII type. Same as prewar model, except made
with 24-inch barrel only, has screw eyes for sling swivels.
Calibers: 250 Sav., 300 Sav., 308 Win., 243 Win. and 358
Win. Made 1946–1960.

Savage Model 99RS (I) **$550**
Pre-WWII type. Same as prewar Model 99r5, except
equipped w/Lyman rear peep sight and folding middle
sight, quick detachable swivels and sling. Made 1936–1942.

Savage Model 99T

Savage Model 99-358

Savage Model 110

Savage Model 110B

Savage Model 110BL

RIFLES

Savage Model 99RS (II) **$440**
Post-WWII type. Same as postwar Model 99r5, except
equipped w/Redfield 70LH receiver sight, blank in middle
sight slot. Made 1946–1958.

Savage Model 99T **$450**
Featherweight. Solid frame. Calibers: 22 Hi-Power, 30/
30, 303 Sav. with 20-inch barrel; 300 Sav. with 22-inch
barrel. Checkered pistol-grip stock and beavertail forearm.
Weight: about 7 pounds. General specifications same as
other Model 99 rifles. Made 1936–1942.

Savage Model 99-358 . . . . **$365**
Similar to current Model 99A, except caliber 358 Win.,
has grooved forearm, recoil pad, swivel studs. Made 1977–
1980.

Savage Model 110 Sporter Bolt Action Repeater . . **$160**
Calibers: 243, 270, 308, 30-06. 4-shot box magazine. 22-
inch barrel. Weight: about 6¾ pounds. Sights: open rear;
ramp front. Standard sporter stock with pistol grip,
checkered. Made 1958–1963.

Savage Model 110B Bolt Action Rifle
Same as Model 110E, except with checkered select walnut
Monte Carlo-style stock (early models) or brown lami-
nated stock (late models). Calibers: 243 Win., 270 Win.,
30-06, 7mm Rem. Mag., 338 Win. Mag. Made 1976 to
date.
Early Model **$225**
Laminated Stock Model **265**

Savage Model 110BL **$275**
Same as Model 110B, except has left-hand action.

Savage Model 110C
Calibers: 22-250, 243, 25-06, 270, 308, 30-06, 7mm Rem. Mag., 300 Win. Mag. 4-shot detachable clip magazine (3-shot in Magnum calibers). 22-inch barrel (24-inch in 22-250 Magnum calibers). Weight: 6¾ lbs.; Magnum, 7¾ to 8 lbs. Sights: open rear; ramp front. Checkered Monte Carlo-style walnut stock (Magnum has recoil pad). Made 1966–1988.

Standard Calibers	**$275**
Magnum Calibers	**295**

Savage Model 110CL
Same as Model 110C, except has left-hand action. (Available only in 243 Win., 30-06, 270 and 7mm Mag.)

Standard Calibers	**$275**
Magnum Calibers	**295**

Savage 110CY Youth/Ladies Rifle **$240**
Same as Model 110 G, except with walnut-finished hardwood stock with 12½-inch pull. Calibers: 243 and 300 Savage. Made 1991 to date.

Savage Model 110D
Similar to Model 110C, except has internal magazine with hinged floorplate. Calibers: 243 Win., 270 Win., 30-06, 7mm Rem. Mag., 300 Win. Mag. Made 1972–1988.

Standard Calibers	**$250**
Magnum Calibers	**295**

Savage Model 110DL
Same as Model 110D, except has left-hand action. Discontinued.

Standard Calibers	**$250**
Magnum Calibers	**295**

Savage Model 110E **$235**
Calibers: 22-250, 223 Rem., 243, 270 Win., 308, 7mm Rem. Mag., 30-06. 4-shot box magazine (3-shot in Magnum).

Savage Model 110E (cont.)
20- or 22-inch barrel (24-inch stainless steel in Magnum). Weight: 6¾ lbs.; Magnum, 7¾ lbs. Sights: open rear; ramp front. Plain Monte Carlo stock on early production; current models have checkered stocks of walnut-finished hardwood (Magnum has recoil pad). Made 1963 to date.

Savage Model 110EL **$235**
Same as Model 110E, except has left-hand action, made in 30-06 and 7mm Rem. Mag. only. Made 1969–1973.

Savage Model 110F/110K Bolt Action Rifle
Same as Model 110E, except **Model 110F** has black Rynite® synthetic stock, swivel studs; made 1988 to date. **Model 110K** has laminated camouflage stock; made 1986 to date.

Model 110F, Adj. Sights	**$270**
Model 110FNS, No Sights	**280**
Model 110K Standard Calibers	**295**
Model 110K Magnum Calibers	**325**

Savage Model 110FP Police Rifle **$300**
Calibers: 223, 308 Win. 4-shot magazine. 24-inch barrel. 45½ inches overall. Weight: 9 lbs. Black Rynite composition stock. Matte blue finish. Made 1990 to date.

Savage 110G Bolt Action Rifle
Calibers: 223, 22-250, 243, 270, 7mm Rem. Mag., 308 Win., 30-06, 300 Win. Mag. 5-shot (standard) or 4-shot magazine (magnum). 22- or 24-inch barrel. 42⅜ overall (standard). Weight: 6¾ to 7½ pounds. Ramp front sight, adj. rear. Checkered walnut-finished hardwood stock with rubber recoil pad. Made 1989 to date.

Model 110G Standard Calibers	**$255**
Model 110G Magnum Calibers	**270**
Model 110GLNS, Left-hand, No Sights	**300**

Savage Model 110C

Savage Model 110DL

Savage Model 110E

Savage Model 110GV Varmint Rifle **$295**
Similar to the Model 110 G, except fitted with medium-weight varmint barrel with no sights. Receiver drilled and tapped for scope mount. Calibers 22-250 and 223 only. Made 1989 to date.

Savage Model 110M Magnum
Same as Model 110MC, except calibers: 7mm Rem. Mag., 264, 300 and 338 Win. 24-inch barrel. Stock with recoil pad. Weight: 7³/₄ to 8 pounds. Made 1963–69.
Model 110M Magnum **$250**
Model 110ML Magnum, Left-Hand Action **265**

Savage Model 110MC
Same as Model 110, except has Monte Carlo-style stock. Calibers: 22-250, 243, 270, 308, 30-06. 24-inch barrel in 22-250. Made 1959–1969.
Model 110MC **$150**
Model 110MCL w/Left-hand Action **160**

Savage Model 110P Premier Grade
Calibers: 243 Win., 7mm Rem. Mag., 30-06. 4-shot magazine (3-shot in Magnum). 22-inch barrel (24-inch stainless steel in Magnum). Weight: 7 lbs.; Magnum, 7³/₄ lbs. Sights: open rear folding leaf; ramp front. French walnut stock w/Monte Carlo comb and cheekpiece, rosewood forend tip and pistol-grip cap, skip checkering, sling swivels (Magnum has recoil pad). Made 1964–1970.
Calibers 243 Win. and 30-06 . . . . **$325**
Caliber 7mm Rem. Mag. **395**

Savage Model 110PE Presentation Grade
Same as Model 110P, except has engraved receiver, floorplate and trigger guard, stock of choice grade French walnut. Made 1968–1970.

Savage Model 110PE Presentation Grade (cont.)
Calibers 243 and 30-06 . . . . **$495**
Caliber 7mm Rem. Mag. **575**

Savage Model 110PEL Presentation Grade
Same as Model 110PE, except has left-hand action.
Calibers 243 and 30-06 . . . . **$670**
Caliber 7mm Rem. Mag. **695**

Savage Model 110PL Premier Grade
Same as Model 110P, except has left-hand action.
Calibers 243 Win. and 30-06 . . . . **$325**
Caliber 7mm Rem. Mag. **375**

Savage Model 110S/110V
Same as Model 110E, except **Model 110S** in 308 Win. only; **Model 110V** in 22-250 and 223 Rem. w/heavy 25-inch barrel, 47 inches overall, 9 pounds. Discont. 1989.
Model 110S **$265**
Model 110V **295**

Savage Model 111 Chieftain Bolt Action Rifle
Calibers: 243 Win., 270 Win., 7×57mm, 7mm Rem. Mag., 30-06. 4-shot clip magazine (3-shot in Magnum). 22-inch barrel (24-inch in Magnum). Weight: 7¹/₂ lbs.; 8¹/₄ lbs., Magnum. Sights: leaf rear; hooded ramp front. Select walnut stock w/Monte Carlo comb and cheekpiece, checkered, pistol-grip cap, QD swivels and sling. Made 1974–79.
Standard calibers **$295**
Caliber 7mm Rem. Mag. **315**

RIFLES

Savage Model 110MCL

Savage Model 110P

Savage Model 110PE

Savage Model 111 Chieftain

Savage Model 112BV Heavy Varmint Rifle $375

Similar to the Model 110G, except fitted with 26-inch heavy barrel. Laminated wood stock with high comb. Calibers 22-250 and 223 only. Made 1993–94.

Savage Model 112FV, 112FVS, 112FVSS Varmint Rifles

Similar to the Model 110G, except fitted with 26-inch heavy barrel and Dupont Rynite stock. Calibers: 22-250, 223 and 220 Swift (112FVS only). Blued or stainless finish. Made 1991–94.

Model 112FV (blued) **$250**
Model 112FVS (blued, single shot) **275**
Model 112FVSS (stainless) **375**

Savage Model 112V Varmint Rifle $305

Bolt action, single shot. Caliber: 220 Swift, 222 Rem., 223 Rem., 22-250, 243 Win., 25-06. 26-inch heavy barrel with scope bases. Supplied w/o sights. Weight: 9¼ pounds. Select walnut stock in varmint style w/checkered pistol grip, high comb, QD sling swivels. Made 1975–79.

Savage 116FSK Kodiak Rifle $395

Similar to the Model 116FSS, except with 22-inch barrel chambered for 338 Win. Mag. only. "Shock Suppressor" recoil reducer. Made 1993 to date.

Savage Model 116FSS Bolt Action Rifle

Improved Model 110 with satin stainless action and barrel. Calibers: 223, 243, 270, 30-06, 7mm Rem. Mag., 300 Win. Mag., 338 Win. Mag. 22- or 24-inch barrel. 4- or 5-shot capacity. Weight: about 7½ pounds. Black Rynite® stock with recoil pad and swivel studs. Receiver drilled and tapped for scope mounts, no sights. Made 1991 to date.

Savage Model 116FSS Bolt Action Rifle (cont.)

Model 116FSS................................ **$375**
Model 116FSC, Detachable Magazine **395**

Savage Model 170 Pump Action Centerfire Rifle . $175

Calibers: 30-30, 35 Rem. 3-shot tubular magazine. 22-inch barrel. Weight: 6¾ pounds. Sights: folding leaf rear; ramp front. Select walnut stock with checkered pistol grip, Monte Carlo comb, grooved slide handle. Made 1970–1981.

Savage Model 170C Carbine $185

Same as Model 170 Rifle, except has 18½-inch barrel, straight comb stock, weighs 6 pounds; caliber 30-30 only. Made 1974–1981.

Savage Model 219 Single Shot Rifle

Hammerless. Takedown. Shotgun-type action with top lever. Calibers: 22 Hornet, 25-20, 32-20, 30-30. 26-inch barrel. Weight: about 6 pounds. Sights: open rear; bead front. Plain pistol-grip stock and forearm. Made 1938–1965.

Model 219 .... **$175**
Model 219L (w/side lever, made 1965–67) **125**

Savage Model 221-229 Utility Guns

Same as Model 219, except in various calibers, supplied in combination with an interchangeable shotgun barrel. All versions discontinued.

Model 221 (30-30, 12-ga. 30-inch bbl.) **$140**
Model 222 (30-30, 16-ga. 28-inch bbl.) **125**
Model 223 (30-30, 20-ga. 28-inch bbl.) **110**
Model 227 (22 Hornet, 12-ga. 30-inch bbl.) **150**
Model 228 (22 Hornet, 16-ga. 28-inch bbl.) **145**
Model 229 (22 Hornet, 20-ga. 28-inch bbl.) **140**

Savage Model 112V

Savage Model 170C Carbine

Savage Model 219

Savage Model 219L

Savage Model 340 Rifle

RIFLES

Savage Model 340 Bolt Action Repeater
Calibers: 22 Hornet, 222 Rem., 223 Rem., 225 Win., 30-30. Clip magazine; 4-shot capacity (3-shot in 30-30). Barrel lengths: originally 20-inch in 30-30, 22-inch in 22 Hornet; later 22-inch in 30-30, 24-inch in other calibers. Weight: 6½ to 7½ pounds depending on caliber and vintage. Sights: open rear (folding leaf on recent production); ramp front. Early models had plain pistol-grip stock; checkered since 1965. Made 1950–1985. (*Note:* 1947–1950 this was 22 Hornet Stevens Model 322 and 30-30 Model 325.)
Pre-1965 with plain stock **$175**
Current model **160**

Savage Model 340C Carbine **$185**
Same as Model 340, except caliber 30-30, 18½-inch barrel. Weight: about 6 pounds. Made 1962–64.

Savage Model 340S Deluxe **$225**
Same as Model 340, except has checkered stock, screw eyes for sling, peep rear sight, hooded front. Made 1955–1960.

Savage Model 342 . . . . **$250**
Designation, 1950 to 1955, of Model 340 22 Hornet.

Savage Model 342S Deluxe **$275**
Designation, 1950 to 1955, of Model 340S 22 Hornet.

Savage Anniversary Model 1895 Lever Action Rifle **$425**
Replica of Savage Model 1895 Hammerless Lever Action Rifle issued to commemorate the 75th anniversary (1895–1970) of Savage Arms. Caliber: 308 Win. 5-shot rotary magazine. 24-inch full-octagon barrel. Engraved receiver. Brass-plated lever. Sights: open rear; brass blade front. Plain straight-grip buttstock, schnabel-type forend; brass medallion inlaid in buttstock, brass crescent-shaped buttplate. 9,999 produced. Made in 1970 only. Value is for new, unfired specimen.

Savage Model 1903 Slide Action Repeater **$225**
Hammerless. Takedown. Caliber: 22 Short, Long, LR. Detachable box magazine. 24-inch octagon barrel. Weight: about 5 pounds. Sights: open rear; bead front. Pistol-grip stock, grooved slide handle. Made 1903–1921.

Savage Model 1904 Bolt Action Single Shot Rifle . **$100**
Takedown. Caliber: 22 Short, Long, LR. 18-inch barrel. Weight: about 3 pounds. Sights: open rear; bead front. Plain, straight-grip, one-piece stock. Made 1904–1917.

Savage Model 1905 Bolt Action Single Shot Rifle . **$100**
Takedown. Caliber: 22 Short, Long, LR. 22-inch barrel. Weight: about 5 pounds. Sights: open rear; bead front. Plain, straight-grip one-piece stock. Made 1905–1919.

Savage Model 1909 Slide Action Repeater **$195**
Hammerless. Takedown. Similar to Model 1903, except has 20-inch round barrel, plain stock and forearm, weighs about 4¾ pounds. Made 1909–1915.

Savage Model 1912 Autoloading Rifle **$325**
Takedown. Caliber: 22 LR only. 7-shot detachable box magazine. 20-inch barrel. Weight: about 4½ pounds. Sights: open rear; bead front. Plain straight-grip stock and forearm. Made 1912–16.

Savage Model 1914 Slide Action Repeater **$265**
Hammerless. Takedown. Caliber: 22 Short, Long, LR. Tubular magazine holds 20 Short, 17 Long, 15 LR. 24-inch octagon barrel. Weight: about 5¾ pounds. Sights: open rear; bead front. Plain pistol-grip stock, grooved slide handle. Made 1914–1924.

Savage Model 1920 Hi-Power Bolt Action Rifle . . **$400**
Short Mauser-type action. Calibers: 250/3000, 300 Sav. 5-shot box magazine. 22-inch barrel in 250 cal.; 24-inch in 300 cal. Weight: about 6 pounds. Sights: open rear; bead front. Checkered pistol-grip stock w/slender forearm and schnabel tip. Made 1920–26.

Savage Model 340C Carbine

Savage Anniversary Model 1895

Savage/Anschutz Mark 10D

NOTE: In 1965, Savage began the importation of rifles manufactured by J. G. Anschutz GmbH, Ulm, West Germany. Models designated "Savage/Anschutz" are listed in this section; those marketed in the U.S. under the "Anschutz" name are included in that firm's listings. Anschutz rifles are now distributed in the U.S. by Precision Sales Int'l., Westfield, Mass.

Savage/Anschutz Mark 10 Bolt Action Target Rifle $295
Single shot. Caliber: 22 LR. 26-inch barrel. Weight: 8½ pounds. Sights: Anschutz micrometer rear; globe front. Target stock w/full pistol grip and cheekpiece, adj. hand stop and swivel. Made 1967–1972.

Savage/Anschutz Mark 10D $300
Same as Mark 10, except has redesigned stock with Monte Carlo comb, different rear sight. Weight: 7¾ pounds. Made 1972.

Savage/Anschutz Model 54 Custom Sporter ... $515
Bolt action. Caliber: 22 LR. 5-shot clip magazine. 24-inch barrel. Weight: 6¾ pounds. Sights: folding leaf rear; hooded ramp front. Select walnut stock w/Monte Carlo comb and rollover cheekpiece, checkered pistol grip and schnabel-type forearm, QD swivel studs. Made 1969–1981. (*Note:* Same as Anschutz Model 1422D.)

Savage/Anschutz Model 54M $550
Same as Model 54, except chambered for 22 WMR, 4-shot clip magazine. Made 1972–1981. (*Note:* Same as Anschutz Model 1522D.)

Savage/Anschutz Model 64 Bolt Action Target Rifle $395
Single shot. Caliber: 22 LR. 26-inch medium-heavy barrel. Weight: 7¾ pounds. Supplied w/o sights (add $40 for Anschutz match sight set). Target stock w/thumb groove, checkered pistol grip, high comb and cheekpiece, adj. buttplate, swivel rail. Model 64L has left-hand stock. Made 1965–1981. (*Note:* Same as Anschutz Model 1403.)

Savage/Anschutz Model 153 Bolt Action Sporter $395
Caliber: 222 Rem. 3-shot clip magazine. 24-inch barrel. Sights: folding leaf open rear; hooded ramp front. Weight: 6¾ pounds. French walnut stock w/cheekpiece, skip checkering, rosewood forend tip and grip cap, swivels. Made 1964–67.

Savage/Anschutz Model 153S $495
Same as Model 153, except has double-set trigger. Made 1965–67.

Savage/Anschutz Model 164 Custom Sporter ... $250
Bolt action. Caliber: 22 LR. 5-shot clip magazine. 23-inch barrel. Weight: 6 pounds. Sights: folding leaf rear; hooded ramp front. Select walnut stock w/Monte Carlo comb and cheekpiece, checkered pistol grip and schnabel-type forearm. Made 1969–1981 (*Note:* Same as Anschutz Model 1416.)

Savage/Anschutz Model 54 Sporter

Savage/Anschutz Model 64

Savage/Anschutz Model 164

Savage-Stevens Model 34

Savage/Anschutz Model 164M **$295**
Same as Model 164, except chambered for 22 WMR, 4-shot clip magazine. Made 1969 to date. (*Note:* Same as Anschutz Model 1516.)

Savage/Anschutz Model 184 Sporter **$315**
Bolt action. Caliber: 22 LR. 5-shot clip magazine. 21½-inch barrel. Weight: 4½ pounds. Sights: folding leaf rear; hooded ramp front. Monte Carlo stock w/checkered pistol grip and schnabel-type forearm. Made 1972–75. (*Note:* Same as Anschutz Model 1441.)

> **NOTE:** Since J. Stevens Arms (see also separate listing) is a division of Savage Industries, certain Savage models carry the "Stevens" name.

Savage-Stevens Model 34 Bolt Action Repeater . **$85**
Caliber: 22 Short, Long, LR. 5-shot clip magazine. 20-inch barrel. Weight: 5½ pounds. Sights: open rear; bead front. Checkered stock w/Monte Carlo comb. Made 1969–1981.

Savage-Stevens Model 34M **$90**
Same as Model 34, except chambered for 22 WMR. Made 1969–1973.

Savage-Stevens Model 35 . . . . **$80**
Bolt-action repeater. Caliber: 22 LR. 6-shot clip magazine. 22-inch barrel. Weight: about 5 pounds. Sights: open rear; ramp front. Monte Carlo stock w/checkered pistol grip and forearm. Made 1982 to date.

Savage-Stevens Model 35M **$90**
Same as Model 35, except chambered for 22 WMR. Made 1982 to date.

Savage-Stevens Model 46 Bolt Action Tubular Repeater **$95**
Caliber: 22 Short, Long, LR. Tubular magazine holds 22 Short, 17 Long, 15 LR. 20-inch barrel. Weight: 5 pounds. Plain pistol-grip stock on early production; later models have Monte Carlo stock w/checkering. Made 1969–1973.

Savage-Stevens Model 65 Bolt Action Repeater . **$90**
Caliber: 22 Short, Long, LR. 5-shot clip magazine. 20-inch barrel. Weight: 5 pounds. Sights: open rear; ramp front. Monte Carlo stock w/checkered pistol grip and forearm. Made 1969–1973.

Savage-Stevens Model 65M **$105**
Same as Model 65, except chambered for 22 WMR, has 22-inch barrel, weighs 5¾ pounds. Made 1969–1981.

Savage-Stevens Model 72 Crackshot Single Shot Lever Action Rifle **$110**
Falling-block action. Casehardened frame. Caliber: 22 Short, Long, LR. 22-inch octagon barrel. Weight: 4½

RIFLES

Savage-Stevens Model 35

Savage-Stevens Model 46

Savage-Stevens Model 65

Savage-Stevens Model 72 Crackshot

Savage-Stevens Model 73

Savage-Stevens Model 80

Savage-Stevens Model 89

Savage-Stevens Model 987-T

Savage-Stevens Model 72 Crackshot (cont.)
pounds. Sights: open rear; bead front. Plain straight-grip stock and forearm of walnut. Made 1972 to date. (*Note:* This is a "Favorite"-type single-shot, unlike the smaller original "Crackshot" made by Stevens 1913–1939.)

Savage-Stevens Model 73 Bolt Action Single Shot $75
Caliber: 22 Short, Long, LR. 20-inch barrel. Weight: 4¾ pounds. Sights; open rear; bead front. Plain pistol-grip stock. Made 1965–1980.

Savage-Stevens 73Y Youth Model $85
Same as Model 73, except has 18-inch barrel, 1½-inch shorter buttstock, weighs 4½ pounds. Made 1965–1980.

Savage-Stevens Model 74 Little Favorite $130
Same as Model 72 Crackshot, except has black-finished frame, 22-inch round barrel, walnut-finished hardwood stock. Weight: 4¾ pounds. Made 1972–74.

Savage-Stevens Model 80 Autoloading Rifle . . . $120
Caliber: 22 LR. 15-shot tubular magazine. 20-inch barrel. Weight: 6 pounds. Sights: open rear; bead front. Monte Carlo stock of walnut with checkered pistol grip and forearm. Made 1976 to date. (*Note:* This rifle is essentially

Savage-Stevens Model 80 Autoloading Rifle (cont.)
the same as Model 60 of 1969–72, except for a different style of checkering, side instead of top safety and plain bead instead of ramp front sight.)

Savage-Stevens Model 88 Autoloading Rifle . . . $125
Similar to Model 60, except has walnut-finished hardwood stock, plain bead front sight; weight, 5¾ pounds. Made 1969–1972.

Savage-Stevens Model 89 Single Shot Lever Action Carbine $100
Martini-type action. Caliber: 22 Short, Long, LR. 18½-inch barrel. Weight: 5 pounds. Sights: open rear; bead front. Western-style carbine stock w/straight grip, forearm with barrel band. Made 1976–1989.

Savage-Stevens Model 987-T Autoloading Rifle . $120
Caliber: 22 LR. 15-shot tubular magazine. 20-inch barrel. Weight: 6 pounds. Sights: open rear; ramp front. Monte Carlo stock w/checkered pistol grip and forearm. Made 1981–89.

Savage "Stevens Favorite"
See Savage Model 71.

V. C. SCHILLING
Suhl, Germany

Schilling Mauser-Mannlicher Bolt Action Sporting Rifle **$650**
Same general specifications as given for the Haenel Mauser-Mannlicher Sporter. See separate listing.

Schilling '88 Mauser Sporter **$505**
Same general specifications as Haenel '88 Mauser Sporter. See separate listing.

SCHULTZ & LARSEN GEVAERFABRIK
Otterup, Denmark

Schultz & Larsen Match Rifle No. 47 . . . . **$595**
Caliber: 22 LR. Bolt action, single shot, set trigger. 28$\frac{1}{2}$-inch heavy barrel. Weight: about 14 pounds. Sights: micrometer receiver; globe front. Free-rifle stock w/cheekpiece, thumbhole, adj. Schuetzen-type buttplate, swivels, palmrest.

Schultz & Larsen Free Rifle Model 54 . . . . **$730**
Calibers: 6.5×55mm or any standard American centerfire caliber. Schultz & Larsen M54 bolt action, single shot, set trigger. 27$\frac{1}{2}$-inch heavy barrel. Weight: about 15$\frac{1}{2}$ pounds. Sights: micrometer receiver; globe front. Free-rifle stock w/cheekpiece, thumbhole, adj. Schuetzen-type buttplate, swivels, palmrest.

Schultz & Larsen Model 54J Sporting Rifle **$695**
Calibers: 270 Win., 30-06, 7×61 Sharpe & Hart. Schultz & Larsen bolt action. 3-shot magazine. 24-inch barrel in 270 and 30-06, 26-inch in 7×61 S&H. Checkered stock w/ Monte Carlo comb and cheekpiece. Value shown is for rifle less sights.

SEARS, ROEBUCK & COMPANY
Chicago, Illinois

The most encountered brands or model designations used by Sears are J. C. Higgins and Ted Williams. Firearms sold under these designations have been mfd. by various firms including Winchester, Marlin, Savage, Mossberg, etc.

Sears Model 2C Bolt Action Rifle **$85**
Caliber: 22RF. 7-shot clip magazine. 21-inch barrel. Weight: 5 pounds. Sights: open rear; ramp front. Plain Monte Carlo stock. Mfd. by Winchester.

Sears Model 42 Bolt Action Repeater **$80**
Takedown. Caliber: 22RF. 8-shot detachable box magazine. 24-inch barrel. Weight: 6 pounds. Sights: open rear; bead front. Plain pistol-grip stock. Mfd. by Marlin.

Sears Model 42DL Bolt Action Repeater **$85**
Same general specifications as Model 42 except fancier grade w/peep sight, hooded front sight and swivels.

Sears Model 44DL Lever Action Rifle **$140**
Caliber: 22RF. Tubular magazine holds 19 LR cartridges. 22-inch barrel. Weight: 6$\frac{1}{4}$ pounds. Sights: open rear; hooded ramp front. Monte Carlo-style stock w/pistol grip. Mfd. by Marlin.

Sears Model 53 Bolt Action Rifle **$195**
Calibers: 243, 270, 308, 30-06. 4-shot magazine. 22-inch barrel. Weight: 6$\frac{3}{4}$ pounds. Sights: open rear; ramp front. Standard sporter stock w/pistol grip, checkered. Mfd. by Savage.

Sears Model 54 Lever Action Rifle **$145**
Similar general specifications as Winchester Model 94 carbine. Made in 30-30 caliber only. Mfd. by Winchester.

Sears Model 103 Series Bolt Action Repeater . . . **$85**
Same general specifications as Model 103.2 with minor changes. Mfd. by Marlin.

Sears Model 103.2 Bolt Action Repeater **$85**
Takedown. Caliber: 22RF. 8-shot detachable box magazine. 24-inch barrel. Weight: 6 pounds. Sights: open rear; bead front. Plain pistol-grip stock. Mfd. by Marlin.

R. F. SEDGLEY, INC.
Philadelphia, Pennsylvania

Sedgley Springfield Sporter **$495**
Springfield '03 bolt action. Calibers: 220 Swift, 218 Bee, 22-3000, R2, 22-4000, 22 Hornet, 25-35, 250-3000, 257 Roberts, 270 Win., 7mm, 30-06. 24-inch barrel. Weight: 7$\frac{1}{2}$ pounds. Sights: Lyman No. 48 receiver; bead front, on matted ramp. Checkered walnut stock, grip cap, sling swivels. Discontinued 1941.

Sedgley Springfield Left-Hand Sporter **$475**
Bolt action reversed for left-handed shooter; otherwise, the same as standard Sedgley Springfield Sporter.

Sedgley Springfield Mannlicher-Type Sporter . . **$540**
Same as the standard Sedgley Springfield Sporter, except has 20-inch barrel, Mannlicher-type full stock w/cheekpiece, weighs 7$\frac{3}{4}$ pounds.

RIFLES

Sedgley Springfield Sporter

Sedgley Springfield Left Hand

Sedgley Springfield Mannlicher

SHILEN RIFLES, INC.
Ennis, Texas

Shilen DGA Benchrest Rifle **$750**
DGA single-shot bolt action. Calibers as listed for Sporter. 26-inch medium-heavy or heavy barrel. Weight: from 10½ pounds. No sights. Fiberglass or walnut stock, classic or thumbhole pattern. Currently manufactured.

Shilen DGA Sporter **$595**
DGA bolt action. Calibers: 17 Rem., 222 Rem., 223 Rem., 22-250, 220 Swift, 6mm Rem., 243 Win., 250 Sav., 257 Roberts, 284 Win., 308 Win., 358 Win. 3-shot blind magazine. 24-inch barrel. Average weight: 7½ pounds. No sights. Select Claro walnut stock w/cheekpiece, pistol grip, sling swivel studs. Currently manufactured.

Shilen DGA Varminter **$575**
Same as Sporter, except has 25-inch medium-heavy barrel. Weight: about 9 pounds.

Shilen DGA Benchrest Rifle

Shilen DGA Sporter

Shilen DGA Varminter

SIG AMT Sporting Rifle

SIG SWISS INDUSTRIAL COMPANY
Neuhausen-Rhine Falls, Switzerland

SIG-AMT Semiautomatic Rifle **$4500**
Caliber: 308 Win.(7.62 NATO). 5, 10, or 20-shot magazine. 18½-inch barrel w/flash suppressor. Weight: 9½ pounds. Sights: adj. aperture rear; post front. Walnut buttstock and forend with synthetic pistol grip. Imported 1980s.

SIG-AMT Sporting Rifle **$2800**
Semiautomatic version of SG510-4 automatic assault rifle based on Swiss Army StGW57. Roller-delayed blowback action. Caliber: 7.62×51mm NATO (308 Win.). 5-, 10- and 20-round magazines. 19-inch barrel. Weight: about 10 pounds. Sights; aperture rear; post front. Wood buttstock and forearm, folding bipod. Made 1960–1974.

SIG-PE57 Semiautomatic Rifle **$3750**
Caliber: 7.65 Swiss. 24-shot magazine. 23¾-inch barrel. Weight: 12½ pounds. Sights: adj. aperture rear; post front. High-impact synthetic stock. Imported from Switzerland during the 1980s.

Smith & Wesson Model 1500DL

Smith & Wesson Model A

SMITH & WESSON
Springfield, Massachusetts
Mfd. by Husqvarna Vapenfabrik A.B., Huskvarna, Sweden

Smith & Wesson Model 1500 . . . . **$285**
Bolt action. Calibers: 243 Win., 270 Win., 30-06, 7mm Rem. Mag. 22-inch barrel (24-inch in 7mm Rem. Mag.). Weight: about 7½ pounds. American walnut stock w/ Monte Carlo comb and cheekpiece, cut checkering. Sights: open rear; hooded ramp, gold bead front. Introduced in 1979, this model was also produced by Mossberg (see separate listings); now discontinued.

Smith & Wesson Model 1500DL Deluxe **$315**
Same as standard model, except w/o sights; has engine-turned bolt, decorative scroll on floorplate, French checkering.

Smith & Wesson Model A Bolt-Action Sporting Rifle **$350**
Similar to Husqvarna Model 9000 Crown Grade. Mauser-type bolt action. Calibers: 22-250, 243 Win., 270 Win., 308 Win., 30-06, 7mm Rem. Mag., 300 Win. Mag. 5-shot magazine, except 3-round capacity in latter two calibers. 23¾-inch barrel. Weight: about 7 pounds. Sights: folding leaf rear; hooded ramp front. Checkered walnut stock w/ Monte Carlo cheekpiece, rosewood forend tip and pistol-grip cap, swivels. Made 1969–1972.

RIFLES

Smith & Wesson Model B

Smith & Wesson Model C

Smith & Wesson Model D

Smith & Wesson Model E

Smith & Wesson Model B $340
Same as Model A, except has 20³/₄-inch extra-light barrel,
Monte Carlo cheekpiece with schnabel-style forearm,
weighs about 6 lbs. 10 oz. Calibers: 243 Win., 30-06.

Smith & Wesson Model C $350
Same as Model B, except has cheekpiece stock with
straight comb.

Smith & Wesson Model D $425
Same as Model C, except has full-length Mannlicher-style
forearm.

Smith & Wesson Model E $475
Same as Model B, except has full-length Mannlicher-style
forearm.

===== **SPRINGFIELD, INC.** =====
Colona, Illinois
(formerly Springfield Armory of Geneseo, Ill.)

This is a private firm, not to be confused with the former
U.S. Government facility in Springfield, Mass.

Springfield Armory BM-59 Semiautomatic Rifle
Gas-operated. Caliber: 308 Win. (7.62mm NATO). 20-shot
detachable box magazine. 19.3-inch barrel with flash suppressor. About 43 inches overall. Weight: 9¹/₄ pounds. Adj.
military aperture rear sight, square post front; direct and
indirect grenade launcher sights. European walnut stock
w/handguard or folding buttstock (Alpine Paratrooper).
Made 1981 to date.
Standard Model $1795
Paratrooper Model   1950

Springfield Armory M-1 Garand Semiautomatic Rifle
Gas-operated. Calibers: 308 Win. (7.62 NATO), 30-06. 8-
shot stripper clip. 24-inch barrel. 43¹/₂ inches overall.
Weight: 9¹/₂ pounds. Adjustable aperture rear sight, mil-
itary sqaure blade front. Standard "Issue-grade" walnut
stock or folding buttstock. Made 1979 to date.
Standard Model . . . . $ 775
National Match   950
Ultra Match   995
Sniper Model 1095
Paratrooper with folding stock   995

Springfield Armory M1A

Springfield Armory Match M1A

Same as Standard M1A, except has National Match grade barrel with modified flash suppressor, National Match sights, turned trigger pull, gas system assembly in one unit, modified mainspring guide, glass-bedded walnut stock. Super Match M1A has premium-grade heavy barrel (weighs 10 pounds).

Match M1A **$1095**
Super Match M1A **1250**

Springfield Armory Standard M1A Semiautomatic

Gas-operated. Similar to U.S. M14 service rifle, except has no provision for automatic firing. Caliber: 7.65mm NATO (308 Win.). 5-, 10- or 20-round detachable box magazine. 25$\frac{1}{16}$-inch barrel with flash suppressor. Weight: about 9 pounds. Sights: adj. aperture rear; blade front. Fiberglass, birch or walnut stock, fiberglass handguard, sling swivels. Made 1974 to date.

W/fiberglass or birch stock **$695**
W/walnut stock **750**

Squires Bingham Model M16

Squires Bingham Model M20D

SQUIRES BINGHAM CO., INC.
Makati, Rizal, Philippines

Squires Bingham Model 14D Deluxe Bolt Action Repeating Rifle **$125**

Caliber: 22 LR. 5-shot box magazine. 24-inch barrel. Sights: V-notch rear; hooded ramp front. Receiver grooved for scope mounting. Pulong Dalaga stock with contrasting forend tip and grip cap, checkered forearm and pistol grip. Weight: about 6 pounds. Currently mfd.

Squires Bingham Model 15 . . . . **$150**

Same as Model 14D, except chambered for 22 WMR. Currently manufactured.

Squires Bingham Model M16 Semiautomatic Rifle **$165**

Styled after U.S. M16 military rifle. Caliber: 22 LR. 15-shot box magazine. 19$\frac{1}{2}$-inch barrel with muzzle brake/flash hider. Rear sight in carrying handle, post front on high ramp. Black-painted mahogany buttstock and forearm. Weight: about 6$\frac{1}{2}$ pounds. Currently mfd.

Squires Bingham Model M20D Deluxe Semiautomatic Rifle **$175**

Caliber: 22 LR. 15-shot box magazine. 19$\frac{1}{2}$-inch barrel with muzzle brake/flash hider. Sights: V-notch rear; blade front. Receiver grooved for scope mounting. Pulong Dalaga stock w/contrasting forend tip and grip cap, checkered forearm/pistol grip. Weight: about 6 lbs. Currently mfd.

Standard Model G

STANDARD ARMS COMPANY
Wilmington, Delaware

Standard Model G Automatic Rifle **$325**
Gas-operated. Autoloading. Hammerless. Takedown. Calibers: 25-35, 30-30, 25 Rem., 30 Rem., 35 Rem. Magazine capacity: 4 rounds in 35 Rem., 5 rounds in other calibers. 22 3/8-inch barrel. Weight: about 7 3/4 pounds. Sights: open sporting rear; ivory bead front. Shotgun-type

Standard Model G Automatic Rifle (cont.)
stock. Made c. 1910. *Note:* This was the first gas-operated rifle manufactured in the U.S. While essentially an autoloader, the gas port can be closed and the rifle operated as a slide-action repeater.

Standard Model M Hand-Operated Rifle **$275**
Slide-action repeater with same general specifications as Model G, except lacks autoloading feature. Weight: about 7 pounds.

Star Rolling Block

STAR
Eibar, Spain
Mfd. by Bonifacio Echeverria, S.A.

Star Rolling Block Carbine **$160**
Single-shot action similar to Remington Rolling Block. Calibers: 30-30, 357 Mag., 44 Mag. 20-inch barrel. Weight: about 6 pounds. Sights: folding leaf rear; ramp front. Walnut straight-grip stock w/crescent buttplate, forearm with barrel band. Made 1973–75.

STERLING
Imported by Lanchester U.S.A., Inc., Dallas, Texas

Sterling Mark 6 Semi-Automatic Carbine **$695**
Caliber: 9mm Parabellum. 34-shot magazine. Barrel: 16.1 inches. Weight: about 7 1/2 pounds. Flip-type rear peep sight, ramp front. Folding metal skeleton stock. Made 1983 to date.

Stevens No. 12 Marksman

Stevens No. 14 1/2 Little Scout

J. STEVENS ARMS CO.
Chicopee Falls, Massachusetts
Div. of Savage Industries, Westfield, Mass.

Since J. Stevens Arms is a division of Savage Industries, the "Stevens" brand name is used for some rifles by Savage; see separate Savage-Stevens listings under Savage.

Stevens No. 12 Marksman Single Shot Rifle **$145**
Lever action, tip-up. Takedown. Calibers: 22 LR, 25 R.F., 32 R.F. 22-inch barrel. Plain straight-grip stock, small tapered forearm.

Stevens No. 14 1/2 Little Scout Single Shot Rifle **$150**
Rolling block. Takedown. Caliber: 22 LR. 18- or 20-inch barrel. Weight: about 2 3/4 pounds. Sights: open rear; blade front. Plain straight-grip stock, small tapered forearm.

Stevens Youth's Model 15Y

Stevens No. 44 Ideal

Stevens Ideal Schuetzen

Stevens No. 70 Visible Loading

Stevens Model 87

RIFLES

Stevens Model 15 . . . . **$130**
Same as Stevens-Springfield Model 15, except has 24-inch barrel, weighs about 5 pounds, has redesigned stock. Made 1948–1965.

Stevens Model 15Y Youth's Rifle **$125**
Same as Model 15, except has 21-inch barrel, short butt-stock, weighs about 4³/₄ pounds. Made 1958–1965.

Stevens No. 44 Ideal Single Shot Rifle **$650**
Rolling block. Lever action. Takedown. Calibers: 22 LR, 25 R.F., 32 R.F., 25-20 S.S., 32-20, 32-40, 38-40, 38-55, 44-40. Barrel lengths: 24-inch, 26-inch (round, half-octagon, full-octagon). Weight: about 7 pounds with 26-inch round bbl. Sights: open rear; Rocky Mountain front. Plain straight-grip stock and forearm. Made 1894–1932.

Stevens No. 44¹/₂ Ideal Single Shot Rifle **$725**
Falling-block lever action. Aside from the new design action introduced in 1903, the specifications of this model are the same as those of Model 44. Model 44¹/₂ discontinued about 1916.

Stevens Nos. 45 to 54 Ideal Single Shot Rifles
These are the higher grade models, differing from the standard No. 44 and No. 44¹/₂ chiefly in finish, engraving, set triggers, levers, barrels, stocks, etc. The Schuetzen types (including the "Stevens-Pope" models) are in this series. Model Nos. 45 to 54 were introduced about 1896

Stevens Nos. 45 to 54 Ideal Single Shot Rifles (cont.)
and originally had the No. 44-type rolling-block action, which was superseded in 1903 by the No. 44¹/₂-type falling-block action. These models were all discontinued about 1916. Generally speaking the 45-54 series rifles, particularly the "Stevens-Pope" and higher grade Schuetzen models, are collector's items, bringing much higher prices than the ordinary No. 44 and 44¹/₂.

Stevens No. 66 Bolt Action Repeating Rifle **$110**
Takedown. Caliber: 22 Short, Long, LR. Tubular magazine holds 13 LR, 15 Long, 19 Short. 24-inch barrel. Weight: about 5 pounds. Sights: open rear; bead front. Plain pistol-grip stock w/grooved forearm. Made 1931–35.

Stevens No. 70 Visible Loading Slide Action
Repeating Rifle **$210**
Exposed hammer. Caliber: 22 LR, Long, Short. Tubular magazine holds 11 LR, 13 Long, 15 Short. 22-inch barrel. Weight: about 4¹/₂ pounds. Sights: open rear; bead front. Plain straight-grip stock, grooved slide handle. Made 1907–1934. *Note:* Nos. 70¹/₂, 71, 71¹/₂, 72, 72¹/₂ are essentially the same as No. 70, differing chiefly in barrel length or sight equipment.

Stevens Model 87 Autoloading Rifle **$150**
Takedown. Caliber: 22 LR. 15-shot tubular magazine. 24-inch barrel (20-inch on current model). Weight: about 6 pounds. Sights: open rear; bead front. Pistol-grip stock. Made 1938 to date. *Note:* This model originally bore the "Springfield" brand name, discontinued in 1948.

Stevens No. 414 Armory Model

Stevens Model 416

Stevens No. 419

Stevens Buckhorn Model 053

Stevens Model 322 Hi-Power Bolt Action Carbine **$225**
Caliber: 22 Hornet. 4-shot detachable box magazine. 21-inch barrel. Weight: about 6¾ pounds. Sights: open rear; ramp front. Pistol-grip stock. Made 1947–1950. (See Savage Models 340, 342.)

Stevens Model 322-S **$275**
Same as Model 325, except has peep rear sight. (See Savage Models 340S, 342S.)

Stevens Model 325 Hi-Power Bolt Action Carbine **$215**
Caliber: 30-30. 3-shot detachable box magazine. 21-inch barrel. Weight: about 6¾ pounds. Sights: open rear; bead front. Plain pistol-grip stock. Made 1947–1950. (See Savage Model 340.)

Stevens Model 325-S **$260**
Same as Model 325, except has peep rear sight. (See Savage Model 340S.)

Stevens No. 414 Armory Model Single Shot Rifle **$425**
No. 44-type lever action. Calibers: 22 LR only, 22 Short only. 26-inch barrel. Weight: about 8 pounds. Sights: Lyman receiver peep; blade front. Plain straight-grip stock, military-type forearm, swivels. Made 1912–1932.

Stevens Model 416 Bolt Action Target Rifle **$200**
Caliber: 22 LR. 5-shot detachable box magazine. 26-inch heavy barrel. Weight: about 9½ pounds. Sights: receiver peep; hooded front. Target stock, swivels, sling. Made 1937–1949.

Stevens No. 419 Junior Target Model Bolt Action Single Shot Rifle **$235**
Takedown. Caliber: 22 LR. 26-inch barrel. Weight: about 5½ pounds. Sights: Lyman No. 55 rear peep; blade front. Plain junior target stock w/pistol grip and grooved forearm, swivels, sling. Made 1932–36.

Stevens Buckhorn Model 053 Bolt Action Single Shot Rifle **$105**
Takedown. Calibers: 22 Short, Long, LR, 22 WMR. 25 Stevens R.F. 24-inch barrel. Weight: about 5½ pounds. Sights: receiver peep; open middle; hooded front. Sporting stock w/pistol grip and black forend tip. Made 1935–1948.

Stevens Buckhorn Model 53 . . . . **$125**
Same as Buckhorn Model 053, except has open rear sight and plain bead front sight.

Stevens Buckhorn Model 056 Bolt Action Repeating Rifle **$130**
Takedown. Caliber: 22 LR, Long, Short. 5-shot detachable box magazine. 24-inch barrel. Weight: about 6 pounds. Sights: receiver peep; open middle; hooded front. Sporting stock w/pistol grip and black forend tip. Made 1935–1948.

Stevens Buckhorn Model 56 . . . . **$115**
Same as Buckhorn Model 056, except has open rear sight
and plain bead front sight.

Stevens Buckhorn No. 057 . . . . **$110**
Same as Buckhorn Model 076, except has 5-shot detachable box magazine. Made 1939–1948.

Stevens Buckhorn No. 57 . . . . **$120**
Same as Buckhorn Model 76, except has 5-shot detachable
box magazine. Made 1939–1948.

**Stevens Buckhorn Model 066 Bolt Action
Repeating Rifle** **$150**
Takedown. Caliber: 22 LR, Long, Short. Tubular magazine
holds 21 Short, 17 Long, 15 LR. 24-inch barrel. Weight:
about 6 pounds. Sights: receiver peep; open middle; hooded
front. Sporting stock w/pistol grip and black forend tip.
Made 1935–1948.

Stevens Buckhorn Model 66 . . . . **$110**
Same as Buckhorn Model 066, except has open rear sight,
plain bead front sight.

Stevens Buckhorn No. 076 Autoloading Rifle . . . **$150**
Takedown. Caliber: 22 LR. 15-shot tubular magazine. 24-
inch barrel. Weight: about 6 pounds. Sights: receiver peep;
open middle; hooded front. Sporting stock w/pistol grip,
black forend tip. Made 1938–1948.

Stevens Buckhorn No. 76 . . . . **$145**
Same as Buckhorn No. 076, except has open rear sight,
plain bead front sight.

Stevens Crack Shot No. 26 Single Shot Rifle . . . **$140**
Lever action. Takedown. Calibers: 22 LR, 32 R.F. 18-inch
or 22-inch barrel. Weight: about $3\frac{1}{4}$ pounds. Sights: open
rear; blade front. Plain straight-grip stock, small tapered
forearm. Made 1913–1939.

Stevens Crack Shot No. 26½ **$175**
Same as Crack Shot No. 26, except has smoothbore barrel
for shot cartridges.

Stevens Favorite No. 17 Single Shot Rifle **$165**
Lever action. Takedown. Calibers: 22 LR, 25 R.F., 32 R.F.
24-inch round barrel, other lengths were available. Weight:
about $4\frac{1}{2}$ pounds. Sights: open rear; Rocky Mountain
front. Plain straight-grip stock, small tapered forearm.
Made 1894–1935.

Stevens Favorite No. 18 . . . . **$245**
Same as Favorite No. 17 except has Vernier peep rear
sight, leaf middle sight, Beach combination front sight.

Stevens Favorite No. 19 . . . . **$265**
Same as Favorite No. 17 except has Lyman combination
rear sight, leaf sight, Lyman front sight.

RIFLES

Stevens Buckhorn Model 066

Stevens Buckhorn Model 66

Stevens Buckhorn No. 076

Stevens Crack Shot No. 26

Stevens Favorite No. 17

Stevens Walnut Hill No. 417-1

Stevens Walnut Hill No. 417½

Stevens Walnut Hill No. 418

Stevens-Springfield Model 15

Stevens-Springfield Model 82

Stevens Favorite No. 20 .... **$175**
Same as Favorite No. 17, except has smoothbore barrel
for 22 R.F. and 32 R.F. shot cartridges.

Stevens Favorite No. 27 .... **$195**
Same as Favorite No. 17, except has octagon barrel.

Stevens Favorite No. 28 .... **$240**
Same as Favorite No. 18, except has octagon barrel.

Stevens Favorite No. 29 .... **$250**
Same as Favorite No. 19, except has octagon barrel.

**Stevens Walnut Hill No. 417-0 Single Shot
Target Rifle** **$625**
Lever action. Calibers: 22 LR only, 22 Short only, 22
Hornet. 28-inch heavy barrel (extra heavy 29-inch barrel
also available). Weight: about 10½ pounds. Sights: Lyman
52L extension rear; 17A front, scope bases. Target stock
with full pistol grip, beavertail forearm, barrel band,
swivels, sling. Made 1932–1947.

Stevens Walnut Hill No. 417-1 .... **$640**
Same as No. 417-0, except has Lyman 48L receiver sight.

Stevens Walnut Hill No. 417-2 .... **$765**
Same as No. 417-0, except has Lyman No. 144 tang sight.

Stevens Walnut Hill No. 417-3 .... **$620**
Same as No. 417-0, except w/o sights.

**Stevens Walnut Hill No. 417½ Single
Shot Rifle** **$675**
Lever action. Calibers: 22 LR, 22 WMR, 25 R.F., 22
Hornet. 28-inch barrel. Weight: about 8½ pounds. Sights:
Lyman No. 144 tang peep; folding middle; bead front.
Sporting stock w/pistol grip, semibeavertail forearm,
swivels, sling. Made 1932–1940.

Stevens Walnut Hill No. 418 Single Shot Rifle ... **$395**
Lever action. Takedown. Calibers: 22 LR only, 22 Short
only. 26-inch barrel. Weight: about 6½ pounds. Sights:
Lyman No. 144 tang peep; blade front. Pistol-grip stock,
semibeavertail forearm, swivels, sling. Made 1932–1940.

Stevens Walnut Hill No. 418½ **$475**
Same as No. 418, except also available in calibers 22 WMR
and 25 Stevens R.F., has Lyman No. 2A tang peep sight,
bead front sight.

**Stevens-Springfield Model 15 Single Shot Bolt
Action Rifle** **$115**
Takedown. Caliber: 22 LR, Long, Short. 22-inch barrel.
Weight: about 4 pounds. Sights: open rear; bead front.
Plain pistol-grip stock. Made 1937–1948.

**Stevens-Springfield Model 82 Bolt Action
Single Shot Rifle** **$110**
Takedown. Caliber: 22 LR, Long, Short. 22-inch barrel.
Weight: 4 pounds. Sights: open rear; gold bead front. Plain
pistol-grip stock w/grooved forearm. Made 1935–39.

RIFLES

Stevens-Springfield Model 83

Stevens-Springfield Model 84

Stevens-Springfield Model 85

Stevens-Springfield Model 86-S

**Stevens-Springfield Model 83 Bolt Action
Single Shot Rifle** **$110**
Takedown. Calibers: 22 LR, Long, Short; 22 WMR, 25
Stevens R.F. 24-inch barrel. Weight: about 4½ pounds.
Sights: peep rear; open middle; hooded front. Plain pistol-
grip stock with grooved forearm. Made 1935–39.

Stevens-Springfield Model 84 . . . . **$130**
Same as Model 86, except has 5-shot detachable box mag-
azine. Pre-1948 rifles of this model were designated
Springfield Model 84, later known as Stevens Model 84.
Made 1940–1965.

Stevens-Springfield Model 84-S (084) **$135**
Same as Model 84, except has peep rear sight and hooded
front sight. Pre-1948 rifles of this model were designated
Springfield Model 084, later known as Stevens Model
84-S. Discontinued.

Stevens-Springfield Model 85 . . . . **$165**
Same as Stevens Model 87, except has 5-shot detachable
box magazine. Made 1939 to date. Pre-1948 rifles of this
model were designated Springfield Model 85, currently
known as Stevens Model 85.

Stevens-Springfield Model 85-S (085) **$150**
Same as Model 85, except has peep rear sight and hooded
front sight. Pre-1948 models were designated Springfield
Model 085, now known as Stevens Model 85-S.

**Stevens-Springfield Model 86 Bolt Action
Repeater** **$110**
Takedown. Caliber: 22 LR, Long, Short. Tubular magazine
holds 15 LR, 17 Long, 21 Short. 24-inch barrel. Weight:
about 6 pounds. Sights: open rear; gold bead front. Pistol-
grip stock, black forend tip on later production. Made
1935–1965. *Note:* The "Springfield" brand name was
discontinued in 1948.

Stevens-Springfield Model 86-S (086) **$125**
Same as Model 86, except has peep rear sight and hooded
front sight. Pre-1948 rifles of this model were designated
as Springfield Model 086, later known as Stevens Model
86-S. Discontinued.

Stevens-Springfield Model 87-S (087) **$145**
Same as Stevens Model 87, except has peep rear sight and
hooded front sight. Pre-1948 rifles of this model were designated as Springfield Model 087, later known as Stevens
Model 87-S. Discontinued.

═══ **STEYR-DAIMLER-PUCH A.-G.** ═══
Steyr, Austria
See also listings under Mannlicher.

Steyr AUG-SA Semiautomatic Rifle **$3500**
Gas-operated. Caliber: 223 Rem. (5.56mm). 30- or 40-shot
magazine. 20-inch barrel standard; optional 16-inch or
24-inch heavy barrel w/folding bipod. 31 inches overall.
Weight: 8½ pounds. Sights: Integral 1.5X scope and
mount. Green high-impact synthetic stock with folding
vertical grip.

Steyr Small Bore Carbine

Steyr Small Bore Carbine **$425**
Bolt-action repeater. Caliber: 22 LR. 5-shot detachable
box magazine. 19½-inch barrel. Sights: leaf rear; hooded
bead front. Mannlicher-type stock, checkered, swivels.
Made 1953–1967.

STOEGER RIFLE
**Mfd. by Franz Jaeger & Co., Suhl, Germany; dist.
in the U.S. by A. F. Stoeger, Inc., New York, N.Y.**

Stoeger Hornet Rifle **$1500**
Same as Herold Rifle. See listing of that rifle for specifications. Imported during the 1930s.

Thompson/Center Contender Carbine

Thompson/Center TCR '83
Single Shot Rifle

Thompson/Center TCR '87 Hunter

THOMPSON/CENTER ARMS
Rochester, New Hampshire

Thompson/Center Contender Carbine
Calibers: 22 LR, 22 Hornet, 222 Rem., 223 Rem., 7mm
T.C.U., 7×30 Waters, 30-30 Win., 35 Rem., 44 Mag., 357
Rem. Max. and .410 bore. 21-inch interchangeable barrels.
35 inches overall. Adjustable iron sights. Checkered
American walnut or Rynite stock and forend. Made 1985
to date.

Standard Model (rifle calibers)	**$345**
Standard Model (.410 bore)	360
Rynite Stock Model (rifle calibers)	315
Rynite Stock Model (.410 bore)	335
Extra Barrels (rifle calibers)	155
Extra Barrels (.410 bore)	175
Youth Model standard calibers, 16¼″ bbl.	300
Youth Model 45/410 Bore	320

**Thompson/Center Contender Carbine Survival
System** **$475**
Similar to the standard Contender Carbine with Rynite

Thompson/Center Contender Carbine Survival (cont.)
stock and forend. Comes with two 16¼-inch barrels
chambered in 223 and 45/.410 bore. Camo Cordura case.

Thompson/Center Stainless Contender Carbine
Same as the standard Contender Carbine Model, except
stainless steel with blued sights. Calibers: 22 LR, 22 Hornet, 223 Rem., 7-30 Waters, 30-30 Win., .410 Ga. Walnut
or Rynite stock and forend. Made 1993 to date.

Walnut Stock Model	**$415**
Rynite Stock Model	390
Youth Stock Model	375

Thompson/Center TCR '83 Single Shot Rifle
Break frame, overlever action. Calibers: 223 Rem., 22/250
Rem., 243 Win., 7mm Rem. Mag., 30-06 Springfield. Interchangeable barrels: 23 inches in length. Weight: 6
pounds, 14 oz. American walnut stock and forearm,
checkered, black rubber recoil pad, cheekpiece. Made
1983–87.

TCR '83 Standard Model	**$295**
TCR '83 Aristocrat	350

Thompson/Center TCR '87 Hunter Rifle
Similar to TCR '83, except in calibers 22 Hornet, 222
Rem., 223 Rem., 22-250 Rem., 243 Win., 270 Win.,

Thompson/Center TCR '87 Hunter Rifle (cont.)
7mm-08, 308 Win., 30-06, 32-40 Win. Also 12-ga. slug and 10- and 12-ga. field barrels. 23-inch standard or 25⅞-inch heavy barrel interchangeable. 39½ to 43⅜ inches overall. Weight: 6 lbs. 14 oz. to 7½ lbs. Iron sights optional. Checkered American black walnut buttstock w/fluted forend. Discontinued 1993.

Standard Model **$375**
Extra Bbl. (rifle calibers and 10- or 12-ga. Field) . **190**
Extra Barrel (12-ga. slug) **205**

=== **TIKKA RIFLES** ===
Produced in Italy by Armi Marocchi
Imported by Stoeger Industries, Inc.

Tikka Model 412S Double Rifle $1025
Formerly Valmet. Caliber: 9.3×74R. 24-inch barrel. 40 inches overall. Weight: 8½ pounds. European walnut stock. Automatic ejectors. Manufactured in Italy from 1990 to date.

Tikka LSA55 Deluxe $365
Same as LSA55 Standard, except has rollover cheekpiece, rosewood grip cap and forend tip, skip checkering, high-luster blue. Made 1965–1988.

Tikka LSA55 Sporter $395
Same as LSA55, except not available in 6mm Rem., has 22.8-inch heavy barrel, no sights, special stock with beavertail forearm, weighs about 9 pounds. Made 1965–1988.

Tikka LSA55 Standard Bolt Action Repeater . . . $350
Mauser-type action. Calibers: 222 Rem., 22-250, 6mm Rem. Mag., 243 Win., 308 Win. 3-shot clip magazine. 22.8-inch barrel. Weight: 6.8 pounds. Sights: folding leaf rear; hooded ramp front. Checkered walnut stock w/Monte Carlo cheekpiece, swivels. Made 1965–1988.

Tikka LSA65 Deluxe $380
Same as LSA65 Standard, except has special features of LSA55 Deluxe. Made 1970–1988.

Tikka LSA65 Standard $330
Same as LSA55 Standard, except calibers: 25-06, 6.5×55, 270 Win., 30-06. 5-shot magazine, 22-inch barrel, weighs 7½ pounds. Made 1970–1988.

Tikka Model M 55
Bolt action. Calibers: 222 Rem., 22-250 Rem., 223 Rem., 243 Win., 308 Win. (6mm Rem. and 17 Rem. available in Standard and Deluxe models only). 23.2-inch barrel (24.8-inch in Sporter and Heavy Barrel models). 42.8 inches

RIFLES

Tikka Model 412S Double Rifle

Tikka LSA55 Deluxe

Tikka LSA65 Deluxe

Tikka Model M 55 Deluxe

Tikka Model M 55 Standard

Tikka Model M 65 Sporter

Tikka Continental/Varmint

Tikka New Generation

Tikka Premium Grade Rifle

Tikka Model M 55 (cont.)

overall (44 inches in Sporter and Heavy Barrel models). Weight: 7¼ to 9 pounds. Monte Carlo-style stock with pistol grip. Sling swivels.

Continental	$495
Deluxe Model	500
Sporter	475
Sporter with sights	495
Standard	450
Super Sporter	540
Super Sporter with sights	575
Trapper	465

Tikka Model M 65

Bolt action. Calibers: 25-06, 270 Win., 308 Win., 30-06, 7mm Rem. Mag., 300 Win. Mag. (Sporter and Heavy Barrel models in 270 Win., 308 Win. and 30-06 only). 22.4-inch barrel (24.8-inch in Sporter and Heavy Barrel models). 43.2 inches overall (44 inches in Sporter, 44.8 inches in Heavy Barrel). Weight: 7½ to 9.9 pounds. Monte Carlo-style stock with pistol grip. Discontinued 1989.

Continental	$530
Deluxe Magnum	540
Deluxe Model	495
Magnum	490
Sporter	490
Sporter with sights	525

Tikka Model M 65 (cont.)

Standard	$460
Super Sporter	575
Super Sporter with sights	595
Super Sporter Master	730

Tikka Model M 65 Wildboar **$530**

Same general specifications as Model M 65, except 20.8-inch barrel, overall length of 41.6 inches and weight of 7½ pounds. Discontinued 1989.

Tikka Continental **$695**

Calibers: 223 Rem., 22-250 Rem., 243 Win., 308 Win. Overall length: 43¾ inches. Weight 8½ pounds. Prone-type stock and extra wide forend for varmint or target shooting. Made 1991 to date.

Tikka New Generation **$565**

Bolt action. Calibers: 223 Rem., 22-250 Rem., 243 Win., 270 Win., 308 Win., 30-06, 7mm Rem. Mag., 300 Win. Mag., and 338 Win. Mag. 3- and 5-round magazines. 22-inch barrel; 24 inches in Magnum. Weight: 7 lbs. 2 oz. Checkered walnut stock. Oversized trigger guard. Made 1989 to date.

Tikka Premium Grade **$625**

Bolt action. Calibers: 223 Rem., 22-250 Rem., 243 Win., 270 Win., 308 Win., 30-06, 7mm Rem. Mag., 300 Win. Mag. and 338 Win. Mag. 3- and 5-round magazine. Hand-

Tikka Whitetail/Battue

Tikka Premium Grade (cont.)
checkered with matte lacquer stock and rollover cheek-piece. Rosewood pistol-grip cap and forend tip. Deep blued barrel. Made 1990 to date.

Tikka Whitetail Battue **$565**
Calibers: 308 Win., 270 Win., 30-06, 7mm Mag., 300 Win. Mag., 338 Win. Mag. 20½-inch barrel. 40½ inches overall. Weight: 7 pounds. Sights: wide V-shaped rear; hooded front. Optional 3-round detachable magazine. Matte lacquer stock. Made 1991 to date.

Ultra-Hi Model 2200

=== **ULTRA-HI PRODUCTS COMPANY** ===
Hawthorne, New Jersey

Ultra-Hi Model 2200 Single Shot Bolt Action Rifle **$100**
Caliber: 22 LR, Long, Short. 23-inch barrel. Weight: about 5 pounds. Sights: open rear; blade front. Monte Carlo stock w/pistol grip. Made in Japan. Introduced 1977; disc.

Ultra Light Arms Model 20 Series

=== **ULTRA LIGHT ARMS COMPANY** ===
Granville, West Virginia

Ultra Light Arms Model 20 Bolt Action Rifle
Calibers: 22-250 Rem., 243 Win., 6mm Rem., 250-3000 Savage, 257 Roberts, 257 Ack., 7mm Mauser, 7mm Ack., 7mm-08 Rem., 284 Win., 300 Savage, 308 Win., 358 Win. Box magazine. 22-inch ultra light barrel. Weight: 4¾ pounds. No sights. Synthetic stock of Kevlar or graphite finished seven different colors. Nonglare matte or bright metal finish. Medium-length action available left-hand models.
Standard Model **$1550**
Left-hand Model **1625**

Ultra Light Arms Model 20S Bolt Action Rifle
Same general specifications as the Model 20, except w/ short action in calibers 17 Rem., 222 Rem., 223 Rem., 22 Hornet only.
Standard Model **$1595**
Left-hand Model **1695**

Ultra Light Arms Model 24 Bolt Action Rifle
Same general specifications as the Model 20, except w/ long action in calibers 25-06, 270 Win., 30-06 and 7mm Express only.
Standard Model **$1625**
Left-hand Model **1700**

Ultra Light Arms Model 28 Bolt Action Rifle . . . **$1850**
Same general specifications as the Model 20, except w/ long Magnum action in calibers 264 Win. Mag., 7mm Rem. Mag., 300 Win. Mag., 338 Win. Mag. only. Offered w/ recoil arrestor. Left-hand model available.

Unique T66 Match

=== **UNIQUE RIFLE** ===
Hendaye, France
Mfd. by Manufacture d'Armes des Pyrénées Francaises

Unique T66 Match Rifle **$415**
Single-shot bolt action. Caliber: 22 LR. 25½-inch barrel. Weight: about 10½ pounds. Sights: micrometer aperture rear; globe front. French walnut target stock w/Monte Carlo comb, bull pistol grip, wide and deep forearm, stippled grip surfaces, adj. swivel on accessory track, adj. rubber buttplate. Made 1966 to date.

U.S. Model 1898 Krag Rifle

U.S. Model 1903 Springfield

U.S. Model 1903 Springfield Sporter

U.S. MILITARY RIFLES

Mfd. by Springfield Armory, Remington Arms Co., Winchester Repeating Arms Co., Inland Mfg. Div. of G.M.C., and other contractors. See notes.

Unless otherwise indicated, the following U.S. Military rifles were mfd. at Springfield Armory, Springfield, Mass.

U.S. Model 1898 Krag-Jorgensen Carbine **$475**
Same general specifications as Model 1898 Rifle, except has 22-inch barrel, weighs about 8 pounds, carbine-type stock. *Note:* The foregoing specifications apply, in general, to Carbine Models 1896 and 1899, which differed from Model 1898 only in minor details.

U.S. Model 1898 Krag-Jorgensen Military Rifle .. **$325**
Bolt action. Caliber: 30-40 Krag. 5-shot hinged box magazine. 30-inch barrel. Weight: about 9 pounds. Sights: adj. rear; blade front. Military-type stock, straight grip. *Note:* The foregoing specifications apply, in general, to Rifle Models 1892 and 1896, which differed from Model 1898 only in minor details. Made 1894–1904.

U.S. Model 1903 Mark I Springfield **$325**
Same as Standard Model 1903, except altered to permit use of the Pedersen Device. This device, officially designated "U.S. Automatic Pistol Model 1918," converted the M/1903 to a semiautomatic weapon firing a 30 caliber cartridge similar to the 32 automatic pistol ammunition. Mark I rifles have a slot milled in the left side of the receiver to serve as an ejection port when the Pedersen Device was in use; these rifles were also fitted with a special sear and cut-off. Some 65,000 of these devices were manufactured and presumably a like number of M/1903 rifles converted to handle them. During the early 1930s all Pedersen Devices were ordered destroyed and the Mark I rifles were reconverted by replacement of the special sear and cut-off with standard components. Some 20-odd specimens are known to have escaped destruction and are in government museums and private collections. Probably more are extant. Rarely is a Pedersen Device offered for sale, so a current value cannot be assigned. However, many of

U.S. Model 1903 Mark I Springfield (cont.)
the altered rifles were bought by members of the National Rifle Association through the Director of Civilian Marksmanship. Value shown is for the Mark I rifle without the Pedersen Device.

U.S. Model 1903 National Match Springfield **$995**
Same general specifications as the Standard Model 1903, except specially selected with star-gauged barrel, Type C pistol-grip stock, polished bolt assembly; early types have headless firing pin assembly and reversed safety lock. Produced especially for target shooting.

U.S. Model 1903 Springfield Military Rifle
Modified Mauser-type bolt action. Caliber: 30-06. 5-shot box magazine. 23.79-inch barrel. Weight: about 8¾ pounds. Sights: adj. rear; blade front. Military-type stock, straight grip. *Note:* M/1903 rifles of Springfield manufacture with serial numbers under 800,000 (1903–1918) have casehardened receivers; those between 800,000 and 1,275,767 (1918–1927) were double-heat-treated; rifles numbered over 1,275,767 have nickel-steel bolts and receivers. Rock Island production from No. 1 to 285,507 have casehardened receivers. Improved heat treatment was adopted in May 1918 with No. 285,207; about three months later with No. 319,921 the use of nickel steel was begun, but the production of some double-heat-treated carbon-steel receivers and bolts continued. Made 1903–1930 at Springfield Armory; during WWI, M/1903 rifles were also made at Rock Island Arsenal, Rock Island, Ill.
W/casehardened receiver **$185**
W/double-heat-treated receiver **225**
W/nickel steel receiver **350**

U.S. Model 1903 Springfield Sporter **$950**
Same general specifications as the National Match, except has sporting design stock, Lyman No. 48 receiver sight.

U.S. Model 1903 Style T Springfield Match Rifle **$995**
Same specifications as the Springfield Sporter, except has heavy barrel (26-, 28- or 30-inch), scope bases, globe front sight, weighs about 12½ pounds with 26-inch barrel.

U.S. Model 1903 Type A Springfield Free Rifle **$1250**
Same as Style T, except made with 28-inch barrel only, has Swiss buttplate, weighs about 13¼ pounds.

U.S. Model 1903-A1 Springfield

U.S. Model 1903-A3 Springfield

U.S. Rifle Cal. 30 M1 (Garand)

U.S. Model 1917 Enfield

RIFLES

U.S. Model 1903 Type B Springfield Free Rifle $1495
Same as Type A, except has cheekpiece stock, palmrest, Woodie double-set triggers, Garand fast firing pin, weighs about 14³/₄ pounds.

U.S. Model 1903-A1 Springfield
Same general specifications as Model 1903, except may have Type C pistol-grip stock adopted in 1930. The last Springfields produced at the Springfield Armory were of this type, final serial number was 1,532,878 made in 1939. *Note:* Late in 1941, the Remington Arms Co., Ilion, N.Y., began production under government contract of Springfield rifles of this type with a few minor modifications. These rifles are numbered 3,000,001–3,348,085 and were manufactured before the adoption of Model 1903-A3.
Springfield manufacture **$295**
Remington manufacture **250**

U.S. Model 1903-A3 Springfield $325
Same general specifications as Model 1903-A1, except modified to permit increased production and lower cost; may have either straight-grip or pistol-grip stock, bolt is not interchangeable with earlier types, has receiver peep sight, many parts are stamped sheet steel, including the trigger guard and magazine assembly. Quality of these rifles, lower than that of other 1903 Springfields, reflects the emergency conditions under which they were produced. Mfd. during WWII by Remington Arms Co. and L. C. Smith Corona Typewriters, Inc.

U.S. Model 1922-M1 22 Springfield Target Rifle $625
Modified Model 1903. Caliber: 22 LR. 5-shot detachable box magazine. 24¹/₂-inch barrel. Weight: about 9 pounds. Sights: Lyman No. 48C receiver; blade front. Sporting-type stock similar to that of the Model 1903 Springfield Sporter. Issued 1927. *Note:* The earlier Model 1922, which is seldom encountered, differs from the foregoing chiefly in the bolt mechanism and magazine.

U.S. M2 22 Springfield Target Rifle $725
Same general specifications as Model 1922-MI, except has speedlock, improved bolt assembly adjustable for headspace. *Note:* These improvements were later incorporated in many rifles of the preceding models (M1922, M1922MI) and arms so converted were marked "M1922M2" or "M1922MII."

U.S. Rifle, Caliber 30, M1 (Garand) Mil. Rifle $695
Clip-fed, gas-operated, air-cooled semiautomatic. Uses a clip containing 8 rounds. 24-inch barrel. Weight: without bayonet, 9¹/₂ pounds. Sights: adj. peep rear; blade front w/guards. Pistol-grip stock, handguards. Made 1937–1957. *Note:* Garand rifles have also been produced by Winchester Repeating Arms Co., Harrington & Richardson Arms Co., and International Harvester Co. Deduct 25% for arsenal-assembled mismatches.

U.S. Rifle, Caliber 30, M1, National Match $1100
Accurized target version of the Garand. Glass-bedded stock; match grade barrel, sights, gas cylinder. "NM" stamped on barrel forward of handguard.

> **NOTE:** The U.S. Model 1917 Enfield was mfd. 1917–18 by Remington Arms Co. of Delaware (later Midvale Steel & Ordnance Co.), Eddystone, PA; Remington Arms Co., Ilion, NY; Winchester Repeating Arms Co., New Haven, CT.

U.S. Model 1917 Enfield Military Rifle $275
Modified Mauser-type bolt action. Caliber: 30-06. 5-shot box magazine. 26-inch barrel. Weight: about 9¹/₄ pounds. Sights: adj. rear; blade front w/guards. Military-type stock w/semi-pistol grip. This design originated in Great Britain as their "Pattern '14" and was mfd. in caliber 303 for the British Government in three U.S. plants. In 1917, the U.S. Government contracted with these firms to produce the same rifle in caliber 30-06; over two million of these Model 1917 Enfields were mfd. While no more were produced after WWI, the U.S. supplied over a million of them to Great Britain during WWII.

U.S. Carbine Cal. 30 M1

U.S. Carbine, Caliber 30, M1 .... $495

Gas-operated (short-stroke piston), semiautomatic. 15- or 30-round detachable box magazine. 18-inch barrel. Weight: about 5½ pounds. Sights: adj. rear; blade front sight w/guards. Pistol-grip stock w/handguard, side-mounted web sling. Made 1942–45. In 1963, 150,000 surplus M1 Carbines were sold at $20 each to members of the National Rifle Assn. by the Dept. of the Army. *Note:* For Winchester and Rock-Ola, add 30%; for Irwin Pedersen, add 80%. Quality Hardware did not complete its production run. Guns produced by other manufacturers were marked "Unquality" & command premium prices.

> **NOTE:** The WWII-vintage 30-caliber U.S. Carbine was mfd. by Inland Mfg. Div. of G.M.C., Dayton, OH; Winchester Repeating Arms Co., New Haven, CT; and other contractors: International Business Machines Corp., Poughkeepsie, NY; National Postal Meter Co., Rochester, NY; Quality Hardware & Machine Co., and Rock-Ola Co., Chicago, IL; Saginaw Steering Gear Div. of G.M.C., Saginaw, MI; Standard Products Co., Port Clinton, OH; Underwood-Elliott-Fisher Co., Hartford, CT.

U.S. REPEATING ARMS CO.
See Winchester Rifle listings.

Universal Deluxe Carbine

Universal Standard M-1 Carbine

Universal Deluxe Carbine $195

Same as standard model, except also available in caliber 256, has deluxe walnut Monte Carlo stock and handguard. Made 1965 to date.

Universal Standard M-1 Carbine $180

Same as U.S. Carbine, Cal. 30, M1, except may have either wood or metal handguard, barrel band with or w/o bayonet lug; 5-shot magazine standard. Made 1964 to date.

UNIVERSAL SPORTING GOODS, INC.
Miami, Florida

Valmet M-62S

Valmet M-71S $750

Same specifications as M-62S, except caliber 5.56mm×45 (223 Rem.), has open rear sight, reinforced resin or wood stock, weighs 7¾ pounds with former. Made 1971 to date.

Valmet M-76 Semiautomatic Rifle

Semiautomatic assault rifle. Gas-operated, rotating bolt action. Caliber: 223 Rem. 15- and 30-shot magazines. Made 1984 to date.

Wooden stock $750
Folding stock 795

Valmet M-78 Semiautomatic Rifle $995

Caliber: 7.62×51 (NATO). 24⅛-inch barrel. Overall length: 43⅛ inches. Weight: 10½ pounds.

VALMET OY
Jyväskylä, Finland

Valmet M-62S Semiautomatic Rifle $895

Semiautomatic version of Finnish M-62 automatic assault rifle based on Russian AK-47. Gas-operated rotating-bolt action. Caliber: 7.62mm × 39 Russian. 15- and 30-round magazines. 16⅝-inch barrel. Weight: about 8 pounds w/ metal stock. Sights: tangent aperture rear; hooded blade front w/luminous flip-up post for low-light use. Tubular steel or wood stock. Introduced 1962, discontinued.

Valmet Model 412 S

Valmet M-82 Semiautomatic Carbine $750
Caliber: 223 Rem. 15- or 30-shot magazine. 17-inch barrel.
27 inches overall. Weight: 7¾ pounds.

Valmet Model 412 S Double Rifle $795
Boxlock. Manual or automatic extraction. Calibers: 243,
308, 30-06, 375 Win., 9.3×74R. Barrels: 24-inch over/un-

Valmet Model 412 S Double Rifle (cont.)
der. Weight: 8⅝ pounds. American walnut checkered
stock and forend.

Valmet Hunter Semiautomatic Rifle $795
Similar to the M-78, except in calibers 223 Rem. (5.56mm),
243 Win., 308 Win. (7.62 NATO) and 30-06. 5-, 9- or 15-
shot magazine. 20½-inch plain barrel. 42 inches overall.
Weight: 8 pounds. Sights: adj. 412 combination scope
mount/rear; blade front, mounted on gas tube. Checkered
European walnut buttstock and extended checkered forend and handguard. Imported since 1986.

Vickers Empire Model

Vickers Jubilee Model

RIFLES

=== **VOERE, VOELTER & COMPANY** ===
Vaehrenbach, Germany

Mauser-Werke acquired Voere in 1987 and all models are
now marketed under new designations.

Voere Model 1007 Biathlon Repeater $245
Caliber: 22 LR. 5-shot magazine. 19½-inch barrel. 39
inches overall. Weight: 5½ pounds. Sights: adj. rear; blade
front. Plain beechwood stock. Imported 1984–86.

Voere Model 1013 Bolt Action Repeater $425
Same as Model 1007, except with military-style stock in
22 WMR caliber. Double-set triggers optional. Imported
1984–86 by KDF, Inc.

Voere Model 2107 Bolt Action Repeater
Caliber: 22 LR. 5 or 8-shot magazine. 19½-inch barrel.
41 inches overall. Weight: 6 pounds. Sights: adj. rear sight,
hooded front. European hardwood Monte Carlo-style
stock. Imported 1986 by KDF, Inc.
Standard Model $175
Deluxe Model 200

=== **VICKERS LTD.** ===
Crayford, Kent, England

Vickers Empire Model $320
Similar to Jubilee Model, except has 27- or 30-inch barrel,
straight-grip stock, weighs about 9¼ pounds with 30-inch
barrel. Made before WWII.

Vickers Jubilee Model Single Shot Target Rifle . $395
Round-receiver Martini-type action. Caliber: 22 LR. 28-
inch heavy barrel. Weight: about 9½ pounds. Sights: Parker-Hale No. 2 front; Perfection rear peep. One-piece target stock w/full forearm and pistol grip. Made before
WWII.

Walther Model 2

=== **WALTHER RIFLES** ===
**Mfd. by the German firms of Waffenfabrik Walther
and Carl Walther Sportwaffenfabrik**

The following Walther rifles were mfd. before WWII by Waffenfabrik Walther, Zella-Mehlis (Thür.), Germany.

Walther Model 1 Autoloading Rifle (Light) $325
Similar to Standard Model 2, but with 20-inch barrel,
lighter stock, weighs about 4½ pounds.

Walther Model 2 Autoloading Rifle $400
Bolt action, may be used as autoloader, manually operated
repeater or single shot. Caliber: 22 LR. 5- or 9-shot detachable box magazine. 24½-inch barrel. Weight: about

Walther Olympic

Walther Model V Meisterbüchse

Walther Model GX-1

Walther Model KKJ

NOTE: The Walther rifles listed below have been mfd. since WWII by Carl Walther Sportwaffenfabrik, Ulm (Donau), Germany.

Walther Model 2 Autoloading Rifle (cont.)
7 pounds. Sights: tangent-curve rear; ramp front. Sporting stock w/checkered pistol grip, grooved forearm, swivels. Discontinued.

Walther Olympic Bolt Action Single Shot Match Rifle **$925**
Caliber: 22 LR. 26-inch heavy barrel. Weight: about 13 pounds. Sights: micrometer extension rear; interchangeable front. Target stock w/checkered pistol grip, thumbhole, full beavertail forearm covered w/corrugated rubber, palmrest, adj. Swiss-type buttplate, swivels. Discontinued.

Walther Model V Bolt Action Single Shot Rifle . . **$360**
Caliber: 22 LR. 26-inch barrel. Weight: about 7 pounds. Sights: open rear; ramp front. Plain pistol-grip stock w/grooved forearm. Discontinued.

Walther Model V Meisterbüchse (Champion) . . . **$425**
Same as standard Model V, except has micrometer open rear sight and checkered pistol grip. Discontinued.

Walther Model GX-1 Free Rifle **$1295**
Bolt action, single shot. Caliber: 22 LR. 25 1/2-inch heavy barrel. Weight: 15.9 pounds. Sights: micrometer aperture rear; globe front. Thumbhole stock w/adjustable cheekpiece and buttplate w/removable hook, accessory rail. Left-hand stock available. Accessories furnished include hand stop and sling swivel, palmrest, counterweight assembly.

Walther Model KKJ Sporter **$525**
Bolt action. Caliber: 22 LR. 5-shot box magazine. 22 1/2-inch barrel. Weight: 5 1/2 pounds. Sights: open rear; hooded ramp front. Stock w/cheekpiece, checkered pistol grip and forearm, sling swivels. Discontinued.

Walther Model KKJ-Ho **$650**
Same as Model KKJ, except chambered for 22 Hornet. Discontinued.

Walther Model KKJ-Ma **$495**
Same as Model KKJ, except chambered for 22 WMR. Discontinued.

Walther Model KKM International Match Rifle . . . **$795**
Bolt action, single shot. Caliber: 22 LR. 28-inch heavy barrel. Weight: 15½ pounds. Sights: micrometer aperture rear; globe front. Thumbhole stock w/high comb, adj. hook buttplate, accessory rail. Left-hand stock available. Discontinued.

Walther Model KKM-S **$795**
Same specifications as Model KKM, except has adj. cheekpiece. Discontinued.

Walther Moving Target Match Rifle **$625**
Bolt action, single shot. Caliber: 22 LR. 23.6-inch barrel w/weight. Weight: 8.6 pounds. Supplied w/o sights. Thumbhole stock w/adj. cheekpiece and buttplate. Left-hand stock available.

Walther Prone 400 Target Rifle **$695**
Bolt action, single shot. Caliber: 22 LR. 25½-inch heavy barrel. Weight: 10¼ pounds. Supplied w/o sights. Prone stock w/adj. cheekpiece and buttplate, accessory rail. Left-hand stock available. Discontinued.

Walther Model SSV Varmint Rifle **$530**
Bolt action, single shot. Calibers: 22 LR, 22 Hornet. 25½-inch barrel. Weight: 6¾ pounds. Supplied w/o sights. Monte Carlo stock w/high cheekpiece, full pistol grip and forearm. Discontinued.

Walther Model U.I.T. Special Match Rifle **$840**
Bolt action, single shot. Caliber: 22 LR. 25½-inch barrel. Weight: 10.2 pounds. Sights: Micrometer aperture rear; globe front. Target stock w/high comb, adj. buttplate, accessory rail. Left-hand stock avail. Discontinued 1993.

RIFLES

Walther Model KKM International Match

Walther Moving Target Match

Walther Prone 400 Target

Walther Model SSV Varmint

Walther Model U.I.T. Special Match

Walther Model U.I.T. Super Match

Walther Model U.I.T. Super Match Rifle **$895**
Bolt action, single shot. Caliber: 22 LR. 25¹/₂-inch heavy barrel. Weight: 10.2 pounds. Micrometer aperture rear; globe front. Target stock w/support for off-hand shooting, high comb, adj. buttplate and swivel. Left-hand stock available. Discontinued 1993.

MONTGOMERY WARD
Chicago, Illinois
Western Field and Hercules Models

Firearms under the "private label" names of Western Field and Hercules are manufactured by such firms as Mossberg, Stevens, Marlin, and Savage for distribution and sale by Montgomery Ward.

Montgomery Ward Model 14M-497B Western Field Bolt Action Rifle **$80**
Caliber: 22 RF. 7-shot detachable box magazine. 24-inch barrel. Weight: about 5 pounds. Sights: receiver peep; open rear; hooded ramp front. Pistol-grip stock. Mfd. by Mossberg.

Montgomery Ward Model M771 Western Field Lever Action Rifle **$155**
Calibers: 30-30, 35 Rem. 6-shot tubular magazine. 20-inch barrel. Weight: 6³/₄ pounds. Sights: open rear; ramp front. Pistol-grip or straight stock, forearm w/barrel band. Mfd. by Mossberg.

Montgomery Ward Model M772 Western Field Lever Action Rifle **$165**
Calibers: 30-30, 35 Rem. 6-shot tubular magazine. 20-inch barrel. Weight: 6³/₄ pounds. Sights: open rear; ramp front. Pistol-grip or straight stock, forearm with barrel band. Mfd. by Mossberg.

Montgomery Ward Model M775 Bolt Action Rifle **$190**
Calibers: 222 Rem., 22-250, 243 Win., 308 Win. 4-shot magazine. Weight: about 7¹/₂ pounds. Sights: folding leaf rear; ramp front. Monte Carlo stock w/cheekpiece, pistol grip. Mfd by Mossberg.

Montgomery Ward Model M776 Bolt Action Rifle **$195**
Calibers: 222 Rem., 22-250, 243 Win., 308 Win. 4-shot magazine. Weight: about 7¹/₂ pounds. Sights: folding leaf rear; ramp front. Monte Carlo stock w/cheekpiece, pistol grip. Mfd. by Mossberg.

Montgomery Ward Model M778 Lever Action Rifle **$160**
Calibers: 30-30, 35 Rem. 6-shot tubular magazine. 20-inch barrel. Weight: 6³/₄ pounds. Sights: open rear; ramp front. Pistol-grip or straight stock, forearm w/barrel band. Mfd. by Mossberg.

Montgomery Ward Model M780 Bolt Action Rifle **$195**
Calibers: 222 Rem., 22-250, 243 Win., 308 Win. 4-shot magazine. Weight: about 7¹/₂ pounds. Sights: folding leaf rear; ramp front. Monte Carlo stock w/cheekpiece, pistol grip. Mfd. by Mossberg.

Montgomery Ward Model M782 Bolt Action Rifle **$195**
Same general specifications as Model M780.

Montgomery Ward Model M808 . . . . **$85**
Takedown. Caliber: 22RF. 15-shot tubular magazine. Barrels: 20- and 24-inch. Weight: about 6 pounds. Sights: open rear; bead front. Pistol-grip stock. Mfd. by Stevens.

Montgomery Ward Model M832 Bolt Action Rifle **$90**
Caliber: 22 RF. 7-shot clip magazine. 24-inch barrel. Weight: 6¹/₂ pounds. Sights: open rear; ramp front. Mfd. by Mossberg.

Montgomery Ward Model M836 . . . . **$95**
Takedown. Caliber: 22RF. 15-shot tubular magazine. Barrels: 20- and 24-inch. Weight: about 6 pounds. Sights: open rear; bead front. Pistol-grip stock. Mfd. by Stevens.

Montgomery Ward Model M865 Lever Action Carbine **$110**
Hammerless. Caliber: 22RF. Tubular magazine. Made with both 18¹/₂-inch and 20-inch barrel, forearm with barrel band, swivels. Weight: about 5 pounds. Mfd. by Mossberg.

Montgomery Ward Model M894 Autoloading Carbine **$105**
Caliber: 22 RF. 15-shot tubular magazine. 20-inch barrel. Weight: about 6 pounds. Sights: open rear; ramp front. Monte Carlo stock w/pistol grip. Mfd. by Mossberg.

Montgomery Ward Model M-SD57 . . . . **$90**
Takedown. Caliber: 22RF. 15-shot tubular magazine. Barrels: 20- and 24-inch. Weight: about 6 lbs. Sights: open rear; bead front. Pistol-grip stock. Mfd. by Stevens.

WEATHERBY, INC.
South Gate, California

Weatherby Classicmark I Rifle
Same general specifications as Mark V, except with checkered select American Claro walnut stock with oil finish and presentation recoil pad. Satin metal finish. Made 1992–93.

Calibers 240 to 300 Wby.	$ 750
Caliber 340 Wby.	795
Caliber 378 Wby.	825
Caliber 416 Wby.	895
Caliber 460 Wby.	950

RIFLES

Weatherby Classicmark II Rifle

Same general specifications as Classicmark I, except with checkered select American walnut stock with oil finish, steel grip cap and Old English recoil pad. Satin metal finish. Right-hand only. Made 1992–93.

Calibers 240 to 340 Wby. (26-inch bbl.)	**$1275**
Caliber 378 Wby.	**1325**
Caliber 416 Wby.	**1425**
Caliber 460 Wby.	**1550**

Weatherby Deluxe 378 Magnum Rifle $1750

Same general specifications as Deluxe Magnum in other calibers, except caliber 378 W. M. Schultz & Larsen action; 26-inch barrel. Discontinued 1958.

Weatherby Deluxe Magnum Rifle $1200

Calibers: 220 Rocket, 257 Weatherby Mag., 270 W.M., 7mm W.M., 300 W.M., 375 W.M. Specially processed FN Mauser action. 24-inch barrel (26-inch in 375 cal.). Monte Carlo-style stock with cheekpiece, black forend tip, grip cap, checkered pistol grip and forearm, quick-detachable sling swivels. Value shown is for rifle without sights. Discontinued 1958.

Weatherby Deluxe Rifle $995

Same general specifications as Deluxe Magnum, except chambered for standard calibers such as 270, 30-06, etc. Discontinued 1958.

Weatherby Fiberguard Rifle $415

Same general specifications as Vanguard except for fiberglass stock and matte metal finish.

Weatherby Fibermark Rifle $895

Same general specifications as Mark V except with molded fiberglass stock, finished in a nonglare black wrinkle finish. The metal is finished in a non-glare matte finish. Discontinued 1993.

Weatherby Mark V Deluxe Bolt Action Sporting Rifle

Mark V action, right or left hand. Calibers: 22-250, 30-06; 224 Weatherby Varmintmaster; 240, 257, 270, 7mm, 300, 340, 378, 416, 460 Weatherby Magnums. Box magazine holds 2 to 5 cartridges depending on caliber. 24- or 26-inch barrel. Weight: 6½ to 10½ pounds. Monte Carlo-style stock with cheekpiece, skip checkering, forend tip, pistol-grip cap, recoil pad, QD swivels. Values shown are for rifles w/o sights. Made in Germany 1958–69; in Japan 1970–1994.

Calibers 22-250, 224	**$795**
Caliber 378 Weatherby Magnum	**895**
Caliber 460 Weatherby Magnum	**995**
Other calibers	**650**
Add for left-hand action	**100**
Deduct 30% if Japanese-made	

Weatherby Deluxe Magnum

Weatherby Fiberguard™

Weatherby Fibermark™

Weatherby Mark V

Weatherby Mark V Euromark

Weatherby Mark V Lazermark

Weatherby Mark V Safari Grade

Weatherby Mark XXII Clip-fed

Weatherby Vanguard

Weatherby Mark V Euromark Bolt Action Rifle .. $995

Same general specifications as other Mark V rifles, except has hand-rubbed, satin oil finish Claro walnut stock and nonglare special process blue matte barreled action. Left-hand models available. Made 1986 to date.

Weatherby Mark V Lazermark Rifle $945

Same general specifications as Mark V except with lazer-carved stock.

Weatherby Mark V Safari Grade Rifle $1595

Same general specifications as Mark V except extra capacity magazine, barrel sling swivel, and express rear sight, typical "Safari" style.

Weatherby Mark XXII Deluxe 22 Automatic Sporter Clip-fed Model $295

Semiautomatic with single-shot selector. Caliber: 22 LR. 5- and 10-shot clip magazines. 24-inch barrel. Weight: 6 pounds. Sights: folding leaf open rear; ramp front. Monte Carlo-type stock w/cheekpiece, pistol grip, forend tip, grip cap, skip checkering, QD swivels. Introduced 1964. Made in Italy 1964–69; in Japan, 1970–1981; in the U.S., 1982–1990.

Weatherby Mark XXII, Tubular Magazine Model $275

Same as Mark XXII, Clip-fed Model, except has 15-shot tubular magazine. Made in Japan 1973–1981; in the U.S., 1982–1990.

Weatherby Vanguard (I) Bolt Action Sporting Rifle

Mauser-type action. Calibers: 243 Win., 25-06, 270 Win., 7mm Rem. Mag., 30-06, 300 Win. Mag. 5-shot magazine

Weatherby Vanguard VGX

Weatherby Vanguard (I) Bolt Action Sporter (cont.)
(3-shot in Magnum calibers). 24-inch barrel. Weight: 7 lbs. 14 oz. No sights. Monte Carlo-type stock w/cheekpiece, rosewood forend tip and pistol-grip cap, checkering, rubber buttpad, QD swivels. Made in Japan 1970–1984.
Vanguard Standard **$320**
Vanguard VGL (w/shorter 20-inch bbl., plain
  checkered stock, matte finish, 6¹/₂ lbs **325**
Vanguard VGS (w/24-inch bbl., plain checkered
  stock, matte finish **345**
Vanguard VGX (w/higher grade finish) **395**

Weatherby Vanguard Classic I Rifle **$375**
Same general specifications as Vanguard VGX Deluxe, except with hand-checkered classic-style stock, black buttpad and satin finish. Calibers 223 Rem., 243 Win., 270 Win., 7mm-08, 7mm Rem. Mag., 30-06 and 308 Win. Made 1989–1994.

Weatherby Vanguard Classic II Rifle **$495**
Same general specifications as Vanguard VGX Deluxe, except custom checkered classic-style American walnut stock with black forend tip, grip cap and solid black recoil pad, satin finish. Made 1989–1994.

Weatherby Vanguard VGX Deluxe **$495**
Calibers: 22-250 Rem., 243 Rem., 270 Wby. Mag., 270 Win., 7mm Rem. Mag., 30-06, 300 Win. Mag., 300 Wby. Mag., 338 Win. Mag. 3- or 5-round capacity. 24-inch barrel. About 44 inches overall. Weight: 7 to 8¹/₂ pounds. Custom checkered American walnut stock with Monte Carlo and recoil pad. Rosewood forend tip and pistol-grip cap. High-luster finish. Discontinued 1994.

Weatherby Weathermark Rifle **$475**
Same general specifications as Classicmark, except with checkered black Weathermark™ composite stock. Mark V bolt action. Calibers: 240, 257, 270, 300, 340, 378, 416 and 460 Weatherby Magnums; plus 270 Win., 7mm Rem. Mag., 30-06 and 375 H&H Mag. Weight: 8 to 10 pounds. Right-hand only. Made 1992 to date.

Weatherby Weathermark Alaskan Rifle **$625**
Same general specifications as the Weathermark, except with nonglare electroless nickel finish. Right-hand only. Made 1992 to date.

WESTERN FIELD RIFLES
See listings under "W" for Montgomery Ward.

RIFLES

Westley Richards Best Quality Double Rifle

Westley Richards Best Quality Magazine Rifle

WESTLEY RICHARDS & CO., LTD.
London, England

Westley Richards Best Quality Double Rifle .. **$25,000**
Box lock, hammerless, ejector. Hand-detachable locks. Calibers: 30-06, 318 Accelerated Express, 375 Mag., 425 Mag. Express, 465 Nitro Express, 470 Nitro Express. 25-inch barrels. Weight: 8¹/₂ to 11 pounds. Sights: leaf rear; hooded front. French walnut stock w/cheekpiece, checkered pistol grip and forend.

**Westley Richards Best Quality Magazine
Rifle** **$5,000**
Mauser or Magnum Mauser action. Calibers: 7mm High Velocity, 30-06, 318 Accelerated Express, 375 Mag., 404 Nitro Express, 425 Mag. Barrel lengths: 24-inch; 7mm, 22-inch; 425 caliber, 25-inch. Weight: 7¹/₄ to 9¹/₄ pounds. Sights: leaf rear; hooded front. French walnut sporting stock w/cheekpiece, checkered pistol grip and forearm, horn forend tip, swivels.

Wickliffe '76 Standard
Single Shot Rifle

WICKLIFFE RIFLES
Wickliffe, Ohio
Mfd. by Triple S Development Co., Inc.

Wickliffe '76 Commemorative Model **$650**
Limited edition of 100. Same as Deluxe Model, except has filled etching on receiver sidewalls, U.S. silver dollar inlaid in stock, 26-inch barrel only, comes in presentation case. Made in 1976 only.

Wickliffe '76 Deluxe Model **$395**
Same as Standard Model, except 22-inch barrel in 30-06 only, has high-luster blued finish, fancy-grade figured American walnut stock with nickel silver grip cap.

Wickliffe '76 Standard Model Single Shot Rifle . . **$340**
Falling-block action. Calibers: 22 Hornet, 223 Rem., 22-250, 243 Win., 25-06, 308 Win., 30-06, 45-70. 22-inch lightweight barrel (243 and 308 only) or 26-inch heavy sporter barrel. Weight: $6\frac{3}{4}$ or $8\frac{1}{2}$ pounds, depending on barrel. No sights. Select American walnut Monte Carlo stock with right or left cheekpiece and pistol grip, semi-beavertail forearm. Introduced 1976; discontinued.

TED WILLIAMS RIFLES
See Sears, Roebuck and Company.

Winchester Model 02

Winchester Model 03

WINCHESTER RIFLES
New Haven, Connecticut

Formerly Winchester Repeating Arms Co. Now mfd. by Winchester Western Div., Olin Corp., and by U.S. Repeating Arms Co. both of New Haven, CT.

NOTE: Thousands of Winchester rifles have been produced throughout the company's long, illustrious history. For ease in finding a particular model, the organization of Winchester rifles follows that of the other manufacturers (i.e., Model Numbers listed first, then Model Names in alphabetical order). The Model 70, however, which enjoyed a history all its own, is divided into Pre-1964, 1964-Type and 1972-Type variations. The Model 94 commemoratives are also grouped separately. In addition, please consult the Index.

Winchester Model 02 Bolt Action Single Shot Rifle **$295**
Takedown. Basically the same as Model 1900 with minor improvements. Calibers: 22 Short and Long, 22 Extra Long, 22 LR. Weight: 3 pounds. Made 1902–1931.

Winchester [Model 02] Thumb Trigger Bolt Action Single Shot Rifle **$595**
Takedown. Same as Model 02 except fired by pressing a button behind the cocking piece. Made 1904–1923.

Winchester Model 03 Self-Loading Rifle **$325**
Takedown. Caliber: 22 Win. Auto Rimfire. 10-shot tubular magazine in buttstock. 20-inch barrel. Weight: $5\frac{3}{4}$ pounds. Sights: open rear; bead front. Plain straight-grip stock and forearm (stock illustrated was extra-cost option). Made 1903–1936.

Winchester Model 04

Winchester Model 05

Winchester Model 06

Winchester Model 07

Winchester Model 10

Winchester Model 04 Bolt Action Single Shot Rifle $225
Similar to Model 02. Takedown. Caliber: 22 Short, Long, Extra Long, LR. 21-inch barrel. Weight: 4 pounds. Made 1904–1931.

Winchester Model 05 Self-Loading Rifle $495
Takedown. Calibers: 32 Win. S.L., 35 Win. S.L. 5- or 10-shot detachable box magazine. 22-inch barrel. Weight: 7½ pounds. Sights: open rear; bead front. Plain pistol-grip stock and forearm. Made 1905–1920.

Winchester Model 06 Slide Action Repeater $475
Takedown. Visible hammer. Caliber: 22 Short, Long, LR. Tubular magazine holds 20 Short, 16 Long or 14 LR. 20-inch barrel. Weight: 5 pounds. Sights: open rear; bead front. Straight-grip stock and grooved forearm. Made 1906–1932.

Winchester Model 07 Self-Loading Rifle $575
Takedown. Caliber: 351 Win. S.L. 5- or 10-shot detachable box magazine. 20-inch barrel. Weight: 7¾ pounds. Sights: open rear; bead front. Plain pistol-grip stock and forearm. Made 1907–1957.

Winchester Model 10 Self-Loading Rifle $595
Takedown. Caliber: 401 Win. S.L. 4-shot detachable box magazine. 20-inch barrel. Weight: 8½ pounds. Sights: open rear; bead front. Plain pistol-grip stock and forearm. Made 1910–1936.

Winchester Model 43 Bolt Action Sporting Rifle $550
Standard Grade. Calibers: 218 Bee, 22 Hornet, 25-20, 32-20 (latter two discontinued 1950). 3-shot detachable box magazine. 24-inch barrel. Weight: 6 pounds. Sights: open rear; bead front on hooded ramp. Plain pistol-grip stock with swivels. Made 1949–1957.

Winchester Model 43 Special Grade

Winchester Model 47

Winchester Model 52 Standard Barrel

Winchester Model 52 International Match

Winchester Model 43 Special Grade **$625**
Same as Standard Model 43, except has checkered pistol grip and forearm, grip cap.

Winchester Model 47 Bolt Action Single Shot Rifle **$220**
Caliber: 22 Short, Long, LR. 25-inch barrel. Weight: 5½ pounds. Sights: peep or open rear; bead front. Plain pistol-grip stock. Made 1949–1954.

Winchester Model 52 Bolt Action Target Rifle
Standard Barrel. First type. Caliber: 22 LR. 5-shot box magazine. 28-inch barrel. Weight: 8¾ pounds. Sights: folding leaf peep rear; blade front sight; standard sights; various other combinations available. Scope bases. Semi-military type target stock w/pistol grip; original model has grasping grooves in forearm; higher comb and semi-beavertail forearm on later models. Numerous changes were made in this model, the most important was the

Winchester Model 52 Bolt Action Target Rifle (cont.)
adoption of the speed lock in 1929; Model 52 rifles produced before this change are generally referred to as "slow lock" models. Last arms of this type bore serial numbers followed by the letter "A." Made 1919–1937.
Slow Lock Model **$525**
Speed Lock Model **595**

Winchester Model 52 Heavy Barrel **$625**
First type. Speed lock. Same general specifications as Standard Model 52 of this type, except has heavier barrel, Lyman 17G front sight, weighs 10 pounds.

Winchester Model 52 International Match Rifle
Similar to Model 52-D Heavy Barrel, except has special lead-lapped barrel, laminated "free rifle" style stock with high comb, thumbhole, hook buttplate, accessory rail, handstop/swivel assembly, palmrest. Weight: 13½ pounds. Made 1969–1978.
With standard trigger **$660**
With Kenyon or I.S.U. trigger **775**

Winchester Model 52
International Prone Target

Winchester Model 52-B Standard Barrel

Winchester Model 52-B Sporter

Winchester Model 52-C Heavy Barrel

Winchester Model 52 International Prone Target Rifle $1010

Similar to Model 52-D Heavy Barrel, except has special lead-lapped barrel, prone stock with fuller pistol grip, rollover cheekpiece removable for bore-cleaning. Weight: 11½ pounds. Made 1975 to date.

Winchester Model 52 Sporting Rifle $1725

First type. Same as Standard Model 52 of this type, except has lightweight 24-inch barrel, Lyman No. 48 receiver sight and gold bead front sight on hooded ramp, deluxe checkered sporting stock with cheekpiece, black forend tip, etc. Weight: 7¾ pounds.

Winchester Model 52-B Bolt Action Rifle

Standard barrel. Extensively redesigned action. Supplied with choice of "Target" stock, an improved version of the previous Model 52 stock, or "Marksman" stock with high comb, full pistol grip and beavertail forearm. Weight: 9 pounds. Offered with a wide choice of target sight combinations (Lyman, Marble-Goss, Redfield, Vaver, Win-

Winchester Model 52-B Bolt Action Rifle (cont.)

chester); value shown is for rifle less sight equipment. Other specifications as shown for first type. Made 1935–1947. Reintroduced by U.S. Repeating Arms Co. in 1993.

Sporting Model $1510
Target Model 595
USRAC Sporting Model 435

Winchester Model 52-B Rifle $595

Same specifications as Standard Model 52-B, except Bull Gun has extra heavy barrel, Marksman stock only, weighs 12 pounds. Heavy Barrel model weighs 11 lbs.

Winchester Model 52-C Bolt Action Rifle

Improved action with "Micro-Motion" trigger mechanism and new-type "Marksman" stock. General specifications same as shown for previous models. Made 1947–1961; Bull Gun from 1952. Value shown is for rifle less sights.

Bull Gun (Extra Heavy Barrel, wt. 12 lbs.) $625
Standard Barrel (Wt. 9¾ lbs.) 610
Target Model (Heavy Barrel) 600

Winchester Model 52-D Heavy Barrel

Winchester Model 53

Winchester Model 54 National Match

Winchester Model 54 Standard Grade Improved Type

Winchester Model 52-D Bolt Action Target Rifle $625
Redesigned Model 52 action, single shot. Caliber: 22 LR. 28-inch standard or heavy barrel, free-floating, with blocks for standard target scopes. Weight: with standard barrel, 9¾ lbs.; with heavy barrel, 11 lbs. Restyled Marksman stock with accessory channel and forend stop, rubber buttplate. Made 1961–1978. Value shown is for rifle without sights.

Winchester Model 53 Lever Action Repeater . . $1550
Modification of Model 92. Solid frame or takedown. Calibers: 25/20, 32/20, 44/40. 6-shot tubular half-magazine in solid frame model. 7-shot in takedown. 22-inch nickel steel barrel. Weight: 5½ to 6½ pounds. Sights: open rear; bead front. Redesigned straight-grip stock and forearm. Made 1924–1932.

Winchester Model 54 Bolt Action High Power Sporting Rifle (I) $525
First type. Calibers: 270 Win., 7×57mm, 30-30, 30-06, 7.65×53mm, 9×57mm. 5-shot box magazine. 24-inch barrel. Weight: 7¾ pounds. Sights: open rear; bead front. Checkered stock w/pistol grip, tapered forearm w/ schnabel tip. This type has two-piece firing pin. Made 1925–1930.

Winchester Model 54 Bolt Action High Power Sporting Rifle (II) $675
Standard Grade. Improved type with speed lock and one-piece firing pin. Calibers: 22 Hornet, 220 Swift, 250/3000, 257 Roberts, 270 Win., 7×57mm, 30-06. 5-shot box magazine. 24-inch barrel, 26-inch in cal. 220 Swift. Weight:

Winchester Model 54 High Power Sporter II (cont.)
about 8 pounds. Sights: open rear; bead front on ramp. NRA-type stock w/checkered pistol grip and forearm. Made 1930–36.

Winchester Model 54 Carbine (I) $660
First type. Same as Model 54 rifle, except has 20-inch barrel, plain lightweight stock with grasping grooves in forearm. Weight: 7¼ pounds.

Winchester Model 54 Carbine (II) $725
Improved type. Same as Model 54 Standard Grade Sporting Rifle of this type, except has 20-inch barrel. Weight: about 7½ pounds. This model may have either NRA-type stock or the lightweight stock found on the first-type Model 54 Carbine.

Winchester Model 54 National Match Rifle $795
Same as Standard Model 54, except has Lyman sights, scope bases, Marksman-type target stock, weighs 9½ pounds. Same calibers as Standard Model.

Winchester Model 54 Sniper's Match Rifle $895
Similar to the earlier Model 54 Sniper's Rifle, except has Marksman-type target stock, scope bases, weighs 12½ pounds. Available in same calibers as Model 54 Standard Grade.

Winchester Model 54 Sniper's Rifle $725
Same as Standard Model 54, except has heavy 26-inch barrel, Lyman #48 rear peep sight and blade front sight, semi-military stock, weighs 11¾ pounds, cal. 30-06 only.

Winchester Model 54 Super Grade **$950**
Same as Standard Model 54 Sporter, except has deluxe stock with cheekpiece, black forend tip, pistol-grip cap, quick detachable swivels, 1-inch sling strap.

Winchester Model 54 Target Rifle **$825**
Same as Standard Model 54, except has 24-inch medium-weight barrel (26-inch in cal. 220 Swift), Lyman sights, scope bases, Marksman-type target stock, weighs 10½ pounds, same calibers as Standard Model.

Winchester Model 55 "Automatic" Single Shot . **$225**
Caliber: 22 Short, Long, LR. 22-inch barrel. Sights: open rear; bead front. One-piece walnut stock. Weight: about 5½ pounds. Made 1958–1960.

Winchester Model 55 Lever Action Repeater
Modification of Model 94. Solid frame or takedown. Calibers: 25/35, 30/30, 32 Win. Special. 3-shot tubular half

Winchester Model 55 Lever Action Repeater (cont.)
magazine. 24-inch nickel steel barrel. Weight: about 7 pounds. Sights: open rear; bead front. Made 1924–1932.
Straight Grip . . . . **$ 895**
Pistol Grip **1700**

Winchester Model 56 Bolt Action Sporting Rifle **$495**
Solid frame. Caliber: 22 LR, 22 Short. 5- or 10-shot detachable box magazine. 22-inch barrel. Weight: 4¾ pounds. Sights: open rear; bead front. Plain pistol-grip stock with schnabel forend. Made 1926–29.

Winchester Model 57 Bolt Action Target Rifle . . **$525**
Solid frame. Same as Model 56, except available (until 1929) in 22 Short as well as LR, has semi-military style target stock, swivels and web sling, Lyman peep rear sight, blade front sight, weighs 5 lbs. Mfd. 1926–1936.

RIFLES

Winchester Model 54 Super Grade

Winchester Model 54 Target

Winchester Model 55 "Automatic" Single Shot

Winchester Model 55 Lever Action

Winchester Model 56

Winchester Model 57 Target

Winchester Model 58

Winchester Model 60A Target

Winchester Model 61 Repeater

Winchester Model 62 Repeater

Winchester Model 63

Winchester Model 58 Bolt Action Single Shot . . . **$245**
Similar to Model 02. Takedown. Caliber: 22 Short, Long, LR. 18-inch barrel. Weight: 3 pounds. Sights; open rear; blade front. Plain, flat, straight-grip stock. Made 1928–1931.

Winchester Model 59 Bolt Action Single Shot . . . **$425**
Improved version of Model 58, has 23-inch barrel, redesigned stock w/pistol grip, weighs 4½ pounds. Made 1930.

Winchester Model 60 Bolt Action Single Shot . . . **$175**
Redesign of Model 59. Caliber: 22 Short, Long, LR. 23-inch barrel (27-inch after 1933). Weight: 4¼ pounds. Sights: open rear; blade front. Plain stock w/pistol grip. Made 1930–34.

Winchester Model 60A Target Rifle **$540**
Essentially the same as Model 60, except has Lyman peep rear sight and square top front sight, semi-military target stock and web sling, weighs 5½ pounds. Made 1932–39.

Winchester Model 61 Hammerless Slide Action Repeater **$495**
Takedown. Caliber: 22 Short, Long, LR. Tubular magazine holds 20 Short, 16 Long, 14 LR. 24-inch round barrel.

Winchester Model 61 Hammerless Slide Action (cont.)
Weight: 5½ pounds. Sights: open rear; bead front. Plain pistol-grip stock, grooved semibeavertail slide handle. Also available with 24-inch full-octagon barrel and only calibers 22 LR, 22 Short or 22 WRF. Made 1932–1963. *Note:* Octagon barrel model commands higher prices (disc. 1943–44); assembled until 1948.

Winchester Model 61 Magnum **$595**
Same as Standard Model 61, except chambered for 22 WMR; magazine holds 12 rounds. Made 1960–63.

Winchester Model 62 Visible Hammer Slide Action Repeater **$380**
Modernized version of Model 1890. Caliber: 22 Short, Long, LR. 23-inch barrel. Weight: 5½ pounds. Plain straight-grip stock, grooved semibeavertail slide handle. Also available in Gallery Model chambered for 22 Short only. Made 1932–1959. *Note:* Pre-WWII model (small forearm) commands 25% higher price.

Winchester Model 63 Self-Loading Rifle **$475**
Takedown. Caliber: 22 LR High Speed only. 10-shot tubular magazine in buttstock. 23-inch barrel. Weight: 5½ pounds. Sights: open rear; bead front. Plain pistol-grip stock and forearm. Originally available with 20-inch barrel as well as 23-inch. Made 1933–1959.

RIFLES

Winchester Model 64 Deer Rifle

Winchester Model 64 (original)

Winchester Model 64, 1972-74 type

Winchester Model 65

Winchester Model 67

Winchester Model 64 Deer Rifle **$1200**
Same as Standard Model 64, calibers 30-30 and 32 Win. Special, except has checkered pistol grip and semibeavertail forearm, swivels and sling, weighs 7¾ pounds. Made 1933–1956.

Winchester Model 64 Lever Action Repeater
Standard Grade. Improved version of Models 94 and 55. Solid frame. Calibers: 25/35, 30-30, 32 Win. Special. 5-shot tubular ⅔ magazine. 20- or 24-inch barrel. Weight: about 7 pounds. Sights: open rear; bead front on ramp w/ sight cover. Plain pistol-grip stock and forearm. Made 1933–1956. Production resumed in 1972 (caliber 30-30, 24-inch barrel); discontinued 1974.
Original model **$615**
1972–74 model **325**

Winchester Model 64—219 Zipper **$1910**
Same as Standard Grade Model 64, except has 26-inch barrel, peep rear sight. Made 1937–1947.

Winchester Model 65 Lever Action Repeater . . **$1295**
Improved version of Model 53. Solid frame. Calibers: 25-20 and 32-20. Six-shot tubular half-magazine. 22-inch barrel. Weight: 6½ pounds. Sights: open rear; bead front on ramp base. Plain pistol-grip stock and forearm. Made 1933–1947.

Winchester Model 65—218 Bee **$1795**
Same as Standard Model 65, except has 24-inch barrel, peep rear sight. Made 1938–1947.

Winchester Model 67 Bolt Action Single Shot Rifle **$145**
Takedown. Calibers: 22 Short, Long, LR, 22 LR shot (smoothbore), 22 WRF. 27-inch barrel. Weight: 5 pounds. Sights: open rear; bead front. Plain pistol-grip stock (original model had grasping grooves in forearm). Made 1934–1963.

Winchester Model 67 Boy's Rifle **$175**
Same as Standard Model 67, except has shorter stock, 20-inch barrel, weighs 4¼ pounds.

Winchester Model 68

Winchester Model 69

Winchester Model 69 Match

Winchester Model 70 Standard
(Pre-1964)

Winchester Model 68 Bolt Action Single Shot . . . **$195**
Same as Model 67, except has rear peep sight. Made 1934–1946.

Winchester Model 69 Bolt Action Single Shot . . . **$165**
Takedown. Caliber: 22 S, L, LR. 5- or 10-shot box magazine. 25-inch barrel. Weight: 5½ pounds. Peep or open rear sight. Plain pistol-grip stock. Rifle cocks on closing motion of the bolt. Made 1935–1937.

Winchester Model 69A Bolt Action Single Shot
Same as the Model 69, except cocking mechanism was changed to cock the rifle by the opening motion of the bolt. Made 1937–1963. *Note:* Models with grooved receivers command 20% higher prices.
Model 69A Standard **$195**
Match Model w/Lyman #57EW receiver sight . . . **325**
Target Model w/Winchester peep rear sight,
swivels, sling **340**

NOTE: Introduced in 1937, the Model 70 Bolt Action Repeater was offered in several styles and calibers. Only minor design changes were made over 27 years, and more than one-half million of these rifles were sold. In 1964, the original Model 70 was superseded by a revised version with redesigned action, improved bolt, swaged barrel, restyled stock (barrel free-floating). This model again underwent major changes in 1972—most visible: new stock with contrasting forend tip and grip cap, cut checkering (instead of impressed as in predecessor), knurled bolt handle. Action (machined from a solid block of steel) and barrel are chrome molybdenum steel.

PRE-1964 MODEL 70

Winchester Model 70 African Rifle **$2950**
Same general specifications as Super Grade Model 70, except has 25-inch barrel, 3-shot magazine, Monte Carlo stock with recoil pad. Weight: about 9½ pounds. Caliber: 458 Winchester Magnum. Made 1956–1963.

Winchester Model 70 Alaskan **$1550**
Same as Standard Model 70, except calibers 338 Win. Mag., 375 H&H Mag.; 3-shot magazine in 338, 4-shot in 375 caliber; 25-inch barrel; stock with recoil pad. Weight: 8 lbs. in 338; 8¾ lbs. in 375 caliber. Made 1960–63.

Winchester Model 70 Bull Gun **$2625**
Same as Standard Model 70, except has heavy 28-inch barrel, scope bases, Marksman stock, weighs 13¼ pounds, caliber 300 H&H Magnum and 30-06 only. Disc. 1963.

Winchester Model 70 Featherweight Sporter . . . **$910**
Same as Standard Model 70, except has redesigned stock and 22-inch barrel, aluminum trigger guard, floorplate and buttplate. Calibers: 243 Win., 264 Win. Mag., 270 Win., 308 Win., 30-06, 358 Win. Weight: about 6½ pounds. Made 1952–1963.

Winchester Model 70 National Match Rifle **$1095**
Same as Standard Model 70, except has scope bases, Marksman-type target stock, weighs 9½ pounds, caliber 30-06 only. Discontinued 1960.

Winchester Model 70 Standard Grade **$875**
Calibers: 22 Hornet, 220 Swift, 243 Win., 250-3000, 257 Roberts, 270 Win., 7×57mm, 30-06, 308 Win., 300 H&H Mag., 375 H&H Mag. 5-shot box magazine (4-shot in Magnum calibers). 24-inch barrel standard; 26-inch in 220

RIFLES

Winchester Model 70 Standard Grade (cont.)
Swift and 300 Mag.; 25-inch in 375 Mag.; at one time a 20-inch barrel was available. Sights: open rear; hooded ramp front. Checkered walnut stock; Monte Carlo comb standard on later production. Weight: from 7¾ pounds depending on caliber and barrel length. Made 1937–1963.

Winchester Model 70 Super Grade **$1895**
Same as Standard Grade Model 70, except has deluxe stock w/cheekpiece, black forend tip, pistol-grip cap, quick detachable swivels, sling. Discontinued 1960.

Winchester Model 70 Super Grade Featherweight **$1695**
Same as Standard Grade Featherweight except has deluxe stock w/cheekpiece, black forend tip, pistol-grip cap, quick detachable swivels, sling. Discontinued 1960. *Note:* SG-FWs are rare but, unless documented, will not command premium price of $2800–$3500; price here reflects "All" (incl. nondocumented transactions).

Winchester Model 70 Target Rifle **$1350**
Same as Standard Model 70, except has 24-inch medium-weight barrel, scope bases, Marksman stock, weight about 10½ pounds. Originally offered in all of the Model 70 calibers, this rifle was available later in calibers 243 Win. and 30-06. Discontinued 1963.

Winchester Model 70 Varmint Rifle **$925**
Same general specifications as Standard Model 70, except has 26-inch heavy barrel, scope bases, special varminter stock. Calibers: 220 Swift, 243 Win. Made 1956–1963.

Winchester Model 70 Westerner **$950**
Same as Standard Model 70, except calibers 264 Win. Mag., 300 Win. Mag.; 3-shot magazine; 26-inch barrel in former caliber, 24-inch in latter. Weight: about 8¼ pounds. Made 1960–63.

Winchester Model 70 African (1964)

Winchester Model 70 Deluxe (1964)

Winchester Model 70 International Army Match (1964)

1964-TYPE MODEL 70

Winchester Model 70 African **$650**
Caliber: 458 Win. Mag. 3-shot magazine. 22-inch barrel. Weight: 8½ pounds. Special "African" sights. Monte Carlo stock with ebony forend tip, hand-checkering, twin stock-reinforcing bolts, recoil pad, QD swivels. Made 1964–1971.

Winchester Model 70 Deluxe **$695**
Calibers: 243, 270 Win., 30-06, 300 Win. Mag. 5-shot box magazine (3-shot in Magnum). 22-inch barrel (24-inch in Magnum). Weight: 7½ pounds. Sights: open rear; hooded ramp front. Monte Carlo stock w/ebony forend tip, hand-checkering, QD swivels, recoil pad on Magnum. Made 1964–1971.

Winchester Model 70 International Army Match Rifle **$725**
Caliber: 308 Win. (7.62 NATO). 5-shot box magazine. 24-inch heavy barrel. Externally adj. trigger. Weight: 11 pounds. ISU stock w/military oil finish, forearm rail for standard accessories, vertically adj. buttplate. Made in 1971. Value shown is for rifle w/o sights.

Winchester Model 70 Magnum
Calibers: 7mm Rem. Mag.; 264, 300, 338 Win. Mag.; 375 H&H Mag. 3-shot magazine. 24-inch barrel. Weight: 7¾ to 8½ pounds. Sights: open rear; hooded ramp front. Monte Carlo stock w/cheekpiece, checkering, twin stock-reinforcing bolts, recoil pad, swivels. Made 1964–1971.
Caliber 375 H&H Mag. **$595**
Other calibers **350**

Winchester Model 70 Mannlicher (1964)

Winchester Model 70 Standard (1964)

Winchester Model 70 Target (1964)

Winchester Model 70 Mannlicher **$495**
Calibers: 243, 270, 308 Win., 30-06. 5-shot box magazine.
19-inch barrel. Sights: open rear; hooded ramp front.
Weight: 7½ pounds. Mannlicher-style stock w/Monte
Carlo comb and cheekpiece, checkering, steel forend cap,
QD swivels. Made 1969–1971.

Winchester Model 70 Standard **$425**
Calibers: 22-250, 222 Rem., 225, 243, 270, 308 Win., 30-
06. 5-shot box magazine. 22-inch barrel. Weight: 7½
pounds. Sights: open rear; hooded ramp front. Monte Carlo
stock w/cheekpiece, checkering, swivels. Made 1964–1971.

Winchester Model 70 Target **$595**
Calibers: 308 Win. (7.62 NATO) and 30-06. 5-shot box
magazine. 24-inch heavy barrel. Blocks for target scope,
no sights. Weight: 10¼ pounds. High-comb Marksman-
style stock, aluminum hand stop, swivels. Made 1964–
1971.

Winchester Model 70 Varmint **$575**
Same as Model 70 Standard, except has 24-inch target
weight barrel, blocks for target scope, no sights, available
in calibers 22-250, 222 Rem., and 243 Win. only. Weight:
9¾ pounds. Made 1964–1971.

Winchester Model 70 African (1972)

1972-TYPE MODEL 70

Winchester Model 70 African **$625**
Similar to Model 70 Magnum, except caliber 458 Win.
Mag.; has 22-inch barrel, special African open rear sight,
reinforced stock with ebony forend tip, detachable swivels
and sling. Weight: about 8½ pounds. Made 1972 to date.

Winchester Model 70 Custom Sharpshooter . . . **$1250**
Calibers: 22-250, 223, 308 Win., 300 Win. Mag. 24- or 26-
inch barrel. 44½ inches overall (24-inch bbl.). Weight: 11

Winchester Model 70 Custom Sharpshooter (cont.)
pounds. Custom fitted, hand-honed action. McMillan
A-2 target-style stock. Matte blue finish. Made 1992 to
date.

**Winchester Model 70 Custom Sporting
Sharpshooter** **$1195**
Similar to the Custom Sharpshooter Model, except has
McMillan sporter-style gray composite stock. Stainless
24- or 26-inch barrel with blued receiver. Calibers: 270,
7mm STW, 300 Win. Mag. Made 1993 to date.

**Winchester Model 70
Golden 50th Anniversary Rifle**

Winchester Model 70 Lightweight

Winchester Model 70 Magnum (1972)

Winchester Model 70 Standard (1972)

RIFLES

Winchester Model 70 Golden 50th Anniversary Edition Bolt Action Rifle $925
Caliber: 300 Win. 3-shot magazine. 24-inch barrel. 44½ inches overall. Weight: 7¾ pounds. Checkered American walnut stock. Hand-engraved American scroll pattern on barrel, receiver, magazine cover, trigger guard and pistol grip cap. Sights: adj. rear; hooded front ramp. Inscription on barrel reads "The Rifleman's Rifle 1937–1987." Only 500 made 1986–87.

Winchester Model 70 Featherweight Classic . . . $395
Similar to the Model 70 XTR Featherweight, except with controlled-round feeding system. Calibers: 270, 280 and 30-06. Made 1992 to date.

Winchester Model 70 International Army Match $750
Caliber: 308 Win. (7.62mm NATO). 5-shot magazine, clip slot in receiver bridge. 24-inch heavy barrel. Weight: 11 pounds. No sights. ISU target stock. Intro. 1973; discont.

Winchester Model 70 Lightweight Bolt Action Rifle $325
Calibers: 22-250 and 223 Rem.; 243, 270 and 308 Win.; 30-06 Springfld. 5-shot mag. capacity (6-shot 223 Rem.).

Winchester Model 70 Lightweight Bolt Action (cont.)
22-inch barrel. 42 to 42½ inches overall. Weight: 6 to 6¼ pounds. Checkered classic straight stock. Sling swivel studs. Made 1986 to date.

Winchester Model 70 Magnum
Same as Model 70, except has 3-shot magazine, 24-inch barrel, reinforced stock with recoil pad. Weight: about 7¾ pounds (except 8½ pounds in 375 H&H Mag.). Calibers: 264 Win. Mag., 7mm Rem. Mag., 300 Win. Mag., 338 Win. Mag., 375 H&H Mag. Made 1972 to date.
375 H&H Magnum **$425**
Other Magnum calibers **375**

Winchester Model 70 Standard **$345**
Same as Model 70A, except has 5-shot magazine, Monte Carlo stock with cheekpiece, black forend tip and pistol-grip cap with white spacers, checkered pistol grip and forearm, detachable sling swivels. Same calibers plus 225 Win. Made 1972 to date.

Winchester Model 70 Sporter DBM
Same general specifications as Model 70 Sporter SSM, except with detachable box magazine. Calibers: 22-250 (discontinued 1994), 223 (discontinued 1994), 243 (discontinued 1994), 270, 7mm Rem. Mag., 308 (discontinued 1994), 30-06, 300 Win. Mag. Made 1992 to date.
Model 70 DBM **$375**
Model 70 DBM-S **385**

Winchester Model 70 Target (1972)

Winchester Model 70 Varmint (1972)

Winchester Model 70 Win-Cam

Winchester Model 70 Win-Tuff

Winchester Model 70 Stainless Sporter SSM ... **$395**
Same general specifications as Model 70 XTR Sporter, except with checkered black composite stock and matte finished receiver and barrel. Calibers: 270, 7mm Rem. Mag., 30-06, 300 Win. Mag., 338 Win. Mag. Weight: 7³/₄ pounds. Made 1992 to date.

Winchester Model 70 Super Grade **$495**
Calibers: 270, 7mm Rem. Mag., 30-06, 300 Win. Mag., 338 Win. Mag. 5-shot magazine (standard), 3-shot (magnum). 24-inch barrel. 44¹/₂ inches overall. Weight: 7³/₄ pounds. Checkered walnut stock with sculptured cheekpiece and tapered forend. Scope bases and rings, no sights. Controlled- round feeding system. Made 1990 to date.

Winchester Model 70 Target **$495**
Calibers: 30-06 and 308 Win. (7.62mm NATO). 5-shot magazine. 26-inch heavy barrel. Weight: 10¹/₂ lbs. No sights. High-comb Marksman-style target stock, aluminum hand stop, swivels. Made 1972 to date.

Winchester Model 70 Ultra Match **$625**
Similar to Model 70 Target, but custom grade; has 26-inch heavy barrel with deep counterbore, glass bedding, externally adj. trigger. Made 1972 to date.

Winchester Model 70 Varmint (Heavy Barrel)
Same as Model 70 Standard, except has medium-heavy, counter-bored 26-inch barrel, no sights, stock with less drop. Weight: 9 pounds. Calibers: 22-250 Rem., 223 Rem.,

Winchester Model 70 Varmint (Heavy Barrel) (cont.)
243 Win., 308 Win. Made 1972 to date. **Model 70 SHB**, in 308 Win. only with black synthetic stock and matte blue receiver/barrel, made 1992 to date.
Model 70 Varmint **$485**
Model 70 SHB (Synthetic Heavy Barrel) **450**

Winchester Model 70 Win-Cam Bolt Action Rifle **$385**
Caliber: 270 Win. and 30-06 Springfield. 24-inch barrel. Camouflage one-piece laminated stock. Recoil pad. Drilled and tapped for scope. Made 1986 to date.

Winchester Model 70 Winlite Bolt Action Rifle .. **$475**
Calibers: 270 Win., 280 Rem., 30-06 Springfield, 7mm Rem., 300 Win. Mag., and 338 Win. Mag. 5-shot magazine; 3-shot for Magnum calibers. 22-inch barrel; 24-inch for Magnum calibers. 42¹/₂ inches overall; 44¹/₂, Magnum calibers. Weight: 6¹/₄ to 7 pounds. Fiberglass stock with rubber recoil pad, sling swivel studs. Made 1986 to date.

Winchester Model 70 Win-Tuff Bolt Action Rifle
Calibers: 22-250, 223, 243, 270, 308 and 30-06 Springfield. 22-inch barrel. Weight: 6¹/₄–7 pounds. Laminated dye-shaded brown wood stock with recoil pad. Barrel drilled and tapped for scope. Swivel studs. FWT Model made 1986–1994. LW Model introduced in 1992.
Featherweight Model **$385**
Lightweight Model (Made 1992–93) **325**

Winchester Model 70 XTR
Featherweight (1972)

Winchester Model 70 XTR Sporter

Winchester Model 70A (1972)

Winchester Model 71 Special

RIFLES

Winchester Model 70 XTR Featherweight $365
Similar to Standard Win. Model 70, except lightweight American walnut stock with classic schnabel forend, checkered. 22-inch barrel, hooded blade front sight, folding leaf rear sight. Stainless-steel magazine follower. Weight: 6³/₄ pounds. Made 1984 to date.

Winchester Model 70 XTR Sporter Rifle $375
Calibers: 264 Win. Mag., 7mm Rem. Mag., 300 Win. Mag., 200 Weatherby Mag., and 338 Win. Mag. 3-shot magazine. 24-inch barrel. 44¹/₂ inches overall. Weight: 7³/₄ pounds. Walnut Monte Carlo stock. Rubber buttpad. Receiver tapped and drilled for scope mounting. Made 1986 to date.

Winchester Model 70 XTR 50th Anniversary $975
Same as XTR Sporter Magnum, except with checkered classic-style walnut stock with early-style Model 70 swivels. Hand-engraved receiver, floorplate, trigger guard and grip cap. "The Rifleman's Rifle 1937–1987" commemorative inscription engraved on barrel. Chambered in 300 Win. Mag. only. 500 produced in 1987.

Winchester Model 70 XTR Sporter Magnum $395
Calibers: 264 Win. Mag., 7mm Rem. Mag., 300 Win. Mag., 338 Win. Mag. 3-shot magazine. 24-inch barrel. 44¹/₂ inches overall. Weight: 7³/₄ pounds. No sights furnished,

Winchester Model 70 XTR Sporter Magnum (cont.)
optional adjustable folding leaf rear; hooded ramp. Receiver drilled and tapped for scope. Checkered American walnut Monte Carlo-style stock with satin finish. Made 1986 to date.

Winchester Model 70 XTR Sporter Varmint $385
Same general specifications as Model 70 XTR Sporter, except in calibers 223, 22-250, 243 only. Checkered American walnut Monte Carlo-style stock w/cheekpiece.

Winchester Model 70A $275
Calibers: 222 Rem., 22-250, 243 Win., 25-06, 270 Win., 30-06, 308 Win. 4-shot magazine. 22-inch barrel (except 24- or 26-inch in 25-06). Weight: about 7¹/₂ pounds. Sights: open rear: hooded ramp front. Monte Carlo stock with checkered pistol grip and forearm, sling swivels. Made 1972 to date.

Winchester Model 70A Magnum $295
Same as Model 70A, except has 3-shot magazine, 24-inch barrel, recoil pad. Weight: about 7³/₄ pounds. Calibers: 264 Win. Mag., 7mm Rem. Mag., 300 Win. Mag. Made 1972 to date.

Winchester Model 71 Special Lever Action
Repeater $1200
Solid frame. Caliber: 348 Win. 4-shot tubular magazine. 20- or 24-inch barrel. Weight: 8 pounds. Sights: open rear; bead front on ramp w/hood. Walnut stock, checkered pistol grip and forearm, grip cap, quick-detachable swivels and sling. Made 1935–1957.

Winchester Model 71 Standard Grade $795
Plain Model. Same as Model 71 Special, except lacks
checkering, grip car, sling and swivels.

Winchester Model 72 Bolt Action Repeater . . . $195
Tubular magazine. Takedown. Caliber: 22 Short, Long,
LR. Magazine holds 20 Short, 16 Long or 15 LR. 25-inch
barrel. Weight: 5¾ pounds. Sights: peep or open rear;
bead front. Plain pistol-grip stock. Made 1938–1959.

Winchester Model 73 Lever Action Carbine . . . $2795
Same as Standard Model 73 Rifle, except has 20-inch barrel, 12-shot magazine, weighs 7¼ pounds.

Winchester Model 73 Lever Action Repeater . . $2600
Calibers: 32-20, 38-40, 44-40; a few were chambered for
22 rimfire. 15-shot magazine, also made with 6-shot half
magazine. 24-inch barrel (round, half-octagon, octagon).
Weight: about 8½ pounds. Sights: open rear; bead or blade
front. Plain straight-grip stock and forearm. Made 1873–
1924. 720,610 rifles of this model were mfd.

**Winchester Model 73 Rifle — One of One
Thousand** . . . . **$50,000+**
During the late 1870s Winchester offered Model 73 rifles
of superior accuracy and extra finish, designated "One of
One Thousand" grade, at $100. These rifles are marked
"1 of 1000" or "One of One Thousand." Only 136 of this
model are known to have been manufactured. This is one
of the rarest of shoulder arms and, because so very few
have been sold in recent years, it is extremely difficult to
assign a value; however, in the author's opinion, an
"excellent" specimen would probably bring a price upward
of $35,000.

Winchester Model 73 Special Sporting Rifle . . . $2750
Same as Standard Model 73 Rifle, except this type has
receiver casehardened in colors, pistol-grip stock of select
walnut, octagon barrel only.

Winchester Model 74 Self-Loading Rifle $185
Takedown. Calibers: 22 Short only, 22 LR only. Tubular
magazine in buttstock holds 20 Short, 14 LR. 24-inch barrel. Weight: 6¼ pounds. Sights: open rear; bead front.
Plain pistol-grip stock, one-piece. Made 1939–1955.

Winchester Model 72

**Winchester Model 73
Lever Action Repeater**

**Winchester Model 73
One of One Thousand**

**Closeup of Barrel Engraving
Winchester Model 73 One of One Thousand**

Winchester Model 74

Winchester Model 75 Bolt Action Target Rifle . . **$425**
Caliber: 22 LR. 5- or 10-shot box magazine. 28-inch barrel.
Weight: 8¾ pounds. Target sights (Lyman, Redfield or
Winchester). Target stock w/pistol grip and semibeav-
ertail forearm, swivels and sling. Made 1938–1959.

Winchester Model 75 Sporting Rifle **$695**
Same as Model 75 Target, except has 24-inch barrel,
checkered sporter stock, open rear sight; bead front on
hooded ramp, weighs 5½ pounds.

Winchester Model 77 Semiautomatic Rifle,
Clip Type **$195**
Solid frame. Caliber: 22 LR. 8-shot clip magazine. 22-inch
barrel. Weight: about 5½ pounds. Sights: open rear; bead
front. Plain, one-piece pistol-grip stock. Made 1955–1963.

Winchester Model 77, Tubular Magazine Type . . **$195**
Same as Model 77. Clip type, except has tubular magazine
holding 15 rounds. Made 1955–1963.

Winchester Model 86 Lever Action Carbine . . . **$7500**
Same as standard Model 86 rifle, except with 22-inch barrel and weighs about 7¾ pounds.

Winchester Model 86 Lever Action Repeater . . **$1895**
Solid frame or takedown style. Calibers: 45/70, 38/56, 45/
90/300, 40/82/260, 40/65/260, 38/56/255, 38/70/255, 40/
70/330, 50/110/300, 50/100/450, 33 Win. All but the first
cartridge listed are now obsolete. 33 Win. and 45/70 were
the last calibers in which this model was supplied. 8-shot
tubular magazine, also 4-shot half-magazine. 22- or 26-
inch barrel (round, half-octagon, octagon). Weight: from
7½ pounds up. Sights: open rear; bead or blade front.
Plain straight-grip stock and forearm. Made 1886–1935.

RIFLES

Winchester Model 75 Target

Winchester Model 75 Sporter

Winchester Model 77 Clip Type

Winchester Model 77 Tubular Magazine

Winchester Model 86
Lever Action Repeater

Winchester Model 88 Carbine

Winchester Model 88 Rifle

Winchester Model 90

Winchester Model 92 Repeater

Winchester Model 88 Carbine $475
Same as Model 88 Rifle, except has 19-inch barrel, plain
carbine-style stock and forearm with barrel band. Weight:
7 pounds. Made 1968–1973.

Winchester Model 88 Lever Action Rifle $465
Hammerless. Calibers: 243 Win., 284 Win., 308 Win., 358
Win. 4-shot box magazine. 3-shot in pre-1963 models and
in current 284. 22-inch barrel. Weight: about 7¼ pounds.
One-piece walnut stock with pistol grip, swivels (1965 and
later models have basket-weave ornamentation instead of
checkering). Made 1955–1973. *Note:* 243 and 358 introduced 1956, latter discontinued 1964; 284 introduced 1963.

Winchester Model 90 Slide Action Repeater $995
Visible hammer. Calibers: 22 Short, Long, LR; 22 WRF.
(not interchangeable). Tubular magazine holds 15 Short,
12 Long, 11 LR; 12 WRF. 24-inch octagon barrel. Weight:

Winchester Model 90 Slide Action Repeater (cont.)
5¾ pounds. Sights: open rear; bead front. Plain straight-
grip stock, grooved slide handle. Originally solid frame,
after No. 15,499 all rifles of this model were takedown
type. Fancy checkered pistol-grip stock, stainless-steel
barrel supplied at extra cost. Made 1890–1932.

Winchester Model 92 Lever Action Carbine . . . $1150
Same as Model 92RR rifle, except has 20-inch barrel, 5-
shot or 11-shot magazine, weighs about 5¾ pounds.

Winchester Model 92 Lever Action Repeater . . $1050
Solid frame or takedown. Calibers: 25/20, 32/20, 38/40,
44/40. 13-shot tubular magazine, also 7-shot half-magazine. 24-inch barrel (round, octagon, half-octagon).
Weight: from 6¾ pounds up. Sights: open rear; bead front.
Plain straight-grip stock and forearm (stock illustrated
was extra cost option). Made 1892–1941.

Winchester Model 94 Antique Carbine

Winchester Model 94 Carbine

Winchester Model 94
Deluxe Carbine

Winchester Model 94
Lever Action Rifle

RIFLES

Winchester Model 94 Antique Carbine **$295**
Same as standard Model 94 Carbine, except has receiver
with decorative scrollwork and casehardened in colors,
brass-plated loading gate, saddle ring; caliber 30-30 only.
Made 1964–1984.

Winchester Model 94 Carbine
Same as Model 94 Rifle, except 20-inch round barrel, 6-
shot full-length magazine. Weight: about 6½ pounds.
Originally made in calibers 25-35, 30-30, 32 Special and
38-55. Currently mfd. in calibers 30-30 and 32 Special,
solid frame only.
Pre-World War II (under No. 1,300,000) **$795**
Postwar, pre-1964 . . . . **550**

Winchester Model 94 Classic Carbine **$295**
Same as Model 67 Carbine, except without commemorative details; has scroll-engraved receiver, gold-plated
loading gate. Made 1968–1970.

Winchester Model 94 Classic Rifle **$295**
Same as Model 67 Rifle, except without commemorative
details; has scroll-engraved receiver, gold-plated loading
gate. Made 1968–1970.

Winchester Model 94 Deluxe Carbine **$345**
Caliber: 30-30. 6-shot magazine. 20-inch barrel. 37¾
inches overall. Weight: 6½ pounds. Semi-fancy American
walnut stock with rubber buttpad, long forearm and specially cut checkering. Engraved with "Deluxe" script.
Made 1987 to date.

Winchester Model 94 Lever Action Rifle **$895**
Solid frame or takedown. Calibers: 25-35, 30-30, 32-40, 32
Special, 38-55. 7-shot tubular magazine or 4-shot half-
magazine. 26-inch barrel (octagon, half-octagon, round).
Weight: about 7¾ pounds. Sights: open rear; bead front.
Plain straight-grip stock and forearm; crescent-shaped or
shotgun-style buttplate. Made 1894–1937.

Winchester Model 94
Long Barrel Rifle

Winchester Model 94 Win-Tuff

Winchester Model 94
Wrangler II Angle Eject

Winchester Model 94 XTR Big Bore

Winchester Model 94 XTR in 7-30 Waters

Winchester Model 94 Long Barrel Rifle **$235**
Caliber: 30-30. 7-round magazine. 24-inch barrel. 41³/₄
inches overall. Weight: 7 pounds. American walnut stock.
Blade front sight. Made 1987 to date.

Winchester Model 94 Trapper **$195**
Same as Winchester Model 94 Carbine, except 16-inch
barrel and weighs 6 lbs. 2 oz. Made 1980 to date.

Winchester Model 94 Win-Tuff Rifle **$225**
Caliber: 30-30. 6-round magazine. 20-inch barrel. 37³/₄
inches overall. Weight: 6¹/₂ pounds. Brown laminated
wood stock. Made 1987 to date.

**Winchester Model 94 Wrangler II Angle Eject
Carbine** **$195**
Same as standard Model 94 Carbine, except has 16-inch
barrel, engraved receiver and chambered for 38-55 Win.
Introduced by U.S. Repeating Arms.

Winchester Model 94 XTR Big Bore
Modified Model 94 action for added strength. Caliber: 375
Win. 20-inch barrel. Rubber buttpad. Checkered stock and
forearm. Weight: 6¹/₂ pounds. Made 1978 to date.
Standard **$225**
Angle Eject **325**

**Winchester Model 94 XTR in 7-30 Waters
Lever Action Rifle** **$225**
Same general specifications as standard Angle Eject M94
except chambered for 7-30 Waters cartridge and has 24-
inch barrel. Weight: 7 pounds. Made 1985 to date by U.S.
Repeating Arms.

MODEL 94 COMMEMORATIVES

Values indicated are for commemorative Winchesters in new condition.

Winchester Model 94 Alaskan Purchase Centennial Commemorative Carbine $1800
Same as Wyoming issue, except different medallion and inscription. 1,501 made in 1967.

Winchester Model 94 Antlered Game $475
Standard Model 94 action. Gold-colored medallion inlaid in stock. Antique gold-plated receiver, lever tang and barrel bands. Medallion and receiver engraved with elk, moose, deer and caribou. 20½-inch barrel. Curved steel buttplate. In 30-30 caliber. 19,999 made in 1978.

Winchester Model 94 Bicentennial '76 Carbine . $595
Same as Standard Model 94 Carbine, except caliber 30-30 only; antique silver-finished, engraved receiver; stock and forearm of fancy walnut, checkered, Bicentennial medallion embedded in buttstock, curved buttplate. 20,000 made in 1976.

Winchester Model 94 Buffalo Bill Commemorative
Same as Centennial '66 Rifle, except receiver is black-chromed, scroll-engraved and bears name "Buffalo Bill"; hammer, trigger, loading gate, saddle ring, forearm cap, and buttplate are nickel-plated; Buffalo Bill Memorial Assn. commemorative medallion embedded in buttstock; "Buffalo Bill Commemorative" inscribed on barrel, facsimile signature "W.F. Cody, Chief of Scouts" on tang. Carbine has 20-inch barrel, 6-shot magazine, 7-pound weight. Made in 1968.

Carbine	**$375**
Rifle	**395**
Matched Carbine/Rifle Set (120,751 made)	**850**

Winchester Canadian Centennial Commemorative (Model 67)
Same as Centennial '66 Rifle, except receiver—engraved with maple leaves—and forearm cap are black-chromed, buttplate is blued, commemorative inscription in gold on barrel and top tang: "Canadian Centennial 1867–1967." Carbine has 20-inch barrel, 6-shot magazine, 7-pound weight. Made in 1967.

Carbine	**$350**
Rifle	**375**
Matched Carbine/Rifle Set (90,398 made)	**795**

RIFLES

Winchester Model 94 Alaskan Purchase Carbine

Winchester Model 94 Bicentennial '76 Carbine

Winchester Model 94 Buffalo Bill Rifle

Winchester Canadian Centennial

MODEL 94 COMMEMORATIVES (cont.)

Winchester Centennial '66 Rifle

Winchester Model 94 Cowboy Carbine

Winchester Colt
Commemorative Set

Winchester Model 94 Golden Spike Carbine

Winchester Centennial '66 Commemorative
Commemorates Winchester's 100th anniversary. Standard Model 94 action. Caliber: 30-30. Full-length magazine holds 8 rounds. 26-inch octagon barrel. Weight: 8 pounds. Gold-plated receiver and forearm cap. Sights: open rear; post front. Saddle ring. Walnut buttstock and forearm with high-gloss finish, solid brass buttplate. Commemorative inscription on barrel and top tang of receiver. Made in 1966.
Carbine **$395**
Rifle 425
Matched Carbine/Rifle Set (100,478 made) 895

Winchester Model 94 Cheyenne Comm. **$695**
Available in Canada only. Same as Standard Model 94 Carbine, except chambered for 44-40. 11,225 made in 1977.

Winchester Model 94 Colt Commemorative Carbine Set **$2595**
Standard Model 94 action. Caliber: 44-40 Win. 20-inch barrel. Weight: 6¼ pounds. Features a horse-and-rider trademark and distinctive WC monogram in gold etching on left side of receiver. Sold in set with Colt Single Action Revolver chambered for same caliber.

Winchester Model 94 Cowboy Commemorative Carbine **$475**
Same as Standard Model 94 Carbine, except caliber 30-30 only; nickel-plated receiver, tangs, lever, barrel bands; engraved receiver, "Cowboy Commemorative" on barrel, commemorative medallion embedded in buttstock; curved buttplate. 20,915 made in 1970.

Winchester Model 94 Golden Spike Commemorative Carbine **$375**
Same as Standard Model 94 Carbine, except caliber 30-30 only; gold-plated receiver, tangs and barrel bands; engraved receiver, commemorative medallion embedded in stock. 64,758 made in 1969.

Winchester Model 94 Illinois Sesquicentennial Commemorative Carbine **$380**
Same as Standard Model 94 Carbine, except caliber 30-30 only; gold-plated buttplate, trigger, loading gate, and saddle ring; receiver engraved with profile of Lincoln, commemorative inscriptions on receiver, barrel; souvenir medallion embedded in stock. 31,124 made in 1968.

MODEL 94 COMMEMORATIVES (cont.)

**Winchester Model 94
Legendary Frontiersmen**

**Winchester Model 94
Legendary Lawmen Carbine**

Winchester Model 94 Lone Star Rifle

Winchester Model 94 NRA Centennial Musket

**Winchester Model 94
Nebraska Centennial Carbine**

RIFLES

Winchester Model 94 Legendary Frontiersmen Commemorative $425
Standard Model 94 action. Caliber: 38-55. 24-inch round barrel. Nickel-silver medallion inlaid in stock. Antique silver-plated receiver engraved with scenes of the old frontier. Checkered walnut stock and forearm. 19,999 made in 1979.

Winchester Model 94 Legendary Lawmen Commemorative $415
Same as Standard Model 94 Carbine, except 30-30 only; antique silver-plated receiver engraved with action law-enforcement scenes. 16-inch Trapper barrel, antique silver-plated barrel bands. 19,999 made in 1978.

Winchester Model 94 Lone Star Commemorative
Same as Theodore Roosevelt Rifle, except yellow-gold plating; "Lone Star" engraving on receiver and barrel, commemorative medallion embedded in buttstock. Made in 1970.
Rifle $395
Matched Carbine/Rifle Set (30,669 made) 850

Winchester Model 94 NRA Centennial Musket $350
Commemorates 100th anniversary of National Rifle Association of America. Standard Model 94 action. Caliber: 30-30. 7-shot magazine. 26-inch barrel. Sights: military folding rear; blade front. Black chrome-finished receiver engraved "NRA 1871–1971" plus scrollwork. Barrel inscribed "NRA Centennial Musket." Musket-style buttstock and full-length forearm; commemorative medallion embedded in buttstock. Weight: 7 1/8 pounds. Made in 1971.

Winchester Model 94 NRA Centennial Rifle $350
Same as Model 94 Rifle, except has commemorative details as in NRA Centennial Musket (barrel inscribed "NRA Centennial Rifle"); caliber 30-30, 24-inch barrel, QD sling swivels. Made in 1971.

Winchester NRA Centennial Matched Set $850
Rifle and musket were offered in sets with consecutive serial numbers. *Note:* Production figures not available. These rifles offered in Winchester's 1972 catalog.

Winchester Model 94 Nebraska Centennial Commemorative Carbine $1195
Same as Standard Model 94 Carbine, except caliber 30-30 only; gold-plated hammer, loading gate, barrel band, and buttplate; souvenir medallion embedded in stock, commemorative inscription on barrel. 2,500 made in 1966.

MODEL 94 COMMEMORATIVES (cont.)

Winchester Model 94 Theodore Roosevelt Commemorative Rifle/Carbine
Standard Model 94 action. Caliber: 30-30. Rifle has 6-shot half-magazine, 26-inch octagon barrel, 7½-pound weight. Carbine has 6-shot full magazine, 20-inch barrel, 7-pound weight. White gold-plated receiver, upper tang, and forend cap; receiver engraved with American Eagle, "26th President 1901–1909," and Roosevelt's signature. Commemorative medallion embedded in buttstock. Saddle ring. Half pistol grip, contoured lever. Made in 1969.

Carbine	**$365**
Rifle	**375**
Matched Set (49,505 made)	**795**

Winchester Model 94 Texas Ranger Association Carbine **$2400**
Same as Texas Ranger Commemorative Model 94, except special edition of 150 carbines, numbered 1 through 150, with hand-checkered full-fancy walnut stock and forearm. Sold only through Texas Ranger Association. Made in 1973.

Winchester Model 94 Texas Ranger Commemorative Carbine **$725**
Same as Standard Model 94 Carbine, except caliber 30-30 only, stock and forearm of semi-fancy walnut, replica of Texas Ranger star embedded in buttstock, curved buttplate. 5,000 made in 1973.

Winchester Model 94 John Wayne Comm. **$825**
Standard Model 94 action. Caliber: 32-40. 18½-inch barrel. Receiver is pewter-plated with engraving of Indian attack and cattle drive scenes. Oversized bow on lever. Nickel-silver medallion in buttstock bears a bas-relief portrait of Wayne. Selected American walnut stock with deep-cut checkering. Introduced by U.S. Repeating Arms.

Winchester Model 94 Wells Fargo & Co. Commemorative Carbine **$450**
Same as Standard Model 94 Carbine, except 30-30 only; antique silver-finished, engraved receiver; stock and forearm of fancy walnut, checkered, curved buttplate. Nickel-silver stagecoach medallion (inscribed "Wells Fargo & Co.—1852–1977—125 Years") embedded in buttstock. 20,000 made in 1977.

Winchester Model 94 Oliver F. Winchester Commemorative **$575**
Standard Model 94 action. Caliber: 38-55. 24-inch octagonal barrel. Receiver is satin gold-plated with distinctive engravings. Stock and forearm semi-fancy American walnut with high grade checkering. 19,999 made in 1980.

Winchester Model 94
Theodore Roosevelt Rifle

Winchester Model 94
Texas Ranger Carbine

Winchester Model 94
John Wayne Carbine

Winchester Model 94
Wells Fargo Carbine

Winchester Model 94
Oliver F. Winchester

RIFLES

Winchester Model 94 Wyoming Diamond Jubilee Commemorative Carbine $1495
Same as Standard Model 94 Carbine, except caliber 30-30 only, receiver engraved and casehardened in colors, brass saddle ring and loading gate, souvenir medallion embedded in buttstock, commemorative inscription on barrel. 1,500 made in 1964.

Winchester Model 95 Lever Action Carbine . . . $1895
Same as Model 95 Standard Rifle, except has 22-inch barrel, carbine-style stock, weighs about 8 pounds, calibers 30-40, 30-03, 30-06 and 303, solid frame only.

Winchester Model 95 Lever Action Repeater . . $1400
Calibers: 30-40 Krag, 30-03, 30-06, 303 British, 35 Win., 405 Win.; original model supplied in the now obsolete 38-72 and 40-72 calibers. 4-shot box magazine, except 30-40 and 303, which have 5-shot magazine. Barrel lengths: 24-, 26-, 28-inches (round, half-octagon, octagon). Weight: about 8½ pounds. Sights: open rear; bead or blade front.

Winchester Model 95 Lever Action Repeater (cont.)
Plain straight-grip stock and forearm (standard). Both solid frame and takedown models were available. Made 1895–1931.

Winchester Model 100 Autoloading Rifle $425
Gas-operated semiautomatic. Calibers: 243, 284, 308 Win. 4-shot clip magazine (3-shot in 284). 22-inch barrel. Weight: 7¼ pounds. Sights: open rear; hooded ramp front. One-piece stock w/pistol grip, basket-weave checkering, grip cap, sling swivels. Made 1961–1973.

Winchester Model 100 Carbine $450
Same as Model 100 Rifle, except has 19-inch barrel, plain carbine-style stock and forearm with barrel band. Weight: 7 pounds. Made 1967–1973.

Winchester Model 95 Carbine

Winchester Model 95 Rifle

Winchester Model 100 Autoloading Rifle

Winchester Model 100 Carbine

Winchester Model 121 Deluxe **$115**
Same as Model 121 Standard, except has ramp front sight, stock with fluted comb and sling swivels. Made 1967–1973.

Winchester Model 121 Standard Bolt Action Single Shot **$120**
Caliber: 22 Short, Long, LR. 20¾-inch barrel. Weight: 5 pounds. Sights: open rear; bead front. Monte Carlo-style stock. Made 1967–1973.

Winchester Model 121 Youth **$125**
Same as Model 121 Standard, except has 1¼-inch shorter stock. Made 1967–1973.

Winchester Model 131 Bolt Action Repeater . . . **$135**
Caliber: 22 Short, Long or LR. 7-shot clip magazine. 20¾-inch barrel. Weight: 5 pounds. Sights: open rear; ramp front. Plain Monte Carlo stock. Made 1967–1973.

Winchester Model 135 . . . . **$125**
Same as Model 131, except chambered for 22 WMR cartridge. Magazine holds 5 rounds. Made in 1967.

Winchester Model 141 Bolt Action Tubular Repeater **$140**
Same as Model 131, except has tubular magazine in buttstock; holds 19 Short, 15 Long, 13 LR. Made 1967–1973.

Winchester Model 145 . . . . **$140**
Same as Model 141, except chambered for 22 WMR; magazine holds 9 rounds. Made in 1967.

Winchester Model 150 Lever Action Carbine . . . **$110**
Same as Model 250, except has straight loop lever, plain carbine-style straight-grip stock and forearm with barrel band. Made 1967–1973.

Winchester Model 190 Carbine **$120**
Same as Model 190 rifle, except has carbine-style forearm with barrel band. Made 1967–1973.

Winchester Model 121 Deluxe

Winchester Model 131

Winchester Model 141

Winchester Model 150 Carbine

Winchester Model 190 Carbine

Winchester Model 250 Standard

Winchester Model 270 Standard

Winchester Model 290 Standard

Winchester Model 190 Semiautomatic Rifle **$135**
Same as current Model 290, except has plain stock and forearm. Made 1966–1978.

Winchester Model 250 Deluxe Rifle **$150**
Same as Model 250 Standard Rifle, except has fancy walnut Monte Carlo stock and forearm, sling swivels. Made 1965–1971.

Winchester Model 250 Standard Lever Action Rifle **$150**
Hammerless. Caliber: 22 Short, Long or LR. Tubular magazine holds 21 Short, 17 Long, 15 LR. 20½-inch barrel. Sights: open rear; ramp front. Weight: about 5 pounds. Plain stock and forearm on early production; later model has checkering. Made 1963–1973.

Winchester Model 255 Deluxe Rifle **$170**
Same as Model 250 Deluxe Rifle, except chambered for 22 WMR cartridge. Magazine holds 11 rounds. Made 1965–1973.

Winchester Model 255 Standard Rifle **$150**
Same as Model 250 Standard Rifle, except chambered for 22 WMR cartridge. Magazine holds 11 rounds. Made 1964–1970.

Winchester Model 270 Deluxe Rifle **$195**
Same as Model 270 Standard Rifle, except has fancy walnut Monte Carlo stock and forearm. Maden 1965–1973.

Winchester Model 270 Standard Slide Action Rifle **$125**
Hammerless. Caliber: 22 Short, Long or LR. Tubular magazine holds 21 Short, 17 Long, 15 LR. 20½-inch barrel. Sights: open rear; ramp front. Weight: about 5 pounds. Early production had plain walnut stock and forearm (slide handle); latter also furnished in plastic (Cycolac); last model has checkering. Made 1963–1973.

Winchester Model 275 Deluxe Rifle **$165**
Same as Model 270 Deluxe Rifle, except chambered for 22 WMR cartridge. Magazine holds 11 rounds. Made 1965–1970.

Winchester Model 275 Standard Rifle **$125**
Same as Model 270 Standard Rifle, except chambered for 22 WMR cartridge. Magazine holds 11 rounds. Made 1964–1970.

Winchester Model 290 Deluxe Rifle **$175**
Same as Model 290 Standard Rifle, except has fancy walnut Monte Carlo stock and forearm. Made 1965–1973.

Winchester Model 290 Standard Semiautomatic Rifle
Caliber: 22 Long or LR. Tubular magazine holds 17 Long, 15 LR. 20½-inch barrel. Sights: open rear; ramp front. Weight: about 5 pounds. Plain stock and forearm on early production; current model has checkering. Made 1963–1977.
W/plain stock/forearm **$185**
W/checkered stock/forearm **210**

Winchester Model 310

Winchester Model 320

Winchester Model 490 Rifle

Winchester Model 670 Rifle

Winchester Model 670 Magnum

Winchester Model 310 Bolt Action Single Shot . . **$175**
Caliber: 22 Short, Long, LR. 22-inch barrel. Weight: 5⅝ pounds. Sights: open rear; ramp front. Monte Carlo stock w/checkered pistol grip and forearm, sling swivels. Made 1972–75.

Winchester Model 320 Bolt Action Repeater . . . **$250**
Same as Model 310, except has 5-shot clip magazine. Made 1972–74.

Winchester Model 490 Semiautomatic Rifle **$240**
Caliber: 22 LR. 5-shot clip magazine. 22-inch barrel. Weight: 6 pounds. Sights: folding leaf rear; hooded ramp front. One-piece walnut stock w/checkered pistol grip and forearm. Made 1975–77.

Winchester Model 670 Bolt Action Sporting Rifle **$260**
Calibers: 225 Win., 243 Win., 270 Win., 30-06, 308 Win. 4-shot magazine. 22-inch barrel. Weight: 7 pounds. Sights: open rear; ramp front. Monte Carlo stock w/checkered pistol grip and forearm. Made 1967–1973.

Winchester Model 670 Carbine **$275**
Same as Model 670 Rifle, except has 19-inch barrel. Weight: 6¾ pounds. Calibers: 243 Win., 270 Win., 30-06. Made 1967–1970.

Winchester Model 670 Magnum **$295**
Same as Model 670 Rifle, except has 24-inch barrel, reinforced stock with recoil pad. Weight: 7¼ pounds. Calibers: 264 Win. Mag., 7mm Rem. Mag., 300 Win. Mag. Made 1967–1970.

Winchester Model 770

Winchester Model 1900

RIFLES

Winchester Model 770 Bolt Action Sporting Rifle $300
Model 70-type action. Calibers: 22-250, 222 Rem., 243, 270 Win., 30-06. 4-shot box magazine. 22-inch barrel. Sights: open rear; hooded ramp front. Weight: 7¹⁄₈ pounds. Monte Carlo stock, checkered, swivels. Made 1969–1971.

Winchester Model 770 Magnum $325
Same as Standard Model 770, except 24-inch barrel, weight 7¹⁄₄ pounds, recoil pad. Calibers: 7mm Rem. Mag., 264 and 300 Win. Mag. Made 1969–1971.

Winchester Model 1900 Bolt Action Single Shot Rifle $360
Takedown. Caliber: 22 Short and Long. 18-inch barrel. Weight: 2³⁄₄ pounds. Sights: open rear; blade front. One-piece, straight-grip stock. Made 1899–1902.

Winchester Model 9422 Boy Scouts of America Commemorative $500
Standard Model 9422 action. Caliber: 22RF. 20¹⁄₂-inch round barrel. Receiver roll-engraved and plated in antique pewter, illustrating the Boy Scout oath and law. Frame carries inscription, "1910–1985." "Boy Scouts of America" inscribed on right side of barrel. Checkered stock and forearm of American walnut with satin finish. A maximum of 15,000 were produced by U.S. Repeating Arms beginning with serial number BSA1.

Winchester Model 9422 Eagle Scout Commemorative $1895
Standard Model 9422 action. Caliber: 22 RF. Same general specifications as Boy Scout model except different engraving, jeweled bolt, antique gold-plated forearm cap and brass magazine tube. Only 1,000 were made by U.S. Repeating Arms bearing serial number Eagle 1 through Eagle 1,000.

Winchester Model 9422
Boy Scouts of America Commemorative

Winchester Model 9422
Eagle Scout Limited Edition

Winchester Model 9422

Winchester Model 9422 XTR Classic

Winchester Model 9422 Lever Action Carbine . . **$245**
Styled after Model 94. Caliber: 22 Short, Long, LR. Tubular magazine holds 21 Short, 17 Long, 15 LR. 20 1/2-inch barrel. Weight: 6 1/4 pounds. Sights: open rear; hooded ramp front. Carbine-style stock and forearm, barrel band. Made 1972 to date.

Winchester Model 9422M **$295**
Same as Model 9422, except chambered for 22 WMR; magazine holds 11 rounds. Stock options: Walnut, WinCam (laminated green), WinTuff (laminated brown). Made 1972 to date.

Winchester Model 9422 Win-Cam **$250**
Caliber: 22 RF. 11-shot magazine. 20 1/2-inch barrel. 37 1/8 inches overall. Weight: 6 1/4 pounds. Laminated non-glare green-shaded stock and forend. Made 1987 to date.

Winchester Model 9422 XTR Classic **$265**
Same general specifications as standard Model 9422, except has pistol-grip stock and weighs 6 1/2 pounds.

Winchester Double Xpress Rifle **$2095**
Over/under double rifle. Caliber: 30-06. 23 1/2-inch barrel. Weight: 8 1/2 pounds. Made for Olin Corp. by Olin-Kodensha in Japan. Introduced 1982.

Winchester Lee Straight-Pull Bolt Action Repeating Rifle—Musket Model **$895**
Commercial version of U.S. Navy Model 1895 Rifle, caliber 6mm (1895–1897). Caliber: 236 U.S.N. 5-shot box magazine, clip-loaded. 28-inch barrel. Weight: 8 1/2 pounds. Sights: folding leaf rear; post front. Military-type full stock w/semi-pistol grip. Made 1897–1902.

Winchester Lee Straight-Pull Sporting Rifle **$950**
Same as Musket Model except has 24-inch barrel, sporter-style stock, open sporting rear sight, bead front sight. Weight: about 7 1/2 pounds. Made 1897–1902.

Winchester Ranger Angle Eject Lever Action Carbine **$180**
Caliber: 30-30. 5-shot tubular magazine. Barrel: 20-inch round. Weight: 6 1/2 pounds. American hardwood stock. Economy version of Model 94. Made 1985 to date by U.S. Repeating Arms.

Winchester Lee Sporting Rifle

**Winchester Ranger Angle Eject
Lever Action Carbine**

Winchester Ranger Bolt Action Carbine

Winchester Ranger Youth
Bolt Action Carbine

Winchester Ranger Bolt Action Carbine **$260**
Calibers: 223 Rem., 243 Win., 270, 30-06, 7mm Rem. (discontinued 1985), Mag. 3- and 4-shot magazine. Barrel: 24-inch in 7mm; 22-inch in 270 and 30-06. Open sights. American hardwood stock. Made 1985 to date by U.S. Repeating Arms.

Winchester Ranger Youth Bolt Action Carbine **$275**
Calibers: 223 (discontinued 1989), 243, and 308 Win. 4- and 5-shot magazine. Barrel: 20-inch. Weight: 5¾ pounds. American hardwood stock. Open rear sight. Made 1985 to date by U.S. Repeating Arms.

Winslow Crown Grade
Plainsmaster Stock

Winslow Regent Grade
Bushmaster Stock

WINSLOW ARMS COMPANY
Camden, South Carolina

Winslow Bolt Action Sporting Rifle
Action: FN Supreme Mauser, Mark X Mauser, Remington 700 and 788, Sako, Winchester 70. *Standard calibers:* 17-222, 17-223, 222 Rem., 22-250, 243 Win., 6mm Rem., 25-06, 257 Roberts, 270 Win., 7×57, 280 Rem., 284 Win., 308 Win., 30-06, 358 Win. *Magnum calibers:* 17-222 Mag., 257 Weatherby, 264 Win., 270 Weath., 7mm Rem., 7mm Weath., 300 H&H, 300 Weath., 300 Win., 308 Norma, 8mm Rem., 338 Win., 358 Norma, 375 H&H, 375 Weath.,

Winslow Bolt Action Sporting Rifle (cont.)
458 Win. 3-shot magazine in standard calibers, 2-shot in magnum. 24-inch barrel in standard calibers, 26-inch in magnum. Weight: with 24-inch barrel, 7 to 7½ lbs.; with 26-inch barrel, 8 to 9 lbs. No sights. Stocks: "Bushmaster" with slender pistol grip and beavertail forearm, "Plainsmaster" with full curl pistol grip and flat forearm; both styles have Monte Carlo cheekpiece; rosewood forend tip and pistol-grip cap, recoil pad, QD swivels; woods used include walnut, maple, myrtle. There are eight grades—Commander, Regal, Regent, Regimental, Royal, Imperial, Emperor—in ascending order of quality of wood, carving, inlays, engraving. Values shown are for basic rifle in each

Winslow Bolt Action Sporting Rifle (cont.)

grade; extras such as special fancy wood, more elaborate carving, inlays and engraving can increase these figures considerably. Made 1962–1989.

Commander Grade	$ 515
Regal Grade	585
Regent Grade	695
Regimental Grade	875
Crown Grade	1200
Royal Grade	1400
Imperial Grade	3000
Emperor Grade	5500

ZEPHYR DOUBLE RIFLES

Manufactured by Victor Sarasqueta Company, Eibar, Spain

Zephyr Double Rifle **$14,000**
Boxlock. Calibers: Available in practically every caliber from .22 Hornet to .505 Gibbs. Barrels: 22 to 28 inches standard, but any lengths were available on special order. Weight: 7 pounds for the smaller caliber up to 12 or more pounds for the larger calibers. Checkered Spanish walnut stock and beavertail forearm. Receiver engraved with scroll patterns. Imported by Stoeger 1938–1951.

Section III
SHOTGUNS

Armalite AR-17

ALDENS SHOTGUN
Chicago, Illinois

Aldens Model 670 Chieftain Slide Action **$155**
Hammerless. Gauges: 12, 20 and others. 3-shot tubular
magazine. Barrel: 26- to 30-inch; various chokes. Weight:
6¼ to 7½ pounds depending on barrel length and gauge.
Walnut-finished hardwood stock.

ARMALITE, INC.
Costa Mesa, California

Armalite AR-17 Golden Gun **$545**
Recoil-operated semiautomatic. High-test aluminum barrel and receiver housing. 12 gauge only. 2-shot. 24-inch
barrel with interchangeable choke tubes: IC/M/F. Weight:
5.6 pounds. Polycarbonate stock and forearm, recoil pad.
Gold anodized finish standard; also made with black finish.
Made 1964–65. Less than 2,000 produced.

**American Arms Derby
Side-by-Side**

American Arms Gentry

American Arms Grulla #2

AMERICAN ARMS
N. Kansas City, Missouri

See also Franchi Shotguns.

American Arms Brittany Hammerless Double . . . **$590**
Boxlock with engraved case-colored receiver. Single selective trigger. Selective automatic ejectors. Gauges: 12,
20. 3-inch chambers. Barrels: 25- or 27-inch with screw-
in choke tubes (IC/M/F). Weight: 6½ pounds (20 ga.).
Checkered English-style walnut stock with semibeavertail
forearm or pistol-grip stock with high-gloss finish. Imported from 1989 to date.

American Arms Camper Special **$85**
Similar to the Single Barrel, except a takedown model
with 21-inch barrel, Mod. choke and pistol-grip stock.
Made in 1989 only.

> **NOTE:** The following abbreviations are used throughout
> this section when referring to chokes: Cyl.=Cylinder; F=Full;
> IC=Improved Cylinder; IM=Improved Modified; M=Modi-
> fied; SK=Skeet.

American Arms Combo **$195**
Similar to the Single Barrel model, except available with
interchangeable rifle and shotgun barrels. 22 LR/20-gauge
shotgun or 22 Hornet/12-gauge shotgun. Rifle barrel has
adj. rear sights; blade-type front sight. Made in 1989.

American Arms Derby Hammerless Double **$795**
Sidelock with engraved sideplates. Single non-selective
trigger. Selective automatic ejectors. Gauges: 12, 20. 3-
inch chambers. Barrels: 26-inch (IC/M) or 28-inch (M/
F). Weight: 6 pounds (20 ga.). Checkered English-style
walnut stock and splinter forearm with hand-rubbed oil
finish. Engraved frame/sideplates w/antique silver finish.

American Arms Gentry Hammerless Double
Color casehardened boxlock receiver with scroll engraving.
Double triggers. Extractors. Gauges: 12, 16, 20, 28, .410.
3-inch chambers (16 and 28 have 2¾-inch). Barrels: 26-
inch (IC/M) or 28-inch (M/F, 12, 16 and 20). Weight: 6¾
pounds (12 ga.). Checkered walnut stock with pistol grip
and beavertail forearm with semi-gloss finish. Imported
from 1987 to date.
12, 16 or 20 Gauge **$475**
28 or .410 Gauge **515**

American Arms Grulla #2 Hammerless Double
True sidelock with engraved detachable sideplates. Double
triggers. Extractors and cocking indicators. Gauges: 12

American Arms Silver I
Over/Under

American Arms Silver Skeet/Trap

American Arms Grulla #2 Hammerless Double (cont.)

and 20 w/2³/₄-inch chambers; 28 and .410 with 3-inch. Barrels: 26-inch (IC/M) or 28-inch (M/F, 12 and 28 ga. only). Weight: 6¹/₄ pounds (12 gauge). English-style walnut stock and splinter forearm w/hand-rubbed oil finish and checkered grip, forearm and butt. Imported 1989 to date.
Standard Model **$2200**
Two-barrel Set **2875**

American Arms Silver I Over/Under

Boxlock. Single selective trigger. Extractors. Gauges: 12, 20 and .410 with 3-inch chambers; 28 with 2³/₄. Barrels: 26-inch (IC/M), 28-inch (M/F, 12 and 20 ga. only). Weight: 6³/₄ pounds (12 ga.). Checkered walnut stock and forearm. Antique-silver receiver with scroll engraving. Imported from 1987 to date.
12 or 20 Gauge **$410**
28 or .410 Gauge **450**

American Arms Silver II Over/Under

Similar to Model Silver I, except with selective automatic ejectors and 26-inch barrels with screw-in tubes (12 and 20 ga.). Fixed chokes (28 and .410).
12 or 20 Gauge **$520**
28 or .410 . . . . **560**
Two-barrel Set **825**

American Arms Silver Lite Over/Under

Similar to Model Silver II, except with blued, engraved alloy receiver. Available in 12 and 20 gauge only. Imported from 1990 to date.
Standard Model **$545**
Two-barrel Set **850**

American Arms Silver Skeet/Trap **$750**

Similar to the Silver II Model, except has 28-inch (Skeet) or 30-inch (Trap) ported barrels with target-style rib and mid-bead sight. Imported from 1992 to date.

American Arms Silver Sporting Over/Under **$620**

Boxlock. Single selective trigger. Selective automatic ejectors. Gauges: 12; 2³/₄-inch chambers. Barrels: 28-inch with Franchoke tubes: SK, IC, M and F. Weight: 7¹/₂ pounds. Checkered walnut stock and forearm. Special broadway rib and vented side ribs. Engraved receiver with chrome-nickel finish. Imported from 1990 to date.

American Arms Single Barrel Shotgun **$85**

Break-open action. Gauges: 12, 20, .410; 3-inch chamber. Weight: about 6¹/₂ pounds. Bead front sight. Walnut-finished hardwood stock with checkered grip and forend. Made from 1988 to date.

American Arms Slugger Single Shot Shotgun **$95**

Similar to the Single Barrel model, except in 12 and 20 gauges only with 24-inch slug barrel. Rifle-type sights and recoil pad. Made from 1989 to date.

American Arms TS/OU 12 Shotgun **$540**

Turkey Special. Boxlock. Single selective trigger. Selective automatic ejectors. Gauge: 12; 3¹/₂-inch chambers. Barrels: 24-inch over/under with screw-in choke tubes (IC, M, F). Weight: 6 lbs. 15 oz. Checkered European walnut stock and beavertail forearm. Matte blue metal finish.

American Arms TS/SS 10 Hammerless Double . **$525**

Turkey Special. Same general specifications as Model WS/ SS 10, except with 26-inch side-by-side barrels and screw-in choke tubes (F/F). Weight: 10 lbs. 13 oz.

American Arms TS/SS 12 Hammerless Double . **$495**

Same general specifications as Model WS/SS 10, except in 12 gauge with 26-inch side-by-side barrels and 3 screw-in choke tubes (IC/M/F). Weight: 7 lbs. 6 oz.

American Arms WS/OU 12 Shotgun **$425**

Waterfowl Special. Boxlock. Single selective trigger. Selective automatic ejectors. Gauge: 12; 3¹/₂-inch chambers. Barrels: 28-inch over/under with screw-in tubes (IC/M/ F). Weight: 7 pounds. Checkered European walnut stock and beavertail forearm. Matte blue metal finish.

American Arms WS/SS 10 Hammerless Double . . **$495**

Waterfowl Special. Boxlock. Double triggers. Extractors. Gauge: 10; 3¹/₂-inch chambers. Barrels: 32-inch side/side choked F/F. Weight: about 11 pounds. Checkered walnut stock and beavertail forearm with satin finish. Parkerized metal finish. Imported from 1987 to date.

American Arms WT/OU 10 Shotgun **$750**

Same general specifications as Model WS/OU 12, except chambered for 10-gauge 3¹/₂-inch shells. Extractors. Satin wood finish and matte blue metal.

ARMSPORT, INC.
Miami, Florida

Armsport Models 1050, 1053, 1054 Hammerless Doubles

Side-by-side with engraved receiver, double triggers and extractors. Gauges: 12, 20, .410; 3-inch chambers. **Model 1050**: 12 ga., 28-inch bbl., M/F choke. **Model 1053**: 20 ga., 26-inch bbl., I/M choke. **Model 1054**: .410 ga., 26-

Armsport Model 1050

Armsport Model 2700
10 Gauge O/U Goose Gun

Armsport Model 2750/2751 Over/Under

Armsport Model 2900 Tri-Barrel

Armsport Models 1050, 1053, 1054 (cont.)

inch bbl., I/M. Weight: 6 pounds (12 ga.). European walnut buttstock and forend. Made in Italy from 1986 to date.

Model 1050	**$625**
Model 1053	**650**
Model 1054	**695**

Armsport Model 2700 Goose Gun

Similar to the 2700 Standard Model, except 10 gauge with 3 1/2-inch chambers. Double triggers with 28-inch barrel choked IC/M or 32-inch barrel, F/F. 12mm wide vent rib. Weight: 9 1/2 pounds. Canada geese engraved on receiver. Antiqued silver-finished action. Checkered European walnut stock w/rubber recoil pad. Made in Italy 1986 to date.

With Fixed Chokes	**$910**
With Choke Tubes	**975**

Armsport Model 2700 Over/Under Series

Hammerless, takedown shotgun with engraved receiver. Selective single or double triggers. Gauges: 10, 12, 20, 28 and .410. Barrel: 26- or 28-inch with fixed chokes or choke tubes. Weight: 8 pounds. Checkered European walnut buttstock and forend. Made in Italy.

Model 2705 (.410, DT, fixed chokes)	**$615**
Model 2730, 2731 (Boss-style action, SST, Choke tubes)	**670**
Model 2733, 2735 (Boss-style action, extractors)	**695**
Model 2741 (Boss-style action, ejectors)	**645**
Model 2742 Sporting Clays (12 ga./choke tubes)	**695**
Model 2744 Sporting Clays (20 ga./choke tubes)	**695**
Model 2750 Sporting Clays (12 ga./sideplates)	**785**
Model 2751 Sporting Clays (20 ga./sideplates)	**785**

Armsport Model 2755 Slide Action Shotgun

Pump action, hammerless shotgun. 12 gauge w/3-inch chamber. Tubular magazine. Barrels: 28- or 30-inch with fixed choke or choke tubes. Weight: 7 pounds; vent rib. European walnut stock. Made in Italy 1986–87.

Standard Model, Fixed Choke	**$315**
Standard Model, Choke Tubes	**360**
Police Model, 20-inch Barrel	**295**

Armsport Model 2900 Tri-Barrel Shotgun $2850

Boxlock. Double triggers with top-tang barrel selector. Extractors. Gauge: 12; 3-inch chambers. Barrels: 28-inch (IC, M and F). Weight: 7 3/4 pounds. Checkered European walnut stock and forearm. Engraved silver receiver. Imported from 1986 to date.

ASTRA SHOTGUNS
Guernica, Spain
Manufactured by Unceta y Compania

Astra Model 650 Over/Under Shotgun

Hammerless, takedown with double triggers. 12 gauge w/ 2 3/4-inch chambers. Barrels: 28-inch (M/F or SK/SK); 30-inch (M/F). Weight: 6 3/4 pounds. Checkered European walnut buttstock and forend.

With Extractors	**$450**
With Ejectors	**545**

Astra Model 750 Over/Under Shotgun

Similar to the Model 650, except with selective single trigger and ejectors. Made in Field, Skeet and Trap configurations since 1980.

Astra Model 750 Over/Under (cont.)

Field Model w/Extractors	$500
Field Model w/Ejectors	595
Trap or Skeet	710

AyA Model 53E

AyA Model 76

AyA Model 117

AYA (AGUIRRE Y ARANZABAL)
Eibar, Spain

AyA Model 2 Hammerless Double

Sidelock action with selective single or double triggers, automatic ejectors and safety. Gauges: 12, 20, 28, (2³/₄-inch chambers); .410 (3-inch chambers). Barrels: 26- or 28-inch with various fixed choke combinations. Weight: 7 pounds (12 ga.). English-style straight walnut buttstock and splinter forend. Made in 1987.

12 or 20 ga. w/Double Triggers	$1450
12 or 20 ga. w/Single Trigger	1525
28 or .410 ga. w/Double Triggers	1600
28 or .410 ga. w/Single Trigger	1750
Two-barrel Set	750

AyA Model 37 Super Over/Under Shotgun $2595

Sidelock. Automatic ejectors. Selective single trigger. Made in all gauges, barrel lengths and chokes. Vent-rib barrels. Elaborately engraved. Checkered stock (with straight or pistol grip) and forend. Discontinued 1985.

AyA Model 53E $1295

Same general specifications as Model 117, except more elaborate engraving and select figured wood. Disc. 1986.

AyA Model 76 Hammerless Double $550

Anson & Deeley boxlock. Auto ejectors. Selective single trigger. Gauges: 12, 20 (3-inch). Barrels: 26-, 28-, 30-inch (latter in 12 gauge only); any standard choke combination. Checkered pistol-grip stock/beavertail forend. Disc.

AyA Model 76—.410 Gauge $610

Same general specifications as 12 and 20 gauge Model 76, except chambered for 3-inch shells in .410, has extractors, double triggers, 26-inch barrels only, English-style stock with straight grip and small forend. Discontinued.

AyA Model 117 Hammerless Double $825

Holland & Holland-type sidelocks, hand-detachable. Engraved action. Automatic ejectors. Selective single trigger. Gauges: 12, 20 (3-inch). Barrels: 26-, 27-, 28-, 30-inch; 27- and 30-inch in 12 gauge only; any standard choke combination. Checkered pistol-grip stock and beavertail forend of select walnut. Manufactured in 1985.

AyA Bolero $450

Same general specifications as Matador except non-selective single trigger and extractors. Gauges: 12, 16, 20, 20 Magnum (3-inch), .410 (3-inch). *Note:* This model, prior to 1956, was designated F. I. Model 400 by the importer. Made 1955–1963.

AyA Matador Hammerless Double $525

Anson & Deeley boxlock. Selective automatic ejectors. Selective single trigger. Gauges: 12, 16, 20, 20 Magnum (3-inch). Barrels: 26-, 28-, 30-inch; any standard choke combination. Weight: 6¹/₂ to 7¹/₂ pounds, depending on gauge and barrel length. Checkered pistol-grip stock and beavertail forend. *Note:* This model, prior to 1956, was

SHOTGUNS

AyA Matador II

AyA Matador Hammerless Double (cont.)
designated F. I. Model 400E by the U.S. importer, Firearms Int'l. Corp. of Washington, D.C. Made 1955–1963.

AyA Matador II **$595**
Improved version of Matador with same general specifications, except has vent-rib barrels. Made 1964–69.

AyA Matador III **$810**
Same general specifications as AyA Matador II. Made 1970–1985.

BAKER SHOTGUNS
Batavia, New York
Made 1903–1933 by Baker Gun Company

Baker Batavia Ejector **$770**
Same general specifications as the Batavia Leader, except higher quality and finer finish throughout; has Damascus or homotensile steel barrels, checkered pistol-grip stock and forearm of select walnut; automatic ejectors standard; 12 and 16 gauge only.

Baker Batavia Leader

Baker Batavia Leader Hammerless Double
Sidelock. Plain extractors or automatic ejectors. Double triggers. Gauges: 12, 16, 20. Barrels: 26- to 32-inch; any standard boring. Weight: about 7¾ pounds (12 gauge with 30-inch barrels). Checkered pistol-grip stock and forearm.
With Plain Extractors **$395**
With Automatic Ejectors 450

Baker Batavia Special

Baker Batavia Special **$345**
Same general specifications as the Batavia Leader, except plainer finish; 12 and 16 gauge only; has plain extractors, homotensile steel barrels.

Baker Black Beauty Special
Same general specifications as the Batavia Leader, except higher quality and finer finish throughout; has line engraving, special steel barrels, select walnut stock with straight, full or half-pistol grip.
With Plain Extractors **$750**
With Automatic Ejectors 835

Baker Grade R

Baker Grade R
High-grade gun with same general specifications as the Batavia Leader, except has fine Damascus or Krupp fluid steel barrels, engraving in line, scroll and game scene designs, checkered stock and forearm of fancy European walnut; 12 and 16 gauges only.
Non-ejector **$1000**
With Automatic Ejectors 1200

Baker Grade S
Same general specifications as the Batavia Leader, except higher quality and finer finish throughout; has Flui-tempered steel barrels, line and scroll engraving, checkered stock with half-pistol grip and forearm of semifancy imported walnut; 10, 12 and 16 gauges.
Non-ejector **$595**
With Automatic Ejectors 745

Baker Paragon, Expert and Deluxe Grades
Made to order only, these are the higher grades of Baker hammerless sidelock double-barrel shotguns. After 1909, the Paragon Grade, as well as the Expert and Deluxe introduced that year, had a cross bolt in addition to the regular Baker system taper wedge fastening. There are early Paragon guns with Damascus barrels and some are non-ejector, but this grade was also produced with automatic ejectors and with the finest fluid steel barrels, in lengths to 34 inches, standard on Expert and Deluxe guns.

Differences among the three models are in overall quality, finish, elaborateness of engraving and grade of fancy figured walnut in the stock and forearm; Expert and Deluxe wood may be carved as well as checkered. Choice of straight, full or half-pistol grip was offered. A single trigger

Baker Paragon Grade

Baker Paragon, Expert and Deluxe Grades (cont.)

was available in the two higher grades. The Paragon was available in 10 gauge (Damascus barrels only); this and the other two models were regularly produced in 12, 16 and 20 gauges.

Paragon Grade, Non-ejector $1525
Paragon Grade, Automatic Ejectors 1600
Expert Grade. 2575
Deluxe Grade 4000
For Single Trigger, **add** 200

BELKNAP SHOTGUNS
Louisville, Kentucky

Belknap Model B-63 Single Shot Shotgun $70
Takedown. Visible hammer. Automatic ejector. Gauges: 12, 20 and .410. Barrels: 26- to 36-inch; F choke. Weight: average 6 pounds. Plain pistol-grip stock and forearm.

Belknap Model B-63E Single Shot Shotgun $70
Same general specifications as Model B-68, except has side lever opening instead of top lever.

Belknap Model B-64 Slide Action Shotgun $145
Hammerless. Gauges: 12, 16, 20 and .410. 3-shot tubular magazine. Various barrel lengths and chokes from 26-inch to 30-inch. Weight: 6$\frac{1}{4}$ to 7$\frac{1}{2}$ pounds. Walnut-finished hardwood stock.

Belknap Model B-65C Autoloading Shotgun $265
Browning-type lightweight alloy receiver. 12 gauge only. 4-shot tubular magazine. Barrel: plain, 28-inch. Weight: about 8$\frac{1}{4}$ pounds. Discontinued 1949.

Belknap Model B-68 Single Shot Shotgun $75
Takedown. Visible hammer. Automatic ejector. Gauges: 12, 16, 20 and .410. Barrels: 26-inch to 36-inch; F choke. Weight: 6 pounds. Plain pistol-grip stock and forearm.

Benelli Model 121 M1 Military/Police Shotgun

Benelli Model M1 Super 90 Defense

BENELLI SHOTGUNS
Urbino, Italy

**Benelli Model 121 M1 Military/Police
Autoloading Shotgun** $350
Gauge: 12. 7-shot magazine. 19$\frac{3}{4}$-inch barrel. 39$\frac{3}{4}$ inches overall. Cylinder choke, 2$\frac{3}{4}$-inch chamber. Weight: 7.4 pounds. Matte black finish and European hardwood stock. Post front sight, fixed buckhorn rear sight. Made in 1985.

Benelli Model Black Eagle Autoloading Shotgun
Two-piece aluminum and steel receiver. Gauge: 12; 3-inch chamber. 4-shot magazine. Screw-in choke tubes (SK, IC, M, IM, F). Barrels: ventilated rib; 21, 24, 26 or 28 inches w/bead front sight; 24-inch rifled slug. 42$\frac{1}{2}$ to 49$\frac{1}{2}$ inches overall. Weight: 7$\frac{1}{4}$ pounds (28-inch bbl.). Matte black lower receiver with blued upper receiver and barrel. Checkered walnut stock with high-gloss finish and drop adjustment. Made from 1989 to date.

Competition Model $795
Slug Model (Discontinued 1992) 705
Standard Model (Discontinued 1992) 635

Benelli Model M1 Super 90 Defense Autoloader
Same general specifications as Model Super 90, except with pistol-grip stock. Available with Ghost Ring sight option. Made from 1986 to date.

Standard Defense Model $565
Defense Model w/Ghost Ring Sights 600

Benelli Model M1 Super 90 Entry Autoloader . . . $575
Same general specifications as Model Super 90, except with 5-shot magazine, 14-inch barrel. 35$\frac{1}{2}$ inches overall. Weight: 6$\frac{1}{2}$ pounds. Standard or pistol-grip stock. Made from 1992 to date.

Benelli Model M3 Super 90 Autoloading/Pump Shotgun
Inertia recoil semiautomatic and/or pump action. Gauge: 12. 7-shot magazine. Cylinder choke. 19$\frac{3}{4}$-inch barrel. 41 inches overall (31 inches folded). Weight: 7 to 7$\frac{1}{2}$ pounds. Matte black finish. Stock: standard synthetic, pistol-grip or folding tubular steel. Standard rifle or Ghost Ring sights. Made from 1989 to date.

Standard Model $675
With Folding Stock 750
Pistol-grip Model 720
For Ghost Ring Sights, **add** 35

SHOTGUNS

Benelli SL 123V Semiautomatic

Benelli Model Super 90 Autoloader

Benelli Super Black Eagle

Benelli Montefeltro Super 90 Semiautomatic

Same general specifications as Model M1 Super 90, except has checkered walnut stock with high-gloss finish. Barrels: 21, 24, 26 or 28 inches, with screw-in choke tubes (IC, M, IM, F). Weight: 7½ pounds. Blued finish. Imported from 1987 to date.

Standard Model	**$625**
Slug Model (Discontinued 1992)	**640**
Turkey Model	**615**
Uplander Model	**625**
Left-hand Model	**650**

Benelli Model SL 121V Semiauto Shotgun $345

Gauge: 12. 5-shot capacity. Barrels: 26-, 28- and 30-inch. 26-inch choked M, IM, IC; 28-inch, F, M, IM; 30-inch, F choke (Mag.). Straight walnut stock with hand-checkered pistol grip and forend. Ventilated rib. Made in 1985.

Benelli Model SL 121V Slug Shotgun $360

Same general specifications as Benelli SL121V, except designed for rifled slugs and equipped with rifle sights. Made in 1985.

Benelli Model SL 123V Semiauto Shotgun $375

Gauge: 12. 26- and 28-inch barrels. 26-inch choked IM, M, IC; 28-inch choked F, IM, M. Made in 1985.

Benelli Model SL 201 Semiautomatic Shotgun .. $320

Gauge: 20. 26-inch barrel. Mod. choke. Weight: 5 lbs., 10 oz. Ventilated rib. Made in 1985.

Benelli Model Super 90 Autoloading Shotgun ... $515

Gauge: 12. 7-shot magazine. Cylinder choke. 19¾-inch barrel. 39¾ inches overall. Weight: 7 lbs. 4 oz. to 7 lbs. 10 oz. Matte black finish. Stock and forend made of fiberglass reinforced polymer. Sights: post front; fixed buckhorn rear, drift adjustable. Made from 1985 to date.

Benelli Super Black Eagle Autoloading Shotgun

Same general specifications as Model Black Eagle, except with 3½-inch chamber that accepts 2¾-, 3- and 3½-inch shells. 2-shot magazine (3½-inch), 3-shot magazine (2¾- or 3-inch). High-gloss or satin finish stock. Matte black or blued metal finish. Made from 1991 to date.

Custom Slug Model	**$760**
Standard Model	**795**

BERETTA USA CORP.
Accokeek, Maryland

Manufactured by Fabbrica D'Armi Pietro Beretta S.p.A. in the Gardone Valtrompia (Brescia), Italy

Beretta Model 57E

Beretta Model 57E Over-and-Under

Same general specifications as Golden Snipe, but higher quality throughout. Made 1955–1967.

With Non-selective Single Trigger	**$755**
With Selective Single Trigger	**825**

Beretta Model 409PB

Beretta Model 409PB Hammerless Double $775

Boxlock. Double triggers. Plain extractors. Gauges: 12, 16, 20, 28. Barrels: 27½-, 28½- and 30-inch; IC/M choke or M/F choke. Weight: from 5½ to 7¾ pounds, depending on gauge and barrel length. Straight or pistol-grip stock and beavertail forearm, checkered. Made 1934–1964.

Beretta Model 410 E

Beretta Model 410E $850
Same general specifications as Model 409PB, except has automatic ejectors and is of higher quality throughout. Made 1934–1964.

Beretta Model 410, 10-Gauge Magnum $1025
Same as Model 410E, except heavier construction. Plain extractors. Double triggers. 10-gauge Magnum, 3½-inch chambers. 32-inch barrels, both F choke. Weight: about 10 pounds. Checkered pistol-grip stock and forearm, recoil pad. Made 1934–1984.

Beretta Model 411E $1395
Same general specifications as Model 409PB except has sideplates, automatic ejectors and is of higher quality throughout. Made 1934–1964.

Beretta Model 424 Hammerless Double $830
Boxlock. Light border engraving. Plain extractors. Gauges: 12, 20; chambers 2¾-inch in former, 3-inch in latter. Barrels: 28-inch M/F choke; 26-inch IC/M choke. Weight: 5 lbs. 14 oz. to 6 lbs. 10 oz., depending on gauge and barrel

Beretta Model 424 Hammerless Double (cont.)
length. English-style straight-grip stock and forearm, checkered. Made 1977–1984.

Beretta Model 426E $1085
Same as Model 424, except action body is finely engraved, silver pigeon inlaid in top lever; has selective automatic ejectors and selective single trigger, stock and forearm of select European walnut. Made 1977–1984.

Beretta Model 452 Hammerless Double
Custom English-style sidelock. Single, single non-selective trigger or double triggers. Manual safety. Selective automatic ejectors. Gauge: 12; 2¾- or 3-inch chambers. Barrels: 26, 28 or 30 inches choked to customers specifications. Weight: 6¾ pounds. Checkered high-grade walnut stock. Receiver with coin-silver finish.
Model 452 Standard **$18,150**
Model 452 EELL **24,000**

Beretta Model 626 S/S Hammerless Double
Field Grade side-by-side. Boxlock action with single selective trigger, extractors and automatic safety. Gauges: 12 (2¾-inch chambers); 20 (3-inch chambers). Barrels: 26- or 28-inch with Mobilchoke® or various fixed-choke combinations. Weight: 6¾ pounds (12 ga.). Bright chrome finish. Checkered European walnut buttstock and forend in straight English style. Made 1985 to date.
Model 626 Field **$1140**
Model 626 Onyx **1490**

Beretta Model 627 S/S Hammerless Double
Same as Model 626 S/S, except with engraved sideplates and pistol-grip or straight English-style stock.
Model 627 EL Field **$2700**
Model 627 EELL **4200**

SHOTGUNS

Beretta Model 424

Beretta Model 426E

Beretta Model 626 Field Grade Side/Side Shotgun

Beretta Model 682 Sporting

Beretta Model 686EL Over/Under

Beretta Model 687L Field

Beretta Model 682 Over/Under Shotgun

Hammerless takedown with single selective trigger. Gauges: 12, 20, 28, .410. Barrels: 26- to 34-inch with fixed chokes or Mobilchoke® tubes. Checkered European walnut buttstock/forend in various grades and configurations.

Model 682 Comp Trap Standard	**$1955**
Model 682 Comp Trap Top Single	**2050**
Model 682 Comp Trap Pigeon	**2290**
Model 682 Comp Trap Combo	**2640**
Model 682 Comp Skeet	**1450**
Model 682 Comp Skeet 2-Barrel Set	**2900**
Model 682 Comp Skeet 4-Barrel Set	**3000**
Model 682 Sporting	**1800**
Model 682 Sporting Combo	**2300**
Model 682 Super Sport	**1895**
Model 682 Super Trap	**2050**
Model 682 Super Trap Combo	**2650**
Model 682 Super Trap Single	**2195**

Beretta Model 686 Over/Under Shotgun

Low-profile improved boxlock. Single selective trigger. Selective automatic ejectors. Gauges: 12, 20, 28 with 3½-, 3- or 2¾-inch chambers. Barrels: 26-, 28-, 30-inch with fixed chokes or Mobilchoke® tubes. Weight: 5¾ to 7½ pounds. Checkered American walnut stock and forearm.

Model 686 Field, Onyx	**$ 925**
Model 686 EL, English	**1495**
Model 686 Sporting, Sporting Onyx	**895**
Model 686 Sporting Combo	**1725**
Model 686 2-barrel Set	**1495**
Model 686 Ultralight	**995**

Beretta Model 687 Over/Under Shotgun

Same as Model 686, except with decorative sideplates and varying grades of engraving and game-scene motifs.

Model 687L Field	**$1250**
Model 687 EL	**1895**
Model 687 EL Small Frame	**2250**
Model 687 EELL	**2850**
Model 687 EELL Combo	**3850**
Model 687 EELL Sporter, Trap, Skeet	**3470**
Model 687 EELL Skeet 4-barrel Set	**6030**
Model 687 Sporting	**1895**
Model 687 Sporting Combo	**2350**

Beretta Model 1200 Semiautoloading Shotgun

Short recoil action. Gauge: 12; 2¾- or 3-inch chamber. 6-shot magazine. 24-, 26- or 28-inch vent-rib barrel with fixed chokes or Mobilchoke® tubes. Weight: 7¼ pounds. Matte black finish. Adjustable technopolymer stock and forend. Made from 1988 to date.

Model 1200 w/Fixed Choke	**$425**
Model 1200 Riot	**475**
Model 1201 w/Mobilchoke®	**470**
Model 1201 Riot	**495**

Beretta Model A-301 Autoloading Shotgun — **$395**

Field Gun. Gas-operated. Scroll-decorated receiver. Gauge: 12 or 20; 2¾-inch chamber in former, 3-inch in latter. 3-shot magazine. Barrel: ventilated rib; 28-inch F or M choke, 26-inch IC. Weight: 6 lbs. 5 oz.–6 lbs. 14 oz., depending on gauge and barrel length. Checkered pistol-grip stock/forearm. Made 1977–1982.

Beretta Model A-301 Magnum — **$425**

Same as Model A-301 Field Gun, except chambered for 12 gauge 3-inch Magnum shells; 30-inch F choke barrel only, stock with recoil pad. Weight: 7¼ pounds.

Beretta Model A-301 Skeet Gun — **$400**

Same as Model A-301 Field Gun, except 26-inch barrel SK choke only, skeet-style stock, gold-plated trigger.

Beretta Model A-301 Slug Gun — **$370**

Same as Model A-301 Field Gun, except has plain 22-inch barrel, slug choke, with rifle sights. Weight: 6 lbs. 14 oz.

Beretta Model A-301 Trap Gun — **$405**

Same as Model A-301 Field Gun, except has 30-inch barrel in F choke only, Monte Carlo stock with recoil pad, gold-plated trigger. Weight: 7 lbs. 10 oz.

Beretta Model A-302 Semiautoloading Shotgun

Similar to gas-operated Model 301. Hammerless, takedown shotgun with tubular magazine and Mag-Action that handles both 2¾- and 3-inch Magnum shells. Gauge: 12 or 20; 2¾- or 3-inch Mag. chambers. Barrel: vent or plain;

Beretta Model A-302 Multi-Choke

Beretta Model A-303 Matte Finish

Beretta Model A390 Field

Beretta Model A390 Super Trap

Beretta Model A-302 Semiautoloading Shotgun (cont.)
22-inch/Slug (12 ga.); 26-inch/IC (12 or 20); 28-inch/M (20 ga.); 28-inch/Multi-choke (12 or 20 ga.); 30-inch/F (12 ga.). Weight: 6½ lbs., 20 ga.; 7¼ lbs., 12 ga. Blued/black finish. Checkered European walnut, pistol-grip stock and forend. Made from 1983 to about 1987.

Standard Model with Fixed Choke	**$410**
Standard Model with Multi-choke	**525**

Beretta Model A-302 Super Lusso **$1895**
A custom A-302 in presentation grade with hand-engraved receiver and custom select walnut stock.

Beretta Model A-303 Semiautoloader
Similar to Model 302, except with target specifications in Trap, Skeet and Youth configurations, and weighs 6½ to 8 pounds. Made from 1983 to date.

Field, Upland and Youth models	**$565**
Skeet and Trap	**555**
Slug Model (Discontinued 1992)	**580**
Sporting Clays	**565**
Super Skeet	**935**
Super Trap	**995**
Waterfowl/Turkey (Discontinued 1992)	**550**
For Mobilchoke®, **add**	**50**

Beretta Model A-390 Semiautoloading Shotgun
Gas-operated, self-regulating action designed to handle any size load. Gauge: 12; 3-inch chamber. 3-shot magazine. Barrel: 24, 26, 28 or 30 inches w/vent rib and Mobilchoke® tubes. Weight: 7¼ pounds. Select walnut stock w/adjustable comb. Blued or matte black finish. Made 1992 to date.

Standard Model	**$560**
Field Model	**580**
Deluxe Model	**735**

Beretta Model A-390 Super Target
Similar to the Model 390 Field, except in 12 gauge only with 2¾-inch chamber. Skeet: 28-inch ported barrel with wide vent rib and fixed choke (SK). Trap: 30- or 32-inch with Mobilchoke® tubes. Weight: 7½ pounds. Fully adjustable buttstock. Made from 1993 to date.

Super Trap Model	**$1000**
Super Skeet Model	**950**

Beretta Model AL-1 Field Gun **$355**
Same as Model AL-2 Field Gun, except has barrel without rib, no engraving on receiver. Made 1971–73.

Beretta Model AL-2 Autoloading Shotgun
Field Gun. Gas-operated. Engraved receiver (1968 version, 12 gauge only, had no engraving). Gauge: 12 or 20. 2¾-inch chamber. 3-shot magazine. Barrels: vent rib; 30-inch F choke; 28-inch F or M choke; 26-inch IC. Weight: 6½

Beretta Model AL-2 Field Gun

Beretta Model BL-1

Beretta Model BL-2/S

Beretta Model AL-2 Autoloading Shotgun (cont.)
to 7¼ pounds, depending on gauge and barrel length. Checkered pistol-grip stock and forearm. Made 1968–1975.
With Plain Receiver **$385**
With Engraved Receiver **440**

Beretta Model AL-2 Magnum **$415**
Same as Model AL-2 Field Gun, except chambered for 12 gauge 3-inch Magnum shells; 30-inch F or 28-inch M choke barrel only. Weight: about 8 lbs. Made 1973–75.

Beretta Model AL-2 Skeet Gun **$395**
Same as Model AL-2 Field Gun, except has wide rib, 26-inch barrel in SK choke only, beavertail forearm. Made 1969–1975.

Beretta Model AL-2 Trap Gun **$415**
Same as Model AL-2 Field Gun, except has wide rib, 30-inch barrel in F choke only, beavertail forearm. Monte Carlo stock with recoil pad. Weight: about 7¾ pounds. Made 1969–1975.

Beretta Model AL-3
Similar to corresponding AL-2 models in design and general specifications. Made 1975–76.
Field Model **$425**
Magnum Model **440**
Skeet Model **450**
Trap Model **495**

Beretta Model AL-3 Deluxe Trap Gun **$775**
Same as standard Model AL-3 Trap Gun, except has fully engraved receiver, gold-plated trigger and safety, stock and forearm of premium grade European walnut, gold monogram escutcheon inlaid in buttstock. Made 1975–76.

Beretta Model ASE 90 Over-and-Under Shotgun
Competition-style receiver with coin-silver finish and gold inlay featuring drop-out trigger group. Gauge: 12; 2¾-inch chamber. Barrels: 28- or 30-inch w/fixed or Mobil-choke® tubes; vent rib. Weight: 8½ pounds (30-inch bbl.).

Beretta Model ASE 90 Over-and-Under Shotgun (cont.)
Checkered high-grade walnut stock. Made 1992 to date.
Pigeon, Skeet, Trap Models **$6100**
Sporting Clays Model **6200**

Beretta Model Asel

Beretta Model Asel Over-and-Under Shotgun . . **$1110**
Boxlock. Single non-selective trigger. Selective automatic ejectors. Gauges: 12, 20. Barrels: 26-, 28-, 30-inch; IC and M choke or M and F choke. Weight: about 5¾ lbs., 20 ga.; about 7 lbs., 12 ga. Checkered pistol-grip stock and forearm. Made 1947–1964.

Beretta Model BL-1/BL-2 Over/Under
Boxlock. Plain extractors. Double triggers. 12 gauge, 2¾-inch chambers only. Barrels: 30- and 28-inch M/F choke; 26-inch IC/M choke. Weight: 6¾–7 pounds, depending on barrel length. Checkered pistol-grip stock and forearm. Made 1968–1973.
Model BL-1 . . . . **$375**
Model BL-2 (Single Selective Trigger) **415**

Beretta Model BL-2/S **$425**
Similar to Model BL-1, except has selective "Speed-Trigger," vent-rib barrels, 2¾- or 3-inch chambers. Weight: 7–7½ pounds. Made 1974–76.

Beretta Model BL-3

Beretta Model BL-6

Beretta Model FS-1

SHOTGUNS

Beretta Model BL-3 . . . . $555
Same as Model BL-1, except has deluxe engraved receiver, selective single trigger, vent-rib barrels; 12 or 20 gauge, 2³/₄-inch or 3-inch chambers in former, 3-inch in latter. Weight: 6–7¹/₂ pounds, depending on gauge and barrel length. Made 1968–1976.

Beretta Models BL-4, BL-5 and BL-6
Higher grade versions of Model BL-3 with more elaborate engraving and fancier wood; Model BL-6 has sideplates. Selective automatic ejectors standard. Made 1968–1976 (Model BL-6 introduced in 1973).
Model BL-4 . . . . **$ 665**
Model BL-5 . . . . **840**
Model BL-6 . . . . **1025**

Beretta Series BL Skeet Guns
Models BL-3, BL-4, BL-5 and BL-6 with standard features of their respective grades plus wider rib and skeet-style stock; 26-inch barrels SK choked. Weight: 6–7¹/₄ pounds, depending on gauge.
Model BL-3 Skeet Gun . . . . **$ 600**
Model BL-4 Skeet Gun **750**
Model BL-5 Skeet Gun **925**
Model BL-6 Skeet Gun **1225**

Beretta Series BL Trap Guns
Models BL-3, BL-4, BL-5 and BL-6 with standard features of their respective grades plus wider rib and Monte Carlo stock with recoil pad; 30-inch barrels, improved M/F or both F choke. Weight: about 7¹/₂ pounds.

Beretta Series BL Trap Guns (cont.)
Model BL-3 Trap Gun . . . . **$ 600**
Model BL-4 Trap Gun **750**
Model BL-5 Trap Gun **980**
Model BL-6 Trap Gun **1250**

Beretta Model FS-1 Folding Single $195
Formerly "Companion." Folds to length of barrel. Hammerless. Underlever. Gauge: 12, 16, 20, 28 or .410. Barrel: 30-inch in 12 ga.; 28-inch in 16 and 20 ga.; 26-inch in 28 and .410 ga.; all F choke. Checkered semipistol-grip stock/forearm. Weight: 4¹/₂–5¹/₂ pounds, depending on gauge. Discontinued 1971.

Beretta Golden Snipe Over-and-Under
Same as Silver Snipe, except has automatic ejectors, ventilated rib is standard feature. Made 1959–1967.
With Non-selective Single Trigger **$650**
Extra for Selective Single Trigger **100**

Beretta Model GR-2 Hammerless Double **$630**
Boxlock. Plain extractors. Double triggers. Gauges: 12, 20; 2³/₄-inch chambers in former, 3-inch in latter. Barrels: vent rib; 30-inch M/F choke (12 ga. only); 28-inch M/F choke; 26-inch IC/M choke. Weight: 6¹/₂ to 7¹/₄ pounds, depending on gauge and barrel length. Checkered pistol-grip stock and forearm. Made 1968–1976.

Beretta Model GR-3 . . . . $750
Same as Model GR-2, except has selective single trigger; chambered for 12-gauge 3-inch or 2³/₄-inch shells. Magnum model has 30-inch M/F choke barrel, recoil pad. Weight: about 8 pounds. Made 1968–1976.

Beretta Model GR-2

Beretta Mark II Trap

Beretta S58 Trap

Beretta Silver Hawk

Beretta Silver Snipe

Beretta Model GR-4 . . . . **$840**
Same as Model GR-2, except has automatic ejectors and
selective single trigger, higher grade engraving and wood.
12 gauge, 2¾-inch chambers only. Made 1968–1976.

Beretta Grade 100 Over-and-Under Shotgun . **$1720**
Sidelock. Double triggers. Automatic ejectors. 12 gauge
only. Barrels: 26-, 28-, 30-inch; any standard boring.
Weight: about 7½ pounds. Checkered stock and forend,
straight or pistol grip. Discontinued.

Beretta Grade 200 . . . . **$2215**
Same general specifications as Grade 100 except higher
quality, bores and action parts hard chrome-plated. Discontinued.

Beretta Mark II Single Barrel Trap Gun **$610**
Boxlock action similar to that of Series "BL" Over-and-
Unders. Engraved receiver. Automatic ejector. 12 gauge
only. 32- or 34-inch barrel with wide vent rib. Weight:
about 8½ pounds. Monte Carlo stock with pistol grip and
recoil pad, beavertail forearm. Made 1972–76.

Beretta Model S55B Over-and-Under Shotgun . . **$515**
Boxlock. Plain extractors. Selective single trigger. Gauges:
12, 20; 2¾- or 3-inch chambers in former, 3-inch in latter.
Barrels: vent rib; 30-inch M/F choke or both F choke in
12-gauge 3-inch Magnum only; 28-inch M/F choke; 26-
inch IC/M choke. Weight: 6½ to 7½ pounds, depending
on gauge and barrel length. Checkered pistol-grip stock
and forearm. Introduced in 1977.

Beretta Model S56E **$595**
Same as Model S55B, except has scroll-engraved receiver,
selective automatic ejectors. Introduced in 1977.

Beretta Model S58 Skeet Gun **$745**
Same as Model S56E, except has 26-inch barrels of Boeh-
ler Antinit Anticorro steel, SK choked, with wide vent
rib; skeet-style stock and forearm. Weight: 7½ pounds.
Introduced in 1977.

Beretta Model S58 Trap Gun **$710**
Same as Model S58 Skeet Gun, except has 30-inch barrels
bored IM/Full Trap, Monte Carlo stock with recoil pad.
Weight: 7 lbs. 10 oz. Introduced in 1977.

**Beretta Silver Hawk Featherweight Hammerless
Double Barrel Shotgun**
Boxlock. Double triggers or non-selective single trigger.
Plain extractor. Gauges: 12, 16, 20, 28, 12 Mag. Barrels:
26- to 32-inch with high matted rib; all standard choke
combinations. Weight: 7 lbs. (12 ga. w/26-inch barrels).
Checkered walnut stock with beavertail forearm. Discon-
tinued 1967.
With Double Triggers **$475**
For Non-selective Single Trigger, **add** **65**

Beretta Silver Snipe Over-and-Under Shotgun
Boxlock. Non-selective or selective single trigger. Plain
extractor. Gauges: 12, 20, 12 Mag., 20 Mag. Barrels: 26-,
28-, 30-inch; plain or vent rib; chokes IC/M, M/F, SK #1
and #2, F/F. Weight: from about 6 pounds in 20 ga. to
8½ pounds in 12 ga. (Trap gun). Checkered walnut pistol-
grip stock and forearm. Made 1955–1967.
With Plain Barrel, Non-selective Trigger **$435**
With Vent-rib Barrel, Non-sel. Single Trigger . . . **575**
For Selective Single Trigger, **add** **65**

Beretta Model SL-2

Beretta Model SL-2 Pump Gun **$300**
Hammerless. Takedown. 12 gauge only. 3-shot magazine.
Barrels: vent rib; 30-inch F choke, 28-inch M, 26-inch IC.
Weight: about 7–7¼ pounds, depending on barrel length.
Checkered pistol-grip stock and forearm. Made 1968–1971.

Beretta Series "SO" Over-and-Under Shotguns
Sidelock. Selective automatic ejectors. Selective single
trigger or double triggers. 12 gauge only, 2¾- or 3-inch
chambers. Barrels: vent rib (wide type on skeet and trap
guns); 26-, 27-, 29-, 30-inch; any combination of standard
chokes. Weight: from about 7 to 7¾ pounds, depending
on barrel length, style of stock and density of wood. Stock
and forearm of select walnut, finely checkered; straight
or pistol grip; field, skeet and trap guns have appropriate
styles of stock and forearm. Models differ chiefly in quality
of wood and grade of engraving. Models SO-3EL, SO-
3EELL, SO-4 and SO-5 have hand-detachable locks. "SO-

Beretta Series "SO" Over-Under Shotguns (cont.)
4" is used to designate current skeet and trap models de-
rived from Model SO-3EL but with less elaborate engraving. Present Models SO-3EL and SO-3EELL are
similar to the earlier SO-4 and SO-5, respectively. Made
1948–1986.
Model SO-2 . . . . **$4025**
Model SO-3 . . . . **6195**
Model SO-4 Skeet or Trap Gun (current) **7000**
Model SO-4 (pre-1977) or SO-3EL **6295**
Model SO-5 or SO-3EELL **9600**

Beretta Models SO-6 and SO-7 Hammerless Doubles
Side-by-side guns with same gen. specifications as Series
"SO" over/unders. Higher grade Model SO-7 has more
elaborate engraving, fancier wood. Made 1948 to date.
Model SO-6 . . . . **$8500**
Model SO-7 . . . . **9500**

**Beretta Model SO-2
Over-and-Under**

Beretta Model SO-3

Beretta Model SO-4

Beretta Model SO-5

Beretta Model SO-7

SHOTGUNS

Beretta Model TR-1

Beretta Model TR-2

Beretta Vittoria

Beretta Model TR-1 Single Barrel Trap Gun **$275**
Hammerless. Underlever action. Engraved frame. 12 gauge
only. 32-inch barrel with vent rib. Weight: about 8¼
pounds. Monte Carlo stock with pistol grip and recoil pad,
beavertail forearm. Made 1968–1971.

Beretta Model TR-2 .... **$295**
Same as Model TR-1, except has extended ventilated rib.
Made 1969–1973.

Beretta Vittoria Semiautoloading Shotgun **$550**
Short recoil action. Gauge: 12; 3-inch chamber. Barrel:
24-inch slug; 24- or 26-inch vent rib w/Mobilchoke® tubes.
Weight: 7 pounds. Checkered walnut stock/forend. Matte
finish on both metal and wood. Made 1993 to date.

Bernardelli Elio

Bernardelli Elio **$1310**
Lightweight game gun, 12 gauge only, with same general
specifications as Standard Gamecock (S. Uberto 1), except
weighs about 6 to 6¼ pounds, has automatic ejectors, fine
English-pattern scroll engraving. No longer imported.

VINCENZO BERNARDELLI
Gardone V.T. (Brescia), Italy

Bernardelli Brescia

Bernardelli Premier Gamecock

Bernardelli Brescia Hammer Double **$1915**
Back-action sidelock. Plain extractors. Double triggers.
Gauges: 12, 20. Barrels: 27½ or 29½-inch M/F choke in
12 gauge, 25½-inch IC/M choke in 20 gauge. Weight: from
5¾ to 7 pounds, depending on gauge and barrel length.
English-style stock and forearm, checkered. Currently
manufactured.

Bernardelli Gamecock, Premier (Roma 3) **$1375**
Same general specifications as Standard Gamecock (S.
Uberto 1), except has sideplates, auto ejectors, single trig-
ger. Currently manufactured.

**Bernardelli Gamecock, Standard (S. Uberto 1)
Hammerless Double Barrel Shotgun** **$1075**
Boxlock. Plain extractors. Double triggers. Gauges: 12,
16, 20; 2¾-inch chambers in 12 and 16, 3-inch in 20 gauge.
Barrels: 25½-inch IC/M choke; 27½-inch M/F choke.

Bernardelli Standard Gamecock

Bernardelli Gamecock, Standard (cont.)

Weight: 5³/₄–6¹/₂ pounds, depending on gauge and barrel length. English-style straight-grip stock and forearm, checkered. No longer imported.

Bernardelli Gardone Hammer Double

Bernardelli Gardone Hammer Double $2065

Same general specifications as Brescia, except for higher grade engraving and wood, but not as high as the Italia. Half-cock safety. Discontinued 1956.

Bernardelli Hemingway Hammerless Double

Boxlock. Single or double triggers with hinged front. Selective automatic ejectors. Gauges: 12 and 20 w/2³/₄- or 3-inch chambers; 16 and 28 w/2³/₄-inch. Barrels: 23¹/₂- to 28-inch with fixed chokes. Weight: 6¹/₄ pounds. Checkered English-style European walnut stock. Silvered and engraved receiver.

Standard Model $1650
Deluxe Model w/Sideplates (Disc. 1993)........ 1875
For Single Trigger, **add** 65

Bernardelli Italia

Bernardelli Italia $2200

Same general specifications as Brescia, except higher grade engraving and wood. Discontinued 1986.

**Bernardelli
Roma 6**

Bernardelli Roma 4 and Roma 6

Same as Premier Gamecock (Roma 3), except higher grade engraving and wood, double triggers. Currently manufactured; Roma 6 discontinued 1993.

Roma 4 .... **$1620**
Roma 6 .... **1635**

**Bernardelli
S. Uberto 2**

**Bernardelli
S. Uberto F.S.**

Bernadelli S. Uberto 2 .... $1225

Same as Standard Gamecock (S. Uberto 1), except higher grade engraving and wood. Currently manufactured.

Bernardelli S. Uberto F.S. $1995

Same as Standard Gamecock, except with higher grade engraving, wood and has auto ejectors. Currently manufactured.

**Bernardelli
V.B. Holland Liscio**

Bernardelli V.B. Holland Liscio Deluxe
Hammerless Double Barrel Shotgun $8195

Holland & Holland-type sidelock action. Auto ejectors. Double triggers. 12 gauge only. Any barrel length, chokes. Checkered stock (straight or pistol grip) and forearm. Currently manufactured.

SHOTGUNS

BOSS & CO.
London, England

Boss Double Barrel

Boss Hammerless Double Barrel Shotgun
Sidelock. Automatic ejectors. Double triggers, non-selective or selective single trigger. Made in all gauges, barrel

Boss Hammerless Double Barrel Shotgun (cont.)
lengths and chokes. Checkered stock and forend, straight or pistol grip.
W/Double Triggers or Non-sel. Single Trigger . **$18,000**
W/Selective Single Trigger **23,000**

Boss Over-Under

Boss Hammerless Over/Under Shotgun $24,500
Sidelock. Automatic ejectors. Selective single trigger. Made in all gauges, barrel lengths and chokes. Checkered stock and forend, straight or pistol grip. Discontinued.

Breda Autoloading Shotgun

ERNESTO BREDA
Milan, Italy

Breda Autoloading Shotgun
Recoil-operated. 12 gauge, 2¾-inch chamber. 4-shell tubular magazine. Barrels: 25½- and 27½-inch; plain, matted or vent rib; IC, M or F choke; current model has 26-inch vent-rib barrel with interchangeable choke tubes. Weight: about 7¼ pounds. Checkered straight or pistol-grip stock and forearm. Discontinued 1988.
W/Plain Barrel **$325**
W/Raised Matted-rib Barrel **375**
W/Ventilated-rib Barrel **395**
W/Vent Rib, Interchangeable Choke Tubes **420**

Breda Magnum
Same general specifications as standard model, except chambered for 12-gauge 3-inch Magnum, 3-shot magazine; latest model has 29-inch vent-rib barrel. Disc. 1988.
W/Plain Barrel **$415**
W/Ventilated-rib Barrel **445**

BRNO SHOTGUNS
Manufactured in Czechoslovakia

Brno 500 Over/Under Shotgun $595
Hammerless boxlock with double triggers and ejectors. 12 gauge w/2¾-inch chambers. 27½-inch barrels choked M/F. Weight: 7 pounds. Checkered walnut stock with classic-style cheekpiece.

Brno CZ 581 Over/Under Shotgun $500
Hammerless boxlock with double triggers, ejectors and automatic safety. 12 gauge w/2¾- or 3-inch chambers. 28-inch barrels choked M/F. Weight: 7½ pounds. Checkered walnut stock.

Brno Super Over/Under Shotgun $795
Hammerless sidelock with selective single or double triggers and ejectors. 12 gauge w/2¾- or 3-inch chambers. 27½-inch barrels choked M and F. Weight: 7¼ pounds. Checkered European walnut stock with classic-style cheekpiece.

Brno ZH 301 Over/Under Shotgun $495
Hammerless boxlock with double triggers. 12 gauge w/2¾- or 3-inch chambers. 27½-inch barrels choked M/F. Weight: 7 pounds. Skip-line checkered walnut stock with classic-style cheekpiece.

Brno ZP 149 Hammerless Double
Sidelock action with double triggers, automatic ejectors and automatic safety. 12 gauge w/2¾- or 3-inch chambers. 28½-inch barrels choked M/F. Weight: 7¼ pounds. Checkered walnut buttstock with cheekpiece.
Standard Model **$465**
Engraved Model **490**

BROWNING SHOTGUNS
Morgan (formerly Ogden), Utah

Designated "American" Browning because they were produced in Ilion, New York, the following Remington-made Brownings are almost identical to the Remington Model 11A and Sportsman and the Browning Auto-5. They are the only Browning shotguns manufactured in the U.S. during the 20th century and were made for Browning Arms when production was suspended in Belgium because of WW II (see *Note* below).

Browning Model 12 Limited Edition Grade I 20 Gauge

Browning Model 12 Limited Edition Grade V 28 Gauge

Browning Model 42 Ltd. Edition Grade V

Browning 2000 Field Model

AMERICAN BROWNING SHOTGUNS

American Browning Grade I Autoloader **$450**
Recoil-operated. Gauges: 12, 16, 20. 2- or 4-shell tubular magazine. Plain barrel, 26- to 32-inch, any standard boring. Weight: about 6⅞ (20 ga.) to 8 pounds (12 ga.). Checkered pistol-grip stock and forearm. Made 1940–49.

American Browning Special
Same general specifications as Grade I, except supplied with raised matted rib or vent rib. Discont. 1949.
With raised matted rib **$495**
With ventilated rib   645

American Browning Special Skeet Model **$595**
Same general specifications as Grade I, except has 26-inch barrel with vent rib and Cutts Compensator. Discontinued in 1949.

American Browning Utility Field Gun **$395**
Same general specifications as Grade I, except has 28-inch plain barrel with Poly Choke. Discontinued in 1949.

> **NOTE:** Fabrique Nationale Herstal (formerly Fabrique Nationale d'Armes de Guerre) of Herstal, Belgium, is the long-time manufacturer of Browning shotguns, dating back to 1900. Miroku Firearms Mfg. Co. of Tokyo, Japan, bought into the Browning company and has, since the early 1970s, undertaken some of the production. The following shotguns were manufactured for Browning by these two firms.

Browning Model 12 Pump Shotgun
Special limited edition Winchester Model 12. Gauge: 20 or 28. Five-shot tubular magazine. 26-inch barrel, M choke. 45 inches overall. Weight: about 7 pounds. Grade I has blued receiver, checkered walnut stock with matte finish. Grade V has engraved receiver, checkered deluxe walnut

Browning Model 12 Pump Shotgun (cont.)
stock with high-gloss finish. Made from 1988 to date.
Grade I, 20 Gauge (8500) . . . . $ 715
Grade I, 28 Gauge   725
Grade V, 20 Gauge (4000) 1125
Grade V, 28 Gauge 1200

Browning Model 42 Limited Edition Shotgun
Special limited edition Winchester Model 42 pump shotgun. Same general specifications as Model 12, except with smaller frame in .410 gauge and 3-inch chamber. Made from 1991 to date.
Grade I (6000 produced) . . . . $ 650
Grade V (6000 produced) 1120

Browning 2000 Buck Special $395
Same as Field Model, except has 24-inch plain barrel bored for rifled slug and buck shot, fitted with rifle sights (open rear, ramp front). 12 gauge, 2¾-inch or 3-inch chamber; 20 gauge, 2¾-inch chamber. Weight: 12 ga., 7 lbs. 8 oz.; 20 ga., 6 lbs. 10 oz. Made 1974–1981 by FN.

Browning 2000 Gas Automatic Shotgun, Field Model
Gas-operated. Gauge: 12 or 20. 2¾-inch chamber. 4-shot magazine. Barrel: 26-, 28-, 30-inch; any standard choke; plain matted barrel (12 ga. only) or vent rib. Weight: 6 lbs. 11 oz.–7 lbs. 12 oz. depending on gauge and barrel length. Checkered pistol-grip stock/forearm. Made 1974–1981 by FN.
With Plain Matted Barrel $450
With Vent-rib Barrel   495

Browning 2000 Magnum Model $410
Same as Field Model, except chambered for 3-inch shells, 3-shot magazine. Barrel: 26- (20 ga. only), 28-, 30- or 32-inch (latter two 12 ga. only); any standard choke; vent rib. Weight: 6 lbs. 11 oz.–7 lbs. 13 oz. depending on gauge and barrel. Made 1974–1981 by FN.

Browning A-500R Semiautomatic

Browning Automatic-5
Buck Special

Browning Automatic-5 Classic

Browning 2000 Skeet Model $395
Same as Field Model, except has skeet-style stock with recoil pad, 26-inch vent-rib barrel, SK choke. 12 or 20 gauge, 2³/₄-inch chamber. Weight: 8 lbs. 1 oz. (12 ga.); 6 lbs. 12 oz.(20 ga.) Made 1974–1981 by FN.

Browning 2000 Trap Model $395
Same as Field Model, except has Monte Carlo stock with recoil pad, 30- or 32-inch barrel w/high-post vent rib and receiver extension; M/I/F chokes. 12 gauge, 2³/₄-inch chamber. Weight: about 8 lbs. 5 oz. Made 1974–1981 by FN.

Browning A-500G Gas-Operated Semiautomatic
Same general specifications as Browning Model A-500R, except gas-operated. Made 1990 to date.
Buck Special $515
Hunting Model 495

Browning A-500G Sporting Clays $545
Same general specifications as Model A-500G, except has matte blued receiver with "Sporting Clays" logo. 28- or 30-inch barrel w/Invector choke tubes. Made 1992 to date.

Browning A-500R Semiautomatic
Recoil-operated. Gauge: 12. 26- to 30-inch vent-rib barrels; 24-inch Buck Special. Invector choke tube system. 2³/₄- or 3-inch Magnum cartridges. Weight: 7 lbs. 3 oz.–8 lbs. 2 oz. Cross-bolt safety. Gold-plated trigger. Scroll-engraved receiver. Gloss-finished walnut stock and forend. Made by FN from 1987 to date.
Hunting Model $495
Buck Special 535

Browning Autoloading Shotguns, Grade III and IV
These higher grade models differ from the Standard or Grade I in general quality, grade of wood, checkering, engraving, etc., otherwise specifications are the same. Grade IV guns, sometimes called Midas Grade, are inlaid with yellow and green gold. Discontinued in 1940.

Browning Autoloaders, Grade III and IV (cont.)
Grade III, Plain Barrel $2300
Grade IV, Plain Barrel 3700
For Raised Matte-rib Barrel, **add** 225
For Vent-rib Barrel, **add** 450

Browning Automatic-5, Buck Special Models
Same as Light 12, Magnum 12, Light 20, Magnum 20, in respective gauges, except 24-inch plain barrel bored for rifled slug and buckshot, fitted with rifle sights (open rear, ramp front). Weight: 6¹/₈–8¹/₄ pounds depending on gauge. Made 1964–1976 by FN, since then by Miroku.
FN Manufacture, with Plain Barrel $590
Miroku Manufacture 455

Browning Automatic-5 Classic $895
Gauge: 12. 5-shot capacity. 28-inch vent-rib barrel/M choke. 2³/₄-inch chamber. Engraved silver grey receiver. Gold-plated trigger. Cross-bolt safety. High-grade, hand-checkered select American walnut stock w/rounded pistol grip. 5,000 issued; made in Japan in 1984, engraved in Belgium.

Browning Automatic-5 Gold Classic

Browning Automatic-5 Gold Classic $3650
Same general specifications as Automatic-5 Classic, except engraved receiver inlaid with gold. Pearl border on stock

Browning Automatic-5 Magnum

Browning Automatic-5 Stalker

Browning Automatic-5 Gold Classic (cont.)
and forend plus fine-line hand-checkering. Each gun numbered "1 of Five Hundred," etc. 500 issued in 1984; made in Belgium.

Browning Automatic-5, Light 12
12 gauge only. Same general specifications as Standard Model, except lightweight (about 7 1/4 pounds), has gold-plated trigger. Guns without rib have striped matting on top of barrel. Fixed chokes or Invector tubes. Made 1948–1976 by FN, since then by Miroku.

FN Manufacture, Plain Barrel	$550
FN Manufacture, Raised Matte Rib	625
FN Manufacture, Ventilated Rib	675
Miroku Manufacture, Vent Rib, Fixed Choke	450
Miroku manufacture, Vent Rib, Invectors	495

Browning Automatic-5, Light 20
Same general specifications as Standard Model, except lightweight and 20 gauge. Barrel: 26- or 28-inch; plain or vent rib. Weight: about 6 1/4–6 1/2 pounds depending on barrel. Made 1958–1976 by FN, since then by Miroku.

FN Manufacture, Plain Barrel	$545
FN Manufacture, Vent-rib Barrel	595
Miroku Manufacture, Vent Rib, Fixed Choke	415
Miroku Manufacture, Vent Rib, Invectors	475

Browning Automatic-5, Magnum 12 Gauge
Same general specifications as Standard Model. Chambered for 3-inch Magnum 12-gauge shells. Barrel: 28-inch M/F, 30- or 32-inch F/F; plain or vent rib. Weight: 8 1/2–9 pounds depending on barrel. Buttstock has recoil pad. Made 1958–1976 by FN, since then by Miroku. Fixed chokes or Invector tubes.

FN Manufacture, Plain Barrel	$635
FN Manufacture, Vent-rib Barrel	680
Miroku Manufacture, Vent Rib, Fixed Chokes . . .	435
Miroku Manufacture, Vent Rib, Invectors	495

Browning Automatic-5, Magnum 20 Gauge
Same general specifications as Standard Model, except chambered for 3-inch Magnum 20-gauge shell. Barrel: 26- or 28-inch, plain or vent rib. Weight: 7 lbs. 5 oz.–7 lbs. 7 oz. depending on barrel. Made 1967–1976 by FN, since then by Miroku.

Browning Automatic-5, Magnum 20 Gauge (cont.)

FN Manufacture, Plain Barrel	$645
FN Manufacture, Vent-rib Barrel	675
Miroku Manufacture, Vent Rib, Invectors	450

Browning Automatic-5, Skeet Model
12 gauge only. Same general specifications as Light 12. Barrel: 26- or 28-inch, plain or vent rib, SK choke. Weight: 7 lbs. 5 oz.–7 lbs. 10 oz. depending on barrel. Made by FN prior to 1976, since then by Miroku.

FN Manufacture, Plain Barrel	$495
FN Manufacture, Vent-rib Barrel	525
Miroku Manufacture, Vent-rib Barrel	425

Browning Automatic-5 Stalker
Same general specifications as Automatic-5 Light and Magnum models, except with matte blue finish and black graphite fiberglass stock and forearm. Made 1992 to date.

Light Model	$540
Magnum Model	560

Browning Automatic-5, Standard (Grade I)
Recoil-operated. Gauge: 12 or 16 (16-gauge guns made prior to WW II were chambered for 2 9/16-inch shells; standard 16 discontinued 1964). 4-shell magazine in five-shot model; prewar guns were also available in three-shot model. Barrels: 26- to 32-inch; plain, raised matted or vent rib; choice of standard chokes. Weight: about 8 pounds, 12 ga.; 7 1/4 pounds, 16 ga. Checkered pistol-grip stock and forearm. (*Note:* Browning Special, discontinued about 1940, is Grade I gun with either vent or raised matted rib.) Made 1900–1973 by FN.

Grade I, Plain Barrel	$575
Grade I or Browning Special, Raised Matted Rib	605
Grade I or Browning Special, Vent Rib	620

Browning Automatic-5, Sweet 16
16 gauge only. Same general specifications as Standard Model, except lightweight (about 6 3/4 pounds), has gold-plated trigger. Guns without rib have striped matting on top of barrel. Made 1937–1976 by FN.

With Plain Barrel	$650
With Raised Matted Rib	675
With Ventilated Rib	795

SHOTGUNS

Browning Automatic-5 Sweet Sixteen New Model

Browning Model B-80 Automatic

Browning B-80 Upland Special

Browning Auto-5, Sweet Sixteen New Model ... $565
Reissue of popular 16-gauge Hunting Model with 5-shot capacity, 2¾-inch chamber, scroll-engraved blued receiver, high-gloss French walnut stock with rounded pistol grip. 26- or 28-inch vent-rib barrel. Full choke tube. Weight: 7 lbs. 5 oz. Reintroduced in 1987.

Browning Automatic-5, Trap Model ... $565
12 gauge only. Same general specifications as Standard Model, except has trap-style stock, 30-inch vent-rib barrel, full choke. Weight: 8½ pounds. Discontinued 1971.

Browning Model B-80 Gas-Operated Automatic
Gauge: 12 or 20; 2¾-inch chamber. 4-shot magazine. Barrel: 26-, 28- or 30-inch; any standard choke; vent-rib barrel with fixed chokes or Invector tubes. Weight: 6 lbs. 12 oz.–8 lbs. 1 oz. depending on gauge and barrel. Checkered pistol-grip stock and forearm. Made 1981–87.
Model B-80 Standard ... $415
Model B-80 Magnum (3-inch Mag.) ... 425

Browning Model B-80 Plus ... $425
Same general specifications as Browning Model B-80, except chambered for 3-inch shotshells. Made in 1988 only.

Browning Model B-80 Superlight ... $425
Same as Standard Model, except weighs 1 pound less.

Browning Model B-80 Upland Special ... $395
Gauge: 12 or 20. 22-inch vent-rib barrel. Invector choke tube system. 2¾-inch chambers. 42 inches overall. Weight: 5 lbs. 7 oz. (20 ga.); 6 lbs. 10 oz. (12 ga.). German nickel-silver sight bead. Cross-bolt safety. Checkered walnut straight-grip stock and forend. Discontinued 1988.

Browning BPS Game Gun Deer Special ... $380
Same general specifications as Standard BPS Model, except has 20½-inch barrel with adjustable rifle-style sights, solid scope mounting system. Checkered walnut stock with sling swivel studs. Made from 1992 to date.

Browning BPS Game Gun Turkey Special ... $360
Same general specifications as Standard BPS Model, except with matte blue metal finish and satin-finished stock. Gauges: 10, 3½-inch chamber; 12, 3- or 3½-inch. Barrels: 22-, 28-, 30-inch with Extra-Full Invector choke system. Receiver drilled and tapped for scope. Made 1992 to date.

Browning BPS Game Gun Deer Special

Browning BPS Game Gun Turkey Special

Browning BPS Pump Invector Stalker

Browning BPS Pump Shotgun

Browning BSA 10 Semiautomatic

Browning BPS Pigeon Grade $450
Same general specifications as Standard BPS Model, except with select grade walnut stock and gold-trimmed receiver. Available in 12 gauge only with 26- or 28-inch vent-rib barrel. Made 1992 to date.

Browning BPS Pump Invector Stalker
Same general specifications as BPS Pump Shotgun, except in 10 and 12 gauge with Invector choke system; 22-, 26-, 28- or 30-inch barrels; matte blue metal finish with matte black stock. Made 1987 to date.

12-Gauge Model	**$345**
10-Gauge Model	**440**

Browning BPS Pump Shotgun
Takedown. Gauges: 10, 12 (3³/₄-inch chamber); 12 or 20 (3-inch); 2³/₄-inch in target models. Barrels: 22-, 24-, 26-, 28-, 30-, or 32-inch; fixed choke or Invector tubes. Weight: 7¹/₂ lbs. (with 28-inch barrel). Checkered select walnut pistol-grip stock and semibeavertail forearm, recoil pad. Introduced in 1977. Made by Miroku.

Hunting Model (10 or 12 ga., 3¹/₂″)	**$450**
Hunting, Upland (12 or 20 ga.)	**350**
Buck Special (10 or 12 ga., 3¹/₂″)	**460**
Buck Special (12 or 20 ga.)	**350**

Browning BPS Youth and Ladies' Model $395
Lightweight (6 lbs. 11 oz.) version of BPS Pump Shotgun in 20 gauge with 22-inch barrel and floating vent rib, full choke (invector) tube. Discontinued 1992.

Browning BSA 10 Semiautomatic Shotgun $675
Gas-operated short-stroke action. 10 gauge; 3¹/₂-inch chamber. 5-shot magazine. Barrels: 26-, 28- or 30-inch with Invector tubes and vent rib. Weight: 10¹/₂ pounds.

Browning BSA 10 Semiautomatic Shotgun (cont.)
Checkered select walnut buttstock and forend. Blued finish. Made 1993 to date.

Browning B-SS Side-by-Side $650
Boxlock. Automatic ejectors. Non-selective single trigger. Gauges: 12, 20; 3-inch chambers. Barrels: 26-, 28-, or 30-inch (latter in 12 gauge only); IC/M, M/F, or F/F chokes; matte solid rib. Weight (w/28-inch barrels): 12 ga., 7 lbs. 5 oz.; 20 ga., 7 lbs. Checkered straight-grip stock and beavertail forearm. Made 1972–1987 by Miroku.

Browning B-SS Side-by-Side Sidelock $1775
Same general specifications as B-SS boxlock models, except sidelock version available in 26- or 28-inch barrel lengths. 26-inch choked IC/M; 28-inch, M/F. Double triggers. Satin greyed receiver engraved with rosettes and scrolls. German nickel-silver sight bead. Weight: 6¹/₄ lbs. to 6 lbs. 11 oz. 12 ga. made in 1983; 20 ga. made in 1984.

Browning B-SS S/S 20 Gauge Sporter $675
Same as standard B-SS 20 gauge, except has selective single trigger, straight-grip stock. Introduced 1977. Discontinued 1987.

Browning BT-99 Competition Trap Special
Same as BT-99, except has super-high wide rib and standard, Monte Carlo or fully adjustable stock. Available with fixed choke or Invector Plus tubes with optional porting. Made 1976 to date.

BT-99 Grade I w/Fixed Choke (Disc. 1992)	**$ 695**
BT-99 Grade I w/Invectors..................	**850**
BT-99 Plus w/Adjustable Stock	**1100**

Browning B-SS 20 Gauge Sporter

Browning BT-99

Browning BT-99 Grade I Single Barrel Trap $585
Boxlock. Automatic ejector. 12 gauge only. 32- or 34-inch vent-rib barrel; M, IM or F choke. Weight: about 8 pounds. Checkered pistol-grip stock and beavertail forearm, recoil pad. Made 1971–76 by Miroku.

Browning BT-99 Plus Micro $1095
Same general specifications as BT-99 Plus, except scaled down for smaller shooters. 30-inch barrel with adjustable rib and Browning's recoil reducer system. Made 1991 to date.

Browning Citori Hunting Over/Under Models ... $795
Boxlock. Gauges: 12, 16, 20, 28 and .410. Barrel lengths: 24-, 26-, 28-, or 30-inch with vent rib. Chokes: M/F or invector (30-inch bbl.); invector, M/F or IC/M (other bbl. lengths). Overall length ranges from 41–47 inches. 2 1/2-, 3- or 3-inch Mag. loads, depending on gauge. Weight: 5 3/4 lbs. to 7 lbs. 13 oz. Single selective, gold-plated trigger. Medium raised German nickel-silver sight bead. Checkered, rounded pistol-grip walnut stock with beavertail forend. Prices vary with the different grades. Made from 1973 to date by Miroku.

Browning Citori Lightning O/U Models
Same general specifications as the Citori Hunting Models, except with classic Browning rounded pistol-grip stock.
Grade I	**$ 850**
Grade III	**1250**
Grade VI	**1795**

Browning Citori Skeet Gun
Same as Hunting Model, except has skeet-style stock and forearm, 26- or 28-inch barrels, both bored SK choke. Available with either standard vent rib or special target-type, high-post, wide vent rib. Weight (with 26-inch barrels): 12 ga., 8 pounds; 20 ga., 7 pounds. Made 1974 to date by Miroku.

Browning Citori Skeet Gun (cont.)
Grade I	**$ 995**
Grade III	**1250**
Grade VI	**1800**
4-Barrel Set, Grade I	**2795**
4-Barrel Set, Grade III	**3190**
4-Barrel Set, Grade VI	**3575**

Browning Citori Sporting Clays
Same general specifications as Hunting Model, except engraved, with gold-filled logos identifying each model.
GTI Model	**$950**
Micro Citori Lightning Model (w/Low Rib)	**895**
Special Model	**940**
For High Rib **add**	**50**
For Ported Barrels **add**	**55**

Browning Citori Superlight O/U Shotguns
Similar to the Citori Hunting Model, except with straight-grip stock and schnabel forend tip. Made by Miroku 1982 to date.
Grade I, Fixed Choke	**$ 740**
Grade I, Invector	**850**
Grade III, 12 and 20 ga.	**1100**
Grade III, 28 and .410 ga.	**1250**
Grade VI, 12 and 20 ga.	**1695**
Grade VI, 28 and .410 ga.	**1800**

Browning Citori Trap Gun
Same as Hunting Model, except 12 gauge only, has Monte Carlo or fully adjustable stock and beavertail forearm, trap-style recoil pad; 30- or 32-inch barrels; M/F, IM/F, or F/F. Available with either standard vent rib or special target-type, high-post, wide vent rib. Weight: 8 pounds. Made from 1974 to date by Miroku.

Browning Citori O/U Hunting Model

Browning Micro Citori Lightning 20 Gauge

**Browning Citori Plus Trap
Pigeon Grade**

**Browning Double Automatic
Standard Grade**

**Browning Liege
Over-and-Under**

Browning Lightning Sporting Clays

Browning Citori Trap Gun (cont.)

Citori Plus Trap	$1185
Citori Plus Trap w/ported barrel	1225
Grade I	975
Grade III	1200
Grade VI	1725

Browning Citori Upland Special O/U Shotgun $825

A shortened version of the Hunting Model, fitted with 24-inch barrels and straight-grip stock.

Browning Double Automatic, Standard Grade (Steel Receiver)

Short recoil system. Takedown. 12 gauge only. Two shots. Barrels: 26-, 28-, 30-inch; any standard choke. Checkered pistol-grip stock and forearm. Weight: about 7¾ pounds. Made 1955–1961.

With plain barrel	$465
With recessed-rib barrel	590

Browning Lightning Sporting Clays

Similar to the standard Citori Lightning Model, except Classic-style stock with rounded pistol grip. 30-inch back-bored barrels with Invector Plus tubes. Receiver with "Lightning Sporting Clays Edition" logo. Made 1989 to date.

Standard Model	$1150
Pigeon Grade	1295

Browning Liege Over-and-Under Shotgun $725

Boxlock. Automatic ejectors. Non-selective single trigger. 12 gauge only. Barrels: 26½-, 28-, or 30-inch; 2¾-inch chambers in 26½- and 28-inch, 3-inch in 30-inch; IC/M,

Browning Liege OVer-and-Under Shotgun (cont.)

M/F, or F/F chokes; vent rib. Weight: 7 lbs. 4 oz. to 7 lbs. 14 oz., depending on barrels. Checkered pistol-grip stock and forearm. Made 1973–75 by FN.

Browning Over/Under Classic $1650

Gauge: 20, 2¾-inch chambers. 26-inch blued barrels choked IC/M. Gold-plated, single selective trigger. Manual, top-tang-mounted safety. Engraved receiver. High-grade, select American walnut straight-grip stock with schnabel forend. Fine-line checkering with pearl borders. High-gloss finish. 5,000 issued in 1986; made in Japan, engraved in Belgium.

**Browning Over/Under
Gold Classic**

Browning Over/Under Gold Classic $3995

Same general specifications as Over/Under Classic, except more elaborate engravings, enhanced in gold, including profile of John M. Browning. Fine oil finish. 500 issued; made in 1986 in Belgium.

Browning Recoilless Trap Shotgun

The action and barrel are driven forward when firing to achieve 70 percent less recoil. 12 gauge; 2¾-inch chamber. 30-inch barrel with Invector Plus tubes; adjustable vent rib. 51⅝ inches overall. Weight: 9 pounds. Adjustable checkered walnut buttstock and forend. Blued finish. Made from 1993 to date.

Standard Model **$1200**
Micro Model (27-inch bbl.) **1250**

Browning Superposed Bicentennial (Left Side)

Browning Superposed Bicentennial (Right Side)

Browning Superposed Bicentennial Commemorative **$12,000**

Special limited edition issued to commemorate U.S. Bicentennial. 51 guns, one for each state in the Union plus one for Washington, D.C. Receiver with sideplates has engraved and gold-inlaid hunter and wild turkey on right side, U.S. flag and bald eagle on left side, together with state markings inlaid in gold, on blued background. Checkered straight-grip stock and schnabel-style forearm of highly figured American walnut. Velvet-lined wooden presentation case. Made in 1976 by FN. Value shown is for gun in new, unfired condition.

Browning Superposed BROADway 12 Trap ... **$1475**

Same as standard Trap Gun, except has 30- or 32-inch barrels with wider BROADway rib. Discontinued 1976.

Pigeon Grade (Prewar)

Diana Grade (Prewar)

Midas Grade (Prewar)

Browning Superposed Shotguns, Hunting Models

Over-and-under. Boxlock. Selective automatic ejectors. Selective single trigger; earlier models (worth 25% less) supplied with double triggers, twin selective triggers or non-selective single trigger. Gauges: 12, 20 (introduced 1949, 3-inch chambers in later production), 28, .410 (latter two gauges introduced 1960). Barrels: 26½-, 28-, 30-, 32-inch; raised matted or vent rib; prewar Lightning Model made without ribbed barrel, postwar version supplied only with vent rib; any combination of standard chokes. Weight (with 26½-inch vent-rib barrels): Standard 12, 7 lbs. 11 oz.; Lightning 12, 7 lbs. 6 oz.; Standard 20, 6 lbs. 8 oz.; Lightning 20, 6 lbs. 4 oz.; Lightning 28, 6 lbs. 7 oz.; Lightning .410, 6 lbs. 10 oz. Checkered pistol-grip stock and forearm. Higher grades—Pigeon, Pointer, Diana, Midas, Grade VI—differ from standard Grade I models in overall quality, engraving, wood and checkering; otherwise, spec-

Browning Superposed BROADway Trap

Browning Superposed Grade I Standard (Prewar)

Browning Superposed Grade I Lightning (Prewar)

Browning Superposed Hunting Models (cont.)

ifications are the same. Midas Grade and Grade VI guns are richly gold-inlaid. Made by FN 1928–1976. Prewar models may be considered as discontinued in 1940 when Belgium was occupied by Germany. Grade VI offered 1955–1960. Pointer Grade discontinued in 1966, Grade I Standard in 1973, Pigeon Grade in 1974. Lightning Grade I, Diana and Midas Grades were not offered after 1976.

Grade I Standard	**$1150**
Grade I Lightning	1425
Grade I Lightning, prewar, matted bbl., no rib	2000
Grade II—Pigeon	2400
Grade III—Pointer	2900
Grade IV—Diana	3600
Grade V—Midas	4625
Grade VI	6000
Add for 28 or .410 gauge	375

Values shown are for models with ventilated rib, if gun has raised matted rib, *deduct* 175

Grade II Pigeon (Postwar)

Grade III Pointer (Postwar)

Grade IV Diana (Postwar)

Grade V Midas (Postwar)

Browning Superposed Lightning and Superlight Models (Reissue)

Reissue of popular 12-and 20-gauge superposed shotguns. Lightning models available in 26½- and 28-inch barrel lengths with 2¾- or 3-inch chambering, full pistol grip. Superlight models available in 26½-inch barrel lengths

Browning Superposed Lightning/Superlight (cont.)

with 2¾-inch chambering only, and straight-grip stock with schnabel forend. Both have hand-engraved receivers, fine-line checkering, gold-plated single selective trigger, automatic selective ejectors, manual safety. Weight: 6 to 7½ pounds. Reintroduced 1985–86.

Grade II, Pigeon	**$2595**
Grade III, Pointer	2995
Grade IV, Diana	3195
Grade V, Midas	4195

Browning Superposed Magnum **$1300**
Same as Grade I, except chambered for 12-gauge 3-inch shells, 30-inch vent-rib barrels, stock with recoil pad. Weight: about 8¼ pounds. Discontinued 1976.

Browning Superposed Ltd. Black Duck Issue . . **$4600**
Gauge: 12. Superposed Lightning action. 28-inch vent-rib barrels. Choked M/F. 2¾-inch chambers. Weight: 7 lbs. 6 oz. Gold inlaid receiver and trigger guard engraved with Black Duck scenes. Gold-plated, single selective trigger. Top-tang mounted manual safety. Automatic, selective ejectors. Front and center ivory sights. High-grade, hand-checkered, hand-oiled select walnut stock and forend. 500 issued in 1983.

Browning Superposed Ltd. Pintail Duck Issue . **$4610**
Same general specifications as Ltd. Black Duck Issue, except Pintail Duck scenes engraved on receiver and trigger guard; stock is of dark French walnut with rounded pistol grip. 500 issued in 1983.

Browning Superposed, Presentation Grades
Custom versions of Super-Light, Lightning Hunting, Trap and Skeet Models, with same general specifications as those of standard guns, but of higher overall quality. The four Presentation Grades differ in receiver finish (greyed or blued), engraving, gold inlays, wood and checkering; Presentation 4 has sideplates. Made by FN, these models were introduced in 1977.

Presentation 1	**$3200**
Presentation 1, gold-inlaid	3600
Presentation 2	3800
Presentation 2, gold-inlaid	4600
Presentation 3, gold-inlaid	5520
Presentation 4	6500
Presentation 4, gold-inlaid	7500

Browning Superposed Skeet Guns, Grade I
Same as standard Lightning 12, 20, 28 and .410 Hunting Models, except has skeet-style stock and forearm, 26½- or 28-inch vent-rib barrels with SK choke. Available also in All Gauge Skeet Set: Lightning 12 with one removable forearm and three extra sets of barrels in 20, 28 and .410 gauge in fitted luggage case. Discontinued 1976.

12 or 20 gauge	**$1495**
28 or .410 gauge	1795
All Gauge Skeet Set	4250

SHOTGUNS

Browning Superposed Ltd. Pintail Duck Issue

Browning Superposed Trap

Browning Twelvette Double Automatic

Browning Twentyweight Double Automatic

Browning Choke Marks. The following markings are used to indicate chokes on Browning shotguns:

Full *	Improved Cylinder **—
Improved Modified *—	Skeet **S
Modified **	Cylinder ***

Browning Superposed Super-Light Model $1425
Ultralight field gun version of Standard Lightning Model has classic straight-grip stock and slimmer forearm. Available only in 12 and 20 gauges (2³/₄-inch chambers), with 26¹/₂-inch vent-rib barrels. Weight: 6¹/₂ pounds, 12 ga.; 6 pounds, 20 ga. Made 1967–1976.

Browning Superposed Trap Gun $1475
Same as Grade I, except has trap-style stock, beavertail forearm, 30-inch vent-rib barrels, 12 gauge only. Discont. 1976.

Browning Twelvette Double Automatic
Lightweight version of Double Automatic with same general specifications except aluminum receiver. Barrel with plain matted top or vent rib. Weight: 6³/₄ to 7 pounds, depending on barrel. Receiver is finished in black w/gold engraving; 1956–1961 receivers were also anodized in grey, brown and green w/silver engraving. Made 1955–1971.
With Plain Barrel **$425**
With Vent-rib Barrel **510**

Browning Twentyweight Double Automatic
Same as Twelvette, but ³/₄ pound lighter. 26¹/₂-inch barrel only. Made 1956–1971.
With Plain Barrel **$450**
With Vent-rib Barrel **495**

E.J. CHURCHILL, LTD.
London, England

Originally made in London, Churchill shotguns are now manufactured in Italy and Spain.

Churchill Automatic Shotgun
Gas-operated. Gauge: 12, 2³/₄- or 3-inch. 5-shot magazine with cut-off. Barrel: 24-, 25-, 26-, 28-inch with ICT Choke tubes. Checkered walnut stock with satin finish. made 1990 to date.
Standard Model **$425**
Turkey Model **450**

Churchill Field Model Hammerless Double
Sidelock hammerless ejector gun with same general specifications as Premiere Model but of lower quality. Discontinued.
With Double Triggers **$8000**
Selective Single Trigger, **add** **400**

Churchill Automatic Shotgun

Churchill Monarch Over/Under Shotgun

Hammerless, takedown with engraved receiver. Selective single or double triggers. Gauges: 12, 20, 28, .410; 3-inch chambers. Barrels: 25- or 26-inch (IC/M); 28-inch (M/F). Weight: 6½–7½ pounds. Checkered European walnut buttstock and forend. Made in Italy 1986–1993.

With Double Triggers **$350**
With Single Trigger **425**

Churchill Premiere Quality Hammerless Double

Sidelock. Automatic ejectors. Double triggers or selective single trigger. Gauges: 12, 16, 20, 28. Barrels: 25-, 28-, 30-, 32-inch; any degree of boring. Weight: 5–8 pounds depending on gauge and barrel length. Checkered stock and forend, straight or pistol grip. Discontinued.

With Double Triggers **$14,000**
Selective Single Trigger, extra **900**

Churchill Premiere

Churchill Premiere Quality Under-and-Over Shotgun

Sidelock. Automatic ejectors. Double triggers or selective single trigger. Gauges: 12, 16, 20, 28. Barrels: 25-, 28-, 30-, 32-inch; any degree of boring. Weight: 5–8 pounds depending on gauge and barrel length. Checkered stock and forend, straight or pistol grip. Discontinued.

With Double Triggers **$14,995**
Selective Single Trigger, **add** **700**
Raised Vent Rib, **add** **400**

Churchill Regent Over/Under Shotguns

Gauges: 12 or 20; 2¾-inch chambers. 27-inch barrels w/ interchangeable choke tubes and wide vent rib. Single selective trigger, selective automatic ejectors. Checkered pistol-grip stock in fancy walnut. Imported from Italy 1984–88.

Regent V **$825**
Regent VII w/Sideplates **950**

Churchill Regent Side-by-Side Shotguns

12 gauge s/s. 25-, 27- or 28-inch barrels w/fixed choke or interchangeable choke tubes. Double triggers. Automatic top tang safety. Double safety sidelock, engraved silver receiver. Automatic selective ejectors. Oil-finished English-style stock of extra select European walnut. Imported from Spain 1984 to date.

Regent Standard **$650**
Regent VI, Sidelock **795**

Churchill Regent Skeet **$820**

12 or 20 gauge with 2¾-inch chambers. Selective automatic ejectors, single-selective trigger. 26-inch over/under barrels w/vent rib. Weight: 7 lbs. Made in Italy 1984–88.

Churchill Regent Trap **$815**

12-gauge competition shotgun w/2¾-inch chambers. 30-inch over/under barrels choked IM/F, vent side ribs. Weight: 8 pounds. Selective automatic ejectors, single-selective trigger. Checkered Monte Carlo stock with Supercushion recoil pad. Made in Italy 1984–88.

Churchill Sporting Clays Over/Under $695

Same general specifications as Windsor IV, except in 12 gauge only with 28-inch ported barrels and choke tubes. Selective automatic ejectors. Weight: 7½ pounds. Made from 1992 to date.

Churchill Monarch Over/Under Shotgun

Churchill Regent VII w/Side Plates

Churchill Regent Trap

Churchill Sporting Clays Over/Under

SHOTGUNS

Churchill Windsor III Over/Under

**Churchill Windsor Grade
Side/Side Flyweight Shotgun**

Churchill Utility Model Hammerless Double Barrel
Anson & Deeley boxlock action. Double triggers or single trigger. Gauges: 12, 16, 20, 28, .410. Barrels: 25-, 28-, 30-, 32-inch; any degree of boring. Weight: 4½–8 pounds depending on gauge and barrel length. Checkered stock and forend, straight or pistol grip. Discontinued.

With Double Triggers	$4125
Selective Single Trigger, **add**	400

Churchill Windsor Over/Under Shotguns
Hammerless, boxlock with engraved receiver, selective single trigger. Extractors or ejectors. Gauges: 12, 20, 28 or .410; 3-inch chambers. Barrels: 24 to 30 inches with fixed chokes or choke tubes. Weight: 6 lbs. 3 oz. (Flyweight) to 7 lbs. 10 oz. (12 ga.). Checkered straight (Flyweight) or pistol-grip stock and forend of European walnut. Imported from Italy 1984 to date.

Windsor III w/Fixed Chokes	$500
Windsor III w/Choke Tubes	565
Windsor IV w/Fixed Chokes (Disc. 1993)	545
Windsor IV w/Choke Tubes	695

Churchill Windsor Side-by-Side Shotguns
Boxlock action with double triggers, ejectors or extractors and automatic safety. Gauges: 10, (3½-inch chambers); 12, 20, 28, .410 (3-inch chambers); 16 (2¾-inch chambers). Barrels: 23 to 32 inches with various fixed choke or choke tube combinations. Weight: 5 lbs. 12 oz. (Flyweight) to 11½ lbs. (10 ga.). European walnut buttstock and forend. Imported from Spain 1984–1990.

Windsor I 10 ga.	$510
Windsor I 12 thru .410 ga.	390
Windsor II 12 or 20 ga.	500

Churchill XXV Premiere Hammerless Double ... $12,500
Sidelock. Assisted opening. Automatic ejectors. Double triggers. Gauges: 12, 20. 25-inch barrels with narrow, quick-sighting rib; any standard choke combination. English-style straight-grip stock and forearm, checkered.

Churchill XXV Imperial $9500
Similar to XXV Premiere, but no assisted opening feature.

Churchill XXV Hercules $7995
Boxlock, otherwise specs same as for XXV Premiere.

Churchill XXV Regal $4200
Similar to XXV Hercules, but without assisted opening feature. Gauges: 12, 20, 28, .410.

COGSWELL & HARRISON, LTD.
London, England

Cogswell & Harrison Ambassador Hammerless Double Barrel Shotgun $3300
Boxlock. Sideplates with game scene or rose scroll engraving. Automatic ejectors. Double triggers. Gauges: 12, 16, 20. Barrels: 26-, 28-, 30-inch; any choke combination. Checkered straight-grip stock and forearm. Currently manufactured.

Cogswell & Harrison Avant Tout Series Hammerless Double Barrel Shotguns
Boxlock. Sideplates (except Avant Tout III Grade). Automatic ejectors. Double triggers or single trigger (selective or non-selective). Gauges: 12, 16, 20. Barrels: 25-, 27½-, 30-inch; any choke combination. Checkered stock and forend, straight grip standard. Made in three models—Avant Tout I or Konor, Avant Tout II or Sandhurst, Avant Tout III or Rex—which differ chiefly in overall quality, engraving, grade of wood, checkering, etc.; general specifications are the same. Discontinued.

Avant Tout I	$2410
Avant Tout II	2325
Avant Tout III	1915
Single Trigger, Non-selective, **add**	225
Single Trigger, Selective, **add**	300

Cogswell & Harrison Best Quality Hammerless—Victor Model

Cogswell & Harrison Best Quality Hammerless Sidelock Double Barrel Shotgun
Hand-detachable locks. Automatic ejectors. Double triggers or single trigger (selective or non-selective). Gauges: 12, 16, 20. Barrels: 25-, 26-, 28-, 30-inch; any choke com-

SHOTGUNS (vertical, right margin)

Cogswell & Harrison Best Quality Hammerless (cont.)

bination. Checkered stock and forend, straight grip standard. Made in two models: Victor (currently manufactured) and Primic (with plainer finish, discontinued), otherwise the same.

Victor Model	**$6950**
Primic Model	**4350**
Single Trigger, Non-selective, **add**	**225**
Single Trigger, Selective, **add**	**300**

Cogswell & Harrison Huntic Model Hammerless Double

Sidelock. Automatic ejectors. Double triggers or single trigger (selective or non-selective). Gauges: 12, 16, 20. Barrels: 25-, 27½-, 30-inch; any choke combination. Checkered stock and forend, straight grip standard. Discontinued.

With Double Triggers	**$3200**
Single Trigger, Non-selective, **add**	**225**
Single Trigger, Selective, **add**	**300**

Cogswell & Harrison Markor Hammerless Double

Boxlock. Non-ejector or ejector. Double triggers. Gauges: 12, 16, 20. Barrels: 27½- or 30-inch; any choke combination. Checkered stock and forend, straight grip standard. Discontinued.

Non-ejector Model	**$1295**
Ejector Model	**1845**

Cogswell & Harrison Regency

Cogswell & Harrison Regency Hammerless
Double **$2650**

Anson & Deeley boxlock action. Automatic ejectors. Double triggers. Gauges: 12, 16, 20. Barrels: 26-, 28-, 30-inch; any choke combination. Checkered straight-grip stock and forearm. Introduced in 1970 to commemorate the firm's bicentenary, this model has deep scroll engraving and the name "Regency" inlaid in gold on the rib. Currently manufactured.

COLT INDUSTRIES
Hartford, Connecticut

Colt Auto Shotguns were made by Luigi Franchi S.p.A. and are similar to corresponding models of that manufacturer.

Colt Auto Shotgun—Magnum

Same as Standard Auto, except steel receiver, handles 3-inch Magnum shells, 30- and 32-inch barrels in 12 gauge, 28-inch in 20 gauge. Weight: 12 ga., about 8¼ pounds. Made 1964–66.

With plain barrel	**$345**
With solid-rib barrel	**375**
With ventilated-rib barrel	**395**

Colt Auto Shotgun—Magnum Custom

Same as Magnum, except has engraved receiver, select walnut stock and forearm. Made 1964–66.

With solid-rib barrel	**$425**
With ventilated-rib barrel	**475**

Colt Auto Shotgun—Ultra Light Custom

Same as Standard Auto, except has engraved receiver, select walnut stock and forearm. Made 1964–66.

With solid-rib barrel	**$350**
With ventilated-rib barrel	**375**

Colt Auto Shotgun—Ultra Light Standard

Recoil-operated. Takedown. Alloy receiver. Gauges: 12, 20. Magazine holds 4 shells. Barrels: plain, solid or vent rib; chrome-lined; 26-inch IC or M choke, 28-inch M or F choke, 30-inch F choke, 32-inch F choke. Weight: 12 ga., about 6¼ pounds. Checkered pistol-grip stock and forearm. Made 1964–66.

With Plain Barrel	**$245**
With Solid-rib Barrel	**275**
With Vent-rib Barrel	**295**

Colt Custom Hammerless Double **$575**

Boxlock. Double triggers. Auto ejectors. Gauges: 12 Mag., 16. Barrels: 26-inch IC/M; 28-inch M/F; 30-inch F/F. Weight: 12 ga., about 7½ pounds. Checkered pistol-grip stock and beavertail forearm. Made in 1961.

Coltsman Custom Pump **$320**

Same as Standard Pump except has checkered stock, vent-rib barrel. Weight: about 6½ pounds. Made 1961–63.

**Colt Auto Shotgun—
Ultra Light Standard**

Colt Custom Hammerless Double

Coltsman Standard Pump

Colt-Sauer Drilling

Coltsman Standard Pump Shotgun **$295**
Takedown. Gauges: 12, 16, 20. Magazine holds 4 shells.
Barrels: 26-inch IC; 28-inch M or F choke; 30-inch F
choke. Weight: about 6 pounds. Plain pistol-grip stock
and forearm. Made 1961–65 by Manufrance.

Colt-Sauer Drilling **$3300**
Three-barrel combination gun. Boxlock. Set rifle trigger.
Tang barrel selector, automatic rear sight positioner. 12

Colt-Sauer Drilling (cont.)
gauge over 30-06 or 243 rifle barrel. 25-inch barrels, F and
M choke. Weight: about 8 pounds. Folding leaf rear sight,
blade front with brass bead. Checkered pistol-grip stock
and beavertail forearm, recoil pad. Made 1974 to date by
J. P. Sauer & Sohn, Eckernförde, Germany.

CVC Classic Field Waterfowler

CVC Classic Sporter

=== **CONNECTICUT VALLEY CLASSICS** ===
Westport, Connecticut

CVC Classic Field Waterfowler **$1495**
Similar to the standard Classic Sporter Model, except with
30-inch barrels only and non-reflective matte blued finish.
Made 1993 to date.

CVC Classic Sporter Over/Under
Gauge: 12; 3-inch chamber. Barrels: 28-, 30- or 32-inch
with screw-in tubes. Weight: 7¾ pounds. Engraved stainless or nitrided receiver; blued barrels. Checkered American black walnut buttstock and forend with low-luster
satin finish. Made from 1993 to date.
Classic Sporter **$1675**
Stainless Classic Sporter **1815**

**Daly Commander
Over-and-Under**

CHARLES DALY, INC.
New York, New York

The pre-WWII Charles Daly shotguns, with the exception of the Commander, were manufactured by various firms in Suhl, Germany. The postwar guns, except for the Novamatic series and the current models distributed by Outdoor Sports Headquarters, were produced by Miroku Firearms Mfg. Co., Tokyo.

Charles Daly Commander Over-and-Under Shotgun

Daly pattern Anson & Deeley system boxlock action. Automatic ejectors. Double triggers or Miller selective single trigger. Gauges: 12, 16, 20, 28, .410. Barrels: 26- to 30-inch, IC/M or M/F choke. Weight: 5$\frac{1}{4}$ to 7$\frac{1}{4}$ pounds depending on gauge and barrel length. Checkered stock and forend, straight or pistol grip. The two models, 100 and 200, differ in general quality, grade of wood, checkering, engraving, etc.; otherwise specs are the same. Made in Belgium c. 1939.

Model 100	**$420**
Model 200	**550**
Miller Single Trigger, **add**	**100**

Daly Diamond Hammerless Double

**Daly Regent Diamond
Hammerless Double**

Daly Superior Hammerless Double

Charles Daly Hammerless Double Barrel Shotgun

Daly pattern Anson & Deeley system boxlock action. Automatic ejectors—except "Superior Quality" is non-ejector. Double triggers. Gauges: 10, 12, 16, 20, 28, .410. Barrels: 26- to 32-inch, any combination of chokes. Weight: from 4 pounds to 8$\frac{1}{2}$ pounds depending on gauge and barrel length. Checkered pistol-grip stock and forend. The four grades—Regent Diamond, Diamond, Empire, Superior—differ in general quality, grade of wood, checkering, engraving, etc.; otherwise specifications are the same. Discontinued about 1933.

Diamond Quality	**$3995**
Empire Quality	**1895**
Regent Diamond Quality	**3495**
Superior Quality	**895**

Charles Daly Hammerless Drilling (Three Barrel Gun)

Daly pattern Anson & Deeley system boxlock action. Plain extractors. Double triggers, front single set for rifle barrel. Gauges: 12, 16, 20, 25-20, 25-35, 30-30 rifle barrel. Supplied in various barrel lengths and weights. Checkered pistol-grip stock and forend. Auto rear sight operated by rifle barrel selector. The three grades—Regent Diamond, Diamond, Superior—differ in general quality, grade of wood, checkering, engraving; otherwise, specs are the same. Discont. about 1933.

Diamond Quality	**$3050**
Regent Diamond Quality	**3875**
Superior Quality	**1995**

Daly Empire Double Barrel

Charles Daly Empire Grade Hammerless Double **$545**

Boxlock. Plain extractors. Non-selective single trigger. Gauges: 12, 16, 20; 3-inch chambers in 12 and 20, 2$\frac{3}{4}$-inch in 16 gauge. Barrels: vent rib; 26-, 28-, 30-inch (latter in 12 gauge only); IC/M, M/F, F/F. Weight: 6 to 7$\frac{3}{4}$ pounds, depending on gauge and barrels. Checkered pistol-grip stock and beavertail forearm. Made 1968-1971.

Charles Daly 1974 Wildlife Commemorative ... **$1715**

Limited issue of 500 guns. Similar to Diamond Grade over/under. 12-gauge trap and skeet models only. Duck scene engraved on right side of receiver, fine scroll on left side. Made in 1974. (*See* photo, next page.)

SHOTGUNS

Daly 1974 Wildlife Commemorative

> **NOTE:** The following Novamatic autoloaders were produced in 1968 by Ernesto Breda, Milan, Italy.

Charles Daly Novamatic Lightweight Autoloader
Same as Breda. Recoil-operated. Takedown. 12 gauge, 2³/₄-inch chamber. 4-shell tubular magazine. Barrels: plain, vent rib; 26-inch IC or Quick-Choke with three interchangeable tubes, 28-inch M or F choke. Weight (with 26-inch vent-rib barrel): 7 lbs. 6 oz. Checkered pistol-grip stock and forearm.

With Plain Barrel **$350**
With Vent-rib Barrel **395**
For Quick-Choke, **add** **20**

Charles Daly Novamatic Super Lightweight
Lighter version of Novamatic Lightweight. Gauges: 12, 20. Weight (with 26-inch vent-rib barrel): 12 ga., 6 lbs. 10 oz.; 20 ga., 6 lbs. SK choke available in 26-inch vent-rib barrel. 28-inch barrels in 12 gauge only. Quick-Choke in 20 gauge with plain barrel.

Charles Daly Novamatic Super Lightweight (cont.)
12 Gauge, Plain Barrel **$345**
12 Gauge, Vent-rib Barrel **375**
20 Gauge, Plain Barrel **310**
20 Gauge, Plain Barrel w/Quick-Choke **325**
20 Gauge, Vent-rib Barrel **345**

Charles Daly Novamatic Super Lightweight 20-Gauge Magnum **$345**
Same as Novamatic Super Lightweight 20, except 3-inch chamber, has 3-shell magazine, 28-inch vent-rib barrel, Full choke.

Charles Daly Novamatic 12-Gauge Magnum **$350**
Same as Novamatic Lightweight, except chambered for 12-gauge Magnum 3-inch shell, has 3-shell magazine, 30-inch vent-rib barrel, Full choke, and stock with recoil pad. Weight: 7³/₄ pounds.

Charles Daly Novamatic Trap Gun **$375**
Same as Novamatic Lightweight, except has 30-inch vent-rib barrel, Full choke and Monte Carlo stock with recoil pad. Weight: 7³/₄ pounds.

Charles Daly Over-and-Under Shotguns (Prewar)
Daly-pattern Anson & Deeley-system boxlock action. Sideplates. Auto ejectors. Double triggers. Gauges: 12, 16, 20. Supplied in various barrel lengths and weights. Checkered pistol-grip stock and forend. The two grades—Diamond and Empire—differ in general quality, grade of wood, checkering, engraving, etc.; otherwise specifications are the same. Discontinued about 1933.
Diamond Quality **$4295**
Empire Quality **3150**

Charles Daly Over-and-Under Shotguns (Postwar)
Boxlock. Auto ejectors or selective auto/manual ejection. Selective single trigger. Gauges: 12, 12 Magnum (3-inch chambers), 20 (3-inch chambers), 28, .410. Barrels: vent rib; 26-, 28-, 30-inch; standard choke combinations.

Daly Novamatic Autoloader

**Daly Over-and-Under
Field Grade (Postwar)**

**Daly Over-and-Under
Venture (Postwar)**

Charles Daly Over-and-Under (Postwar) (cont.)

Weight: 6 to 8 pounds depending on gauge and barrels. Select walnut stock with pistol grip, fluted forearm, checkered; Monte Carlo comb on trap guns; recoil pad on 12-ga. Mag. and trap models. The various grades differ in quality of engraving and wood. Made 1963–1976.

Diamond Grade	**$925**
Field Grade	**530**
Superior Grade	**625**
Venture Grade	**520**

Daly Sextuple Trap

Charles Daly Sextuple Model Single Barrel Trap Gun

Daly pattern Anson & Deeley system boxlock action. Six locking bolts. Auto ejector. 12 gauge only. Barrels: 30-, 32-, 34-inch, vent rib. Weight: 7½ to 8¼ pounds. Checkered pistol-grip stock and forend. The two models made—Empire and Regent Diamond—differ in general quality, grade of wood, checkering, engraving, etc.; otherwise specs are the same. Discontinued about 1933.

Regent Diamond Quality	**$2650**
Empire Quality	**1995**

Daly Single Barrel Trap

Charles Daly Single Barrel Trap Gun

Daly pattern Anson & Deeley system boxlock action. Auto ejector. 12 gauge only. Barrels: 30-, 32-, 34-inch, vent rib. Weight: 7½ to 8¼ pounds. Checkered pistol-grip stock and forend. This model was made in Empire Quality only. Discontinued about 1933.

Diamond Grade	**$2750**
Empire Grade	**2095**

Charles Daly Superior Grade Single Barrel Trap $625

Boxlock. Automatic ejector. 12 gauge only. 32- or 34-inch vent-rib barrel, full choke. Weight: about 8 pounds. Monte Carlo stock with pistol grip and recoil pad, beavertail forearm, checkered. Made 1968–1976.

> **NOTE:** The following Charles Daly shotguns are distributed in the U.S. by Outdoor Sports Headquarters, Dayton, Ohio. The Daly semiauto guns are currently manufactured in Japan, while the over/under models are produced in Italy.

Charles Daly Diamond Grade Over/Under

Boxlock. Single selective trigger. Selective automatic ejectors. Gauges: 12 and 20; 3-inch chambers (2¾ target grade). Barrels: 26-, 27- or 30-inch with fixed chokes or screw-in tubes. Weight: 7 pounds. Checkered European walnut stock and forearm with oil finish. Engraved antique silver receiver and blued barrels. Made 1984–1990.

Standard Model	**$750**
Skeet Model	**770**
Trap Model	**775**

Charles Daly DSS Hammerless Double $525

Boxlock. Single selective trigger. Selective automatic ejectors. Gauges: 12 and 20; 3-inch chambers. 26-inch barrels with screw-in choke tubes. Weight: 6¾ pounds. Checkered walnut pistol-grip stock and semibeavertail forearm with recoil pad. Engraved antique silver receiver and blued barrels. Made from 1990 to date.

Charles Daly Field Grade Over/Under $375

Boxlock. Single selective trigger. Extractors. Gauges: 12 and 20; 3-inch chambers. Barrels: 26-inch, IC/M; 28-inch, M/F. Weight: 6¾ pounds (12 ga.). Checkered walnut stock and forearm with semi-gloss finish and recoil pad. Engraved color-casehardened receiver and blued barrels. Made from 1989 to date.

Charles Daly Field Semiauto Shotgun $300

Recoil-operated. Takedown. 12-gauge and 12-gauge Magnum. Barrels: 27- and 30-inch; vent rib. Made 1982–88.

Charles Daly Field III Over/Under Shotgun $410

Boxlock. Plain extractors. Non-selective single trigger. Gauges: 12 or 20. Barrels: vent rib; 26- and 28-inch; IC/M, M/F. Weight: 6 to 7¾ pounds depending on gauge and barrels. Chrome-molybdenum steel barrels. Checkered pistol-grip stock and forearm. Made from 1982 to date.

SHOTGUNS

Daly Field Semi-Auto

Daly Field III

Daly Presentation Grade

Daly Superior II

Charles Daly Lux Over/Under **$545**
Similar to the Field Grade, except with selective automatic
ejectors and choke tubes. Gauges: 12, 20, 28 and .410. Receiver with antique silver finish and blued barrels. Made
from 1989 to date.

Charles Daly Multi-XII Self-loading Shotgun **$395**
Similar to the gas-operated field semiauto, except with
new Multi-Action gas system designed to shoot all loads
without adjustment. 12 gauge w/3-inch chamber. 27-inch
barrel with Invector choke tubes, vent rib. Made in Japan
from 1987 to date.

Charles Daly Over/Under Presentation Grade . . **$795**
Purdey double cross-bolt locks. Single selective trigger.
Gauges: 12 or 20. Barrels: chrome-molybdenum steel, rec-
tified, honed and internally chromed; 27-inch vent rib.
Hand-checkered deluxe European walnut stock. Made
1982–86.

Charles Daly Over/Under Superior II Shotgun . . . **$530**
Boxlock. Plain extractors. Non-selective single trigger.
Gauges: 12 or 20. Barrels: chrome-molybdenum vent rib;
26-, 28-, 30-inch; latter in Magnum only; assorted chokes.
Silver engraved receiver. Checkered pistol-grip stock and
forearm. Made from 1982 to date.

Darne Model V22

Darne Model V
Hors Série No. 1

DARNE S.A.
Saint-Etienne, France

Darne Model R11

Darne Hammerless Double Barrel Shotguns
Sliding-breech action with fixed barrels. Auto ejectors.
Double triggers. Gauges: 12, 16, 20, 28; also 12 and 20
Magnum with 3-inch chambers. Barrels: 27½-inch standard, 25½- to 31½-inch lengths available; any standard
choke combination. Weight: 5½ to 7 pounds, depending
on gauge and barrel length. Checkered straight-grip or

Darne Hammerless Double Barrel Shotguns (cont.)
pistol-grip stock and forearm. The various models differ
in grade of engraving and wood. Currently manufactured.
Model R11 (Bird Hunter) . . . . **$ 850**
Model R15 (Pheasant Hunter) **2000**
Model R16 (Magnum) **1525**
Model V19 (Quail Hunter) **2800**
Model V22 . . . . **5800**
Model V Hors Série No. 1 . . . . **7200**

DAVIDSON GUNS
**Mfd. by Fabrica de Armas ILJA, Eibar, Spain; dis-
tributed by Davidson Firearms Co., Greensboro,
North Carolina**

Davidson Model 63B Double Barrel Shotgun . . . **$275**
Anson & Deeley boxlock action. Frame-engraved and
nickel plated. Plain extractors. Auto safety. Double triggers. Gauges: 12, 16, 20, 28, .410. Barrel lengths: 25 (.410
only), 26, 28, 30 inches (latter 12 ga. only). Chokes: IC/

Davidson Model 63B

Davidson Model 63B Double Barrel Shotgun (cont.)
M, M/F, F/F. Weight: 5 lb. 11 oz. (.410) to 7 lbs. (12 ga.).
Checkered pistol-grip stock and forearm of European
walnut. Made from 1963 to date.

Davidson Model 63B Magnum
Similar to standard Model 63B, except chambered for 10
ga. 3½-inch, 12 and 20 ga. 3-inch Magnum shells; 10 gauge
has 32-inch barrels, choked F/F. Weight: 10 lb. 10 oz.
Made from 1963 to date.
12-and 20-gauge Magnum **$350**
10-gauge Magnum **400**

Davidson Model 69SL Double Barrel Shotgun . . **$405**
Sidelock action with detachable sideplates, engraved and
nickel-plated. Plain extractors. Auto safety. Double triggers. 12 and 20 gauge. Barrels: 26-inch IC/M, 28-inch
M/F. Weight: 12 ga., 7 pounds; 20 ga., 6½ pounds. Pistol-
grip stock and forearm of European walnut, checkered.
Made 1963–1976.

Davidson Model 73 Stagecoach
Hammer Double **$265**
Sidelock action with detachable sideplates and exposed
hammers. Plain extractors. Double triggers. Gauges: 12,
20; 3-inch chambers. 20-inch barrels, M/F chokes. Weight:
7 lbs., 12 ga.; 6½ lbs., 20 ga. Checkered pistol-grip stock
and forearm. Made from 1976 to date.

EXEL ARMS OF AMERICA
Gardner, Massachusetts

Exel Series 100 Over/Under Shotguns
Gauge: 12. Single selective trigger. Selective auto ejectors.
Hand-checkered European walnut stock with full pistol
grip, tulip forend. Black metal finish. Chambered for 2¾-
inch shells (Model 103 for 3-inch). Weight: 6⅞ to 7⅞
pounds. Discontinued 1988.
Model 101, 26-inch bbl., IC/M **$360**
Model 102, 28-inch bbl., IC/IM **360**
Model 103, 30-inch bbl., M/F **375**
Model 104, 28-inch bbl., IC/IM **395**
Model 105, 28-inch bbl., 5 choke tubes **495**
Model 106, 28-inch bbl., 5 choke tubes **645**
Model 107 Trap, 30-inch bbl., Full +5 tubes **675**

Exel Series 200 Side-by-Side Shotgun **$375**
Gauges: 12, 20, 28 and .410. Barrels: 26-, 27- and 28-inch;
various choke combinations. Weight: 7 pounds average.
American or European-style stock and forend. Made 1985
to date.

Exel Model 101 Shotgun

Exel Model 103 Shotgun

Exel Model 107 Trap

Exel Series 200 Side-By-Side

SHOTGUNS

Exel Series 300 Over/Under

Exel Series 300 Over/Under Shotgun **$450**
Gauge: 12. Barrels: 26-, 28- and 29-inch. Non-glare black-chrome matte finish. Weight: 7 pounds average. Selective auto ejectors, engraved receiver. Hand-checkered European walnut stock and forend. Made 1985–86.

FOX SHOTGUNS

Made by A. H. Fox Gun Co., Philadelphia, Penn., 1903 to 1930, and since then by Savage Arms, originally of Utica, N.Y., now of Westfield, Mass.

Values shown are for 12 and 16 gauge doubles made by A. H. Fox. Twenty gauge guns often are valued up to 75% higher. Savage-made Fox models generally bring prices 25% lower. With the exception of Model B, production of Fox shotguns was discontinued about 1942.

Fox Model B Hammerless Double **$235**
Boxlock. Double triggers. Plain extractor. Gauges: 12, 16, 20, .410. 24- to 30-inch barrels; vent rib on current production; chokes: M/F, C/M, F/F (.410 only). Weight: about 7½ pounds, 12 ga. Checkered pistol-grip stock and forearm. Made about 1940–1985.

Fox Model B-DE **$295**
Same as Model B-ST except frame finished in satin chrome, select walnut buttstock with checkered pistol grip and beavertail forearm. Made 1965–66.

Fox Model B-DL **$320**
Same as Model B-ST except frame finished in satin chrome, select walnut buttstock with checkered pistol grip, side panels, beavertail forearm. Made 1962–66.

Fox Model B-SE **$365**
Same as Model B except has selective ejectors and single trigger. Made 1966–1989.

Fox Model B

Fox Model B-DE

Fox Model B-DL

Fox Model B-ST

Fox Model B-ST **$255**
Same as Model B except has non-selective single trigger. Made 1955–1966.

Fox Grade A

Fox Grade AE

Fox Grade CE

Fox Grade XE

Fox Hammerless Double Barrel Shotguns

The higher grades have the same general specifications as the standard Sterlingworth model with differences chiefly in workmanship and materials. Higher grade models are stocked in fine select walnut; quantity and quality of engraving increases with price. Except for Grade A, all have auto ejectors.

Grade A	$ 1,195
Grade AE	1,495
Grade BE	2,595
Grade CE	2,550
Grade DE	7,495
Grade FE	15,250
Grade XE	4,495
Fox-Kautzky selective single trigger, extra	200
Ventilated rib, extra	300
Beavertail forearm, extra	200

Fox Single Barrel Trap Guns

Boxlock. Auto ejector. 12 gauge only. 30- or 32-inch vent-rib barrel. Weight: 7½ to 8 pounds. Trap-style stock and forearm of select walnut, checkered, recoil pad optional. The four grades differ chiefly in quality of wood and engraving; Grade M guns, built to order, have finest Circassian walnut. Stock and receiver are elaborately engraved and inlaid with gold. Discontinued 1942. *Note:* In 1932 the Fox Trap Gun was redesigned and those manufactured

Fox Single Barrel Trap Guns (cont.)

after that date have a stock with full pistol grip and Monte Carlo comb; at the same time frame was changed to permit the rib line to extend across it to the rear.

Grade JE	$1795
Grade KE	2650
Grade LE	3595
Grade ME	8995

Fox "Skeeter" Double Barrel Shotgun $2495

Boxlock. Gauge: 12 or 20. Barrels: 28 inches w/full-length vent rib. Weight: approx. 7 pound. Buttstock and beavertail forend of select American walnut, finely checkered. Soft rubber recoil pad and ivory bead sights. Made in early 1930s.

Fox Sterlingworth Deluxe

Same general specifications as Sterlingworth, except 32-inch barrel also available; recoil pad, ivory bead sights.

With plain extractors	$1145
With automatic ejectors	1295

Fox Sterlingworth

Fox Sterlingworth Hammerless Double

Boxlock. Double triggers (Fox-Kautzky selective single trigger extra). Plain extractors (auto ejectors extra). Gauges: 12, 16, 20. Barrel lengths: 26-, 28-, 30-inch; chokes F/F, M/F, C/M (any combination of C to F choke borings was available at no extra cost). Weight: 12 ga., 6⅞ to 8¼ lbs.; 16 ga., 6 to 7 lbs.; 20 ga., 5¾ to 6¾ lbs. Checkered pistol-grip stock and forearm.

With plain extractors	$ 995
With automatic ejectors	1150
Selective single trigger, extra	300

Fox Sterlingworth Skeet and Upland Game Gun

Same general specifications as the standard Sterlingworth, except has 26- or 28-inch barrels with skeet boring only, straight-grip stock. Weight: 7 pounds, 12 ga.

With plain extractors	$1550
With automatic ejectors	1895

Super Fox HE

Super Fox HE Grade $1945

Long-range gun made in 12 gauge only (chambered for 3-inch shells on order), 30- or 32-inch Full choke barrels, auto ejectors standard. Weight: 8¾ to 9¾ pounds. General specifications same as standard Sterlingworth.

SHOTGUNS

Franchi 48/AL Hunter Model

Franchi Model 500 Standard Autoloader

Franchi Model 520 Deluxe

Franchi 2004 Trap

LUIGI FRANCHI S.P.A.
Brescia, Italy

Franchi 48/AL Ultra Light Shotgun
Recoil-operated, takedown, hammerless shotgun with tubular magazine. Gauges: 12 or 20 (2³/₄-inch); 12-ga. Magnum (3-inch chamber). Barrels: 24- to 32-inch w/various choke combinations. Weight: 5 lbs. 2 oz. (20 ga.) to 6¼ lbs. (12 ga.). Checkered pistol-grip walnut stock and forend with high-gloss finish.
Standard Model **$365**
Hunter or Magnum Models **395**

Franchi Model 500 Standard Autoloader **$295**
Gas-operated. 12 gauge. 4-shot magazine. Barrels: 26-, 28-inch; vent rib; IC, M, IM, F chokes. Weight: about 7 pounds. Checkered pistol-grip stock and forearm. Made 1976–1980.

Franchi Model 520 Deluxe **$360**
Same as Model 500, except higher grade with engraved receiver. Made 1975–79.

Franchi Model 520 Eldorado Gold **$775**
Same as Model 520, except custom grade with engraved and gold-inlaid receiver, finer quality wood. Intro. 1977.

Franchi Model 2003 Trap Over-and-Under **$1050**
Boxlock. Auto ejectors. Selective single trigger. 12 gauge. Barrels: 30-, 32-inch; IM/F, F/F; high vent rib. Weight (with 30-inch barrel): 8¼ pounds. Checkered walnut beavertail forearm and stock with straight or Monte Carlo comb, recoil pad. Luggage-type carrying case. Made 1976 to date.

Franchi Model 2004 Trap Single Barrel **$1095**
Same as Model 2003, except single barrel, 32- or 34-inch, Full choke. Weight (with 32-inch barrel): 8¼ pounds. Made 1976 to date.

Franchi Model 2005 Combination Trap **$1550**
Model 2004/2005 type gun with two sets of barrels, single and over-and-under. Made 1976 to date.

Franchi Model 2005/3 Combination Trap **$1995**
Model 2004/2005 type gun with three sets of barrels, any combination of single and over/under. Made 1976 to date.

Franchi Model 3000/2 Combination Trap **$2500**
Boxlock. Automatic ejectors. Selective single trigger. 12 gauge. Barrels: 32-inch over/under choked F/IM; 34-inch underbarrel M choke; high vent rib. Weight (with 32-inch barrels): 8 lbs. 6 oz. Choice of six different castoff buttstocks. Made 1979 to date.

Franchi Airone

Franchi Airone Hammerless Double **$950**
Boxlock. Anson & Deeley system action. Auto ejectors. Double triggers. 12 gauge. Various barrel lengths, chokes, weights. Checkered straight-grip stock and forearm. Made 1940–1950.

Franchi Alcione Over/Under Shotgun **$1015**
Hammerless, takedown shotgun with engraved receiver. Selective single trigger and ejectors. 12 gauge w/3-inch chambers. Barrels: 26-inch (IC/M; 28-inch (M/F). Weight: 6³/₄ pounds. Checkered French walnut buttstock and forend. Imported from Italy since 1982.

Franchi Aristocrat Field Model Over/Under **$550**
Boxlock. Selective auto ejectors. Selective single trigger. 12 gauge. Barrels: 26-inch IC/M; 28- and 30-inch M/F choke; vent rib. Weight (w/26-inch barrels): 7 pounds. Checkered pistol-grip stock and forearm. Made 1960–69.

Franchi Aristocrat Deluxe and Supreme Grades
Available in Field, Skeet and Trap Models with the same general specifications as standard guns of these types. Deluxe and Supreme Grades are of higher quality with stock and forearm of select walnut, elaborate relief engraving on receiver, trigger guard, tang and top lever. Supreme game birds inlaid in gold. Made 1960–66.
Deluxe Grade . . . . **$ 850**
Supreme Grade **1195**

Franchi Aristocrat Imperial and Monte Carlo Grades
Custom guns made in Field, Skeet and Trap Models with the same general specifications as standard for these types. Imperial and Monte Carlo Grades are of highest quality with stock and forearm of select walnut, fine engraving—elaborate on the latter grade. Made 1967–69.
Imperial Grade **$2195**
Monte Carlo Grade **3095**

Franchi Aristocrat Magnum Model **$475**
Same as Field Model, except chambered for 3-inch shells, has 32-inch barrels choked F/F; stock has recoil pad. Weight: about 8 pounds. Made 1962–65.

Franchi Aristocrat Silver King **$550**
Available in Field, Magnum, Skeet and Trap models with the same general specifications as standard guns of these types. Silver King has stock and forearm of select walnut, more elaborately engraved silver-finished receiver. Made 1962–69.

Franchi Aristocrat Skeet Model **$525**
Same general specifications as Field Model, except made only with 26-inch vent-rib barrels with SK chokes #1 and #2; skeet-style stock and forearm. Weight: about 7¹/₂ pounds. Later production had wider (10mm) rib. Made 1960–69.

Franchi Aristocrat Trap Model **$545**
Same general specifications as Field Model, except made only with 30-inch vent-rib barrels, M/F choke; trap-style stock with recoil pad, beavertail forearm. Later production had Monte Carlo comb, 10mm rib. Made 1960–69.

Franchi Astore

Franchi Astore Hammerless Double **$795**
Boxlock. Anson & Deeley system action. Plain extractors. Double triggers. 12 gauge. Various barrel lengths, chokes, weights. Checkered straight-grip stock and forearm. Made 1937–1960.

Franchi Astore II **$1095**
Similar to Astore S, but not as high grade. Furnished with either plain extractors or auto ejectors, double triggers, pistol-grip stock. Barrels: 27-inch IC/IM; 28-inch M/F chokes. Currently manufactured for Franchi in Spain.

Franchi Aristocrat Deluxe

Franchi Aristocrat Supreme

SHOTGUNS

Franchi Astore S

Franchi Astore S $1795

Same as Astore, except has higher grade wood, fine engraving. Automatic ejectors, single trigger, 28-inch barrel (M/F or IM/F choke) are standard on current production.

Franchi Crown Grade

Franchi Diamond Grade

Franchi Crown, Diamond and Imperial Grade Autoloaders

Same general specifications as Standard Model, except these are custom guns of the highest quality. Crown Grade has hunting scene engraving; Diamond Grade has silver-inlaid scroll engraving; Imperial Grade has elaborately engraved hunting scenes with figures inlaid in gold. Stock and forearm of fancy walnut. Made 1954–1975.

Crown Grade	**$1395**
Diamond Grade	**1795**
Imperial Grade	**2100**

Franchi Dynamic-12

Same general specifications and appearance as Standard Model, except 12 gauge only, has heavier steel receiver. Weight: about 7¼ pounds. Made 1965–1972.

With plain barrel	**$310**
With ventilated rib	**340**

Franchi Dynamic-12 Slug Gun $320

Same as standard Slug Gun, except 12 gauge only, has heavier steel receiver. Made 1965–1972.

Franchi Dynamic-12 Skeet Gun $375

Same general specifications and appearance as Standard Model, except has heavier steel receiver; made only in 12 gauge with 26-inch vent-rib barrel, SK choke; stock and forearm of extra fancy walnut. Made 1965–1972.

Franchi Eldorado Model $450

Same general specifications as Standard Model except highest grade with gold-filled engraving, stock and forearm of select walnut; furnished with vent-rib barrel only. Made 1954 to date.

Franchi Falconet International Skeet Model $895

Similar to Standard Skeet Model, but higher grade. Made 1970–74.

Franchi Falconet International Trap Model $915

Similar to Standard Trap Model, but higher grade; with straight or Monte Carlo comb stock. Made 1970–74.

Franchi Falconet Over-and-Under Field Models

Boxlock. Auto ejectors. Selective single trigger. Gauges: 12, 16, 20, 28, .410. Barrels: 24-, 26-, 28-, 30-inch; vent

Franchi Eldorado

Franchi Falconet Buckskin

Franchi Falconet Ebony

Franchi Falconet Over/Under Field Models (cont.)

rib. Chokes: C/IC, IC/M, M/F. Weight: from about 6 pounds. Engraved lightweight alloy receiver; light-colored in Buckskin Model, blued in Ebony Model, pickled silver in Silver Model. Checkered walnut stock and forearm. Made 1968–1975.

Buckskin or Ebony Model **$495**
Silver Model **550**

Franchi Falconet Standard Skeet Model **$850**

Same general specifications as Field Models, except made only with 26-inch barrels with SK chokes #1 and #2, wide vent rib, color-casehardened receiver, skeet-style stock and forearm. Weight: 12 ga., about 7¾ lbs. Made 1970–74.

Franchi Falconet Standard Trap Model **$850**

Same general specifications as Field Models, except made only in 12 gauge with 30-inch barrels, choked M/F; wide vent rib, color-casehardened receiver, Monte Carlo trap-style stock and forearm, recoil pad. Weight: about 8 pounds. Made 1970–74.

Franchi Hammerless Condor Grade

**Franchi Hammerless Imperiale
Montecarlo Extra**

Franchi Imperiale "S"

Franchi Hammerless Side Lock Doubles

Hand-detachable locks. Self-opening action. Auto ejectors. Double triggers or single trigger. Gauges: 12, 16, 20. Barrel lengths, chokes, weights according to customer's specifications. Checkered stock and forend, straight or pistol grip. Made in six grades—Condor, Imperiale, Imperiale S, Imperiale Montecarlo No. 5, Imperiale Montecarlo No. 11, Imperiale Montecarlo Extra—which differ chiefly in overall quality, engraving, grade of wood, checkering, etc.; general specifications are the same. Only the Imperiale Montecarlo Extra Grade is currently manufactured.

Condor Grade . . . . **$ 6,395**
Imperiale, Imperiale S Grades **8,500**
Imperiale Montecarlo Grades No. 5, 11 . . . . **12,500**
Imperiale Montecarlo Extra Grade **14,500**

Franchi Hunter Model

Same general specifications as Standard Model except higher grade with engraved receiver; furnished with ribbed barrel only. Made 1950 to date.

With solid rib **$325**
With ventilated rib **340**

Franchi Hunter Model Magnum **$395**

Same as Standard Model Magnum, except higher grade with engraved receiver, vent-rib barrel only. Formerly designated "Wildfowler Model." Made 1954–73.

Franchi Peregrine Model 400 . . . . **$475**

Same general specifications as Model 451, except has steel receiver. Weight (with 26½-inch barrel): 6 lbs. 15 oz. Made 1975–78.

Franchi Peregrine Model 451 Over-and-Under **$530**

Boxlock. Lightweight alloy receiver. Automatic ejectors. Selective single trigger. 12 gauge. Barrels: 26½-, 28-inch; choked C/IC, IC/M, M/F; vent rib. Weight (with 26½-inch barrels): 6 lbs. 1 oz. Checkered pistol-grip stock and forearm. Made 1975–78.

SHOTGUNS

Franchi Hunter

Franchi Hunter Magnum

Franchi PG-80 Prestige Model

Franchi Standard Autoloader

Franchi Standard Magnum

Franchi PG-80 Gas-Operated Semiautomatic Shotgun
Gas-operated, takedown, hammerless shotgun with tubular magazine. 12 gauge w/2³/₄-inch chamber. 5-shot magazine. Barrels: 24 to 30 inches w/vent rib. Weight: 7¹/₂ pounds. Gold-plated trigger. Checkered pistol-grip stock and forend of European walnut. Imported from Italy since 1985.
Prestige Model $425
Elite Model 475

Franchi Skeet Gun $395
Same general specifications and appearance as Standard Model, except made only with 26-inch vent-rib barrel, SK choke. Stock and forearm of extra fancy walnut. Made 1972–74.

Franchi Slug Gun $345
Same as Standard Model, except has 22-inch plain barrel, Cyl. bore, folding leaf open rear sight, gold bead front sight. Made 1960 to date.

Franchi Standard Model Autoloader
Recoil operated. Light alloy receiver. Gauges: 12, 20. 4-shot magazine. Barrels: 26-, 28-, 30-inch; plain, solid or vent rib; IC, M, F chokes. Weight: 12 ga., about 6¹/₄ lbs.; 20 ga., 5¹/₈ lbs. Checkered pistol-grip stock and forearm. Made 1950 to date.
With plain barrel $300
With solid rib 325
With ventilated rib 340

Franchi Standard Model Magnum
Same general specifications as Standard Model, except has 3-inch chamber, 32-inch (12 ga.) or 28-inch (20 ga.) F choke barrel, recoil pad. Weight: 12 ga., 8¹/₄ lbs.; 20 ga., 6 lbs. Formerly designated "Superange Model." Made 1954–1988.
With plain barrel $345
With ventilated rib 365

Franchi Turkey Gun $400
Same as Standard Model Magnum, except higher grade with turkey scene engraved receiver, 12 gauge only, 36-inch matted-rib barrel, Extra Full choke. Made 1963–65.

> **NOTE:** The following Franchi shotguns are currently imported by American Arms, Inc.

Franchi Black Magic 48/AL Semiautomatic
Similar to the Franchi Model 48/AL, except with Franchoke screw-in tubes and matte black receiver with Black Magic logo. Gauge: 12 or 20; 2³/₄-inch chamber. Barrels: 24-, 26-, 28-inch with vent rib; 24-inch rifled slug with sights. Weight: 5.2 pounds (20 ga.). Checkered walnut buttstock and forend. Blued finish.
Standard Model $425
Slug Barrel Model 455

Franchi Falconet 2000 Over/Under $1050
Boxlock. Single selective trigger. Selective automatic ejectors. Gauge: 12; 2³/₄-inch chambers. Barrels: 26-inch

Franchi Black Magic 48 AL

Franchi Falconet 2000

Franchi LAW Shotgun

Franchi SPAS Shotgun

Franchi Sporting 2000 O/U

Franchi Falconet 2000 Over/Under (cont.)
with Franchoke tubes; IC/M/F. Weight: 6 pounds.
Checkered walnut stock and forearm. Engraved silver receiver with gold-plated game scene. Imported from 1992 to date.

Franchi LAW-12 Shotgun **$455**
Similar to the SPAS-12 Model, except gas-operated semiautomatic action only, ambidextrous safety, decocking lever and adjustable sights. Made 1983 to date.

Franchi SPAS-12 Shotgun
Selective operating system functions as a gas-operated semiautomatic or pump action. Gauge: 12; 2¾-inch chamber. 7-shot magazine. Barrel: 21½ inches with cylinder bore and muzzle protector or optional screw-in choke tubes; matte finish. 41 inches overall with fixed stock. Weight: 8¾ pounds. Blade front sight, aperture rear sight. Folding or black nylon buttstock with pistol grip and forend; non-reflective anodized finish. Made 1983 to date.
Fixed Stock Model **$495**
Folding Stock Model (Discontinued) 525
Optional choke tubes, **Add** 50

Franchi Sporting 2000 Over/Under **$895**
Same general specifications as Falconet 2000, except with blued receiver, ported 28-inch barrels. Weight: 7¾ pounds. Imported from 1992 to date.

=== **AUGUSTE FRANCOTTE & CIE., S.A.** ===
Liège, Belgium

Francotte shotguns for many years were distributed in the U.S. by Abercrombie & Fitch of New York City. This firm has used a series of model designations for Francotte guns which do not correspond to those of the manufacturer. Because so many Francotte owners refer to their guns by the A & F model names and numbers, the A & F series is included in a listing separate from that of the standard Francotte numbers.

Francotte Box Lock Hammerless Doubles
Anson & Deeley system. Side clips. Greener crossbolt on Models 6886, 8446, 4996 and 9261; square crossbolt on Model 6930; Greener-Scott crossbolt on Model 8457; Purdey bolt on Models 11/18E and 10/18E/628. Auto ejectors. Double triggers. Made in all standard gauges, barrel

Francotte Model 6886

Francotte Model 8446

Francotte Model 9261

Francotte Model 10/18E/628

Francotte Box Lock Hammerless
A&F Series—No. 20

Francotte No. 30

Francotte No. 45 Eagle

Francotte Knockabout

Francotte Box Lock Hammerless Doubles (cont.)

lengths, chokes, weights. Checkered stock and forend, straight or pistol grip. The eight models listed vary chiefly in fastening as described above, finish and engraving, etc.; general specifications are the same. All except Model 10/18E/628 are discontinued.

Model 6886	$2500
Model 8446 ("Francotte Special"), 6930, 4996	2995
Model 8457, 9261 ("Francotte Original"), 11/18E	3650
Model 10/18E/628	4895

Francotte Box Lock Hammerless Doubles—A & F Series

Boxlock, Anson & Deeley type. Crossbolt. Sideplate on all except Knockabout Model. Side clips. Auto ejectors. Double triggers. Gauges: 12, 16, 20, 28, .410. Barrels: 26- to 32-inch in 12 gauge, 26- and 28-inch in other gauges; any boring. Weight: 4¾ to 8 pounds depending on gauge and barrel length. Checkered stock and forend; straight, half or full pistol grip. The seven grades—No. 45 Eagle Grade, No. 30, No. 25, No. 20, No. 14, Jubilee Model, Knockabout Model—differ chiefly in overall quality, engraving, grade of wood, checkering, etc.; general specifications are the same. Discontinued.

No. 45 Eagle Grade	$5295
No. 30	4550
No. 25	2995
No. 20	2595
No. 14	1695
Jubilee Model	4100
Knockabout Model	1495

**Francotte Box Lock Hammerless
Model 6982**

**Francotte Half-Fine O/U
Model SOB.E/11082**

Francotte Box Lock Hammerless Doubles With Sideplates

Anson & Deeley system. Reinforced frame with side clips. Purdey-type bolt except on Model 8455 which has Greener crossbolt. Auto ejectors. Double triggers. Made in all standard gauges, barrel lengths, chokes, weights. Checkered stock and forend, straight or pistol grip. Models 10594, 8455 and 6982 are of equal quality, differing chiefly in style of engraving; Model 9/40E/38321 is a higher grade gun in all details and has fine English-style engraving. Currently manufactured.

Models 10594, 8455, 6982 . . . . $3895
Model 9/40E/38321   4750

**Francotte Fine O/U
Model 9/40.SE**

Francotte Fine Over-and-Under Shotgun $9000

Model 9/40.SE. Boxlock, Anson & Deeley system. Auto ejectors. Double triggers. Made in all standard gauges; barrel length, boring to order. Weight: about 6³/₄ pounds, 12 ga. Checkered stock and forend, straight or pistol grip. Currently manufactured.

Francotte Fine Side Lock Hammerless Double $18,250

Model 120.HE/328. Automatic ejectors. Double triggers. Made in all standard gauges; barrel length, boring, weight to order. Checkered stock and forend, straight or pistol grip. Currently manufactured.

Francotte Half-Fine Over-and-Under Shotgun . . $7650

Model SOB.E/11082. Boxlock, Anson & Deeley system. Auto ejectors. Double triggers. Made in all standard gauges; barrel length, boring to order. Checkered stock and forend, straight or pistol grip. *Note:* This model is quite similar to No. 9/40.SE except general quality is not as high and frame is not fully engraved or scalloped. Discontinued.

GALEF SHOTGUNS

Manufactured for J. L. Galef & Son, Inc., New York, New York, by M.A.V.I., Gardone V.T., Italy, by Zabala Hermanos, Elquetta, Spain, and by Antonio Zoli, Gardone V.T., Italy

Galef Companion

Galef Companion Folding Single Barrel Shotgun

Hammerless. Underlever. Gauges: 12 Mag., 16, 20 Mag., 28, .410. Barrels: 26-inch (.410 only), 28-inch (12, 16, 20, 28), 30-inch (12 gauge only); Full choke; plain or vent rib. Weight: 4¹/₂ lbs. for .410 to 5 lbs. 9 oz. for 12 gauge. Checkered pistol-grip stock and forearm. Made by M.A.V.I. from 1968 to date.

With plain barrel . . . . $ 95
With ventilated rib 115

Galef Golden Snipe $445

Same as Silver Snipe, except has selective automatic ejectors. Made by Antonio Zoli 1968 to date.

Galef Monte Carlo Trap Single Barrel Shotgun . . $185

Hammerless. Underlever. Plain extractor. 12 gauge. 32-inch barrel, Full choke, vent rib. Weight: about 8¹/₄ pounds. Checkered pistol-grip stock with Monte Carlo comb and recoil pad, beavertail forearm. Made by M.A.V.I. from 1968 to date.

Galef Monte Carlo Trap

Galef Silver Hawk

Galef Silver Snipe

Galef Zabala

Galef Silver Hawk Hammerless Double **$385**
Boxlock. Plain extractors. Double triggers. Gauges: 12, 20; 3-inch chambers. Barrels: 26-, 28-, 30-inch (latter in 12 gauge only); IC/M, M/F chokes. Weight: 12 ga. with 26-inch barrels, 6 lbs. 6 oz. Checkered walnut pistol-grip stock and beavertail forearm. Made by Antonio Zoli 1968–1972.

Galef Silver Snipe Over-and-Under Shotgun **$415**
Boxlock. Plain extractors. Single trigger. Gauges: 12, 20; 3-inch chambers. Barrels: 26-, 28-, 30-inch (latter in 12 gauge only); IC/M, M/F chokes; vent rib. Weight: 12 gauge with 28-inch barrels, 6½ pounds. Checkered walnut pistol-grip stock and forearm. Made by Antonio Zoli 1968 to date.

Galef Zabala Hammerless Double Barrel Shotgun
Boxlock. Plain extractors. Double triggers. Gauges: 10 Mag., 12 Mag., 16, 20 Mag., 28, .410. Barrels: 22-, 26-, 28-, 30-, 32-inch; IC/IC, IC/M, M/F, F/F chokes. Weight: 12 gauge with 28-inch barrels, 7¾ pounds. Checkered walnut pistol-grip stock and beavertail forearm, recoil pad. Made by Zabala from 1972 to date.
10 gauge **$235**
Other gauges **180**

GAMBA S.p.A.
Gardone V.T. (Brescia), Italy

Gamba Daytona Competition Over/Under
Boxlock with Boss-style locking system. Anatomical single trigger; optional adjustable, single-selective release trigger. Selective automatic ejectors. Gauge: 12 or 20; 2¾- or 3-inch chambers. Barrels: 26¾-, 28-, 30- or 32-inch choked SK/SK, IM/F or M/F. Weight: 7½ to 8½ pounds. Black or chrome receiver with blued barrels. Checkered select walnut stock and forearm with oil finish. Imported by Heckler & Koch until 1992.
American Trap Model . . . . **$ 4,045**
Pigeon, Skeet, Trap Models **3,745**
Sporting Model **3,595**
Sideplate Model **8,625**
Engraved Models . . . . **7500 to 10,000**
Sidelock Model **18,750**

GARBI SHOTGUNS
Eibar, Spain

Garbi Model 100 Sidelock

Garbi Model 100 Sidelock Shotgun **$2495**
Gauges: 12, 16, 20 and 28. Barrels: 25-, 28-, 30-inch. Action: Holland & Holland pattern sidelock; automatic ejectors and double trigger. Weight: 5 lbs. 6 oz. to 7 lbs. 7 oz. English-style straight grip stock with fine-line hand-checkered butt; classic forend. Made 1985 to date.

Garbi Model 101 Sidelock Shotgun $3295
Same general specifications as Model 100, except the sidelocks are handcrafted with hand-engraved receiver; select walnut straight-grip stock.

Garbi Model 103 Hammerless Double
Similar to Model 100, except with Purdey-type, higher
grade engraving.

Garbi Model 103 Hammerless Double (cont.)
Model 103A **$3895**
Model 103B 5750

Garbi Model 200 Hammerless Double **$5895**
Similar to Model 100, except with double heavy-duty locks.
Continental-style floral and scroll engraving. Checkered
deluxe walnut stock and forearm.

Garcia Bronco 22/410

Garcia Bronco 410

GARCIA CORPORATION
Teaneck, New Jersey

Garcia Bronco 22/.410 O/U Combination **$95**
Swing-out action. Takedown. 18½-inch barrels; 22 LR
over, .410 gauge under. Weight: 4½ pounds. One-piece
stock and receiver, crackle finish. Introduced in 1976.
Discontinued.

Garcia Bronco .410 Single Shot **$70**
Swing-out action. Takedown. .410 gauge. 18½-inch barrel.
Weight: 3½ pounds. One-piece stock and receiver, crackle
finish. Introduced in 1967. Discontinued.

GOLDEN EAGLE FIREARMS INC.
Houston, Texas
Mfd. by Nikko Firearms Ltd., Tochigi, Japan

Golden Eagle Model 5000 Grade I Field O/U . . . **$750**
Receiver engraved and inlaid with gold eagle head. Boxlock. Auto ejectors. Selective single trigger. Gauges: 12,
20; 2¾- or 3-inch chambers, 12 ga., 3-inch, 20 ga. Barrels:
26-, 28-, 30-inch (latter only in 12-gauge 3-inch Magnum);
IC/M, M/F chokes; vent rib. Weight: 6¼ lbs., 20 ga.; 7¼
lbs., 12 ga.; 8 lbs., 12-ga. Magnum. Checkered pistol-grip
stock and semibeavertail forearm. Made 1975 to date.
Note: Guns marketed 1975-76 under the Nikko brand
name have white receivers; since 1976 are blued.

Golden Eagle Model 5000 Grade I Skeet **$795**
Same as Field Model, except has 26- or 28-inch barrels
with wide (11mm) vent rib, SK choked. Intro. 1975.

Golden Eagle Model 5000 Grade I Trap **$815**
Same as Field Model, except has 30- or 32-inch barrels
with wide (11mm) vent rib (M/F, IM/F, F/F chokes), trap-
style stock with recoil pad. Made 1975 to date.

Golden Eagle Model 5000 Grade II Field **$795**
Same as Grade I Field Model, except higher grade with
fancier wood, more elaborate engraving and "screaming
eagle" inlaid in gold. Made 1975 to date.

SHOTGUNS

Golden Eagle Model 5000
Grade I Field

Golden Eagle Model 5000
Grade II Field

**Golden Eagle Model 5000
Grade III Grandee**

Golden Eagle Model 5000 Grade II Skeet **$850**
Same as Grade I Skeet Model, except higher grade with fancier wood, more elaborate engraving and "screaming eagle" inlaid in gold; inertia trigger, vent side ribs. Made 1975 to date.

Golden Eagle Model 5000 Grade II Trap **$855**
Same as Grade I Trap Model, except higher grade with fancier wood, more elaborate engraving and "screaming eagle" inlaid in gold; inertia trigger, vent side ribs. Made 1975 to date.

Golden Eagle Model 5000 Grade III Grandee .. **$1950**
Best grade, available in Field, Skeet and Trap Models with same general specifications as lower grades. Has sideplates with game scene engraving, scroll on frame and barrels, fancy wood (Monte Carlo comb, full pistol grip and recoil pad on Trap Model). Made 1976 to date.

Gorosabel Model 503 Shotgun

Gorosabel Model 504 Shotgun

GOROSABEL SHOTGUNS
Spain

Gorosabel Model 503 Shotgun **$675**
Gauges: 12, 16, 20 and .410. Action: Anson & Deeley-style boxlock. Barrels: 26-, 27- and 28-inch. Select European walnut, English or pistol grip, silver or beavertail forend, hand-checkering. Scalloped frame and scroll engraving. Intro. 1985; discontinued.

Gorosabel Model 504 Shotgun **$710**
Gauge: 12 or 20. Action: Holland & Holland-style sidelock. Barrel: 26-, 27- or 28-inch. Select European walnut, English or pistol grip, sliver or beavertail forend, hand-checkering. Holland-style large scroll engraving. Intro. 1985; discontinued.

Gorosabel Model 505 Shotgun **$945**
Gauge: 12 or 20. Action: Holland & Holland-style sidelock. Barrels: 26-, 27- or 28-inch. Select European walnut, English or pistol grip, sliver or beavertail forend, hand-checkering. Purdey-style fine scroll and rose engraving. Intro. 1985; discontinued.

STEPHEN GRANT
London, England

Grant Best Quality Self-Opener Double Barrel Shotgun **$9995**
Sidelock, self-opener. Gauges: 12, 16 and 20. Barrels: 25 to 30 inches standard. Highest grade English or European walnut straight-grip buttstock and forearm with Greener type lever. Imported by Stoeger in the 1950s.

Grant Best Quality Side-Lever Double Barrel Shotgun **$9995**
Sidelock, self-lever. Gauges: 12, 16 and 20. Barrels: 25 to 30 inches standard. Highest grade English or European walnut straight-grip buttstock and forearm with Greener type lever. Imported by Stoeger in the 1950s.

W. W. GREENER, LTD.
Birmingham, England

Greener Empire

Greener Empire Model Hammerless Doubles
Boxlock. Non-ejector or with automatic ejectors. Double triggers. 12 gauge only ($2\frac{3}{4}$-inch or 3-inch chamber). Barrels: 28- to 32-inch; any choke combination. Weight: from $7\frac{1}{4}$ to $7\frac{3}{4}$ pounds depending on barrel length. Checkered stock and forend, straight- or half-pistol grip. Also furnished in "Empire Deluxe Grade," this model has same general specs, but deluxe finish.

Empire Model, non-ejector **$1550**
Empire Model, ejector **1725**
Empire Deluxe Model, non-ejector **1750**
Empire Deluxe Model, ejector **1950**

Greener Far-Killer

Greener Sovereign

Greener Far-Killer Model Grade FH35 Hammerless Double Barrel Shotgun

Boxlock. Non-ejector or with automatic ejectors. Double triggers. Gauges: 12 (2³/₄-inch or 3-inch), 10, 8. Barrels: 28-, 30- or 32-inch. Weight: 7¹/₂–9 pounds in 12 gauge. Checkered stock, forend; straight or half-pistol grip.

Non-ejector, 12 gauge	**$2250**
Ejector, 12 gauge	**2900**
Non-ejector, 10 or 8 gauge	**2400**
Ejector, 10 or 8 gauge	**3140**

Greener G. P. (General Purpose) Single Barrel .. $395

Greener Improved Martini Lever Action. Takedown. Ejector. 12 gauge only. Barrel lengths: 26-, 30-, 32-inch. M or F choke. Weight: 6¹/₄ to 6³/₄ pounds depending on barrel length. Checkered straight-grip stock and forearm.

Greener Jubilee

Greener Royal

Greener Hammerless Ejector Double Barrel Shotguns

Boxlock. Auto ejectors. Double triggers, non-selective or selective single trigger. Gauges: 12, 16, 20, 28, .410 (two latter gauges not supplied in Grades DH40 and DH35). Barrels: 26-, 28-, 30-inch; any choke combination. Weight: from 4³/₄ to 8 pounds depending on gauge and barrel length. Checkered stock and forend, straight- or half-pistol grip. The Royal, Crown, Sovereign and Jubilee Models differ in quality, engraving, grade of wood, checkering,

Greener Hammerless Ejector Doubles (cont.)

etc. General specifications are the same.

Royal Model Grade DH75	**$3995**
Crown Model Grade DH55	**2950**
Sovereign Model Grade DH40	**2595**
Jubilee Model Grade DH35	**2150**
Selective single trigger, extra	**330**
Non-selective single trigger, extra	**250**

GREIFELT & COMPANY
Suhl, Germany

Greifelt Grade No. 1 Over/Under

Greifelt Grade No. 1 Over-and-Under Shotgun

Anson & Deeley boxlock, Kersten fastening. Auto ejectors. Double triggers or single trigger. Elaborately engraved. Gauges: 12, 16, 20, 28, .410. Barrels: 26- to 32-inch, any combination of chokes, vent or solid matted rib. Weight: 4¹/₄ to 8¹/₄ pounds depending on gauge and barrel length. Straight- or pistol-grip stock, Purdey-type forend, both checkered. Manufactured prior to World War II.

With solid matted-rib barrel, except .410	**$2995**
With solid matted-rib barrel, .410 gauge	**3500**
Extra for ventilated rib	**380**
Extra for single trigger	**425**

Greifelt Grade No. 3 Over-and-Under Shotgun

Same general specifications as Grade No. 1 except not as fancy engraving. Manufactured prior to World War II.

With solid matted-rib barrel, except .410	**$2695**
With solid matted-rib barrel, .410 gauge	**2795**
Extra for ventilated rib	**380**
Extra for single trigger	**425**

Greifelt Model 22 Hammerless Double $1695

Anson & Deeley boxlock. Plain extractors. Double triggers. Gauges: 12 and 16. Barrels: 28- or 30-inch, M/F choke. Checkered stock and forend, pistol grip and cheekpiece standard, English-style stock also supplied. Manufactured since World War II.

SHOTGUNS

Greifelt Model 22E Hammerless Double **$2050**
Same as Model 22, except has automatic ejectors.

Greifelt Model 103 Hammerless Double **$1645**
Anson & Deeley boxlock. Plain extractors. Double triggers. Gauges: 12 and 16. Barrels: 28- or 30-inch, M and F choke. Checkered stock and forend, pistol grip and cheekpiece standard, English-style stock also supplied. Manufactured since World War II.

Greifelt Model 103E Hammerless Double **$1695**
Same as Model 103, except has automatic ejectors.

Greifelt Model 143E Over-and-Under Shotgun
General specifications same as prewar Grade No. 1 Over-and-Under except this model is not supplied in 28 and .410 gauge or with 32-inch barrels. Model 143E is not as high quality as the Grade No. 1 gun. Mfd. since World War II.
With raised matted rib, double triggers **$1950**
With ventilated rib, selective single trigger **2795**

Greifelt Hammerless Drilling (Three Barrel Combination Gun) **$2950**
Boxlock. Plain extractors. Double triggers, front single set for rifle barrel. Gauges: 12, 16, 20; rifle barrel in any caliber adapted to this type of gun. 26-inch barrels. Weight: about 7½ pounds. Auto rear sight operated by rifle barrel selector. Checkered stock and forearm, pistol grip and cheekpiece standard. Manufactured prior to WW II. *Note:* Value shown is for guns chambered for cartridges readily obtainable; if rifle barrel is an odd foreign caliber, value will be considerably less.

Greifelt Over-and-Under Combination Gun
Similar in design to this maker's over-and-under shotguns. Gauges: 12, 16, 20, 28, .410; rifle barrel in any caliber adapted to this type of gun. Barrels: 24- or 26-inch, solid matted rib. Weight: from 4¾ to 7¼ pounds. Folding rear sight. Manufactured prior to WW II. *Note:* Values shown are for gauges other than .410, with rifle barrel chambered for a cartridge readily obtainable; if in an odd foreign caliber, value will be considerably less. .410 gauge increases in value by about 50%.
With nonautomatic ejector **$4800**
With automatic ejector **5200**

= **HARRINGTON & RICHARDSON ARMS CO.** =
Gardner, Massachusetts
Now H&R 1871, Inc.

In 1986, all H&R operations were discontinued. In 1992, the firm was purchased by New England Firearms of Gardner, Mass., and the H&R line was divided. Models are now manufactured under that banner as well as H&R 1871, Inc.

H&R No. 3 Hammerless

Harrington & Richardson No. 3 Hammerless Single Shot Shotgun **$90**
Takedown. Automatic ejector. Gauges: 12, 16, 20, .410. Barrels: plain, 26- to 32-inch, F choke. Weight: 6½ to 7¼ pounds depending on gauge and barrel length. Plain pistol-grip stock and forend. Discontinued 1942.

H&R No. 5 Standard Lightweight

Harrington & Richardson No. 5 Standard Light Weight Hammer Single **$100**
Takedown. Auto ejector. Gauges: 24, 28, .410, 14mm. Barrels: 26- or 28-inch, F choke. Weight: about 4 to 4¾ pounds. Plain pistol-grip stock/forend. Discontinued 1942.

H&R No. 6 Heavy Breech

Harrington & Richardson No. 6 Heavy Breech Single Shot Hammer Shotgun **$100**
Takedown. Automatic ejector. Gauges: 10, 12, 16, 20. Barrels: plain, 28- to 36-inch, F choke. Weight: about 7 to 7¼ pounds. Plain stock and forend. Discontinued 1942.

H&R No. 7 Bay State

Harrington & Richardson No. 7 or 9 Bay State Single Shot Hammer Shotgun **$110**
Takedown. Automatic ejector. Gauges: 12, 16, 20, .410. Barrels: plain, 26- to 32-inch, Full choke. Weight: 5½ to 6½ pounds depending on gauge and barrel length. Plain pistol-grip stock and forend. Discontinued 1942.

H&R No. 8 Single Barrel

Harrington & Richardson No. 8 Standard Single Shot Hammer Shotgun **$135**
Takedown. Automatic ejector. Gauges: 12, 16, 20, 24, 28, .410. Barrels: plain, 26- to 32-inch, Full choke. Weight: 5½ to 6½ pounds depending on gauge and barrel length. Plain pistol-grip stock and forend. Made 1908–1942.

H&R Model 400

H&R Model 403

H&R Model 404C

H&R Model 440

H&R Model 442

Harrington & Richardson Model 348 Gamester Bolt Action Shotgun **$95**
Takedown. 12 and 16 gauge. 2-shot tubular magazine, 28-inch barrel, Full choke. Plain pistol-grip stock. Weight: about 7¹/₂ pounds. Made 1949–1954.

Harrington & Richardson Model 349 Gamester Deluxe **$110**
Same as Model 348, except has 26-inch barrel with adjustable choke device, recoil pad. Made 1953–55.

Harrington & Richardson Model 351 Huntsman Bolt Action Shotgun **$125**
Takedown. 12 and 16 gauge. 2-shot tubular magazine. Pushbutton safety. 26-inch barrel with H&R variable choke. Weight: about 6³/₄ pounds. Monte Carlo stock with recoil pad. Made 1956–58.

Harrington & Richardson Model 400 Pump **$175**
Hammerless. Gauges: 12, 16, 20. Tubular magazine holds 4 shells. 28-inch barrel, Full choke. Weight: about 7¹/₄ pounds. Plain pistol-grip stock (recoil pad in 12 and 16 ga.), grooved slide handle. Made 1955–1967.

Harrington & Richardson Model 401 . . . . **$175**
Same as Model 400, except has H&R variable choke. Made 1956–1963.

Harrington & Richardson Model 402 . . . . **$185**
Similar to Model 400, except .410 gauge, weighs about 5¹/₂ pounds. Made 1959–1967.

Harrington & Richardson Model 403 Autoloading Rifle **$200**
Takedown. .410 gauge. Tubular magazine holds four shells. 26-inch barrel, Full choke. Weight: about 5³/₄ pounds. Plain pistol-grip stock and forearm. Made in 1964.

Harrington & Richardson Model 404 Double **$225**
Boxlock. Plain extractors. Double triggers. Gauges: 12, 20, .410. Barrels: 28-inch in 12 ga. (M/F choke), 26-inch in 20 ga. (IC/M) and .410 (F/F). Weight: 5¹/₂ to 7¹/₄ pounds. Plain walnut-finished hardwood stock and forend. Made in Brazil by Amadeo Rossi 1969–1972.

Harrington & Richardson Model 404C **$195**
Same as Model 404, except has checkered stock and forend. Made 1969–1972.

Harrington & Richardson Model 440 Pump **$145**
Hammerless. Gauges: 12, 16, 20. 2³/₄-inch chamber in 16 gauge, 3-inch in 12 and 20 gauges. 3-shot magazine. Barrels: 26-, 28-, 30-inch; IC, M, F choke. Weight: 6¹/₄ pounds. Plain pistol-grip stock and slide handle, recoil pad. Made 1968–1973.

Harrington & Richardson Model 442 . . . . **$185**
Same as Model 440, except has vent-rib barrel, checkered stock and forearm, weighs 6³/₄ pounds. Made 1969–1973.

H&R Model 1212 Field

H&R Model 1212 Waterfowl

H&R Golden Squire
Model 159

H&R Harrich No. 1

Harrington & Richardson Model 1212 Over/Under Field Gun **$295**
Boxlock. Plain extractors. Selective single trigger. 12 gauge, 2³/₄-inch chambers. 28-inch barrels, IC/IM, vent rib. Weight: 7 pounds. Checkered walnut pistol-grip stock and fluted forearm. Made 1976–1980 by Lanber Arms S.A., Zaldibar (Vizcaya), Spain.

Harrington & Richardson Model 1212 Waterfowl Gun **$350**
Same as Field Gun, except chambered for 12-gauge 3-inch Magnum shells, has 30-inch barrels, M/F chokes, stock and recoil pad, weighs 7¹/₂ pounds. Made 1976–1980.

Harrington & Richardson Model 1908 Single Shot Shotgun **$115**
Takedown. Automatic ejector. Gauges: 12, 16, 24 and 28. Barrels: 26- to 32-inch, Full choke. Weight: 5¹/₄ to 6¹/₂ lbs., depending on gauge and barrel length. Casehardened receiver. Plain pistol-grip stock. Bead front sight. Made 1908–1934.

Harrington & Richardson Model 1908 .410 (12mm) Single Shot Shotgun **$125**
Same general specifications as standard Model 1908, except chambered for .410 or 12mm shot cartridge with barrel milled down at receiver to give a more pleasing contour.

Harrington & Richardson Model 1915 Single Shot Shotgun **$130**
Takedown. Both nonauto and auto ejectors available. Gauges: 24, 28, .410, 14mm and 12mm. Barrels: 26- or 28-inch, Full choke. Weight: 4 to 4³/₄ lbs., depending on gauge and barrel length. Plain black walnut stock with semi-pistol grip.

Harrington & Richardson Folding Gun **$135**
Single barrel hammer shotgun hinged at the front of the frame, the barrel folds down against the stock. *Light Frame Model:* gauges—28, 14mm, .410; 22-inch barrel; weighs about 4¹/₂ pounds. *Heavy Frame Model:* gauges—12, 16, 20, 28, .410; 26-inch barrel; weighs from 5³/₄ to 6¹/₂ pounds. Plain pistol-grip stock and forend. Discontinued 1942.

Harrington & Richardson Golden Squire Model 159 Single Barrel Hammer Shotgun **$100**
Hammerless. Side lever. Automatic ejection. Gauges: 12, 20. Barrels: 30-inch in 12 ga., 28-inch in 20 ga., both F choke. Weight: about 6¹/₂ pounds. Straight-grip stock with recoil pad, forearm with schnabel. Made 1964–66.

Harrington & Richardson Golden Squire Jr. Model 459 . . . . **$100**
Same as Model 159, except gauges 20 and .410, 26-inch barrel, youth-size stock. Made in 1964.

Harrington & Richardson Harrich No. 1 Single Barrel Trap Gun **$1750**
Anson & Deeley-type locking system with Kersten top locks and double underlocking lugs. Sideplates engraved with hunting scenes. 12 gauge. Barrels: 32-, 34-inch; Full choke; high vent rib. Weight: 8¹/₂ pounds. Checkered Monte Carlo stock with pistol grip and recoil pad, beavertail forearm, of select walnut. Made in Ferlach, Austria, 1971–75.

Harrington & Richardson "Top Rib" Single Barrel Shotgun **$165**
Takedown. Auto ejector. Gauges: 12, 16 and 20. Barrels: 28- to 30-inch, Full choke with full-length matted top rib. Weight: 6¹/₂ to 7 lbs. depending on gauge and barrel length. Black walnut pistol-grip stock (capped) and forend; both checkered. Flexible rubber buttplate. Made during 1930s.

H&R Topper Model 099 Deluxe

H&R Topper Model 158 (058)

H&R Topper Model 162 Slug Gun

H&R Topper Model 176

H&R Topper No. 48

Harrington & Richardson Topper No. 48 Single Barrel Hammer Shotgun $125
Similar to old Model 8 Standard. Takedown. Top lever. Auto ejector. Gauges: 12, 16, 20, .410. Barrels: plain; 26- to 30-inch; M or F choke. Weight: 5½ to 6½ pounds depending on gauge and barrel length. Plain pistol-grip stock and forend. Made 1946–1957.

Harrington & Richardson Topper Model 099 Deluxe $110
Same as Model 158, except has matte nickel finish, semi-pistol grip walnut-finished American hardwood stock; semibeavertail forearm; 12, 16, 20, and .410 gauges. Made 1982–86.

Harrington & Richardson Topper Model 148 Single Shot Hammer Shotgun $110
Takedown. Side lever. Auto ejection. Gauges: 12, 16, 20, .410. Barrels: 12 ga., 30-, 32- and 36-inch; 16 ga., 28- and

Harrington & Richardson Topper Model 148 (cont.)
30-inch; 20 and .410 ga., 28-inch; F choke. Weight: 5 to 6½ pounds. Plain pistol-grip stock and forend, recoil pad. Made 1958–1961.

Harrington & Richardson Topper Model 158 (058) Single Shot Hammer Shotgun $110
Takedown. Side lever. Automatic ejection. Gauges: 12, 20, .410 (2¾-inch and 3-inch shells); 16 (2¾-inch). Barrel length and choke combinations: 12 ga., 36-inch/F, 32-inch/F, 30-inch/F, 28-inch/F or M; .410, 28-inch/F. Weight: about 5½ pounds. Plain pistol-grip stock and forend, recoil pad. Made 1962–1981. *Note:* Designation changed to 058 in 1974.

Harrington & Richardson Topper Model 162 Slug Gun $135
Same as Topper Model 158, except has 24-inch barrel, Cyl. bore, with rifle sights. Made 1968–1986.

Harrington & Richardson Topper Model 176 10 Gauge Magnum $145
Similar to Model 158, but has 36-inch heavy barrel chambered for 3½-inch 10-gauge Magnum shells, weighs 10 pounds; stock with Monte Carlo comb and recoil pad, longer and fuller forearm. Made 1977–1986.

Harrington & Richardson Topper Model 188 Deluxe $125
Same as standard Topper Model 148, except has chromed frame, stock and forend in black, red, yellow, blue, green, pink, or purple colored finish. .410 gauge only. Made 1958–1961.

H&R Topper Model 198 (098)

H&R Model 490 Greenwing

**Harrington & Richardson Topper Model 198 (098)
Deluxe** **$130**
Same as Model 158, except has chrome-plated frame, black
finished stock and forend; 12, 20 and .410 gauges. Made
1962–1981. *Note:* Designation changed to 098 in 1974.

Harrington & Richardson Topper Jr. Model 480 . **$115**
Similar to No. 48 Topper, except has youth-size stock,
26-inch barrel, .410 gauge only. Made 1958–1961.

**Harrington & Richardson Topper No. 488
Deluxe** **$110**
Same as standard No. 48 Topper, except chrome-plated
frame, black lacquered stock and forend, recoil pad.
Discontinued 1957.

Harrington & Richardson Topper Model 490 . . . . **$115**
Same as Model 158, except has youth-size stock (3 inches
shorter), 26-inch barrel; 20 and 28 gauge (M choke), .410
(F). Made 1962–1986.

**Harrington & Richardson Topper Model 490
Greenwing** **$130**
Same as the Model 490, except has a special high-polished
finish. Made 1981–86.

Harrington & Richardson Topper Jr. Model 580 . **$100**
Same as Model 480, except has colored stocks as on Model
188. Made 1958–1961.

Harrington & Richardson Topper Model 590 . . . . **$105**
Same as Model 490, except has chrome-plated frame, black
finished stock and forend. Made 1962–63.

> **NOTE:** The following models are manufactured and distrib-
> uted by the reorganized company of H&R 1871, Inc.

H&R Model N.W.T.F. Turkey Mag **$120**
Same as Model 098 Single Shot Hammer, except with 24-
inch barrel, 3½-inch chamber with screw-in choke tube.
Weight: 6 pounds. American hardwood stock with Mossy
Oak camo finish.

**H&R Topper Model 098 Single Shot Hammer
Shotgun** **$80**
Side lever. Automatic ejector. Gauges: 12, 20 and .410 with
3-inch chamber. Barrels: 28-inch, (12 ga./M); 26-inch, (20
ga./M); 26-inch (.410/F). Weight: 5 to 6 pounds. Satin
nickel receiver, blued barrel. Plain pistol-grip stock and
semibeavertail forend w/black finish. Reintroduced 1992.

H&R Topper Model 098 Deluxe **$95**
Same as Model 098 Single Barrel Hammer, except with
12 gauge, 3-inch chamber only. 28-inch barrel; Mod. choke
tube. Made 1992 to date.

H&R N.W.T.F. Turkey Mag

H&R Topper Model 098 Deluxe

H&R Topper Junior Model 098

H&R Topper Classic Youth

H&R Topper Classic Youth Shotgun **$105**
Same as Topper Junior, except has checkered American black walnut stock/forend with satin finish and recoil pad.

H&R Topper Junior Model 098 . . . . **$85**
Same as Model 098, except has youth-size stock and 22-inch barrel. 20 or .410 gauge only.

HERCULES SHOTGUNS
See listings under "W" for Montgomery Ward.

Heym Model 55 BF Shotgun/Rifle

HEYM SHOTGUNS
Münnerstadt, Germany

Heym Model 22S "Safety" Shotgun/Rifle Combination **$2195**
Gauges: 16 and 20. Calibers: 22 Mag., 22 Hornet, 222 Rem., 222 Rem. Mag., 5.6 × 50 R Mag., 6.5 × 57 R, 7 × 57 R, 243 Win. 24-inch barrels. 40 inches overall. Weight: about 5½ pounds. Single-set trigger. Left-side barrel selector. Integral dovetail base for scope mounting. Arabesque engraving. Walnut stock. Discontinued 1993.

Heym Model 55 BF Shotgun/Rifle Combo **$4750**
Gauges: 12, 16 and 20. Calibers: 5.6 × 50 R Mag., 6.5 × 57 R, 7 × 57 R, 7 × 65 R, 243 Win., 308 Win., 30-06. 25-inch barrels. 42 inches overall. Weight: about 6¾ pounds. Black satin-finished, corrosion-resistant barrels of Krupps special steel. Hand-checkered walnut stock with long pistol grip. Hand-engraved leaf scroll. German cheekpiece. Discontinued 1988.

J. C. HIGGINS SHOTGUNS
See Sears, Roebuck & Company.

HIGH STANDARD SPORTING ARMS
East Hartford, Connecticut
Formerly High Standard Mfg. Corp.
of Hamden, Conn.

In 1966, High Standard introduced new series of Flite-King pumps and Supermatic autoloaders, both readily identifiable by the damascened bolt and restyled checkering. To avoid confusion, these models are designated "Series II" in this text. This is *not* an official factory designation. Operation of this firm was discontinued in 1984.

High Standard Flite-King Brush—12 Gauge **$200**
Same as Flite-King Field 12, except has 18- or 20-inch barrel (cylinder bore) with rifle sights. Made 1962–64.

High Standard Flite-King Brush Deluxe **$255**
Same as Flite-King Brush, except has adjustable peep rear sight, checkered pistol grip, recoil pad, fluted slide handle, swivels and sling. Not available with 18-inch barrel. Made 1964–66.

High Standard Flite-King Brush

SHOTGUNS

High Standard Flite-King
Deluxe Rib—12 Gauge

High Standard Flite-King
Deluxe Rib—20 (II), Adjustable Choke

High Standard Flite-King Field—12 Gauge

High Standard Flite-King Field—20 Gauge

High Standard Flite-King Brush (Series II) $235
Same as Flite-King Deluxe 12 (II), except has 20-inch
barrel, cylinder bore, with rifle sights. Weight: 7 pounds.
Made 1966–1975.

High Standard Flite-King Brush Deluxe (II) $260
Same as Flite-King Brush (II), except has adjustable peep
rear sight, swivels and sling. Made 1966–1975.

High Standard Flite-King Deluxe—12 Ga. (Series II)
Hammerless. 5-shot magazine. Barrels: plain; 27-inch with
adjustable choke. 26-inch IC, 28-inch M or F, 30-inch Full
choke. Weight: about 7¼ pounds. Checkered pistol-grip
stock and forearm, recoil pad. Made 1966–1975.
With adjustable choke **$275**
Without adjustable choke **250**

**High Standard Flite-King Deluxe—20, 28, .410
Gauge (Series II)** **$235**
Same as Flite-King Deluxe 12 (II), except chambered for
20 and .410 gauge 3-inch shell, 28 gauge 2¾-inch shell;
plain barrel in IC (20), M (20, 28), F choke (20, 28, .410).
Weight: about 6 pounds. Made 1966–1975.

High Standard Flite-King Deluxe Rib—12 Ga. . . **$295**
Same as Flite-King Field 12, except vent-rib barrel (28-
inch M or F, 30-inch F), checkered stock and forearm.
Made 1961–66.

High Standard Flite-King Deluxe Rib—12 Gauge (II)
Same as Flite-King Deluxe 12 (II), except has vent-rib
barrel; available in 27-inch with adjustable choke, 28-inch
M or F, 30-inch F choke. Made 1966–1975.
With adjustable choke **$300**
Without adjustable choke **295**

High Standard Flite-King Deluxe Rib—20 Ga. . . **$275**
Same as Flite-King Field 20, except vent-rib barrel (28-

High Standard Flite-King Deluxe Rib—20 Ga. (cont.)
inch M or F), checkered stock and slide handle. Made
1962–66.

**High Standard Flite-King Deluxe Rib—20, 28, .410 Ga.
(Series II)**
Same as Flite-King Deluxe 20, 28, .410 (II), except 20
gauge available with 27-inch adjustable choke, 28-inch M
or F choke. Weight: about 6¼ pounds. Made 1966–1975.
With adjustable choke **$300**
Without adjustable choke **295**

**High Standard Flite-King Deluxe Skeet Gun—
12 Gauge (Series II)** **$275**
Same as Flite-King Deluxe Rib 12 (II), except available
only with 26-inch vent-rib barrel, skeet choke; recoil pad
optional. Made 1966–1975.

**High Standard Flite-King Deluxe Skeet Gun—
20, 28, 410 Gauge (Series II)** **$305**
Same as Flite-King Deluxe Rib 20, 28, .410 (II) except
available only with 26-inch vent-rib barrel, skeet choke.
Made 1966–1975.

High Standard Flite-King Deluxe Trap Gun (II) . . **$275**
Same as Flite-King Deluxe Rib 12 (II), except available
only with 30-inch vent-rib barrel, Full choke; trap-style
stock. Made 1966–1975.

High Standard Flite-King Field Pump—12 Ga. . . **$225**
Hammerless. Magazine holds 5 shells. Barrels: 26-inch
IC, 28-inch M or F, 30-inch F choke. Weight: 7¼ pounds.
Plain pistol-grip stock and slide handle. Made 1960–66.

High Standard Flite-King Field Pump—20 Ga. . . **$205**
Hammerless. Chambered for 3-inch Magnum shells, also
handles 2¾-inch. Magazine holds four shells. Barrels: 26-
inch IC, 28-inch M or F choke. Weight: about 6 pounds.
Plain pistol-grip stock and slide handle. Made 1961–66.

High Standard Flite-King Trophy—20 Gauge

High Standard Supermatic Deluxe—12 Gauge (II)

High Standard Supermatic Deluxe—20 Ga. (II), Adjustable Choke

High Standard Supermatic Deluxe Deer (II)

High Standard Flite-King Pump Shotguns—16 Gauge
Same general specifications as Flite-King 12, except not available in Brush, Skeet and Trap Models, or 30-inch barrel. Values same as for 12-gauge guns. Made 1961–65.

High Standard Flite-King Pump Shotguns—.410 Ga.
Same general specifications as Flite-King 20, except not available in Special and Trophy Models, or with other than 26-inch Full choke barrel. Values same as for 20-gauge guns. Made 1962–66.

High Standard Flite-King Skeet—12 Gauge $310
Same as Flite-King Deluxe Rib, except 26-inch vent-rib barrel, with SK choke. Made 1962–66.

High Standard Flite-King Special—12 Gauge . . . $225
Same as Flite-King Field 12, except has 27-inch barrel with adjustable choke. Made 1960–66.

High Standard Flite-King Special—20 Gauge . . . $230
Same as Flite-King Field 20, except has 27-inch barrel with adjustable choke. Made 1961–66.

High Standard Flite-King Trap—12 Gauge $325
Same as Flite-King Deluxe Rib 12, except 30-inch vent-rib barrel, Full choke; special trap stock with recoil pad. Made 1962–66.

High Standard Flite-King Trophy—12 Gauge . . . $310
Same as Flite-King Deluxe Rib 12, except has 27-inch vent-rib barrel with adjustable choke. Made 1960–66.

High Standard Flite-King Trophy—20 Gauge . . . $325
Same as Flite-King Deluxe Rib 20, except has 27-inch vent-rib barrel with adjustable choke. Made 1962–66.

High Standard Supermatic Deer Gun $300
Same as Supermatic Field 12, except has 22-inch barrel (cylinder bore) with rifle sights, checkered stock and forearm, recoil pad. Weight: 7¾ pounds. Made in 1965.

High Standard Supermatic Deluxe—12 Ga. (Series II)
Gas-operated autoloader. 4-shot magazine. Barrels: plain; 27-inch with adjustable choke (discontinued about 1970); 26-inch IC, 28-inch M or F, 30-inch F choke. Weight: about 7½ pounds. Checkered pistol-grip stock and forearm, recoil pad. Made 1966–1975.
With adjustable choke $310
Without adjustable choke 275

High Standard Supermatic Deluxe—20 Ga. (Series II)
Same as Supermatic Deluxe 12 (II), except chambered for 20 gauge 3-inch shell; barrels available in 27-inch with adjustable choke (discontinued about 1970), 26-inch IC, 28-inch M or F choke. Weight: about 7 pounds. Made 1966–1975.
With adjustable choke $295
Without adjustable choke 275

High Standard Supermatic Deluxe Deer Gun (II) . . $310
Same as Supermatic Deluxe 12 (II), except has 22-inch barrel, cylinder bore, with rifle sights. Weight: 7¾ pounds. Made 1966–1974.

High Standard Supermatic Deluxe Duck— 12 Gauge Magnum (Series II) $225
Same as Supermatic Deluxe 12 (II), except chambered for 3-inch Magnum shell, 3-shot magazine; 30-inch plain barrel, Full choke. Weight: 8 pounds. Made 1966–1974.

High Standard Supermatic Deluxe Duck Rib— 12 Gauge Magnum (Series II) **$245**
Same as Supermatic Deluxe Rib 12 (II), except chambered for 3-inch Magnum shell, 3-shot magazine; 30-inch vent-rib barrel, Full choke. Weight: 8 pounds. Made 1966–1975.

High Standard Supermatic Deluxe Rib—12 Ga. . . . **$215**
Same as Supermatic Field 12, except vent-rib barrel (28-inch M or F, 30-inch F), checkered stock and forearm. Made 1961–66.

High Standard Supermatic Deluxe Rib—12 Gauge (II)
Same as Supermatic Deluxe 12 (II), except has vent-rib barrel; available in 27-inch with adjustable choke, 28-inch M or F, 30-inch F choke. Made 1966–1975.
With adjustable choke **$275**
Without adjustable choke **250**

High Standard Supermatic Deluxe Rib—20 Ga. . . . **$275**
Same as Supermatic Field 20, except vent-rib barrel (28-inch M or F), checkered stock and forearm. Made 1963–66.

High Standard Supermatic Deluxe Rib—20 Ga. (II)
Same as Supermatic Deluxe 20 (II), except has vent-rib barrel. Made 1966–1975.
With adjustable choke **$275**
Without adjustable choke **245**

High Standard Supermatic Deluxe Skeet Gun— 12 Gauge (Series II) **$265**
Same as Supermatic Deluxe Rib 12 (II), except available only with 26-inch vent-rib barrel, SK choke. Made 1966–1975.

High Standard Supermatic Deluxe Skeet Gun— 20 Gauge (Series II) **$275**
Same as Supermatic Deluxe Rib 20 (II), except available only with 26-inch vent-rib barrel, SK choke. Made 1966–1975.

High Standard Supermatic Deluxe Trap Gun (Series II) **$280**
Same as Supermatic Deluxe Rib 12 (II), except available only with 30-inch vent-rib barrel, Full choke; trap-style stock. Made 1966–1975.

High Standard Supermatic Duck—12 Ga. Mag. . . . **$245**
Same as Supermatic Field 12, except chambered for 3-inch Magnum shell, 30-inch Full choke barrel, recoil pad. Made 1961–66.

High Standard Supermatic Duck Rib—12 Gauge Magnum **$265**
Same as Supermatic Duck 12 Magnum, except has vent-rib barrel, checkered stock and forearm. Made 1961–66.

High Standard Supermatic Field Autoloading Shotgun—12 Gauge **$195**
Gas-operated. Magazine holds four shells. Barrels: 26-inch IC, 28-inch M or F choke, 30-inch F choke. Weight: about 7½ pounds. Plain pistol-grip stock and forearm. Made 1960–66.

High Standard Supermatic Deluxe Duck Rib—12 Gauge (II)

High Standard Supermatic Deluxe Rib—12 Gauge

High Standard Supermatic Duck—12 Gauge Magnum

High Standard Supermatic Duck Rib—12 Gauge

High Standard Supermatic Field Autoloading Shotgun—20 Gauge **$205**
Gas-operated. Chambered for 3-inch Magnum shells, also handles 2³/₄-inch. Magazine holds three shells. Barrels: 26-inch IC, 28-inch M or F choke. Weight: about 7 pounds. Plain pistol-grip stock and forearm. Made 1963–66.

High Standard Supermatic Shadow Automatic . . **$290**
Gas-operated. Gauge: 12, 20, 2³/₄- or 3-inch chamber in 12 gauges, 3-inch in 20 gauge. Magazine holds four 2³/₄-inch shells, three 3-inch. Barrels: full-size airflow rib; 26-inch (IC or SK choke); 28-inch (M, IM or F); 30-inch (trap or F choke); 12-gauge 3-inch Magnum available only in 30-inch F choke; 20 gauge not available in 30-inch. Weight: 12 ga., 7 pounds. Checkered walnut stock and forearm. Made 1974–75 by Caspoll Int'l., Inc., Tokyo.

High Standard Supermatic Shadow Indy O/U . . . **$750**
Boxlock. Fully engraved receiver. Selective auto ejectors. Selective single trigger. 12 gauge. 2³/₄-inch chambers. Barrels: full-size airflow rib; 27¹/₂-inch both SK choke, 29³/₄-inch IM/F or F/F. Weight: with 29³/₄-inch barrels, 8 lbs. 2 oz. Pistol-grip stock with recoil pad, ventilated

High Standard Supermatic Shadow Indy (cont.)
forearm, skip checkering. Made 1974–75 by Caspoll Int'l., Inc., Tokyo.

High Standard Supermatic Shadow Seven **$625**
Same general specifications as Shadow Indy, except has conventional vent rib, less elaborate engraving, standard checkering; forearm is not vented, no recoil pad. 27¹/₂-inch barrels also available in IC/M, M/F choke. Made 1974–75.

High Standard Supermatic Skeet—12 Gauge . . . **$205**
Same as Supermatic Deluxe Rib 12, except 26-inch vent-rib barrel with SK choke. Made 1962–66.

High Standard Supermatic Skeet—20 Gauge . . . **$230**
Same as Supermatic Deluxe Rib 20, except 26-inch vent-rib barrel with SK choke. Made 1964–66.

High Standard Supermatic Special—12 Gauge . **$210**
Same as Supermatic Field 12, except has 27-inch barrel with adjustable choke. Made 1960–66.

High Standard Supermatic
Shadow Automatic

High Standard Supermatic
Shadow Indy

High Standard Supermatic
Shadow Seven

High Standard Supermatic
Special—12 Gauge

High Standard Supermatic
Special—20 Gauge

SHOTGUNS

High Standard Supermatic Special—20 Gauge . **$220**
Same as Supermatic Field 20, except has 27-inch barrel with adjustable choke. Made 1963–66.

High Standard Supermatic
Trophy—12 Gauge

High Standard Supermatic
Trophy—20 Gauge

High Standard Supermatic Trap—12 Gauge ... **$225**
Same as Supermatic Deluxe Rib 12, except 30-inch vent-rib barrel, Full choke, special trap stock with recoil pad. Made 1962–66.

High Standard Supermatic Trophy—12 Gauge . . **$225**
Same as Supermatic Deluxe Rib 12, except has 27-inch vent-rib barrel with adjustable choke. Made 1961–66.

High Standard Supermatic Trophy—20 Gauge . . **$230**
Same as Supermatic Deluxe Rib 20, except has 27-inch vent-rib barrel with adjustable choke. Made 1963–66.

Holland & Holland Badminton

Holland & Holland Dominion

HOLLAND & HOLLAND, LTD.
London, England

Holland & Holland Badminton Model Hammerless Double Barrel Shotgun. Originally No. 2 Grade
General specifications same as Royal Model except without self-opening action. Made as a Game Gun or Pigeon and Wildfowl Gun. Made from 1902 to date.
With double triggers **$8250**
With single trigger 8750

Holland & Holland Centenary Model Hammerless Double Barrel Shotgun
Lightweight (5½ lbs.). 12 gauge game gun designed for 2-inch shell. Made in four grades—Model Deluxe, Royal, Badminton, Dominion—values same as shown for standard guns in those grades. Discontinued 1962.

Holland & Holland Dominion Model Hammerless Double Barrel Shotgun **$4695**
Game Gun. Sidelock. Auto ejectors. Double triggers. Gauges: 12, 16, 20. Barrels: 25- to 30-inch, any standard boring. Checkered stock and forend, straight grip standard. Discontinued 1967.

Holland & Holland Model Deluxe Hammerless Double
Same as Royal Model, except has special engraving and exhibition grade stock and forearm. Currently mfd.
With double triggers **$15,000**
With single trigger 16,000

Holland & Holland Northwood

Holland & Holland Northwood Model Hammerless Double Barrel Shotgun **$7295**
Anson & Deeley system boxlock. Auto ejectors. Double triggers. Gauges: 12, 16, 20, 28 in Game Model; 28 gauge not offered in Pigeon Model; Wildfowl Model in 12 gauge only (3-inch chambers available). Barrels: 28-inch standard in Game and Pigeon Models, 30-inch in Wildfowl

Holland & Holland Royal Double Barrel

Holland & Holland Royal Under-and-Over

Holland & Holland Northwood Model (cont.)
Model; other lengths, any standard choke combination available. Weight: from 5 to 7¾ pounds depending on gauge and barrels. Checkered straight-grip or pistol-grip stock and forearm. Discontinued.

Holland & Holland Riviera Model Pigeon Gun . . . **$10,500**
Same as Badminton Model but supplied with two sets of barrels, double triggers. Discontinued 1967.

Holland & Holland Royal Model Hammerless Double
Self-opening. Sidelocks, hand-detachable. Auto ejectors. Double triggers or single trigger. Gauges: 12, 16, 20, 28, .410. Built to customer's specifications as to barrel length, chokes, etc. Made as a Game Gun or Pigeon and Wildfowl Gun, the latter having treble-grip action and side clips. Checkered stock and forend, straight grip standard. Made from 1885 to date.
With double triggers **$23,950**
With single trigger **25,250**

Holland & Holland Royal Model Under-and-Over
Sidelocks, hand-detachable. Auto ejectors. Double triggers or single trigger. 12 gauge. Built to customer's specifications as to barrel length, chokes, etc. Made as a Game Gun or Pigeon and Wildfowl Gun. Checkered stock and forend, straight grip standard. *Note:* In 1951 Holland & Holland introduced its New Model Under/Over with an improved, narrower action body. Discont. 1960.
New Model with double triggers **$25,000**
New Model with single trigger **27,500**
Old Model with double triggers **12,500**
Old Model with single trigger **13,500**

Holland & Holland Single Shot Super Trap Gun
Anson & Deeley system boxlock. Auto ejector. No safety. 12 gauge. Barrels: wide vent rib, 30- or 32-inch, with Extra Full choke. Weight: about 8¾ pounds. Monte Carlo stock with pistol grip and recoil pad, full beavertail forearm. Models differ in grade of engraving and wood. Discontinued.
Standard Grade . . . . **$ 4,750**
Deluxe Grade **6,850**
Exhibition Grade **10,000**

HUNTER ARMS COMPANY
Fulton, New York

Hunter Fulton

Hunter Fulton Hammerless Double Barrel Shotgun
Boxlock. Plain extractors. Double triggers or non-selective single trigger. Gauges: 12, 16, 20. Barrels: 26- to 32-inch, various choke combinations. Weight: about 7 pounds. Checkered pistol-grip stock and forearm. Discont. 1948.
With double triggers **$325**
With single trigger **550**

Hunter Special

Hunter Special Hammerless Double Barrel Shotgun
Boxlock. Plain extractors. Double triggers or non-selective single trigger. Gauges: 12, 16, 20. Barrels: 26- to 30-inch, various choke combinations. Weight: 6½ to 7¼ pounds depending on barrel length and gauge. Checkered full pistol-grip stock and forearm. Discont. 1948.
With double triggers **$525**
With single trigger **610**

SHOTGUNS

IGA SHOTGUNS
South Hackensack, New Jersey
Distributed by Stoeger Industries, Inc.

IGA Coach Gun **$195**
Gauges: 12, 20 and .410. 20-inch side-by-side barrels of chrome-molybdenum steel. Chokes: IC/M, 3-inch chambers. Weight: 6½ pounds. Double triggers. Automatic safety. Hand-rubbed, oil-finish pistol grip hardwood stock and forend with hand-checkering. Made from 1983 to date.

IGA Condor I O/U Single Trigger Shotgun
Gauge: 12 or 20. 26- or 28-inch barrels of chrome-molybdenum steel. Chokes: Fixed—M/F or IC/M; screw-in choke tubes (12 ga. only). 3-inch chambers. Weight: 6¾ to 7 pounds. Sighting rib with anti-glare surface. Hand-checkered, hardwood pistol grip stock and forend. Made from 1983 to date.
With Fixed Chokes **$395**
With Screw-in Tubes **425**

IGA Condor II O/U Double Trigger Shotgun **$295**
Same general specifications as the Condor I Over/Under, except with double triggers and fixed chokes only.

IGA Era 2000 O/U Shotgun **$460**
Gauge: 12 with 3-inch chambers. 26- or 28-inch barrels of chrome-molybdenum steel with screw-in choke tubes. Extractors. Manual safety. (Mechanical triggers.) Weight: 7 pounds. Checkered Brazilian hardwood stock with oil finish. Made from 1992 to date.

IGA Reuna Single Shot Shotgun **$80**
Visible hammer. Under-lever release. Gauges: 12, 20 and .410; 3-inch chambers. 26- or 28-inch barrels with fixed chokes or screw-in choke tubes (12 gauge only). Extractors. Weight: 5¼ to 6½ pounds. Plain Brazilian hardwood stock and semibeavertail forend. Made from 1992 to date.

IGA Uplander Side-by-Side Shotgun
Gauges: 12, 20, 28 and .410. 26- or 28-inch barrels of chrome-molybdenum steel. Various fixed-choke combinations; screw-in choke tubes (12 ga. only). 3-inch chambers (2¾-inch in 28 ga.). Weight: 6¼ to 7 pounds. Double triggers. Automatic safety. Matte-finished solid sighting rib. Hand-rubbed, oil-finish pistol grip stock and forend with hand-checkering. Made from 1983 to date.
With Fixed Chokes **$240**
With Screw-in Tubes **265**

IGA Coach Gun

IGA Condor I Over/Under
Single Trigger Shotgun

IGA Era 2000 Over/Under

IGA Reuna Single Shot

IGA Uplander Side-by-Side
Shotgun

ITHACA GUN COMPANY
King Ferry (formerly Ithaca), New York
Now Ithaca Acquisition Corp./Ithaca Gun Co.

In 1988 Ithaca Gun Company was reorganized as Ithaca Acquisition Corporation. While some models were discontinued, others have been reintroduced and updated.

Ithaca Model 37 Bicentennial Commemorative . . **$395**
Limited to issue of 1976. Similar to Model 37 Supreme, except has special Bicentennial design etched on receiver, full-fancy walnut stock and slide handle. Serial numbers U.S.A. 0001 to U.S.A. 1976. Comes in presentation case with cast pewter belt buckle. Made in 1976. Value is for gun in new, unfired condition.

Ithaca Model 37 English Ultra **$375**
Same general specifications as Model 37 Ultralite, except straight buttstock, 25-inch Rot-Forged vent-rib barrel. Made 1984–87.

Ithaca Model 37 Featherlight Standard Grade Slide Action Repeating Shotgun
Adaptation of the earlier Remington Model 17, a Browning design patented in 1915. Hammerless. Takedown. Gauges: 12, 16 (discontinued 1973), 20. 4-shell magazine. Barrel lengths: 26-, 28-, 30-inch (the latter in 12 gauge only); standard chokes. Weight: from 5¾ to 7½ pounds depending on gauge and barrel length. Checkered pistol-grip stock and slide handle. Some guns made in the 1950s and 1960s have grooved slide handle; plain or checkered

Ithaca Model 37 Featherlight Standard (cont.)
pistol grip. Made 1937–1984.
Standard w/checkered pistol grip	**$230**
Standard w/plain stock	**205**
Model 37D Deluxe (1954–1977)	**285**
Model 37DV Deluxe Vent Rib (1962–1984)	**315**
Model 37R Deluxe Solid Rib (1955–1961)	**305**
Model 37V Standard Vent Rib (1962–1984)	**265**

Ithaca Model 37 Field Grade Mag. w/Tubes **$310**
Same general specifications as Model 37 Featherlight, except 32-inch barrel and detachable choke tubes. Vent-rib barrel. Made 1984–87.

Ithaca Model 37 $5000 Grade **$5795**
Custom built, elaborately engraved and inlaid with gold, hand-finished working parts, stock and forend of select figured walnut. General specifications same as standard Model 37. *Note:* The same gun was designated the $1000 Grade prior to World War II. Made 1937–1967.

Ithaca Model 37 Standard Deerslayer **$285**
Same as Model 37 Standard, except has 20- or 26-inch barrel bored for rifled slugs, rifle-type open rear sight and ramp front sight. Weight: 5¾ to 6½ pounds depending on gauge and barrel length. Made 1959 to date.

Ithaca Model 37 Super Deluxe Deerslayer **$315**
Formerly "Deluxe Deerslayer." Same as Model 37 Standard Deerslayer, except has stock and slide handle of fancy walnut. Made from 1962 to date.

Ithaca Model 37 Supreme Grade **$425**
Available in Skeet or Trap Gun, similar to Model 37T. Made from 1967 to date.

Ithaca Model 37
English Ultra

Ithaca Model 37
Field Grade Mag. w/Tubes

Ithaca Model 37
Super Deluxe Deerslayer

Ithaca Model 37 Supreme

SHOTGUNS

**Ithaca Model 37R
Deluxe Solid Rib**

Ithaca Model 37T Target

Ithaca Model 37 Ultralite
Same general specifications as Model 37 Featherlight, except streamlined forend, gold trigger, Sid Bell grip cap and vent rib. Weight: 5 to 5¾ pounds. Made 1984–87.
Standard **$315**
With Choke Tubes **355**

Ithaca Model 37R Solid Rib Grade
Same general specifications as the Model 37 Featherlight, except has a raised solid rib, adding about ¼ pound of weight. Made 1937–1967.
With checkered grip and slide handle **$300**
With plain stock **295**

Ithaca Model 37S Skeet Grade **$465**
Same general specifications as the Model 37 Featherlight, except has vent rib and large extension-type forend; weighs about ½ pound more. Made 1937–1955.

Ithaca Model 37T Target Grade **$395**
Same general specifications as Model 37 Featherlight, except has vent-rib barrel, checkered stock and slide handle of fancy walnut (choice of skeet- or trap-style stock). *Note:* This model replaced Model 37S Skeet and Model 37T Trap. Made 1955–1961.

Ithaca Model 37T Trap Grade **$385**
Same general specifications as Model 37S, except has straighter trap-style stock of select walnut, recoil pad; weighs about ½ pound more. Made 1937–1955.

Ithaca Model 51 Deerslayer **$295**
Same as Model 51 Standard, except has 24-inch plain barrel with slug boring, rifle sights, recoil pad. Weight: about 7¼ pounds. Made 1972–1984.

Ithaca Model 51 Deluxe Skeet Grade **$375**
Same as Model 51 Standard, except 26-inch vent-rib barrel only, SK choke, skeet-style stock, semi-fancy wood. Weight: about 8 pounds. Made 1970–1987.

Ithaca Model 51 Deluxe Trap Grade
Same as Model 51 Standard, except 12 gauge only, 30-inch barrel with broad floating rib, F choke, trap-style stock w/straight or Monte Carlo comb, semifancy wood, recoil pad. Weight: about 8 lbs. Made 1970–1987.
With straight stock **$295**
With Monte Carlo stock **340**

Ithaca Model 51 Standard Automatic Shotgun
Gas-operated. Gauges: 12, 20. 3-shot. Barrels: plain or vent rib; 30-inch F choke (12 gauge only), 28-inch F or M, 26-inch IC. Weight: 7¼–7¾ pounds depending on gauge and barrel. Checkered pistol-grip stock, forearm. Made 1970–1980. Still avail. in 12 and 20 ga., 28-inch M choke only.
With plain barrel **$230**
With ventilated rib **275**

Ithaca Model 51 Deerslayer

Ithaca Model 51 Deluxe Trap

Ithaca Model 51 Standard

Ithaca Model 51A Turkey Gun

Ithaca Model 51 Standard Magnum
Same as Model 51 Standard, except has 3-inch chamber, handles Magnum shells only; 30-inch barrel in 12 gauge, 28-inch in 20 gauge, F or M choke, stock with recoil pad. Weight: 7³/₄–8 pounds. Made 1972 to date.
With plain barrel (discontinued 1976) **$250**
With ventilated rib **295**

Ithaca Model 51A Turkey Gun **$325**
Same general specifications as standard Model 51 Magnum, except 26-inch barrel and matte finish. Disc. 1986.

Ithaca Model 66 Long Tom **$100**
Same as Model 66 Standard, except has 36-inch Full choke barrel, 12 gauge only, checkered stock and recoil pad standard. Made 1969–1974.

Ithaca Model 66 Standard Supersingle Lever
Single shot. Hand-cocked hammer. Gauges: 12 (discont. 1974), 20, .410; 3-inch chambers. Barrels: 12 ga., 30-inch Full choke, 28-inch F or M; 20 ga., 28-inch F or M; .410, 26-inch F. Weight: about 7 pounds. Plain or checkered straight-grip stock, plain forend. Made 1963–1978.
Standard Model **$125**
Vent Rib Model (20 ga., checkered stock, recoil
  pad, 1969–1974) **145**
Youth Model (20 & .410 ga., 26-inch bbl., shorter
  stock, recoil pad, 1965–1978) **105**

Ithaca Model 66RS Buckbuster **$150**
Same as Model 66 Standard, except has 22-inch barrel, cylinder bore with rifle sights; later version has recoil pad.

Ithaca Model 66RS Buckbuster (cont.)
Originally offered in 12 and 20 gauges; the former was discontinued in 1970. Made 1967–1978.

> **NOTE:** Previously issued as the Ithaca Model 37, the Model 87 listed below is now made available through the Ithaca Acquisition Corp.

Ithaca Model 87 Deerslayer Shotgun
Gauges: 12 or 20, 3-inch chamber. Barrels: 18¹/₂-, 20- or 25-inch (w/special or rifled bore). Weight: 6 to 6³/₄ pounds. Ramp blade front sight, adjustable rear. Receiver grooved for scope. Checkered American walnut pistol-grip stock and forearm. Made from 1988 to date.
Basic Model **$285**
Basic Field Combo (w/extra 28-inch bbl.) **345**
Deluxe Model **320**
Deluxe Combo (w/extra 28-inch bbl.) **410**
DSPS Model (8-shot) **280**
Field Model **240**
Monte Carlo Model **255**
Ultra Model (discontinued 1991) **295**

Ithaca Model 87 Deerslayer II Rifled Shotgun **$360**
Similar to the Standard Deerslayer Model, except with solid frame construction and 25-inch rifled barrel. Monte Carlo stock. Made from 1988 to date.

Ithaca Model 87 Ultralite Field Pump Shotgun . . . **$295**
Gauges: 12 and 20; 2³/₄-inch chambers. 25-inch barrel with choke tube. Weight: 5 to 6 pounds. Made 1988–1990.

SHOTGUNS

Ithaca Model 66 Long Tom

Ithaca Model 66 Standard Supersingle

Ithaca Model 66RS Buckbuster

Ithaca Model 87 Field Grade

Gauge: 12 or 20; 3-inch chamber. 5-shot magazine. Fixed chokes or screw-in choke tubes (IC, M, F). Barrels: 18½-inch (M&P); 20- and 25-inch (Combo); 26-, 28-, 30-inch vent rib. Weight: 5 to 7 pounds. Made from 1988 to date.

Basic Field Model	**$290**
Camo Model	365
Deluxe Model	340
Deluxe Combo Model	375
English Model	295
Hand Grip Model (w/polymer pistol-grip)	285
M&P Model	280
Supreme Model	595
Turkey Model	295
Ultra Deluxe Model (discontinued 1992)	365
Ultra Field Model (discontinued 1992)	335

Ithaca Field Grade

Ithaca No. 1

Ithaca No. 2

Ithaca No. 3

Ithaca No. 4E

Ithaca No. 5E

Ithaca No. 7E

Ithaca Hammerless Double Barrel Shotguns

Boxlock. Plain extractors, auto ejectors standard on the "E" grades. Double triggers, non-selective or selective single trigger extra. Gauges: Magnum 10, 12; 12, 16, 20, 28, .410. Barrels: 26- to 32-inch, any standard boring. Weight: 5¾ (.410) to 10½ pounds (Magnum 10). Checkered pistol-grip stock and forearm standard. Higher grades differ from Field Grade in quality of workmanship, grade of wood, checkering, engraving, etc.; general specifications are the same. Ithaca doubles made before 1925 had underbolts and a bolt thru the rib extension. In 1925 (serial number 425,000) the rotary bolt and a stronger frame were adopted. Values shown are for this latter type; earlier

Ithaca Hammerless Doubles (cont.)

models valued about 50 percent lower. Smaller gauge guns often command up to 75 percent higher. Discontinued 1948.

Field Grade	$	650
No. 1 Grade		595
No. 2 Grade		895
No. 3 Grade		1,200
No. 4E Grade (ejector)		2,395
No. 5E Grade (ejector)		2,850
No. 7E Grade (ejector)		7,500
$2000 (prewar $1000) Grade (ejector and selective single trigger standard)		12,000

Extras:

Magnum 10 or 12 gauge (in other than the four highest grades), **add**	**$200**
Automatic ejectors (Grades No. 1, 2, 3, with ejectors are designated No. 1E, 2E, 3E), **add**	200
Selective single trigger, **add**	150
Non-selective single trigger, **add**	100
Beavertail forend (Field No. 1 or 2), **add**	150
Beavertail forend (No. 3 or 4), **add**	175
Beavertail forend (No. 5, 7 or $2000 Grade), **add**	250
Ventilated rib (No. 4, 5, 7 or $2000 Grade), **add**	250
Ventilated rib (lower grades), **add**	175

Ithaca LSA-55 Turkey Gun

Ithaca LSA-55 Turkey Gun $525

Over-and-under shotgun/rifle combination. Boxlock. Exposed hammer. Plain extractor. Single trigger. 12 gauge/ 222 Rem. 24½-inch ribbed barrels (rifle barrel has muzzle

Ithaca LSA-55 Turkey Gun (cont.)

brake). Weight: about 7 pounds. Folding leaf rear sight, bead front sight. Checkered Monte Carlo stock and forearm. Made 1970–77 by Oy Tikkakoski AB, Tikkakoski, Finland.

Ithaca Mag-10 Standard
Ventilated Rib

Ithaca Single Barrel Trap
Model 5-E

Ithaca Single Barrel Trap
"Dollar Grade"

Ithaca Single Barrel Super Trap

SHOTGUNS

Ithaca Mag-10 Automatic Shotgun
Gas-operated. 10 gauge. 3$\frac{1}{2}$-inch Magnum. 3-shot. 32-inch plain (Standard Grade only) or vent-rib barrel. Full choke. Weight: 11 lbs., plain barrel; 11$\frac{1}{2}$ lbs., vent rib. Standard Grade has plain stock and forearm. Deluxe and Supreme Grades have checkering, semi-fancy and fancy wood respectively, and stud swivel. All have recoil pad. Deluxe and Supreme Grades made 1974–1982. Standard Grade introduced in 1977. All grades discontinued 1986.

Camo Model	**$650**
Deluxe Grade	695
Roadblocker	595
Standard Grade, plain barrel	550
Standard Grade, ventilated rib	650
Standard Grade, with tubes	695
Supreme Grade	840

Ithaca Single Shot Trap, Flues and Knick Models
Boxlock. Hammerless. Ejector. 12 gauge only. Barrel lengths: 30-, 32-, 34-inch (32-inch only in Victory Grade). Vent rib. Weight: about 8 pounds. Checkered pistol-grip stock and forend. Grades differ only in quality of workmanship, engraving, checkering, wood, etc. Flues Model, serial numbers under 400,000, made 1908–1921. Triple-bolted Knick Model, serial numbers above 400,000, made since 1921. Victory Model discontinued in 1938, No. 7-E in 1964, No. 4-E in 1976, No. 5-E in 1986. $5000 Grade currently manufactured. Values shown are for Knick Model; Flues Model guns bring prices about 50% lower.

Ithaca Single Shot Trap
Victory Grade

Ithaca Single Shot Trap, Flues and Knick (cont.)

Victory Grade	$ 895
No. 4-E	1,295
No. 5-E	2,595
No. 7-E	3,500
$5000 Grade (prewar $1000 Grade)	8,700
Sousa Grade	10,000

> **NOTE:** The following Ithaca-Perazzi shotguns were manufactured by Manifattura Armi Perazzi, Brescia, Italy. See also separate Perazzi listings.

Ithaca-Perazzi Competition I Skeet $1950
Same as Competition I Trap, except has 26$\frac{3}{4}$-inch barrels with integral muzzle brakes, skeet choke, skeet-style stock and forearm. Weight: 7$\frac{3}{4}$ pounds. Made 1969–1974.

Ithaca-Perazzi Competition I Skeet

Ithaca-Perazzi Competition I Trap

Ithaca-Perazzi Competition IV

Ithaca-Perazzi Competition I Trap O/U **$1995**
Boxlock. Auto ejectors. Single trigger. 12 gauge. 30- or 32-inch vent-rib barrels, IM/F choke. Weight: about 8½ pounds. Checkered pistol-grip stock, forearm; recoil pad. Made 1969–1974.

Ithaca-Perazzi Competition I Trap Single Barrel **$1850**
Boxlock. Auto ejection. 12 gauge. 32- or 34-inch barrel, vent rib, Full choke. Weight: 8½ pounds. Checkered Monte Carlo stock and beavertail forearm, recoil pad. Made 1973–78.

Ithaca-Perazzi Competition IV Trap Gun **$2125**
Boxlock. Auto ejection. 12 gauge. 32- or 34-inch barrel with high, wide vent rib, four interchangeable choke tubes (Extra Full, F, IM, M). Weight: about 8¾ pounds. Checkered Monte Carlo stock and beavertail forearm, recoil pad. Fitted case. Made 1977–78.

Ithaca-Perazzi Light Game O/U Field **$2095**
Boxlock. Auto ejectors. Single trigger. 12 gauge. 27½-inch vent-rib barrels, M/F or IC/M choke. Weight: 6¾ pounds. Checkered field-style stock and forearm. Made 1972–74.

Ithaca-Perazzi Mirage Live Bird **$2895**
Same as Mirage Trap, except has 28-inch barrels, Mod. and Extra Full choke, special stock and forearm for live bird shooting. Weight: about 8 pounds. Made 1973–78.

Ithaca-Perazzi Mirage Skeet **$2750**
Same as Mirage Trap, except has 28-inch barrels with integral muzzle brakes, SK choke, skeet-style stock and forearm. Weight: about 8 pounds. Made 1973–78.

Ithaca-Perazzi Mirage Trap **$2850**
Same general specifications as MX-8 Trap, except has tapered rib. Made 1973–78.

Ithaca-Perazzi MT-6 Skeet **$2795**
Same as MT-6 Trap, except has 28-inch barrels with two skeet choke tubes instead of Extra Full and Full, skeet-style stock and forearm. Weight: about 8 pounds. Made 1976–78.

Ithaca-Perazzi MT-6 Trap Combo **$3595**
MT-6 with extra single under barrel with high-rise aluminum vent rib, 32- or 34-inch; seven interchangeable choke tubes (IC through Extra Full). Fitted case. Made 1977–78.

Ithaca-Perazzi Light Game Model

Ithaca-Perazzi Mirage Trap

Ithaca-Perazzi MT-6

Ithaca-Perazzi MX-8 Trap

Ithaca-Perazzi
Single Barrel Trap

Ithaca-Perazzi MT-6 Trap Over-and-Under **$2250**
Boxlock. Auto selective ejectors. Non-selective single
trigger. 12 gauge. Barrels separated, wide vent rib, 30- or
32-inch, five interchangeable choke tubes (Extra Full, F,
IM, M, IC). Weight: about 8½ lbs. Checkered pistol-grip
stock/forearm, recoil pad. Fitted case. Made 1976–78.

Ithaca-Perazzi MX-8 Trap Combo **$3795**
MX-8 with extra single barrel, vent rib, 32- or 34-inch,
Full choke, forearm; two trigger groups included. Made
1973–78.

Ithaca-Perazzi MX-8 Trap Over-and-Under **$2895**
Boxlock. Auto selective ejectors. Non-selective single
trigger. 12 gauge. Barrels: high vent rib; 30- or 32-inch,
IM/F choke. Weight: 8¼–8½ pounds. Checkered Monte
Carlo stock and forearm, recoil pad. Made 1969–1978.

Ithaca-Perazzi Single Barrel Trap Gun **$1795**
Boxlock. Auto ejection. 12 gauge. 34-inch vent-rib barrel,
Full choke. Weight: about 8½ pounds. Checkered pistol-
grip stock, forearm; recoil pad. Made 1971–72.

NOTE: The following Ithaca-SKB shotguns, manufactured
by SKB Arms Company, Tokyo, Japan, were distributed in
the U.S. by Ithaca Gun Company 1966–1976. See also
listings under SKB.

Ithaca-SKB Model 100 Side-by-Side **$435**
Boxlock. Plain extractors. Selective single trigger. Auto
safety. Gauges: 12 and 20; 2¾-inch and 3-inch chambers
respectively. Barrels: 30-inch, F/F (12 ga. only); 28-inch,
F/M; 26-inch, IC/M (12 ga. only); 25-inch, IC/M (20 ga.
only). Weight: 12 ga., about 7 lbs.; 20 ga., about 6 lbs.
Checkered stock and forend. Made 1966–1976.

Ithaca-SKB Model 150 Field Grade **$475**
Same as Model 100, except has fancier scroll engraving,
beavertail forearm. Made 1972–74.

Ithaca-SKB Model 200E Field Grade S/S **$565**
Same as Model 100, except auto selective ejectors, engraved and silver-plated frame, gold-plated nameplate and
trigger, beavertail forearm. Made 1966–1976.

Ithaca-SKB Model 200E Skeet Gun **$595**
Same as Model 200E Field Grade, except 26-inch (12 ga.)
and 25-inch (20 ga./2¾-inch chambers) barrels, SK choke;
nonautomatic safety and recoil pad. Made 1966–1976.

Ithaca-SKB Model 100

Ithaca-SKB Model 200E Field

Ithaca-SKB Model 280 English **$650**
Same as Model 200E, except has scrolled game scene engraving on frame, English-style straight-grip stock; 30-
inch barrels not available; special quail gun in 20 gauge
has 25-inch barrels, both bored IC. Made 1971–76.

Ithaca-SKB Model 280 English

Ithaca-SKB Model 300

Ithaca-SKB Model 500 Field

Ithaca-SKB Model 300 Standard Automatic Shotgun
Recoil-operated. Gauges: 12, 20 (3-inch). 5-shot. Barrels: plain or vent rib; 30-inch Full choke (12 gauge only), 28-inch F or M, 26-inch IC. Weight: about 7 pounds. Checkered pistol-grip stock and forearm. Made 1968–1972.
With plain barrel **$235**
With ventilated rib **265**

Ithaca-SKB Model 500 Field Grade O/U **$465**
Boxlock. Auto selective ejectors. Selective single trigger. Nonautomatic safety. Gauges: 12 and 20; 2³/4-inch and 3-inch chambers respectively. Vent-rib barrels: 30-inch M/F (12 ga. only); 28-inch M/F; 26-inch IC/M. Weight: 12 ga., about 7¹/2 lbs.; 20 ga., about 6¹/2 lbs. Checkered stock and forearm. Made 1966–1976.

Ithaca-SKB Model 500 Magnum **$495**
Same as Model 500 Field Grade, except chambered for 3-inch 12 gauge shells, has 30-inch barrels, IM/F choke. Weight: about 8 pounds. Made 1973-76.

Ithaca-SKB Model 600 Doubles Gun **$585**
Same as Model 600 Trap Grade, except specially choked for 21-yard first target, 30-yard second. Made 1973–75.

Ithaca-SKB Model 600 Field Grade **$525**
Same as Model 500, except has silver-plated frame, higher grade wood. Made 1969–1976.

Ithaca-SKB Model 600 Magnum **$555**
Same as Model 600 Field Grade, except chambered for 3-inch 12 gauge shells; has 30-inch barrels, IM/F choke. Weight: 8¹/2 pounds. Made 1969-72.

Ithaca-SKB Model 600 Skeet Grade
Same as Model 500, except also available in 28 and .410 gauge, has silver-plated frame, higher grade wood, recoil pad, 26- or 28-inch barrels (28-inch only in 28 and .410), skeet choke. Weight: 7 to 7³/4 pounds depending on gauge and barrel length. Made 1966–1976.
12 or 20 gauge **$550**
28 or .410 gauge **625**

Ithaca-SKB Model 600 Skeet Combo Set **$1495**
Model 600 Skeet Grade with matched set of 20, 28 and .410 gauge barrels, 28-inch, fitted case. Made 1970-76.

Ithaca-SKB Model 600 Trap Grade O/U **$565**
Same as Model 500, except 12 gauge only, has silver-plated frame, 30- or 32-inch barrels choked F/F or F/IM, choice of Monte Carlo or straight stock of higher grade wood, recoil pad. Weight: about 8 pounds. Made 1966–1976.

Ithaca-SKB Model 680 English **$595**
Same as Model 600 Field Grade, except has intricate scroll engraving, English-style straight-grip stock and forearm of extra-fine walnut; 30-inch barrels not available. Made 1973–76.

Ithaca-SKB Model 600 Field

Ithaca-SKB Model 600 Trap

Ithaca-SKB Model 680 English

Ithaca-SKB Model 700 Skeet Grade

Ithaca-SKB Model 900 Deluxe

Ithaca-SKB Model 700 Doubles Gun **$775**
Same as Model 700 Trap Grade, except choked for 21-yard first target, 30-yard second target. Made 1973–75.

Ithaca-SKB Model 700 Skeet Combo Set **$1595**
Model 700 Skeet Grade with matched set of 20, 28 and .410 gauge barrels, 28-inch, fitted case. Made 1970–71.

Ithaca-SKB Model 700 Skeet Grade **$750**
Same as Model 600 Skeet Grade, except not available in 28 and .410 gauge, has more elaborate scroll engraving, extra-wide rib, higher grade wood. Made 1969–1975.

Ithaca-SKB Model 700 Trap Grade **$765**
Same as Model 600 Trap Grade, except has more elaborate scroll engraving, extra-wide rib, higher grade wood. Made 1969–1975.

Ithaca-SKB Model 900 Deluxe Automatic **$315**
Same as Model 300, except has game scene etched and gold-filled on receiver, vent rib standard. Made 1968–1972.

Ithaca-SKB Model 900 Slug Gun **$275**
Same as Model 900 Deluxe, except has 24-inch plain barrel with slug boring, rifle sights. Weight: about 6½ pounds. Made 1970–72.

Ithaca-SKB Century Single Shot Trap Gun **$515**
Boxlock. Auto ejector. 12 gauge. Barrels: 32- or 34-inch, vent rib, Full choke. Weight: about 8 pounds. Checkered walnut stock with pistol grip, straight or Monte Carlo comb, recoil pad, beavertail forearm. Made 1973–74. *Note:* Current SKB Century is same as Ithaca-SKB Century II.

Ithaca-SKB Century II **$575**
Improved version of Century. Same general specifications, except has higher stock, reverse-taper beavertail forearm with redesigned locking iron. Made 1975–76.

Ithaca-SKB Model XL300 Standard Automatic
Gas-operated. Gauges: 12, 20 (3-inch). 5-shot. Barrels: plain or vent rib; 30-inch Full choke (12 gauge only), 28-inch F or M, 26-inch IC. Weight: 6 to 7½ pounds depending on gauge and barrel. Checkered pistol-grip stock, forearm. Made 1972–76.
With plain barrel **$215**
With ventilated rib 235

Ithaca-SKB Century Trap

Ithaca-SKB Century II Trap

Ithaca-SKB Model XL300

SHOTGUNS

Ithaca-SKB Model XL900 Deluxe

Ithaca-SKB Model XL900 Slug Gun

Ithaca-SKB Model XL900 Deluxe Automatic **$265**
Same as Model XL300, except has game scene finished in silver on receiver, vent rib standard. Made 1972–76.

Ithaca-SKB Model XL900 Skeet Grade **$325**
Same as Model XL900 Deluxe, except has scrolled receiver finished in black chrome, 26-inch barrel only, skeet choke, skeet-style stock. Weight: 7 or 7½ pounds depending on gauge. Made 1972–76.

Ithaca-SKB Model XL900 Slug Gun **$295**
Same as Model XL900 Deluxe, except has 24-inch plain barrel with slug boring, rifle sights. Weight: 6½ or 7 pounds depending on gauge. Made 1972–76.

Ithaca-SKB Model XL900 Trap Grade **$335**
Same as Model XL900 Deluxe, except 12 gauge only, has scrolled receiver finished in black chrome, 30-inch barrel only, IM or F choke, trap style with straight or Monte Carlo comb, recoil pad. Weight: about 7¾ pounds. Made 1972–76.

Iver Johnson Champion
Single Shot Hammer Shotgun

Iver Johnson Hercules Hammerless
Double Barrel Shotgun

Iver Johnson Matted Rib

IVER JOHNSON'S ARMS
Jacksonville, Arkansas

Formerly Iver Johnson's Arms & Cycle Works of Fitchburg, Mass., and Middlesex, N.J. Now a division of the American Military Arms Corporation.

Iver Johnson Champion Grade Single Shot Hammer Shotgun **$150**
Auto ejector. Gauges: 12, 16, 20, 28 and .410. Barrels: 26- to 36-inch, Full choke. Weight: 5¾ to 6½ pounds depending on gauge and barrel length. Plain pistol-grip stock and forend. Extras include checkered stock and forend, pistol-grip cap and knob forend. Known as Model 36. Also made in a Semi-Octagon Breech, Top Matted and Jacketed Breech (extra heavy) model. Made in Champion Lightweight as Model 39 in gauges 24, 28, 32 and .410; 44 and 45 caliber; 12 and 14mm with same extras—$200; add $100 in the smaller and obsolete gauges. Made 1909–1973.

Iver Johnson Hercules Grade Hammerless Double
Boxlock. (Some made with false sideplates.) Plain extractors and auto ejectors. Double or Miller Single triggers (both selective or non-selective). Gauges: 12, 16, 20 and .410. Barrel lengths: 26- to 32-inch, all chokes. Weight: 5¾ to 7¾ pounds depending on gauge and barrel length. Checkered stock and forend. Straight grip in .410 gauge

Iver Johnson Hercules Hammerless Double (cont.)
with both 2½ and 3-inch chambers. Extras include Miller Single Trigger, Jostam Anti-Flinch Recoil Pad and Lyman Ivory Sights at extra cost. Discont. 1946.
With double triggers, extractors **$510**
With double triggers, automatic ejectors **595**
Extra for non-selective single trigger **100**
Extra for selective single trigger **135**
Extra for .410 gauge **185**

Iver Johnson Matted Rib Single Shot Hammer Shotgun in smaller gauges **$220**
Same general specifications as Champion Grade except has solid matted top rib, checkered stock and forend. Weight: 6 to 6¾ pounds. Discont. 1948.

Iver Johnson Silver Shadow Over-and-Under Shotgun
Boxlock. Plain extractors. Double triggers or non-selective single trigger. 12 gauge, 3-inch chambers. Barrels: 26-inch IC/M; 28-inch IC/M; 28-inch M/F; 30-inch both F choke; vent rib. Weight: with 28-inch barrels, 7½ pounds. Checkered pistol-grip stock and forearm. Made by F.

Iver Johnson Silver Shadow

Iver Johnson Special Trap

Iver Johnson Super Trap

Iver Johnson Silver Shadow Over/Under (cont.)
Marocchi, Brescia, Italy, 1973–78.

Model 412 with double triggers	$400
Model 422 with single trigger	440

Iver Johnson Skeeter Model Hammerless Double
Boxlock. Plain extractors or selective auto ejectors. Double triggers or Miller Single Trigger (selective or non-selective). Gauges: 12, 16, 20, 28 and .410. 26- or 28-inch barrels, skeet boring standard. Weight: about 7½ pounds; less in smaller gauges. Pistol- or straight-grip stock and beavertail forend, both checkered, of select fancy figured black walnut. Extras include Miller Single Trigger, selective or non-selective, Jostam Anti-Flinch Recoil Pad and Lyman Ivory Rear Sight at additional cost. Discont. 1942.

With double triggers, plain extractors	$ 895
With double triggers, automatic ejectors	1050
Extra for non-selective single trigger	100
Extra for selective single trigger	135
Extra for .410 gauge	200
Extra for 28 gauge	300

Iver Johnson Special Trap Single Shot
Hammer Shotgun **$320**
Auto ejector. 12 gauge only. 32-inch barrel with vent rib, Full choke. Checkered pistol-grip stock and forend. Weight: about 7½ pounds. Discontinued 1942.

Iver Johnson Super Trap Hammerless Double
Boxlock. Plain extractors. Double triggers or Miller Single Trigger (selective or non-selective), 12 gauge only, 32-inch Full choke barrels, vent rib. Weight: about 8½ pounds. Checkered pistol-grip stock and beavertail forend, recoil pad. Discontinued 1942.

With double triggers	$895
Extra for non-selective single trigger	200
Extra for selective single trigger	200

SHOTGUNS

KBI/Baikal Hammerless Double

KBI/Baikal Over/Under

KBI/KASSNAR SHOTGUNS
Harrisburg, Pennsylvania

KBI/Baikal Hammerless Double **$250**
Boxlock. Double triggers with extractors. 12 gauge; 2¾-inch chambers. Barrels: 26-inch, IC/M; 28-inch, M/F with fixed chokes. Weight: 6¾ pounds. Made in Russia.

KBI/Baikal Over/Under
Boxlock. Single selective trigger with automatic ejectors or double triggers with extractors. Gauge: 12 or 20; 2¾-inch chambers. Barrels: 26-inch, IC/M; 28-inch, M/F; fixed chokes or screw-in choke tubes. Weight: 7 pounds. Checkered European walnut stock and forearm. Made in Russia.

12 Gauge	$295
20 Gauge	325

KBI/Baikal Single Shot $265
Hammerless. Automatic ejector. Manual safety. Gauges: 12 (2³/₄-inch chamber), 20 or .410 with 3-inch. Barrels: 26-, 28-inch with fixed chokes (IC, M, F). Weight: 5¹/₂ to 6 pounds. Made in Russia.

KBI/Fias Grade I Over/Under
Boxlock. Single selective trigger. Gauges: 12, 20, 28, .410; 3-inch chambers. Barrels: 26-inch IC/M; 28-inch M/F; screw-in choke tubes. Weight: 6¹/₂ to 7¹/₂ pounds. Checkered European walnut stock and forearm. Engraved receiver and blued finish.

12 Gauge Model	$375
20 Gauge Model	450
28 and .410 Models.......................	560

KBI/Kassnar Grade II Side-by-Side Shotgun $415
Gauges: 10, 12, 20, 28 and .410. 26- to 32-inch chromed barrels. Weight: 5 pounds (.410 ga.) to 9 pounds (10 ga.). Double-hinged triggers. Automatic top tang safety. Extractors. Casehardened antique silver receiver with fine scroll engraving. Checkered European walnut stock. Discontinued 1990.

KBI/Omega Over-Under
Boxlock. Single selective trigger. Gauges: 12, 20, 28, .410; 3-inch chambers. Barrels: 26- or 28-inch vent-rib with fixed chokes (IC/M or M/F). Automatic safety. Weight: 6 to 7¹/₂ pounds. Checkered European walnut stock and forearm. Discontinued 1992.

Deluxe Model (12 gauge only)	$350
Standard Model	305

=== **KESSLER ARMS CORP.** ===
Silver Creek, New York

Kessler Lever-Matic Repeating Shotgun $135
Lever action. Takedown. Gauges: 12, 16, 20; three-shot magazine. Barrels: 26-, 28-, 30-inch; F choke. Plain pistol-grip stock, recoil pad. Weight: 7 to 7³/₄ pounds. Discont. 1953.

Kessler Three Shot Bolt Action Repeater $75
Takedown. Gauges: 12, 16, 20. Two-shell detachable box magazine. Barrels: 28-inch in 12 and 16 gauge; 26-inch in 20 gauge; Full choke. Weight: 6¹/₄ to 7¹/₄ pounds depending on gauge and barrel length. Plain one-piece pistol-grip stock, recoil pad. Made 1951-53.

=== **H. KRIEGHOFF JAGD UND** ===
SPORTWAFFENFABRIK
Ulm (Donau), West Germany

Krieghoff Model 32 Monte Carlo

Krieghoff Model 32 San Remo

Krieghoff Model 32 Four-barrel Skeet Set
Over-and-under gun with four sets of matched barrels in 12, 20, 28 and .410 gauge, in fitted case. Available in six grades that differ in quality of engraving and wood. Discontinued 1979.

Standard Grade	$ 4,595
München Grade	6,595
San Remo Grade	7,525
Monte Carlo Grade	13,950
Crown Grade.........................	15,925
Super Crown Grade	17,550
Exhibition Grade	29,950

Krieghoff Model 32 Standard Grade Over/Under
Similar to prewar Remington Model 23. Boxlock. Auto ejector. Single trigger. Gauges: 12, 20, 28, .410. Barrels: vent rib, 26¹/₂- to 32-inch, any chokes. Weight: 12 gauge field gun with 28-inch barrels, about 7¹/₂ pounds. Checkered pistol-grip stock and forearm of select walnut; available in field, skeet and trap styles. Made 1958–1981.

With one set of barrels	$1795
Low-rib Two-barrel Trap Combo..............	2995
Vandalia (high-rib) Two-barrel Trap Combo	3995

Krieghoff Model 32 Standard Field Gun

Krieghoff Model 32 Standard Single Shot Trap

Krieghoff Model 32 Standard Grade Single Shot Trap Gun $1595
Same action as over-and-under. 12 gauge. 32- or 34-inch barrel with high vent rib; M, IM, or F choke. Monte Carlo stock with recoil pad, beavertail forearm. Disc. 1979.

Krieghoff Model K-80
Over/Under Trap

Krieghoff Model S-5
Single Shot Trap

Krieghoff Teck
Over-and-Under

Krieghoff Model K-80
Refined and enhanced version of the Model 32. Single selective mechanical trigger, adjustable for position; release trigger optional. Fixed chokes or screw-in choke tubes. Interchangeable front barrel hangers to adjust point of impact. Quick-removable stock. Color casehardened or satin grey finished receiver; aluminum alloy receiver on lightweight models. Available in standard plus five engraved grades. Made 1980 to date. Standard grade shown except where noted.

SKEET MODELS

Skeet International	$4950
Skeet Special	4595
Skeet Standard Model	4295
Skeet w/Tubla Chokes	4750

SKEET SETS

Standard Grade 2-Barrel Set	$ 6,950
Standard Grade 4-Barrel Set	9,895
Bavaria Grade 4-Barrel Set	12,250
Danube Grade 4-Barrel Set	15,295
Gold Target Grade 4-Barrel Set	18,750

SPORTING MODELS

Pigeon	$4595
Sporting Clays	4950

TRAP MODELS

Trap Combo	$6995
Trap Single	4950
Trap Standard	4595
Trap Unsingle	5145
RT Models (Removable Trigger) **Add**	1385

Krieghoff Model KS-5 Single Shot Trap
Boxlock with no sliding top-latch. Adjustable or optional release trigger. Gauge: 12 with 2 3/4-inch chamber. Barrel: 32-, 34-inch with fixed choke or screw-in tubes. Weight: 8 1/2 pounds. Adjustable or Monte Carlo European walnut stock. Blue or nickeled receiver. Made from 1980 to date.

Standard Model w/Fixed Chokes	$2150
Standard Model w/Tubes	2595
Special Model w/Adjustable Rib & Stock	2850

Krieghoff Neptun Drilling $8795
Same general specifications as Trumpf model, except has sidelocks with hunting scene engraving. Currently manufactured.

Krieghoff Neptun-Primus Drilling $10,250
Deluxe version of Neptun model; has detachable sidelocks, higher grade engraving and fancier wood. Currently manufactured.

Krieghoff Teck Over/Under Rifle-Shotgun $4550
Boxlock. Kersten double crossbolt system. Steel or dural receiver. Split extractor or ejector for shotgun barrel. Single or double triggers. Gauges: 12, 16, 20; latter with either 2 3/4- or 3-inch chamber. Calibers: 22 Hornet, 222 Rem., 222 Rem. Mag., 7×57r5, 7×64, 7×65r5, 30-30, 300 Win. Mag., 30-06, 308, 9.3×74R. 25-inch barrels with solid rib, folding leaf rear sight, post or bead front sight; over barrel is shotgun, under barrel rifle (later fixed or interchangeable; extra rifle barrel, $175). Weight: 7.9 to 9.5 pounds depending on type of receiver and caliber. Checkered pistol-grip stock with cheekpiece and semibeavertail forearm of figured walnut, sling swivels. Made 1967 to date. *Note:* This combination gun is similar in appearance to the same model shotgun.

Krieghoff Teck Over-and-Under Shotgun $3550
Boxlock. Kersten double crossbolt system. Auto ejector. Single or double triggers. Gauges: 12, 16, 20; latter with either 2 3/4- or 3-inch chambers. 28-inch vent-rib barrel, M/F choke. Weight: about 7 pounds. Checkered walnut pistol-grip stock and forearm. Made 1967–1989.

Krieghoff Trumpf Drilling $5195
Boxlock. Steel or dural receiver. Split extractor or ejector for shotgun barrels. Double triggers. Gauges: 12, 16, 20; latter with either 2 3/4- or 3-inch chambers. Calibers: 243,

Krieghoff Trumpf Drilling

Krieghoff Ulm Over-and-Under

Krieghoff ULM-P Live Pigeon

Krieghoff Trumpf Drilling (cont.)
6.5×57r5, 7×57r5, 7×65r5, 30-06; other calibers available. 25-inch barrels with solid rib, folding leaf rear sight, post or bead front sight; rifle barrel soldered or free floating. Weight: 6.6 to 7.5 pounds depending on type of receiver, gauge and caliber. Checkered pistol-grip stock with cheekpiece and forearm of figured walnut, sling swivels. Made 1953 to date.

Krieghoff Ulm Over/Under Rifle-Shotgun $8595
Same general specifications as Teck model, except has sidelocks with leaf arabesque engraving. Made from 1963 to date. *Note:* This combination gun is similar in appearance to the same model shotgun.

Krieghoff Ulm Over-and-Under Shotgun $7395
Same general specifications as Teck model, except has sidelocks with leaf arabesque engraving. Made 1958 to date.

Krieghoff ULM-P Live Pigeon Gun
Sidelock. Gauge: 12. 28- and 30-inch barrels. Chokes: F/IM Weight: 8 pounds. Oil-finished, fancy English walnut stock with semibeavertail forearm. Light scrollwork engraving. Tapered, vent rib. Made from 1983 to date.
Bavaria **$9950**
Standard **8550**

Krieghoff Ulm-Primus Over-and-Under $7995
Deluxe version of Ulm model; detachable sidelocks, higher grade engraving and fancier wood. Made 1958 to date.

Krieghoff Ulm-Primus O/U Rifle-Shotgun $8595
Deluxe version of Ulm model; has detachable sidelocks, higher grade engraving and fancier wood. Made 1963 to date. *Note:* This combination gun is similar in appearance to the same model shotgun.

Krieghoff ULM-S Skeet Gun
Sidelock. Gauge: 12. Barrel: 28-inch. Chokes: skeet/skeet. Other specifications similar to the Model ULM-P. Made 1983–86.
Bavaria **$6995**
Standard **5695**

Krieghoff ULM-T O/U Live Trap Gun
Over/under sidelock. Gauge: 12. 30-inch barrel. Tapered vent rib. Chokes: IM/F.; optional screw-in choke. Custom grade versions command a higher price. Discontinued 1986.
Bavaria **$6950**
Standard **5700**

Lanber Model 844 MST
Magnum Over/Under

LANBER SHOTGUNS
Spain

Lanber Model 844 MST Magnum O/U $350
Field grade. Gauge: 12. 3-inch Mag. chambers. 30-inch flat vent-rib barrels. Chokes: M/F. Weight: 7 lbs. 7 oz. Single selective trigger. Blued barrels and engraved receiver. European walnut stock with hand-checkered pistol grip and forend. Made from 1984 to date.

**Lanber Model 2004 LCH
Field Grade Over/Under**

Lanber Model 2008 LCH Skeet

Lanber Model 2009 LCH Trap

Lanber Model 2004 LCH O/U **$525**
Field grade. Gauge: 12. 2³/₄-inch chambers. 28-inch flat
vent-rib barrels. 5 interchangeable choke tubes: cyl., IC,
M, IM, F. Weight: about 7 pounds. Single selective trigger.
Engraved silver receiver with fine-line scroll. Walnut stock
with checkered pistol grip and forend. Rubber recoil pad.
Made from 1984 to date.

Lanber Model 2008 LCH O/U Skeet **$630**
Gauge: 12. 28-inch vent-rib barrels. 5 interchangeable
choke tubes: same as Model 2004 LCH. Single selective
trigger. Auto safety. Blued barrels and engraved receiver.
Hand-checkered European walnut stock with pistol grip.
Made from 1984 to date.

Lanber Model 2009 LCH O/U Trap **$675**
Gauge: 12. 30-inch vent-rib barrels. 3 interchangeable
choke tubes: M, IM, F. Manual safety. Other specifications
same as Model 2008 LCH Skeet. Made from 1984 to date.

CHARLES LANCASTER
London, England

**Lancaster "Twelve-Twenty" Double Barrel
Shotgun** **$12,250**
Sidelock, self-opener. Gauge: 12. Barrels: 24 to 30 inches
standard. Weight: about 5³/₄ pounds. Elaborate metal
engraving. Highest quality English or French walnut buttstock and forearm. Imported by Stoeger in the 1950s.

JOSEPH LANG & SONS
London, England

Highest Quality Over/Under Shotgun **$14,600**
Sidelock. Gauges: 12, 16, 20, 28 and .410. Barrels: 25 to
30 inches standard. Highest grade English or French walnut buttstock and forearm. Selective single trigger. Imported by Stoeger in 1950s.

LAURONA SHOTGUNS
Spain

Laurona Grand Trap Combo
Same general specifications as Model 300, except supplied
with 29-inch over/under barrels, screw-in choke tubes and
34-inch single barrel. Discontinued 1992.
Model GTO (top single) **$1695**
Model GTU (bottom single) 1695
Extra Field O/U barrels (12 or 20 ga.), **add** 560

Laurona Silhouette 300 Over/Under
Boxlock. Single selective trigger. Selective automatic
ejectors. Gauge: 12; 2³/₄-, 3- or 3¹/₂-inch chambers. 28- or
29-inch vent-rib barrels with flush or knurled choke tubes.
Weight: 7³/₄ to 8 pounds. Checkered pistol-grip European
walnut stock and beavertail forend. Engraved receiver with
silvered finish and black chrome barrels. Made 1988–1992.
Model 300 Sporting Clays . . . . **$ 995**
Model 300 Trap 1015
Model 300 Ultra-Magnum 975

SHOTGUNS

Laurona Grand Trap-GTO

Laurona Model 82 Super Game

Laurona Model 83M Multichoke

Laurona Model 84S Super Trap

Laurona Super Model Over/Under Shotguns
Boxlock. Single selective or twin single triggers. Selective automatic ejectors. Gauges: 12 or 20; 2³/₄- or 3-inch chambers. 26-, 28- or 29-inch vent-rib barrels with fixed chokes or screw-in choke tubes. Weight: 7 to 7¹/₄ pounds. Checkered pistol-grip European walnut stock. Engraved receiver with silvered finish and black chrome barrels. Made from 1985 to date.

Model 82 Super Game (discontinued)	$ 795
Model 83 MG Super Game	925
Model 84 S Super Trap	1025
Model 85 MG Super Game	935
Model 85 MG 2-Barrel Set	1325
Model 85 MS Special Sporting (discontinued)	950
Model 85 MS Super Trap	1025
Model 85 MS Pigeon	995
Model 85 S Super Skeet	995

LEBEAU-COURALLY SHOTGUNS
Belgium

Lebeau-Courally Boxlock Side-by-Side
Shotguns **$8595**
Gauges: 12, 16, 20 and 28. barrels. 26- to 30-inch. Weight: 6¹/₂ pounds average. Checkered, hand-rubbed, oil-finished, straight-grip stock of French walnut. Classic forend. Made from 1986 to date.

LEFEVER ARMS COMPANY
Syracuse and Ithaca, N.Y.

Lefever sidelock hammerless double-barrel shotguns were made by Lefever Arms Company of Syracuse, New York, from about 1885–1915 (serial numbers 1 to 70,000) when the firm was sold to Ithaca Gun Company of Ithaca, New York. Production of these models was continued at the Ithaca plant until 1919 (serial numbers 70,001 to 72,000). Grades listed are those that appear in the last catalog of the Lefever Gun Company, Syracuse. In 1921, Ithaca introduced the boxlock Lefever Nitro Special double, followed in 1934 by the Lefever Grade A; there also were two single barrel Lefevers made from 1927–1942. Manufacture of Lefever brand shotguns was discontinued in 1948. *Note:* "New Lefever" boxlock shotguns made circa 1904–1906 by D. M. Lefever Company, Bowling Green, Ohio, are included in a separate listing.

Lefever A Grade

Lefever A Grade Hammerless Double Barrel Shotgun
Boxlock. Plain extractors or auto ejector. Single or double triggers. Gauges: 12, 16, 20, .410. Barrels: 26- to 32-inch, standard chokes. Weight: about 7 pounds in 12 gauge. Checkered pistol-grip stock and forearm. Made 1934–1942.

With plain extractors, double triggers	**$750**
Extra for automatic ejector	**100**
Extra for single trigger	**100**
Extra for beavertail forearm	**75**

Lefever A Grade Skeet

Lefever A Grade Skeet Model **$1095**
Same as A Grade, except standard features include auto ejector, single trigger, beavertail forearm; 26-inch barrels, skeet boring. Discontinued 1942.

Lefever Single Shot Trap

Lefever Hammerless Single Shot Trap Gun $425

Boxlock. Ejector. 12 gauge only. Barrel lengths: 30- or 32-inch. Vent rib. Weight: about 8 pounds. Checkered pistol-grip stock and forend, recoil pad. Made 1927–1942.

Lefever Long Range

Lefever Long Range Hammerless Single Barrel Field Gun $275

Boxlock. Plain extractor. Gauges: 12, 16, 20, .410. Barrel lengths: 26- to 32-inch. Weight: 5½ to 7 pounds depending on gauge and barrel length. Checkered pistol-grip stock and forend. Made 1927–1942.

Lefever Nitro Special

Lefever Nitro Special Hammerless Double

Boxlock. Plain extractors. Single or double triggers. Gauges: 12, 16, 20, .410. Barrels: 26- to 32-inch, standard chokes. Weight: about 7 pounds in 12 gauge. Checkered pistol-grip stock and forend. Made 1921–1948.
With double triggers $495
With single trigger 625

Lefever F Grade

Lefever EE Grade

Lefever DS Grade

Lefever DE Grade

Lefever CE Grade

Lefever BE Grade

Lefever Side Lock Hammerless Doubles

Plain extractors or auto ejectors. Double triggers or selective single trigger. Gauges: 10, 12, 16, 20. Barrels: 26- to 32-inch, standard choke combinations. Weight: 5¾ to 10½ pounds depending on gauge and barrel length. Checkered walnut straight-grip or pistol-grip stock and forearm. Grades differ chiefly in quality of workmanship, engraving, wood, checkering, etc.; general specifications are the same. DS and DSE Grade guns lack the cocking indicators found on all other models. Suffix "E" means model has auto ejector; also standard on A, AA, Optimus, and Thousand Dollar Grade guns.

H Grade	$ 1195
HE Grade	1550
G Grade	1325
GE Grade	1650
F Grade	1450
FE Grade	1825
E Grade	1650
EE Grade	2100
D Grade	1995
DE Grade	2595
DS Grade	995
DSE Grade	1295
C Grade	3150
CE Grade	5250

SHOTGUNS

Lefever A Grade

Lefever Optimus Grade

D. M. Lefever No. 5, B Grade

D. M. Lefever No. 8, E Grade

Lefever Side Lock Hammerless Doubles (cont.)

B Grade	$ 4,895
BE Grade	7,995
A Grade	15,000
AA Grade	20,000
Optimus Grade	25,000
Thousand Dollar Grade	35,000
Extra for single trigger	500

D. M. LEFEVER COMPANY
Bowling Green, Ohio

In 1901, D. M. "Uncle Dan" Lefever, founder of the Lefever Arms Company, withdrew from that firm to organize D. M. Lefever, Sons & Company (later D. M. Lefever Company) to manufacture the "New Lefever" boxlock double and single barrel shotguns. These were produced at Bowling Green, Ohio, from about 1904–1906, when Dan Lefever died and the factory closed permanently. Grades listed are those that appear in the last catalog of D. M. Lefever Co.

D. M. Lefever O Excelsior Grade

D. M. Lefever Hammerless Double Barrel Shotguns

"New Lefever." Boxlock. Auto ejector standard on all grades except O Excelsior, which was regularly supplied with plain extractors (auto ejector offered as an extra). Double triggers or selective single trigger (latter standard on Uncle Dan Grade, extra on all others). Gauges: 12, 16, 20. Barrels: any length and choke combination. Weight: 5½ to 8 pounds depending on gauge and barrel length. Checkered walnut straight-grip or pistol-grip stock and forearm. Grades differ chiefly in quality of workmanship, engraving, wood, checkering, etc.; general specifications are the same.

O Excelsior Grade with plain extractors	$ 2,495
O Excelsior Grade with automatic ejectors	2,895
No. 9, F Grade	3,430
No. 8, E Grade	4,375
No. 6, C Grade	5,195
No. 5, B Grade	6,895
No. 4, AA Grade	10,000
Uncle Dan Grade	15,000
Extra for single trigger	400

D. M. Lefever Single Barrel Trap Gun $4995

Boxlock. Auto ejector. 12 gauge only. Barrels: 26- to 32-inches, Full choke. Weight: 6½ to 8 pounds, depending on barrel length. Checkered walnut pistol-grip stock and forearm.

D. M. Lefever Single Trap

Marlin Model 17 Standard

MARLIN FIREARMS CO.
North Haven (formerly New Haven), Conn.

Marlin Model 16 Visible Hammer Slide Action Repeater
Takedown. 16 gauge. 5-shell tubular magazine. Barrels: 26- or 28-inch, standard chokes. Weight: about 6¼ pounds. Pistol-grip stock, grooved slide handle; checkering on higher grades. Difference among grades is in quality of wood, engraving on Grades C and D. Made 1904–1910.

Grade A	$ 315
Grade B	395
Grade C	525
Grade D	1095

Marlin Model 17 Brush Gun **$350**
Same as Model 17 Standard, except has 26-inch barrel, cylinder bore. Weight: about 7 pounds. Made 1906–1908.

Marlin Model 17 Riot Gun **$325**
Same as Model 17 Standard, except has 20-inch barrel, cylinder bore. Weight: about 6⅞ pounds. Made 1906–1908.

Marlin Model 17 Standard Visible Hammer Slide Action Repeater **$315**
Solid frame. 12 gauge. 5-shot tubular magazine. Barrels: 30- or 32-inch, Full choke. Weight: about 7½ pounds. Straight-grip stock, grooved slide handle. Made 1906–1908.

Marlin Model 19 Visible Hammer Slide Action Repeater
Similar to Model 1898, but improved, lighter weight, with two extractors, matted sighting groove on receiver top. Weight: about 7 pounds. Made 1906–1907.

Grade A	$ 295
Grade B	395
Grade C	525
Grade D	1095

Marlin Model 21 Trap Visible Hammer Slide Action Repeater
Similar to Model 19 with same general specifications, except has straight-grip stock. Made 1907–1909.

Grade A	$ 325
Grade B	435
Grade C	550
Grade D	1125

Marlin Model 24 Visible Hammer Slide Action Repeater
Similar to Model 19, but has improved takedown system and auto recoil safety lock, solid matted rib on frame. Weight: about 7½ pounds. Made 1908–1915.

Grade A	$ 315
Grade B	415
Grade C	575
Grade D	1150

Marlin Model 26 Brush Gun **$235**
Same as Model 26 Standard, except has 26-inch barrel, cylinder bore. Weight: about 7 pounds. Made 1909–1915.

Marlin Model 26 Riot Gun **$210**
Same as Model 26 Standard, except has 20-inch barrel, cylinder bore. Weight: about 6⅞ pounds. Made 1909–1915.

Marlin Model 26 Standard Visible Hammer Slide Action Repeater **$230**
Similar to Model 24 Grade A, except solid frame and straight-grip stock. 30- or 32-inch Full choke barrel. Weight: about 7⅛ pounds. Made from 1909–1915.

Marlin Model 28 Hammerless Slide Action Repeater
Takedown. 12 gauge. 5-shot tubular magazine. Barrels: 26-, 28-, 30-, 32-inch, standard chokes; matted-top barrel except on Model 28D which has solid matted rib. Weight: about 8 pounds. Pistol-grip stock, grooved slide handle; checkering on higher grades. Grades differ in quality of wood, engraving on Models 28C and 28D. Made 1913–1922; all but Model 28A discont. in 1915.

Model 28A	$ 300
Model 28B	400
Model 28C	500
Model 28D	1195

Marlin Model 28T Trap Gun **$515**
Same as Model 28, except has 30-inch matted-rib barrel, Full choke, straight-grip stock with high-fluted comb of fancy walnut, checkered. Made in 1915.

Marlin Model 28TS Trap Gun **$295**
Same as Model 28T, except has matted-top barrel, plainer stock. Made in 1915.

Marlin Model 30 Field Gun **$285**
Same as Model 30 Grade B, except has 25-inch barrel, Mod. choke, straight-grip stock. Made 1913–1914.

SHOTGUNS

Marlin Model 28B

Marlin Model 30 Grade D

Marlin Model 30 Visible Hammer Slide Action Repeater
Similar to Model 16, but with Model 24 improvements. Made 1910–1914.

Grade A	$ 295
Grade B	420
Grade C	545
Grade D	1210

Marlin Models 30A, 30B, 30C, 30D
Same as Model 30; designations were changed in 1915. Also available in 20 gauge with 25- or 28-inch barrel; matted-top barrel on all grades. Suffixes "A," "B," "C" and "D" correspond to former grades. Made in 1915.

Model 30A	$ 320
Model 30B	400
Model 30C	595
Model 30D	1075

Marlin Model 31 Hammerless Slide Action Repeater
Similar to Model 28, except scaled down for 16 and 20 gauges. Barrels: 25-inch (20 gauge only), 26-inch (16 gauge only), 28-inch; all with matted top; standard chokes. Weight: 16 ga., about 6¾ pounds; 20 ga., about 6 pounds. Pistol-grip stock, grooved slide handle; checkering on higher grades; straight-grip stock optional on Model 31D. Made 1915–1917; Model 31A until 1922.

Model 31A	$ 305
Model 31B	445
Model 31C	560
Model 31D	1215

Marlin Model 31F Field Gun $425
Same as Model 31B, except has 25-inch barrel, Modified choke, straight- or pistol-grip stock. Made 1915–17.

Marlin Model 42A Visible Hammer Slide Action Repeater $245
Similar to pre-World War I Model 24 Grade A with same general specifications, but not of as high quality. Made from 1922–1934.

Marlin Model 43 Hammerless Slide Action Repeater
Similar to pre-World War I Models 28A, 28T and 28TS, with same general specifications, but not of as high quality. Made 1923–1930.

Model 43A	$260
Model 43T	500
Model 43TS	525

Marlin Model 44 Hammerless Slide Action Repeater
Similar to pre-World War I Model 31A, with same general specifications, but not of as high quality. 20 gauge only. Model 44A is a standard grade field gun. Model 44S Special Grade has checkered stock and slide handle of fancy walnut. Made 1923–1935.

Model 44A	$310
Model 44S	415

Marlin Model 49 Visible Hammer Slide Action Repeating Shotgun $375
Economy version of Model 42A, offered as a bonus on the purchase of four shares of Marlin stock. About 3000 were made 1925–28.

Marlin Model 42A

Marlin Model 43A

Marlin Model 43T

Marlin Model 53

Marlin Model 55 Hunter

Marlin Model 55 Goose Gun

Marlin Model 55
Swamp Gun

SHOTGUNS

Marlin Model 53 Hammerless Slide Action Repeater $305
Similar to Model 43A, with same general specifications. Made 1929–1930.

Marlin Model 55 Goose Gun $175
Same as Model 55 Hunter, except chambered for 12-gauge 3-inch Magnum shell, has 36-inch barrel, Full choke, swivels and sling. Weight: about 8 pounds. Made 1962 to date.

Marlin Model 55 Hunter Bolt Action Repeater
Takedown. Gauges: 12, 16, 20. 2-shot clip magazine. 28-inch barrel (26-inch in 20 ga.), Full or adjustable choke. Plain pistol-grip stock; 12 ga. has recoil pad. Weight: about $7\frac{1}{4}$ pounds; 20 ga., $6\frac{1}{2}$ pounds. Made 1954–1965.
With plain barrel .... **$ 95**
With adjustable choke **115**

Marlin Model 55 Swamp Gun $125
Same as Model 55 Hunter except chambered for 12-gauge 3-inch Magnum shell, has $20\frac{1}{2}$-inch barrel with adjustable choke, sling swivels. Weight: about $6\frac{1}{2}$ pounds. Made 1963–65.

Marlin Model 55S Slug Gun $140
Same as Model 55 Goose Gun, except has 24-inch barrel, cylinder bore, rifle sights. Weight: about $7\frac{1}{2}$ pounds. Made 1974–79.

Marlin Model 59 Auto-Safe Bolt Action Single ... $85
Takedown. Auto thumb safety. 410 gauge. 24-inch barrel, Full choke. Weight: about 5 pounds. Plain pistol-grip stock. Made 1959–1961.

Marlin Model 60 Single Shot Shotgun $220
Visible hammer. Takedown. Boxlock. Automatic ejector. 12 gauge. 30- or 32-inch barrel, Full choke. Weight: about $6\frac{1}{2}$ pounds. Pistol-grip stock, beavertail forearm. *Note:* Only about 600 were produced in 1923.

Marlin Model 59
Bolt Action Single

Marlin Model 60
Single Shot

**Marlin Model 90
Standard Over-and-Under**

Marlin Model 120 Magnum

Marlin Model 410

Marlin Model 63 Hammerless Slide Action Repeater
Similar to Models 43A and 43T with same general specifications. Model 63TS Trap Special is same as Model 63T Trap Gun except stock style and dimensions to order. Made 1931–35.

Model 63A **$245**
Model 63T or 63TS **350**

Marlin Model 90 Standard Over-and-Under Shotgun
Hammerless. Boxlock. Double triggers; non-selective single trigger was available as an extra on prewar guns except .410. Gauges: 12, 16, 20, .410. Barrels: plain; 26-, 28- or 30-inch; chokes IC/M or M/F; barrel design changed in 1949, eliminating full-length rib between barrels. Weight: 12 ga., about 7½ lbs.; 16 and 20 ga., about 6¼ lbs. Checkered pistol-grip stock and forearm, recoil pad standard on prewar guns. Postwar production: Model 90-DT (double trigger), Model 90-ST (single trigger). Made 1937–1958.

With double triggers **$395**
With single trigger **475**

Marlin Model 120 Magnum Slide Action Repeater **$225**
Hammerless. Takedown. 12 gauge (3-inch). 4-shot tubular magazine. Barrels: 26-inch vent rib, IC; 28-inch vent rib, M choke; 30-inch vent rib, Full choke; 38-inch plain, Full choke; 40-inch plain, Full choke; 26-inch slug barrel with rifle sights, IC. Weight: about 7¾ pounds. Checkered pistol-grip stock and forearm, recoil pad. Made 1971–1985.

Marlin Model 120 Slug Gun **$200**
Same general specifications as Model 120 Magnum, except with 20-inch barrel and about ½ pound lighter in weight. No vent rib. Adjustable rear rifle sights; hooded front sight. Discontinued 1990.

Marlin Model 410 Lever Action Repeater **$525**
Action similar to that of Marlin Model 93 rifle. Visible hammer. Solid frame. .410 gauge (2½-inch shell). 5-shot tubular magazine. 22- or 26-inch barrel, Full choke. Weight: about 6 pounds. Plain pistol-grip stock and grooved beavertail forearm. Made 1929–1932.

Marlin Model 1898 Visible Hammer Slide Action Repeater
Takedown. 12 gauge. 5-shell tubular magazine. Barrels: 26-, 28-, 30-, 32-inch; standard chokes. Weight: about 7¼ pounds. Pistol-grip stock, grooved slide handle; checkering on higher grades. Difference among grades is in quality of wood, engraving on Grades C and D. Made 1898–1905. *Note:* This was the first Marlin shotgun.

Grade A (Field) . . . . **$ 350**
Grade B **495**
Grade C **695**
Grade D **1650**

Marlin Model 5510 Super Goose 10 . . . . **$175**
Similar to Model 55 Goose Gun, except chambered for 10 gauge 3½-inch Magnum shell, has 34-inch heavy barrel, Full choke. Weight: about 10½ pounds. Made 1976–1985.

Marlin Premier Mark I Slide Action Repeater . . . **$175**
Hammerless. Takedown. 12 gauge. Magazine holds 3 shells. Barrels: 30-inch Full choke, 28-inch M, 26-inch IC

**Marlin Model 5510
Super Goose 10**

Marlin Premier Mark I

Marlin Premier Mark IV

Marlin-Glenfield Model 50

Marlin Premier Mark I Slide Action (cont.)
or SK choke. Weight: about 6 pounds. Plain pistol-grip stock and forearm. Made in France 1960–63.

Marlin Premier Mark II and IV
Same as Premier Mark I, except engraved receiver (Mark IV is more elaborate), checkered stock and forearm, fancier wood. Made 1960–63.

Premier Mark II **$205**
Premier Mark IV (plain barrel) **275**
Premier Mark IV (vent-rib barrel) **325**

Marlin-Glenfield Model 50 Bolt Action Repeater . . **$65**
Similar to Model 55 Hunter, except chambered for 12-or 20-gauge, 3-inch Magnum shell; has 28-inch barrel in 12 gauge, 26-inch in 20 gauge, Full choke. Made 1966–1974.

Marlin-Glenfield 778 Slide Action Repeater
Hammerless. 12 gauge 2¾-inch or 3-inch. 4-shot tubular magazine. Barrels: 26-inch IC, 28-inch M, 30-inch Full, 38-inch MXR, 20-inch slug barrel. Weight: 7¾ pounds. Checkered pistol grip. Made from 1979–1984.
With plain barrel **$140**
With vent-rib barrel **175**

Maverick Model 60
Turkey/Deer Combo

MAVERICK ARMS, INC.
Eagle Pass, Texas

Maverick Model 60 Autoloading Shotgun
Gauge: 12; 2¾- or 3-inch chamber. 5-round capacity. Barrels: Magnum or non-Magnum; 24- or 28-inch with fixed choke or screw-in tubes; plain or vent rib; blued. Weight: 7¼ pounds. Black synthetic buttstock and forend. Made from 1993 to date.
Standard Model **$210**
Combo Model w/extra 18½″ bbl. **235**
Turkey/Deer Model (w/Ghost Ring sights) **245**

Maverick Model 88 Bullpup **$295**
Gauge: 12; 3-inch chamber. Barrel: 18½-inch with fixed choke; blued. Weight: 9½ pounds. Dual safeties: grip style and crossbolt. Fixed sights in carrying handle. High-impact black synthetic stock; trigger-forward bullpup configuration with twin pistol-grip design. Made from 1991 to date.

Maverick Model 88 Bullpup

Maverick Model 88 Pump Shotgun
Gauge: 12; 2¾- or 3-inch chamber. Barrel: 28 inches/M or 30 inches/F with fixed choke or screw-in tubes; plain or vent rib; blued. Weight: 7¼ pounds. Bead front sight. Black synthetic or wood buttstock and forend. Made from 1989 to date.
Synthetic stock w/plain bbl. **$150**

SHOTGUNS

**Maverick Model 88 Pump
Vent Rib**

Maverick Model 88 Pump Shotgun (cont.)
Synthetic stock w/vent-rib bbl.	**$160**
Synthetic Combo w/18½" bbl.	**180**
Wood stock w/vent-rib bbl./tubes	**175**
Wood Combo w/vent-rib bbl./tubes	**200**

Maverick Model 91 Pump Shotgun
Same as Model 88, except with 2¾-, 3- or 3½-inch chamber, 28-inch barrel with ACCU-full choke, crossbolt safety and synthetic stock only.
Synthetic stock w/plain bbl.	**$180**
Synthetic stock w/vent-rib bbl.	**210**

Maverick Model HS410 Pump Shotgun
Similar to the Model 88, except in .410 bore with 3-inch chamber. Blued 18½-inch barrel with muzzle brake. Weight: 6¼ pounds. Optional laser sight. Synthetic stock. Made from 1993 to date. A similar gun is marketed by Mossberg under the same model designation.
Standard Model	**$170**
Laser Model	**275**

══ GEBRÜDER MERKEL ══
Suhl, Germany

Merkel Model 8 Hammerless Double **$895**
Anson & Deeley boxlock action with Greener double-barrel hook lock. Double triggers. Extractors. Automatic safety. Gauges: 12, 16, 20; 2¾- or 3-inch chambers. 26- or 28-inch barrels with fixed standard chokes. Checkered European walnut stock, pistol-grip or English-style with or without cheek-piece. Scroll engraved receiver with tinted marble finish.

Merkel Model 100

Merkel Model 100 Over-and-Under Shotgun
Hammerless. Boxlock. Greener crossbolt. Plain extractor. Double triggers. Gauges: 12, 16, 20. Made with plain or ribbed barrels in various lengths and chokes. Plain finish, no engraving. Checkered forend and stock with pistol grip and cheekpiece or English style. Made prior to WWII.
With plain barrel	**$1095**
With ribbed barrel	**1150**

Merkel Model 101

Merkel Models 101 and 101E Over/Unders
Same as Model 100, except ribbed barrel standard, has separate extractors (ejectors on Model 101E), English engraving. Made prior to World War II.
Model 101	**$1250**
Model 101E	**1350**

Merkel Model 127

Merkel Model 127 Hammerless Sidelock Double **$15,750**
Holland & Holland system, hand-detachable locks. Auto ejectors. Double triggers. Made in all standard gauges, barrel lengths and chokes. Checkered forend and stock with pistol grip and cheekpiece or English style. This is a highest quality deluxe gun, elaborately engraved in arabesque or hunting scene pattern. Made prior to WW II.

Merkel Model 130

Merkel Model 130 Hammerless Boxlock Double **$8500**
Anson & Deeley system. Sideplates. Auto ejectors. Double triggers. Elaborate hunting scene or arabesque engraving. Made in all standard gauges, various barrel lengths and chokes. Checkered forend and stock with pistol grip and cheekpiece or English style. Made prior to WW II.

Merkel Model 147E

Merkel Model 147S

Merkel Model 47S

Merkel Model 147E Hammerless Boxlock Double Barrel Shotgun **$1595**

Anson & Deeley system. Auto ejectors. Double triggers. Gauges: 12, 16, 20 (3-inch chambers available in 12 and 20 gauge). Barrels: 26-inch standard, other lengths available; any standard choke combination. Weight: about 6½ pounds. Checkered straight-grip stock and forearm. Discontinued 1989.

Merkel Model 147S/47S & S Series Hammerless Doubles

Same general specifications as Model 147E, except has sidelocks engraved with arabesques, borders, scrolls or game scenes in varying degrees of elaborateness.

Model 47S	**$2995**
Model 147S	3795
Model 247S	4195
Model 347S	4550
Model 447S	4895

Merkel Models 200/200E, 201/201E, 202/202E (cont.)

pounds depending on barrel length and gauge. Checkered forend and stock with pistol grip and cheekpiece or English style. The 200, 201, and 202 differ in overall quality, engraving, wood, checkering, etc.; aside from the faux sideplates on Models 202 and 202E, general specifications are the same. Models 200, 201, 202, and 202E, all made before WW II, are discontinued.

Model 200	**$1295**
Model 200E	1595
Model 201	1625
Model 201E	1895
Model 202	2495
Model 202E	2795

SHOTGUNS

Merkel Model 201

Merkel Model 203E

Merkel Models 200, 200E, 201, 201E, 202 and 202E Over-and-Under Shotguns

Hammerless. Boxlock. Kersten double crossbolt. Scalloped frame. Sideplates on Models 202 and 202E. Arabesque or hunting engraving supplied on all except Models 200 and 200E. "E" models have ejectors, others have separate extractors. Signal pins. Double triggers. Gauges: 12, 16, 20, 24, 28, 32 (last three not available in postwar guns). Ribbed barrels in various lengths and chokes. Weight: 5¾ to 7½

Merkel Model 203E Over-and-Under Shotgun . . **$3495**

Hammerless. Hand-detachable sidelocks, Kersten fastening, auto ejectors, double triggers. Arabesque engraving standard, hunting engraving optional. Gauges: 12, 16, 20. Ribbed barrels in various lengths and chokes. Checkered forend and stock with pistol grip and cheekpiece or English style. Currently manufactured.

Merkel Model 204E Over-and-Under Shotgun . . **$4500**
Similar to Model 203E; has Merkel sidelocks, fine English engraving. Made prior to World War II.

Merkel Model 300E

Merkel Model 302

Merkel Models 300, 300E, 301, 301E and 302 O/U
Merkel-Anson system boxlock. Kersten double crossbolt, two underlugs, scalloped frame, sideplates on Model 302. Arabesque or hunting engraving. "E" models and Model 302 have auto ejectors, others have separate extractors. Signal pins. Double triggers. Gauges: 12, 16, 20, 24, 28, 32. Ribbed barrels in various lengths and chokes. Checkered forend and stock with pistol grip and cheekpiece or English style. Grades 300, 301 and 302 differ in overall quality, engraving, wood, checkering, etc.; aside from the dummy sideplates on Model 302, general specifications are the same. Manufactured prior to World War II.

Model 300	**$1850**
Model 300E	**1995**
Model 301	**3750**
Model 301E	**4875**
Model 302	**6495**

Merkel Model 303E Over/Under Shotgun **$10,500**
Similar to Model 203E. Has Kersten crossbolt, double underlugs, Holland & Holland-type hand-detachable sidelocks, auto ejectors. This is a finer gun than Model 203E. Currently manufactured.

Merkel Model 304E

Merkel Model 304E Over/Under Shotgun **$12,950**
Special version of the Model 303E-type, but higher quality throughout. This is the top grade Merkel over/under. Currently manufactured.

Merkel Model 400

Merkel Models 400, 400E, 401, 401E Over/Unders
Similar to Model 101 except have Kersten double crossbolt, arabesque engraving on Models 400 and 400E, hunting engraving on Models 401 and 401E, finer general quality. "E" models have Merkel ejectors, others have separate extractors. Made prior to World War II.

Model 400	**$1250**
Model 400E	**1395**
Model 401	**1450**
Model 401E	**1725**

Merkel O/U Combination
Model 210

**Merkel Over-and-Under Combination Guns
("Bock-Büchsflinten")**
Shotgun barrel over, rifle barrel under. Gauges: 12, 16, 20; calibers: 5.6×35 Vierling, 7×57r5, 8×57JR, 8×60R Magnum, 9.3×53r5, 9.3×72r5, 9.3×74R and others. Various barrel lengths, chokes and weights. Other specifications and values correspond to those of Merkel over/under shotguns listed below. Currently manufactured. Model 210 & 211 series discontinued 1992.

Models 410, 410E, 411E . . . . **see shotgun Models 400, 400E, 401, 401E respectively**
Models 210, 210E, 211, 211E, 212, 212E . . **see shotgun Models 200, 200E, 201, 201E, 202, 202E**

> **NOTE:** Merkel over/under guns were often supplied with accessory barrels, interchangeable to convert the gun into an arm of another type; for example, a set might consist of one pair each of shotgun, rifle and combination gun barrels. Each pair of interchangeable barrels has a value of approximately one-third that of the gun with which they are supplied.

**Merkel Anson Drilling
Model 144**

Merkel Anson Drillings

Three-barrel combination guns; usually made with double shotgun barrels, over rifle barrel, although "Doppel-büchsdrillingen" were made with two rifle barrels over and shotgun barrel under. Hammerless. Boxlock. Anson & Deeley system. Side clips. Plain extractors. Double triggers. Gauges: 12, 16, 20; rifle calibers: 7×57r5, 8×57JR and 9.3×74R are most common, but other calibers from 5.6mm to 10.75mm available. Barrels: standard drilling, 25.6 inches; short drilling, 21.6 inches. Checkered pistol-grip stock and forend. The three models listed differ chiefly in overall quality, grade of wood, etc.; general specifications are the same. Made prior to WW II.

Model 144 . . . . $7000
Model 142 5500
Model 145 5500

MIIDA SHOTGUNS

Manufactured for Marubeni America Corp., New York, N.Y., by Olin-Kodensha Co., Tochigi, Japan

Miida Model 612 Field Grade Over-and-Under . . $750
Boxlock. Auto ejectors. Selective single trigger. 12 gauge. Barrels: vent rib; 26-inch, IC/M; 28-inch, M/F choke. Weight: with 26-inch barrel, 6 lbs. 11 oz. Checkered pistol-grip stock and forearm. Made 1972–74.

Miida Model 2100 Skeet Gun **$850**
Similar to Model 612, except has more elaborate engraving on frame (50 percent coverage), skeet-style stock and forearm of select grade wood; 27-inch vent-rib barrels, SK choke. Weight: 7 lbs. 11 oz. Made 1972–74.

**Miida Model 2200T Trap Gun, Model 2200S
Skeet Gun** **$895**
Similar to Model 612, except more elaborate engraving on frame (60 percent coverage), trap- or skeet-style stock and semibeavertail forearm of fancy walnut, recoil pad on trap stock. Barrels: wide vent rib; 29¾-inch, IM/F choke on Trap Gun; 27-inch, SK choke on Skeet Gun. Weight: Trap, 7 lbs. 14 oz.; Skeet, 7 lbs. 11 oz. Made 1972–74.

**Miida Model 2300T Trap Gun, Model 2300S
Skeet Gun** **$950**
Same as Models 2200T and 2200S, except more elaborate engraving on frame (70% coverage). Made 1972–74.

Miida Model 612

Miida Model 2100

Miida Model 2200T

Miida Model 2300T

SHOTGUNS

Miida Grandee Model GRT

Miida Grandee Model GRT Trap Gun, Model IRS Skeet Gun $2195
Boxlock with sideplates. Frame, breech ends of barrels, trigger guard and locking lever fully engraved and gold inlaid. Auto ejectors. Selective single trigger. 12 gauge. Barrels: wide vent rib; 29-inch, Full choke on Trap Gun; 27-inch, SK choke on Skeet Gun. Weight: Trap, 7 lbs. 14 oz.; Skeet, 7 lbs. 11 oz. Trap- or skeet-style stock and semibeavertail forearm of extra fancy wood, recoil pad on trap stock. Made 1972–74.

MONTGOMERY WARD
See shotgun listings under "W."

MORRONE SHOTGUN
Manufactured by Rhode Island Arms Company, Hope Valley, R.I.

Morrone Standard Model 46 Over-and-Under . . . $725
Boxlock. Plain extractors. Non-selective single trigger. Gauges: 12, 20. Barrels: plain, vent rib; 26-inch IC/M; 28-inch M/F choke. Weight: about 7 lbs., 12 ga.; 6 lbs., 20 ga. Checkered straight- or pistol-grip stock and forearm. Made 1949–1953. *Note:* Less than 500 of these guns were produced, about 50 in 20 gauge; a few had vent-rib barrels. Value shown is for 12 gauge with plain barrels; the rare 20 ga. and vent-rib types should bring considerably more.

Mossberg Model 83D

Mossberg Model 85D

Mossberg Model 183K

Mossberg Model 185K

O. F. MOSSBERG & SONS, INC.
North Haven, Connecticut
Formerly of New Haven, Conn.

Mossberg Model 83D or 183D $100
3-shot. Takedown. .410-bore only. 2-shell fixed, top-loading magazine. 23-inch barrel with two interchangeable choke tubes (M/F). Later production had 24-inch barrel. Plain one-piece, pistol-grip stock. Weight: about 5½ pounds. Originally designated Model 83D, changed in 1947 to Model 183D. Made 1940–1971.

Mossberg Model 85D or 185D Bolt Action Repeating Shotgun $85
Takedown. 3-shot. 20 gauge only. 2-shell detachable box magazine. 25-inch barrel, three interchangeable choke tubes (F, M, IC). Later production had 26-inch barrel with F/IC choke tubes. Weight: about 6¼ pounds. Plain one-piece, pistol-grip stock. Originally designated Model 85D, changed in 1947 to Model 185D. Made 1940–1971.

Mossberg Model 183K $95
Same as Model 183D, except has 25-inch barrel with variable C-Lect-Choke instead of interchangeable choke tubes. Made 1953–1986.

Mossberg Model 185K $100
Same as Model 185D, except has variable C-Lect-Choke instead of interchangeable choke tubes. Made 1950–1963.

Mossberg Model 190D

Mossberg Model 195D

Mossberg Model 200K

Mossberg Model 395K

Mossberg Model 500 Accu-Steel
Pump Shotgun

Mossberg Model 190D **$95**
Same as Model 185D, except in 16 gauge. Weight: about
6 pounds. Made 1955–1971.

Mossberg Model 190K **$100**
Same as Model 185K, except in 16 gauge. Weight: about
6³/₄ pounds. Made 1956–1963.

Mossberg Model 195D **$100**
Same as Model 185D, except in 12 gauge. Weight: about
6³/₄ pounds. Made 1955–1971.

Mossberg Model 195K **$100**
Same as Model 185K, except in 12 gauge. Weight: about
7¹/₂ pounds. Made 1956–1963.

Mossberg Model 200D **$115**
Same as Model 200K, except with two interchangeable
choke tubes instead of C-Lect-Choke. Made 1955–59.

Mossberg Model 200K Slide Action Repeater . . . **$115**
12 gauge. 3-shot detachable box magazine. 28-inch barrel.
C-Lect-Choke. Plain pistol-grip stock. Black nylon slide
handle. Weight: about 7¹/₂ pounds. Made 1955–59.

Mossberg Model 385K **$100**
Same as Model 395K, except 20 gauge (3-inch), 26-inch
barrel with C-Lect-Choke. Weight: about 6¹/₄ pounds.
Made 1963–1983.

Mossberg Model 390K **$115**
Same as Model 395K, except 16 gauge (2³/₄-inch). Made
1963–1974.

Mossberg Model 395K Bolt Action Repeater . . . **$100**
Takedown. 3-shot (detachable-clip magazine holds two
shells). 12 gauge (3-inch chamber). 28-inch barrel with C-
Lect-Choke. Weight: about 7¹/₂ pounds. Monte Carlo stock
with recoil pad. Made 1963–1983.

Mossberg Model 395S Slugster **$130**
Same as Model 395K, except has 24-inch barrel, cylinder
bore, rifle sights, swivels and web sling. Weight: about 7
pounds. Made 1968–1981.

Mossberg Model 500 Accu-Steel Shotgun **$265**
Pump. Gauge: 12. 24- or 28-inch barrel. Weight: 7¹/₄
pounds. Checkered walnut-finished woodstock with ventilated recoil pad. Available with synthetic field or Speedfeed stocks. Drilled and tapped receivers, swivels and camo
sling on camo models. Made from 1987 to date.

Mossberg Model 500 Bantam Shotgun **$185**
Same as Model 500 Sporting Pump, except 20 or .410
gauge only. 22-inch w/ACCU-Choke tubes or 24-inch w/
F choke; vent rib. Scaled-down checkered hardwood stock.
Made from 1992 to date.

Mossberg Model 500 Bullpup Shotgun **$350**
Pump. Gauge: 12. 6- or 8-shot capacity. Barrel: 18¹/₂ to
20 inches. 26¹/₂ and 28¹/₂ inches overall. Weight: about
9¹/₂ pounds. Multiple independent safety systems. Dual
pistol grips, rubber recoil pad. Fully enclosed rifle-type
sights. Synthetic stock. Ventilated barrel heat shield.
Made 1987–1990.

Mossberg Model 500A Field

Mossberg Model 500AK
Field Grade

Mossberg Model 500AS
Field Grade Slugster

Mossberg Model 500ALDR
"L" Series

Mossberg Model 500 Camo Pump
Same as Model 500 Sporting Pump, except 12 gauge only. Receiver drilled and tapped. QD swivels and camo sling. Special camouflage finish.

Standard Model	**$195**
Combo Model (w/extra Slugster bbl.)	**250**

Mossberg Model 500 Field Grade Hammerless Slide Action Repeater
Pre-1977 type. Takedown. Gauges: 12, 16, 20, .410. 3-inch chamber (2³/₄-inch in 16 gauge). Tubular magazine holds five 2³/₄-inch shells or four three-inch. Barrels: plain; 30-inch regular or heavy Magnum, Full choke (12 ga. only); 28-inch, M or F; 26-inch, IC or adj. C-Lect-Choke; 24-inch Slugster, cylinder bore, with rifle sights. Weight: 5³/₄ to 8 pounds. Plain pistol-grip stock with recoil pad, grooved slide handle. After 1973, these guns have checkered stock and slide handle, Models 500AM and 500AS have receivers etched with game scenes. The latter has swivels and sling. Made 1962–1976.

Model 500A, 12 gauge	**$200**
Model 500AM, 12 gauge, heavy Magnum barrel	**200**
Model 500AK, 12 gauge, C-Lect-Choke	**225**
Model 500AS, 12 gauge, Slugster	**220**
Model 500B, 16 gauge	**200**
Model 500BK, 16 gauge, C-Lect-Choke	**235**
Model 500BS, 16 gauge, Slugster	**225**
Model 500C, 20 gauge	**200**
Model 500CK, 20 gauge, C-Lect-Choke	**240**
Model 500CS, 20 gauge, Slugster	**225**
Model 500E, .410 gauge	**240**
Model 500EK, .410 gauge, C-Lect-Choke	**275**

Mossberg Model 500 "L" Series
"L" in model designation. Same as pre-1977 Model 500 Field Grade, except not available in 16 gauge, has receiver etched with different game scenes; Accu-Choke with three interchangeable tubes (IC, M, F) standard, restyled stock and slide handle. Barrels: plain or vent rib; 30- or 32-inch, heavy, F choke (12 ga. Magnum and vent rib only); 28-inch, Accu-Choke (12 and 20 ga.); 26-inch F choke (.410 bore only); 18¹/₂-inch (12 ga. only), 24-inch (12 and 20 ga.) Slugster with rifle sights, cylinder bore. Weight: 6 to 8¹/₂ pounds. Intro. 1977.

Model 500ALD, 12 gauge, plain barrel (Disc. 1980)	**$210**
Model 500ALDR, 12 gauge, vent rib	**250**
Model 500ALMR, 12 ga., Heavy Duck Gun (Disc. 1980)	**250**
Model 500ALS, 12 gauge, Slugster (Disc. 1981)	**200**
Model 500CLD, 20 gauge, plain barrel (Disc. 1980)	**200**
Model 500CLDR, 20 gauge, vent rib	**250**
Model 500CLS, 20 gauge, Slugster (Disc. 1980)	**250**
Model 500EL, .410 gauge, plain barrel (Disc. 1980)	**200**
Model 500ELR, .410 gauge, vent rib	**250**

Mossberg Model 500 Mariner Shotgun   **$265**
Slide action. Gauge: 12. 18¹/₂ or 20-inch barrel. 6-shot and 8-shot respectively. Weight: 7¹/₄ pounds. High-strength synthetic buttstock and forend. Available in extra round-carrying speedfeed synthetic buttstock. All metal treated for protection against saltwater corrosion. Intro. 1987.

Mossberg Model 500 Muzzleloader Combo **$270**
Same as Model 500 Sporting Pump, except with extra 24-inch rifled 50-caliber muzzleloading barrel and ram rod. Made from 1992 to date.

Mossberg Model 500ATP6 Persuader

Mossberg Model 500 ATP6CN Persuader

Mossberg Model 500 ATP8S

Mossberg Model 500 Security Combo 6-S

Mossberg Model 500 Persuader Law Enforcement Shotgun

Similar to pre-1977 Model 500 Field Grade, except 12 gauge only, 6- or 8-shot, has 18½- or 20-inch plain barrel, cylinder bore, either shotgun or rifle sights, plain pistol-grip stock and grooved slide handle, sling swivels. Special Model 500ATP8-SP has bayonet lug, Parkerized finish. Currently manufactured.

Model 500ATP6, 6-shot, 18½-inch barrel, shotgun sights	**$185**
Model 500ATP6CN, 6-shot, nickel finish, "Cruiser" pistol grip	**190**
Model 500ATP6N, 6-shot, nickel finish, 2¾- or 3-inch Mag. shells	**190**
Model 500ATP6S, 6-shot, 18½" barrel, rifle sights	**185**
Model 500ATP8, 8-shot, 20-inch bbl., shotgun sights	**200**

Mossberg Model 500 Cruiser

Mossberg Model 500 Persuader (cont.)

Model 500ATP8S, 8-shot, 20-inch barrel, rifle sights	**$200**
Model 500ATP8-SP Special Enforcement	**250**
Model 500 Bullpup	**350**
Model 500 Security Combo Pack	**150**
Model 500 Cruiser with pistol grip	**155**

Mossberg Model 500APR
Pigeon Grade

Mossberg Model 500APTR
Pigeon Grade Trap

Mossberg Model 500 Regal

Mossberg Model 500AKR
Super Grade

Mossberg Model 500 Pigeon Grade

Same as Model 500 Super Grade, except higher quality with fancy wood, floating vent rib; field gun hunting dog etching, trap and skeet guns have scroll etching. Barrels: 30-inch, F choke (12 gauge only); 28-inch, M choke; 26-inch, SK choke or C-Lect-Choke. Made 1971–75.

Model 500APR, 12 gauge, Field, Trap or Skeet	**$350**
Model 500APKR, 12 gauge, Field Gun, C-Lect-Choke	**360**
Model 500 APTR, 12 gauge, Trap Gun, Monte Carlo stock	**425**
Model 500CPR, 20 gauge, Field or Skeet Gun	**375**
Model 500EPR, .410 gauge, Field or Skeet Gun	**375**

Mossberg Model 500 Pump Combo Shotgun ... $210

Gauges: 12 and 20. 24- and 28-inch barrel with adjustable rifle sights. Weight: 7 to 7¼ pounds. Available with blued or camo finish. Drilled and tapped receiver with sling swivels and a camo web sling. Made from 1987 to date.

Mossberg Model 500 Pump Slugster Shotgun

Gauge: 12. 24-inch barrel with adjustable rifle sights. Weight: 7 pounds. Camo finish. Drilled and tapped receiver with camo sling and swivels. Made 1987 to date.

Standard Barrel Model	**$195**
Rifled Barrel Model	**220**
Rifled Barrel w/Integral Scope Mount	**240**

Mossberg Model 500 Regal Slide Action Repeater

Similar to regular Model 500 except higher quality workmanship throughout. Gauges: 12 and 20. Barrels: 26- and 28-inch with various chokes, or Accu-Choke. Weight: 6¾ to 7½ pounds. Checkered walnut stock and forearm. Made 1985 to date.

Model 500 with Accu-Choke	**$185**
Model 500 with fixed choke	**170**

Mossberg Model 500 Sporting Pump

Gauges: 12, 20 or .410; 2¾- or 3-inch chamber. Barrels: 22 to 28 inches with fixed choke or screw-in tubes; plain or vent rib. Weight: 6¼ to 7¼ pounds. White bead front sight, brass mid-bead. Checkered hardwood buttstock and forend with walnut finish.

Standard Model	**$190**
Field Combo (w/extra Slugster bbl.)	**240**

Mossberg Model 500 Super Grade

Same as pre-1977 Model 500 Field Grade, except not made in 16 gauge, has vent-rib barrel, checkered pistol grip and slide handle. Made 1965–1976.

Model 500AR, 12 gauge	**$195**
Model 500AMR, 12 gauge, heavy Magnum bbl.	**220**
Model 500AKR, 12 gauge, C-Lect-Choke	**225**
Model 500CR, 20 gauge	**210**
Model 500CKR, 20 gauge, C-Lect-Choke	**295**
Model 500ER, .410 gauge	**190**
Model 500EKR, .410 gauge, C-Lect-Choke	**240**

**Mossberg Model 500 Turkey/Deer
Combination**

**Mossberg Model 500/410
Camper**

Mossberg Model 500 Turkey/Deer Combo **$255**
Pump. Gauge: 12. 20- and 24-inch barrels. Weight: 7¼ pounds. Drilled and tapped receiver, camo sling and swivels. Adjustable rifle sights and camo finish. Vent rib. Made from 1987 to date.

Mossberg Model 500 Turkey Gun **$260**
Same as Model 500 Camo Pump, except with 24-inch ACCU-Choke barrel with Extra Full choke tube and Ghost Ring sights. Made from 1992 to date.

Mossberg Model 500 Waterfowl/Deer Combo . . **$265**
Same general specifications as the Turkey/Deer Combo, except with either 28- or 30-inch barrel along with the 24-inch barrel. Made from 1987 to date.

Mossberg Model 500ATR Super Grade Trap . . . **$290**
Same as pre-1977 Model 500 Field Grade, except 12 gauge only with vent-rib barrel; 30-inch Full choke, checkered Monte Carlo stock with recoil pad, beavertail forearm (slide handle). Made 1968–1971.

**Mossberg Model 500DSPR Duck Stamp
Commemorative** **$645**
Limited edition of 1000 to commemorate the Migratory Bird Hunting Stamp Program. Same as Model 500DSPR Pigeon Grade 12-Gauge Magnum Heavy Duck Gun with heavy 30-inch vent-rib barrel, Full choke; receiver has special Wood Duck etching. Gun accompanied by a special wall plaque. Made in 1975. *Note:* Value is for gun in new, unfired condition.

Mossberg Model 500/410 Camper **$180**
Similar to regular Model 500 action, except in .410 only. Barrel: 18½-inch; IC choke. Synthetic pistol-grip stock, ribbed forearm. Made from 1985 to date.

Mossberg Model 590 Military Security Shotgun . **$275**
Same general specifications as the Model 590 Military, except there is no heat shield and gun has short pistol-grip style instead of buttstock. Weight: about 6¾ lbs. Made from 1987 to date.

Mossberg Model 590 Military Shotgun
Slide-action. Gauge: 12. 9-shot capacity. 20-inch barrel. Weight: about 7 pounds. Synthetic or hardwood buttstock and forend. Ventilated barrel heat shields. Equipped with bayonet lug. Blue or Parkerized finish. Made from 1987 to date.

Synthetic Model, blued	**$265**
Synthetic Model, Parkerized	285
Speedfeed Model, blued	280
Speedfeed Model, Parkerized	285
Intimidator Model w/Laser Sight, blued	365
Intimidator Model w/Laser Sight, Parkerized	375
For Ghost Ring Sight, **add**	50

Mossberg Model 595 Bolt Action Repeater **$135**
12 gauge only. 4-shot detachable magazine. 18½-inch barrel. Weight: about 7 pounds. Walnut finished stock with recoil pad and sling swivels. Made 1985–86.

SHOTGUNS

**Mossberg Model 590 Military
Shotgun**

**Mossberg Model 595
Bolt Action**

Mossberg Model 712 Slugster

Mossberg Model 835 "NWTF" Ulti-Mag™

Mossberg Model 5500
Accu-Choke

Mossberg Model 712 Autoloading Shotgun $250
Gas-operated, takedown, hammerless shotgun with 5-shot (4-shot w/3-inch chamber) tubular magazine. 12 gauge. Barrels: 28-inch vent rib or 24-inch plain barrel Slugster with rifle sights; ACCU-Choke tube system. Weight: 7½ pounds. Plain alloy receiver, top-mounted ambidextrous safety. Checkered walnut stained hardwood stock with recoil pad. Imported from Japan 1988–1990

Mossberg Model 835 Field Pump Shotgun
Similar to the Model 9600 Regal, except has walnut-stained hardwood stock and one ACCU-Choke tube only.
Standard Model $210
Turkey Model 205
Combo Model (24- & 28-inch bbls.) 240

Mossberg Model 835 "NWTF" Ulti-Mag™
Shotgun $375
National Wild Turkey Federation pump-action. Gauge: 12; 3½-inch chamber. 24-inch vent-rib barrel with four ACCU-MAG chokes. Realtree® Camo finish. QD swivel and post. Made 1989–1993.

Mossberg Model 835 Regal Ulti-Mag Pump
Gauge: 12; 3½-inch chamber. Barrels: 24- or 28-inch vent-rib with ACCU-Choke screw-in tubes. Weight: 7¾ pounds. White bead front, brass mid-bead. Checkered hardwood or synthetic stock with camo finish.
Special Model $210
Standard Model 280
Camo Synthetic Model 300
Combo Model 325

Mossberg Model 1000 Autoloading Shotgun
Gas-operated, takedown, hammerless shotgun with tubular magazine. Gauges: 12, 20; 2¾- or 3-inch chamber. Barrels: 22- to 30-inch vent rib w/fixed choke or ACCU-Choke tubes; or 22-inch plain barrel Slugster with rifle sights. Weight: 6½ to 7½ pounds. Scroll-engraved alloy receiver, crossbolt-type safety. Checkered American walnut buttstock and forend. Imported from Japan.
Junior Model, 20 ga., 22-inch bbl. $340
Standard Model with Fixed Choke 345
Standard Model with Choke Tubes 375

Mossberg Model 1000 Super Autoloading Shotgun
Similar to Model 1000, but in 12 gauge only with 3-inch chamber and new gas metering system. Barrels: 26-, 28- or 30-inch vent rib with ACCU-Choke tubes.
Standard Model w/Choke Tubes $395
Waterfowler Model (Parkerized) 425

Mossberg Model 1000S Super Skeet $495
Similar to Model 1000 in 12 or 20 gauge, except with all-steel receiver and vented jug-type choke for reduced muzzle jump. Bright-point front sight and brass mid-bead. 1 and 2 oz. forend cap weights.

Mossberg Model 5500 Autoloading Shotgun
Gas-operated. Takedown. 12 gauge only. 4-shot magazine (3-shot with 3-inch shells). Barrels: 18½- to 30-inch; various chokes. Checkered walnut finished hardwood. Made 1985–86.
Model 5500 w/ACCU-Choke $250
Model 5500 Modified Junior 255
Model 5500 Slugster 265
Model 5500 12 gauge 225
Model 5500 Guardian 215

Mossberg Model 5500 MKII Autoloading Shotgun
Same as Model 5500, except equipped with two Accu-Choke barrels: 26-inch ported for non-Magnum 2¾-inch shells; 28-inch for Magnum loads. Made 1988–1993.
Standard Model $270
Camo Model 285
NTWF Mossy Oak Model 295

Mossberg Model 6000 Auto Shotgun $240
Similar to the Model 9200 Regal, except has 28-inch vent-rib barrel with mod. ACCU-Choke tube only. Made from 1993 to date.

Mossberg Model 9200 Camo Shotgun
Similar to the Model 9200 Regal, except has synthetic stock and forend and is completely finished in camouflage pattern (incl. barrel). Made from 1993 to date.
Standard Model (OFM Camo) $295
Turkey Model (Mossy Oak® camo) 325
Combo Model (24- & 28-inch bbls. w/OFM Camo) 375

Mossberg Model 9200 Regal

Mossberg Model HS410 Home
Security Shotgun

Mossberg Model 9200 Regal Autoloader
Gauge: 12; 3-inch chamber. Barrels: 24- to 28-inch w/
ACCU-Choke tubes; plain or vent rib. Weight: 7¼ to 7½
pounds. Checkered hardwood buttstock and forend with
walnut finish. Made from 1992 to date.

Model 9200 w/ACCU-Choke **$280**
Model 9200 w/rifled barrel **295**
Model 9200 Combo (w/extra Slugster bbl.) **330**

Mossberg Model 9200 USST Autoloader **$280**
Similar to the Model 9200 Regal, except has 26-inch vent-
rib barrel w/ACCU-Choke tubes. "United States Shooting
Team" engraved on receiver. Made from 1993 to date.

Mossberg Model HS410 Home Security Pump Shotgun
Gauge: .410; 3-inch chamber. Barrel: 18½-inch with muzzle brake; blued. Weight: 6¼ pounds. Synthetic stock and
pistol-grip slide. Optional laser sight. Made from 1990 to
date. A similar version of this gun is marketed by Maverick
Arms under the same model designation.

Standard Model **$190**
Laser Model **340**

Mossberg "New Haven Brand" Shotguns
Promotional models, similar to their standard guns but
plainer in finish, are marketed by Mossberg under the
"New Haven" brand name. Values generally are about 20
percent lower than for corresponding standard models.

Navy Arms Model 83

Navy Arms Model 100/150

NAVY ARMS SHOTGUNS
Ridgefield, New Jersey

Navy Arms Model 83/93 Bird Hunter Over/Under
Hammerless. Boxlock, engraved receiver. Gauges: 12 and
20; 3-inch chambers. Barrels: 28-inch chrome lined with
double vent-rib construction. Checkered European walnut
stock and forearm. Gold plated triggers. Made 1984–1990.

Model 83 w/Extractors **$235**
Model 93 w/Ejectors **275**

Navy Arms Model 95/96 Over/Under Shotgun
Same as the Model 83/93, except with five interchangeable
choke tubes. Imported from Italy. Discontinued 1990.

Model 95 w/Extractors **$325**
Model 96 w/Ejectors **395**

Navy Arms Model 100/150 Field Hunter Double Barrel Shotgun
Boxlock. Gauges: 12 and 20. Barrels: 28-inch chrome lined.
Checkered European walnut stock and forearm. Made
1984–1990.

Model 100 . . . . **$275**
Model 150 (auto ejectors) **375**

Navy Arms Model 410 Over/Under Shotgun **$240**
Hammerless, takedown shotgun with engraved chrome
receiver. Single trigger. .410 gauge w/3-inch chambers.
Barrels: 26-inch (F/F or SK/SK); vent rib. Weight: 6¼
pounds. Checkered European walnut buttstock and forend.
Imported from Italy since 1986.

SHOTGUNS

New England Firearms
NWTF Turkey Special

New England Firearms
Tracker II Rifled Slug Gun

New England Firearms
Turkey/Goose Shotgun

NEW ENGLAND FIREARMS
Gardner, Massachusetts

New England Firearms NWTF Turkey Special .. **$150**
Similar to Turkey and Goose Model, except has 24-inch plain barrel with screw-in Turkey Full choke tube. Mossy Oak Camo finish on entire gun. Made from 1992 to date.

New England Firearms Pardner Shotgun
Takedown. Side lever. Single barrel. Gauges: 12, 20 and .410 w/3-inch chamber; 16 and 28 w/2³/4-inch chamber. Barrel: 26- or 28-inch, plain; fixed choke. Weight: 5–6 pounds. Bead front sight. Pistol grip-style hardwood stock with walnut finish. Made from 1988 to date.
Standard Model **$75**
Youth Model **80**

New England Firearms Tracker Slug Gun
Similar to Pardner Model, except in 12 or 20 gauge only. Barrel: 24-inch with cylinder choke or rifled slug (Tracker II). Weight: 6 pounds. American hardwood stock with walnut or camo finish, schnabel forend, sling swivel studs. Made from 1992 to date.
Tracker Slug .... **$ 95**
Tracker II (rifled bore) **100**

New England Firearms Turkey and Goose Gun
Similar to Pardner Model, except chambered in 10 gauge w/3¹/2-inch chamber. 28-inch plain barrel w/F choke. Weight: 9¹/2 pounds. American hardwood stock with walnut or camo finish. Made from 1992 to date.
Standard Model **$110**
Camo Model **120**

NIKKO FIREARMS LTD.
Tochigi, Japan
See listings under Golden Eagle Firearms, Inc.

Noble Model 65

NOBLE MANUFACTURING CO.
Haydenville, Massachusetts

Noble Series 602 and 70 are similar in appearance to the corresponding Model 66 guns.

Noble Model 40 Hammerless Slide Action
Repeating Shotgun **$110**
Solid frame. 12 gauge only. 5-shell tubular magazine. 28-inch barrel with ventilated Multi-Choke. Weight: about 7¹/2 pounds. Plain pistol-grip stock, grooved slide handle. Made 1950–55.

Noble Model 50 .... **$100**
Same as Model 40, except without Multi-Choke. M or F choke barrel. Made 1953–55.

Noble Model 60 Hammerless Slide Action
Repeating Shotgun **$155**
Solid frame. 12 and 16 gauge. 5-shot tubular magazine. 28-inch barrel with adjustable choke. Plain pistol-grip stock with recoil pad, grooved slide handle. Weight: about 7¹/2 pounds. Made 1955–1966.

Noble Model 65 .... **$135**
Same as Model 60, except without adjustable choke and recoil pad. M or F choke barrel. Made 1955–1966.

Noble Model 66RCLP

Noble Model 66XL

Noble Model 80

Noble Model 66CLP $125
Same as Model 66RCLP, except has plain barrel. Introduced in 1967. Discontinued.

Noble Model 66RCLP Hammerless Slide Action Repeating Shotgun $165
Solid frame. Key lock fire control mechanism. Gauges: 12, 16. 3-inch chamber in 12 gauge. 5-shot tubular magazine. 28-inch barrel, vent rib, adjustable choke. Weight: about 7 1/2 pounds. Checkered pistol-grip stock and slide handle, recoil pad. Made 1967–1970.

Noble Model 66RLP $145
Same as Model 66RCLP, except with F or M choke. Made 1967–1970.

Noble Model 66XL $125
Same as Model 66RCLP, except has plain barrel, F or M choke, slide handle only checkered, no recoil pad. Made 1967–1970.

Noble Model 70CLP Hammerless Slide Action Repeating Shotgun $150
Solid frame. .410 gauge. Magazine holds 5 shells. 26-inch barrel with adjustable choke. Weight: about 6 pounds. Checkered buttstock and forearm, recoil pad. Made 1958–1970.

Noble Model 70RCLP $165
Same as Model 70CLP, except has vent rib. Made 1967–1970.

Noble Model 70RLP $150
Same as Model 70CLP, except has vent rib and no adjustable choke. Made 1967–1970.

Noble Model 70XL $105
Same as Model 70CLP, except without adjustable choke and checkering on buttstock. Made 1958–1970.

Noble Model 80 Autoloading Shotgun $225
Recoil-operated. .410 gauge. Magazine holds three 3-inch shells, four 2 1/2-inch shells. 26-inch barrel, Full choke. Weight: about 6 pounds. Plain pistol-grip stock and fluted forearm. Made 1964–1966.

Noble Key Lock
Fire Control Mechanism
Model 166L Deergun

Noble Model 166L Deergun $230
Solid frame. Key lock fire control mechanism. 12 gauge. 2 3/4-inch chamber. 5-shot tubular magazine. 24-inch plain barrel, specially bored for rifled slug. Lyman peep rear sight, post ramp front sight. Receiver dovetailed for scope mounting. Weight: about 7 1/4 pounds. Checkered pistol-grip stock and slide handle, swivels and carrying strap. Made 1967–1970.

Noble Model 420 Hammerless Double $310
Boxlock. Plain extractors. Double triggers. Gauges: 12 ga. 3-inch mag.; 16 ga.; 20 ga. 3-inch mag.; .410 ga. Barrels:

Noble Model 166L Deergun

SHOTGUNS

Noble Model 420

Noble Model 420 Hammerless Double (cont.)
28-inch, except .410 in 26-inch, M/F choke. Weight: about
6¾ pounds. Engraved frame. Checkered walnut stock and
forearm. Made 1958–1970.

Noble Model 450E

Noble Model 450E Hammerless Double $395
Boxlock. Engraved frame. Selective auto ejectors. Double
triggers. Gauges: 12, 16, 20. 3-inch chambers in 12 and 20
gauge. 28-inch barrels, M/F choke. Weight: about 6 lbs.
14 oz., 12 ga. Checkered pistol-grip stock and beavertail
forearm, recoil pad. Made 1967–1970.

Noble Model 602CLP $155
Same as Model 602RCLP, except has plain barrel. Made
1958–1970.

Noble Model 602RCLP Hammerless Slide Action
Repeating Shotgun $185
Solid frame. Key lock fire control mechanism. 20 gauge. 3-
inch chamber. 5-shot tubular magazine. 28-inch barrel, vent
rib, adjustable choke. Weight: about 6½ pounds. Checkered
pistol-grip stock/slide handle, recoil pad. Made 1967–1970.

Noble Model 602RLP $165
Same as Model 602RCLP, except without adjustable
choke, bored F or M choke. Made 1967–1970.

Noble Model 602XL $125
Same as Model 602RCLP, except has plain barrel, F or
M choke, slide handle only checkered, no recoil pad. Made
1958–1970.

Noble Model 662 .... $175
Same as Model 602CLP, except has aluminum receiver
and barrel. Weight: about 4½ pounds. Made 1966–1970.

Omega Single Shot Shotgun

OMEGA SHOTGUNS
Brescia, Italy, and Korea

Omega Folding Over/Under Shotgun $295
Hammerless. Single trigger with automatic safety. Gauges:
12, 20, 28 and .410; 3-inch chambers. Barrels: 26- or 28-
inch with various fixed choke combinations. Weight: 5½–
6 pounds. Checkered European walnut buttstock and forend. Imported from Italy since 1986.

Omega Over/Under Shotgun, Deluxe $320
Gauges: 20, 28 and .410. 26- or 28-inch vent-rib barrels.
40½ inches overall (42½ inches, 20 ga., 28-inch bbl.).
Chokes: IC/M, M/F or F/F (.410). Weight: about 5½–6
pounds. Single trigger. Automatic safety. European walnut
stock with checkered pistol grip and tulip forend. Made
in Italy from 1984 to date.

Omega Side-by-Side Shotgun, Deluxe $190
Same general specifications as the Standard Side-by-Side,
except has checkered European walnut stock and low barrel rib. Made in Italy from 1984 to date.

Omega Side-by-Side Shotgun, Standard $165
Gauge: .410. 26-inch barrel. 40½ inches overall. Choked
F/F. Weight: 5½ pounds. Double trigger. Manual safety.
Checkered beechwood stock and semi-pistol grip. Made
in Italy from 1984 to date.

Omega Single Shot Shotgun, Deluxe $105
Same general specifications as the Standard Single Barrel,
except has checkered walnut stock, top lever break, fully
blued receiver, vent rib. Made in Korea from 1984 to date.

Omega Single Shot Shotgun, Standard
Gauges: 12, 16, 20, 28 and .410. Barrel lengths: 26-, 28- or
30-inch. Weight: 5 lbs. 4 oz.–5 lbs. 11 oz. Indonesian wal-
nut stock. Matte-chromed receiver and top lever break.
Made in Korea from 1984 to date.
Standard Fixed .... $ 80
Standard Folding 125
Deluxe Folding 175

Parker G.H.E.

Parker D.H.E.

Parker C.H.E.

Parker B.H.E.

Parker A.H.E.

PARKER BROTHERS
Meriden, Connecticut

This firm was taken over by Remington Arms Company in 1934 and its production facilities removed to Remington's Ilion, New York, plant.

Parker Hammerless Double Barrel Shotguns

Grades V.H.E. through A-1 Special. Boxlock. Auto ejectors. Double triggers or selective single trigger. Gauges: 10, 12, 16, 20, 28, .410. Barrels: 26- to 32-inch, any standard boring. Weight: 6⁷⁄₈–8¹⁄₂ pounds, 12 ga. Stock and forearm of select walnut, checkered; straight, half or full pistol grip. Grades differ only in quality of workmanship, grade of wood, engraving, checkering, etc.; general specifications are the same for all. Discontinued about 1940.

V.H.E. Grade, 12 or 16 gauge	$ 1,995
V.H.E. Grade, 20 gauge	3,350
V.H.E. Grade, 28 gauge	5,595
V.H.E. Grade, .410 gauge	13,500
G.H.E. Grade, 12 or 16 gauge	2,895
G.H.E. Grade, 20 gauge	3,250
G.H.E. Grade, 28 gauge	6,200
G.H.E. Grade, .410 gauge	15,500
D.H.E. Grade, 12 or 16 gauge	4,995
D.H.E. Grade, 20 gauge	4,895
D.H.E. Grade, 28 gauge	12,500
D.H.E. Grade, .410 gauge	19,500
C.H.E. Grade, 12 or 16 gauge	7,425
C.H.E. Grade, 20 gauge	8,450
C.H.E. Grade, 28 gauge	17,500
C.H.E. Grade, .410 gauge	35,250
B.H.E. Grade, 12 or 16 gauge	7,995
B.H.E. Grade, 20 gauge	11,995
B.H.E. Grade, 28 gauge	18,500
B.H.E. Grade, .410 gauge	32,500
A.H.E. Grade, 12 or 16 gauge	15,500
A.H.E. Grade, 20 gauge	19,750
A.H.E. Grade, 28 gauge	28,500
A.A.H.E. Grade, 12 or 16 gauge	25,950
A.A.H.E. Grade, 20 gauge	45,000
A.A.H.E. Grade, 28 gauge	70,500
A-1 Special Grade, 12 or 16 gauge	68,000
A-1 Special Grade, 20 gauge	90,000
A-1 Special Grade, 28 gauge	130,000

For non-ejector guns, deduct 30 percent from values shown. Vent-rib barrels, add 20 percent to values shown.

Parker Single Shot Trap Guns

Hammerless. Boxlock. Ejector. 12 gauge only. Barrel lengths: 30-, 32-, 34-inch; any boring. vent rib. Weight: 7¹⁄₂–8¹⁄₂ pounds. Stock and forearm of select walnut, checkered; straight, half or full pistol grip. The five grades differ only in quality of workmanship, grade of wood, checkering, engraving, etc.; general specifications same for all. Discontinued about 1940.

S.C. Grade	$ 2,000
S.B. Grade	3,000
S.A. Grade	3,750
S.A.A. Grade	5,500
S.A.1 Special	17,000

SHOTGUNS

Parker Single Shot Trap

Parker Skeet Gun

Same as other Parker doubles from Grade V.H.E. up, except selective single trigger and beavertail forearm are standard on this model, as are 26-inch barrels, SK choke. Discontinued about 1940. Values are 20 percent higher.

Parker Trojan

Parker Trojan Hammerless Double Barrel Shotgun

Boxlock. Plain extractors. Double trigger or single trigger. Gauges: 12, 16, 20. Barrels: 30-inch both F choke (12 ga. only), 26- or 28-inch M and F choke. Weight: 6¼–7¾ pounds. Checkered pistol-grip stock and forearm. Discont. 1939.

12 or 16 gauge	$1400
20 gauge	2800

PARKER-HALE SHOTGUNS
Mfd. by Ignacio Ugartechea, Spain

Parker-Hale Model 645A (American) Side-by-Side Shotgun **$695**
Gauges: 12, 16 and 20. Boxlock action. 26- and 28-inch barrels. Chokes: IC/M, M/F. Weight: 6 pounds average. Single non-selective trigger. Automatic safety. Hand-checkered pistol grip walnut stock with beavertail forend.

PARKER REPRODUCTIONS
Middlesex, New Jersey

Parker Hammerless Double Barrel Shotguns

Reproduction of the original Parker boxlock. Single selective trigger or double triggers. Selective automatic ejectors. Automatic safety. Gauges: 12, 16, 20 or 28; 2¾- or 3-inch chambers. Barrels: 26- or 28-inch choked SK/SK, IC/M, M/F. Weight: 5½–7 pounds. Checkered English-style or pistol-grip American walnut stock with beavertail or splinter forend and checkered skeleton buttplate. Color casehardened receiver with game scenes and scroll engraving. Imported from Japan 1984 to date.

D Grade	$ 2,295
D Grade 2-barrel set	3,550
B Grade Bank Note Limited Edition	3,295
B Grade 2-barrel set	4,750
B Grade 3-barrel set	5,595
A-1 Special Grade	6,995
A-1 Special Grade 2-barrel set	7,950
A-1 Special Grade Custom Engraved	8,995
A-1 Special Grade 3-barrel set	10,500

Parker-Hale Model 645A

Parker-Hale Model 645A (American) S/S (cont.)

Raised matted rib. English scroll-design engraved receiver. Discontinued 1990.

Parker-Hale Model 645E (English) Side-by-Side Shotgun

Same general specifications as the Model 645A, except double triggers, straight grip, splinter forend, checkered butt and concave rib. Discontinued 1990.

MODEL 645E	
12, 16, 20 ga. with 26- or 28-inch bbl.	$750
28, .410 ga. with 27-inch bbl.	795
MODEL 645E-XXV	
12, 16, 20 ga. with 25-inch bbl.	715
28, .410 ga. with 25-inch bbl.	795

Pedersen Model 1000, Grade I

Pedersen Model 1000, Grade II

Pedersen Model 1000 Over/Under Hunting Shotgun

Boxlock. Auto ejectors. Selective single trigger. Gauges: 12, 20. 2¾-inch chambers in 12 gauge, 3-inch in 20 gauge. Barrels: vent rib; 30-inch M/F (12 ga. only); 28-inch IC/M (12 ga. only), M/F; 26-inch IC/M. Checkered pistol-grip stock and forearm. Grade I is the higher quality gun with custom stock dimensions, fancier wood, more elaborate engraving, silver inlays. Made 1973–75.

Grade I	$1850
Grade II	1525

PEDERSEN CUSTOM GUNS
North Haven, Connecticut
Division of O. F. Mossberg & Sons, Inc.

Pedersen Model 1500 Trap

Pedersen Model 2500

Pedersen Model 4000

SHOTGUNS

Pedersen Model 1000 Magnum
Same as Model 1000 Hunting Gun, except chambered for 12-gauge Magnum 3-inch shells, 30-inch barrels, IM/F choke. Made 1973–75.
Grade I **$1950**
Grade II 1595

Pedersen Model 1000 Skeet Gun
Same as Model 1000 Hunting Gun, except has skeet-style stock; 26- and 28-inch barrels (12 gauge only), SK choke. Made 1973–75.
Grade I **$1995**
Grade II 1550

Pedersen Model 1000 Trap Gun
Same as Model 1000 Hunting Gun, except 12 gauge only, has Monte Carlo trap-style stock, 30- or 32-inch barrels, M/F or IM/F choke. Made 1973–75.
Grade I **$1995**
Grade II 1550

Pedersen Model 1500 O/U Hunting Shotgun **$550**
Boxlock. Auto ejectors. Selective single trigger. 12 gauge. 2³/₄- or 3-inch chambers. Barrels: vent rib; 26-inch IC/M; 28- and 30-inch M/F; Magnum has 30-inch, IM/F choke. Weight: 7–7¹/₂ pounds, depending on barrel length. Checkered pistol-grip stock and forearm. Made 1973–75.

Pedersen Model 1500 Skeet Gun **$595**
Same as Model 1500 Hunting Gun, except has skeet-style stock, 27-inch barrels, SK choke. Made 1973–75.

Pedersen Model 1500 Trap Gun **$595**
Same as Model 1500 Hunting Gun, except has Monte Carlo trap-style stock, 30- or 32-inch barrels, M/F or IM/F chokes. Made 1973–75.

Pedersen Model 2000 Hammerless Double
Boxlock. Auto ejectors. Selective single trigger. Gauges: 12, 20. 2³/₄-inch chambers in 12 gauge, 3-inch in 20 gauge. Barrels: vent rib; 30-inch M/F (12 gauge only); 28-inch M/F; 26-inch IC/M choke. Checkered pistol-grip stock and forearm. Grade I is the higher quality gun with custom dimensions, fancier wood, more elaborate engraving, silver inlays. Made 1973–74.

Pedersen Model 2000 Hammerless Double (cont.)
Grade I **$1595**
Grade II 1295

Pedersen Model 2500 Hammerless Double **$380**
Boxlock. Auto ejectors. Selective single trigger. Gauges: 12, 20. 2³/₄-inch chambers in 12 gauge, 3-inch in 20 gauge. Barrels: vent rib; 28-inch M/F; 26-inch IC/M choke. Checkered pistol-grip stock and forearm. Made 1973–74.

Pedersen Model 4000 Hammerless Slide Action Repeating Shotgun **$380**
Custom version of Mossberg Model 500. Full-coverage floral engraving on receiver. Gauges: 12, 20, .410. 3-inch chamber. Barrels: vent rib; 26-inch IC or SK choke; 28-inch F or M; 30-inch F. Weight: 6–8 pounds depending on gauge and barrel. Checkered stock and slide handle of select wood. Made in 1975.

Pedersen Model 4000 Trap Gun **$395**
Same as standard Model 4000, except 12 gauge only, has 30-inch F choke barrel, Monte Carlo trap-style stock with recoil pad. Made in 1975.

Pedersen Model 4500 . . . . **$325**
Same as Model 4000, except has simpler scroll engraving. Made in 1975.

Pedersen Model 4500 Trap Gun **$350**
Same as Model 4000 Trap Gun, except has simpler scroll engraving. Made in 1975.

J. C. PENNEY CO., INC.
Dallas, Texas

J. C. Penney Model 4011 Autoloading Shotgun . **$175**
Hammerless. 5-shot magazine. Barrels: 26-inch IC; 28-inch M or F; 30-inch F choke. Weight: 7¹/₄ lbs. Plain pistol-grip stock and slide handle.

J. C. Penney Model 6610 Single Shot Shotgun . . . **$80**
Hammerless. Takedown. Auto ejector. Gauges: 12, 16, 20 and .410. Barrel length: 28–36 inches. Weight: about 6 pounds. Plain pistol-grip stock and forearm.

J. C. Penney Model 6630 Bolt Action Shotgun . . $110
Takedown. Gauges: 12, 16, 20. 2-shot clip magazine. 26- and 28-inch barrel lengths; with or without adjustable choke. Plain pistol-grip stock. Weight: about 7 1/4 pounds.

J. C. Penney Model 6670 Slide Action Shotgun . $130
Hammerless. Gauges: 12, 16, 20, and .410. 3-shot tubular magazine. Barrels: 26- to 30-inch; various chokes. Weight: 6 1/4–7 1/2 pounds. Walnut finished hardwood stock.

J. C. Penney Model 6870 Slide Action Shotgun . $195
Hammerless. Gauges: 12, 16, 20, .410. 4-shot magazine. Barrels: vent rib; 26- to 30-inch, various chokes. Weight: average 6 1/2 pounds. Plain pistol-grip stock.

PERAZZI SHOTGUNS
Manufactured by Manifattura Armi Perazzi, Brescia, Italy. See also listings under Ithaca-Perazzi.

Perazzi DB81 Over/Under Trap $4650
Gauge: 12; 2 3/4-inch chambers. 29 1/2- or 31 1/2-inch barrels with wide vent rib; M/F chokes. Weight: 8 lbs. 6 oz. Detachable and interchangeable trigger with flat V-springs. Bead front sight. Interchangeable and custom-made checkered stock; beavertail forend. Made from 1988 to date.

Perazzi DB81 Single Shot Trap $3850
Same general specifications as the DB81 Over/Under, except in single barrel version with 32- or 34-inch wide vent-rib barrel, Full choke. Made from 1988 to date.

> **NOTE:** Prices shown reflect Standard Grade values, except where noted. For SC3 Grade add 70%, for SCO Grade add 190% and for SHO Grade add 500%.

Perazzi Grand American 88 Special Single Trap
Same general specifications as MX8 Special Single Trap, except with high ramped rib. Fixed choke or screw-in choke tubes.

Perazzi Grand American 88 Special Single Trap (cont.)
Model 88 Standard	$4125
Model 88 w/Interchangeable Choke Tubes	4425

Perazzi Mirage Over/Under Shotgun
Gauge: 12; 2 3/4-inch chambers. Barrels: 27 5/8-, 29 1/2 or 31 1/2-inch vent-rib w/fixed chokes or screw-in choke tubes. Single selective trigger. Weight: 7 to 7 3/4 pounds. Interchangeable and custom-made checkered buttstock and forend.
Competition Trap, Skeet, Pigeon, Sporting . . .	$ 4,700
Skeet 4-Barrel Sets	12,400
Competition Special (w/adj. 4-position trigger)	
add	400

Perazzi MX1 Over/Under Shotgun
Similar to Model MX8, except with a ramp-style, tapered rib and modified stock configuration.
Competition Trap, Skeet, Pigeon & Sporting. . . .	$3600
MX1C (w/Choke Tubes)	3750
MX1B (w/Flat Low-Rib)	3560

Perazzi MX2 Over/Under Shotgun
Similar to Model MX8, except with broad high-ramped competition rib.
Competition-Trap, Skeet, Pigeon & Sporting . . .	$3750
MX2C (w/choke tubes)	3750

Perazzi MX3 Over/Under Shotgun
Similar to Model MX8, except with a ramp-style, tapered rib and modified stock configuration.
Competition Trap, Skeet, Pigeon & Sporting. . . .	$3295
Competition Special (w/adj. 4-position trigger)	
Add	300
Game Models	3195
Combo O/U plus SB	3950
SB Trap 32- or 34-inch	2695
Skeet 4-barrel sets	8950
Skeet Special 4-barrel sets	9395

Perazzi MX3 Special Pigeon Shotgun $5100
Gauge: 12; 2 3/4-inch chambers. 29 1/2- or 31 1/2-inch vent-rib barrel; IC/M and Extra Full chokes. Weight: 8 lbs. 6 oz. Detachable and interchangeable trigger group with flat V-springs. Bead front sight. Interchangeable and custom-made checkered stock for live pigeon shoots; splinter forend. Made from 1991 to date.

Perazzi DB81 Over/Under Trap

Perazzi Mirage Over/Under

Perazzi MX3 Special Pigeon Shotgun

Perazzi Model MX7 Over/Under

Perazzi MX8 Special Skeet Shotgun

Perazzi Model MX9 O/U Combo

Perazzi MX20 O/U Game Gun

Perazzi MX4 Over/Under Shotgun
Similar to Model MX3 in appearance and shares the MX8 locking system. Detachable, adjustable 4-position trigger standard. Interchangeable choke tubes optional.

Competition Trap, Skeet, Pigeon & Sporting....	**$3650**
MX4C (w/Choke Tubes)	3895

Perazzi MX5 Over/Under Game Gun
Similar to Model MX8, except in hunting configuration chambered in 12 or 20 gauge. Non-detachable single selective trigger.

MX5 Standard	**$2495**
MX5C (w/Choke Tubes)	2750

Perazzi MX7 Over/Under Shotgun $4575
Similar to Model MX12, except with MX3-style receiver and top-mounted trigger selector. Barrels: $28^3/4$-, $29^1/2$-, $31^1/2$-inch w/vent rib; screw-in choke tubes. Made from 1992 to date.

Perazzi MX8 Over/Under Shotgun
Gauge: 12; $2^3/4$-inch chambers. Barrels: $27^5/8$-, $29^1/2$- or $31^1/2$-inch vent-rib w/fixed chokes or screw-in choke tubes. Weight: 7 to $8^1/2$ pounds. Interchangeable and custom-made checkered stock; beavertail forend. Special models have detachable and interchangeable 4-position trigger group with flat V-springs. Made from 1988 to date.

MX8 Standard	**$3695**
MX8 Special (adj. 4-pos. trigger)	3795
MX8 Special Single (32- or 34-inch bbl.)	3595
MX8 Special Combo	7390

Perazzi MX8/20 Over/Under Shotgun $3750
Similar to the Model MX8, except with smaller frame and custom stock. Available in sporting or game configurations with fixed chokes or screw-in tubes. Made from 1993 to date.

Perazzi MX9 Over/Under Shotgun $5995
Gauge: 12; $2^3/4$-inch chambers. Barrels: $29^1/2$- or $30^1/2$-inch with choke tubes and vent side rib. Selective trigger. Checkered walnut stock with adjustable cheekpiece. Available in single barrel, combo, O/U trap, skeet, pigeon and sporting models. Made from 1993 to date.

Perazzi MX10 Over/Under Shotgun $7495
Similar to the Model MX9, except with fixed chokes and different rib configuration. Made from 1993 to date.

Perazzi MX12 Over/Under Game Gun
Gauge: 12; $2^3/4$-inch chambers. Barrels: 26-, $27^5/8$-, $28^3/8$- or $29^1/2$-inch, vent-rib, fixed chokes or screw-in choke tubes. Non-detachable single selective trigger group with coil springs. Weight: $7^1/4$ pounds. Interchangeable and custom-made checkered stock; schnabel forend.

MX12 Standard	**$3850**
MX12C (w/Choke Tubes)	4250

Perazzi MX20 O/U Game Gun
Gauges: 20, 28 and .410; $2^3/4$- or 3-inch chambers. 26-inch vent-rib barrels; M/F chokes or screw-in chokes. Auto selective ejectors. Selective single trigger. Weight: 6 lbs. 6 oz. Non-detachable coil-spring trigger. Bead front sight.

Perazzi MX20 O/U Game Gun (cont.)

Interchangeable and custom-made checkered stock with schnabel forend. Made from 1988 to date.

Standard Grade	$ 3,995
Standard Grade w/Gold Outline	6,950
MX20C w/Choke Tubes	4,295
SC3 Grade	7,500
SCO Grade	10,350

Perazzi MX28 Over/Under Game Gun $10,950

Similar to the Model MX12, except chambered in 28 gauge with 26-inch barrels fitted to smaller frame. Made from 1993 to date.

Perazzi MX410 Over/Under Game Gun $10,950

Similar to the Model MX12, except in .410 bore w/3-inch chambers, 26-inch barrels fitted to smaller frame. Made from 1993 to date.

Perazzi TM1 Special Single Shot Trap **$3295**

Gauge: 12; 2¾-inch chambers. 32- or 34-inch barrel with wide vent rib; Full choke. Weight: 8 lbs. 6 oz. Detachable and interchangeable trigger group with coil springs. Bead front sight. Interchangeable and custom-made stock with checkered pistol grip and beavertail forend. Made from 1988 to date.

Perazzi TMX Single Barrel Trap

Perazzi TMX Special Single Shot Trap $3350

Same general specifications as Model TM1 Special, except with ultra-high rib. Interchangeable choke tubes optional.

Piotti Piuma Boxlock

PIOTTI SHOTGUNS
Italy

Piotti King No. 1 Sidelock **$12,995**

Gauges: 10, 12, 16, 20, 28 and .410. 25- to 30-inch barrels (12 ga.); 25- to 28-inch (other gauges). Weight: about 5 lbs. (.410) to 8 lbs. (12 ga.) Holland & Holland pattern sidelock. Double triggers standard. Coin finish or color casehardened. Level file-cut rib. Full-coverage scroll engraving, gold inlays. Hand-rubbed, oil-finished, straight-grip stock with checkered butt, splinter forend.

Piotti King Extra Side-by-Side Shotgun **$19,500**

Same general specifications as the Piotti King No. 1, except has choice of engraving, gold inlays plus stock is of exhibition grade wood.

Piotti Lunik Sidelock Shotgun **$12,500**

Same general specifications as the Monte Carlo model, except has level, file-cut rib. Renaissance-style, large scroll engraving in relief, gold crown in top lever, gold name, and gold crest in forearm, finely figured wood.

Piotti Monte Carlo Sidelock Shotgun **$7995**

Gauges: 10, 12, 16, 20, 28 or .410. Barrels: 25- to 30-inch. Holland & Holland pattern sidelock. Weight: 5–8 pounds. Automatic ejectors. Double triggers. Hand-rubbed oil-finished straight-grip stock with checkered butt. Choice of Purdey-style scroll and rosette or Holland & Holland-style large scroll engraving.

Piotti Piuma Boxlock Side-by-Side Shotgun ... **$8250**

Same general specifications as the Monte Carlo model, except has Anson & Deeley boxlock action with demi-bloc barrels, scalloped frame. Standard scroll and rosette engraving. Hand-rubbed, oil-finished straight-grip stock.

WILLIAM POWELL & SON LTD.
Birmingham, England

**Powell No. 1 Best Grade Double-Barrel
Shotgun** **$25,000**

Sidelock. Gauges: Made to order, with 12, 16 and 20 the most common. Barrels: Made to order in any length, but 28 inches was recommended. Highest grade French walnut buttstock and forearm with fine checkering. Metal elaborately engraved. Imported by Stoeger about 1938–1951.

Powell No. 2 Best Grade Double **$20,000**

Same general specifications as the Powell No. 1, except plain finish without engraving. Imported by Stoeger about 1938–1951.

Powell No. 6 Crown Grade Double **$8000**

Boxlock. Gauges: Made to order, with 12, 16 and 20 the most common. Barrels: Made to order, but 28 inches was recommended. Highest grade French walnut buttstock and forearm with fine checkering. Metal elaborately engraved. Uses Anson & Deeley locks. Imported by Stoeger about 1938–1951.

Powell No. 7 Aristocrat Grade Double **$2500**

Same general specifications as the Powell No. 6, except with lower quality wood and metal engraving.

PRECISION SPORTS SHOTGUNS
Cortland, New York
Manufactured by Ignacio Ugartechea, Spain

**Precision Sports 600 Series American
Hammerless Doubles**

Boxlock. Single selective trigger. Selective automatic ejectors. Automatic safety. Gauges: 12, 16, 20, 28, .410; 2¾- or 3-inch chambers. Barrels: 26-, 27- or 28-inch with raised matte rib; choked IC/M or M/F. Weight: 5¾–7

SHOTGUNS

Precision Sports 600 Series American (cont.)

pounds. Checkered pistol-grip walnut buttstock with beavertail forend. Engraved silvered receiver with blued barrels. Imported from Spain 1986 to date.

640A (12, 16, 20 ga. w/extractors)	**$625**
640A (28, .410 ga. w/extractors)	**750**
640 Slug Gun (12 ga. w/extractors)	**735**
645A (12, 16, 20 ga. w/ejectors)	**695**
645A (28, .410 ga. w/ejectors)	**850**
645A (20/28 ga. two-bbl. set)	**995**
650A (12 ga. w/extractors, choke tubes)	**655**
655A (12 ga. w/ejectors, choke tubes)	**725**

Precision Sports 600 Series English Hammerless Doubles

Same general specifications as American 600 Series, except with double triggers and concave rib. Checkered English-style walnut stock with splinter forend, straight grip and oil finish.

640E (12, 16, 20 ga. w/extractors)	**$535**
640E (28, .410 ga. w/extractors)	**625**

Precision Sports 600 Series English (cont.)

640 Slug Gun (12 ga. w/extractors)	**$735**
645E (12, 16, 20 ga. w/ejectors)	**750**
645E (28, .410 ga. w/ejectors)	**715**
645E (20/28 ga. two-bbl. set)	**945**
650E (12 ga. w/extractors, choke tubes)	**650**
655E (12 ga. w/ejectors, choke tubes)	**695**

Precision Sports Model 640M Magnum 10 Hammerless Double

Similar to Model 640E, except in 10 gauge with 3½-inch Mag. chambers. Barrels: 26-, 30-, 32-inch choked F/F. Model 640M Big Ten, Turkey or Goose Gun **$655**

Precision Sports Model 645E-XXV Hammerless Double

Similar to Model 645E, except with 25-inch barrel and Churchill-style rib.

645E-XXV (12, 16, 20 ga. w/ejectors)	**$715**
645E-XXV (28, .410 ga. w/ejectors)	**795**

Premier Ambassador

Premier Continental

Premier Monarch

═══ PREMIER SHOTGUNS ═══

Premier shotguns have been produced by various gunmakers in Europe.

Premier Ambassador Model Field Grade Hammerless Double Barrel Shotgun **$350**

Sidelock. Plain extractors. Double triggers. Gauges: 12, 16, 20, .410. 3-inch chambers in 20 and .410 gauge, 2¾-inch in 12 and 16 gauge. Barrels: 26-inch in .410 gauge, 28 inch in other gauges; choked M/F. Weight: 6 lbs. 3 oz.–7 lbs. 3 oz. depending on gauge. Checkered pistol-grip stock and beavertail forearm. Intro. in 1957; discontinued.

Premier Brush King **$250**

Same as standard Regent Model, except chambered for 12 (2¾-inch) and 20 gauge (3-inch) only; has 22-inch barrels, IC/M choke, straight-grip stock. Weight: 6 lbs. 3 oz. in 12 gauge; 5 lbs. 12 oz. in 20 gauge. Introduced in 1959; discontinued.

Premier Continental Model Field Grade Hammer Double Barrel Shotgun **$350**

Sidelock. Exposed hammers. Plain extractors. Double triggers. Gauges: 12, 16, 20, .410. 3-inch chambers in 20 and .410 gauge, 2¾-inch in 12 and 16 gauge. Barrels: 26-inch in .410 gauge; 28-inch in other gauges; choked M/F. Weight: 6 lbs. 3 oz.–7 lbs. 3 oz. depending on gauge. Checkered pistol-grip stock and English-style forearm. Introduced in 1957; discontinued.

Premier Monarch Supreme Grade Hammerless Double Barrel Shotgun **$375**

Boxlock. Auto ejectors. Double triggers. Gauges: 12, 20. 2¾-inch chambers in 12 gauge, 3-inch in 20 gauge. Barrels: 28-inch M/F; 26-inch IC/M choke. Weight: 6 lbs. 6 oz.–7 lbs. 2 oz. depending on gauge and barrel. Checkered pistol-grip stock and beavertail forearm of fancy walnut. Introduced in 1959; discontinued.

Premier Presentation Custom Grade **$895**

Similar to Monarch model, but made to order; of higher quality with hunting scene engraving gold and silver inlaid, fancier wood. Introduced in 1959; discontinued.

Premier Regent

Premier Regent 10-Gauge Magnum Express . . . $295
Same as standard Regent Model, except chambered for 10-gauge Magnum 3½-inch shells, has heavier construction, 32-inch barrels choked F/F, stock with recoil pad. Weight: 11¼ pounds. Introduced in 1957; discontinued.

Premier Regent 12-Gauge Magnum Express . . . $265
Same as standard Regent Model, except chambered for 12-gauge Magnum 3-inch shells, has 30-inch barrels

Premier Regent 12-Gauge Magnum Express (cont.)
choked F and F, stock with recoil pad. Weight: 7¼ pounds. Introduced in 1957; discontinued.

Premier Regent Model Field Grade Hammerless Double Barrel Shotgun $225
Boxlock. Plain extractors. Double triggers. Gauges: 12, 16, 20, 28, .410. 3-inch chambers in 20 and .410 gauge, 2¾-inch in other gauges. Barrels: 26-inch IC/M, M/F (28 and .410 gauge only); 28-inch M/F; 30-inch M/F (12 ga. only). Weight: 6 lbs. 2 oz.–7 lbs. 4 oz. depending on gauge and barrel. Checkered pistol-grip stock and beavertail forearm. Introduced in 1955; discontinued.

Purdey Over-and-Under

Purdey Single Barrel Trap

JAMES PURDEY & SONS, LTD.
London, England

Purdey Hammerless Double Barrel

Purdey Hammerless Double Barrel Shotgun
Sidelock. Auto ejectors. Single or double triggers. Gauges: 12, 16, 20. Barrels: 26-, 27-, 28-, 30-inch (latter in 12 gauge only); any boring, any shape or style of rib. Weight: 5¼–6½ pounds depending on model, gauge and barrel length.

Purdey Hammerless Double Barrel Shotgun (cont.)
Checkered stock and forearm, straight grip standard, pistol-grip also available. Purdey guns of this type have been made from about 1880 to date. Models include: Game Gun, Featherweight Game Gun, Two-Inch Gun (chambered for 12 gauge 2-inch shells), Pigeon Gun (with 3rd fastening and side clips); values of all models are the same.
With double triggers **$31,500**
With single trigger **34,550**

Purdey Over-and-Under Gun
Sidelock. Auto ejectors. Single or double triggers. Gauges: 12, 16, 20. Barrels: 26-, 27-, 28-, 30-inch (latter in 12 gauge only); any boring, any style rib. Weight: 6–7½ pounds depending on gauge and barrel length. Checkered stock and forend, straight or pistol grip. Prior to WW II, the Purdey Over-and-Under Gun was made with a Purdey action; since the war James Purdey & Sons have acquired the business of James Woodward & Sons and all Purdey over/under guns are now built on the Woodward principle. General specifications of both types are the same.
With Purdey action, double triggers **$45,000**
With Woodward action, double triggers **48,000**
Single trigger, extra **1,000**

Purdey Single Barrel Trap Gun **$9,000**
Sidelock. Mechanical features similar to those of the over-and-under model with Purdey action. 12 gauge only. Built to customer's specifications. Made prior to World War II.

Remington Model 10A
Standard Repeater

Remington Model 11A
Autoloader

Remington Model 11-87 Premier
12-Gauge Autoloader

REMINGTON ARMS CO.
Ilion, New York

Eliphalet Remington Jr. began making long arms with his father in 1816. In 1828 they moved their facility to Ilion, N.Y., where it remained a family-run business for decades. As the family died, other people bought controlling interests and today, still a successful gunmaking company, it is a subsidiary of the du Pont Corporation.

Remington Model 10A Standard Grade Slide Action Repeating Shotgun $275
Hammerless. Takedown. 6-shot. 12 gauge only. 5-shell tubular magazine. Barrels: plain; 26- to 32-inch; choked F, M or Cyl. Weight: about 7½ pounds. Plain pistol-grip stock, grooved slide handle. Made 1907–1929.

Remington Model 11 Special, Tournament, Expert and Premier Grade Guns
These higher grade models differ from the Model 11A in general quality, grade of wood, checkering, engraving, etc. General specifications are the same.

Model 11B Special Grade	$ 425
Model 11D Tournament Grade	850
Model 11E Expert Grade	1250
Model 11F Premier Grade	2195

Remington Model 11A Standard Grade Autoloader
Hammerless Browning type. 5-shot. Takedown. Gauges: 12, 16, 20. Tubular magazine holds four shells. Barrels: plain, solid or vent rib; lengths from 26–32 inches; F, M, IC, Cyl., SK chokes. Weight: about 8 pounds, 12 ga.; 7½ pounds, 16 ga.; 7¼ pounds, 20 ga. Checkered pistol grip and forend. Made 1905–1949.

With plain barrel	$255
With solid-rib barrel	345
With ventilated-rib barrel	365

Remington Model 11R Riot Gun $265
Same as Model 11A Standard Grade, except has 20-inch plain barrel, 12 gauge only.

Remington Model 11-48.
See Remington Sportsman-48 Series.

Remington Model 11-87 Premier Autoloader
Gas-operated. Hammerless. Gauge: 12; 3-inch chamber. Barrel: 26-, 28- or 30-inch with REM choke. Weight: 8⅛–8⅜ pounds, depending on barrel length. Checkered walnut stock and forend in satin finish. Made 1987 to date.

Premier Deer Gun	$415
Premier Deer Gun w/Cantilever scope mount	470
Premier Skeet	650
Premier Sporting Clays	520
Premier Standard Autoloader	425
Premier Trap	475
For Left-Hand Models, **add**	50

Remington Model 11-87 Special Purpose Magnum
Same general specifications Model 11-87 Premier, except with non-reflective wood finish and Parkerized metal. 21-, 26- or 28-inch vent-rib barrel with REM Choke tubes. Made 1987–1993.

Model 11-87 SP Field Magnum	$470
Model 11-87 SP Deer Gun (w/21-inch bbl.)	450
Model 11-87 SP Deer Gun w/cantilever scope mount	495

Remington 11-87 SPS Magnum
Same general specifications Model 11-87 Special Purpose Magnum, except with synthetic stock and forend. 21-, 26- or 28-inch vent-rib barrel with REM Choke tubes. Matte black or Mossy Oak Camo finish (except NWTF Turkey Gun). Made 1990 to date.

Model 11-87 SPS Magnum (Matte black)	$450
Model 11-87 SPS Camo (Mossy Oak Camo)	495
Model 11-87 NWTF Turkey Gun (Brown Trebark) Discontinued 1993	520
Model 11-87 SPST Turkey Gun (Matte black) . . .	475

Remington Model 17A Standard Grade Slide Action Repeating Shotgun $365
Hammerless. Takedown. 5-shot. 20 gauge only. 4-shell tubular magazine. Barrels: plain; 26- to 32-inch; choked F, M or Cyl.. Weight: about 5¾ pounds. Plain pistol-grip

Remington Model 17A

Remington Model 29A

Remington Model 31A

Remington Model 17A Standard Grade Slide (cont.)
stock, grooved slide handle. Made 1921–1933. *Note:* The present Ithaca Model 37 is an adaptation of this Browning design.

Remington Model 29A Standard Grade Slide Action Repeating Shotgun **$350**
Hammerless. Takedown. 6-shot. 12 gauge only. 5-shell tubular magazine. Barrels: plain; 26- to 32-inch; choked F, M or Cyl. Weight: about 7½ pounds. Checkered pistol-grip stock and slide handle. Made 1929–1933.

Remington Model 29T Target Grade **$360**
Same general specifications as Model 29A, except has trap-style stock with straight grip, extension slide handle, vent-rib barrel. Discontinued 1933.

Remington Model 31 Skeet Grade
Same general specifications as Model 31A, except has 26-inch barrel with raised solid or vent rib, SK choke, checkered pistol-grip stock and beavertail forend. Weight: about 8 pounds, 12 ga.
With raised solid rib **$395**
With ventilated rib **495**

Remington Model 31 Special, Tournament, Expert and Premier Grade Guns
These higher grade models differ from the Model 31A in general quality, grade of wood, checkering, engraving, etc. General specifications are the same.
Model 31B Special Grade . . . . **$ 450**
Model 31D Tournament Grade **775**
Model 31E Expert Grade **1095**
Model 31F Premier Grade **1200**

Remington Model 31A Standard Grade Slide Action Repeater
Hammerless. Takedown. 3- or 5-shot. Gauges: 12, 16, 20. Tubular magazine holds two or four shells. Barrels: plain, solid or vent rib; lengths from 26 –32 inches; F, M, IC, C or SK choke. Weight: about 7½ lbs., 12 ga.; 6¾ lbs., 16 ga.; 6½ lbs., 20 ga. Earlier models have checkered pistol-grip stock and slide handle; later models have plain stock and grooved slide handle. Made 1931–1949.

Remington Model 31A Standard Grade (cont.)
Model 31A with plain barrel **$315**
Model 31A with solid-rib barrel **395**
Model 31A with vent-rib barrel **425**
Model 31H Hunters' Special w/sporting-style stock **375**
Model 31R Riot Gun w/20-inch plain bbl., 12 ga. . . **225**

Remington Model 31S Trap Special/31TC Trap Grade
Same general specifications as Model 31A, except 12 gauge only, has 30- or 32-inch vent-rib barrel, Full choke, checkered trap stock with full pistol grip and recoil pad, checkered extension beavertail forend. Weight: about 8 pounds. (Trap Special has solid-rib barrel, half-pistol grip stock with standard walnut forend).
Model 31S Trap Special **$425**
Model 31TC Trap Grade **595**

Remington Model 32 Skeet Grade
Same general specifications as Model 32A, except 26- or 28-inch barrel, SK choke, beavertail forend, selective single trigger only. Weight: about 7½ pounds. Made 1932–1942.
With plain barrels **$1495**
With raised solid rib **1650**
With ventilated rib **1750**

Remington Model 32 Tournament, Expert and Premier Grade Guns
These higher grade models differ from the Model 32A in general quality, grade of wood, checkering, engraving, etc. General specifications are the same. Made 1932–1942.
Model 32D Tournament Grade . . . . **$ 2,995**
Model 32E Expert Grade **3,795**
Model 32F Premier Grade **10,000**

Remington Model 32A Standard Grade Over/Under
Hammerless. Takedown. Auto ejectors. Early model had double triggers, later built with selective single trigger only. 12 gauge only. Barrels: plain, raised matted solid or vent rib; 26-, 28-, 30-, 32-inch; F/M choke standard, option of any combination of F, M, IC, C, SK choke. Weight: about 7¾ pounds. Checkered pistol-grip stock and forend. Made 1932–1942.
With double triggers **$1595**
With selective single trigger **1795**

Remington Model 32A

Remington Model 870 Competition Trap

Remington Model 870 Deer Gun—Brushmaster

Remington Model 870 Deer Gun—Brushmaster (1980 Design)

Remington Model 32A Standard Grade O/U (cont.)
Extra for raised solid rib $200
Extra for ventilated rib 250

Remington Model 32TC Target (Trap) Grade
Same general specifications as Model 32A, except 30- or 32-inch vent-rib barrel, Full choke, trap-style stock with checkered pistol-grip and beavertail forend. Weight: about 8 pounds. Made 1932–1942.
With double triggers **$2395**
With selective single trigger 3595

Remington Model 89 . . . . $850
Hammers. Circular action. Gauges: 10, 12, 16. 28- to 32-inch barrels; steel or damascus twist. Weight 7–10 pounds. Made 1889–1908.

Remington Model 90-T Single Shot Trap $2200
Gauge: 12; 2³/4-inch chambers. 30-, 32- or 34-inch vent-rib barrel with fixed chokes or screw-in REM Chokes; ported or non-ported. Weight: 8¹/4 pounds. Checkered American walnut standard or Monte Carlo stock with low-luster finish. Engraved sideplates and drop-out trigger group optional. Made 1990 to date.

> **NOTE:** In 1980 Remington changed the stock styling for all Model 870 shotguns.

Remington Model 870 "All American" Trap Gun $725
Same as Model 870TB, except custom grade with engraved receiver, trigger guard and barrel; Monte Carlo or straight-comb stock and forend of fancy walnut; available only with 30-inch Full choke barrel. Made 1972–77.

Remington Model 870 "All American" Trap

Remington Model 870 Competition Trap $495
Based on standard Model 870 receiver, except is single-shot with gas-assisted recoil-reducing system, new choke design, a high step-up vent rib and redesigned stock and forend with cut checkering and a satin finish. Weight: 8¹/2 pounds. Made 1981 to date.

Remington Model 870 Deer Gun Brushmaster Deluxe
Same as Model 870 Standard Deer Gun, except available in 20 gauge as well as 12, has cut-checkered, satin-finished American walnut stock and forend, recoil pad.
Right-Hand Model $295
Left-Hand Model 345

Remington Model 870 Deer Gun Standard $295
Same as Model 870 Wingmaster Riot Gun, except has rifle-type sights.

Remington Model 870 Express
Same general specifications Model 870 Wingmaster, except has low-luster walnut-finished hardwood stock with pressed checkering and black recoil pad. Gauges: 12, 20 or .410; 3-inch chambers. Barrels: 26- or 28-inch vent-rib with REM Choke; 25-inch vent-rib with fixed Full choke (.410 only). Black oxide metal finish. Made 1987 to date.

Remington Model 870
Express

Remington Model 870
Magnum Duck Gun

Remington Model 870
Marine Magnum

Remington Model 870
Mississippi Magnum Duck

Remington Model 870 Express (cont.)

Model 870 Express (12 or 20 ga., REM Choke) . . . **$200**
Model 870 Express (.410 w/fixed choke) **215**
Express Combo (w/extra 20-inch Deer Barrel) . . . **270**

Remington Model 870 Express Deer Gun

Same general specifications as Model 870 Express, except in 12 gauge only, 20-inch barrel with fixed IC choke, adj. rifle sights and Monte Carlo stock. Made 1991 to date.
Express Deer Gun w/standard barrel **$205**
Express Deer Gun w/fully rifled barrel **230**

Remington Model 870 Express Turkey Gun **$220**

Same general specifications as Model 870 Express, except has 21-inch vent-rib barrel and Turkey Extra-Full REM choke. Made 1991 to date.

Remington Model 870 Express Youth Gun **$250**

Same general specifications as Model 870 Express, except has scaled-down stock with 12½-inch pull and 21-inch vent-rib barrel with REM choke. Made 1991 to date.

Remington Model 870 Lightweight

Same as standard Model 870, but with scaled-down receiver and lightweight mahogany stock; 20 gauge only. 2¾-inch chamber. Barrels: plain or vent rib; 26-inch, IC; 28-inch, M or F choke. REM choke available from 1987. Weight: 5¾ pounds w/26-inch plain barrel. American walnut stock and forend with satin or Hi-gloss finish. Made 1972 to date.
With plain barrel **$235**
With ventilated-rib barrel **260**
With REM choke barrel **340**

Remington Model 870 Lightweight Magnum

Same as Model 870 Lightweight, but chambered for 20 gauge Magnum 3-inch shell; 28-inch barrel, plain or vent rib, Full choke. Weight: 6 pounds with plain barrel. Made 1972 to date.

Remington Model 870 Lightweight Magnum (cont.)

With plain barrel **$295**
With ventilated-rib barrel **325**

Remington Model 870 Magnum Duck Gun

Same as Model 870 Field Gun, except has 3-inch chamber, 12 and 20 gauge Magnum only. 28- or 30-inch barrel, plain or vent rib, M or F choke; recoil pad. Weight: about 7½ or 6¾ pounds. Made 1964 to date.
With plain barrel **$295**
With ventilated-rib barrel **310**

Remington Model 870 Marine Magnum **$295**

Same general specifications as Model 870 Wingmaster, except has 7-shot magazine, 18-inch plain barrel with fixed IC choke, bead front sight and electroless nickel finish. Made 1992 to date.

Remington Model 870 Mississippi Magnum Duck Gun **$320**

Same as Remington Model 870 Magnum Duck Gun except has 32-inch barrel. Engraved receiver, "Ducks Unlimited." Made in 1983.

Remington Model 870 SA Skeet Gun, Small Bore **$295**

Similar to Wingmaster Model 870SA, except chambered for 28 and .410 gauge (2½-inch chamber for latter); 25-inch vent-rib barrel, SK choke. Weight: 6 lbs., 28 ga.; 6½ lbs., .410. Made 1969–1982.

Remington Model 870 Special Field Shotgun . . . **$325**

Pump action. Hammerless. Gauge: 12 or 20. 21-inch vent-rib barrel with REM choke. 41½ inches overall. Weight: 6–7 pounds. Straight-grip checkered walnut stock and forend. Made 1987 to date.

Remington Model 870 Special Purpose Deer Gun

Similar to Special Purpose Magnum, except with 20-inch, IC choke, rifle sights. Matte black oxide and Parkerized finish. Oil-finished, checkered buttstock and forend with recoil pad. Made 1986 to date.
Model 870 SP Deer Gun **$330**
Model 870 SP Deer Gun, cantilever scope mount . . . **375**

Remington Model 870 Special Purpose Magnum $295

Similar to the 870 Magnum Duck Gun, except with 26-, 28- or 30-inch vent-rib REM Choke barrel. 12 gauge only; 3-inch chamber. Oil-finished field-grade stock with recoil pad, QD swivels and Cordura sling. Made 1985 to date.

Remington Model 870 SPS Magnum

Same general specifications Model 870 Special Purpose Magnum, except with synthetic stock and forend. 26- or 28-inch vent-rib barrel with REM Choke tubes. Matte black or Mossy Oak Camo finish. Made 1991 to date.

Model 870 SPS Magnum (black syn. stock) **$270**
Model 870 SPS-T Camo (Mossy Oak Camo) **280**

Remington Model 870 Wingmaster Field Gun

Same general specifications as Model 870AP, except checkered stock and forend. Later models have REM choke systems in 12 ga. Made 1964 to date.

With plain barrel **$270**
With ventilated-rib barrel **295**

Remington Model 870 Wingmaster Field Gun, Small Bore

Same as standard Model 870, but scaled down. Gauges: 20, 28, .410. 25-inch barrel, plain or vent rib; IC, M or F choke; 26-, 28-inch (20 ga.) vent rib with REM Choke tubes. Weight: 5½–6¼ pounds depending on gauge and barrel. Made 1969 to date.

With plain barrel **$325**
With ventilated-rib barrel **340**
With REM Choke **350**

Remington Model 870 Wingmaster Magnum Deluxe Grade $310

Same as Model 870 Magnum Standard Grade, except has checkered stock and extension beavertail forearm, barrel with matted top surface. Discontinued in 1963.

Remington Model 870 Wingmaster Magnum Standard Grade $275

Same as Model 870AP, except chambered for 12 gauge 3-inch Magnum, 30-inch Full choke barrel, recoil pad. Weight: about 8¼ pounds. Made 1955–1963.

Remington Model 870 Wingmaster REM Choke Series

Hammerless, takedown with blued all-steel receiver. Gauges: 12, 20; 3-inch chamber. Tubular magazine. Barrels: 21-, 26-, 28-inch vent-rib with REM Choke. Weight: 7½ pounds (12 ga.). Satin-finished, checkered walnut buttstock and forend with recoil pad. Right- or left-hand models. Made 1986 to date.

Standard Model, 12 ga. **$305**
Standard Model, 20 ga. **315**
Youth Model, 21-inch barrel **310**

Remington Model 870ADL Wingmaster Deluxe Grade

Same general specifications as Wingmaster Model 870AP, except has pistol-grip stock and extension beavertail forend, both finely checkered; matted top surface or vent-rib barrel. Made 1950–1963.

With matted top-surface barrel **$220**
With ventilated-rib barrel **245**

Remington Model 870AP Wingmaster Standard Grade 5-Shot Slide Action Repeater

Hammerless. Takedown. Gauges: 12, 16, 20. Tubular magazine holds four shells. Barrels: plain, matted top surface or vent rib; 26-inch IC, 28-inch M or F choke, 30-inch F choke (12 ga. only). Weight: about 7 pounds, 12 ga.; 6¾ pounds, 16 ga.; 6½ pounds, 20 ga. Plain pistol-grip stock, grooved forend. Made 1950–1963.

With plain barrel **$200**
With matted top-surface barrel **210**
With ventilated-rib barrel **230**
Left-hand model **240**

Remington Model 870BDL Wingmaster Deluxe Special

Same as Model 870ADL, except select American walnut stock and forend. Made 1950–1963.

With matted top-surface barrel **$275**
With ventilated-rib barrel **305**

Remington Model 870D, 870F Wingmaster Tournament and Premier Grade Guns

These higher grade models differ from the Model 870AP in general quality, grade of wood, checkering, engraving, etc. Gen. specifications are the same. Made 1950 to date.

SHOTGUNS

**Remington Model 870
Wingmaster Field Gun**

**Remington Model 870
Wingmaster Field Gun (1980 Design)**

**Remington Model 870ADL
Wingmaster Deluxe**

Remington Model 870F
Wingmaster Premier Grade

Remington Model 870TC
Wingmaster Trap

Remington Model 878A

Remington Model 870D, 870F Wingmaster (cont.)

Model 870D Tournament Grade **$1895**
Model 870F Premier Grade **4250**
Model 870F Premier Grade with gold inlay **5500**

Remington Model 870R Wingmaster Riot Gun . . **$280**

Same as Model 870AP, except 20-inch barrel, IC, 12 gauge only.

Remington Model 870SA Wingmaster Skeet Gun

Same general specifications as Model 870AP, except has 26-inch vent-rib barrel, SK choke, ivory bead front sight, metal bead rear sight, pistol-grip stock and extension beavertail forend. Weight: 6¾ to 7½ pounds depending on gauge. Made 1950–1982.
Model 870SA Skeet Grade (Disc. 1982) . . . . **$ 275**
Model 870SC Skeet Target Grade (Disc 1980) . . . **425**
Model 870SD Skeet Tournament Grade **1250**
Model 870SF Skeet Premier Grade **2495**

Remington Model 870TB Wingmaster
Trap Special **$335**

Same general specifications as Model 870AP Wingmaster, except has 28- or 30-inch vent-rib barrel, Full choke, metal bead front sight, no rear sight. "Special" grade trap-style stock and forend, both checkered, recoil pad. Weight: about 8 pounds. Made 1950–1981.

Remington Model 870TC Trap

Same general specifications Model 870TC Wingmaster, except with REM Choke high-rib vent barrel. Redesigned satin finished stock and forend with cut-checkering. Made 1987 to date.
Model 870 TC Trap (Standard) **$460**
Model 870 TC Trap (Monte Carlo) **475**

Remington Model 870TC Wingmaster Trap Grade

Same as Model 870TB, except higher grade walnut in stock and forend, has both front and rear sights. Made 1950–1979. Model 870 TC reissued in 1987. See separate listing.
Model 870TC Trap Grade . . . . **$ 420**
Model 870TD Trap Tournament Grade **1295**
Model 870TF Trap Premier Grade **2550**

Remington Model 878A Automaster **$225**

Gas-operated Autoloader. 12 gauge, 3-shot magazine. Barrels: 26-inch IC, 28-inch M choke, 30-inch F choke. Weight: about 7 pounds. Plain pistol-grip stock and forearm. Made 1959–1962.

NOTE: New stock checkering patterns and receiver scroll markings were incorporated on all standard Model 1100 field, magnum, skeet and trap models in 1979.

Remington Model 1100 Automatic Field Gun

Gas-operated. Hammerless. Takedown. Gauges: 12, 16, 20. Barrels: plain or vent. rib; 30-inch F, 28-inch M or F, 26-inch IC; or REM choke tubes. Weight: average 7¼–7½ pounds depending on gauge and barrel length. Checkered walnut pistol-grip stock and forearm in high-gloss finish. Made 1963 to date. 16 ga. discontinued.
With plain barrel **$295**
With ventilated-rib barrel **335**
REM choke model **375**
REM chokes, Left-hand action **395**

Remington Model 1100 Field
Left-hand Action

Remington Model 1100 Deer Gun (1979 Model)

Remington Model 1100 Ducks Unlimited Atlantic Commemorative

Remington Model 1100 Ducks Unlimited "The Chesapeake" Commemorative

Remington Model 1100 Lightweight (1979 Model)

Remington Model 1100 Deer Gun $405
Same as Model 1100 Field Gun, except has 22-inch barrel, IC, with rifle-type sights; 12 and 20 gauge only; recoil pad. Weight: about 7¼ pounds. Made 1963 to date.

Remington Model 1100 Ducks Unlimited Atlantic Commemorative $660
Limited production for one year. Similar specifications to Model 1100 Field, except with 32-inch Full choke, vent-rib barrel. 12-gauge Magnum only. Made in 1982.

Remington Model 1100 Ducks Unlimited "The Chesapeake" Commemorative $475
Limited edition 1 to 2400. Same general specifications as Model 1100 Field, except sequentially serial numbered with markings "The Chesapeake." 12-gauge Magnum with 30-inch Full choke, vent-rib barrel. Made in 1981.

Remington Model 1100 Field Grade, Small Bore
Same as standard Model 1100, but scaled down. Gauges: 28, .410. 25-inch barrel, plain or vent rib; IC, M or F choke. Weight: 6¼–7 pounds depending on gauge and barrel. Made 1969 to date.
With plain barrel $380
With ventilated rib 425

Remington Model 1100 Lightweight
Same as standard Model 1100, but scaled-down receiver and lightweight mahogany stock; 20 gauge only, 2¾-inch chamber. Barrels: plain or vent rib; 26-inch IC; 28-inch M and F choke. Weight: 6¼ pounds. Made 1971 to date.
With plain barrel $380
With ventilated rib 400

Remington Model 1100 Lightweight Magnum
Same as Model 1100 Lightweight, but chambered for 20 gauge Magnum 3-inch shell; 28-inch barrel, plain or vent rib, Full choke. Weight: 6½ pounds. Made 1971 to date.
With plain barrel $405
With ventilated rib 420
With choke tubes 450

Remington Model 1100 LT-20 Ducks Unlimited Special Commemorative $495
Limited edition 1 to 2400. Same general specifications as Model 1100 Field, except sequentially serial numbered with markings "The Chesapeake." 20-gauge only. 26-inch IC, vent-rib barrel. Made in 1981.

Remington Model 1100 LT-20 Series
Same as Model 1100 Field Gun, except in 20 gauge with shorter 23-inch vent-rib barrel, straight-grip stock. REM

Remington Model 1100 LT-20 Ducks Unlimited Special

SHOTGUNS

Remington Model 1100 LT-20
Special

Remington Model 1100
Magnum Duck Gun

Remington Model 1100D
Tournament Grade

Remington Model 1100 LT-20 Series (cont.)

choke series has 21-inch vent-rib barrel, choke tubes. Weight: 6¼ pounds. Checkered grip and forearm. Made 1983 to date.

Model 1100 LT-20 Special	**$430**
Model 1100 LT-20 Deer Gun	**395**
Model 1100 LT-20 Youth	**425**

Remington Model 1100 Magnum **$350**

Limited production. Similar to the Model 1100 Field, except with 26-inch Full choke, vent-rib barrel and 3-inch chamber. Made in 1981.

Remington Model 1100 Magnum Duck Gun

Same as Model 1100 Field Gun, except has 3-inch chamber, 12 and 20 gauge magnum only. 30-inch plain or vent-rib barrel in 12 gauge, 28-inch in 20 gauge; M or F choke. Recoil pad. Weight: about 7¾ pounds. Made 1963 to date.

With plain barrel	**$295**
With ventilated-rib barrel	**335**

Remington Model 1100 One of 3000 Field **$895**

Limited edition, numbered 1 to 3000. Similar to Model 1100 Field, except with fancy wood and gold-trimmed etched hunting scenes on receiver. 12 gauge with 28-inch Mod., vent-rib barrel. Made in 1980.

Remington Model 1100 Special Field Shotgun . . **$410**

Gas-operated. 5-shot. Hammerless. Gauges: 12 and 20. 21-inch vent-rib barrel with REM choke. Weight: 6½–7¼ pounds. Straight-grip checkered walnut stock and forend. Made 1987 to date.

Remington Model 1100 SP Magnum

Same as Model 1100 Field, except 12 gauge only with 3-inch chambers. Barrels: 26- or 30-inch F choke; or 26-inch with REM Choke tubes; vent rib. Non-reflective, matte black, Parkerized barrel and receiver. Satin-finished stock and forend. Made 1981 to date.

With Fixed Choke	**$395**
With REM Choke	**410**

Remington Model 1100 Tournament and Premier

These higher grade guns differ from standard models in overall quality, grade of wood, checkering, engraving, gold inlays, etc. General specifications are the same. Made 1963 to date.

Model 1100D Tournament	**$1450**
Model 1100F Premier	**2995**
Model 1100F Premier with gold inlay	**4295**

Remington Model 1100 Tournament Skeet **$425**

Similar to Model 1100 Field, except with 26-inch barrel, SK choke. Gauges: 12, LT-20, 28, and .410. Features select walnut stocks and new cut-checkering patterns. Made 1979–1989.

Remington Model 1100 Tournament Trap

Similar to Model 1100 Field Gun, except with 30-inch Full or mod. trap barrels. 12-gauge. Features select walnut stocks with cut-checkering patterns. Made 1979 to date.

D Grade	**$1495**
F Grade	**2995**
F Grade w/Gold Inlay	**4150**

Remington Model 1100SA Skeet Gun

Same as Model 1100 Field Gun, 12 and 20 gauge, except has 26-inch vent-rib barrel, SK choke or with Cutts Compensator. Weight: 7¼–7½ pounds. Made 1963 to date.

With skeet-choked barrel	**$390**
With Cutts Comp	**410**
Left-hand action	**425**

Remington Model 1100SA Lightweight Skeet . . . **$375**

Same as Model 1100 Lightweight, except has skeet-style stock and forearm, 26-inch vent-rib barrel, SK choke. Made 1971 to date.

Remington Model 1100SA Skeet Small Bore . . . **$415**

Similar to standard Model 1100SA, except chambered for 28 and .410 gauge (2½-inch chamber for latter); 25-inch vent-rib barrel, SK choke. Weight: 6¾ pounds, 28 ga.; 7¼ pounds, .410. Made 1969 to date.

**Remington Model 1100SA Skeet Gun
Left-hand Action**

Remington Model 1100TB Trap

Remington Model 1900

Remington Model 1100SB Lightweight Skeet . . . **$395**
Same as Model 1100SA Lightweight, except has select wood. Introduced in 1977.

Remington Model 1100SB Skeet Gun **$375**
Same as Model 1100SA, except has select wood. Made 1963 to date.

Remington Model 1100TA Trap Gun **$360**
Similar to Model 1100TB Trap Gun, except with regular-grade stocks. Available in both left- and right-hand versions. Made 1979 to date.

Remington Model 1100TB Trap Gun
Same as Model 1100 Field Gun, except has special trap stock, straight or Monte Carlo comb, recoil pad; 30-inch vent-rib barrel, F or mod. trap choke; 12 gauge only. Weight: 8 1/4 pounds. Made 1963–1979.
With straight stock **$395**
With Monte Carlo stock **415**

Remington Model 1900 Hammerless Double . . . **$595**
Improved version of Model 1894. Boxlock. Auto ejector. Double triggers. Gauges: 10, 12, 16. Barrels: 28 to 32 inches. Value shown is for standard grade with ordnance steel barrels. Made 1900–1910.

Remington Model 3200 Competition Skeet Gun . . **$1400**
Same as Model 3200 Skeet Gun, except has gilded scrollwork on frame, engraved forend latch plate and trigger guard, select fancy wood. Made 1973–1984.

Remington Model 3200 Competition Skeet Set . . **$4500**
Similar specifications to Model 3200 Field. 12-gauge over-and-under with additional, interchangeable barrels in 20, 28, and .410 gauges. Cased. Made 1980–84.

Remington Model 3200 Competition Trap Gun . . . **$1595**
Same as Model 3200 Trap Gun, except has gilded scrollwork on frame, engraved forend latch plate and trigger guard, select fancy wood. Made 1973–1984.

Remington Model 3200 Field Grade Magnum . . . **$1500**
Same as Model 3200 Field Grade, except chambered for 12 gauge magnum 3-inch shell; 30-inch barrels, M and F or both F choke. Made 1975–1984.

Remington Model 3200 Field Grade O/U **$995**
Boxlock. Auto ejectors. Selective single trigger. 12 gauge. 2 3/4-inch chambers. Barrels: vent rib; 26- and 28-inch M/F; 30-inch IC/M. Weight: about 7 3/4 pounds with 26-inch barrels. Checkered pistol-grip stock/forearm. Made 1973–78.

Remington Model 3200 "One of 1000" Skeet . . . **$2150**
Same as Model 3200 "One of 1000" Trap Gun, except has 26- or 28-inch barrels, SK choke, skeet-style stock and forearm. Made in 1974.

Remington Model 3200 "One of 1000" Trap **$2495**
Limited edition numbered 1 to 1000. Same general specifications as Model 3200 Trap Gun, but has frame, trigger guard and forend latch elaborately engraved (designation "One of 1,000" on frame side), stock and forearm of high grade walnut. Supplied in carrying case. Made in 1973.

Remington Model 3200 Skeet Gun **$1150**
Same as Model 3200 Field Grade, except skeet-style stock and full beavertail forearm; 26- or 28-inch barrels, SK choke. Made 1973–1980.

Remington Model 3200 Special Trap Gun **$995**
Same as Model 3200 Trap Gun, except has select wood. Made 1973–1984.

SHOTGUNS

Remington Model 3200 Field

**Remington Model 3200
"One of 1000" Skeet**

Remington Model 3200 Trap

Remington Model 3200 Trap Gun **$1175**
Same as Model 3200 Field Grade, except trap-style stock w/Monte Carlo or straight comb, beavertail forearm; 30- or 32-inch barrels, IM/F or F/F chokes. Made 1973–77.

Remington Rider No. 9 Single Shot Shotgun **$295**
Improved version of No. 3 Single Barrel Shotgun made in the late 1800s. Semihammerless. Gauges 10, 12, 16, 20, 24, 28. 30- to 32-inch plain barrel. Weight: about 6 pounds. Plain pistol-grip stock and forearm. Auto ejector. Made 1902–1910.

Remington SP-10 Magnum **$695**
Takedown. Gas-operated with stainless steel piston. 10 gauge; 3½-inch chamber. Barrels: 26- or 30-inch vent-rib with REM Choke screw-in tubes. Weight: 11 to 11¼ pounds. Metal bead front. Checkered walnut stock with satin finish. Made 1989 to date.

Remington SP-10 Magnum Turkey Combo **$765**
Same general specifications as Model SP-10 Magnum, except has extra 22-inch REM Choke barrel with M, F and Turkey Extra-Full tubes. Rifle sights. QD swivels and camo sling. Made 1991 to date.

Remington Sportsman A Standard Grade Autoloader
Same general specifications as Model 11A, except magazine holds two shells. Also available in "B" Special Grade, "D" Tournament Grade, "E" Expert Grade, "F" Premier Grade. Made 1931–1948. Same values as for Model 11A.

Remington Sportsman Skeet Gun
Same general specifications as the Sportsman A, except has 26-inch barrel (plain, solid or vent rib), SK choke, beavertail forend. Discont. 1949.
With plain barrel **$350**
With solid-rib barrel **435**
With ventilated-rib barrel **465**

Remington Sportsman-48A Standard Grade 3-Shot Autoloader
Streamlined receiver. Hammerless. Takedown. Gauges: 12, 16, 20. Tubular magazine holds two shells. Barrels: plain, matted top surface or vent rib; 26-inch IC, 28-inch M or F choke, 30-inch F choke (12 ga. only). Weight: about 7½ pounds, 12 ga.; 6¾ pounds, 16 ga.; 6½ pounds, 20 ga. Pistol-grip stock, grooved forend, both checkered. Made 1949–1959.
With plain barrel **$295**
With matted top-surface barrel **310**
With ventilated-rib barrel **325**

Remington Sportsman 48D Tournament Grade

Remington Sportsman-48 B, D, F Special, Tournament and Premier Grade Guns
These higher grade models differ from the Sportsman-48A in general quality, grade of wood, checkering, engraving, etc. General specifications are the same. Made 1949–1959.
Sportsman-48B Special Grade . . . . **$ 355**
Sportsman-48D Tournament Grade **725**
Sportsman-48F Premier Grade **1550**

Remington Sportsman-48SA Skeet Gun
Same general specifications as Sportsman-48A, except has 26-inch barrel with matted top surface or vent rib, SK choke, ivory bead front sight, metal bead rear sight. Made 1949–1960.
With matted top-surface barrel . . . . **$ 265**
With ventilated-rib barrel **325**

Remington Rider No. 9

Remington Sportsman Autoloader

Remington Sportsman-48SC Skeet Target Grade

**Remington Model 11-48A
Standard**

Remington Model 11-48A, .410 & 28

Remington Sportsman-58ADL

SHOTGUNS

Remington Sportsman-48SA Skeet Gun (cont.)

Sportsman-48SC Skeet Target Grade	**405**
Sportsman-48SD Skeet Tournament Grade	**595**
Sportsman-48SF Skeet Premier Grade	**1695**

Remington Model 11-48A Riot Gun $245

Same as Model 11-48A, except 20-inch plain barrel and 12 gauge only. Discontinued in 1969.

Remington Model 11-48A Standard Grade 4-Shot Autoloader. 410 & 28 Gauge

Same general specifications as Sportsman-48A, except gauge, 3-shell magazine, 25-inch barrel. Weight: about 6¼ pounds. 28 gauge introduced 1952, .410 in 1954. Discontinued in 1969. Prices same as shown for Sportsman-48A.

Remington Model 11-48A Standard Grade 5-Shot Autoloader

Same general specifications as Sportsman-48A, except magazine holds four shells, forend not grooved. Also available in Special Grade (11-48B), Tournament Grade (11-48D) and Premier Grade (11-48F). Made 1949–1969. Prices same as shown for Sportsman-48A.

Remington Model 11-48SA 28 Gauge Skeet $320

Same general specifications as Model 11-48A 28 Gauge, except has 25-inch vent-rib barrel, SK choke. 28 gauge introduced 1952, .410 in 1954.

Remington Sportsman-58 Skeet Target, Tournament and Premier Grades

These higher grade models differ from the Sportsman-58SA in general quality, grade of wood, checkering, engraving, etc. General specifications are the same.

Sportsman-58C Skeet Target Grade	**$ 510**
Sportsman-58D Skeet Tournament Grade	**695**
Sportsman-58SF Skeet Premier Grade	**1195**

Remington Sportsman-58 Tournament and Premier

These higher grade models differ from the Sportsman-58ADL with vent-rib barrel in general quality, grade of wood, checkering, engraving, etc. General specifications are the same.

Sportsman-58D Tournament Grade	**$ 800**
Sportsman-58F Premier Grade	**1400**

Remington Sportsman-58ADL Autoloader

Deluxe Grade. Gas-operated. 12 gauge. 3-shot magazine. Barrels: plain or vent rib; 26-, 28- or 30-inch; IC, M or F choke, or Remington Special Skeet choke. Weight: about 7 pounds. Checkered pistol-grip stock and forearm. Made 1956–1964.

With plain barrel	**$295**
With ventilated-rib barrel	**325**

Remington Sportsman-58BDL Deluxe Special Grade

Same as Model 58ADL, except select grade wood.

With plain barrel	**$300**
With ventilated-rib barrel	**345**

Remington Sportsman-58SA Skeet Grade $330

Same general specifications as Model 58ADL with vent-rib barrel, except special skeet stock and forearm.

REVELATION SHOTGUNS
See Western Auto listings.

RICHLAND ARMS COMPANY
Blissfield, Michigan
Manufactured in Italy and Spain

Richland Model 200 Field Grade Double $295

Hammerless, boxlock, Anson & Deeley-type. Plain extractors. Double triggers. Gauges: 12, 16, 20, 28, .410 (3-

**Richland Model 200
Field Grade Double**

Richland Model 202
Field Grade Double

Richland Model 707 Deluxe
Field Gun

Richland Model 711 Long Range
Waterfowl Magnum

Richland Model 808
Over-and-Under

Richland Model 200 Field Grade Double (cont.)
inch chambers in 20 and .410; others have 2³/₄-inch). Barrels: 28-inch M/F choke; 26-inch IC/M; .410 with 26-inch M/F only; 22-inch IC/M in 20 ga. only. Weight: 6 lbs. 2 oz. to 7 lbs. 4 oz. Checkered walnut stock with cheekpiece, pistol grip, recoil pad; beavertail forend. Made in Spain 1963 to date.

Richland Model 202 All-Purpose Field Gun $355
Same as Model 200, except has two sets of barrels same gauge. 12 gauge: 30-inch barrels F/F, 3-inch chambers; 26-inch barrels IC/M, 2³/₄-inch chambers. 20 gauge: 28-inch barrels M/F; 22-inch barrels IC/M, 3-inch chambers. Made 1963 to date.

Richland Model 707 Deluxe Field Gun $310
Hammerless, boxlock, triple bolting system. Plain extractors. Double triggers. Gauges: 12, 2³/₄-inch chambers; 20, 3-inch chambers. Barrels: 12 gauge, 28-inch M/F, 26-inch IC/M; 20 gauge, 30-inch F/F, 28-inch M/F, 26-inch IC/M. Weight: 6 lbs. 4 oz. to 6 lbs. 15 oz. Checkered walnut stock and forend, recoil pad. Made 1963–1972.

Richland Model 711 Long Range Waterfowl Magnum Double Barrel Shotgun
Hammerless, boxlock, Anson & Deeley-type, Purdey triple lock. Plain extractors. Double triggers. Auto safety. Gauges: 10, 3¹/₂-inch chambers; 12, 3-inch chambers. Barrels: 10 ga., 32-inch; 12 ga., 30-inch; F/F. Weight: 10 ga., 11 pounds; 12 ga., 7³/₄ pounds. Checkered walnut stock and beavertail forend; recoil pad. Made in Spain 1963 to date.
10 Gauge Magnum $345
12 Gauge Magnum 275

Richland Model 808 Over-and-Under Gun $375
Boxlock. Plain extractors. Non-selective single trigger. 12 gauge only. Barrels (Vickers steel): 30-inch F/F; 28-inch M/F; 26-inch IC/M. Weight: 6 lbs. 12 oz. to 7 lbs. 3 oz. Checkered walnut stock/forend. Made in Italy 1963–68.

JOHN RIGBY & CO.
London, England

Rigby Hammerless Box Lock Double Barrel Shotguns
Auto ejectors. Double triggers. Made in all gauges, barrel lengths and chokes. Checkered stock and forend, straight grip standard. Made in two grades: Sackville and Chatsworth. These guns differ in general quality, engraving, etc.; specifications are the same.
Sackville Grade $5125
Chatsworth Grade 3750

Rigby Regal Side Lock

Rigby Hammerless Side Lock Double Barrel Shotguns
Auto ejectors. Double triggers. Made in all gauges, barrel lengths and chokes. Checkered stock and forend, straight grip standard. Made in two grades: Regal (best quality) and Sandringham; these guns differ in general quality, engraving, etc.; specifications are the same.
Regal Grade $9050
Sandringham Grade 6595

Rossi Hammerless Double

Rossi Overland

Rossi Hammerless Double Barrel Shotgun (cont.)
beavertail forearm, uncheckered. Made 1974 to date. *Note:*
H&R Model 404 (1969-72) is same gun.

Rossi Overland Hammer Double **$225**
Sidelock. Plain extractors. Double triggers. Gauges: 12,
.410; 3-inch chambers. Barrels: 20-inch, IC/M in 12 gauge;
26-inch, F/F choke in .410. Weight: 7 lbs., 12 ga.; 6 lbs.,
.410. Pistol-grip stock and beavertail forearm, uncheckered. *Note:* Because of its resemblance to the short-barreled doubles carried by guards riding shotgun on 19th-
century stagecoaches, the 12 gauge version originally was
called the "Coach Gun." Made 1968–1989.

AMADEO ROSSI, S.A.
Sao Leopoldo, Brazil

Rossi Hammerless Double Barrel Shotgun **$265**
Boxlock. Plain extractors. Double triggers. 12 gauge. 3-
inch chambers. Barrels: 26-inch IC/M; 28-inch M/F
choke. Weight: 7 to 7½ pounds. Pistol-grip stock and

Rottweil American Skeet

ROTTWEIL SHOTGUNS
West Germany

Rottweil Model 72 Over/Under Shotgun **$1595**
Hammerless, takedown with engraved receiver. 12 gauge;
2¾-inch chambers. 26¾-inch barrels with SK/SK chokes.
Weight: 7½ pounds. Interchangeable trigger groups and
buttstocks. Checkered French walnut buttstock and forend. Imported from West Germany.

Rottweil Model 650 Field O/U Shotgun **$650**
Breech action. Gauge: 12. 28-inch barrels. Six screw-in
choke tubes. Automatic ejectors. Engraved receiver.
Checkered pistol grip stock. Made 1984–86.

Rottweil American Skeet **$1550**
Boxlock action. Gauge: 12. 27-inch vent-rib barrels. 44½
inches overall. SK chokes. Weight: 7½ pounds. Designed
for tube sets. Hand-checkered European walnut stock with
modified forend. Made 1984–87.

Rottweil International Trap Shotgun **$1575**
Boxlock action. Gauge: 12. 30-inch barrels. 48½ inches
overall. Weight: 8 pounds. Choked IM/F. Selective single
trigger. Metal bead front sight. Checkered European walnut stock w/pistol grip. Engraved action. Made 1984–87.

SHOTGUNS

Ruger Red Label O/U Stainless

Ruger Red Label—12 Gauge
(1982)

RUGER SHOTGUN
Southport, Connecticut
Manufactured by Sturm, Ruger & Company

Ruger Plain Grade Red Label Over/Under **$725**
Boxlock. Auto ejectors. Selective single trigger. 20 gauge.
3-inch chambers. 26-inch vent-rib barrel, IC/M or SK

Ruger Plain Grade Red Label Over/Under (cont.)
choke. Weight: about 7 pounds. Checkered pistol-grip
stock and forearm. Introduced in 1977; 12 gauge version,
1982. Chambers: 2¾- and 3-inch. Barrels: 26-, 28- and
30-inch. Weight: about 7½ pounds.

Ruger Red Label Over/Under Stainless
Gauges: 12 and 20; 3-inch chambers. Barrels: 26- or 28-
inch. Various chokes, fixed or screw-in tubes. Weight: 7
to 7½ pounds. Single selective trigger. Selective automatic
ejectors. Automatic top safety. Standard gold bead front

Ruger Red Label O/U Stainless (cont.)

sight. Pistol-grip or English-style American walnut stock with hand-cut checkering. Made 1985 to date.

With Fixed Chokes	$800
With Screw-in Tubes	895

Ruger Sporting Clays Over/Under Stainless $880

Similar to the Red Label O/U Stainless, except in 12 gauge only with 30-inch vent-rib barrels, no side ribs; back-bored with screw-in choke tubes (not interchangeable with other Red Label O/U models). Brass front and mid-rib beads. Made 1992 to date.

VICTOR SARASQUETA, S. A.
Eibar, Spain

Sarasqueta Model 3

Sarasqueta Model 3 Hammerless Box Lock Double Barrel Shotgun

Plain extractors or auto ejectors. Double triggers. Gauges: 12, 16, 20. Made in various barrel lengths, chokes and weights. Checkered stock and forend, straight grip standard. Currently manufactured.

Model 3, plain extractors	$495
Model 3E, automatic ejectors	550

Sarasqueta Model 6E

Sarasqueta Model 11E

Sarasqueta Hammerless Side Lock Doubles

Automatic ejectors (except on Models 4 and 203 which have plain extractors). Double triggers. Gauges: 12, 16,

Sarasqueta Model 12E

Sarasqueta Hammerless Side Lock Doubles (cont.)

20. Barrel lengths, chokes and weights made to order. Checkered stock and forend, straight grip standard. Models differ chiefly in overall quality, engraving, grade of wood, checkering, etc.; general specifications are the same. Currently manufactured.

Model 4	$ 575
Model 4E	625
Model 203	575
Model 203E	615
Model 6E	705
Model 7E	750
Model 10E	1525
Model 11E	1650
Model 12E	1825

J. P. SAUER & SOHN
Eckernförde, Germany
Formerly located in Suhl, Germany

Sauer Model 66
Field, Grade II

Sauer Model 66
Field, Grade III

Sauer Model 66 Over-and-Under Field Gun

Purdey-system action with Holland & Holland-type sidelocks. Selective single trigger. Selective auto ejectors. Automatic safety. Available in three grades of engraving.

Sauer Model 66 Field, Grade I

Sauer Model 66 Trap, Grade II

Sauer Model 66 Over-and-Under Field Gun (cont.)

12 gauge only. Krupp-Special steel barrels with vent rib, 28-inch, M/F choke. Weight: about 7¼ pounds. Checkered walnut stock and forend; recoil pad. Made 1966–1975.

Grade I	**$1600**
Grade II	**2100**
Grade III	**2900**

Sauer Model 66 Over-and-Under Skeet Gun

Same as Model 66 Field Gun, except 26-inch barrels with wide vent rib, SK choked; skeet-style stock and ventilated beavertail forearm; nonautomatic safety. Made 1966–1975.

Grade I	**$1595**
Grade II	**2000**
Grade III	**2895**

Sauer Model 66 Over-and-Under Trap Gun

Same as Model 66 Skeet Gun, except has 30-inch barrels choked F/F or M/F; trap-style stock. Values same as for Skeet Model. Made 1966–1975.

Sauer Model 3000E Drilling

Combination rifle and double barrel shotgun. Blitz action with Greener crossbolt, double underlugs, separate rifle cartridge extractor, front set trigger, firing pin indicators, Greener side safety, sear slide selector locks right shotgun barrel for firing rifle barrel. Gauge/calibers: 12 gauge (2¾-inch chambers); 222, 243, 30-06, 7×65R. 25-inch Krupp-Special steel barrels; M/F choke, automatic folding leaf rear rifle sight. Weight: 6½ to 7¼ pounds depending on rifle caliber. Checkered walnut stock and forend; pistol grip, M Monte Carlo comb and cheekpiece, sling swivels. Standard Model with arabesque engraving; Deluxe Model with hunting scenes engraved on action. Currently manufactured. *Note:* Also see listing under Colt.

Standard Model	**$2495**
Deluxe Model	**3250**

Sauer Model 3000E Drilling, Standard

Sauer Artemis Double Barrel Shotgun

Holland & Holland-type sidelock with Greener crossbolt, double underlugs, double sear safeties, selective single trigger, selective auto ejectors. Grade I with fine-line engraving; Grade II with full English arabesque engraving. 12 gauge (2¾-inch chambers). Krupp-Special steel barrels, 28-inch, M/F choke. Weight: about 6½ pounds. Checkered walnut pistol-grip stock and beavertail forend; recoil pad. Made 1966–1977.

Grade I	**$3995**
Grade II	**4950**

Sauer BBF Over/Under Combination Rifle/Shotgun

Blitz action with Kersten lock, front set trigger fires rifle barrel, slide-operated sear safety. Gauge/calibers: 16 gauge; 30-30, 30-06, 7×65R. 25-inch Krupp-Special steel barrels; shotgun barrel Full choke, folding-leaf rear sight. Weight:

Sauer Artemis, Grade II

SHOTGUNS

Sauer Royal Double

Sauer BBF Combination, Standard Model

Sauer BBF Over/Under Combo (cont.)

about 6 pounds. Checkered walnut stock and forend; pistol grip, mod. Monte Carlo comb and cheekpiece, sling swivels. Standard Model with arabesque engraving; Deluxe Model with hunting scenes engraved on action. Currently manufactured.

Standard Model **$1850**
Deluxe Model **2295**

Sauer Royal Double Barrel Shotguns

Anson & Deeley action (boxlock) with Greener crossbolt, double underlugs, signal pins, selective single trigger, selective auto ejectors, auto safety. Scalloped frame with arabesque engraving. Krupp-Special steel barrels. Gauges: 12, 2³/₄-inch chambers; 20, 3-inch chambers. Barrels: 30-inch (12 ga. only) and 28-inch, M/F; 26-inch (20 ga. only), IC/M. Weight: 12 ga., about 6¹/₂ pounds; 20 ga., 6 pounds. Checkered walnut pistol-grip stock and beavertail forend; recoil pad. Made 1955–1977.

Standard Model **$1295**
20 Gauge **1740**

Savage Model 24D

Savage Model 24F-12T Turkey Gun

SAVAGE ARMS
Westfield, Massachusetts
Formerly located in Utica, New York

Savage Model 24 22-.410 O/U Combination **$130**
Same as Stevens No. 22-.410, has walnut stock and forearm. Made 1950–1965.

Savage Model 24C Camper's Companion **$145**
Same as Model 24FG, except made in 22 Magnum/20 gauge only; has 20-inch barrels, shotgun tube Cyl. bore. Weight: 5³/₄ pounds. Trap in butt provides ammunition storage; comes with carrying case. Made 1972–1989.

Savage Model 24D **$185**
Same as Models 24DL and 24MDL, except frame has black or casehardened finish. Game scene decoration of frame eliminated in 1974; forearm uncheckered after 1976. Made 1970–1988.

Savage Model 24DL **$195**
Same general specifications as Model 24S, except top lever opening; satin-chrome-finished frame decorated with game scenes, checkered Monte Carlo stock and forearm. Made 1965–69.

Savage Model 24F-12T Turkey Gun **$255**
12- or 20-gauge shotgun barrel/22 Hornet, 223 or 30-30 caliber rifle. 24-inch blued barrels; 3-inch chambers; extra removable Full choke tube. Hammer block safety. Color casehardened frame. du Pont Rynite® camo stock. Swivel studs. Made 1989 to date.

Savage Model 24FG Field Grade **$125**
Same general specifications as Model 24S, except top lever opening. Made 1972 to date.

Savage Model 24MDL **$140**
Same as Model 24DL, except rifle barrel chambered for 22 WMR. Made 1965–69.

Savage Model 24MS **$125**
Same as Model 24S, except rifle barrel chambered for 22 WMR. Made 1965–1971.

Savage Model 24S

Savage Model 24V

Savage Model 24-VS Camper/Survival

Savage Model 28A

Savage Model 30 Solid Frame

Savage Model 30 Takedown Slug

SHOTGUNS

Savage Model 24S Over/Under Combination ... **$140**
Boxlock. Visible hammer. Side lever opening. Plain extractors. Single trigger. 20 ga. or .410 bore shotgun barrel under 22 LR barrel; 24-inch. Open rear sight, ramp front, dovetail for scope mounting. Weight: about 6¾ pounds. Plain pistol-grip stock and forearm. Made 1965–1971.

Savage Model 24V **$235**
Similar to Model 24D, except 20 gauge under 222 Rem., 22 Rem., 357 Mag., 22 Hornet or 30-30 rifle barrel. Made 1971–1989.

**Savage Model 24-VS Camper/Survival/
Centerfire Rifle/Shotgun** **$155**
Similar to Model 24V except 357 Rem. Mag. over 20 gauge. Nickel finish, full-length stock and accessory pistol-grip stock. Overall length: 36 inches with full stock; 26 inches w/pistol grip. Weight: about 6½ pounds. Made 1983–88.

**Savage Model 28A Standard Grade Slide Action
Repeating Shotgun** **$215**
Hammerless. Takedown. 12 gauge. 5-shell tubular magazine. Plain barrel; lengths: 26-, 28-, 30-, 32-inches; choked C/M/F. Weight: about 7½ pounds with 30-inch barrel. Plain pistol-grip stock, grooved slide handle. Made 1928–1931.

Savage Model 28B **$235**
Raised matted rib; otherwise the same as Model 28A.

Savage Model 28D Trap Grade **$300**
Same general specifications as Model 28A, except has 30-inch Full choke barrel with matted rib, trap-style stock with checkered pistol grip, checkered slide handle of select walnut.

**Savage Model 30 Solid Frame Hammerless
Slide Action Shotgun** **$180**
Gauges: 12, 16, 20, .410. 2¾-inch chamber in 16 gauge, 3-inch in other gauges. Magazine holds four 2¾-inch shells or three 3-inch shells. Barrels: vent rib; 26-, 28-, 30-inch; IC, M, F choke. Weight: average 6¼ to 6¾ pounds depending on gauge. Plain pistol-grip stock (checkered on later production), grooved slide handle. Made 1958–1970.

Savage Model 30 Takedown Slug Gun **$175**
Same as Model 30FG, except 21-inch Cyl. bore barrel with rifle sights. Made 1971–79.

Savage Model 30AC Solid Frame **$190**
Same as Model 30 Solid Frame, except has 26-inch barrel with adjustable choke; 12 gauge only. Made 1959–1970.

Savage Model 30AC Takedown

Savage Model 30FG Takedown

Savage Model 69-RXL

Savage Model 220

Savage Model 30AC Takedown **$170**
Same as Model 30FG, except has 26-inch barrel with adjustable choke; 12 and 20 gauge only. Made 1971–72.

Savage Model 30ACL Solid Frame **$195**
Same as Model 30AC Solid Frame, except left-hand model with ejection port and safety on left side; 12 gauge only. Made 1960–64.

Savage Model 30D Takedown **$175**
Deluxe Grade. Same as Model 30FG, except has receiver engraved with game scene, vent-rib barrel, recoil pad. Made 1971 to date.

**Savage Model 30FG Takedown Hammerless Slide
Action Shotgun** **$145**
Field Grade. Gauges: 12, 20, .410. 3-inch chamber. Magazine holds four 2¾-inch shells or three 3-inch shells. Barrels: plain; 26-inch Full choke (.410 ga. only); 28-inch M/F choke; 30-inch Full choke (12 ga. only). Weight: average 7 to 7¾ pounds depending on gauge. Checkered pistol-grip stock, fluted slide handle. Made 1970–79.

Savage Model 30L Solid Frame **$170**
Same as Model 30 Solid Frame, except left-handed model with ejection port and safety on left side; 12 gauge only. Made 1959–1970.

Savage Model 30T Solid Frame Trap and Duck . **$195**
Same as Model 30 Solid Frame, except only in 12 gauge with 30-inch Full choke barrel; has Monte Carlo stock with recoil pad, weighs about 8 pounds. Made 1963–1970.

Savage Model 30T Takedown Trap Gun **$175**
Same as Model 30D, except only in 12 gauge with 30-inch Full choke barrel. Monte Carlo stock with recoil pad. Made 1970–73.

Savage Model 69-RXL Slide Action Shotgun . . . **$160**
Hammerless, side ejection, top tang safe for left- or right-hand use. 12 gauge, chambered for 2¾- and 3-inch magnum shells. 18¼-inch barrel. Tubular magazine holds 6 rounds (one less for 3-inch mag). Walnut finish hardwood stock with recoil pad, grooved operating handle. Weight: about 6½ pounds. Made 1982 to date.

Savage Model 220 Single Barrel Shotgun **$125**
Hammerless. Takedown. Auto ejector. Gauges: 12, 16, 20, .410. Single shot. Barrel lengths: 12 ga., 28- to 36-inch; 16 ga., 28- to 32-inch; 20 ga., 26- to 32-inch; .410 bore, 26- and 28-inch. Full choke. Weight: about 6 pounds. Plain pistol-grip stock and wide forearm. Made 1938–1965.

Savage Model 220AC **$150**
Same as Model 220, except has Savage adjustable choke.

Savage Model 220L **$120**
Same general specifications as Model 220, except has side lever opening instead of top lever. Made 1965–1972.

Savage Model 220P **$135**
Same as Model 220, except has Poly Choke built integrally with barrel; made in 12 gauge with 30-inch barrel, 16 and 20 gauge with 28-inch barrel, not made in .410 bore; has recoil pad.

Savage Model 242 Over-and-Under Shotgun . . . **$285**
Similar to Model 24D, except both barrels .410 bore, Full choke. Weight: about 7 pounds. Made 1977–1980.

Savage Model 312 Field Grade O/U **$495**
Gauge: 12; 2¾- or 3-inch chambers. 26- or 28-inch barrels w/vent rib; F/M/IC chokes. 43 or 45 inches overall. Weight: 7 pounds. Internal hammers. Top tang safety. American walnut stock with checkered pistol grip and recoil pad. Made 1990–93.

Savage Model 312 Sporting Clays O/U **$525**
Same as Model 312 Field Grade, except furnished with #1 and #2 skeet tubes and 28-inch barrels only. Made 1990–93.

Savage Model 312 Trap Over/Under **$530**
Same as Model 312 Field Grade, except with 30-inch barrels only, Monte Carlo buttstock and weight of 7½ pounds. Made 1990–93.

> **NOTE:** Savage Models 330, 333T, 333, and 2400 were manufactured by Valmet Oy, Helsinki, Finland.

Savage Model 330 Over-and-Under Shotgun . . . **$425**
Boxlock. Plain extractors. Selective single trigger. Gauges: 12, 20. 2¾-inch chambers in 12 gauge, 3-inch in 20 gauge. Barrels: 26-inch IC/M; 28-inch M/F; 30-inch M/F choke (12 ga. only). Weight: 6¼ to 7¼ pounds, depending on gauge. Checkered pistol-grip stock and forearm. Made 1969–1978.

Savage Model 333 Over-and-Under Shotgun . . . **$525**
Boxlock. Auto ejectors. Selective single trigger. Gauges: 12, 20. 2¾-inch chambers in 12 gauge, 3-inch in 20 gauge. Barrels: vent rib; 26-inch SK choke, IC/M; 28-inch M/F; 30-inch M/F choke (12 ga. only). Weight: average 6¼ to 7¼ pounds. Checkered pistol-grip stock and forearm. Made 1973–79.

Savage Model 242

Savage Model 312 Field Grade O/U

Savage Model 312 Trap Over/Under

Savage Model 330

**Savage Model 333
20 Gauge**

SHOTGUNS

Savage Model 333T Trap Gun **$495**
Similar to Model 330, except only in 12 gauge with 30-inch vent-rib barrels, IM/F choke; Monte Carlo stock with recoil pad. Weight: 7¾ pounds. Made 1972–79.

Savage Model 420 Over-and-Under Shotgun
Boxlock. Hammerless. Takedown. Automatic safety. Double triggers or non-selective single trigger. Gauges: 12, 16, 20. Barrels: plain; 26- to 30-inch (the latter in 12 gauge only); choked M/F, C/IC. Weight with 28-inch barrels: 12 ga., 7¾ lbs.; 16 ga., 7½ lbs.; 20 ga., 6¾ lbs. Plain pistol-grip stock and forearm. Made 1938–1942.
With double triggers **$495**
With single trigger **575**

Savage Model 430
Same as Model 420, except has matted top barrel, checkered stock of select walnut with recoil pad, checkered forearm. Made 1938–1942.
With double triggers **$550**
With single trigger **600**

Savage Model 440 Over-and-Under Shotgun . . . **$475**
Boxlock. Plain extractors. Selective single trigger. Gauges: 12, 20. 2¾-inch chambers in 12 gauge, 3-inch in 20 gauge. Barrels: vent rib; 26-inch SK choke, IC/M; 28-inch M/F; 30-inch M/F choke (12 ga. only). Weight: average 6 to 6½ pounds depending on gauge. Made 1968–1972.

Savage Model 440T Trap Gun **$465**
Similar to Model 440, except only in 12 gauge with 30-inch barrels, extra-wide vent rib, IM/F choke. Trap-style Monte Carlo stock and semibeavertail forearm of select walnut, recoil pad. Weight: 7½ pounds. Made 1969–1972.

Savage Model 444 Deluxe Over/Under Shotgun . . **$510**
Similar to Model 440, except has auto ejectors, select walnut stock and semibeavertail forearm. Made 1969–1972.

Savage Model 550 Hammerless Double **$225**
Boxlock. Auto ejectors. Non-selective single trigger. Gauges: 12, 20. 2¾-inch chamber in 12 gauge, 3-inch in 20 gauge. Barrels: vent rib; 26-inch IC/M; 28-inch M/F; 30-inch M/F choke (12 ga. only). Weight: 7 to 8 lbs. Checkered pistol-grip stock and semibeavertail forearm. Made 1971–73.

Savage Model 333T

Savage Model 430

Savage Model 440

Savage Model 440T

Savage Model 550

Savage Model 720

Savage Model 726

Savage Model 750

Savage Model 775

Savage Model 775-SC

Savage Model 720 Standard Grade 5-Shot Autoloading Shotgun $250
Browning type. Takedown. 12 and 16 gauge. 4-shell tubular magazine. Barrel: plain; 26- to 32-inch (the latter in 12 gauge only); choked C, M, F. Weight: about 8¼ pounds, 12 ga. with 30-inch barrel; 16 ga., about ½ pound lighter. Checkered pistol-grip stock and forearm. Made 1930–1949.

Savage Model 726 Upland Sporter Grade 3-Shot Autoloading Shotgun $240
Same as Model 720, except has 2-shell magazine capacity. Made 1931–1949.

Savage Model 740C Skeet Gun $295
Same as Model 726, except has special skeet stock and full beavertail forearm, equipped with Cutts Compensator, barrel length overall with spreader tube is about 24½ inches. Made 1936–1949.

Savage Model 745 Lightweight Autoloader $210
Three- or five-shot model. Same general specifications as Model 720, except has lightweight alloy receiver, 12 gauge only, 28-inch plain barrel. Weight: about 6¾ pounds. Made 1940–49.

Savage Model 750 Automatic Shotgun $210
Browning-type autoloader. Takedown. 12 gauge. 4-shot tubular magazine. Barrels: 28-inch F or M choke; 26-inch IC. Weight: about 7¼ pounds. Checkered walnut pistol-grip stock and grooved forearm. Made 1960–67.

Savage Model 750-AC $275
Same as Model 750, except has 26-inch barrel with adjustable choke. Made 1964–67.

Savage Model 750-SC $250
Same as Model 750, except has 26-inch barrel with Savage Super Choke. Made 1962–63.

Savage Model 755 Standard Grade Autoloader $210
Streamlined receiver. Takedown. 12 and 16 gauge. 4-shell tubular magazine (a three-shot model with magazine capacity of two shells was also produced until 1951). Barrel: plain; 30-inch F choke (12 ga. only), 28-inch F or M, 26-inch IC. Weight: about 8¼ pounds, 12 ga. Checkered pistol-grip stock and forearm. Made 1949–1958.

Savage Model 755-SC $200
Same as Model 755, except has 26-inch barrel with recoil-reducing, adjustable Savage Super Choke.

Savage Model 775 Lightweight $210
Same general specifications as Model 755, except has lightweight alloy receiver and weighs about 6¾ pounds. Made 1950–1965.

Savage Model 775-SC $210
Same as Model 775, except has 26-inch barrel with Savage Super Choke.

Savage Model 2400
Over/Under Combination

Savage Model 2400 Over/Under Combination .. **$595**
Boxlock action similar to that of Model 330. Plain extractors. Selective single trigger. 12-gauge (2³/₄-inch chamber) shotgun barrel, Full choke, over 308 Win. or 222 Rem. rifle barrel; 23¹/₂-inch; solid matted rib with blade front sight and folding leaf rear, dovetail for scope mounting. Weight: about 7¹/₂ pounds. Monte Carlo stock with pistol grip and recoil pad, semibeavertail forearm, checkered. Made 1975–79 by Valmet.

SEARS, ROEBUCK & COMPANY
Chicago, Illinois
J. C. Higgins and Ted Williams Models

Although they do not correspond to specific models below, the names Ted Williams and J. C. Higgins have been used to designate various Sears shotguns at various times.

Sears Model 18 Bolt Action Repeater **$80**
Takedown. 3-shot top-loading magazine. Gauge: .410 only. Barrel: 25-inch with variable choke. Weight: about 5³/₄ pounds.

Sears Model 20 Slide Action Repeater **$160**
Hammerless. 5-shot magazine. Barrels: 26- to 30-inch with various chokes. Weight: 7¹/₄ pounds. Plain pistol-grip stock and slide handle.

Sears Model 21 Slide Action Repeater **$185**
Same general specifications as the Model 20 except vent rib and adjustable choke.

Sears Model 30 Slide Action Repeater **$175**
Hammerless. Gauges: 12, 16, 20 and .410. 4-shot magazine. Barrels: 26- to 30-inch, various chokes. Weight: 6¹/₂ pounds. Plain pistol-grip stock, grooved slide handle.

Sears Model 97 Single Shot Shotgun **$65**
Takedown. Visible hammer. Automatic ejector. Gauges: 12, 16, 20 and .410. Barrels: 26- to 36-inch, Full choke. Weight: average 6 pounds. Plain pistol-grip stock and forearm.

Sears Model 97-AC Single Shot Shotgun **$80**
Same general specifications as Model 97 except fancier stock and forearm.

Sears Model 101.7 Double Barrel Shotgun **$160**
Boxlock. Double triggers. Gauges: 12, 16, 20, .410. Barrels: 26- to 32-inch, choked M and F. Weight: from 6 to 7¹/₂ pounds. Plain stock and forend.

Sears Model 101.7C Double Barrel Shotgun **$175**
Same general specifications as Model 101.7, except checkered stock and forearm.

Sears Model 101.25 Bolt Action Shotgun **$80**
Takedown. .410 gauge. 5-shell tubular magazine. 24-inch barrel, Full choke. Weight: about 6 pounds. Plain, one-piece pistol-grip stock.

Sears Model 101.40 Single Shot Shotgun **$65**
Takedown. Visible hammer. Automatic ejector. Gauges: 12, 16, 20 and .410. Barrels: 26- to 36-inch, Full choke. Weight: average 6 pounds. Plain pistol-grip stock and forearm.

Sears Model 101.1120 Bolt Action Repeater **$80**
Takedown. .410 gauge. 24-inch barrel, Full choke. Weight: about 5 pounds. Plain one-piece pistol-grip stock.

Sears Model 101.1380 Bolt Action Repeater **$90**
Takedown. Gauges: 12, 16, 20. 2-shell detachable box magazine. 26-inch barrel, Full choke. Weight: about 7 pounds. Plain one-piece pistol-grip stock.

Sears Model 101.1610 Double Barrel Shotgun .. **$235**
Boxlock. Double triggers. Plain extractors. Gauges: 12, 16, 20 and .410. Barrels: 24- to 30-inch. Various chokes, but mostly M and F. Weight: about 7¹/₂ pounds, 12 ga. Checkered pistol-grip stock and forearm.

Sears Model 101.1701 Double Barrel Shotgun .. **$245**
Same general specifications as Model 101.1610 except satin chrome frame and select walnut stock and forearm.

Sears Model 101.5350-D Bolt Action Repeater ... **$80**
Takedown. Gauges: 12, 16, 20. 2-shell detachable box magazine. 26-inch barrel, Full choke. Weight: about 7¹/₄ pounds. Plain one-piece pistol-grip stock.

Sears Model 101.5410 Bolt Action Repeater **$80**
Same general specifications as Model 101.5350-D.

Sears Model 103.720 Bolt Action Repeater **$75**
Takedown. Automatic thumb safety. .410 gauge. 24-inch barrel, Full choke. Weight: about 5 pounds. Plain pistol-grip stock.

Sears Model 103.740 Bolt Action Repeater **$75**
Same general specifications as Model 103.720.

Sears Model 200 Slide Action Repeater **$165**
Front-locking rotary bolt. Takedown. 4-shot magazine. Gauges: 12, 16 and 20. Barrel: plain or vent rib. Weight: 6¹/₂ to 7¹/₄ pounds. Checkered pistol grip and forearm.

Sears Model 300 Autoloading Shotgun **$195**
Gas-operated. Front-locking rotary bolt. Takedown. 2-shot magazine. Gauges: 12, 16, 20. Barrel: plain or vent rib. Various chokes. Weight: 6¹/₂ to 7¹/₂ pounds. Checkered pistol-grip stock and forearm, recoil pad.

Sears Model 5100 Double Barrel Shotgun **$150**
Boxlock. Double triggers. Gauges: 12, 16, 20, .410. Barrels: 26- to 32-inch, various chokes. Weight: 6 to 7¹/₂ pounds.

SKB Model 880

SKB ARMS COMPANY
Tokyo, Japan

SKB Models 300 and 400 Side-by-Side Doubles
Similar to Model 200E, except higher grade. Models 300 and 400 differ in that the latter has more elaborate engraving and fancier wood.
Model 300 . . . . **$595**
Model 400 . . . . **795**

SKB Model 400 Skeet **$810**
Similar to Model 200E Skeet, except higher grade with more elaborate engraving and full fancy wood.

SKB Model 480 English **$850**
Similar to Model 280 English, except higher grade with more elaborate engraving and full fancy wood.

SKB Model 500 Small Gauge O/U Shotgun **$550**
Similar to Model 500, except gauges 28 and .410; has 28-inch vent-rib barrels, M/F chokes. Weight: about 6½ pounds.

SKB Model 585 Deluxe Over/Under Shotgun
Boxlock. Gauges: 12, 20, 28 and .410; 2¾-or 3-inch chambers. Barrels: 26-, 28-, 30-, 32- or 34-inch with vent rib; fixed chokes or Inter-choke tubes. Weight: 6½ to 8½ pounds. Single selective trigger. Selective automatic ejectors. Manual safety. Checkered walnut stock in standard or Monte Carlo style. Silver nitride finish with engraved game scenes. Made 1987 to date.
Field, Skeet, Trap Grade . . . . **$ 790**
Field Grade, two-barrel set **1395**
Skeet Set (20, 28, .410 ga.) **1850**
Sporting Clays **825**
Trap Combo (two-bbl.) **1350**

SKB Model 600 Small Gauge **$625**
Same as Model 500 Small Gauge, except higher grade with more elaborate engraving and fancier wood.

SKB Model 685 Deluxe Over/Under
Similar to the 585 Deluxe, except with semi-fancy American walnut stock. Gold trigger and jeweled barrel block. Silvered receiver with fine engraving.
Field, Skeet, Trap Grade . . . . **$ 895**
Field Grade, two-bbl. set **1395**
Skeet Set **1995**

SKB Model 685 Deluxe Over/Under (cont.)
Sporting Clays . . . . **$ 925**
Trap Combo, two bbl. **1595**

SKB Model 800 Skeet/Trap Over/Under
Similar to Model 700 Skeet and Trap, except higher grade with more elaborate engraving and fancier wood.
Model 800 Skeet **$850**
Model 800 Trap **875**

SKB Model 880 Skeet/Trap
Similar to Model 800 Skeet, except has sideplates.
Model 880 Skeet **$1050**
Model 880 Trap **1125**

SKB Model 885 Deluxe Over/Under
Similar to the 685 Deluxe, except with engraved sideplates.
Field, Skeet, Trap Grade . . . . **$ 995**
Field Grade, two-bbl. set **1395**
Skeet Set **2595**
Sporting Clays **1025**
Trap Combo **1695**

> **NOTE:** The following SKB shotguns were distributed by Ithaca Gun Co. 1966–1976. For specific data, please see corresponding listings under Ithaca.

SKB Century Single Barrel Trap Gun
The SKB catalog does not differentiate between Century and Century II; however, specifications of current Century are those of Ithaca-SKB Century II.
Century **$495**
Century II **595**

SKB Gas-operated Automatic Shotguns
Model XL300 with plain barrel **$265**
Model XL300 with vent rib **295**
Model XL900 . . . . **315**
Model XL900 Trap **350**
Model XL900 Skeet **345**
Model XL900 Slug **290**
Model 1300 Upland, Slug **375**
Model 1900 Field, Trap, Slug **425**

SKB Over-and-Under Shotguns
Model 500 Field **$525**
Model 500 Magnum **540**

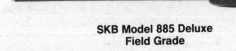

**SKB Model 885 Deluxe
Field Grade**

SHOTGUNS

SKB Model 600 Field

SKB Over-and-Under Shotguns (cont.)

Model 600 Field	$ 630
Model 600 Magnum	640
Model 600 Trap	650
Model 600 Doubles	650
Model 600 Skeet—12 or 20 gauge	635
Model 600 Skeet—28 or .410	650
Model 600 Skeet Combo	1900
Model 600 English	650
Model 700 Trap	810
Model 700 Doubles	810
Model 700 Skeet	810
Model 700 Skeet Combo	2100

SKB Recoil-operated Automatic Shotguns

Model 300—with plain barrel	$225
Model 300—with vent rib	250
Model 900	325
Model 900 Slug	295

SKB Side-by-Side Double Barrel Shotguns

Model 100	$385
Model 150E	395
Model 200E	525
Model 200E Skeet	540
Model 280 English	595

L. C. Smith Ideal

L. C. SMITH SHOTGUNS

Made 1890–1945 by Hunter Arms Company, Fulton, N.Y.; 1946–1951 and 1968–1973 by Marlin Firearms Company, New Haven, Conn.

L. C. Smith Crown

L. C. Smith Field

L. C. Smith Monogram

L. C. Smith Olympic

L. C. Smith Premier

L. C. Smith Double Barrel Shotguns

Values shown are for L. C. Smith doubles made by Hunter. Those of 1946–1951 Marlin manufacture generally bring prices about 1/3 lower. Smaller gauge models, especially in the higher grades, command premium prices: up to 50 percent more for 20 gauge, up to 200 percent for .410 gauge.

L. C. Smith Double Barrel Shotguns (cont.)

Crown Grade, double triggers, automatic ejectors	$ 4,500
Crown Grade, selective single trigger, automatic ejectors	4,800
Deluxe Grade, selective single trigger, automatic ejectors	14,995
Field Grade, double triggers, plain extractors	995
Field Grade, double triggers, auto ejectors	1,100
Field Grade, non-selective single trigger, plain extractors	1,025
Field Grade, selective single trigger, automatic ejectors	1,150
Ideal Grade, double triggers, plain extractors	1,400
Ideal Grade, double triggers, automatic ejectors	1,595
Ideal Grade, selective single trigger, automatic ejectors	1,900
Monogram Grade, selective single trigger, automatic ejectors	9,500
Olympic Grade, selective single trigger, automatic ejectors	1,750
Premier Grade, selective single trigger, automatic ejectors	11,500

L. C. Smith Skeet

L. C. Smith Specialty

L. C. Smith Trap

L. C. Smith Double Barrel Shotguns (cont.)

Skeet Special, non-selective single trigger, automatic ejectors	$ 1,600
Skeet Special, sel. single trigger, auto ejectors	1,595
.410 Gauge	12,000
Specialty Grade, double triggers, auto ejectors	2,795
Specialty Grade, selective single trigger, automatic ejectors	3,000
Trap Grade, sel. single trigger, auto ejectors	1,250

L. C. Smith Hammerless Double Barrel Shotguns

Sidelock. Auto ejectors standard on higher grades, extra on Field and Ideal Grades. Double triggers or Hunter single trigger (non-selective or selective). Gauges: 12, 16, 20, .410. Barrels: 26- to 32-inch, any standard boring. Weight: 6½ to 8¼ pounds, 12 ga. Checkered stock and forend; choice of straight, half or full pistol grip, beavertail or standard-type forend. Grades differ only in quality of workmanship, wood, checkering, engraving, etc. Same general specifications apply to all. Manufacture of these L. C. Smith guns was discontinued in 1951. Production of Field Grade 12 gauge was resumed 1968–1973. *Note:* L. C. Smith Shot-

L. C. Smith Hammerless Doubles (cont.)

guns manufactured by the Hunter Arms Co. 1890–1913 were designated by numerals to indicate grade, with the exception of Pigeon and Monogram.

00 Grade	$ 995
0 Grade	1,350
1 Grade	1,500
2 Grade	1,700
3 Grade	2,350
Pigeon	3,000
4 Grade	5,500
5 Grade	5,750
Monogram	8,500
A1	3,500
A2	8,400
A3	+15,000

L. C. Smith Hammerless Double Model 1968 Field Grade $595

"Re-creation" of the original L. C. Smith double. Sidelock. Plain extractors. Double triggers. 12 gauge. 28-inch vent-rib barrels, M/F choke. Weight: about 6¾ pounds. Checkered pistol-grip stock and forearm. Made 1968–1973.

L. C. Smith Hammerless Double Model 1968 Deluxe $625

Same as 1968 Field Grade, except has Simmons floating vent rib, beavertail forearm. Made 1971–73.

L. C. Smith Single Shot Trap
Olympic Grade

L. C. Smith Single Shot Trap Guns

Boxlock. Hammerless. Auto ejector. 12 gauge only. Barrel lengths: 32- or 34-inch. Vent rib. Weight: 8 to 8¼ pounds. Checkered pistol-grip stock and forend, recoil pad. Grades vary in quality of workmanship, wood, engraving, etc.; general specifications are the same. Discont. 1951. *Note:* Values shown are for L. C. Smith single barrel trap guns made by Hunter. Those of Marlin manufacture generally bring prices about one-third lower.

Olympic Grade	$ 1275
Specialty Grade	1595
Crown Grade	2995
Monogram Grade	4300
Premier Grade	7000
Deluxe Grade	11,995

L. C. Smith Model 1968
Field Grade

L. C. Smith Model 1968 Deluxe

SHOTGUNS

Smith & Wesson Model 916, Vent Rib

Smith & Wesson Model 1000 Magnum

Smith & Wesson Model 3000

SMITH & WESSON SHOTGUNS
Springfield, Massachusetts
Mfd. by Howa Machinery, Ltd., Nagoya, Japan

In 1985 Smith and Wesson sold its shotgun operation to O. F. Mossberg & Sons, Inc.

Smith & Wesson Model 916 Slide Action Repeater
Hammerless. Solid frame. Gauges: 12, 16, 20. 3-inch chamber in 12 and 20 gauge. 5-shot tubular magazine. Barrels: plain or vent rib; 20-inch C (12 ga., plain only); 26-inch IC; 28-inch M or F; 30-inch F choke (12 ga. only). Weight: with 28-inch plain barrel, 7¼ pounds. Plain pistol-grip stock, fluted slide handle. Made 1972–1981.
With plain barrel **$145**
With ventilated-rib barrel **175**

Smith & Wesson Model 916T
Same as Model 916, except takedown, 12 gauge only. Not available with 20-inch barrel. Made 1976–1981.
With plain barrel **$165**
With ventilated-rib barrel **195**

Smith & Wesson Model 1000 Autoloader **$315**
Gas-operated. Takedown. Gauges: 12, 20. 2¾-inch chamber in 12 ga., 3-inch in 20 ga. 4-shot magazine. Barrels: vent rib; 26-inch SK choke, IC; 28-inch M or F; 30-inch F choke (12 ga. only). Weight: with 28-inch barrel, 6½ lbs. in 20 ga., 7½ lbs. in 12 ga. Checkered pistol-grip stock and forearm. Made 1972 to date.

Smith & Wesson Model 1000 Magnum **$375**
Same as standard Model 1000, except chambered for 12 gauge magnum, 3-inch shell; 30-inch barrel only, M or F choke; stock with recoil pad. Weight: about 8 pounds. Introduced in 1977.

Smith & Wesson Model 1000P **$295**
Same general specifications as Model C 3000 Slide Action, but an earlier version.

Smith & Wesson Model 3000 Slide Action **$275**
Hammerless. 20-gauge. Barrels: 26-inch IC; 28-inch M or F. Chambered for 3-inch magnum and 2¾-inch loads. American walnut stock and forearm. Checkered pistol grip and forearm. Intro. 1982.

SPRINGFIELD ARMS
Built by Savage Arms Company, Utica, New York

Springfield Double-Barrel Hammer Shotgun **$295**
Gauges: 12 and 16. Barrels: 28 to 32 inches. In 12 ga., 32-inch model, both barrels have Full choke. All other gauges and barrel lengths are left barrel Full, right barrel Mod. Weight: 7¼ to 8¼ lbs., depending on gauge and barrel length. Black walnut checkered buttstock and forend. Discontinued 1934.

Squires Bingham Model 30
Pump Shotgun

SQUIRES BINGHAM CO., INC.
Makati, Rizal, Philippines

Squires Bingham Model 30 Pump Shotgun **$150**
Hammerless. 12 gauge. 5-shot magazine. Barrels: 20-inch Cyl.; 28-inch M; 30-inch Full choke. Weight: about 7 pounds. Pulong Dalaga stock and slide handle. Currently manufactured.

Stevens Model 51

Stevens Model 58

Stevens Model 58-410

Stevens Model 59

Stevens Model 67 Pump Shotgun

J. STEVENS ARMS COMPANY
Chicopee Falls, Massachusetts
Division of Savage Arms Corporation

Stevens No. 20 "Favorite" Shotgun **$350**
Calibers: 22 and 32 Shot. Smoothbore barrel. Blade front sight; no rear. Made 1893–1939.

Stevens No. 39 New Model Pocket Shotgun **$525**
Gauge: .410. Calibers: 38-40 Shot, 44-40 Shot. Barrels: 10, 12, 15 or 18 inches, half-octagonal smoothbore. Shotgun sights. Made 1895–1906.

Stevens No. 22-.410 Over-and-Under Combination Gun
22 caliber rifle barrel over .410 bore shotgun barrel. Visible hammer. Takedown. Single trigger. 24-inch barrels, shotgun barrel Full choke. Weight: about 6 pounds. Open rear sight and ramp front sight of sporting rifle type. Plain pistol-grip stock and forearm; originally supplied with walnut stock and forearm. "Tenite" (plastic) was used in later production. Made 1938–1950. *Note:* This gun is now manufactured as the Savage Model 24.
With wood stock and forearm **$175**
With Tenite stock and forearm **140**

Stevens Model 51 Bolt Action Shotgun **$80**
Single shot. Takedown. .410 gauge. 24-inch barrel, Full choke. Weight: about $4\frac{3}{4}$ pounds. Plain one-piece pistol-grip stock, checkered on later models. Made 1962–1971.

Stevens Model 58 Bolt Action Repeater **$95**
Takedown. Gauges: 12, 16, 20. 2-shell detachable box magazine. 26-inch barrel, Full choke. Weight: about $7\frac{1}{4}$ pounds. Plain one-piece pistol-grip stock. Made 1933–1981. *Note:* Later production models have 3-inch chamber in 20 gauge, checkered stock with recoil pad.

Stevens Model 58-.410 Bolt Action Repeater **$85**
Takedown. .410 gauge. 3-shell detachable box magazine. 24-inch barrel, Full choke. Weight: about $5\frac{1}{2}$ pounds. Plain one-piece pistol-grip stock, checkered on later production. Made 1937–1981.

Stevens Model 59 Bolt Action Repeater **$125**
Takedown. .410 gauge. 5-shell tubular magazine. 24-inch barrel, Full choke. Weight: about 6 pounds. Plain, one-piece pistol-grip stock, checkered on later production. Made 1934–1973.

Stevens Model 67 Pump Shotgun
Hammerless, side-ejection solid steel receiver. Gauges: 12, 20 and .410; $2\frac{3}{4}$- or 3-inch shells. Barrels: 21-, 26-, 28-, 30-inch with fixed chokes or interchangeable choke tubes; plain or vent rib. Weight: $6\frac{1}{4}$ to $7\frac{1}{2}$ pounds. Optional rifle sights. Walnut-finished hardwood stock with corn cob-style forend.
Standard Model, Plain Barrel **$200**
Standard Model, Vent Rib **215**
Standard Model, w/Choke Tubes **225**
Slug Model, w/Rifle Sights **195**
Lobo Model, Matte Finish **205**
Youth Model, 20 ga. **175**
Camo Model, w/Choke Tubes **250**

SHOTGUNS

Stevens Model 67
Waterfowl Gun

Stevens Model 77

Stevens Model 94C

Stevens Model 94Y

Stevens Model 95

Stevens Model 107

Stevens Model 67 Waterfowl Shotgun $225
Hammerless. Gauge: 12. 3-shot tubular magazine. Walnut finished hardwood stock. Weight: about 7½ pounds. Made 1972–1989.

Stevens Model 77 Slide Action Repeater $210
Solid frame. Gauges: 12, 16, 20. 5-shot tubular magazine. Barrels: 26-inch IC; 28-inch M or F choke. Weight: about 7½ pounds. Plain pistol-grip stock with recoil pad, grooved slide handle. Made 1954–1971.

Stevens Model 77-AC $225
Same as Model 77, except has Savage Super Choke.

Stevens Model 79-VR Super Value $215
Hammerless, side ejection. Barrel: chambered for 2¾-inch and 3-inch mag. shells. 12, 20, and .410 gauge. vent rib. Walnut finished hardwood stock with checkering on grip. Weight: 6¾-7 pounds. Made 1979 to date.

Stevens Model 94 Single Shot Shotgun $100
Takedown. Visible hammer. Auto ejector. Gauges: 12, 16, 20, 28, .410. Barrels: 26-, 28-, 30-, 32-, 36-inch; Full choke. Weight: about 6 pounds depending on gauge and barrel. Plain pistol-grip stock and forearm. Made 1939–1961.

Stevens Model 94C $125
Same as Model 94, except has checkered stock, fluted forearm on late production. Made 1965 to date.

Stevens Model 94Y Youth Gun $130
Same as Model 94, except made in 20 and .410 gauge only; has 26-inch Full choke barrel, 12½-inch buttstock with recoil pad; checkered pistol grip and fluted forearm on late production. Made 1959 to date.

Stevens Model 95 Single Shot Shotgun $90
Solid frame. Visible hammer. Plain extractor. 12 gauge. 3-inch chamber. Barrels: 28-inch M; 30-inch Full choke. Weight: about 7¼ pounds. Plain pistol-grip stock, grooved forearm. Made 1965–69.

Stevens Model 107 Single Shot Hammer Shotgun $85
Takedown. Auto ejector. Gauges: 12, 16, 20, .410. Barrel lengths: 28- and 30-inch (12 and 16 ga.), 28-inch (20 ga.), 26-inch (.410); Full choke only. Weight: about 6 pounds, 12 bore ga. Plain pistol-grip stock and forearm. Made about 1937–1953.

Stevens Model 124

Stevens Model 258

Stevens Model 311-R

Stevens Model 124 Cross Bolt Repeater **$140**
Hammerless. Solid frame. 12 gauge only. 2-shot tubular magazine. 28-inch barrel; IC, M or F choke. Weight: about 7 pounds. Tenite stock and forearm. Made 1947–1952.

Stevens Model 240 Over-and-Under Shotgun . . . **$510**
Visible hammer. Takedown. Double triggers. .410 gauge. 26-inch barrels, Full choke. Weight: 6 lbs. Tenite (plastic) pistol-grip stock and forearm. Made 1940–49.

Stevens Model 258 Bolt Action Repeater **$95**
Takedown. 20-gauge. 2-shell detachable box magazine. 26-inch barrel, Full choke. Weight: about 6 1/4 pounds. Plain one-piece pistol-grip stock. Made 1937–1965.

Stevens Model 311-R Hammerless Double **$245**
Same general specifications as Stevens-Springfield Model 311 except compact design for law enforcement use. Barrels: 18 1/4-inch 12 gauge with solid rib, chambered for 2 3/4- and 3-inch Mag. shells. Double triggers and auto top tang safety. Walnut finished hardwood stock with recoil pad and semibeavertail forend. Weight: about 6 3/4 pounds. Made 1982–89.

Stevens Model 530 Hammerless Double **$265**
Boxlock. Double triggers. Gauges: 12, 16, 20, .410. Barrel lengths: 26- to 32-inch; choked M/F, C/M, F/F. Weight: 6 to 7 1/2 pounds depending on gauge and barrel length. Checkered pistol-grip stock and forearm; some early models with recoil pad. Made 1936–1954.

Stevens Model 530M **$230**
Same as Model 530, except has Tenite (plastic) stock and forearm. Discontinued about 1947.

Stevens Model 530ST Double Gun **$250**
Same as Model 530, except has non-selective single trigger. Discontinued.

Stevens Model 620 Hammerless Slide Action Repeating Shotgun **$215**
Takedown. Gauges: 12, 16, 20. 5-shell tubular magazine. Barrel lengths: 26-, 28-, 30-, 32-inch; choked F, M, IC, C. Weight: about 7 3/4 lbs., 12 ga.; 7 1/4 lbs., 16 ga.; 6 lbs., 20 ga. Checkered pistol-grip stock and slide handle. Made 1927–1953.

Stevens Model 621 . . . . **$265**
Same as Model 620, except has raised solid matted-rib barrel. Discontinued.

Stevens Model 820 Hammerless Slide Action Repeating Shotgun **$200**
Solid frame. 12 gauge only. 5-shell tubular magazine. 28-inch barrel; IC, M or F choke. Weight: about 7 1/2 pounds. Plain pistol-grip stock, grooved slide handle. Made 1949–1954.

Stevens Model 820-SC **$225**
Same as Model 820, except has Savage Super Choke.

SHOTGUNS

Stevens Model 530ST

Stevens Model 620

Stevens Model 940

Stevens Model 9478

Stevens-Springfield Model 311

Stevens Model 940 Single Barrel Shotgun **$85**
Same general specifications as Model 94, except has side
lever opening instead of top lever. Made 1961–1970.

Stevens Model 940Y Youth Gun **$90**
Same general specifications as Model 94Y, except has side
lever opening instead of top lever. Made 1961–1970.

Stevens Model 9478 . . . . **$95**
Takedown. Visible hammer. Automatic ejector. Gauges:
12, 20, .410. Barrels: 26-, 28-, 30-, 36-inch; Full choke.
Weight: average 6 pounds depending on gauge and barrel.
Plain pistol-grip stock and forearm. Made 1978–1985.

Stevens-Springfield Model 311 Hammerless Double
Same general specifications as Stevens Model 530, except
earlier production has plain stock and forearm; checkered

Stevens-Springfield Model 311 Hammerless (cont.)
on current guns. Originally produced as a "Springfield"
gun, this model became a part of the "Stevens" line in
1948 when the "Springfield" brand name was discontinued. Made 1931–1989.
Pre-WWII **$325**
Post-WWII **295**

STOEGER SHOTGUNS
See IGA Shotguns

TECNI-MEC SHOTGUNS
Italy

Tecni-Mec Model SPL 640 Folding Shotgun **$345**
Gauges: 12, 16, 20, 24, 28, 32 and .410 bore. 26-inch barrel.
Chokes: IC/IM Weight: 6½ pounds. Checkered walnut
pistol grip stock and forend. Engraved receiver. Available
with double triggers. Made 1988 to date.

Thompson/Center Contender
.410 Gauge Carbine

Thompson/Center Model '87
Hunter Slug Barrel

THOMPSON/CENTER ARMS
Rochester, New Hampshire

Thompson/Center Contender .410 Ga. Carbine . . **$315**
Gauge: .410 smoothbore. 21-inch vent-rib barrel. 34¾
inches overall. Weight: about 5¼ pounds. Bead front sight.
Rynite® stock and forend. Made 1991 to date.

Thompson/Center Model '87 Hunter Shotgun **$295**
Single shot. Gauge: 10 or 12; 3½-inch chamber. 25-inch
field barrel with Full choke. Weight 8 pounds. Bead front
sight. American black walnut stock with recoil pad. Drop
at heel ⅞ inch. Made 1987 to date.

Thompson/Center Model '87 Hunter Slug **$325**
Gauge: 10 (3½-inch chamber) or 12 (3-inch chamber).
Same general specifications as Model '87 Hunter Shotgun,
except with 22-inch slug (rifled) barrel and rifle sights.
Made 1987 to date.

Tikka M 07 Shotgun/Rifle

Tikka M 77 Over/Under

Tikka Model 412S Over/Under
Field Grade

TIKKA SHOTGUNS
Riihimaki, Finland
Manufactured by Sako; formerly by Valmet

Tikka M 07 Shotgun/Rifle Combination **$795**
Gauge/caliber: 12/222 Rem. Shotgun barrel: about 25 inches; rifle barrel: about 22³/₄ inches. 40²/₃ inches overall. Weight: about 7 pounds. Dovetailed for telescopic sight. Single trigger with selector between the barrels. Vent rib. Monte Carlo-style walnut stock with checkered pistol grip and forend. Made 1965–1987.

Tikka M 77 Over/Under Shotgun **$995**
Gauge: 12. 27-inch vent-rib barrels. Approx. 44 inches overall. Weight: about 7¹/₄ pounds. Barrel selector. Ejectors. Monte Carlo-style walnut stock with checkered pistol grip and forend; rollover cheekpiece. Made 1977–1987.

Tikka Model 412S Over/Under
Gauge: 12; 3-inch chambers. 24-, 26-, 28- or 30-inch blued chrome-lined barrels with five integral stainless steel choke tubes. Weight: 7¹/₄ to 7¹/₂ pounds. Matte nickel receiver. Select American walnut stock with checkered pistol grip and forend. (Same as the former Valmet Model 412.) Manufactured in Italy by arrangement with Marocchi from 1990 to date.
Field Model **$850**
Sporting Clays Model **925**

Tikka M 77K Shotgun/Rifle Combination **$1050**
Gauge: 12/70. Calibers: 222 Rem., 5.6×52r5, 6.5×55, 7×57r5, 7×65r5, 308 Win. Vent-rib barrels: about 25 inches (shotgun); almost 23 inches (rifle). 42.3 inches overall. Weight: about 7¹/₂ pounds. Double triggers. Monte Carlo-style walnut stock with checkered pistol grip and forend; rollover cheekpiece. Made 1977–1986.

SHOTGUNS OF ULM
Ulm, West Germany
See listings under Krieghoff.

U.S. REPEATING ARMS CO.
New Haven, Connecticut
See Winchester Shotgun listings.

VALMET OY
Jyväskylä, Finland

See also Savage Models 330, 333T, 333 and 2400, which are Valmet guns.

Valmet Lion Over-and-Under Shotgun **$395**
Boxlock. Selective single trigger. Plain extractors. 12 gauge only. Barrels: 26-inch IC/M; 28-inch M/F; 30-inch M/F, F/F. Weight: about 7 pounds. Checkered pistol-grip stock and forearm. Made 1947–1968.

SHOTGUNS

Valmet Lion Over-Under

Valmet Model 412 K

Valmet Model 412 K Combination Shotgun/Rifle

Valmet Model 412 KE Skeet

Valmet Model 412 K Over/Under Field Shotgun . . . $625
Hammerless. 12-gauge, 3-inch chamber. 36-inch barrel, F/ F chokes. Amer. walnut Monte Carlo stock. Made 1982–87.

Valmet Model 412 K Shotgun/Rifle Combination . . $795
Similar to Model 412 K, except bottom barrel chambered for either 222 Rem., 223 Rem., 243 Win., 308 Win. or 30-06. 12-gauge shotgun barrel with IM choke. Monte Carlo American walnut stock, recoil pad.

Valmet Model 412 KE Over/Under Field Shotgun . . $625
12-gauge chambered for 2³/₄-inch shells; 26-inch barrel, IC/ M chokes; 28-inch barrel, M/F chokes; 12-gauge chambered for 3-inch shells, 30-inch barrel, M/F chokes. 20-gauge (3-inch shells); 26-inch barrel IC/M chokes; 28-inch barrel, M/ F chokes. American walnut Monte Carlo stock.

Valmet Model 412 KE Skeet $685
Similar to Model 412 K, except Skeet stock and chokes. 12 and 20 gauges. Discontinued 1989.

Valmet Model 412 KE Trap $695
Similar to Model 412 K Field, except trap stock, recoil pad. 30-inch barrels, IM/F chokes. Discontinued 1989.

Valmet 3-Barrel Set $1795

MONTGOMERY WARD
Chicago, Illinois
Western Field and Hercules Models

Although they do not correspond to specific models below, the names Western Field and Hercules have been used to designate various Montgomery Ward shotguns at various times.

Wards Model 25 Slide Action Repeater $150
Solid frame. 12 gauge only. 5-shot tubular magazine. 28-inch barrel, various chokes. Weight: about 7¹/₂ pounds. Plain pistol-grip stock, grooved slide handle.

Wards Model 40 Over-and-Under Shotgun $595
Hammerless. Boxlock. Double triggers. Gauges: 12, 16, 20, .410. Barrels: plain; 26- to 30-inch, various chokes. Checkered pistol-grip stock and forearm.

Wards Model 40N Slide Action Repeater $165
Same general specifications as Model 25.

Wards Model 172 Bolt Action Shotgun $85
Takedown. 2-shot detachable clip magazine. 12 gauge. 28-inch barrel with variable choke. Weight: about 7¹/₂ pounds. Monte Carlo stock with recoil pad.

Wards Model 550A Slide Action Repeater $215
Takedown. Gauges: 12, 16, 20, .410. 5-shot tubular magazine. Barrels: plain, 26- to 30-inch, various chokes. Weight: 6 to 8 pounds. Plain pistol-grip stock and grooved slide handle.

Wards Model SB300 Double Barrel Shotgun $230
Same general specifications as Model SD52A.

Wards Model SB312 Double Barrel Shotgun $250
Boxlock. Double triggers. Plain extractors. Gauges: 12, 16, 20, .410. Barrels: 24- to 30-inch. Various chokes. Weight, about 7¹/₂ pounds in 12 gauge. Checkered pistol-grip stock and forearm.

Wards Model SD52A Double Barrel Shotgun . . . $195
Boxlock. Double triggers. Gauges: 12, 16, 20, .410. Barrels: 26- to 32-inch, various chokes. Weight: 6 to 7¹/₂ pounds.

WEATHERBY, INC.
South Gate, California

Weatherby Model 82 Autoloading Shotgun
Hammerless, gas-operated. 12 gauge only. Barrels: 22- to 30-inch, various integral chokes. Weight: 7¹/₂ pounds.

Weatherby Model 82 Autoloading

Weatherby Model 92 Pump

Weatherby Athena

Weatherby Centurion Field Grade

Weatherby Centurion Deluxe

Weatherby Orion

Weatherby Model 82 Autoloading Shotgun (cont.)

Checkered walnut stock and forearm. Made 1982–89.

Standard Autoloading Shotgun **$375**
BuckMaster Auto Slug w/rifle sights (1986–90) . . **400**

Weatherby Model 92 Slide Action Shotgun

Hammerless, short-stroke action. 12 gauge; 3-inch chamber. Tubular magazine. Barrels: 22-, 26-, 28-, 30-inch with fixed choke or IMC choke tubes; plain or vent rib with rifle sights. Weight: 7^1/$_2$ pounds. Engraved, matte black receiver and blued barrel. Checkered high-gloss buttstock and forend. Imported from Japan since 1982.

Standard Model 92 . . . . **$275**
BuckMaster Pump Slug w/rifle sights (intro.
1986) **295**

Weatherby Athena Over/Under Shotgun

Engraved boxlock action with Greener crossbolt and sideplates. Gauges: 12, 20, 28 and .410; 2^3/$_4$- or 3^1/$_2$-inch chambers. Barrels: 26-, 28-, 30- or 32-inch with fixed or IMC Multi-choke tubes. Weight: 6^3/$_4$ to 7^3/$_8$ pounds. Single selective trigger. Selective auto ejectors. Top tang safety. Checkered Claro walnut stock and forearm with high lus-

Weatherby Athena Over/Under Shotgun (cont.)

ter finish. Made 1982 to date.

Field Model w/IMC Multi-choke (12 or 20 ga.) . . **$1150**
Field Model w/Fixed Chokes (28 or .410 ga.) **1295**
Skeet Model w/Fixed Chokes (12 or 20 ga.) **1275**
Skeet Model w/Fixed Chokes (28 or .410 ga.) . . . **1425**
Master Skeet Tube Set **2195**
Trap Model w/IMC Tubes **1195**
Grade V **1595**

Weatherby Centurion Automatic Shotgun

Gas-operated. Takedown. 12 gauge. 2^3/$_4$-inch chamber. 3-shot magazine. Barrels: vent ribs; 26-inch SK, IC or M; 28-inch M or F; 30-inch Full choke. Weight: with 28-inch barrel, 7 lbs. 10^1/$_2$ oz. Checkered pistol-grip stock and forearm, recoil pad. Made in Japan 1972–1981.

Centurion Field Grade **$325**
Centurion Trap Gun (30-inch Full choke bbl.) . . . **320**
Centurion Deluxe (etched receiver, fancy grade
wood, made 1972 to date) **360**

Weatherby Ducks Unlimited Shotgun **$495**

Weatherby Orion Over/Under Shotgun

Boxlock with Greener crossbolt. Gauges: 12, 20, 28 and .410; 2^3/$_4$- or 3-inch chambers. Barrels: 26-, 28-, 30-, 32- or

Weatherby Patrician Field Grade

Weatherby Regency Field Grade

Weatherby Regency Trap

Weatherby Orion Over/Under Shotgun (cont.)

34-inch with fixed or IMC Multi-choke tubes. Weight: 6$\frac{1}{2}$ to 9 pounds. Single selective trigger. Selective auto ejectors. Top tang safety. Checkered, high-gloss pistol-grip Claro walnut stock and forearm. Finish: Grade I, plain blued receiver; Grade II, engraved blued receiver; Grade III, silver gray receiver. Made 1982 to date.

Orion I Field w/IMC (12 or 20 ga.)	$750
Orion II Field w/IMC (12 or 20 ga.)	825
Orion III Field w/IMC (12 or 20 ga.)	850
Skeet II w/Fixed Chokes	895
Sporting Clays II	925
Trap II	900

Weatherby Patrician Slide Action Shotgun

Hammerless. Takedown. 12 gauge. 2$\frac{3}{4}$-inch chamber. 4 shot tubular magazine. Barrels: vent rib; 26-inch, SK, IC, M; 28-inch, M, F; 30-inch, Full choke. Weight: with 28-inch barrel, 7 lbs. 7 oz. Checkered pistol-grip stock and slide handle, recoil pad. Made in Japan 1972–1982.

Patrician Field Grade	$250
Patrician Deluxe (etched receiver, fancy grade wood)	295
Patrician Trap Gun (30-inch Full choke bbl.)	260

Weatherby Regency Field Grade O/U Shotgun ... $750

Boxlock with sideplates, elaborately engraved. Auto ejectors. Selective single trigger. Gauges: 12, 20. 2$\frac{3}{4}$-inch chamber in 12 gauge, 3-inch in 20 gauge. Barrels: vent rib; 26-inch SK, IC/M, M/F (20 ga. only); 28-inch SK, IC/M, M/F; 30-inch M/F (12 ga. only). Weight with 28-inch barrels: 7 lbs. 6 oz., 12 ga.; 6 lbs. 14 oz., 20 ga. Checkered pistol-grip stock and forearm of fancy walnut. Made in Italy 1965–1982.

Weatherby Regency Trap Gun ... $795

Similar to Regency Field Grade, except has trap-style stock with straight or Monte Carlo comb. Barrels have vent side ribs and high, wide vent top rib; 30- or 32-inch, M/F, IM/F or F/F chokes. Weight: with 32-inch barrels, 8 pounds. Made in Italy 1965–1982.

WESTERN ARMS CORP.
Ithaca, New York
Division of Ithaca Gun Company

Western Long Range

Western Long Range Hammerless Double

Boxlock. Plain extractors. Single or double triggers. Gauges: 12, 16, 20, .410. Barrels: 26- to 32-inch, M/F choke standard. Weight: 7$\frac{1}{2}$ pounds, 12 ga. Plain pistol-grip stock and forend. Made 1929–1946.

With double triggers	$265
With single trigger	340

WESTERN AUTO SHOTGUNS
Kansas City, Missouri

Revelation Model 300H Slide Action Repeater .. $195

Gauges: 12, 16, 20, .410. 4-shot tubular magazine. Barrels: 26- to 30-inch, various chokes. Weight: about 7 pounds. Plain pistol-grip stock, grooved slide handle.

Revelation Model 310A Slide Action Repeater .. $195

Takedown. 12 gauge. 5-shot tubular magazine. Barrels: 28- and 30-inch. Weight: about 7$\frac{1}{2}$ pounds. Plain pistol-grip stock.

Revelation Model 310B Slide Action Repeater .. $165

Same general specifications as Model 310A except chambered for 16 gauge.

Revelation Model 310C Slide Action Repeater .. $200

Same general specifications as Model 310A except chambered for 20 gauge.

**Westley Richards Modele
Deluxe Box Lock**

Revelation Model 310E Slide Action Repeater . . **$200**
Same general specifications as Model 310A except chambered for .410 bore.

Revelation Model 325BK Bolt Action Repeater . . . **$80**
Takedown. 2-shot detachable clip magazine. 20 gauge. 26-inch barrel with variable choke. Weight: 6¼ pounds.

═══ WESTERN FIELD SHOTGUNS ═══
See "W" for listings under Montgomery Ward.

═══ WESTLEY RICHARDS & CO., LTD. ═══
Birmingham, England

The Pigeon and Wildfowl Gun, available in all of the Westley Richards models except the Ovundo, has the same general specifications as the corresponding standard field gun, except has magnum action of extra strength and treble bolting; chambered for 12 gauge only (2¾- or 3-inch); 30-inch Full choke barrels standard. Weight: about 8 pounds. The manufacturer warns that 12-gauge magnum shells should not be used in their standard weight double barrel shotguns.

Westley Richards Best Quality Box Lock Hammerless Double Barrel Shotgun
Boxlock. Hand-detachable locks and hinged cover plate. Selective ejectors. Double triggers or selective single trigger. Gauges: 12, 16, 20. Barrel lengths and boring to order. Weight: 5½ to 6¼ pounds depending on gauge and barrel length. Checkered stock and forend, straight or half-pistol grip. Also supplied in Pigeon and Wildfowl Model with same values. Made from 1899 to date.
With double triggers **$10,435**
With selective single trigger **11,000**

Westley Richards Best Quality Side Lock Hammerless Double Barrel Shotgun
Hand-detachable sidelocks. Selective ejectors. Double triggers or selective single trigger. Gauges: 12, 16, 20, 28,

Westley Richards Best Quality Side Lock (cont.)
.410. Barrel lengths and boring to order. Weight: 4¾ to 6¾ pounds depending on gauge and barrel length. Checkered stock and forend, straight or half-pistol grip. Also supplied in Pigeon and Wildfowl Model with same values. Currently manufactured.
With double triggers **$18,995**
With selective single trigger **20,000**

Westley Richards Modele Deluxe Box Lock Hammerless Double Barrel Shotgun
Same general specifications as standard Best Quality gun, except higher quality throughout. Has Westley Richards top-projection and treble-bite lever-work, hand-detachable locks. Also supplied in Pigeon and Wildfowl Model with same values. Currently manufactured.
With double triggers . . . . **$ 8,950**
With selective single trigger **10,000**

Westley Richards Modele Deluxe Side Lock
Same as Best Quality Side Lock, except higher grade engraving and wood. Currently manufactured.
With double triggers **$20,000**
With single trigger **24,000**

Westley Richards Model E Hammerless Double
Anson & Deeley-type boxlock action. Selective ejector or non-ejector. Double triggers. Gauges: 12, 16, 20. Barrel lengths and boring to order. Weight: 5½ to 7¼ pounds depending on type, gauge and barrel length. Checkered stock and forend, straight or half-pistol grip. Also supplied in Pigeon and Wildfowl Model with same values. Currently manufactured.
Ejector model **$3795**
Non-ejector model **3300**

Westley Richards Ovundo (Over/Under) **$14,995**
Hammerless. Boxlock. Hand-detachable locks. Dummy sideplates. Selective ejectors. Selective single trigger. 12 gauge. Barrel lengths and boring to order. Checkered stock/forend, straight or half-pistol grip. Mfd. before WW II.

SHOTGUNS

**Westley Richards
Best Quality Side Lock**

Westley Richards Model E

**Westley Richards Modele
Deluxe Side Lock**

Winchester Model 12 Classic
Ltd. Edition (Grade I)

Winchester Model 12 Field
(1972 Type)

Winchester Model 12 Pigeon

Winchester Model 12 Skeet
(1972 Type)

TED WILLIAMS SHOTGUNS
See Sears shotguns.

WINCHESTER SHOTGUNS
New Haven, Connecticut

Formerly Winchester Repeating Arms Co. Now mfd. by Winchester-Western Div., Olin Corp., and by U.S. Repeating Arms Co.

Winchester Model 12 Classic Limited Edition
Gauge: 20; 2³/₄-inch chamber. Barrel: 26-inch vent rib; IC. Weight: 7 pounds. Checkered walnut buttstock and forend. Polished blue finish (Grade I) or engraved with gold inlays (Grade IV). Made 1993 to date.
Grade I (4000) . . . . $ 660
Grade IV (1000) 1070

Winchester Model 12 Featherweight $450
Same as Plain Barrel Model 12 Standard, except has alloy guard, modified takedown. 12 gauge only. Barrels: 26-inch IC; 28-inch M or F; 30-inch F choke. Weight: about 6³/₄ pounds. Made 1959–1962.

Winchester Model 12 Field Gun, 1972 Type $575
Same general specifications as Standard Model 12. 12 gauge only. 26-, 28- or 30-inch vent-rib barrel, standard chokes. Engine-turned bolt and carrier. Hand-checkered stock/slide handle of semi-fancy walnut. Made 1972–75.

Winchester Model 12 Heavy Duck Gun $695
12 gauge only, chambered for 3-inch shells. Same general specifications as Standard Grade, except 30- or 32-inch plain Full choke barrel only, 3-shot magazine, recoil pad. Weight: about 8³/₄ pounds. Discont. 1964.

**Winchester Model 12 Heavy Duck Gun,
Matte Rib** $850
Same as Plain Barrel Model 12 Heavy Duck Gun, except has solid raised matted rib. Discont. 1959.

Winchester Model 12 Pigeon Grade
Deluxe versions of the regular Model 12 Standard or Field Gun, Duck Gun, Skeet Gun and Trap Gun made on special order. This grade has finer finish throughout, hand-smoothed action, engine-turned breech bolt and carrier, stock and extension slide handle of high grade walnut, fancy checkering, stock dimensions to individual specifications. Engraving and carving available at extra cost ranging from about $35 to over $200. Discont. 1965.
Field Gun, plain barrel $1150
Field Gun, vent rib 1395
Skeet Gun, matted rib 1450
Skeet Gun, vent rib 1595
Skeet Gun, Cutts Compensator 995
Trap Gun, matted rib 1350
Trap Gun, vent rib 1425

Winchester Model 12 Riot Gun $550
Same general specifications as Plain Barrel Model 12 Standard, except has 20-inch cylinder bore barrel, 12 gauge only. Made 1918–1963.

Winchester Model 12 Skeet Gun $850
Gauges: 12, 16, 20, 28. 5-shot tubular magazine. 26-inch matted rib barrel, SK choke. Weight: about 7³/₄ lbs., 12 ga.; 6³/₄ lbs., other gauges. Bradley red or ivory bead front sight. Winchester 94B middle sight. Checkered pistol-grip stock and extension slide handle. Discont. after WWII.

**Winchester Model 12 Skeet Gun,
Cutts Compensator** $775
Same general specifications as standard Model 12 Skeet Gun, except has plain barrel fitted with Cutts Compensator, 26 inches overall. Discont. 1954.

Winchester Model 12 Skeet Gun, Plain Barrel . . $745
Same general specifications as standard Model 12 Skeet Gun, except has plain barrel. Made 1937–1947.

Winchester Model 12 Skeet Gun, Vent Rib **$1095**
Same general specifications as standard Model 12 Skeet
Gun, except has 26-inch barrel with vent rib, 12 and 20
gauge. Discontinued in 1965.

Winchester Model 12 Skeet Gun, 1972 Type . . . **$725**
Same gen. specifications as Standard Model 12. 12 ga.
only. 26-inch vent-rib barrel, SK choke. Engine-turned
bolt and carrier. Hand-checkered skeet-style stock and
slide handle of choice walnut, recoil pad. Made 1972–75.

Winchester Model 12 Standard Gr., Matted Rib . **$750**
Same general specifications as Plain Barrel Model 12
Standard, except has solid raised matted rib. Discontinued
after World War II.

Winchester Model 12 Standard Gr., Vent Rib . . . **$825**
Same general specifications as Plain Barrel Model 12
Standard, except has vent rib. 26¾- or 30-inch barrel, 12
gauge only. Discont. after World War II.

Winchester Model 12 Standard Slide Action Repeater
Hammerless. Takedown. Gauges: 12, 16, 20, 28. 6-shell
tubular magazine. Plain barrel. Lengths: 26- to 32-inches;
choked F to Cyl. Weight: about 7½ lbs., 12 ga. 30-inch;
6½ lbs. in other gauges with 28-inch barrel. Plain pistol-
grip stock, grooved slide handle. Made 1912–1964.
28 gauge **$2995**
12-ga., 28-inch barrel (Full) 595
Other gauges, etc. 575

Winchester Model 12 Super Pigeon Grade **$1995**
Custom version of Model 12 with same general specifications as standard models. 12 gauge only. 26-, 28- or 30-

Winchester Model 12 Super Pigeon Grade (cont.)
inch vent-rib barrel, any standard choke. Engraved receiver. Hand-smoothed and fitted action. Full fancy walnut stock and forearm made to individual order. Made
1965–1972.

Winchester Model 12 Trap Gun
Same general specifications as standard Model 12, except
has straighter stock, checkered pistol grip and extension
slide handle, recoil pad, 30-inch matted-rib barrel, F choke,
12 gauge only. Discont. after World War II; vent-rib model
discontinued 1965.
Matted-rib barrel **$850**
With straight stock, vent rib 950
With Monte Carlo stock, vent rib 995

Winchester Model 12 Trap Gun, 1972 Type **$695**
Same general specifications as Standard Model 12. 12
gauge only. 30-inch vent-rib barrel, Full choke. Engine-
turned bolt and carrier. Hand-checkered trap-style stock
(straight or Monte Carlo comb) and slide handle of select
walnut, recoil pad. Intro. in 1972. Discont.

Winchester Model 20 Single Shot Hammer Gun . . **$375**
Takedown. .410 bore. 2½-inch chamber. 26-inch barrel, Full
choke. Checkered pistol-grip stock and forearm. Weight:
about 6 pounds. Made 1919–1924.

Winchester Model 21 Custom, Pigeon, Grand American
Since 1959, the Model 21 has been offered only in deluxe
models: Custom, Pigeon, Grand American—on special
order. General specifications same as for Model 21 standard models, except these custom guns have full fancy
American walnut stock and forearm with fancy checkering, finely polished and hand-smoothed working parts,

SHOTGUNS

Winchester Model 12
Standard

Winchester Model 12
Super Pigeon Trap

Winchester Model 12 Trap
(1972 Type)

Winchester Model 20

Winchester Model 21
Grand American

Winchester Model 21 Pigeon

Winchester Model 21 Field

Winchester Model 24

Winchester Model 25 Repeater

Winchester Model 21 Custom, Pigeon (cont.)
etc.; engraving inlays, carved stocks and other extras are available at additional cost. Made 1960 to date.

Custom Grade	**$ 5,500**
Pigeon Grade	**7,500**
Grand American	**16,500**

Winchester Model 21 Double Barrel Field Gun
Hammerless. Boxlock. Automatic safety. Double triggers or selective single trigger, selective or non-selective ejection (all postwar Model 21 shotguns have selective single trigger and selective ejection). Gauges: 12, 16, 20. Barrels: raised matted rib or vent rib; 26-, 28-, 30-, 32-inch, the latter in 12 gauge only; F, IM, M, IC, SK chokes. Weight: 7 1/2 pounds, 12 ga. w/30-inch barrel; about 6 1/2 pounds, 16 or 20 ga. w/28-inch barrel. Checkered pistol- or straight-grip stock, regular or beavertail forend. Made 1930–1958.

With double trigger, non-selective ejection	**$2795**
With double trigger, selective ejection	**2995**
With selective single trigger, non-selective ejection	**3250**
With selective single trigger, selective ejection	**3400**
Extra for vent rib	**500**

Winchester Model 21 Duck Gun
Same general specifications as Model 21 Field Gun, except chambered for 12 gauge 3-inch shells, 30- or 32-inch barrels only, Full choke, selective single trigger, selective ejection, pistol-grip stock with recoil pad, beavertail forearm, both checkered. Discont. 1958.

With matted-rib barrels	**$2995**
With vent-rib barrels	**3250**

Winchester Model 21 Skeet Gun
Same general specifications as Model 21 Standard, except has 26- or 28-inch barrels only, SK chokes No. 1 and 2, Bradley red bead front sight, selective single trigger, selective ejection, nonauto safety, checkered pistol- or straight-grip stock without buttplate or pad (wood butt checkered), checkered beavertail forearm. Discont. 1958.

Winchester Model 21 Skeet Gun (cont.)

With matted-rib barrels	**$3600**
With vent-rib barrels	**4200**

Winchester Model 21 Trap Gun
Same general specifications as Model 21 Standard, except has 30- or 32-inch barrels only, Full choke, selective single trigger, selective ejection, nonauto safety, checkered pistol- or straight-grip stock with recoil pad, checkered beavertail forearm. Discont. 1958.

With matted-rib barrels	**$3575**
With vent-rib barrels	**4200**

Winchester Model 23 Side-by-Side Shotgun
Boxlock. Single trigger. Automatic safety. Gauges: 12, 20, 28, .410. Barrels: 25 1/2-, 26-, 28-inch with fixed chokes or Winchoke tubes. Weight: 5 7/8 to 7 pounds. Checkered American walnut buttstock and forend. Made 1979 to date for Olin at its Olin-Kodensha facility, Japan.

Classic 23—Gold inlay, Engraved	**$1500**
Custom 23—Plain receiver, Winchoke system	**895**
Heavy Duck 23—Standard	**1225**
Lightweight 23—Classic Style	**1215**
Light Duck 23—Standard	**1150**
Light Duck 23—12 ga. Golden Quail	**1350**
Light Duck 23—.410 Golden Quail	**1995**
Custom Set 23—20 & 28 gauge	**3560**

Winchester Model 24 Hammerless Double **$495**
Boxlock. Double triggers. Plain extractors. Auto safety. Gauges: 12, 16, 20. Barrels: 26-inch IC/M; 28-inch M/F (also IC/M in 12 ga. only); 30-inch M and F in 12 ga. only. Weight: about 7 1/2 pounds, 12 ga. Metal bead front sight. Plain pistol-grip stock, semibeavertail forearm. Made 1939–1957.

Winchester Model 25 Riot Gun **$345**
Same as Model 25 Standard, except has 20-inch cylinder bore barrel, 12 gauge only. Made 1949–1955.

Winchester Model 25 Slide Action Repeater **$410**
Hammerless. Solid frame. 12 gauge only. 4-shell tubular magazine. 28-inch plain barrel; IC, M or F choke. Weight:

Winchester Model 36

Winchester Model 37

Winchester Model 37A

Winchester Model 37A Youth

Winchester Model 25 Slide Action Repeater (cont.)
about 7½ pounds. Metal bead front sight. Plain pistol-grip stock, grooved slide handle. Made 1949–1955.

Winchester Model 36 Single Shot Bolt Action . . . **$295**
Takedown. Uses 9mm Short or Long shot or ball cartridges interchangeably. 18-inch barrel. Plain stock. Weight: about 3 pounds. Made 1920–27.

Winchester Model 37 Single Shot Shotgun
Semi-hammerless. Auto ejection. Takedown. Gauges: 12, 16, 20, 28, .410. Barrel lengths: 28-, 30-, 32-inch in all gauges except .410; 26- or 28-inch in .410; all barrels plain with Full choke. Weight: about 6½ pounds, 12 ga. Made 1937–1963.
12 Gauge **$225**
28 Gauge 795
Other Gauges 150

Winchester Model 37A Single Shot Shotgun **$125**
Similar to Model 370, except has engraved receiver and gold trigger, checkered pistol-grip stock, fluted forearm; 16 gauge available with 30-inch barrel only. Made 1973–1980.

Winchester Model 37A Youth **$135**
Similar to Model 370 Youth, except has engraved receiver and gold trigger, checkered pistol-grip stock, fluted forearm. Made 1973–1980.

Winchester Model 40 Skeet Gun **$795**
Same general specifications as Model 40 Standard, except has 24-inch plain barrel with Cutts Compensator, checkered forearm and pistol grip, grip cap. Made 1940–41.

Winchester Model 40 Standard Autoloader **$545**
Streamlined receiver. Hammerless. Takedown. 12 gauge only. 4-shell tubular magazine. 28- or 30-inch barrel; M or F choke. Weight: about 8 pounds. Bead sight on ramp. Plain pistol-grip stock, semibeavertail forearm. Made 1940–41.

Winchester Model 41 Single Shot Bolt Action . . . **$525**
Takedown. .410 bore. 2½-inch chamber (chambered for 3-inch shells after 1932). 24-inch barrel, Full choke. Plain straight stock standard. Made 1920–1934.

Winchester Model 40 Skeet

Winchester Model 41

Winchester Model 42 Classic Limited Edition

Winchester Model 42 Standard Slide Action Repeater

Winchester Model 50 Skeet

Winchester Model 59

Winchester Model 42 Classic Ltd. Edition **$1250**
Gauge: .410 with 2³/₄-inch chamber. Barrel: 26-inch vent rib; Full choke. Weight: 7 pounds. Checkered walnut buttstock and forend. Engraved blue with gold inlays. Limited production of 850. Made 1993 to date.

Winchester Model 42 Deluxe **$2100**
Same general specifications as the Model 42 Standard, except has vent rib, finer finish throughout, hand-smoothed action, engine-turned breech bolt and carrier, stock and extension slide handle of high grade walnut, fancy checkering, stock dimensions to individual specifications. Engraving and carving were offered at extra cost. Made 1933–1963.

Winchester Model 42 Skeet Gun **$1750**
Same general specifications as Model 42 Standard, except has checkered straight or pistol-grip stock and extension slide handle, 26- or 28-inch matted-rib barrel, SK choke. *Note:* Some Model 42 Skeet Guns are chambered for 2¹/₂-inch shells only. Discont. 1963.

Winchester Model 42 Standard Grade, Matt Rib **$1450**
Same general specifications as Plain Barrel Model 42, except has solid raised matted rib. Discont. 1963.

Winchester Model 42 Standard Slide Action Repeating Shotgun **$995**
Hammerless. Takedown. .410 bore (3- or 2¹/₂-inch shell). Tubular magazine holds five 3-inch or six 2¹/₂-inch shells. 26- or 28-inch plain barrel; cylinder bore, M or F choke.

Winchester Model 42 Standard Slide Action (cont.)
Weight: about 6 pounds. Plain pistol-grip stock; grooved slide handle. Made 1933–1963.

Winchester Model 50 Field Gun, Vent Rib **$375**
Same as Model 50 Standard, except has vent rib.

Winchester Model 50 Skeet Gun **$460**
Same as Model 50 Standard, except has 26-inch vent-rib barrel with SK choke, skeet-style stock of select walnut.

Winchester Model 50 Standard Grade Autoloader **$360**
Non-recoiling barrel and independent chamber. Gauges: 12 and 20. 2-shot tubular magazine. Barrels: 12 ga.—26-, 28-, 30-inch; 20 ga.—26-, 28-inch; IC, SK, M, F choke. Checkered pistol-grip stock and forearm. Weight: about 7³/₄ pounds. Made 1954–1961.

Winchester Model 50 Trap Gun **$475**
Same as Model 50 Standard, except 12 gauge only, has 30-inch vent-rib barrel with F choke, Monte Carlo stock of select walnut.

Winchester Model 59 Autoloading Shotgun **$435**
12 gauge. Magazine holds two shells. Alloy receiver. Win-Lite steel and fiberglass barrel: 26-inch IC, 28-inch M or F choke, 30-inch F choke; also furnished with 26-inch barrel with Versalite choke (interchangeable F, M, IC tubes; one supplied with gun). Weight: about 6¹/₂ pounds. Checkered pistol-grip stock and forearm. Made 1959–1965.

Winchester Model 97 Riot Gun **$495**
Takedown or solid frame. Same general specifications as standard Model 97, except 12 gauge only, 20-inch cylinder bore barrel. Made 1897–1957.

**Winchester Model 97
Visible Hammer**

Winchester Model 97 Trap, Tournament and Pigeon

These higher grade models offer higher overall quality than the standard grade. Discont. 1939.

Trap Gun **$695**
Tournament Grade 825
Pigeon Grade 995

Winchester Model 97 Trench Gun **$1295**

Solid frame. Same as Model 97 Riot Gun, except has handguard and is equipped with a bayonet. World War I government issue, 1917–1918.

Winchester Model 97 Visible Hammer Slide
Action Repeating Shotgun **$395**

Standard Grade. Takedown or solid frame. Gauges: 12 and 16. 5-shell tubular magazine. Barrel: plain; 26 to 32 inches, the latter in 12 ga. only; choked F to Cyl. Weight: about 7¾ pounds (12 ga./28-inch barrel). Plain pistol-grip stock, grooved slide handle. Made 1897–1957.

> **NOTE:** All Winchester Model 101s are mfd. for Olin Corp. at its Olin-Kodensha facility in Tochigi, Japan.

Winchester Model 101 Diamond Grade Target . . **$1295**

Similar to Model 101 Standard except silvered frame and Winchoke interchangeable choke tubes. Made 1981–1990.

Winchester Model 101 Field Gun Over/Under

Boxlock. Engraved receiver. Auto ejectors. Single selective trigger. Combination barrel selector and safety. Gauges: 12 and 28, 2¾-inch chambers; 20 and .410, 3-inch chambers. Vent-rib barrels: 30- (12 ga. only) and 26½-inch, IC/M. Weight: 6¼ to 7¾ pounds depending on gauge and barrel length. Hand-checkered French walnut stock and forearm. Made 1963–1981; gauges other than 12 intro. 1966.

Winchester Model 101 Field Gun Over/Under (cont.) $695

12 and 20 gauge **$695**
28 and .410 gauge 875

Winchester Model 101 Grand European **$1295**

Similar to Model 101 Pigeon Grade except silvered frame and Winchoke interchangeable choke tubes. Made 1981–1987.

Winchester Model 101 Magnum Field Gun **$710**

Same as Model 101 Field Gun, except chambered for 12 or 20 ga. 3-inch magnum shells only, 30-inch barrels (F/F or M/F), recoil pad. Made 1966–1981.

Winchester Model 101 Pigeon Grade

Same general specifications as standard Model 101 Field and Skeet, except higher grade with more elaborately engraved satin gray steel receiver, fancier wood and finer checkering. 12 and 20 gauge only. Made 1974–1981.

Field Gun . . . . **$ 875**
Skeet Gun 995
Trap Gun with straight stock 995
Trap Gun with Monte Carlo stock 1295

Winchester Model 101 Skeet Gun

Same as Model 101 Field Gun, except skeet-style stock and forearm. Barrels: 12 ga., 26-inch; 20 ga., 26½-inch; 28 and .410 ga., 28-inch; all SK choked. Made 1966–1981.

12 and 20 gauge **$795**
28 and .410 gauge 810

Winchester Model 101 Waterfowl **$1025**

Similar to Model 101 Magnum Field, except silvered frame and Winchoke interchangeable choke tubes. Made 1981 to date.

SHOTGUNS

Winchester Model 101 Field

**Winchester Model 101 Pigeon Trap
Monte Carlo Stock**

Winchester Model 101 Skeet

Winchester Model 370

Winchester Model 370 Single Shot Shotgun $95

Visible hammer. Auto ejector. Takedown. Gauges: 12, 16, 20, 28, .410. 2³/₄-inch chambers in 16 and 28 gauge, 3-inch in other gauges. Barrels: 12 ga., 30-, 32- or 36-inch; 16 ga., 30- or 32-inch; 20 and 28 ga., 28-inch; .410 bore, 26-inch; all Full choke. Weight: 5¹/₂ to 6¹/₄ pounds depending on gauge and barrel. Plain pistol-grip stock and forearm. Made 1968–1973.

Winchester Model 370 Youth $105

Same as standard Model 370, except has 26-inch barrel and 12¹/₂-inch stock with recoil pad; 20 gauge with IM choke, .410 bore with Full choke. Made 1968–1973.

Winchester Model 1001 O/U Shotgun

Boxlock. 12 gauge; 2³/₄- or 3-inch chambers. Barrels: 28- or 30-inch vent rib; WinPlus choke tubes. Weight: 7–7³/₄ pounds. Checkered walnut buttstock and forend. Blued finish with scroll engraved receiver. Made 1993 to date.
Field Model (28″ bbl., 3″) $795
Sporting Clays I (28″ bbl.) 895
Sporting Clays II (30″ bbl.) 895

Winchester Model 1200 Deer Gun $200

Same as standard Model 1200, except has special 22-inch barrel with rifle-type sights, for rifled slug or buckshot; 12 gauge only. Weight: 6¹/₂ pounds. Made 1965–1974.

Winchester Model 1200 Defender Slide Action Security Shotgun $195

Hammerless. 12 and 20 gauge (3-inch chambers). 18-inch barrel. 8-shot capacity. Low-glare blued finish. Weight: 6³/₄ pounds. Made 1984 to date by U. S. Repeating Arms.

Winchester Model 1200 Field Gun—Magnum

Same as standard Model 1200, except chambered for 3-inch 12 and 20 gauge magnum shells; plain or vent-rib barrel, 28- or 30-inch, Full choke. Weight: 7³/₈ to 7⁷/₈ pounds. Made 1964–1983.
With plain barrel **$200**
With vent-rib barrel **210**
Add for Winchester Recoil Reduction System **50**

Winchester Model 1200 Pistol Grip Defender . . . $195

Same general specifications as standard Model 1200, except has 18-inch barrel, 7-shot magazine and pistol grip. Mfd. by U. S. Repeating Arms.

Winchester Model 1001 O/U Field

Winchester Model 1200 Defender

Winchester Model 1200 Field Magnum, Plain Barrel

Winchester Model 1200 Field Ventilated Rib

Winchester Model 1200 Pistol Grip Defender

Winchester Model 1200 Skeet

Winchester Model 1200 Trap With Recoil Reduction System

Winchester Model 1300 Featherweight w/Winchoke

Winchester Model 1300 Ranger 22″ Rifled Deer Combo

Winchester Model 1200 Police $195
Same general specifications as 1200 Defender, except has rifle-type front and rear sights. Stainless-steel barrel and satin chrome finish on all external metal parts.

Winchester Model 1200 Skeet Gun $195
Same as standard Model 1200, except 12 and 20 gauge only; has 2-shot magazine, specially tuned trigger, 26-inch vent-rib barrel SK choke, semi-fancy walnut stock and forearm. Weight: 7¼ to 7½ pounds. Made 1965–1973. Also avail. 1966–70 with Winchester Recoil Reduction System (add $50 to value).

Winchester Model 1200 Slide Action Field Gun
Front-locking rotary bolt. Takedown. 4-shot magazine. Gauges: 12, 16, 20 (2¾-inch chamber). Barrel: plain or vent rib; 26-, 28-, 30-inch; IC, M, F choke or with Winchoke (interchangeable tubes IC-M-F). Weight: 6½ to 7¼ pounds. Checkered pistol-grip stock and forearm (slide handle), recoil pad; also avail. 1966–70 w/Winchester Recoil Reduction System (Cycolac stock). Made 1964–1983.
With plain barrel **$185**
With vent-rib barrel 205
Add for Winchester Recoil Reduction System 50
Add for Winchoke 25

Winchester Model 1200 Stainless $260
Same as standard Model 1200 Defender, except has stainless-steel barrel and special bright chrome finish on external metal parts.

Winchester Model 1200 Trap Gun
Same as standard Model 1200, except 12 gauge only. Has 2-shot magazine, 30-inch vent-rib barrel, Full choke or 28-inch with Winchoke. Semi-fancy walnut stock, straight or Monte Carlo trap style. Weight: about 8¼ pounds.

Winchester Model 1200 Trap Gun (cont.)
Made 1965–1973. Also available 1966–70 with Winchester Recoil Reduction System.
With straight-trap stock **$275**
With Monte Carlo stock 325
Add for Winchester Recoil Reduction System 50
Add for Winchoke 25

Winchester Model 1300 CamoPack $325
Gauge: 12. 3-inch Magnum. 5-shot magazine. Barrels: 30- and 22-inch with Winchoke system. Weight: 7 pounds. Laminated stock with Win-Cam camouflage green, cut checkering, recoil pad, swivels and sling. Made 1987.

Winchester Model 1300 Deer Gun $295
Same as standard Model 1300, except has special 24⅛-inch barrel with rifle-type sights, for rifled slug or buckshot; 12 gauge only. Weight: 6½ pounds.

Winchester Model 1300 Deluxe Slide Action Pump
Gauges: 12 and 20; 3-inch chamber. 5-shot magazine. Barrel: 22, 26 or 28 inches with vent rib; Winchoke tubes. Weight: 6½ pounds. Checkered walnut buttstock and forend. Polished blued finish with roll-engraved receiver. Made 1984 to date.
Model 1300 Deluxe . . . . **$ 280**
Model 1300 Ladies/Youth (22-inch bbl.) 235

Winchester Model 1300 Featherweight Slide Action Shotgun $265
Hammerless. Takedown. 4-shot magazine. Gauges: 12 and 20 (3-inch chambers). Barrel: 22-inch vent rib. Weight: 6⅜ pounds. Checkered walnut buttstock, rib slide handled. Made 1985 to date.

Winchester Model 1300 Ranger Series
Gauges: 12 and 20; 3-inch chamber. 5-shot magazine. Barrel: 22 (Rifled), 26 or 28 inches with vent rib; Winchoke

Winchester Model 1300
Slug Hunter

Winchester Model 1300
Turkey Win-Cam Shotgun

Winchester Model 1300 XTR
w/Winchoke

Winchester Model 1300 Ranger Series (cont.)

tubes. Weight: 7¹/₄ pounds. Walnut-finished hardwood buttstock and forend. Blued finish. Made 1984 to date.

Standard Model	$220
Combo Model	275
Rifled Deer Combo (D&T w/rings & bases)	290

Winchester Model 1300 Slug Hunter

Similar to the Model 1300, except has 22-inch rifled barrel with rifle sights and walnut stock.

Hunter Model	$335
Whitetails Unlimited Model	340

Winchester Model 1300 Turkey Slide Action ... $250

Same general specifications as Model 1300 Featherweight, except low-luster finish on walnut stock and forearm; non-glare matte finish on receiver, barrel and exterior metal surfaces.

Winchester Model 1300 Turkey Win-Cam $295

Same as Model 1300 CamoPack, except has only one 22-inch barrel. Made 1987 to date.

Winchester Model 1300 Waterfowl Slide Action Shotgun ... $275

Same general specifications as Model 1300 Featherweight, except 30-inch barrel. Weight: 7 pounds. Made 1985–1992.

Winchester Model 1300 XTR Slide Action $305

Hammerless. Takedown. 4-shot magazine. Gauges: 12 and 20 (3-inch chambers). Barrel: plain or vent rib; 28-inch

Winchester Model 1300 XTR Slide Action (cont.)

barrels; Winchoke (interchangeable tubes IC-M-F). Weight: about 7 pounds.

> **NOTE:** Model 1400 shotguns were available in left-hand versions (ejection port and safety on left side), with values the same as for right-hand models. In 1968, Model 1400 was replaced by Model 1400 Mark II, which is the same gun with an improved action release and restyled checkering on stock and forearm. Winchester dropped the "Mark II" designation in 1972; however, to distinguish between the two types, it has been retained in the following listings. Until 1973, the Mark II shotguns were available in left-hand versions (ejection port and safety on left side), with values the same as for right-hand models.

Winchester Model 1400 Automatic Field Gun

Gas-operated. Front-locking rotary bolt. Takedown. 2-shot magazine. Gauges: 12, 16, 20 (2³/₄-inch chamber). Barrel: plain or vent rib; 26-, 28-, 30-inch; IC, M, F choke, or with Winchoke (interchangeable tubes IC-M-F). Weight: 6¹/₂ to 7¹/₄ pounds. Checkered pistol-grip stock and forearm, recoil pad; also available with Winchester Recoil Reduction System (Cycolac stock). Made 1964–68.

With plain barrel	$250
With vent-rib barrel	275
Add for Winchester Recoil Reduction System	75
Add for Winchoke	25

Winchester Model 1400 Deer Gun $225

Same as standard Model 1400, except has special 22-inch barrel with rifle-type sights, for rifle slug or buckshot; 12 gauge only. Weight: 6¹/₂ pounds. Made 1965–68.

**Winchester Model 1400 Field
Left Hand, Ventilated Rib**

Winchester Model 1400 Deer Gun

**Winchester Model 1400 Mark II
Ventilated Rib, Winchoke**

**Winchester Model 1400 Trap
Monte Carlo Stock**

Winchester Model 1400 Mark II Deer Gun $275
Same general specifications as Model 1400 Deer Gun. Made 1968–1973.

Winchester Model 1400 Mark II Field Gun
Same general specifications as Model 1400 Field Gun, except not chambered for 16 gauge; Winchester Recoil Reduction System not available after 1970; only 28-inch barrels w/Winchoke offered after 1973. Made 1968–1978.

With plain barrel	$240
With plain barrel and Winchoke	260
With vent-rib barrel	275
With vent-rib barrel and Winchoke	295
Add for Winchester Recoil Reduction System	75

Winchester Model 1400 Mark II Skeet Gun $340
Same general specifications as Model 1400 Skeet Gun. Made 1968–1973.

Winchester Model 1400 Mark II Trap Gun
Same general specifications as Model 1400 Trap Gun, except also furnished with 28-inch barrel and Winchoke. Winchester Recoil Reduction System not available after 1970. Made 1968–1973.

With straight stock	$340
With Monte Carlo stock	375
Add for Winchester Recoil Reduction System	75
Add for Winchoke	25

Winchester Model 1400 Mark II Utility Skeet $245
Same general specifications as Model 1400 Mark II Skeet Gun, except has stock and forearm of field grade walnut. Made 1970–73.

Winchester Model 1400 Mark II Utility Trap $265
Same as Model 1400 Mark II Trap Gun, except has Monte Carlo stock/forearm of field grade walnut. Made 1970–73.

Winchester Model 1400 Skeet Gun $275
Same as standard Model 1400, except 12 and 20 gauge only, 26-inch vent-rib barrel, SK choke, semi-fancy walnut stock and forearm. Weight: $7\frac{1}{4}$ to $7\frac{1}{2}$ pounds. Made 1965–1968. Also available with Winchester Recoil Reduction System (add $50 to value).

Winchester Model 1400 Trap Gun
Same as standard Model 1400, except 12 gauge only with 30-inch vent-rib barrel, Full choke. Semi-fancy walnut stock, straight or Monte Carlo trap style. Also available with Winchester Recoil Reduction System. Weight: about $8\frac{1}{4}$ pounds. Made 1965–68.

With straight stock	$325
With Monte Carlo stock	360
Add for Winchester Recoil Reduction System	75

Winchester Model 1500 XTR Semiautomatic . . . $305
Gas-operated. Gauges: 12 and 20 ($2\frac{3}{4}$-inch chambers). Barrel: plain or vent rib; 28-inch; Winchoke (interchangeable tubes IC-M-F). American walnut stock and forend; checkered grip and forend. Weight: $7\frac{1}{4}$ pounds.

Winchester Model 1901 Lever Action Repeater $1195
Same general specifications as Model 1887 of which this is a redesigned version. 10 gauge only. Made 1901–1920.

Winchester Model 1911 Autoloading Shotgun . . $425
Hammerless. Takedown. 12 gauge only. 4-shell tubular magazine. Barrels: plain, 26- to 32-inch, standard borings. Weight: about $8\frac{1}{2}$ pounds. Plain or checkered pistol-grip stock and forearm. Made 1911–1925.

SHOTGUNS

Winchester Model 1901

Winchester Model 1911

**Winchester Pistol Grip
Stainless Marine**

**Winchester Ranger
Deer Semiautomatic**

**Winchester Ranger Youth
With Winchoke**

**Winchester Single Shot
Lever Action**

Winchester Pistol Grip Stainless Marine **$225**
Same general specifications as standard Model 1200, ex-
cept has 18-inch barrel, 6-shot magazine and pistol grip.
Mfd. by U. S. Repeating Arms.

Winchester Pistol Grip Stainless Police **$225**
Same general specifications as standard Model 1200, ex-
cept has 18-inch barrel, 6-shot magazine and pistol grip.
Mfd. by U. S. Repeating Arms.

Winchester Quail Special O/U Small Frame . . . **$1295**
Same Specifications as small-frame Model 101, except in
28 and .410 ga. with 3-inch chambers. 25$\frac{1}{2}$-inch barrels
with choke tubes (28 ga.) or M/F chokes (.410). Imported
from Japan in 1987.

Winchester Ranger Combination Shotgun **$225**
Same as Ranger Deer Combination, except has one 28-
inch vent-rib barrel with M choke and one 18-inch Police
Cyl. bore. Made 1987 to date.

Winchester Ranger Deer Combination **$240**
Gauge: 12; 3-inch Magnum. 3-shot magazine. Barrels: 24-
inch Cyl. bore deer barrel and 28-inch vent-rib barrel with
Winchoke system. Weight: 7$\frac{1}{4}$ pounds. Made 1987 to date.

Winchester Ranger Semiautomatic **$195**
Gauges: 12, 20. 2-shot magazine. 28-inch vent-rib barrel
with Full choke. Overall length: 48$\frac{5}{8}$ inches. Weight: 7
to 7$\frac{1}{4}$ pounds. Walnut finish, hardwood stock and forearm

Winchester Ranger Semiautomatic (cont.)
with cut checkering. Made 1984 to date by U. S. Repeating
Arms.

Winchester Ranger Semiauto Deer Shotgun **$210**
Same general specifications as Ranger Semiautomatic,
except 24$\frac{1}{8}$-inch plain barrel with rifle sights. Mfd. by
U.S. Repeating Arms.

Winchester Ranger Slide Action Shotgun **$180**
Hammerless. 12 and 20 gauge; 3-inch chambers. Walnut
finished hardwood stock, ribbed forearm. 28-inch vent-
rib barrel; Winchoke system. Weight: 7$\frac{1}{4}$ pounds. Made
1982 to date by U. S. Repeating Arms.

Winchester Ranger Youth Slide Action **$175**
Same general specifications as standard Ranger Slide Action except chambered for 20 gauge only, has 4-shot magazine, recoil pad on buttstock and weighs 6$\frac{1}{2}$ pounds.
Mfd. by U. S. Repeating Arms.

Winchester Shotgun/Rifle Combination **$1995**
12-gauge Winchoke barrel on top and rifle barrel chambered for 30-06 on bottom (over/under). 25-inch barrels.
Engraved receiver. Hand checkered walnut stock and forend. Weight: 8$\frac{1}{2}$ pounds. Mfd. for Olin Corp. in Japan.

Winchester Single Shot Lever Action Shotgun . . **$1150**
Falling-block action, same as in Single Shot Rifle. High-
wall receiver. Solid frame or takedown. 20 gauge. 3-inch
chamber. 26-inch barrel; plain, matted or matted rib; Cyl.
bore, M or Full choke. Weight: about 5$\frac{1}{2}$ pounds. Straight-
grip stock and forearm. Made 1914–1916.

Winchester Stainless Police

Winchester Super-X Model I Field

Winchester Xpert Model 96 Field

Winchester Stainless Marine Slide Action Security Shotgun $275
Hammerless. 12 gauge only. 18-inch barrel of ordnance stainless steel. 7-shot capacity. Weight: 7 pounds. Made 1984 to date by U. S. Repeating Arms.

Winchester Stainless Police Slide Action Security Shotgun $275
Hammerless. 12 gauge only. 18-inch ordnance stainless steel barrel accommodates gas launchers. Rifle-type sights. Made from 1984 to date by U.S. Repeating Arms.

Winchester Super-X Model I Auto Field Gun $375
Gas-operated. Takedown. 12 gauge. 2³/₄-inch chamber. 4-shot magazine. Barrels: vent rib; 26-inch IC; 28-inch M or F; 30-inch Full choke. Weight: about 7 pounds. Checkered pistol-grip stock and forearm. Made 1974–1984.

Winchester Super-X Model I Skeet Gun $495
Same as Super-X Field Gun, except has 26-inch barrel, SK choke, skeet-style stock and forearm of select walnut. Made 1974–1984.

Winchester Super-X Model I Trap Gun
Same as Super-X Field Gun, except has 30-inch barrel, IM or F choke, trap-style stock (straight or Monte Carlo

Winchester Super-X Model I Trap Gun (cont.)
comb) and forearm of select walnut, recoil pad. Made 1974–1984.

With straight stock	$395
With Monte Carlo stock	450

Winchester Xpert Model 96 O/U Field Gun $575
Boxlock action similar to Model 101. Plain receiver. Auto ejectors. Selective single trigger. Gauges: 12, 20. 3-inch chambers. Barrels: vent rib; 26-inch IC/M; 28-inch M/F; 30-inch F/F choke (12 ga. only). Weight: 6¹/₄ to 8¹/₄ pounds depending on gauge and barrels. Checkered pistol-grip stock and forearm. Made 1976–1981 for Olin Corp. at its Olin-Kodensha facility in Japan.

Winchester Xpert Model 96 Skeet Gun $600
Same as Xpert Field Gun, except has 2³/₄-inch chambers, 27-inch barrels, SK choke, skeet-style stock and forearm. Made 1976–1981.

Winchester Xpert Model 96 Trap Gun
Same as Xpert Field Gun, except 12 gauge only, 2³/₄-inch chambers, has 30-inch barrels, IM/F or F/F choke, trap-style stock (straight or Monte Carlo comb) with recoil pad. Made 1976–1981.

With straight stock	$580
With Monte Carlo stock	595

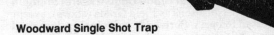

Woodward Single Shot Trap

═══ JAMES WOODWARD & SONS ═══
London, England
The business of this firm was acquired by James Purdey & Sons after World War II.

Woodward Best Quality Hammerless Double
Sidelock. Automatic ejectors. Double triggers or single trigger. Built to order in all standard gauges, barrel lengths, boring and other specifications; made as a field gun, pigeon and wildfowl gun, skeet gun or trap gun. Manufactured prior to World War II.

Woodward Best Quality Hammerless Double (cont.)

With double triggers	$19,250
With single trigger	20,500

Woodward Best Quality Single Shot Trap $10,925
Sidelock. Mechanical features of the Under and Over Gun. vent-rib barrel. 12 gauge only. Built to customers' specifications. Made prior to World War II.

SHOTGUNS

Woodward Best Quality Under-and-Over Shotgun

Sidelock. Automatic ejectors. Double triggers or single trigger. Built to order in all standard gauges, barrel lengths, boring and other specifications, including Special Trap Grade with vent rib. Woodward introduced this type of gun in 1908. Made until World War II. See listing of Purdey Over-and-Under Gun.

With double triggers **$24,500**
Single trigger, extra **1,000**

**Woodward Best Quality
Under-and-Over**

**Woodward Under-and-Over
Special Trap Grade**

ZEPHYR SHOTGUNS

**Manufactured by Victor Sarasqueta Company,
Eibar, Spain**

Zephyr Model 1 Over/Under Shotgun **$895**
Same general specifications as Field Model O/U, except with more elaborate engraving, finer wood and checkering. Imported by Stoeger 1930s–1951.

Zephyr Model 2 Over/Under Shotgun **$1145**
Sidelock. Auto ejectors. Gauges: 12, 16, 20, 28 and .410. Barrels: 25 to 30 inches most common. Modest scroll engraving on receiver and sideplates. Checkered, straight-grain select walnut buttstock and forend. Imported by Stoeger 1930s–1951.

Zephyr Model 3 Over/Under Shotgun **$1595**
Same general specifications as Zephyr Model 2 O/U, except with more elaborate engraving, finer wood and checkering. Imported by Stoeger 1930s–1951.

Zephyr Model 400E Field Grade Double Barrel Shotgun
Anson & Deeley boxlock system. Gauges: 12, 16, 20, 28 and .410. Barrels: 25 to 30 inches. Weight: 4½ lbs. (.410) to 6¼ lbs. (12 ga.). Checkered French walnut buttstock and forearm. Modest scroll engraving on barrels, receiver and trigger guard. Imported by Stoeger 1930s–1950s.
12, 16 or 20 gauge **$1100**
28 or .410 gauge **1250**
Add for selective single trigger **200**

Zephyr Model 401E Skeet Grade Double Barrel Shotgun
Same general specifications as Field Grade (above), except with beavertail forearm. Barrels: 25 to 28 inches. Imported by Stoeger 1930s–1950s.
12, 16 or 20 gauge **$1400**
28 or .410 gauge **1500**
Extra for selective single trigger.............. **350**
Extra for nonselective single trigger **250**

Zephyr Model 402E Deluxe Double Barrel Shotgun **$1700**
Same general specifications as Model 400E Field Grade, except for custom refinements. The action was carefully

Zephyr Model 402E Deluxe Double (cont.)
hand-honed for smoother operation; finer, elaborate engraving throughout plus higher quality wood in stock and forearm. Imported by Stoeger 1930s–1950s.

Zephyr Crown Grade

Zephyr Crown Grade **$1200**
Boxlock. Gauges: 12, 16, 20, 28 and .410. Barrels: 25 to 30 inches standard, but any lengths could be ordered. Weight: 6 lbs. 4 oz. (.410) to 7 lbs. 4 oz. (12 ga.). Checkered Spanish walnut stock and beavertail forearm. Receiver engraved with scroll patterns. Imported by Stoeger 1938–1951.

Zephyr Field Model Over/Under Shotgun **$625**
Anson & Deeley boxlock. Auto ejectors. Gauges: 12, 16 and 20. Barrels: 25 to 30 inches standard; full-length matt rib. Double triggers. Checkered buttstock and forend. Light scroll engraving on receiver. Imported by Stoeger 1930s–1951.

Zephyr Honker Single-Shot Shotgun **$895**
Sidelock. Gauge: 10; 3½-inch magnum. 36-inch vent-rib barrel w/Full choke. Weight: 10½ pounds. Checkered select Spanish walnut buttstock and beavertail forend; recoil pad. Imported by Stoeger 1950s–1972.

Zephyr Pinehurst Double Barrel Shotgun **$895**
Boxlock. Gauges: 12, 16, 20, 28 and .410. Barrels: 25 to 28 inches most common. Checkered, select walnut buttstock and forend. Selective single trigger and auto ejectors. Imported by Stoeger 1950s–1972.

Zephyr Premier Grade

Zephyr Premier Grade Double Barrel Shotgun . $2000
Sidelock. Gauges: 12, 16, 20, 28 and .410. Barrels: any length, but 25 to 30 inches most popular. Weight: 4½ lbs. (.410) to 7 lbs. (12 ga.). Checkered high-grade French walnut buttstock and forend. Imported by Stoeger 1930s-1951.

Zephyr Royal Grade

Zephyr Royal Grade Double Barrel Shotgun . . . $3000
Same general specifications as the Premier Grade, except with more elaborate engraving, finer checkering and wood. Imported by Stoeger 1930s-1951.

Zephyr Sterlingworth II Double Barrel Shotgun . . $995
Action: genuine sidelocks with color-casehardened sideplates. Gauges: 12, 20, 20 and .410. Barrels: 25 to 30 inches. Weight: 6 lbs. 4 oz. (.410) to 7 lbs. 4 oz. (12 ga.). Select Spanish walnut buttstock and beavertail forearm. Light scroll engraving on receiver and sideplates. Automatic, sliding-tang safety. Imported by Stoeger 1950s-1972.

Zephyr Thunderbird Double Barrel Shotgun . . . $1150
Sidelock. Gauges: 12 and 10 Magnum. Barrels: 32-inch, both Full choke. Weight: 8 lbs. 8 oz. (12 ga.); 12 lbs. (10 ga.). Receiver elaborately engraved with waterfowl scenes. Checkered select Spanish walnut buttstock and beavertail forend. Plain extractors, double triggers. Imported by Stoeger 1950-1972.

Zephyr Upland King Double Barrel Shotgun . . . $1125
Sidelock. Gauges: 12, 16, 20, 28 and .410. Barrels: 25 to 28 inches most popular. Checkered buttstock and forend of select walnut. Selective single trigger and auto ejectors. Imported by Stoeger 1950-1972.

Zephyr Uplander Double Barrel Shotgun $1050
Same general specifications as the Zephyr Sterlingworth II, except with selective auto ejectors and highly polished sideplates. Imported by Stoeger 1951-1972.

Zephyr Woodlander II Double Barrel Shotgun . . . $545
Boxlock. Gauges: 12, 20 and .410. Barrels: 25 to 30 inches. Weight: 6 lbs. 4 oz. (.410) to 7 lbs. 4 oz. (12 ga.). Checkered Spanish walnut stock and beavertail forearm. Receiver engraved with Moorish patterns and game scenes. Imported by Stoeger 1950-1972.

**Angelo Zoli Apache O/U
Field Shotgun**

**Angelo Zoli Daino I
Folding Single Shot**

ANGELO ZOLI
Mississauga, Ontario, Canada

Angelo Zoli Alley Cleaner S/S Shotgun $550
Gauges: 12 and 20. 20-inch barrel. 26½ inches overall. Weight: 7 pounds average. Chokes: F/M, F, IM, M, IC, SK. Chrome-lined barrels. Walnut stock and engraved action. Made 1986-87.

Angelo Zoli Apache O/U Field Shotgun $425
Gauge: 12. Chokes: F/M, F, IM, M, IC, SK. 20-inch barrel. Short vent rib. Weight: 7½ pounds. Checkered walnut stock and forearm. Lever action. Pistol grip. Made 1986-88.

Angelo Zoli Daino I Folding Single Shot $135
Gauges: 12, 20 and .410. 28- or 30-inch barrel. Weight: 6 pounds average. Choke: Full. Chrome-lined barrel, vent rib. Pistol-grip walnut stock. Engraved action. Made 1986-88.

SHOTGUNS

**Angelo Zoli HK 2000
Semiautomatic**

**Angelo Zoli Patricia
Side-by-Side**

**Angelo Zoli Z43 Standard
Over/Under Shotgun**

Angelo Zoli HK 2000 Semiautomatic Shotgun **$525**
Gauge: 12. 5-shot capacity. Barrels: 24-, 26-, 28- and 30-inch; vent rib. Weight: 6 1/2 to 7 1/2 pounds. Checkered walnut stock and forearm. Glossy finish. Pistol grip. Engraved receiver. Made 1988.

Angelo Zoli Patricia Side-by-Side Shotguns **$1200**
Gauge: .410 only. 28-inch barrel. Choke: F/M. Weight: 5 1/2 lbs. Automatic ejectors; Zoli single selective trigger, boxlock. Hand-checkered walnut stock with English straight grip, splinter forearm. Made 1986–88.

Angelo Zoli Saint George O/U Competition Trap Combo **$1050**
Gauge: 12. 30- and 32-inch vent rib barrels. Weight: 8 pounds. Single selective trigger. Oil-finished, pistol-grip walnut stock. Made 1986–88.

Angelo Zoli Silver Snipe Over/Under Shotgun . . **$695**
Purdey-type boxlock with crossbolt. Selective single trigger. Gauges: 12, 20; 3-inch chambers. Barrels: 26-, 28- or 30-inch with a variety of choke combinations. Weight: 5 3/4 to 6 3/4 pounds. Checkered European walnut buttstock and forend. Made in Italy.

Angelo Zoli Z43 Standard O/U Shotgun **$410**
Gauge: 12 or 20. 26-, 28- or 30-inch barrels. Chokes: F/M, M/IC Weight: 6 3/4 to 8 pounds. vent lateral ribs, standard extractors,, single non-selective trigger. Glossy-finished walnut stock and forearm. Automatic safety. Made 1986–88.

**Antonio Zoli
Silver Falcon O/U**

**Antonio Zoli
Uplander Side/Side Shotgun**

ANTONIO ZOLI, U.S.A., INC.
Fort Wayne, Indiana
Manufactured in Italy

Antonio Zoli Silver Falcon O/U **$775**
Gauges: 12 and 20; 3-inch chambers. 26- or 28-inch blued barrels. Weight: 6 1/4 to 7 1/4 pounds. Antiqued silver finish on receiver. Pistol-grip stock of Turkish Circassian walnut with polyurethane-type finish. Imported 1989–1990.

Antonio Zoli Uplander Side/Side Shotgun **$725**
Gauges: 12 and 20. Casehardened receiver. Checkered oil-finished, hand-rubbed stock of Turkish Circassian walnut; splinter forend. Imported 1989–1990.

INDEX

18TH EDITION — 571